Koren Talmud Bavli

THE NOÉ EDITION

YEVAMOT

Steinsaltz Center

KOREN

תלמוד בבלי

KOREN TALMUD BAVLI

THE NOÉ EDITION

יבמות

YEVAMOT

Daf 70a through Daf 87b

COMMENTARY BY

Rabbi Adin Even-Israel Steinsaltz

EDITOR-IN-CHIEF

Rabbi Dr Tzvi Hersh Weinreb

SENIOR CONTENT EDITOR

Rabbi Dr Shalom Z Berger

EXECUTIVE EDITOR

Rabbi Joshua Schreier

•

STEINSALTZ CENTER

KOREN PUBLISHERS JERUSALEM

Supported by the Matanel Foundation

Koren Talmud Bavli, The Noe Edition
Vol. 14e: Tractate Yevamot, Daf 70a through Daf 87b
Paperback, ISBN, 978-965-7765-68-5

First Hebrew/English paperback edition, 2021

Koren Publishers Jerusalem Ltd.
PO Box 4044, Jerusalem 91040, ISRAEL
PO Box 8531, New Milford, CT 06776, USA
www.korenpub.com

Steinsaltz Center

Steinsaltz Center is the parent organization of institutions established by Rabbi Adin Even-Israel Steinsaltz

PO Box 45187, Jerusalem 91450 ISRAEL
Telephone: +972 2 646 0900, Fax +972 2 624 9454
www.steinsaltz-center.org

הִנֵּה יָמִים בָּאִים, נְאֻם אֲדֹנָי יֱהוִה, וְהִשְׁלַחְתִּי רָעָב בָּאָרֶץ,
לֹא־רָעָב לַלֶּחֶם וְלֹא־צָמָא לַמַּיִם, כִּי אִם־לִשְׁמֹעַ אֵת דִּבְרֵי יהוה.

Behold, days are coming – says the Lord God – I will send a hunger to the land, not a hunger for bread nor a thirst for water, but to hear the words of the Lord. (AMOS 8:11)

The Noé edition of the Koren Talmud Bavli
with the commentary of Rabbi Adin Even-Israel Steinsaltz
is dedicated to all those who open its covers
to quench their thirst for Jewish Knowledge,
in our generation of Torah renaissance.

This beautiful edition is for the young, the aged,
the novice and the savant alike,
as it unites the depth of Torah knowledge
with the best of academic scholarship.

Within its exquisite and vibrant pages,
words become worlds.

It will claim its place in the library of classics,
in the bookcases of the Beit Midrash,
the classrooms of our schools,
and in the offices of professionals and business people
who carve out precious time to grapple with its timeless wisdom.

For the Student and the Scholar

DEDICATED BY LEO AND SUE NOÉ

Steinsaltz Center

Executive Director, Steinsaltz Center

Rabbi Meni Even-Israel

Managing Editor

Rabbi Jason Rappoport

Senior Content Editor

Rabbi Dr. Shalom Z. Berger

Editors

Rabbi Joshua Amaru, *Coordinating Editor*
Amy Kaplan Benoff
Menucha Chwat
Rabbi Yoel Domb
Rabbi Yonatan Shai Freedman
Rabbi Alan Haber
Rabbi Tzvi Chaim Kaye
Catriel Lev
Elisha Loewenstern
Adina Luber
Rabbi Avishai Magence, *Content Curator*
Gavriel Reiss
Rabbi David Sedley
Shira Shmidman
Rabbi Michael Siev
Avi Steinhart
Rabbi Binyamin Zimmerman

Copy Editors

Aliza Israel, *Coordinator*
Bracha Hermon
Ita Olesker
Debbie Ismailoff
Shira Finson
Ilana Sobel
Deena Nataf
Eliana Kurlantzick Yorav
Nava Wieder

Language Consultants

Dr. Stephanie E. Binder, *Greek & Latin*
Rabbi Yaakov Hoffman, *Arabic*
Dr. Shai Secunda, *Persian*
Shira Shmidman, *Aramaic*

KOREN

Design & Typesetting

Raphaël Freeman, *Design & Typography*
Dena Landowne Bailey, *Typesetting*
Tani Bayer, *Jacket Design*

Images

Eliahu Misgav, *Illustration & Image Acquisition*

Introduction by the Publisher

The Talmud has sustained and inspired Jews for thousands of years. Throughout Jewish history, an elite cadre of scholars has absorbed its learning and passed it on to succeeding generations. The Talmud has been the fundamental text of our people.

Beginning in the 1960s, Rabbi Adin Even-Israel Steinsaltz שליט״א created a revolution in the history of Talmud study. His translation of the Talmud, first into modern Hebrew and then into other languages, as well the practical learning aids he added to the text, have enabled millions of people around the world to access and master the complexity and context of the world of Talmud.

It is thus a privilege to present the *Koren Talmud Bavli*, an English translation of the talmudic text with the brilliant elucidation of Rabbi Steinsaltz. The depth and breadth of his knowledge are unique in our time. His rootedness in the tradition and his reach into the world beyond it are inspirational.

Working with Rabbi Steinsaltz on this remarkable project has been not only an honor, but a great pleasure. Never shy to express an opinion, with wisdom and humor, Rabbi Steinsaltz sparkles in conversation, demonstrating his knowledge (both sacred and worldly), sharing his wide-ranging interests, and, above all, radiating his passion. I am grateful for the unique opportunity to work closely with him, and I wish him many more years of writing and teaching.

Our intentions in publishing this new edition of the Talmud are threefold. First, we seek to fully clarify the talmudic page to the reader – textually, intellectually, and graphically. Second, we seek to utilize today's most sophisticated technologies, both in print and electronic formats, to provide the reader with a comprehensive set of study tools. And third, we seek to help readers advance in their process of Talmud study.

To achieve these goals, the *Koren Talmud Bavli* is unique in a number of ways:

- The classic *tzurat hadaf* of Vilna, used by scholars since the 1800s, has been reset for great clarity, and opens from the Hebrew "front" of the book. Full *nikkud* has been added to both the talmudic text and Rashi's commentary, allowing for a more fluent reading with the correct pronunciation; the commentaries of *Tosafot* have been punctuated. Upon the advice of many English-speaking teachers of Talmud, we have separated these core pages from the translation, thereby enabling the advanced student to approach the text without the distraction of the translation. This also reduces the number of volumes in the set. At the bottom of each *daf*, there is a reference to the corresponding English pages. In addition, the Vilna edition was read against other manuscripts and older print editions, so that texts which had been removed by non-Jewish censors have been restored to their rightful place.
- The English translation, which starts on the English "front" of the book, reproduces the *menukad* Talmud text alongside the English translation (in bold) and commentary and explanation (in a lighter font). The Hebrew and Aramaic text is presented in logical paragraphs. This allows for a fluent reading of the text for the non-Hebrew or non-Aramaic reader. It also allows for the Hebrew reader to refer easily to the text alongside. Where the original text features dialogue or poetry, the English text is laid out in a manner appropriate to the genre. Each page refers to the relevant *daf*.

- Critical contextual tools surround the text and translation: personality notes, providing short biographies of the Sages; language notes, explaining foreign terms borrowed from Greek, Latin, Persian, or Arabic; and background notes, giving information essential to the understanding of the text, including history, geography, botany, archaeology, zoology, astronomy, and aspects of daily life in the talmudic era.
- Halakhic summaries provide references to the authoritative legal decisions made over the centuries by the rabbis. They explain the reasons behind each halakhic decision as well as the ruling's close connection to the Talmud and its various interpreters.
- Photographs, drawings, and other illustrations have been added throughout the text – in full color in the Standard and Electronic editions, and in black and white in the Daf Yomi edition – to visually elucidate the text.

This is not an exhaustive list of features of this edition, it merely presents an overview for the English-speaking reader who may not be familiar with the "total approach" to Talmud pioneered by Rabbi Steinsaltz.

Several professionals have helped bring this vast collaborative project to fruition. My many colleagues are noted on the Acknowledgments page, and the leadership of this project has been exceptional.

RABBI MENACHEM EVEN-ISRAEL, DIRECTOR OF THE STEINSALTZ CENTER, was the driving force behind this enterprise. With enthusiasm and energy, he formed the happy alliance with Koren and established close relationships among all involved in the work.

RABBI DR. TZVI HERSH WEINREB שליט״א, EDITOR-IN-CHIEF, brought to this project his profound knowledge of Torah, intellectual literacy of Talmud, and erudition of Western literature. It is to him that the text owes its very high standard, both in form and content, and the logical manner in which the beauty of the Talmud is presented.

RABBI JOSHUA SCHREIER, EXECUTIVE EDITOR, assembled an outstanding group of scholars, translators, editors, and proofreaders, whose standards and discipline enabled this project to proceed in a timely and highly professional manner.

RABBI MEIR HANEGBI, EDITOR OF THE HEBREW EDITION OF THE STEINSALTZ TALMUD, lent his invaluable assistance throughout the work process, supervising the reproduction of the Vilna pages.

RAPHAËL FREEMAN, EXECUTIVE EDITOR OF KOREN, created this Talmud's unique typographic design which, true to the Koren approach, is both elegant and user friendly.

It has been an enriching experience for all of us at Koren Publishers Jerusalem to work with the Steinsaltz Center to develop and produce the *Koren Talmud Bavli*. We pray that this publication will be a source of great learning and, ultimately, greater *avodat Hashem* for all Jews.

Matthew Miller, Publisher
Koren Publishers Jerusalem
Jerusalem 5772

Contents

For the vocalized Vilna Shas layout, please open as a Hebrew book.

Introduction to **Perek VIII**

A man wounded with crushed testicles or a severed penis shall not enter into the congregation of the Lord. A mamzer shall not enter into the congregation of the Lord; even to the tenth generation shall not of his enter into the congregation of the Lord. An Ammonite or a Moabite shall not enter into the congregation of the Lord; even to the tenth generation shall none of them enter into the congregation of the Lord forever; because they did not meet you with bread and with water on the way, when you came forth out of Egypt; and because they hired against you Balaam, son of Beor, from Pethor of Aram Naharaim, to curse you.

(Deuteronomy 23:2–5)

You shall not abhor an Edomite, for he is your brother; you shall not abhor an Egyptian, because you were a stranger in his land. The sons of the third generation that are born to them may enter into the congregation of the Lord.

(Deuteronomy 23:8–9)

This chapter continues the discussion in the previous chapter and addresses a number of issues related to women who, as a result of their marriages, are entitled to eat *teruma* or are disqualified from doing so. Parallel to the case where it is permitted for a man to eat *teruma* while his wife is disqualified because their union itself is forbidden, there is a case where it is prohibited for the priest himself to eat *teruma*, but nevertheless he enables his wife to eat *teruma* on his account.

The Gemara then clarifies the *halakhot* governing those who are prohibited from entering into the congregation of the Lord, i.e., marrying an individual who is fit and Jewish from birth. These restrictions may result from a physical injury, e.g., crushed testicles; from the individual's Ammonite, Moabite, Egyptian, or Edomite origins; or from his status as a child born of an incestuous or adulterous union [*mamzer*]. This chapter also discusses the differences between these cases and the implications for the status of their descendants.

When the Torah speaks of a man with crushed testicles or a severed penis, it is referring to one whose sexual organs were impaired as a result of accident or injury. However, there are also others who are unable to have children due to a flaw in their sexual development. This includes both a man who is infertile due to natural causes [*seris ḥamma*] and a sexually underdeveloped woman [*aylonit*]. A significant portion of this chapter is dedicated to defining these cases and establishing their halakhic status on different counts, including determining the point at which they reach maturity and their eligibility for ordinary and levirate marriages. The discussion expands to include other cases of abnormal sexual development: A *tumtum*, one whose external sexual organs are indeterminate and it is unclear whether the person is male or female; and a hermaphrodite, who possesses both male and female genitals. Since the gender of such people is in doubt, this discussion is relevant to many areas of *halakha*. This chapter deals primarily with their standing with respect to marriage and the implications of their sexual relations.

מתני׳ הֶעָרֵל וְכָל הַטְּמֵאִים לֹא יֹאכְלוּ בִּתְרוּמָה, נְשֵׁיהֶן וְעַבְדֵיהֶן יֹאכְלוּ בִּתְרוּמָה.

MISHNA An uncircumcised priest,[N] e.g., one for whom circumcision was considered too dangerous, **and all** those **who are ritually impure** with any type of impurity, **may not partake of *teruma*,**[H] the portion of produce that must be set aside for the priests. However, **their wives and their slaves may partake of *teruma*.**[H]

פְּצוּעַ דַּכָּא וּכְרוּת שָׁפְכָה, הֵן וְעַבְדֵיהֶן – יֹאכְלוּ, וּנְשֵׁיהֶן – לֹא יֹאכְלוּ, וְאִם לֹא יְדָעָהּ מִשֶּׁנַּעֲשָׂה פְּצוּעַ דַּכָּא וּכְרוּת שָׁפְכָה – הֲרֵי אֵלּוּ יֹאכְלוּ.

With regard to both **a man with crushed testicles** or with other wounds to his genitals [*petzua dakka*] **and one whose penis has been severed** [*kerut shofkha*], it is prohibited for them to marry a woman who was born Jewish. If they are priests **they and their slaves may partake** of *teruma*, as this condition does not disqualify them or their property. However, **their wives may not partake**[N] of *teruma*, because if a priest has relations with his wife after suffering his injury, he renders her a *ḥalala*, a woman who is disqualified from marrying a priest, as he has engaged in forbidden sexual relations with her. **If** such a priest **did not know** his wife, i.e., did not engage in sexual relations with her, **after his testicles were crushed or his penis was severed, she may partake** of *teruma*, as she had married the priest in a permitted manner.[H]

וְאֵי זֶהוּ פְּצוּעַ דַּכָּא – כָּל שֶׁנִּפְצְעוּ הַבֵּיצִים שֶׁלּוֹ, וַאֲפִילּוּ אַחַת מֵהֶן. וּכְרוּת שָׁפְכָה – כָּל שֶׁנִּכְרַת הַגִּיד. וְאִם נִשְׁתַּיֵּיר מֵעֲטָרָה אֲפִילּוּ כְּחוּט הַשַּׂעֲרָה – כָּשֵׁר.

And who is deemed **a man with crushed testicles?**[H] It is **anyone whose testicles have been wounded, even one of them. And one whose penis has been severed** is **anyone whose** sexual **member has been cut off.** As for the measure that renders him unfit, **if there remains** a portion **of the corona, even** as much **as a hairsbreadth,** he is still **fit.** However, if nothing at all is left of the corona, he is considered as one with a severed penis, for whom it is prohibited by Torah law to marry a Jewish woman.

גמ׳ תַּנְיָא, אָמַר רַבִּי אֶלְעָזָר: מִנַּיִן לְעָרֵל שֶׁאֵין אוֹכֵל בִּתְרוּמָה – נֶאֱמַר ״תּוֹשָׁב וְשָׂכִיר״ בְּפֶסַח, וְנֶאֱמַר ״תּוֹשָׁב וְשָׂכִיר״ בִּתְרוּמָה, מָה ״תּוֹשָׁב וְשָׂכִיר״ הָאָמוּר בְּפֶסַח עָרֵל אָסוּר בּוֹ, אַף ״תּוֹשָׁב וְשָׂכִיר״ הָאָמוּר בִּתְרוּמָה עָרֵל אָסוּר בּוֹ.

GEMARA It is taught in a *baraita* that **Rabbi Elazar said: From where** is it derived **that an** uncircumcised priest **may not partake of *teruma*? It is stated: "A sojourner and a hired servant** shall not eat thereof" (Exodus 12:45) **with regard to the Paschal lamb, and it is stated: "A sojourner** of a priest **and a hired servant** shall not eat of the holy thing" (Leviticus 22:10) **with regard to *teruma*. Just as "a sojourner and a hired servant" stated with regard to the Paschal lamb** indicates that **an uncircumcised** man **is prohibited** from eating **it, so too, "a sojourner and a hired servant" stated with regard to *teruma*** teaches that **an uncircumcised** man **is prohibited** from eating **it.**

רַבִּי עֲקִיבָא אוֹמֵר: אֵינוֹ צָרִיךְ, הֲרֵי הוּא אוֹמֵר ״אִישׁ אִישׁ״ לְרַבּוֹת הֶעָרֵל.

Rabbi Akiva says: This proof **is not necessary, as the** verse **states:** "Any man [*ish ish*] from the seed of Aaron who is a leper or a *zav* shall not eat of the holy things until he be pure" (Leviticus 22:4). The repetition of the word *ish*, meaning man, comes **to include an uncircumcised** man, indicating that he is like one who is ritually impure and therefore may not partake of consecrated food.

NOTES

An uncircumcised priest – הֶעָרֵל: According to Rashi, this refers to one whose brothers died as a result of circumcision and therefore it was considered too dangerous to circumcise him. Rabbeinu Tam, however, maintains that since in such a case he is not obligated to circumcise himself, he does not fall into the category of the uncircumcised, and he may therefore eat *teruma*. Instead, the mishna is dealing with one who is afraid of being circumcised (see Ramban and Rashba).

Their wives may not partake – נְשֵׁיהֶן לֹא יֹאכְלוּ: The early authorities inquire as to why in fact the wife of a man with crushed testicles or a severed penis may not eat *teruma*. Rashi explains that these women are considered *ḥalalot*, women who are disqualified from marrying a priest, but his opinion is questioned by several commentaries, as the conclusion of the Gemara is that a woman is made a *ḥalala* only by one who was prohibited to her from the outset, and a man with crushed testicles does not fall into this category. Rashba and others explain that this limitation applies only to those disqualified from the priesthood, whereas a man with crushed testicles is forbidden to the entire congregation. Others suggest that since he suffered his injury in the meantime, it is as though his body had changed, and therefore he is considered as prohibited to her from the outset (*Tosafot Yeshanim*); a similar idea is mentioned by the Rashash. According to the Rambam, it is prohibited for this woman to eat *teruma*, not because she is a *ḥalala*, but because she is deemed a *zona*, as she has engaged in relations with a man forbidden to her.

HALAKHA

An uncircumcised priest may not partake of *teruma* – עָרֵל אָסוּר בִּתְרוּמָה: It is prohibited for an uncircumcised priest to partake of *teruma* (Rambam *Sefer Zera'im*, *Hilkhot Terumot* 7:10).

The wife of an uncircumcised priest – אֵשֶׁת כֹּהֵן עָרֵל: It is permitted for the wife and slaves of an uncircumcised or ritually impure priest to eat *teruma* (Rambam *Sefer Zera'im*, *Hilkhot Terumot* 7:12).

A priest with crushed testicles – כֹּהֵן פְּצוּעַ דַּכָּא: A priest with crushed testicles or a severed penis may eat *teruma*, and the same applies to his slaves. It is also permitted for his wife to eat *teruma*, provided that she has not had relations with him since he suffered his injury (Rambam *Sefer Zera'im*, *Hilkhot Terumot* 7:13).

Who is deemed a man with crushed testicles – אֵי זֶהוּ פְּצוּעַ דַּכָּא: A man with crushed testicles is one whose testicles have been wounded. A man with a severed penis is one whose sexual member has been cut off. If part of his member has been removed but a portion of the corona remains, even as little as a hairsbreadth around the member, he is deemed fit (Rambam *Sefer Kedusha*, *Hilkhot Issurei Bia* 16:3–4; *Shulḥan Arukh*, *Even HaEzer* 5:2).

אֲמַר מָר: רַבִּי אֱלִיעֶזֶר אוֹמֵר נֶאֱמַר ״תּוֹשָׁב וְשָׂכִיר״ בְּפֶסַח וְנֶאֱמַר ״תּוֹשָׁב וְשָׂכִיר״ בִּתְרוּמָה, מַה ״תּוֹשָׁב וְשָׂכִיר״ הָאָמוּר בְּפֶסַח עָרֵל אָסוּר בּוֹ, אַף ״תּוֹשָׁב וְשָׂכִיר״ הָאָמוּר בִּתְרוּמָה עָרֵל אָסוּר בּוֹ.

The Gemara analyzes this *baraita* in detail. **The Master said: Rabbi Eliezer**[N] says that **it is stated: "A sojourner and a hired servant" with regard to the Paschal lamb, and it is stated: "A sojourner and a hired servant" with regard to** ***teruma*****. Just as "a sojourner and a hired servant" stated with regard to the Paschal lamb** indicates that **an uncircumcised** man **is prohibited** from eating **it, so too, "a sojourner and a hired servant" stated with regard to** ***teruma*** teaches that **an uncircumcised** man **is prohibited** from eating **it.**

מוּפְנֶה, דְּאִי לָאו מוּפְנֶה – אִיכָּא לְמִיפְרַךְ: מַה לְּפֶסַח – שֶׁכֵּן חַיָּיבִין עָלָיו מִשּׁוּם פִּיגּוּל וְנוֹתָר וְטָמֵא. לָאֵיי, אַפְנוּיֵי מוּפְנֶה.

With regard to this verbal analogy the Gemara comments: The phrase "a sojourner and a hired servant" must be **available,** i.e., superfluous in its context and therefore available for the purpose of establishing a verbal analogy. **As, if it is not available,** the verbal analogy **can be refuted** logically, as it is possible to say: **What is unique to the Paschal lamb?** It is **that one is liable** to receive *karet* **for** eating **it due to** its being ***piggul*****,** an offering that was sacrificed with the intent to consume it after its appointed time, or due to its being ***notar*****,** the flesh of an offering that is left over beyond its allotted time, **or** due to the one consuming it being **ritually impure.**[N] Therefore, it could be argued that it is owing to the Paschal lamb's special sanctity and severity that an uncircumcised man may not partake of it. But from where is it derived that an uncircumcised priest may not eat *teruma*? The Gemara concludes: This is **not so** [*la'ei*],[L] as the phrase **is** in fact **available** for establishing the verbal analogy.

הֵי מוּפְנֶה? אִי דִּתְרוּמָה – מִצְרָךְ צְרִיכִי, דְּתַנְיָא: ״תּוֹשָׁב״ זֶה קְנוּי קִנְיַן עוֹלָם, ״שָׂכִיר״ זֶה קְנוּי קִנְיַן שָׁנִים.

The Gemara asks: **Which** of the instances of the phrase "a sojourner and a hired servant" **is** not needed in its own context and is therefore **available** for establishing a verbal analogy? **If** one would claim that it is that which is stated with regard to ***teruma*****,** certainly those words **are necessary, as it is taught** in a *baraita*: **"A sojourner"; this is** referring to a Hebrew slave who was **acquired as a permanent acquisition** until the Jubilee Year, i.e., a slave who did not wish to terminate his servitude and underwent a ceremony in which his ear was pierced with an awl. **"A hired servant"; this is** referring to a Hebrew slave who was **acquired as an acquisition for** a period of six **years.**

וְיֹאמַר ״תּוֹשָׁב״ וְאַל יֹאמַר ״שָׂכִיר״, וַאֲנִי אוֹמַר: קְנוּי קִנְיַן עוֹלָם אֵינוֹ אוֹכֵל, קְנוּי קִנְיַן שָׁנִים – לֹא כׇּל שֶׁכֵּן?!

The *baraita* asks: **And let** the verse **state** only that **"a sojourner"** may not eat *teruma*, **and not state** anything about **"a hired servant," and I** would **say** by way of an *a fortiori* inference: If a slave who was **acquired as a permanent acquisition may not partake** of *teruma*, then with regard to one who was **acquired as an acquisition for** only six **years, all the more so** is it **not** clear that he should be prohibited from eating it?

אִילּוּ כֵּן, הָיִיתִי אוֹמֵר: ״תּוֹשָׁב״ זֶה קְנוּי קִנְיַן שָׁנִים, אֲבָל קְנוּי קִנְיַן עוֹלָם אוֹכֵל – בָּא ״שָׂכִיר״ וְלִימֵּד עַל תּוֹשָׁב, שֶׁאַף עַל פִּי שֶׁקָּנוּי קִנְיַן עוֹלָם – אֵין אוֹכֵל.

The *baraita* answers: **If it was** written **so, I would have said** with regard to **"a sojourner"** that **this** is referring to a slave who was **acquired as an acquisition for** a period of six **years,** as he may not eat *teruma*; **but** one who was **acquired as a permanent acquisition may** in fact **partake** of *teruma*. Therefore, the term **"a hired servant" comes and teaches** that **"a sojourner"** is referring to a slave who had his ear pierced and must now remain with his master until the Jubilee Year, and **that although he was acquired as a permanent acquisition,** he **may not partake** of *teruma.*

אֶלָּא דְּפֶסַח מוּפְנֵי. הַאי ״תּוֹשָׁב וְשָׂכִיר״ דִּכְתַב רַחֲמָנָא בְּפֶסַח מַאי נִיהוּ? אִי נֵימָא תּוֹשָׁב וְשָׂכִיר מַמָּשׁ – מִשּׁוּם דַּהֲוָה לֵיהּ תּוֹשָׁב וְשָׂכִיר אִיפְּטַר לֵיהּ מִפֶּסַח?! וְהָא קַיְימָא לַן גַּבֵּי תְּרוּמָה דְּלָא אָכֵיל,

The Gemara proposes: **Rather,** it is the phrase with regard to **the Paschal lamb** that **is available** for establishing a verbal analogy. **This** phrase: **"A sojourner and a hired servant," that the Merciful One writes with regard to the Paschal lamb,** to **what is it** referring? **If we say** that the verse is referring to **an actual sojourner and** to **a hired servant,** i.e., a Hebrew slave who was acquired permanently or for a fixed number of years, can it possibly be that **because he is a sojourner or a hired servant he is exempt from** the mitzva of **the Paschal lamb?** If one answers in the affirmative and argues that a Hebrew slave, like his Canaanite counterpart, is considered his master's property and is therefore no longer obligated in all the mitzvot like a freeman, this conclusion is difficult, **as we maintain with regard to** ***teruma*** **that** a Hebrew slave **may not partake** of it on account of his priestly master.[H]

NOTES

Rabbi Eliezer – **רַבִּי אֱלִיעֶזֶר:** The reference here is clearly to Rabbi Elazar, who is mentioned in the *baraita* from which this is a quote. The names Eliezer and Elazar differ in only one letter in Hebrew and are often confused, both in manuscripts and in printed editions of the Talmud.

What is unique to the Paschal lamb? It is that one is liable to receive ***karet*** **for eating it due to…being ritually impure** – **מַה לְּפֶסַח שֶׁכֵּן חַיָּיבִין עָלָיו מִשּׁוּם...טָמֵא:** *Tosafot* note that some authorities omit from this list one who is impure, as the prohibition with regard to impurity applies to *teruma* as well. Some point out that there is still a difference between the two cases: If one who is ritually impure partakes of the Paschal lamb, he is liable to receive *karet*, whereas if he eats *teruma* he is liable only to receive death at the hand of Heaven. It is also cited in the name of Rashi, and explained in further detail by the Meiri, that one who inadvertently eats of the Paschal lamb in a state of impurity must bring a sin-offering, which is not the case with regard to *teruma*. The Meiri adds that in the case of the Paschal lamb one is liable even if it is the offering that is impure and he himself is ritually pure, whereas with regard to *teruma* a ritually pure individual who eats impure *teruma* is not liable.

LANGUAGE

Not so [*la'ei*] – **לָאֵיי:** The source and precise meaning of this word are unclear. Rashi explains that it means: In truth (*Shabbat* 64a). The *Arukh* proposes that it is a combination of the Aramaic word *la*, meaning no, and *ei*, from the Greek υἱός, *huios*, meaning son. The meaning of the expression is therefore roughly parallel to: No, my son. Alternatively, *la* may be understood as a prefix meaning certainly or indeed, while *ei* means yes. In any event, the expression introduces an inescapable conclusion that the statement that follows must be accepted as true.

HALAKHA

It is prohibited for a sojourner and a hired servant to partake of ***teruma*** – **תּוֹשָׁב וְשָׂכִיר אֲסוּרִים בִּתְרוּמָה:** It is prohibited for all non-priests to eat *teruma*, even a sojourner or the hired servant of a priest (Rambam *Sefer Zera'im*, *Hilkhot Terumot* 6:5).

אַלְמָא – לָא קָנֵי לֵיהּ רַבֵּיהּ, הָכָא נַמִי לָא קָנֵי לֵיהּ רַבֵּיהּ. אֶלָּא לְאַפְנוֹיֵי.

Apparently his master does not acquire his body[N] and thereby effect a change in his personal status; rather, he remains a Jew in every sense. **Here too,** then, with regard to the Paschal lamb, **his master does not acquire his** body as a slave, and so he is obviously obligated in the mitzva of the Paschal lamb. **Rather,** the phrase is superfluous and was written only **to be available** to teach a different matter.

וְאַכַּתִּי, מוּפְנֶה מִצַּד אֶחָד הוּא, וְשָׁמְעִינַן לֵיהּ לְרַבִּי אֶלְעָזָר דְּאָמַר: מוּפְנֶה מִצַּד אֶחָד לְמֵדִין – וּמְשִׁיבִין!

The Gemara poses a question: **And** yet there is **still** a difficulty: The verbal analogy **is available from** only **one side,** as only the phrase with regard to the Paschal lamb is superfluous in its context, **and we heard Rabbi Elazar, who said** with regard to a verbal analogy **available from** only **one side** that **one** can **derive** from it, **and one** can also **refute** it logically if there is reason to distinguish between the two cases. Since there are grounds here for differentiating between the two *halakhot* in this case, why is the verbal analogy upheld?

כֵּיוָן דִּלְגוּפֵיהּ לָא צְרִיךְ, שְׁדֵי חַד אַלָּמֵד וּשְׁדֵי חַד אַמְלַמֵּד וַהֲוָה לֵיהּ גְּזֵירָה שָׁוָה מוּפְנָה מִשְּׁנֵי צְדָדִין.

The Gemara answers: **Since** the phrase “a sojourner and a hired servant” is **not needed for its own** matter, there are two superfluous terms, and one may **cast one** superfluous term **on the** *halakha* with regard to which **it is learned** that *teruma* may not be eaten by one who is uncircumcised, **and** one may **cast** the other **one on the** *halakha* with regard to the Paschal lamb that **teaches** this, **and** in this manner **it is** like **a verbal analogy** that is **available from both sides,**[B] which cannot be refuted.

אִי מַה פֶּסַח אוֹנֵן אָסוּר בּוֹ אַף תְּרוּמָה אוֹנֵן אָסוּר בָּהּ!

The Gemara raises a question: There is a principle that there cannot be half a verbal analogy. Consequently, **if** this verbal analogy is accepted, the following *halakha* that can be derived by way of the same analogy should be accepted as well: **Just as** with regard to **the Paschal lamb,** one who is **an acute mourner,** i.e., whose relative died that same day and has not yet been buried, **is prohibited** from eating **it, so too,** with regard to ***teruma*, an acute mourner** should be **prohibited** from eating **it,** but in fact this is not the case.

אָמַר רַבִּי יוֹסֵי בַּר חֲנִינָא: אָמַר קְרָא (״זָר״) ״וְכָל זָר״ זָרוּת אָמַרְתִּי לְךָ, וְלֹא אֲנִינוּת. אֵימָא: וְלֹא עֲרֵלוּת! הָא כְּתִיב ״תּוֹשָׁב וְשָׂכִיר״,

Rabbi Yosei bar Ḥanina said: The verse states: “No foreigner may eat of the holy thing” (Leviticus 22:10), which indicates: A disqualification stemming from **foreignness I told you** prevents one from eating *teruma*, **but not** a disqualification based on **acute mourning.**[H] The Gemara asks: **Say** that the verse comes to teach that a disqualification stemming from foreignness prevents one from eating *teruma*, **but not** a disqualification based on a priest’s **lack of circumcision,** and so it should be permitted for an uncircumcised priest to partake of *teruma*. The Gemara answers: **Isn’t it written** with regard to both *teruma* and the Paschal lamb: **“A sojourner and a hired servant”?** From this it is derived by way of a verbal analogy that it is prohibited for an uncircumcised priest to eat *teruma*.

וּמָה רָאִיתָ? מִסְתַּבְּרָא, עֲרֵלוּת הֲוָה לֵיהּ לְרַבּוּיֵי שֶׁכֵּן (מעשי״ם כרותי״ם בדב״ר העב״ד) מְחוּסַּר מַעֲשֶׂה, וּמַעֲשֶׂה בְּגוּפוֹ, וְעָנוּשׁ כָּרֵת, וְיֶשְׁנוֹ לִפְנֵי הַדִּבּוּר, וּמִילַת זְכָרָיו וַעֲבָדָיו מְעַכֶּבֶת.

The Gemara asks: **And what did you see** that led you to include an uncircumcised priest in the prohibition against eating *teruma* and exclude an acute mourner? Perhaps just the opposite is true. The Gemara answers: **It stands to reason** that **lack of circumcision should be included** and should prevent a priest from eating *teruma*, as the *halakhot* governing an uncircumcised man are stringent in several respects, as alluded to by the following mnemonic of key words: **Acts;** ***karetim*****; the** divine **word; the slave.** The Gemara spells out these stringencies: An uncircumcised man **lacks the act** of circumcision, **and** this **act** is performed **on his body;** the failure to perform circumcision is **punishable by *karet*;**[H] circumcision **existed before the** divine **word** was spoken at Mount Sinai, as the mitzva of circumcision had already been given to Abraham; **and the** lack of **circumcision of one’s male** children **and slaves precludes** one’s eating the Paschal lamb, as is explicitly stated in the Torah (Exodus 12:48).

NOTES

Apparently his master does not acquire his body – אַלְמָא לָא קָנֵי לֵיהּ רַבֵּיהּ: The early authorities are puzzled as to the validity of this argument: Even if a Hebrew slave belongs to his master, why should he not eat of the Paschal lamb? After all, a Canaanite slave may also partake of this offering. The Ra’avad explains that this passage is in accordance with the opinion that women and slaves are not obligated in the mitzva of the Paschal lamb (see *Tosafot*). The Ritva proposes that the Gemara was not suggesting that it should be prohibited for a Hebrew slave to eat the Paschal lamb, but rather that he is not obligated to do so. However, the Ramban and others maintain that the formulation of the Gemara’s difficulty is imprecise, and that it merely wishes to emphasize that there is no possibility of deriving, by way of an *a fortiori* inference, that a Hebrew slave is not obligated to partake of the Paschal lamb.

BACKGROUND

A verbal analogy available from both sides – גְּזֵירָה שָׁוָה מוּפְנָה מִשְּׁנֵי צְדָדִין: A verbal analogy is a fundamental rabbinic principle of biblical interpretation appearing in all standard lists of exegetical principles. If the same word or phrase appears in two places in the Torah and a certain *halakha* is stated explicitly in one of these places, the Sages may infer on the basis of verbal analogy that the same *halakha* must apply in the other case as well. In its simplest form, the verbal analogy is a type of linguistic interpretation by means of which the meaning of an obscure word or phrase is inferred on the basis of another occurrence of the same word or phrase in a clearer context. However, it is often used not only to determine the meaning of obscure words and phrases, but to transfer entire *halakhot* from one context to another.

Verbal analogies are unique among the exegetical principles in that they are based on verbal, rather than conceptual, similarity. For this reason there are a number of limitations placed on their use. One of the limitations imposed is the principle that one cannot expound a verbal analogy on his own; rather, he must have received a tradition to this effect from his teachers, who in turn learned it from their teachers, all the way back to Moses at Sinai. Furthermore, according to many, the analogy can be drawn only if the key words are available, meaning that they are superfluous, i.e., not needed as a source for some other *halakha*. If the key words are not superfluous, the verbal analogy may be refuted logically.

HALAKHA

Acute mourning with regard to *teruma* – אֲנִינוּת בִּתְרוּמָה: The state of acute mourning does not render the mourner disqualified from eating *teruma* (Rambam *Sefer Zera’im*, *Hilkhot Bikkurim* 3:5).

The punishment of *karet* for failure to perform circumcision – עוֹנֶשׁ כָּרֵת עַל מִילָה: Circumcision is a positive mitzva whose lack of fulfillment is punishable by *karet* (Rambam *Sefer Ahava*, *Hilkhot Mila* 1:1).

אַדְּרַבָּה, אֲנִינוּת הֲוָה לֵיהּ לְרַבּוּיֵי, שֶׁכֵּן: יֶשְׁנָהּ בְּכָל שָׁעָה, וְנוֹהֶגֶת בַּאֲנָשִׁים וְנָשִׁים, וְאֵין בְּיָדוֹ לְתַקֵּן אֶת עַצְמוֹ! הָנָךְ נְפִישָׁן.

The Gemara counters: **On the contrary, acute mourning should be included** and should prevent a priest from eating *teruma*, as acute mourning is also subject to several stringencies: **It is** relevant **at any time**[N] after the death of a close relative, unlike circumcision, which is performed only once in a lifetime; **it applies to** both **men and women,** unlike circumcision, which is restricted to men; **and it is not in** the mourner's **power to render himself fit** until after the deceased is buried, unlike an uncircumcised man, who can render himself fit at any time by undergoing circumcision. The Gemara responds: Even so, **these** arguments for including an uncircumcised priest in the prohibition **are** more **numerous.**

רָבָא אֲמַר: בְּלָא הָנָךְ נְפִישָׁן נַמִי לָא מָצֵית אָמְרַתְּ, שָׁבְקִינַן עֲרֵלוּת דִּכְתִיב בְּגוּפֵיהּ דְּפֶסַח וְיָלְפִינַן אֲנִינוּת מִפֶּסַח?! דְּפֶסַח גּוּפֵיהּ מִמַּעֲשֵׂר גָּמְרִינַן.

Rava said: Even **without** the rationale that **these** arguments **are** more **numerous, you still could not say** that the verbal analogy renders it prohibited for an acute mourner to eat *teruma*. As, is it possible to say that **we should leave out the lack of circumcision** from the prohibition against eating *teruma* even though **it is written** explicitly **with regard to the Paschal lamb itself, and learn** the *halakha* that **acute mourning** is included in the prohibition by way of a verbal analogy **from the Paschal lamb**[N] when this *halakha* that an acute mourner is barred from bringing the Paschal lamb is never stated explicitly? **As** the prohibition against acute mourning with respect to **the Paschal lamb itself we learn** only **from** the *halakha* governing **tithes.**

אִי מַה פֶּסַח – מִילַת זְכָרָיו וַעֲבָדָיו מְעַכֶּבֶת, אַף תְּרוּמָה – מִילַת זְכָרָיו וַעֲבָדָיו מְעַכֶּבֶת!

The Gemara raises another question: **If** the verbal analogy is valid, then the following *halakha* that can be derived by way of the same analogy should be accepted as well: **Just as** with regard to the **Paschal lamb, the** lack of **circumcision of one's male** children **and slaves prevents** one from eating of the offering[H] until he ensures that all of the male members of his household have been circumcised, **so too,** with regard to *teruma*, **the** lack of **circumcision of one's male** children **and slaves** should **prevent** one from partaking of *teruma*. However, in reality this is not the *halakha*.

אָמַר קְרָא ״וּמַלְתָּה אוֹתוֹ אָז יֹאכַל בּוֹ״, מִילַת זְכָרָיו וַעֲבָדָיו מְעַכֶּבֶת בּוֹ מִלֶּאֱכוֹל בְּפֶסַח, וְאֵין מִילַת זְכָרָיו וַעֲבָדָיו מְעַכֶּבֶת בִּתְרוּמָה.

The Gemara rejects this argument: **The verse states** with regard to the Paschal lamb: **"When you have circumcised him, then he shall eat from it"** (Exodus 12:44). The words "from it" teach that **the** lack of **circumcision of one's male** children **and slaves prevents one from eating the Paschal lamb,** but **the** lack of **circumcision of one's male** children **and slaves does not prevent one from** eating ***teruma***, if he himself is eligible to eat it.

אִי הָכִי אֵימָא: ״כׇּל עָרֵל לֹא יֹאכַל בּוֹ״, בּוֹ אֵינוֹ אוֹכֵל, אֲבָל אוֹכֵל הוּא בִּתְרוּמָה! הָא כְּתִיב ״תּוֹשָׁב וְשָׂכִיר״.

The Gemara raises a difficulty: **If so,** that the words "from it" come to exclude any other case, **say** a similar exposition with regard to the uncircumcised. As it is stated with regard to the Paschal lamb: **"No uncircumcised person shall eat from it"** (Exodus 12:48), indicating that **"from it,"** the Paschal lamb, an uncircumcised man **may not eat, but he may eat from *teruma*.** The Gemara answers: **Isn't it written** with regard to both *teruma* and the Paschal lamb: **"A sojourner and a hired servant"?** From this it is derived by way of a verbal analogy that an uncircumcised priest may not partake of *teruma*.

וּמָה רָאִיתָ? מִסְתַּבְּרָא: עֲרֵלוּת דְּגוּפֵיהּ הֲוָה לֵיהּ לְרַבּוּיֵי, שֶׁכֵּן מַעֲשֶׂה בְּגוּפוֹ, וְעָנוּשׁ כָּרֵת. אַדְּרַבָּה, מִילַת זְכָרָיו וַעֲבָדָיו הֲוָה לֵיהּ לְרַבּוּיֵי, שֶׁכֵּן יֶשְׁנָהּ בְּכָל שָׁעָה!

The Gemara asks: **And what did you see** that led you to include an uncircumcised priest in the prohibition against eating *teruma*, and not one whose male children and slaves have not been circumcised? The Gemara answers: **It stands to reason** that **one's own lack of circumcision should be included** and should preclude his eating *teruma*, as an uncircumcised man lacks an **act** that is performed **on his own body, and** the failure to perform circumcision **is punishable by *karet*.** The Gemara counters: **On the contrary, the** lack of **circumcision of one's male** children **and slaves should be included** and should preclude a priest's eating *teruma*, **as it is** relevant **at any time,** since whenever one has a male child or slave under his authority he is commanded to circumcise him.

NOTES

It is relevant at any time – שֶׁכֵּן יֶשְׁנָהּ בְּכָל שָׁעָה: One explanation is that the mitzva of circumcision must be performed during the day, whereas acute mourning applies at night as well. The Meiri notes that this interpretation is not in accordance with the accepted *halakha* that acute mourning applies at night only by rabbinic decree.

Acute mourning with regard to the Paschal lamb – אֲנִינוּת בְּפֶסַח: *Tosafot* conclude that the *halakha* governing the Paschal lamb is derived from tithes by verbal analogy, whereas the Meiri maintains that it is derived by an *a fortiori* inference. Although this dispute has no direct practical ramifications, it does affect the manner in which the *halakha* of other offerings is derived from the Paschal lamb.

HALAKHA

The lack of circumcision of one's male children and slaves prevents – מִילַת זְכָרָיו וַעֲבָדָיו מְעַכֶּבֶת: One who has not circumcised all of his male children and slaves may not offer the Paschal lamb. If the offering was slaughtered before they were circumcised, it is invalid (Rambam *Sefer Korbanot, Hilkhot Korban Pesaḥ* 5:5).

הָנָךְ נְפִישָׁן. וְאִיבָּעֵית אֵימָא: בְּלֹא [הָנָךְ] נְפִישָׁן נַמִי לָא מָצֵית אָמְרַתְּ, מִי אִיכָּא מִידֵּי דַּעֲרֵלוּת דְּגוּפֵיהּ לָא מְעַכְּבָא בֵּיהּ, עֲרֵלוּת דַּאֲחֵרִינֵי מְעַכְּבָא בֵּיהּ?!

The Gemara answers: **These** arguments for including one's own circumcision in the prohibition **are more numerous. And if you wish, say:** Even **without** the rationale that **these** arguments **are** more **numerous, you still could not say** that the verbal analogy comes to include in the prohibition against eating *teruma* one whose male children or slaves have not been circumcised. As, **is there anything that his own lack of circumcision**[N] **does not preclude him** from doing but **the lack of circumcision of others does preclude him** from doing? Rather, it must be that the verbal analogy comes to teach that the priest's own lack of circumcision precludes his eating *teruma*, while that of his male children and slaves does not.

הַשְׁתָּא דְּאָמְרַתְּ "בּוֹ" לִדְרָשָׁה הוּא דְּאָתָא, "כׇּל בֶּן נֵכָר לֹא יֹאכַל בּוֹ" לָמָּה לִי? "בּוֹ"

The Gemara poses a question: **Now that you have said** that the phrase **"from it"** used in this context **comes for an exposition** and serves to exclude other cases, with regard to the phrase "from it" in the verse **"No stranger shall eat from it"** (Exodus 12:43), **why do I** need it? The Gemara answers: This, too, teaches that it is only **from it,** eating the Paschal lamb,

NOTES

Is there anything that his…lack of circumcision, etc. – מִי אִיכָּא מִידֵּי דַּעֲרֵלוּת וכו׳: This point is so obvious that some commentaries are puzzled as to the Gemara's initial line of thought: How could it have been considered possible that the lack of circumcision of others is more problematic than one's own? The Ritva suggests that one could claim that this is a kind of penalty, as, if the *halakha* is not stringent with regard to such an individual, he will be lax and never circumcise those under his authority. *Tosefot HaRosh* and the Meiri explain that since a man who remains uncircumcised usually does so due to circumstances beyond his control, one might have thought that he should not be prohibited from eating *teruma*, whereas no such excuse applies to his failure to circumcise others.

מְשׁוּמָּדוּת פּוֹסֶלֶת, וְאֵין מְשׁוּמָּדוּת פּוֹסֶלֶת בְּמַעֲשֵׂר.

that **apostasy** [*meshumadut*][L] **disqualifies,**[H] as the term "stranger" in this context is understood to refer to a Jew whose conduct makes him estranged from God, and he is disqualified from eating the Paschal lamb, **but apostasy does not disqualify** one from eating **tithe.**[N]

"כׇּל עָרֵל לֹא יֹאכַל בּוֹ" לָמָּה לִי? "בּוֹ" אֵינוֹ אוֹכֵל, אֲבָל אוֹכֵל הוּא בְּמַצָּה וּמָרוֹר.

The Gemara asks further: If so, with regard to the phrase "from it" in the verse **"No uncircumcised person**[N] **shall eat from it"** (Exodus 12:48), which again emphasizes "from it" and not from another item, **why do I** need it? The Gemara answers: This teaches that only **from it,** the Paschal lamb, one who is uncircumcised **may not eat, but he eats *matza* and bitter herbs.**[H] One who is uncircumcised is obligated to eat *matza* and bitter herbs on Passover, just like any other Jew.

וְאִיצְטְרִיךְ לְמִכְתַּב "עָרֵל", וְאִיצְטְרִיךְ לְמִכְתַּב "כׇּל בֶּן נֵכָר". דְּאִי כָּתַב רַחֲמָנָא "עָרֵל" מִשּׁוּם דְּמָאִיס, אֲבָל בֶּן נֵכָר דְּלָא מָאִיס, אֵימָא לָא, וְאִי כָּתַב רַחֲמָנָא "כׇּל בֶּן נֵכָר" מִשּׁוּם דְּאֵין לִבּוֹ לַשָּׁמַיִם, אֲבָל עָרֵל, דְּלִבּוֹ לַשָּׁמַיִם, אֵימָא לָא, צְרִיכָא.

The Gemara continues: **And it was necessary** for the Torah **to write** the prohibition with regard to **an uncircumcised** man, **and it was necessary** for the Torah **to write** a separate prohibition with regard to **any stranger. As, if the Merciful One had written** only about **an uncircumcised** man, one might have thought that only for him is it prohibited to eat from the Paschal lamb **because** the foreskin **is repulsive, but** with regard to **a stranger,** who **is not repulsive, say** that it is **not** prohibited. **And if the Merciful One had written** only about **any stranger,** one might have concluded that only for him is it prohibited to eat from the Paschal lamb **because his heart is not** directed **toward Heaven** due to his apostasy, **but** with regard to **an uncircumcised** man, **whose heart is** directed **toward Heaven,** and it is only on account of unavoidable circumstances that he has not undergone circumcision, **say** that there is **no** prohibition against his eating the Paschal lamb. Therefore, **it is necessary** to teach both cases.

HALAKHA

Apostasy disqualifies – מְשׁוּמָּדוּת פּוֹסֶלֶת: One who feeds an olive-bulk of the Paschal lamb to an apostate guilty of idolatry has transgressed a negative mitzva (Rambam *Sefer Korbanot, Hilkhot Korban Pesaḥ* 9:7).

He eats *matza* – אוֹכֵל הוּא בְּמַצָּה: An uncircumcised man is obligated to eat *matza* and bitter herbs on Passover (Rambam *Sefer Korbanot, Hilkhot Korban Pesaḥ* 9:8).

NOTES

But apostasy does not disqualify one from eating tithe – וְאֵין מְשׁוּמָּדוּת פּוֹסֶלֶת בְּמַעֲשֵׂר: *Tosafot* state that apostasy does not disqualify a priest from eating *teruma* either, and they explain how both *halakhot* can be derived from the same exclusion. However, Rashba, who apparently had a different reading of the Gemara in *Pesaḥim*, maintains that apostasy does disqualify a priest from eating *teruma*. Since there is a verbal analogy between the Paschal lamb and *teruma*, they are equated in every possible manner.

No uncircumcised person – כׇּל עָרֵל: One issue concerning the prohibition against gentiles eating from the Paschal lamb is the question: To whom does the prohibition apply? If one claims that it applies to Jews in that they may not feed gentiles from the offering, there is no need for a special teaching with regard to a circumcised Arab, as this prohibition itself is a novelty. For this reason some commentaries say that the prohibition applies to the gentile himself. *Tosefot HaRosh* points out that it is unusual for the Torah to state a special *halakha* that applies only to gentiles and not to Jews.

LANGUAGE

Apostasy [*meshumadut*] – מְשׁוּמָּדוּת: There are various opinions as to the etymology of this word. Some understand the original meaning of the word as connected to the root *sh-m-d*, in the sense of a decree enacted against the Jews that they must change their religion. Therefore, the primary sense of the word *meshumad* is: One who was forced to convert to another religion. Rav Hai Gaon argues that the word is derived from the ancient Aramaic *amad*, meaning immersed, and a *meshumad*, the abbreviated form of *meshuamad*, is one who has been baptized. From here the word was taken to mean anyone who converted to another religion. The Ramban, however, suggests that the word is a shortened form of *meshumada*, from the Aramaic *eshtamoda*, meaning alienate. Therefore, a *meshumad* is anyone alienated from his religion. Others are of the opinion that the term is derived from the word *shemad* in the sense of excision, close in meaning to the root *sh-m-t*, meaning: Place under a ban. According to this opinion, *meshumad* means one who is cursed and cut off from the Jewish people.

״מִמֶּנּוּ״ ״מִמֶּנּוּ״ לָמָּה לִי? לְכִדְרַבָּה אָמַר רַבִּי יִצְחָק.

The Gemara asks: With regard to the phrase **"of it"** in the verse "Do not eat of it raw, nor boiled in water, but roasted in fire" (Exodus 12:9), and the phrase **"of it"** in the verse "And you shall let nothing of it remain until the morning" (Exodus 12:10), both of which are terms of exclusion, **why do I need them?** The Gemara answers that they are necessary **for that which Rabba said** that **Rabbi Yitzḥak said,** as will be explained later (74a).[N]

אָמַר מָר, רַבִּי עֲקִיבָא אוֹמֵר: אֵינוֹ צָרִיךְ, הֲרֵי הוּא אוֹמֵר ״אִישׁ אִישׁ״ לְרַבּוֹת אֶת הֶעָרֵל. וְאֵימָא לְרַבּוֹת אֶת הָאוֹנֵן! אָמַר רַבִּי יוֹסֵי בְּרַבִּי חֲנִינָא: אָמַר קְרָא ״וְכָל זָר״ זָרוּת אָמַרְתִּי לְךָ וְלֹא אֲנִינוּת.

The Master said above in the *baraita*: **Rabbi Akiva says** that it **is not necessary** to derive by way of a verbal analogy the *halakha* that an uncircumcised priest may not eat *teruma*, **as the verse says:** "**Any man** [*ish ish*] from the seed of Aaron who is a leper or a *zav* shall not eat of the holy things" (Leviticus 22:4). The repetition of the word *ish* comes **to include an uncircumcised** man and indicate that he too may not partake of consecrated food. The Gemara asks: **But say** that the verse comes **to include an acute mourner**[N] in the prohibition against eating *teruma*. **Rabbi Yosei, son of Rabbi Ḥanina, said: The verse states: "No foreigner** may eat of the holy thing" (Leviticus 22:10), which indicates: A disqualification stemming from **foreignness I told you** prevents one from eating *teruma*, **but not** a disqualification based on **acute mourning.**

אֵימָא: וְלֹא עֲרֵלוּת! הָא כְּתִיב ״אִישׁ אִישׁ״.

The Gemara asks: **Say** that the verse comes to teach that a disqualification stemming from foreignness prevents one from eating *teruma*, **but not** a disqualification based on the priest's **lack of circumcision,** and so it should be permitted for an uncircumcised priest to partake of *teruma*. The Gemara answers: **Isn't it written: "Any man** [*ish ish*]," where the repetition of the word *ish* comes to include an uncircumcised priest in the prohibition?

וּמָה רָאִיתָ? מִסְתַּבְּרָא, עֲרֵלוּת הֲוָה לֵיהּ לְרַבּוֹיֵי, שֶׁכֵּן מעשי״ם כרותי״ם בדב״ר העב״ד: מְחוּסַּר מַעֲשֶׂה, וּמַעֲשֶׂה בְּגוּפוֹ, וְעָנוּשׁ כָּרֵת, וְיֶשְׁנוֹ לִפְנֵי הַדִּבּוּר, וּמִילַת זְכָרָיו וַעֲבָדָיו מְעַכֶּבֶת.

The Gemara asks: **And what did you see** that led you to include an uncircumcised priest in the prohibition against eating *teruma* and exclude an acute mourner? The Gemara answers: **It stands to reason** that **lack of circumcision should be included** and should preclude a priest's eating *teruma*, as the *halakhot* governing an uncircumcised man are stringent in several respects, as alluded to by the following mnemonic of key words: **Acts; *karetim*; the** divine **word; the slave.** The Gemara explains: An uncircumcised man **lacks** the **act** of circumcision, **and** this **act** is performed **on his body;** the failure to perform circumcision is **punishable by *karet*;** circumcision **existed before the** divine **word** was spoken at Mount Sinai, as the mitzva of circumcision had already been given to Abraham; **and the** lack of **circumcision of one's male** children **and slaves precludes** one's eating the Paschal lamb.

אַדְּרַבָּה, אֲנִינוּת הֲוָה לֵיהּ לְרַבּוֹיֵי, שֶׁכֵּן יֶשְׁנָהּ בְּכָל שָׁעָה, וְנוֹהֶגֶת בַּאֲנָשִׁים וְנָשִׁים, וְאֵין בְּיָדוֹ לְתַקֵּן עַצְמוֹ.

The Gemara counters: **On the contrary, acute mourning should be included** and it should prevent a priest from eating *teruma*, **as** acute mourning **is** relevant **at any time, it applies to** both **men and women, and it is not in** the mourner's **power to render himself fit** until after the deceased is buried.

הָנָךְ נְפִישָׁן. רָבָא אָמַר: בְּלֹא הָנָךְ נְפִישָׁן נַמִי לָא מָצֵית אָמְרַתְּ, אָמַר קְרָא ״אִישׁ אִישׁ״, אֵיזֶהוּ דָּבָר שֶׁיֶּשְׁנוֹ בְּאִישׁ וְאֵינוֹ בְּאִשָּׁה – הֱוֵי אוֹמֵר: זֶה עֲרֵלוּת.

The Gemara answers: **These** arguments for including an uncircumcised priest in the prohibition **are** more **numerous. Rava said:** Even **without** the rationale that **these** arguments **are more numerous, you still cannot say** that an acute mourner should be included and an uncircumcised priest should be excluded, as **the verse states: "Any man** [*ish ish*]," emphasizing maleness. Now, **what matter applies to a man and not to a woman? You must say** that **it is lack of circumcision,** and therefore it cannot be that the phrase comes to include acute mourning in the prohibition.

וְרַבִּי עֲקִיבָא, הַאי ״תּוֹשָׁב וְשָׂכִיר״ מַאי עָבֵיד לֵיהּ? אָמַר רַב שְׁמַעְיָא: לְאֵתוֹיֵי עֲרָבִי מָהוּל וְגִבְעוֹנִי מָהוּל.

The Gemara asks: **And what does Rabbi Akiva do with this** phrase: **"A sojourner and a hired servant,"** as it is not needed for the Paschal lamb? **Rav Shemaya said:** It serves **to include a circumcised Arab**[N] **and a circumcised Gibeonite**[B] in the prohibition against the eating of the Paschal lamb. Although they have been circumcised, it is prohibited for them to partake of the offering.

NOTES

Rabba said that Rabbi Yitzḥak said – רַבָּה אָמַר רַבִּי יִצְחָק: On 74a the statement is that of Rava, citing Rabbi Yitzḥak. Rabba and Rava are actually the same name; they are spelled slightly differently in order to distinguish between two very important *amora'im*: Rabba bar Naḥmani and his student, Rava, the son of Rav Yosef bar Ḥama. Despite this convention, the names are often confused, both in manuscripts and in printed editions of the Talmud.

An acute mourner – אוֹנֵן: The *halakhot* of acute mourning are derived from the verses describing Aaron on the day his sons died. The verse "Behold, this day have they offered their sin-offering" (Leviticus 10:19), teaches that by Torah law, the period of acute mourning applies only on the day of death (Rabbeinu Yehonatan). The Gemara further derives from the verse "And its end as a bitter day" (Amos 8:10), that the *halakhot* of acute mourning apply for the entire day, but only during the day. The extension of the *halakhot* of acute mourning to the night following the first day is by rabbinic decree. Although the mourning rites continue into the following seven- and then thirty-day periods, only the period of acute mourning involves prohibitions related to the Temple and offerings.

To include a circumcised Arab – לְאֵתוֹיֵי עֲרָבִי מָהוּל: If this Arab is a gentile, how is he better than a "stranger," an apostate Jew? The early authorities suggest that it might have been argued that although the stranger was originally a Jew, since he renounced and abandoned his religion he may be lower in status than a gentile (Ramban; Rashba). The *Halakhot Gedolot* explains that this is referring to an Arab who converted but there was as yet no dripping of covenantal blood, the procedure used in the case of a convert who converted when already circumcised (see Meiri).

BACKGROUND

Gibeonite – גִּבְעוֹנִי: The Gibeonites mentioned here are apparently not the Gibeonites mentioned in the Bible. The *Arukh* and others read: Gavnoni, which Rabbeinu Ḥananel understands as a reference to the Gavnonim, meaning: The nation that lives in the mountains, from the word *giva*, meaning mountain. According to some commentaries, they live in the mountains on the east bank of the Jordan, while others propose that they are members of a nation that lived in the Gubia district in the mountains south of Caucasia. According to Rashi, it is the name of a talmudic-era nation that practiced circumcision.

וְהָנֵי מוּלִין נִינְהוּ?! וְהָא תְּנַן: ״קוֹנָם שֶׁאֲנִי נֶהֱנֶה לַעֲרֵלִים״ מוּתָּר בְּעַרְלֵי יִשְׂרָאֵל, וְאָסוּר בְּמוּלֵי אוּמּוֹת הָעוֹלָם. ״קוֹנָם שֶׁאֲנִי נֶהֱנֶה לְמוּלִין״ מוּתָּר בְּמוּלֵי אוּמּוֹת הָעוֹלָם, וְאָסוּר בְּעַרְלֵי יִשְׂרָאֵל.

The Gemara poses a question: **And are these** considered **circumcised? But didn't we learn** in a mishna (*Nedarim* 31b): If one vowed: **The benefit that I** might gain **from the uncircumcised is *konam***[N] to me,[H] i.e., forbidden to me like consecrated property, then it **is permitted** for him to derive benefit **from uncircumcised Jews, and it is prohibited** for him to derive benefit **from the circumcised of the nations of the world,** as gentiles are considered uncircumcised even if they have their foreskins removed. And conversely, if he vowed: **The benefit that I** might gain **from the circumcised is *konam*** to me,[H] it is **permitted** for him to derive benefit **from the circumcised of the nations of the world,** as they are not considered circumcised, **and it is prohibited** for him to derive benefit **from uncircumcised Jews.** This indicates that the circumcision of gentiles is disregarded.

אֶלָּא, לְאַתּוּיֵי גֵּר שֶׁמָּל וְלֹא טָבַל, וְקָטָן שֶׁנּוֹלַד כְּשֶׁהוּא מָהוּל, וְקָסָבַר: צָרִיךְ לְהַטִּיף מִמֶּנּוּ דַּם בְּרִית.

Rather, the phrase "a sojourner and a hired servant" comes **to include** in the prohibition against eating of the Paschal lamb **a convert** to Judaism **who was circumcised but did not** yet **immerse**[NH] in a ritual bath, **and a child who was born circumcised,**[H] i.e., without a foreskin. Although he does not have a foreskin, he is still seen as lacking the act of circumcision. **And he,** Rabbi Akiva, **maintains that it is necessary to drip covenantal blood from him,** in lieu of circumcision, in order to usher him into the covenant of Abraham, even though he has no foreskin that can be removed.

וְרַבִּי אֱלִיעֶזֶר, לְטַעֲמֵיהּ, דְּאָמַר: גֵּר שֶׁמָּל וְלֹא טָבַל גֵּר מַעַלְיָא הוּא, וְקָסָבַר: קָטָן כְּשֶׁנּוֹלַד מָהוּל אֵין צָרִיךְ לְהַטִּיף מִמֶּנּוּ דַּם בְּרִית.

And Rabbi Eliezer, who uses the words "a sojourner and a hired servant" for a verbal analogy, conforms **to his** standard line of **reasoning, as he said: A convert who was circumcised but did not** yet **immerse is a proper convert** in every way. Therefore, the verse cannot come to exclude such an individual. **And he maintains** that in the case of **a child who was born circumcised, it is not necessary to drip covenantal blood from him.** Since he was born without a foreskin, no additional procedure is necessary.

וְרַבִּי אֱלִיעֶזֶר, הַאי ״אִישׁ אִישׁ״ מַאי עָבֵיד לֵיהּ? דִּבְּרָה תוֹרָה כִּלְשׁוֹן בְּנֵי אָדָם.

The Gemara asks: **And what does Rabbi Eliezer do with this** inclusive phrase **"any man [*ish ish*]"?** The Gemara answers: He maintains that **the Torah spoke in the language of men,** meaning that no special *halakha* is derived from this expression, as it is common biblical vernacular.

בָּעֵי רַב חָמָא בַּר עוּקְבָא: קָטָן עָרֵל, מַהוּ לְסוּכוֹ בְּשֶׁמֶן שֶׁל תְּרוּמָה? עַרְלוּת שֶׁלֹּא בִּזְמַנָּהּ מְעַכְּבָא אוֹ לָא מְעַכְּבָא?

Rav Ḥama bar Ukva raises a dilemma: With regard to **an uncircumcised child** who is less than eight days old and not yet fit for circumcision, **what is the** *halakha* with respect **to anointing him**[N] **with oil of *teruma*?**[H] The Gemara explains the two sides of the question: Does **lack of circumcision not at its** appointed **time,**[N] meaning before the obligation of circumcision goes into effect, **preclude** the infant's benefiting from *teruma*, as he has the status of an one who is uncircumcised, **or** perhaps **it does not preclude** his benefiting from *teruma*, as he is not considered uncircumcised until the mitzva of circumcision is applicable?

NOTES

Konam – קוֹנָם: A *konam* is a type of vow, the *halakhot* of which are explained at length in tractate *Nedarim*. The word *konam* refers to an offering; one renders an item prohibited to himself as though it were an offering. One of the basic principles of a *konam* is that it cannot apply to an action or an abstract state, but only to an object the likes of which can be consecrated. Therefore, the phrase: The benefit is *konam* to me, in essence means: I shall be prohibited by a *konam* from deriving benefit (see *Tosafot*).

To include a convert who was circumcised but did not yet immerse – לְאַתּוּיֵי גֵּר שֶׁמָּל וְלֹא טָבַל: The early authorities are puzzled as to why a special verse is required for this *halakha*. Since a convert who was circumcised but did not yet immerse is not a Jew, he certainly may not partake of the Paschal lamb, like any other gentile. They explain that once he has undergone circumcision for the purpose of conversion, he is no longer classified as a gentile, and since his heart is directed toward Heaven and he is not uncircumcised, one might have thought that he may eat of the Paschal lamb (Ramban; Rashba).

What is the *halakha* with respect to anointing him – מַהוּ לְסוּכוֹ: The later authorities discuss which prohibition might be violated by this anointment. One explanation is that while the child himself is not obligated in mitzvot, an adult may not act in a manner that will cause the boy to benefit from a prohibition. According to this opinion, it is prohibited for an adult to feed a minor non-kosher food, despite the fact that the latter is not obligated in mitzvot (*Arukh LaNer*). Others maintain that there is no such prohibition; rather, the question here relates to the loss of *teruma* and the possible theft involved: If the child is considered uncircumcised and *teruma* oil is used on his account, the *teruma* has been misused (*Mei Neftoaḥ*).

Lack of circumcision not at its appointed time – עַרְלוּת שֶׁלֹּא בִּזְמַנָּהּ: Many early authorities are of the opinion that this question with regard to lack of circumcision not at its appointed time is left unresolved by the Gemara, as Rabbi Zeira's proof is ultimately refuted. Therefore, the ruling with regard an uncircumcised newborn is unknown (Rabbeinu Ḥananel; Rid; Rashba). Others maintain that the problem is resolved concerning uncircumcised males under one's authority, and therefore the question concerning one's own uncircumcised state may be answered as well (see Meiri and *Kesef Mishne* on the Rambam). Yet others claim that although in the Babylonian Talmud the dilemma is left unresolved, in the Jerusalem Talmud it is explained that an uncircumcised male prior to the time of obligation is not considered uncircumcised, and the Jerusalem Talmud is relied upon when it is not contradicted by the Babylonian Talmud (see *Yam shel Shlomo*). In the Jerusalem Talmud the following question is raised as well: On the eve of the eighth day, is the child considered an uncircumcised male not at its appointed time, in light of the *halakha* that circumcision is not performed at night? The Gemara there concludes that since he is considered uncircumcised on the eighth day, he has the status of an uncircumcised male the night before as well.

HALAKHA

One who vows not to benefit from the uncircumcised – הַנּוֹדֵר הֲנָאָה מֵעֲרֵלִים: It is prohibited for one who vows not to derive benefit from the uncircumcised to derive benefit from gentiles, even if they underwent circumcision, and it is permitted for him to derive benefit from Jews, even if they are uncircumcised (Rambam *Sefer Hafla'a, Hilkhot Nedarim* 9:22; *Shulḥan Arukh, Yoreh De'a* 217:41).

One who vows not to benefit from the circumcised – הַנּוֹדֵר מִן הַמּוּלִים: It is prohibited for one who vows not to derive benefit from the circumcised to derive benefit from Jews, even if they are uncircumcised, and it is permitted for him to derive benefit from gentiles, even if they underwent circumcision (Rambam *Sefer Hafla'a, Hilkhot Nedarim* 9:22; *Shulḥan Arukh, Yoreh De'a* 217:42).

A convert who was circumcised but did not yet immerse – גֵּר שֶׁמָּל וְלֹא טָבַל: If a gentile undergoing conversion was circumcised but did not yet immerse, or he immersed but was not yet circumcised, he is not a convert until he undergoes circumcision and immerses himself, in accordance with the Rabbis (Rambam *Sefer Kedusha, Hilkhot Issurei Bia* 13:6).

A child who was born circumcised – קָטָן שֶׁנּוֹלַד...מָהוּל: If a child was born without a foreskin, it is necessary to drip covenantal blood from him, as the *halakha* is ruled in accordance with the opinion of Rabbi Akiva against that of Rabbi Eliezer. Although Rav disagrees with Shmuel in tractate *Shabbat* and rules in accordance with the opinion of Rabbi Eliezer, a ruling accepted by the *Halakhot Gedolot* and *Tosafot*, nevertheless, since Rabba and Rav Yosef agree with Shmuel, the *halakha* is ruled in accordance with Shmuel's view (Vilna Gaon; Rambam *Sefer Ahava, Hilkhot Mila* 1:7; *Shulḥan Arukh, Yoreh De'a* 263:4).

An uncircumcised child with regard to *teruma* – קָטָן עָרֵל בִּתְרוּמָה: A priestly infant of less than eight days old may be anointed with *teruma* oil even though he is uncircumcised, in accordance with Rava's resolution of Rav Ḥama's dilemma (Rambam *Sefer Zera'im, Hilkhot Terumot* 11:7).

אָמַר רַבִּי זֵירָא, תָּא שְׁמַע: אֵין לִי אֶלָּא מִילַת זְכָרָיו בִּשְׁעַת עֲשִׂיָּה, וַעֲבָדָיו בִּשְׁעַת אֲכִילָה, מִנַּיִן לִיתֵּן אֶת הָאָמוּר שֶׁל זֶה בְּזֶה וְאֶת הָאָמוּר שֶׁל זֶה בְּזֶה – תַּלְמוּד לוֹמַר "אָז" "אָז" לִגְזֵירָה שָׁוָה.

Rabbi Zeira said: Come and hear a proof from the following *baraita*: **I have** derived **only** the *halakha* concerning **the circumcision of one's male** children **at the time of the preparation,**[H] i.e., the slaughter, of the Paschal lamb, as it is stated: "Let all his males be circumcised, and then let him come near and keep it" (Exodus 12:48), **and** the *halakha* concerning the circumcision of **one's slaves at the time of the eating** of the Paschal lamb, as it is stated: "But every man's servant…when you have circumcised him, then shall he eat from it" (Exodus 12:44). **From where** do I derive that it is proper **to apply** the prohibition **that was stated about this** case **to that** case, **and** the prohibition **that was said about that** case **to this** case, i.e., that the circumcision of both one's male children and one's slaves is indispensable both at the time of the preparation of the Paschal lamb and at the time of its consumption? The *tanna* answers that **the verse states** the term **"then"** with regard to male children and the term **"then"** with regard to slaves **as a verbal analogy.**

בִּשְׁלָמָא עֲבָדָיו, מַשְׁכַּחַתְּ לָהּ דְּאִיתְנְהוּ בִּשְׁעַת אֲכִילָה וְלֵיתְנְהוּ בִּשְׁעַת עֲשִׂיָּה – כְּגוֹן דִּזְבַנִינְהוּ בֵּינֵי בֵּינֵי.

The Gemara comments: **Granted,** with regard to **one's slaves you find** a case **where they are present at the time of eating but they were not present at the time of preparation; for example, if he purchased them in the meantime,** i.e., they did not belong to him when the Paschal lamb was slaughtered but he bought them immediately afterward, before it was time to eat it.

אֶלָּא זְכָרָיו דְּאִיתְנְהוּ בִּשְׁעַת אֲכִילָה וְלֵיתְנְהוּ בִּשְׁעַת עֲשִׂיָּה – הֵיכִי מַשְׁכַּחַתְּ לָהּ? לָאו דְּאִתְיְלוּד בֵּין עֲשִׂיָּה לַאֲכִילָה? שְׁמַע מִינָּהּ: עֲרֵלוּת שֶׁלֹּא בִּזְמַנָּהּ הָוְיָא עֲרֵלוּת.

However, with regard to **his male** children, **how can you find** a case **where they are present at the time of eating, but they were not present at the time of preparation?** Does it **not** involve a situation **where they were born between** the time of the Paschal lamb's **preparation** and the time of its **eating? Learn from this** that **lack of circumcision,** even **not at,** i.e., before, **its** appointed **time, is** nevertheless considered **lack of circumcision** that prevents the father from partaking of the offering.

אֲמַר רָבָא: וְתִסְבְּרָא? "הִמּוֹל לוֹ כָל זָכָר" אָמַר רַחֲמָנָא "וְאָז יִקְרַב לַעֲשׂוֹתוֹ", וְהַאי לָאו בַּר מְהִילָא הוּא! אֶלָּא, הָכָא בְּמַאי עָסְקִינַן – כְּגוֹן שֶׁחֲלָצַתּוּ חַמָּה.

Rava said: And how can **you understand** it that way? How can you think that the lack of circumcision of a newborn child precludes his father's eating from the Paschal lamb? Doesn't **the Merciful One state: "Let all his males be circumcised,"** followed by **"and then let him come near and keep it"** (Exodus 12:48), **and** as **this** infant **is not** yet **fit for circumcision** he cannot possibly preclude the father's partaking of the offering? **Rather, with what** case **are we dealing here?** With the case, **for example,** of a baby who was exempt from circumcision at the time of the preparation of the Paschal lamb because he was sick with a high fever, and subsequently **the fever left him** and he recovered. In such a case, failure to immediately circumcise his son precludes the father's eating from the Paschal lamb.

וְנֵיתוּב לֵיהּ כָּל שִׁבְעָה, דְּאָמַר שְׁמוּאֵל: חֲלָצַתּוּ חַמָּה נוֹתְנִין לוֹ כָּל שִׁבְעָה! דִּיהָבִינַן לֵיהּ כָּל שִׁבְעָה. וְנִימְהֲלֵיהּ מִצַּפְרָא! בָּעֵינַן

The Gemara raises a difficulty: If the case is one of a child recovering from an illness, **let us give him the full seven** days that he needs to recuperate properly. **As Shmuel said:** In the case of a baby that was sick with a high fever, and subsequently **the fever left him,**[H] **one gives him a full seven days** to heal and only then is he circumcised, but not before. The Gemara answers: The case is in fact one where **we** already **gave him a full seven** days to heal, but they culminated on the eve of Passover. The Gemara asks: **But** if the seven-day recovery period ended on the eve of Passover, why did the father wait until the time of eating the Paschal lamb, i.e., the first night of Passover? **He should have circumcised him** already **in the morning,** before the time of the preparation of the Paschal lamb. The Gemara answers: **We require**

HALAKHA

The circumcision of one's male children at the time of the preparation – מִילַת זְכָרָיו בִּשְׁעַת עֲשִׂיָּה: The circumcision of one's male children and slaves is an indispensable requirement both at the time of the preparation of the Paschal lamb and at the time of its consumption. Therefore, if one acquired a slave after the Paschal lamb was slaughtered, or if the obligation to circumcise his son began only after it was slaughtered, e.g., if the infant recovered from illness seven days beforehand, and he did not circumcise the slave or infant, it is prohibited for him to eat the Paschal lamb (Rambam *Sefer Korbanot, Hilkhot Korban Pesaḥ* 9:9).

The fever left him – חֲלָצַתּוּ חַמָּה: As long as a child is ill, he is not circumcised. After he recuperates, he is given a full seven days, and only then does he undergo circumcision. This *halakha* applies only to a sickness that took hold of his entire body, but if he was experiencing minor and localized pains, e.g., in his eyes, he is circumcised immediately upon his recovery. The *halakha* is ruled in accordance with the opinion of Shmuel, Rabba, and Rav Pappa. The Rema notes that severe pain in the eyes is treated like a sickness of the whole body (Rambam *Sefer Ahava, Hilkhot Mila* 1:16; *Shulḥan Arukh, Yoreh De'a* 262:2).

מֵעֵת לְעֵת.

that during the recovery period one must wait **from** the **time** the seven days began **to** the exact same **time** seven days later, i.e., seven complete twenty-four-hour periods. Therefore, if the child recovered in the afternoon of a particular day, one is required to wait until that same time of day a week later, and only then is he circumcised.

וְהָתְנֵי לוּדָאָה: יוֹם הַבְרָאָתוֹ כְּיוֹם הוּלַּדְתּוֹ, מַאי לָאו, מָה יוֹם הוּלַּדְתּוֹ לָא בָּעֵינַן מֵעֵת לְעֵת אַף יוֹם הַבְרָאָתוֹ לָא בָּעֵינַן מֵעֵת לְעֵת!

The Gemara asks: **Didn't** the Sage **from Lod teach** that **the day of his healing is like the day of his birth? What, is it not** that **just as** with regard to **the day of his birth we need not** wait **from** the **time** he is born **to** the same **time** on the eighth day to circumcise him, **so too,** with regard to **the day of his healing we need not** wait **from** the **time** he heals **to** the same **time** seven days later?

לֹא, עָדִיף יוֹם הַבְרָאָתוֹ מִיּוֹם הוּלַּדְתּוֹ. דְּאִילּוּ יוֹם הוּלַּדְתּוֹ לָא בָּעֵינַן מֵעֵת לְעֵת, וְאִילּוּ יוֹם הַבְרָאָתוֹ – בָּעֵינַן מֵעֵת לְעֵת.

The Gemara refutes this argument: **No, the day of his healing is superior to the day of his birth: While** from **the day of his birth** until circumcision **we need not** wait **from** the **time** he is born **to** the same **time** on the eighth day to circumcise him, i.e., the child may be circumcised already at the start of the eighth day, from **the day of his healing we need** to wait seven complete days **from** the **time** he heals **to** the same **time** seven days later.

רַב פָּפָּא אָמַר: כְּגוֹן דִּכְאִיב לֵיהּ עֵינֵיהּ לְיָנוֹקָא, וְאִיתְפַּח בֵּינֵי וּבֵינֵי.

The Gemara suggests other circumstances where a male child may be present at the time of the eating of the Paschal lamb but absent at the time of its preparation. **Rav Pappa said:** This would take place, **for example, if the baby's eye hurt him**[N] on the eighth day following his birth, which occurred on the eve of Passover, **and he recovered in the meantime** between the time of the preparation of the Paschal lamb and the time of its eating. In the case of a minor ailment such as eye pain, circumcision is not performed as long as the pain persists, but it may be performed as soon as the child has recovered, without first waiting seven days.

רָבָא אָמַר: כְּגוֹן שֶׁהָיוּ אָבִיו וְאִמּוֹ חֲבוּשִׁין בְּבֵית הָאֲסוּרִין.

Rava said: This would occur, **for example, if** the infant's **father and mother were incarcerated in a prison** at the time of the preparation of the Paschal lamb, and they slaughtered their offering by way of an agent, and there was no one available to circumcise the infant, and the parents were released from prison before the time for eating the Paschal lamb arrived.

רַב כָּהֲנָא בְּרֵיהּ דְּרַב נְחֶמְיָה אָמַר: כְּגוֹן טוּמְטוּם, שֶׁנִּקְרַע וְנִמְצָא זָכָר בֵּינֵי וּבֵינֵי.

Rav Kahana, son of Rav Neḥemya, said: This would occur, **for example,** if the infant was **a *tumtum*,**[B] one whose external sexual organs are indeterminate and it is unclear whether the infant is male or female, and **in the meantime** between the time of the preparation of the Paschal lamb and the time of its eating, **he was torn** open, his gender was revealed, **and he was found** to be **a male,** so that the obligation to circumcise him went into effect.

רַב שֵׁרֵבְיָא אָמַר: כְּגוֹן שֶׁהוֹצִיא רֹאשׁוֹ חוּץ לַפְּרוֹזְדוֹר.

Rav Sherevya said: This would occur, **for example, if** seven days earlier the baby had already **extended his head,** but not the rest of his body, **out of the corridor**[L] to his mother's womb. In such a situation he is considered born, but he is fit for circumcision only after his entire body has emerged. If this occurs between the time of the preparation of the Paschal lamb and the time of its eating, the child's father may not eat of the offering until he has circumcised his son.

וּמִי חָיֵי? וְהָתַנְיָא: כֵּיוָן שֶׁיָּצָא לַאֲוִיר הָעוֹלָם נִפְתַּח הַסָּתוּם וְנִסְתַּם הַפָּתוּחַ, שֶׁאִלְמָלֵא כֵּן אֵין יָכוֹל לִחְיוֹת אֲפִילּוּ שָׁעָה אַחַת!

The Gemara poses a question: **But** in a case such as this, **can** the child **live** for such a long period with only his head outside? **Isn't it taught** in a *baraita*: **Once** a baby **emerges into the air of the world,** that which had been **closed,** the mouth and nostrils, **open, and** that which had been **open,** the umbilical cord, from which the child had previously received its sustenance, **closes, as, if this** did **not** occur **it could not live for even an hour,** as it has no other way to receive nutrition. If so, this child whose head alone emerged from his mother's womb would certainly starve, as it cannot take in any sustenance.

NOTES

For example, if the baby's eye hurt him – כְּגוֹן דִּכְאִיב לֵיהּ עֵינֵיהּ לְיָנוֹקָא: The Rashba and others explain that this *halakha* was not stated specifically with respect to discomfort in the eye, even though it is recorded that the Sages were especially concerned about eye pain. Rather, if the baby suffers from pain of any kind, his circumcision is delayed until he recovers. A similar interpretation is attributed to the *ge'onim*.

BACKGROUND

Tumtum – טוּמְטוּם: A *tumtum* is one whose external sexual organs are indeterminate, and it is unclear whether the individual is male or female. In certain cases the gender of a *tumtum* can be established through a surgical procedure in which the genitals are exposed. Once the gender of the *tumtum* is revealed, he or she is considered a full-fledged member of that gender.

LANGUAGE

Corridor [*prozdor*] – פְּרוֹזְדוֹר: Many maintain that the proper spelling of this word is *prozdod*. In any event, the word is derived from the Greek, apparently from the word πρόστας, *prostas*, meaning entrance room or gatehouse. This word is used by the Sages in reference to certain structures, and also euphemistically for a woman's vagina and labia.

הָכָא בְּמַאי עָסְקִינַן – כְּגוֹן דְּזָנְתֵיהּ אִישְׁתָּא. אִישְׁתָּא דְּמַאן? אִילֵימָא אִישְׁתָּא דִּידֵיהּ – אִי הָכִי כָּל שִׁבְעָה בָּעֵי, אֶלָּא דְּזָנְתֵיהּ אִישְׁתָּא דְּאִימֵּיהּ. וְאִיבָּעֵית אֵימָא: הָנֵי מִילֵּי – הֵיכָא דְּלָא מְעַוֵּי, אֲבָל הֵיכָא דִּמְעַוֵּי – מִחְיָא חַיֵּי.

The Gemara answers: **With what** case **are we dealing here?** It is, **for example,** a case **where he was sustained by** the heat of a **fever**[B] and therefore did not need to eat. The Gemara asks: **Whose fever? If we say** it is **his own fever,** i.e., the baby himself had a fever, **if so,** it should be **necessary** to wait **a full seven** days after his entire body exits the womb before he can be circumcised, in accordance with the *halakha* governing an infant who was ill. **Rather,** it must be **that he was sustained by his mother's fever. And if you wish, say** that **this** principle that a child cannot survive in such conditions **applies only when he does not cry,**[N] **but when he cries he** can **live,** as his crying indicates that he has already started to breathe.

אָמַר רַבִּי יוֹחָנָן מִשּׁוּם רַבִּי בְּנָאָה: עָרֵל מְקַבֵּל הֲזָאָה, שֶׁכֵּן מָצִינוּ בַּאֲבוֹתֵינוּ שֶׁקִּבְּלוּ הֲזָאָה כְּשֶׁהֵן עֲרֵלִים, שֶׁנֶּאֱמַר "וְהָעָם עָלוּ מִן הַיַּרְדֵּן בֶּעָשׂוֹר לַחֹדֶשׁ הָרִאשׁוֹן".

§ **Rabbi Yoḥanan said in the name of Rabbi Bena'a: An uncircumcised** man **may receive** the **sprinkling**[HN] of the water mixed with the ashes of a red heifer in order to purify himself from ritual impurity imparted by a human corpse, as we do not say that this sprinkling is ineffective as long as he is uncircumcised. **As we found that our forefathers received** the **sprinkling when they were uncircumcised, as it is stated: "And the people came up**[N] **out of the Jordan on the tenth day of the first month"** (Joshua 4:19), and the verses go on to relate that the men were all later circumcised before sacrificing the Paschal lamb on the fourteenth (see Joshua 5:10).

בַּעֲשָׂרָה לָא מְהִילִי מִשּׁוּם חוּלְשָׁא דְּאוֹרְחָא, הֲזָאָה אֵימַת עָבֵיד לְהוּ לָאו כְּשֶׁהֵן עֲרֵלִים?!

The Gemara clarifies: **On the tenth** day itself **they did not circumcise** themselves **due to the weariness** caused by **their journey. When,** then, **was the sprinkling done to them** in order to remove the ritual impurity resulting from contact with a corpse, so that they would be fit to bring the Paschal lamb on the fourteenth? The first sprinkling must have taken place no later than the tenth, as there is a four-day waiting period between the first and second sprinklings. In that case, **wasn't** the initial sprinkling performed **when they were** still **uncircumcised?** This proves that an one who is uncircumcised may receive the sprinkling of the purification waters.

וְדִלְמָא לָא עֲבוּד פֶּסַח כְּלָל? לָא סָלְקָא דַּעְתָּךְ, דִּכְתִיב "וַיַּעֲשׂוּ אֶת הַפֶּסַח".

The Gemara counters: **But perhaps they did not sacrifice** the **Paschal lamb at all.**[N] The Gemara answers: **This cannot enter your mind, as it is written: "And they kept the Passover"** (Joshua 5:10), meaning they brought the Paschal lamb.

מַתְקִיף לַהּ מָר זוּטְרָא: וְדִלְמָא פֶּסַח הַבָּא בְּטוּמְאָה הָיָה! אָמַר לֵיהּ רַב אַשִׁי: תַּנְיָא בְּהֶדְיָא, מָלוּ וְטָבְלוּ וְעָשׂוּ פִּסְחֵיהֶן בְּטָהֳרָה.

Mar Zutra strongly objects to this: But perhaps it was a Paschal lamb that comes in a state of **impurity?** If the majority of the community is ritually impure due to contact with a corpse, they may all sacrifice their Paschal lambs even though they are ritually impure, and there is no need for any sprinkling. **Rav Ashi said to him: It is taught explicitly** in a *baraita* that **they circumcised** themselves, **immersed** in a ritual bath, **and performed** the ritual of **their Paschal lambs in** a state of **purity.**

BACKGROUND

He was sustained by a fever – דְּזָנְתֵיהּ אִישְׁתָּא: One who does not consume any food receives his nourishment through the breakdown of fatty tissue in his body. If he has a fever, this process of fat breakdown is accelerated. Therefore, it can maintain an individual for only a short period of time, as the more rapid loss of body fluids can be fatal.

HALAKHA

An uncircumcised man may receive the sprinkling – עָרֵל מְקַבֵּל הֲזָאָה: If an uncircumcised man contracted ritual impurity from contact with a corpse, and purifying water was sprinkled upon him on the third and seventh days, he is purified from this impurity. After he is circumcised, he must immerse himself, and then he may eat sacrificial foods in the evening, in accordance with the opinion of Rabbi Bena'a (Rambam *Sefer Tahara, Hilkhot Para Aduma* 11:3).

NOTES

When he does not cry [*me'avei*] – דְּלָא מְעַוֵּי: Rabbeinu Ḥananel reads this as *ma'arei*, which is apparently the reading of *Tosafot* as well. This refers to a case where the baby is no longer mingled [*me'ureh*] and connected to his mother by the umbilical cord. However, if he is still attached to his mother, he receives his sustenance from her. The preceding phrase in the Gemara: "He was sustained by his mother's fever," indicates likewise, as he can receive nourishment from his mother only if he is still connected to her.

An uncircumcised man may receive the sprinkling – עָרֵל מְקַבֵּל הֲזָאָה: The early authorities inquire as to why one might think that an uncircumcised man is ineligible for sprinkling. They answer that according to Rabbi Akiva's opinion that one who is uncircumcised is like one who is ritually impure, one might have thought that he may not receive the sprinkling due to this impurity (*Tosafot Yeshanim*). The *Tosefot HaRosh* adds that although most impure individuals may receive the sprinkling and are thereby purified from ritual impurity contracted through contact with the dead, sprinkling is ineffective for certain types of impurity, e.g., leprosy.

As it is stated: And the people came up – שֶׁנֶּאֱמַר וְהָעָם עָלוּ: Rabbi Avraham *Av Beit Din* asks why the Gemara does not cite a more straightforward proof from the instruction given after the war against Midian: "You shall purify yourselves on the third day and on the seventh day, you and your captives" (Numbers 31:19). He answers that this proof can be refuted, as it could be argued that those who fought in that war were from the older, circumcised generation, who had themselves been part of the exodus from Egypt (*Tosefot HaRosh*). The Ramban cites the above question and answer and adds a different resolution of his own: It is possible that although Moses issued these instructions with regard to their purification, in practice they were unable to carry them out and had to wait until they were circumcised.

But perhaps they did not sacrifice the Paschal lamb at all – וְדִלְמָא לָא עֲבוּד פֶּסַח כְּלָל: The Ritva is puzzled by this suggestion, as the verse states explicitly that they did sacrifice the Paschal lamb. One answer is that the verses might be referring to the second *Pesaḥ*, but this appears unlikely. The Ritva himself states that it is possible to explain that only those who were circumcised offered the Paschal lamb, but not the rest of the people.

אָמַר רַבָּה בַּר יִצְחָק אָמַר רַב: לֹא נִיתְּנָה פְּרִיעַת מִילָה לְאַבְרָהָם אָבִינוּ, שֶׁנֶּאֱמַר: ״בָּעֵת הַהִיא אָמַר ה׳ אֶל יְהוֹשֻׁעַ עֲשֵׂה לְךָ חַרְבוֹת צֻרִים״ וגו׳.

Rabba bar Yitzḥak said that Rav said: The mitzva of **uncovering** the corona during **circumcision was not given to our Patriarch Abraham.**[N] The command given to Avraham included only the mitzva of circumcision itself, i.e., the removal of the foreskin, but not the uncovering of the corona, i.e., the folding back of the thin membrane that lies under the foreskin. **As it is stated: "At that time the Lord said to Joshua: Make yourself knives of flint,** and circumcise again the children of Israel a second time" (Joshua 5:2). Why was it necessary to circumcise them? Apparently, it is because before the Torah was given on Mount Sinai, some of them had been circumcised in the manner of Abraham, without uncovering the corona, and therefore they needed to be circumcised a second time in accordance with the Torah law that requires uncovering the corona.

וְדִלְמָא הָנָךְ דְּלָא מְהוּל, דִּכְתִיב ״כִּי מֻלִים הָיוּ כָּל הָעָם הַיֹּצְאִים וְכָל הָעָם הַיִּלֹּדִים״ וגו׳?

The Gemara asks: How may it be inferred that those who were already circumcised required a second circumcision? **Perhaps** the verse is referring to **those who had not been circumcised at all, as it is written: "For all the people who came out were circumcised; but all the people who were born** in the wilderness… had not been circumcised" (Joshua 5:5)?

אִם כֵּן, מַאי ״שׁוּב״? אֶלָּא לָאו – לִפְרִיעָה, וּמַאי ״שֵׁנִית״?

The Gemara responds: **If so,** that it was only those who had never been circumcised who required circumcision, **what is** the meaning of "circumcise **again,**" which indicates that they had to be circumcised a second time? **Rather, is it not** referring **to uncovering** the corona? **And what is** the meaning of **"a second time,"** stated in the same verse? This phrase appears redundant, as the verse already stated: "Circumcise again."

לְאַקּוּשֵׁי סוֹף מִילָה לִתְחִלַּת מִילָה, מַה תְּחִלַּת מִילָה מְעַכֶּבֶת, אַף סוֹף מִילָה מְעַכְּבִין בּוֹ. דִּתְנַן, אֵלּוּ הֵן צִיצִין הַמְעַכְּבִין אֶת הַמִּילָה: בָּשָׂר הַחוֹפֶה אֶת [רוֹב] הָעֲטָרָה, וְאֵין אוֹכֵל בִּתְרוּמָה.

The Gemara explains: It comes **to equate the end of circumcision,** when it is necessary to circumcise a second time in order to correct an improperly performed circumcision, **with the beginning of circumcision: Just as** an incomplete performance at **the beginning of circumcision invalidates** the circumcision, **so too,** incomplete performance at **the end of circumcision,** i.e., the foreskin not being fully removed, **invalidates** the circumcision. **As we learned** in a mishna (*Shabbat* 137a): **These are the shreds** of flesh **that invalidate the circumcision**[H] if they are not cut. The essential element of circumcision is the removal of **the flesh that covers most of the corona,** and a child who was not circumcised in this manner is considered uncircumcised, **and he does not partake of *teruma*.**

אָמַר רָבִינָא, וְאִיתֵּימָא רַב יִרְמְיָה בַּר אַבָּא, אָמַר רַב: בָּשָׂר הַחוֹפֶה אֶת רוֹב גּוֹבְהָהּ שֶׁל עֲטָרָה.

With regard to this issue **Ravina said, and some say** it was **Rav Yirmeya bar Abba** who said that **Rav said:** When the mishna mentioned most of the corona, it meant **the flesh that covers most of the height of the corona** as well as most of its circumference.

וּבְמִדְבָּר מַאי טַעֲמָא לָא מְהוּל? אִיבָּעֵית אֵימָא: מִשּׁוּם חוּלְשָׁא דְּאוֹרְחָא.

The Gemara returns to the incident involving Joshua. **And what is the reason** that **they did not circumcise** themselves **in the wilderness**[N] after the Torah had already been given? The Gemara answers: **If you wish, say** it was **due to the weariness** caused by **their journey.** Since they were traveling continuously, they were too weak to undergo circumcision.

HALAKHA

The shreds that invalidate the circumcision – צִיצִין הַמְעַכְּבִין אֶת הַמִּילָה: If there remains of the foreskin flesh that covers most of the height of the corona, even only in one place, the circumcision is incomplete, and it is as though the individual had not been circumcised at all. However, if the remaining flesh does not cover most of the height of the corona, the circumcision is valid. Nevertheless, all large shreds of flesh should be removed *ab initio*, even those that do not invalidate the circumcision (Rema; Rambam *Sefer Ahava*, *Hilkhot Mila* 2:3; *Shulḥan Arukh*, *Yoreh De'a* 264:5).

NOTES

Uncovering the corona during circumcision was not given to our Patriarch Abraham – לֹא נִיתְּנָה פְּרִיעַת מִילָה לְאַבְרָהָם אָבִינוּ: The early authorities ask: If the mitzva of uncovering the corona is not clearly stated in the verses concerning Abraham, how could Joshua have introduced this requirement? *Tosafot* suggest that Joshua received it as a *halakha* transmitted to Moses from Sinai. The *Halakhot Gedolot* explains that the command "circumcise again…a second time" refers to the manner in which circumcision had been performed by Moses. Moses had earlier circumcised the people in Egypt with the uncovering of the corona, as that is the fundamental *halakha*, but in the wilderness the practice had been stopped. *Tosafot* suggest a somewhat similar explanation. Another explanation is that it was Moses who instructed them to uncover the corona, but in practice they could not perform the mitzva until they arrived in Eretz Yisrael (Rashba; Ritva). In the Jerusalem Talmud it is indicated that this *halakha* is derived either from the verse: "He must surely be circumcised [*himmol yimmol*]" (Genesis 17:13), which includes both circumcision and uncovering of the corona; or from the phrase: "A bridegroom of bloods in regard to circumcision" (Exodus 4:26), the plural term "bloods" indicating that there are two stages of circumcision: The circumcision itself and uncovering the corona.

What is the reason they did not circumcise themselves in the wilderness – בְּמִדְבָּר מַאי טַעֲמָא לָא מְהוּל: The idea that circumcision was not practiced at all in the wilderness is puzzling for several reasons, as mentioned by the early authorities (see *Tosafot*). A novel opinion of the *ge'onim* is that it does not mean that the entire people did not circumcise themselves in the wilderness; rather, it is referring only to those born after Moses' passing until their entrance into Eretz Yisrael.

וְאִיבָּעֵית אֵימָא: מִשּׁוּם דְּלָא נָשֵׁיב לְהוּ רוּחַ צְפוֹנִית. דְּתַנְיָא: כָּל אוֹתָן אַרְבָּעִים שָׁנָה שֶׁהָיוּ יִשְׂרָאֵל בַּמִּדְבָּר לֹא נָשְׁבָה לָהֶם רוּחַ צְפוֹנִית.

And if you wish, say instead that it was **because** the **north wind did not blow for them,** and the hot weather was likely to lead to medical complications following the procedure. **As it is taught** in a *baraita*: **All those forty years that the Jewish people were in the wilderness,** the **north wind did not blow for them.**

מַאי טַעְמָא? אִיבָּעֵית אֵימָא: מִשּׁוּם דִּנְזוּפִים הֲווֹ, וְאִי בָּעֵית אֵימָא: דְּלָא נִבְדּוּר עֲנָנֵי כָבוֹד.

The Gemara asks: **What is the reason** that this wholesome wind did not blow all those years? **If you wish, say** it was **because they were under censure**[N] following the sin of the spies and were therefore undeserving of this salutary wind. **And if you wish, say** instead that it was so **that** the **clouds of glory** covering the Tabernacle **should not disperse.**

אָמַר רַב פַּפָּא: הִלְכָּךְ, יוֹמָא דְּעֵיבָא וְיוֹמָא דְּשׁוּתָא – לָא מְהַלִּינַן בֵּיהּ, וְלָא מְסוֹכְרִינַן בֵּיהּ. וְהָאִידָּנָא דְּדָשׁוּ בָּהּ רַבִּים – "שׁוֹמֵר פְּתָאִים ה׳".

Rav Pappa said: Therefore, learn from here that on **a cloudy day or** on **a day** that **a south wind** [*shuta*][L] blows, **we may neither circumcise nor let** blood [*mesokhrinan*],[L] owing to the danger involved. **But nowadays, when many are accustomed to** ignoring these safeguards, the verse **"The Lord preserves the simple"** (Psalms 116:6)[N] is applied, and it is assumed that they will come to no harm.

תָּנוּ רַבָּנַן: כָּל אוֹתָן אַרְבָּעִים שָׁנָה שֶׁהָיוּ יִשְׂרָאֵל בַּמִּדְבָּר לֹא הָיָה יוֹם שֶׁלֹּא נָשְׁבָה בּוֹ רוּחַ צְפוֹנִית בַּחֲצִי הַלַּיְלָה, שֶׁנֶּאֱמַר "וַיְהִי בַּחֲצִי הַלַּיְלָה וַה׳ הִכָּה כָל בְּכוֹר" וגו׳. מַאי תַּלְמוּדָא? הָא קָא מַשְׁמַע לַן דְּעֵת רָצוֹן מִילְּתָא הִיא.

The Sages taught in a *baraita*: **All those forty years that the Jewish people were in the wilderness there was not a day in which** the **north wind did not blow at midnight, as it is stated: "And it came to pass at midnight, that the Lord smote all the firstborn** in the land of Egypt" (Exodus 12:29). The Gemara asks: **What is the biblical derivation?** How is it derived from this verse that speaks of the exodus from Egypt that a north wind blew at midnight during the forty years that the Jewish people wandered in the wilderness? The Gemara answers: **This** comes to **teach us that a time of favor is a** significant **matter.**[N] Since midnight had once been a time of divine favor at the beginning of the exodus from Egypt, it continued to be a time of favor throughout the forty years that the Jewish people sojourned in the wilderness.

אָמַר רַב הוּנָא: דְּבַר תּוֹרָה מָשׁוּךְ אוֹכֵל בִּתְרוּמָה, וּמִדִּבְרֵיהֶם גָּזְרוּ עָלָיו, מִפְּנֵי שֶׁנִּרְאֶה כְּעָרֵל.

§ **Rav Huna said: By Torah law,** if one had been circumcised, but subsequently the residual foreskin was **drawn forward**[B] by itself or manually so that it covered the corona, he may **partake of *teruma*,** as he is considered circumcised. **However, from the words of the Sages, they decreed** that he must be circumcised again **because he looks** as if he were **uncircumcised.**

מֵיתִיבִי: מָשׁוּךְ צָרִיךְ שֶׁיָּמוּל! מִדְּרַבָּנַן. וּדְקָאָרֵי לַהּ מַאי קָאָרֵי לַהּ? הָא צָרִיךְ קָתָנֵי!

The Gemara **raises an objection** based on the following *baraita*: One whose residual foreskin was **drawn forward** so that it covers the corona **requires** a second **circumcision,** indicating that he is not considered circumcised. The Gemara explains: This requirement is **by rabbinic law,** and by Torah law he is considered circumcised. The Gemara asks: **And the** *amora* **who asked** this question, **why did he ask it** in the first place? The *baraita* merely **teaches** that such an individual **requires** circumcision, and does not indicate that it is a Torah obligation.

NOTES

They were under censure – נְזוּפִים הֲווֹ: Most commentaries accept the explanation of *Tosafot* that this is referring to the sin of the spies, as the Torah states that the sin involving the Golden Calf was forgiven and the Divine Presence rested upon the nation despite that transgression. Furthermore, the people sacrificed the Paschal lamb in the second year in the wilderness, after the sin of the Golden Calf (Ramban). The Meiri explains, based on Rashi, that although the sin of the Golden Calf was essentially forgiven, complete pardon and atonement were not granted. The *Otzar HaShitot* likewise cites the Gemara's teaching that every retribution visited upon the Jewish people includes some punishment for the Golden Calf, which indicates that the incident was not entirely forgiven.

The Lord preserves the simple – שׁוֹמֵר פְּתָאִים ה׳: This principle that God preserves the simple applies only to an action that presents not a clear danger but merely a possible concern. In such a case one may rely on the fact that God will not allow many individuals to come to harm. The Ritva, however, cites a view that if despite this teaching one is worried and does not wish to rely on it, it is permitted for him to refrain from circumcision. The Ran cites a similar opinion (see *Yam shel Shlomo*).

That a time of favor is a significant matter – דְּעֵת רָצוֹן מִילְּתָא הִיא: The question still remains: What proof does this verse provide with regard to the northern wind? The Riaf explains that it is natural for the northern wind to blow at midnight. The fact that this wind continued unabated even during the plague of the firstborn, which was an hour of retribution, indicates that this time of goodwill will never cease.

LANGUAGE

South wind [*shuta*] – שׁוּתָא: According to Rashi, a *shuta* is a southerly wind, but the *Arukh* maintains that it is an easterly wind. Some see the word as an abridged form of *shuḥta*, meaning a destructive [*mashḥita*] wind, with the guttural *ḥ* sound swallowed. This accords with the understanding of the *Arukh*, as in many places the eastern wind blows in the form of a hot blast coming in from the desert.

Let blood [*mesokhrinan*] – מְסוֹכְרִינַן: The *Arukh* reads this as *mesovrinan*, whose root is connected to the Arabic سبر, *sabar*, meaning a special knife. The word is used here to indicate a knife used for bloodletting.

Bloodletting depicted on an ancient Greek urn

BACKGROUND

A foreskin that was drawn forward – מָשׁוּךְ: After a child is properly circumcised and the shreds of foreskin that disqualify the circumcision are removed, he remains circumcised. However, during certain periods there were those who wished to hide the fact that they had been circumcised, drawing forward the skin of the penis to create the appearance of a foreskin. Even if this extension lasted for a period of time, one could later restore himself to his former state, provided that he did so in such a way so as not to cause a wound or infection that might endanger his chances of fathering children.

קְטָעֵי בְּסֵיפָא: רַבִּי יְהוּדָה אוֹמֵר: לֹא יִמּוֹל, מִפְּנֵי שֶׁסַּכָּנָה הִיא לוֹ. אָמְרוּ לוֹ: וַהֲלֹא הַרְבֵּה מָלוּ בִּימֵי בֶּן כּוֹזִיבָא וְהוֹלִידוּ בָּנִים וּבָנוֹת, שֶׁנֶּאֱמַר ״הִמּוֹל יִמּוֹל״ אֲפִילּוּ מֵאָה פְּעָמִים, וְאוֹמֵר ״אֶת בְּרִיתִי הֵפַר״ לְרַבּוֹת אֶת הַמָּשׁוּךְ.

The Gemara explains: The *amora* who raised the question **erred due to the latter clause**[N] of that same *baraita*, which states: **Rabbi Yehuda says: He should not be circumcised because it would be dangerous for him** to do so. His colleagues **said to him: But weren't** there **many** who had drawn their residual foreskins forward and subsequently **were circumcised** a second time **in the days of ben Koziva,**[B] otherwise known as bar Kokheva, **and they fathered sons and daughters.** Such re-circumcision is necessary, **as it is stated: "He must surely be circumcised** [*himmol yimmol*]" (Genesis 17:13), the double verb form indicating: **Even one hundred times. And** furthermore, **it says: "He has broken My covenant"** (Genesis 17:14), which comes **to include one** whose foreskin was **drawn forward.**

מַאי ״וְאוֹמֵר״? וְכִי תֵּימָא, הַאי ״הִמּוֹל יִמּוֹל״ לְרַבּוֹת צִיצִין הַמְעַכְּבִים אֶת הַמִּילָה, תָּא שְׁמַע: ״אֶת בְּרִיתִי הֵפַר״ לְרַבּוֹת אֶת הַמָּשׁוּךְ.

The Gemara comments: **What is** the meaning of: **And** furthermore, **it says?** Why was it necessary to cite two verses in support of the same *halakha*? The Gemara answers: The additional verse is necessary, **lest you say** that **this** first verse: **"He shall surely be circumcised,"** comes only **to include the shreds** of flesh **that invalidate the circumcision** if they are not cut and to indicate that they must be removed. If so, **come** and **hear** a second verse: **"He has broken My covenant,"** which comes **to include one** whose foreskin was **drawn forward.**

הוּא סָבַר: מִדְּקָא נָסֵיב לָהּ תַּלְמוּדָא קְרָא דְּאוֹרַיְיתָא הִיא, וְלָא הִיא, מִדְּרַבָּנַן, וּקְרָא אַסְמַכְתָּא בְּעָלְמָא.

Now **he,** the *amora* who raised an objection based on the first part of the *baraita*, **thought** that **since** at the end of the *baraita* the *tanna* **brings a derivation** from **a verse,** this *halakha* must be **by Torah law. But** in fact **that is not so.** It is only **by rabbinic law, and the verse** quoted is **a mere support** but not the source of the *halakha*.

מֵיתִיבֵי: טוּמְטוּם אֵין אוֹכֵל בִּתְרוּמָה, נָשָׁיו וַעֲבָדָיו אוֹכְלִין. מָשׁוּךְ, וְנוֹלַד כְּשֶׁהוּא מָהוּל, הֲרֵי אֵלּוּ אוֹכְלִים. אַנְדְּרוֹגִינוֹס אוֹכֵל בִּתְרוּמָה וְאֵין אוֹכֵל בְּקָדָשִׁים, טוּמְטוּם אֵינוֹ אוֹכֵל לֹא בִּתְרוּמָה וְלֹא בְּקָדָשִׁים.

The Gemara **raises an objection** from a different source: A priest who is a ***tumtum* may not partake of *teruma*,**[H] but **his wives and slaves may partake** of it.[H] A priest who had been circumcised, but subsequently the residual foreskin was **drawn forward, and** similarly **one who was born circumcised,**[H] i.e., without a foreskin, **may partake** of *teruma*.[H] A priest who is **a hermaphrodite** [***androginos***],[BL] possessing both male and female genitals, and was circumcised **may partake of *teruma*,**[H] as whether he is male or female he is entitled to eat *teruma*, **but he may not partake of sacrificial food,**[H] which is permitted only to male priests, as he might not be a male. A priest who is **a *tumtum* may not partake of *teruma* or sacrificial food,**[H] as he might be a male, and since his member is hidden he cannot be circumcised.

NOTES

He erred due to the latter clause – קְטָעֵי בְּסֵיפָא: If one whose foreskin was drawn forward is obligated by Torah law to undergo a second circumcision, how could Rabbi Yehuda have exempted him from this duty due to the danger? One answer is that according to this opinion, the dispute between Rabbi Yehuda and the Rabbis is precisely whether or not the second circumcision of such a man is a Torah obligation.

BACKGROUND

In the days of ben Koziva – בִּימֵי בֶּן כּוֹזִיבָא: The man who is usually referred to as bar Koziva in talmudic sources, and also known as bar Kokheva, based on the nickname given to him by Rabbi Akiva, is called in his recently discovered letters Shimon ben Kosba. His supporters changed his name to bar Kokheva based on the verse: "A star [*kokhav*] shall go forth from Jacob" (Numbers 24:17). His opponents, especially after his failed revolt, called him bar Koziva, from the word *kazav*, meaning deception.

One of the reasons for the bar Kokheva revolt was the decree issued by the emperor Hadrian in the year 130 CE banning circumcision. This decree, which apparently was not initially directed against the Jews, caused tremendous resentment. According to the Gemara here, it seems that some men succumbed to the pressure of the rulers and restored their foreskins using a device known as a *kynodesme*. Subsequently, when bar Kokheva assumed power they circumcised themselves again.

Letter found in the Judean Desert in which bar Kokheva refers to himself as ben Kosba

A *tumtum* and a hermaphrodite – טוּמְטוּם וְאַנְדְּרוֹגִינוֹס: A *tumtum* and a hermaphrodite are often discussed together, as both are neither male nor female. However, there is a fundamental difference between them: A *tumtum* is a case of unresolved uncertainty, which can sometimes be resolved one way or the other. A hermaphrodite, by contrast, might be an entity in and of itself, constituting a third, unique gender.

HALAKHA

A *tumtum* may not partake of *teruma* – טוּמְטוּם אֵין אוֹכֵל בִּתְרוּמָה: A priest who is a *tumtum* may not eat *teruma*, as there is uncertainty with regard to whether he is uncircumcised (Rambam *Sefer Zera'im, Hilkhot Terumot* 7:11).

His wives and slaves may partake of it – נָשָׁיו וַעֲבָדָיו אוֹכְלִין: If a priest is a hermaphrodite or a *tumtum*, his wife may not eat *teruma*. This is the *halakha* even if his testicles are evident, as the *halakha* is ruled in accordance with the opinion of Rava against that of Abaye (*Mishne LaMelekh*). It is permitted, however, for his slaves to eat *teruma* (Rambam *Sefer Zera'im, Hilkhot Terumot* 7:14).

One who was born circumcised – נוֹלַד כְּשֶׁהוּא מָהוּל: A child who was born without a foreskin may eat *teruma* (Rambam *Sefer Zera'im, Hilkhot Terumot* 7:11).

A priest whose foreskin was drawn forward may partake of *teruma* – מָשׁוּךְ אוֹכֵל בִּתְרוּמָה: It is permitted for a priest whose foreskin was drawn forward to eat *teruma* even though he looks uncircumcised. By rabbinic law, he must circumcise himself a second time in order to correct his appearance. The *halakha* is not ruled in accordance with Rav Huna's opinion, as it is ultimately rejected by the Gemara (Radbaz; Rambam *Sefer Zera'im, Hilkhot Terumot* 7:10).

A hermaphrodite may partake of *teruma* – אַנְדְּרוֹגִינוֹס אוֹכֵל בִּתְרוּמָה: A priest who is a hermaphrodite may eat *teruma* after he has been circumcised (Rambam *Sefer Zera'im, Hilkhot Terumot* 7:11).

A hermaphrodite…may not partake of sacrificial food – אַנְדְּרוֹגִינוֹס...אֵין אוֹכֵל בְּקָדָשִׁים: A priest who is a hermaphrodite may partake of the meat of offerings of minor sanctity, as the statement that he may not eat from sacrificial food refers to offerings of the most sacred order (Rambam *Sefer Avoda, Hilkhot Ma'aseh Korbanot* 10:9 and *Kesef Mishne* there).

A *tumtum* may not partake of…sacrificial food – טוּמְטוּם אֵינוֹ אוֹכֵל...בְּקָדָשִׁים: It is prohibited for a *tumtum* to eat from sacrificial food, as there is uncertainty as to whether he is uncircumcised (Rambam *Sefer Avoda, Hilkhot Ma'aseh Korbanot* 10:9).

LANGUAGE

Hermaphrodite [*androginos*] – אַנְדְּרוֹגִינוֹס: From the Greek ἀνδρόγυνος, *androgynos*, meaning a man-woman, i.e., a being with attributes of both genders.

קָתָנֵי מִיהַת: מָשׁוּךְ, וְנוֹלַד כְּשֶׁהוּא מָהוּל – הֲרֵי אֵלּוּ אוֹכְלִין. תְּיוּבְתָּא דְּרַב הוּנָא! תְּיוּבְתָּא.

In any event, this *baraita* **teaches** that a priest whose foreskin was **drawn forward and** one who was **born circumcised may partake** of *teruma*. This would seem to be **a conclusive refutation of** the opinion of **Rav Huna**[N] that a priest whose foreskin was drawn forward may not eat *teruma* at least by rabbinic law. The Gemara concludes: This is in fact **a conclusive refutation**[N] of his opinion.

אֲמַר מָר: טוּמְטוּם אֵינוֹ אוֹכֵל בִּתְרוּמָה, נָשָׁיו וַעֲבָדָיו אוֹכְלִים. נָשָׁיו לְטוּמְטוּם מְנָא לֵיהּ? אִילֵימָא דְּקָדֵישׁ, דְּתַנְיָא: טוּמְטוּם שֶׁקִּידֵּשׁ קִדּוּשָׁיו קִדּוּשִׁין, נִתְקַדֵּשׁ קִדּוּשָׁיו קִדּוּשִׁין?

The Master said above in the *baraita*: A priest who is a ***tumtum*** **may not partake of *teruma*,** but **his wives** [*nashav*] **and slaves may partake** of it. The Gemara is puzzled by this teaching: **From where does a *tumtum* have wives?** If he does not have a visible male organ, how can he marry a woman? **If we say that he** merely **betrothed** a woman, **as it is taught** in another *baraita*: If **a *tumtum* betrothed**[N] a woman **his betrothal is** considered **a valid betrothal,** as he might be a male, and similarly if **he was betrothed** by a man, **his betrothal is** deemed **a valid betrothal**[H] as he might be a female, there is a difficulty.

אֵימַר דַּאֲמַר – לְחוּמְרָא, לְקוּלָּא מִי אָמְרִינַן? סָפֵק אִשָּׁה הוּא, וְאֵין אִשָּׁה מְקַדֶּשֶׁת אִשָּׁה!

One could **say that** the *tanna* **said** that the betrothal of a *tumtum* is valid only **as a stringency,** i.e., out of concern that he might be a male, and therefore the woman cannot leave without a proper bill of divorce. But **should we say** that his betrothal is valid also **as a leniency,** to allow his wife to eat *teruma*? There is an **uncertainty** here that perhaps **he is a woman, and** one **woman cannot betroth** another **woman.**

אֲמַר אַבַּיֵי: כְּשֶׁבֵּיצָיו נִיכָּרוֹת מִבַּחוּץ.

Abaye said: The *tanna* is referring to a *tumtum* whose male organ is hidden, but he is speaking of a situation **where his testicles are visible externally.**[B] Since it is evident that he is a male, he can betroth a woman even though he cannot have relations with her.

רָבָא אָמַר: מַאי נָשָׁיו – אִמּוֹ. אִמּוֹ, פְּשִׁיטָא! מַהוּ דְּתֵימָא: מוֹלִיד מַאֲכִיל, שֶׁאֵין מוֹלִיד אֵינוֹ מַאֲכִיל, קָא מַשְׁמַע לַן.

Rava said a different answer: **What is** meant here by the word *nashav*, which was translated earlier as his wives, but which can also be understood as **his women?** It refers here to the priest's **mother,**[NH] who, after her husband the priest has passed away, may continue to eat *teruma* by virtue of her son. The Gemara questions this interpretation of the *baraita*: **His mother?** It is **obvious** that she may eat *teruma* on his account, as he is her offspring by a priest. The Gemara explains: This statement is nevertheless necessary, **lest you say** that only if the priest **is capable of having children** does he **enable** his mother **to eat** *teruma*, but if he **is incapable of having children** he **does not enable** his mother **to eat** *teruma*, and therefore a *tumtum*, who cannot have children, should not enable his mother to eat *teruma*. Therefore, the *tanna* **teaches us** that this is not so, as a woman may eat *teruma* by virtue of the child she bore a priest, even if that child is incapable of having children.

תָּא שְׁמַע: טוּמְטוּם אֵינוֹ אוֹכֵל לֹא בִּתְרוּמָה וְלֹא בְּקָדָשִׁים. בִּשְׁלָמָא לְאַבַּיֵי – תָּנָא רֵישָׁא עָרֵל וַדַּאי, וְקָתָנֵי סֵיפָא סָפֵק עָרֵל.

Come and hear a proof in support of Abaye's opinion from that which is taught in the latter part of the *baraita*: A priest who is **a *tumtum* may not partake of *teruma* or sacrificial food.** There is a difficulty here, as the *halakha* that a *tumtum* may not partake of *teruma* was already taught in the first part of the *baraita*. **Granted, according to Abaye,** the *tanna* **teaches** in the **first clause** of the *baraita* the *halakha* governing a *tumtum* who is **definitely uncircumcised,** i.e., one whose testicles are visible externally, so that he is definitely male but cannot undergo circumcision because his member itself is hidden. **And** then **he teaches** in **the latter clause** of the *baraita* the *halakha* governing a *tumtum* about whom there is **uncertainty** as to whether he is **uncircumcised,** i.e., one whose genitalia are completely hidden, so that he might not even be a male.

אֶלָּא לְרָבָא, טוּמְטוּם דְּסֵיפָא לָמָּה לִי? מַאי טוּמְטוּם – עָרֵל.

But according to Rava, why do I need the repetition of the *halakha* governing a ***tumtum*** in **the latter clause?** The *tanna* already stated this *halakha* in the first part of the *baraita*. The Gemara answers: **What is** this ***tumtum*** referred to in the latter clause? It is a man who is definitely **uncircumcised.**

NOTES

A conclusive refutation of the opinion of Rav Huna – תְּיוּבְתָּא דְּרַב הוּנָא: Rashi cites a reading according to which the Gemara actually cites a proof in support of Rav Huna's opinion that one whose foreskin was drawn forward is not prohibited from eating *teruma* by Torah law but only by a decree of the Sages. The Ramban and Rashba accept this opinion.

A conclusive refutation – תְּיוּבְתָּא: One could suggest that this *baraita* is in accordance with the opinion of Rabbi Yehuda, who exempts from a second circumcision one whose foreskin was drawn forward, whereas Rav Huna follows the opinion of the Sages. The *Keren Ora* answers that the context proves otherwise, as this *halakha* is stated alongside that of a child born circumcised, with regard to whom it certainly cannot be said that he is entirely exempt from circumcision even by rabbinic law.

If a *tumtum* betrothed – טוּמְטוּם שֶׁקִּידֵּשׁ: The *ge'onim* note that this discussion with regard to the betrothal of a *tumtum* is relevant to the issue of forbidden relations. If his betrothal is valid, then his relatives are forbidden to his wife, and the same applies to the relatives of a *tumtum* who accepted a betrothal. The Rambam states this *halakha* in connection with the requirement to give a bill of divorce in a case of an uncertain betrothal (see Ritva).

What is his women? His mother – מַאי נָשָׁיו אִמּוֹ: If the *tanna* is referring to his mother, why does he say: His women, in the plural? One answer is that he enables both his mother and his mother's mother to partake of *teruma* (*Arukh LaNer*; see Meiri).

HALAKHA

The betrothal of a *tumtum* is valid – טוּמְטוּם קִדּוּשָׁיו קִדּוּשִׁין: If a *tumtum* betrothed a woman or was betrothed by a man, there is uncertainty as to whether the betrothal is valid. Owing to that uncertainty, a bill of divorce is required (Rambam *Sefer Nashim*, *Hilkhot Ishut* 4:11; *Shulḥan Arukh*, *Even HaEzer* 44:5).

What is his women? His mother – מַאי נָשָׁיו אִמּוֹ: If an Israelite woman has a child with a priest, she may eat *teruma* on the child's account, even if it is a *tumtum* or a hermaphrodite (Rambam *Sefer Zera'im*, *Hilkhot Terumot* 6:12).

BACKGROUND

His testicles are visible externally – כְּשֶׁבֵּיצָיו נִיכָּרוֹת מִבַּחוּץ: Such a situation is possible in a case where the child was born with his penis entirely covered by skin. Such a child, despite the fact that his penis is not visible externally, is essentially a male, although he cannot have intercourse with a female.

הָשְׁתָּא סָפֵק עָרֵל לָא אָכֵיל, וַדַּאי עָרֵל אָכֵיל?! מַה טַּעַם קָאָמַר. מַה טַּעַם טוּמְטוּם אֵינוֹ אוֹכֵל בִּתְרוּמָה – מִפְּנֵי שֶׁסָּפֵק עָרֵל הוּא, וְעָרֵל אֵינוֹ אוֹכֵל לֹא בִּתְרוּמָה וְלֹא בְּקָדָשִׁים.

The Gemara asks: **Now, if a** *tumtum*, about whom there is **uncertainty** as to whether he is **uncircumcised, may not partake** of *teruma*, as stated in the first clause of the *baraita*, can it be supposed that a man who is **definitely uncircumcised** may eat *teruma*, so that it was necessary for the *baraita* to teach in the latter clause that he may not do so? The Gemara answers: **He is saying: What is the reason.** The *baraita* should be understood as follows: **What is the reason** that **a** ***tumtum*** **may not partake of** ***teruma*****?** It is **because** there is **uncertainty** as to whether he is **uncircumcised, and an uncircumcised** priest **may not partake of** ***teruma*** **or sacrificial food.**

לֵימָא כְּתַנָּאֵי: מָשׁוּךְ, (וְנוֹלַד כְּשֶׁהוּא מָהוּל), וְגֵר שֶׁנִּתְגַּיֵּיר כְּשֶׁהוּא מָהוּל, וְקָטָן שֶׁעָבַר זְמַנּוֹ, וּשְׁאָר כׇּל הַנִּימּוֹלִים, לְאֵיתוֹיֵי מִי שֶׁיֵּשׁ לוֹ שְׁתֵּי עֲרָלוֹת – אֵינָן נִימּוֹלִין אֶלָּא בַּיּוֹם. רַבִּי אֶלְעָזָר בַּר שִׁמְעוֹן אוֹמֵר: בִּזְמַנּוֹ

The Gemara suggests: **Let us say** that this amoraic dispute as to whether or not one who had been circumcised but his residual foreskin was drawn forward is considered uncircumcised by Torah law is **parallel to** the following dispute between ***tanna'im***. As it is taught in the *Tosefta* (*Shabbat* 16:7): One whose foreskin was **drawn forward, and** similarly, **one who was born circumcised, and a convert who converted when he was** already **circumcised, and a child whose** appropriate **time** for circumcision already **passed** and he was still uncircumcised, **and all others** who require **circumcision,** which, as the Gemara parenthetically adds, comes **to include one who has two foreskins,** both of which must be removed, **may be circumcised only during the day.**[H] **Rabbi Elazar bar Shimon says:** If the circumcision is performed **at its** appropriate **time,** i.e., on the eighth day,

HALAKHA

Circumcision during the day – **מִילָה בַּיּוֹם**: Circumcision must always be performed during the day, even when not done on the eighth day, and even when it is required only by rabbinic law, in accordance with the opinion of the first *tanna*. If one underwent circumcision at night, it is necessary to drip covenantal blood from him during the day (Rambam *Sefer Ahava, Hilkhot Mila* 1:8; *Shulḥan Arukh, Yoreh De'a* 262:1).

Perek **VIII**
Daf **72** Amud **b**

אֵין נִימּוֹלִין אֶלָּא בַּיּוֹם, שֶׁלֹּא בִּזְמַנּוֹ – נִימּוֹלִין בַּיּוֹם וּבַלַּיְלָה. מַאי לָאו בְּהָא קָמִיפַּלְגִי, דְּמָר סָבַר: מָשׁוּךְ דְּאוֹרָיְיתָא, וּמָר סָבַר: מָשׁוּךְ דְּרַבָּנַן.

they may be circumcised only during the day. However, if the circumcision is performed **not at its** appropriate **time, they may be circumcised** either **during the day or at night. What, is it not** the case that **they disagree about the following: One Sage,** the Rabbis, **holds** that the obligation to circumcise one whose foreskin was **drawn forward** is **by Torah law,** and therefore he must be circumcised during the day despite the fact that the procedure is not performed at the proper time, **and one Sage,** Rabbi Elazar bar Shimon, **holds** that the circumcision of one whose foreskin was **drawn forward** is **by rabbinic law.**

וְתִסְבְּרָא? קָטָן שֶׁעָבַר זְמַנּוֹ מִי אִיכָּא לְמַאן דְּאָמַר דְּרַבָּנַן?!

The Gemara rejects this suggestion: **And** how can **you understand** the disagreement in that way? With regard to **a child whose** appropriate **time** for circumcision **has** already **passed, is there anyone who says that** the obligation to circumcise him is only **by rabbinic law?** Even after the eighth day, there is certainly a Torah obligation to circumcise him, and yet the *tanna'im* disagree about this case as well.

אֶלָּא, דְּכוּלֵּי עָלְמָא: מָשׁוּךְ דְּרַבָּנַן, וְקָטָן שֶׁעָבַר זְמַנּוֹ דְּאוֹרָיְיתָא, וְהָכָא בְּהָא קָמִיפַּלְגִי, מָר סָבַר: דָּרְשִׁינַן ״וּבַיּוֹם״, וּמָר סָבַר: לָא דָּרְשִׁינַן ״וּבַיּוֹם״.

Rather, **everyone** agrees that the obligation to circumcise one whose foreskin was **drawn forward** is **by rabbinic law,**[N] **and** that the obligation to circumcise **a child whose** appropriate **time** for circumcision **has** already **passed** is **by Torah law. And here they disagree with regard to the following: One Sage holds** that **we expound** the phrase **"and on the day"** in the verse "And on the eighth day the flesh of his foreskin shall be circumcised" (Leviticus 12:3). The superfluous word "and" indicates that even if the child was not circumcised on the eighth day, the procedure must still be performed during the day. **And one Sage,** Rabbi Elazar bar Shimon, **holds** that **we do not expound** the phrase **"and on the day,"** and therefore a circumcision must be performed during the day only when it takes place on the eighth day, but afterward it may be performed even at night.

NOTES

Everyone agrees that one whose foreskin was drawn forward is by rabbinic law – **דְּכוּלֵּי עָלְמָא מָשׁוּךְ דְּרַבָּנַן**: The early authorities note that it could equally have been argued that everyone agrees that one whose foreskin was drawn forward must be circumcised by Torah law, but the Gemara wished to establish the *baraita* in accordance with the opinion of Rav Huna, especially as that is the accepted conclusion (Rashba; Ritva).

כִּי הָא דְּיָתֵיב רַבִּי יוֹחָנָן, וְקָדָרֵישׁ: נוֹתָר, בִּזְמַנּוֹ – אֵינוֹ נִשְׂרָף אֶלָּא בַּיּוֹם, שֶׁלֹּא בִּזְמַנּוֹ – נִשְׂרָף בֵּין בַּיּוֹם בֵּין בַּלַּיְלָה,

As in the case where **Rabbi Yoḥanan was sitting and he expounded:** ***Notar***, the flesh of an offering that is left over beyond its allotted time, requires burning. If it is burnt **at its** appropriate **time,** i.e., on the same day that it became *notar*, it **may be burned only during the day.**[H] If it is burnt **not at its** appropriate **time,** it **may be burned either during the day or at night.**

וְאֵיתִיבֵיהּ רַבִּי אֶלְעָזָר לְרַבִּי יוֹחָנָן: אֵין לִי אֶלָּא נִימּוֹל לִשְׁמִינִי שֶׁאֵין נִימּוֹל אֶלָּא בַּיּוֹם, מִנַּיִן לְרַבּוֹת לְתִשְׁעָה, לַעֲשָׂרָה, לְאַחַד עָשָׂר, לִשְׁנֵים עָשָׂר (מִנַּיִן) – תַּלְמוּד לוֹמַר: ״וּבַיּוֹם״.

And Rabbi Elazar raises an objection to the opinion of **Rabbi Yoḥanan** from the following *baraita*: **I have** derived **only** that a child who **is circumcised on the eighth** day **may be circumcised only during the day. From where** do I derive **to include** in this *halakha* a child who is circumcised **on the ninth, tenth,**[N] **eleventh,** or **twelfth** day? **From where** is it derived that he, too, may be circumcised only during the day? Therefore, **the verse states: "And on the day,"** which teaches that the obligation to circumcise during the day extends beyond the eighth day itself.

וַאֲפִילּוּ לְמַאן דְּלָא דָּרֵישׁ וא״ו וא״ו וְה״י דָּרֵישׁ! אִישְׁתִּיק.

And even the Sage **who does not expound** the letter *vav*, meaning "and," as superfluous, **expounds** the letters ***vav* and *heh***[N] when they come together and understands them as alluding to cases not explicitly mentioned in the biblical text. Regarding *notar* the verse states: "And that which remains [*vehanotar*] of the flesh of the offering on the third day shall be burnt with fire" (Leviticus 7:17), where the letters *vav* and *heh* teach that the obligation to burn *notar* during the day extends beyond the third day itself. Rabbi Yoḥanan **was silent,** as he had no response.

בָּתַר דְּנָפַק אָמַר לֵיהּ רַבִּי יוֹחָנָן לְרֵישׁ לָקִישׁ: רָאִיתִי לְבֶן פְּדָת שֶׁיּוֹשֵׁב וְדוֹרֵשׁ כְּמֹשֶׁה מִפִּי הַגְּבוּרָה. אָמַר לֵיהּ רֵישׁ לָקִישׁ: דִּידֵיהּ הִיא? מַתְנִיתָא הִיא! הֵיכָא תָּנָא לֵיהּ? בְּתוֹרַת כֹּהֲנִים. נְפַק, תַּנְיָיהּ בִּתְלָתָא יוֹמֵי, וְסָבְרָהּ בִּתְלָתָא יַרְחֵי.

After Rabbi Elazar **left, Rabbi Yoḥanan,** who was impressed with Rabbi Elazar's exposition, **said to Reish Lakish: I saw that** Rabbi Elazar, **son of Pedat, was sitting and expounding** the Torah **as Moses** had received it directly **from the mouth of the Almighty. Reish Lakish said to him:** Was this exposition **his own? It is a *baraita*.** Rabbi Yoḥanan inquired: **Where is this *baraita* taught?** Reish Lakish replied: It is **in *Torat Kohanim*,**[BN] otherwise known as *Sifra*, a work of halakhic midrash on the book of Leviticus. Rabbi Yoḥanan **went out** and **learned** the entire *Torat Kohanim* **in three days, and reached** a full **understanding of it in three months.**

אָמַר רַבִּי אֶלְעָזָר: עָרֵל שֶׁהִזָּה – הַזָּאָתוֹ כְּשֵׁרָה, מִידֵּי דַּהֲוָה אַטְּבוּל יוֹם, שֶׁאַף עַל פִּי שֶׁאָסוּר בִּתְרוּמָה כָּשֵׁר בְּפָרָה.

§ **Rabbi Elazar said:** If **an uncircumcised** priest **sprinkled** the purification waters[H] containing the ashes of a red heifer in order to purify someone who had contracted ritual impurity imparted by a corpse, **his sprinkling is valid, just as it is** in the case of a priest **who immersed himself that day** but does not become completely purified until nightfall. **As, although** such an individual **is prohibited from** eating ***teruma***,[H] he **is fit for** all the rites connected to the red **heifer.**

HALAKHA

The burning of *notar* – שְׂרֵיפַת נוֹתָר: The leftover flesh of offerings must be burned during the day. Even the leftover parts of a peace-offering, which may not be eaten from the beginning of the night of the third day, must be burned only during the day, whether on that third day or any time later. The *halakha* is in accordance with the opinion of Rabbi Elazar, as it appears that Rabbi Yoḥanan accepted his view (Rambam *Sefer Avoda*, *Hilkhot Pesulei HaMukdashin* 19:4).

An uncircumcised priest with regard to the sprinkling of the purification waters – עָרֵל בְּהַזָּאַת מֵי חַטָּאת: An uncircumcised priest may sprinkle the purification waters containing the ashes of a red heifer. The *halakha* is ruled in accordance with the opinion of Rabbi Elazar rather than that of Rabbi Akiva (Rambam *Sefer Tahara*, *Hilkhot Para Aduma* 10:6).

One who immersed himself that day with regard to *teruma* – טְבוּל יוֹם בִּתְרוּמָה: One who was ritually impure may not partake of *teruma* until the sun has set after he immersed and purified himself (Rambam *Sefer Zera'im*, *Hilkhot Terumot* 7:2).

BACKGROUND

***Torat Kohanim* – תּוֹרַת כֹּהֲנִים:** *Torat Kohanim* is a work of halakhic midrash on the book of Leviticus; it is also known as the book of the school of Rav. The work consists primarily of tannaitic statements that derive various *halakhot* from verses. According to the Talmud, unattributed statements in the book were taught in accordance with the opinion of Rabbi Yehuda. The final redaction of the work was apparently completed by Rav, who also taught it extensively. It was regularly studied by the *amora'im* and became the halakhic midrash quoted most often in the Talmud.

NOTES

On the ninth, tenth – לְתִשְׁעָה, לַעֲשָׂרָה: Another mishna (*Shabbat* 137a) explains why these particular numbers are specified: The *tanna* is not dealing with a simple case of a delay in circumcision due to illness or the like. Rather, he is referring to a situation where an infant is born during the twilight period between the end of the day and the beginning of the night, a period of uncertain status with regard to whether it belongs to the previous day or the day that follows, and the eighth day following the birth occurs on Shabbat or a Festival. If the child's date of birth was definitely eight days earlier, his circumcision would take place even on Shabbat or the Festival. However, since the day of his birth is uncertain, Shabbat and the Festival are not desecrated for his circumcision. Instead, he is circumcised on the next day, after Shabbat or the Festival. Consequently, if the child was born during the twilight period on the eve of Shabbat, so that his eighth day is either Friday or Shabbat, his circumcision is postponed until Sunday, the tenth day, and if that Sunday is a Festival he is circumcised only on Monday, the eleventh day after his birth. If that Festival is the two-day festival of Rosh HaShana, he may be circumcised only on Tuesday, twelve days after his birth.

Expounds *vav* and *heh* – וא״ו וְה״י דָּרֵישׁ: Most commentaries explain this in a straightforward manner: While there are differences of opinion with regard to the additional *vav* of "and on the eighth day," as not all Sages expound a *vav* as an inclusive expression, if a *vav* and *heh* appear together, as in "and that which remains [*vehanotar*]," everyone agrees that this serves as an inclusive expression. According to this opinion, the Gemara is offering a proof concerning the basis of the dispute between the Rabbis and Rabbi Elazar bar Shimon. However, some early authorities also cite a different interpretation, according to which there is a superfluous *vav* and *heh* in the context of circumcision as well. Accordingly, the Gemara is attempting to prove that almost all of the Sages concur that circumcision may be performed only by day, and any dissenting opinion is that of an individual Sage and should be disregarded (*Arukh LaNer*). What remains unclear is where there are in fact a superfluous *vav* and *heh* in connection with circumcision. *Arukh LaNer* suggests that since the word *uvayom*, meaning "and on the day" in the verse, includes a definite article, it is as though the letter *heh*, meaning "the," were written explicitly. Rabbeinu Ḥananel accepts the interpretation that the superfluous *vav* in the context of circumcision is in the word *uvayom*, but he explains that the superfluous *heh* is in the word *hashemini*, meaning "the eighth."

Where is this taught; it is in *Torat Kohanim* – הֵיכָא תָּנָא לֵיהּ, בְּתוֹרַת כֹּהֲנִים: Rav Sherira Gaon writes in his famous epistle that this is one of the proofs that halakhic *midrashim*, despite their importance as early sources, were not as widely studied as the Mishna, in which all Sages were fluent. This can be seen from the fact that even a Sage of Rabbi Yoḥanan's stature was unfamiliar with the *Torat Kohanim*. As for the time it took him to study it, this is recorded as a reflection of his greatness in Torah, as this halakhic midrash is considered particularly difficult and complex, so much so that the *tanna'im* themselves would learn it only a little at a time, and yet Rabbi Yoḥanan was able to complete it in a very short period.

מַה לִּטְבוּל יוֹם – שֶׁכֵּן מוּתָּר בְּמַעֲשֵׂר! אַטּוּ אֲנַן לַאֲכִילָה קָאָמְרִינַן? אֲנַן לִנְגִיעָה קָאָמְרִינַן: וּמַה טְּבוּל יוֹם שֶׁאָסוּר בִּנְגִיעָה דִּתְרוּמָה – מוּתָּר בְּפָרָה, עָרֵל שֶׁמּוּתָּר בִּנְגִיעָה – אֵינוֹ דִּין שֶׁמּוּתָּר בְּפָרָה.

The Gemara raises a difficulty: If **one who immersed himself that day** is fit for all the rites connected to the red heifer, that is because **he is** at least **permitted to** eat **tithes,**[H] and so he is treated more leniently than one who is uncircumcised, for whom it is prohibited to partake of second tithe. The Gemara answers: **Is that to say that we are speaking about eating? We spoke** in reference **to touching,** and the proof was as follows: **If one who immersed himself that day** and **who is forbidden to touch** ***teruma***, as he invalidates *teruma* by touch, is nevertheless **permitted** to participate **in** all the rites connected to the red **heifer;**[H] then with regard to one who is **uncircumcised, who is permitted to touch** *teruma* according to all opinions, **is it not right that** he should be **permitted** to participate **in** the rites connected to **the** red **heifer?**

תַּנְיָא נַמִּי הָכִי: עָרֵל שֶׁהִזָּה הַזָּאָתוֹ כְּשֵׁרָה. וּמַעֲשֶׂה הָיָה וְהִכְשִׁירוּ חֲכָמִים הַזָּאָתוֹ.

The Gemara comments: **That** opinion **is also taught** in a *baraita*: If **an uncircumcised** priest **sprinkled** the purification waters, **his sprinkling is valid. And an incident occurred** in which such an individual sprinkled the purification waters **and the Sages validated his sprinkling.**

מֵיתִיבֵי: טוּמְטוּם שֶׁקִּידֵּשׁ – קִידּוּשׁוֹ פָּסוּל, מִפְּנֵי שֶׁהוּא סְפֵק עָרֵל, וְעָרֵל פָּסוּל לְקַדֵּשׁ. וְאַנְדְּרוֹגִינוֹס שֶׁקִּידֵּשׁ – קִידּוּשׁוֹ כָּשֵׁר, רַבִּי יְהוּדָה אוֹמֵר: אַף אַנְדְּרוֹגִינוֹס שֶׁקִּידֵּשׁ – קִידּוּשָׁיו פְּסוּלִים, מִפְּנֵי שֶׁסָּפֵק אִשָּׁה, וְאִשָּׁה פְּסוּלָה מִלְּקַדֵּשׁ. קָתָנֵי מִיהָא: עָרֵל וּסְפֵק עָרֵל פָּסוּל מִלְּקַדֵּשׁ!

The Gemara **raises an objection** from that which was taught in the *Tosefta* (*Para* 5:5): If **a** ***tumtum*** **sanctified** the purification waters by placing a small amount of ashes from the red heifer into springwater that had been placed into a container for that purpose, **his sanctification is invalid because** there is **uncertainty** as to whether he is **uncircumcised, and an uncircumcised** man **is disqualified from sanctifying** the purification waters. **But** if **a hermaphrodite sanctified** the purification waters, **his sanctification is valid. Rabbi Yehuda** disagrees and **says: Even** if **a hermaphrodite sanctified** the purification waters, **his sanctification is invalid, because** there is **uncertainty** as to whether a hermaphrodite is **a woman, and a woman is disqualified from sanctifying** the purification waters. **In any event,** the *baraita* **teaches** that one who is definitely **uncircumcised, and** even one about whom there is **uncertainty** as to whether he is **uncircumcised, is disqualified from sanctifying** the purification waters.

אָמַר רַב יוֹסֵף: הַאי תַּנָּא – תַּנָּא דְּבֵי רַבִּי עֲקִיבָא הוּא, דִּמְרַבֵּי לֵיהּ לְעָרֵל כְּטָמֵא, דְּתַנְיָא: רַבִּי עֲקִיבָא אוֹמֵר: ״אִישׁ אִישׁ״ – לְרַבּוֹת הֶעָרֵל.

Rav Yosef said: This ***tanna*** of the *baraita*, who disqualifies one who is uncircumcised from sanctifying the purification waters, **is a** ***tanna*** **from the school of Rabbi Akiva, who includes the uncircumcised** in the same *halakha* **as** that which governs **the ritually impure. As it is taught** in a *baraita*: **Rabbi Akiva says** that the words "any man" in the verse "**Any man** from the seed of Aaron who is a leper or a *zav* shall not eat of the holy things until he be pure" (Leviticus 22:4), come **to include** one who is **uncircumcised,** and it is prohibited for him as well to partake of consecrated food. And so too, with regard to other matters as well, e.g., sanctifying the purification waters, one who is uncircumcised has the same status as one who is ritually impure.

אָמַר רָבָא: הֲוָה יָתֵיבְנָא קַמֵּיהּ דְּרַב יוֹסֵף, וְקַשְׁיָא לִי: לָא לִישְׁתַּמֵּיט תַּנָּא וְלִיתְנֵי ״הֶעָרֵל וְהַטָּמֵא״ וְלֵימָא רַבִּי עֲקִיבָא הִיא?

Rava said: I was sitting at the time **before Rav Yosef, and I had** the following **difficulty:** If so, according to Rav Yosef's opinion that the uncircumcised and the ritually impure have the same status, should one **not** be able **to find a** ***tanna*** **who teaches** the *halakha* of **the uncircumcised and** that of **the ritually impure** together,[N] **and we should say** that this is the opinion of **Rabbi Akiva?** There should be some source that reflects this view.

HALAKHA

One who immersed himself that day with regard to tithes – טְבוּל יוֹם בְּמַעֲשֵׂר: It is permitted for one who immersed that day to eat second tithe immediately following his immersion, even before the sun sets (Rambam *Sefer Zera'im*, *Hilkhot Ma'aser Sheni* 3:4).

One who immersed himself that day with regard to the red heifer – טְבוּל יוֹם בְּפָרָה: It is permitted for one who immersed that day to participate in all the rites connected to the red heifer, including the sanctification and sprinkling of the purification waters (Rambam *Sefer Tahara*, *Hilkhot Para Aduma* 1:13).

NOTES

Who teaches the ***halakha*** **of the uncircumcised and that of the ritually impure together – וְלִיתְנֵי הֶעָרֵל וְהַטָּמֵא:** Rava sought a source in which the *halakha* of an uncircumcised man is derived from that of one who is ritually impure. In fact, the *halakha* of a pilgrim's appearance in the Temple is a proof of this kind, as there is no biblical source for the exemption of one who is uncircumcised, whereas with regard to one who is impure it is derived from the verses that one who cannot bring an offering is exempt from the pilgrimage. This shows that the *halakha* of an uncircumcised man is derived from the *halakha* of one who is ritually impure (Meiri).

ולא? והא קתני: הערל והטמא פטורים מן הראייה! התם משום דמאיס.

The Gemara asks: **And** is there **not** such a source? **But isn't it taught** in a *baraita*: One who is **uncircumcised and** one who is **ritually impure are exempt from** making an **appearance** in the Temple on each of the three pilgrim Festivals. The Gemara refutes this argument: This is no proof, as **there** it can be argued that one who is uncircumcised is exempt from appearing in the Temple **because he is repulsive,**[N] and it is unbefitting that one who is uncircumcised appear in the Temple courtyard, but this does not mean that with regard to other matters as well he is treated like one who is ritually impure.

ואזדו לטעמייהו, דתניא: הכל כשרים לקדש, חוץ מחרש שוטה וקטן, רבי יהודה מכשיר בקטן ופוסל באשה ובאנדרוגינוס.

The Gemara comments: **And** the Rabbis and Rabbi Yehuda **follow their** usual line of **reasoning** with regard to a hermaphrodite. **As it is taught** in a *baraita*: **All are fit to sanctify** the purification waters **except for a deaf-mute, an imbecile, and a minor.**[H] **Rabbi Yehuda deems a minor fit** for the task, **but deems a woman and a hermaphrodite unfit.**

מאי טעמא דרבנן – דכתיב ״ולקחו לטמא מעפר שריפת החטאת״ הנך דפסלי באסיפה – פסולין בקידוש, הנך דכשרין באסיפה – כשרים בקידוש.

The Gemara explains: **What is the reasoning of the Rabbis? As it is written: "And they shall take for the impure of the ashes of the burning of the sin-offering,** and he shall place on it running water in a vessel" (Numbers 19:17). The juxtaposition of the placement of the water to the gathering of the ashes indicates that they are governed by the same *halakha*. Therefore, **those who are unfit for gathering** the ashes **are** likewise **unfit for sanctification,** whereas **those who are fit for gathering** the ashes **are** likewise **fit for sanctification.** Since a woman is fit to gather the ashes of the red heifer, she may also sanctify its waters.

ורבי יהודה אמר לך: אם כן נימא קרא ״ולקח״ מאי ״ולקחו״ דאפילו הנך דפסולין התם, כשרים הכא.

And Rabbi Yehuda could have **said to you: If so,** then **let the verse state: And he shall take. What** is the significance of the shift to the plural form: **"And they shall take"**? It teaches **that even those who are unfit there are fit here.** As the *halakhot* of the two cases are not identical, Rabbi Yehuda deems a minor fit to perform the sanctification.

אי הכי אשה נמי! ״ונתן״, ולא ״ונתנה״. ורבנן, אי כתיב ״ולקח, ונתן״ הוה אמינא שקיל חד ויהיב חד, כתב רחמנא ״ולקחו״.

The Gemara raises a difficulty: **If so,** according to Rabbi Yehuda **a woman** should **also** be fit to sanctify the purification waters. The Gemara answers: Rabbi Yehuda reads the verse precisely. It says: **"And he shall place** on it," **and not: And she shall place** on it. The Gemara asks: **And** how do **the Rabbis** respond to this claim? **If** the verse **was written: And he shall take… and he shall place, I would say** that **one** individual must **take** the ashes **and** the same **one** must also **place**[H] the water on them. **The Merciful One** therefore **writes: "And they shall take,"** indicating that the ritual is valid even when performed by two different individuals.

ואי כתב רחמנא ״ולקחו ונתנו״ – הוה אמינא: דשקלי תרי ויהבי תרי, כתב רחמנא ״ולקחו ונתן״ דאפילו שקלי תרי ויהיב חד.

And if the Merciful One had written: And they shall take… and they shall place, I would say that two people must **take** the ashes **and two** must **place** the water on them, but if these rites are performed by fewer than two people they are invalid. **The Torah** therefore **states: "And they shall take… and he shall place,"** to teach **that even** if **two** people **take** the ashes **and one** person **places** the water on them, the ritual is valid. Since the verse had to be formulated precisely in this manner in order to teach that *halakha*, the words "and he shall place" cannot be understood as coming to exclude a woman.

HALAKHA

Who is fit to sanctify the purification waters – מי הם הכשרים לקדש: Everyone is fit to sanctify the purification waters by adding the ashes of the red heifer, apart from a deaf-mute, an imbecile, and a minor, in accordance with the opinion of the Rabbis (Rambam *Sefer Tahara, Hilkhot Para Aduma* 6:2).

One must take and the same one must place – שקיל חד ויהיב חד: One who draws the water to be sanctified need not be the one who sanctifies and sprinkles it on the one who is ritually impure, as each of these actions may be performed by a different individual (Rambam *Sefer Tahara, Hilkhot Para Aduma* 10:1).

NOTES

There it is because he is repulsive – התם משום דמאיס: The Ramban and others note that the Gemara in tractate *Ḥagiga* differs from the passage here, as it is clear to the Sages there that this *halakha* equating one who is uncircumcised and one who is ritually impure reflects the view of Rabbi Akiva. For this reason the Rashba explains that the *halakha* should ultimately be ruled in accordance with the Gemara there, based on the principle that whenever there are contradictory passages like these, the accepted version is that which appears in the tractate dedicated to the subject matter at hand. As for the repulsive nature of an uncircumcised man, this is based on the verse: "For it is a reproach to us" (Genesis 34:14). In tractate *Nedarim* (31b) the Sages discuss the repulsive character of the uncircumcised state and how it serves as a derogatory epithet throughout the Bible.

״וְהִזָּה הַטָּהוֹר עַל הַטָּמֵא״, טָהוֹר – מִכְּלָל שֶׁהוּא טָמֵא, לִימֵּד עַל טְבוּל יוֹם שֶׁכָּשֵׁר בְּפָרָה.

It is further stated: **“And the pure person shall sprinkle upon the impure”** (Numbers 19:19). The verse states **“pure”**; this indicates **by inference that he is** in some way **ritually impure.**[N] In other words, the verse speaks of one who is pure only in relation to one who is impure. Were this not the case, there would have been no need at all to mention his purity, as it would have been understood that since the red heifer is called a sin-offering, with regard to which purity is paramount, the one performing the ritual must be pure. Of necessity, then, this “pure” individual is not completely pure in all regards. This **teaches that one who immersed himself that day is fit to** perform the rites connected to the red **heifer.**[H]

בָּעוּ מִינֵּיהּ מֵרַב שֵׁשֶׁת: עָרֵל מַהוּ בְּמַעֲשֵׂר? כִּי הֵיכִי דְּיָלֵיף פֶּסַח מִמַּעֲשֵׂר לְעִנְיַן אֲנִינוּת – יָלֵיף נַמִּי מַעֲשֵׂר מִפֶּסַח לְעִנְיַן עֲרֵלוּת,

The Gemara returns to the previous discussion. **They raised a dilemma before Rav Sheshet:** In the case of **an uncircumcised** man, **what is the** *halakha* **with regard to** his eating second **tithe?** Can one claim that **just as the** *halakha* governing the **Paschal lamb is derived from** the *halakha* governing second **tithe with regard to acute mourning,** in that an acute mourner, who may not eat second tithe, is likewise prohibited from partaking of the Paschal lamb, so **too,** the *halakha* concerning second **tithe is derived from** the *halakha* concerning the **Paschal lamb with regard to lack of circumcision,** in that an uncircumcised man, who may not partake of the Paschal lamb, is likewise prohibited from eating second tithe?

אוֹ דִּלְמָא: חָמוּר מִקַּל יָלֵיף, קַל מֵחָמוּר – לָא יָלֵיף?

Or perhaps the *halakha* governing the **stringent** case of the Paschal lamb **is derived from** the *halakha* governing the **lenient**[N] case of second tithe, but the *halakha* concerning the **lenient** case of second tithe **is not derived from** the *halakha* concerning the **stringent** case of the Paschal lamb, and therefore it is prohibited for an uncircumcised man to partake of the Paschal lamb, but he may eat second tithe.

אֲמַר לְהוּ: תְּנֵיתוּהָ. הַתְּרוּמָה וְהַבִּכּוּרִים חַיָּיבִים עֲלֵיהֶן מִיתָה וְחוֹמֶשׁ וַאֲסוּרִין לְזָרִים,

Rav Sheshet **said to them: You** already **learned** the answer to this question in a mishna (*Ḥalla* 1:9): The following *halakhot* apply to both ***teruma***[B] **and the first fruits**[B] of the new harvest, which must be given to the priests: If a priest ate of them while in a state of ritual impurity, **he is liable** to the punishment of **death** at the hand of Heaven; **and** if a non-priest ate of them unintentionally, he must restore the value of the produce he ate, adding **one-fifth** of its value as a fine; **and they are** both **forbidden to non-priests.**[NH]

BACKGROUND

Teruma – **תְּרוּמָה:** When the term *teruma* appears without qualification, it refers to *teruma gedola*, which is given to the priest. The Torah commands that *teruma* from grain, wine, and oil, and the Sages extended the scope of this mitzva to include all produce. This mitzva applies only in Eretz Yisrael. The Torah does not specify the amount of *teruma* that must be set aside; one may theoretically fulfill his obligation by giving even a single kernel of grain from an entire crop. The Sages established the following measures: One-fortieth of the produce is a generous gift, one-fiftieth is an average gift, and one-sixtieth is a miserly gift. One should not set aside the other tithes until he has set aside *teruma*. *Teruma* is considered sanctified and may be eaten only by a priest and his household while they are in a state of ritual purity (see Leviticus 22:9–15). To emphasize that *teruma* be eaten only in a state of purity, the Sages obligated the priests to wash their hands before partaking of it. This is the source for the practice of washing one’s hands before eating bread. A ritually impure priest or a non-priest who eats *teruma* is subject to the penalty of death at the hand of Heaven. If *teruma* contracts ritual impurity, it may no longer be eaten and must be burned. Nevertheless, it remains the property of the priest, and he may benefit from its burning. Nowadays, *teruma* is not given to the priests because they have no definite proof of their priestly lineage. The obligation to separate it remains, but only a small portion of the produce is separated.

First fruits – **בִּיכּוּרִים:** The first fruits of the new harvest are given to the priests (Deuteronomy 26:1–11). When the Temple stood, a farmer would select the first fruits of the seven types of fruit with which Eretz Yisrael is specially favored (see Deuteronomy 8:8). By rabbinic decree, at least one-sixtieth of the harvest was to be brought as first fruits. The farmer would bring these fruits to the Temple in a basket, place them before the altar, and recite prayers of appreciation to God. Afterward, the fruit was given to the priests and eaten under the same provisions that govern *teruma*. The first fruits were brought to the Temple between the festivals of *Shavuot* and *Sukkot*. If they were not brought within this period, an extension was granted until Hanukkah. An entire tractate of the Mishna, *Bikkurim*, is devoted to the *halakhot* and practices governing this mitzva.

NOTES

Pure, by inference that he is ritually impure – טָהוֹר מִכְּלָל שֶׁהוּא טָמֵא: This exposition is based on the superfluous word “pure,” which is taken to mean that he is not completely pure but only relatively pure in comparison to one who contracted ritual impurity through contact with the dead.

With regard to the teaching that one who immersed that day may perform any part of the red heifer ritual, *Tosafot* raise two problems that are also addressed by other early authorities. First, why is it assumed that this verse refers to one who immersed that day; perhaps it is speaking of one who lacks atonement, i.e., one who has completed his entire process of purification apart from the offerings he is obligated to bring? The Rashba answers that the fact that the verse speaks of a “pure” person, without further elaboration, indicates that it is referring to anyone who can be called pure, including one who immersed that day. Furthermore, the person who immersed that day is at the first stage of purification, which precedes other special actions, e.g., the placing of oil and blood in the case of a leper, or the sacrifice of offerings. The second problem concerns how all aspects of the heifer ritual are derived from the *halakha* of sprinkling. *Tosafot* suggest that it is learned by way of a kind of *a fortiori* inference, whereas the Ritva claims that the case of sprinkling is considered a matter that is singled out from a generalization, which teaches not only about itself but about the entire category.

Or perhaps the stringent is derived from the lenient – אוֹ דִּילְמָא חָמוּר מִקַּל יָלֵיף: *Tosafot* ask: If the exposition is based on a verbal analogy there should be no difference between the lenient and the stringent, and if it is learned by way of an *a fortiori* inference one certainly cannot apply a stringency to a lenient case based on the more stringent one. Either way, the Gemara’s suggestion has no place. They answer that this is the very question raised by the Gemara, albeit worded slightly differently: Is this *halakha* derived through an *a fortiori* inference or by way of a verbal analogy (Ramban; Rashba)?

And they are forbidden to non-priests – וַאֲסוּרִין לְזָרִים: *Tosafot* ask why it is necessary for the *tanna* to state that *teruma* and first fruits are forbidden to non-priests after he has already written that a non-priest must pay the added fine of one-fifth if he eats of them. This question was already raised by Rashi on *Bava Metzia* 53a, where he explains that the *tanna* is stressing the difference between these cases and tithes, which are not prohibited to non-priests at all. While *Tosafot* challenge this interpretation, the Ramban accepts it. The *Arukh* explains that this comes to teach that they are forbidden even after they have been redeemed; in other words, they cannot be redeemed. It is stated in the Jerusalem Talmud in tractate *Bikkurim* that they are forbidden to non-priests, even if they are less than the usual minimal measure that is considered significant. The Meiri adds that non-priests may not benefit from them even while they are being destroyed, e.g., during burning.

HALAKHA

One who immersed himself that day is fit for the red heifer – טְבוּל יוֹם בְּפָרָה: It is permitted for one who had been ritually impure and immersed himself that day to perform all the rites connected to the red heifer, including the sanctification and sprinkling of the purification waters (Rambam *Sefer Tahara*, *Hilkhot Para Aduma* 1:13).

***Teruma* and first fruits are forbidden to non-priests – תְּרוּמָה וּבִכּוּרִים אֲסוּרִים לְזָרִים:** *Teruma* and first fruits are forbidden to non-priests. If a non-priest ate *teruma* or first fruits after the first fruits were brought to Jerusalem, he is liable to the penalty of death at the hand of Heaven (Rambam *Sefer Zera’im*, *Hilkhot Bikkurim* 3:1).

והן נכסי כהן, ועולין באחד ומאה, וטעונין רחיצת ידים והערב שמש, הרי אלו בתרומה ובבכורים, מה שאין כן במעשר.

The mishna continues: **And they are** considered in all regards **the** private **property of the priest**[NH] to whom they were given; **and they are nullified,** i.e., rendered permitted for consumption by non-priests, **in a mixture of one hundred and one,**[N] when there are at least one hundred parts of permitted food for each part of *teruma* or first fruits; **and they** both **require washing of the hands** before they may be eaten; **and** if a priest is ritually impure, he may not eat of *teruma* or first fruits, even after immersion, until after **sunset** on the day of his immersion. All of **these** *halakhot* apply **to *teruma* and first fruits, which is not** the case **with** regard to second **tithe.**[B]

ואם איתא – ניתני: ערל אסור בהן, מה שאין כן במעשר!

Rav Sheshet resumes his argument: **And if it is so** that one who is uncircumcised may eat second tithe, **let** the *tanna* also **teach: It is prohibited for an uncircumcised man** to eat of *teruma* and first fruits, **which is not** the case **with** regard to second **tithe.**

תנא ושייר! ומאי שייר דהאי שייר?

The Gemara rejects this argument: This is no proof, as the *tanna* of the mishna **taught** only some of the differences between *teruma* and first fruits on the one hand and second tithe on the other, **and he omitted** others. The Gemara asks: The mishna is sometimes not exhaustive, but it never omits only one case. **What** other difference **did he omit that** you say that **he** also **omitted this** difference?

שייר דקא תני סיפא: יש במעשר ובבכורים מה שאין כן בתרומה: שהמעשר והבכורים טעונין הבאת מקום, וטעונין וידוי, ואסור לאונן, ורבי שמעון מתיר. וחייבין בביעור, ורבי שמעון פוטר.

The Gemara answers: **He omitted** the following, **as he teaches in the latter clause** of the mishna: **There are** *halakhot* that apply to second **tithe and first fruits, which is not** the case **with** regard to ***teruma*.** As second **tithe**[H] **and first fruits**[H] **require** that they be **brought to** a particular **place,** Jerusalem, where they must be eaten, whereas *teruma* may be consumed in all places; **and they** both **require a declaration,**[H] as a declaration must be made on the last day of Passover in the fourth and seventh years of the Sabbatical cycle, stating that one's agricultural obligations with regard to tithes have been fulfilled properly, and so too a declaration must be made when first fruits are brought to the Temple;[H] **and they are forbidden to an acute mourner;**[H] **and Rabbi Shimon permits** an acute mourner to partake of first fruits.[H] **And they** both **require eradication**[H] before Passover in the fourth and seventh years of the Sabbatical cycle if one failed to bring them beforehand; **and Rabbi Shimon exempts** first fruits from the obligation of eradication.

ואילו אסור לבער מהן בטומאה

And yet second tithe and first fruits differ from *teruma* in that **it is prohibited to burn** the former and benefit from the burning, even when the produce is **in** a state of **ritual impurity**[H] and therefore unfit to be eaten, e.g., one may not burn impure oil for light;

NOTES

And they are the property of the priest – והן נכסי כהן: The Ramban explains that it was necessary to emphasize that they are the property of the priest in order to prevent a possible *a fortiori* inference from second tithe, which the owner is certainly not permitted to use as he sees fit. The difference is that these portions that are given to the priests, although they are consecrated and forbidden to non-priests, nevertheless belong to the priests themselves, whereas the second tithe is given to the owners from the table of the Most High, i.e., they may consume it as guests at God's table, but it does not belong to them.

And they are nullified in a mixture of one hundred and one – ועולין באחד ומאה: Although this *halakha* is derived hermeneutically from the verses, the conclusion of the Gemara is that this is not a Torah law, as by Torah law all forbidden items are nullified by a simple majority. The *tanna*, however, also includes in his list differences that are based on rabbinic law (Rashba).

BACKGROUND

Second tithe – מעשר שני: When the Temple stood, the second tithe was set aside after the *teruma* had been given to the priests and the first tithe had been given to the Levites. Second tithe was separated during the first, second, fourth, and fifth years of the Sabbatical cycle. After the second tithe was set aside, it was brought to Jerusalem to be consumed there by its owner. If the journey to Jerusalem was too long, so that it would be difficult to carry all of the second tithe there, or if the produce became ritually impure, it could be redeemed for an equivalent sum of money. If the owner redeemed his own produce he was required to add one-fifth of its value. This redemption money was brought to Jerusalem, where it could be spent only to purchase food. Nowadays second tithe is separated but may not be eaten. Therefore, it is redeemed, but only for a nominal sum.

HALAKHA

***Teruma* and first fruits are the property of the priest – תרומה והבכורים נכסי כהן:** *Teruma* and first fruits, and similarly *ḥalla* and the other gifts to the priesthood, belong to the priest. He may therefore use them to purchase property of any kind, or to betroth a woman. A creditor may collect them as payment for his debt, and a wife may take them as payment for her marriage contract (Rambam *Sefer Zera'im, Hilkhot Bikkurim* 4:14).

Second tithe requires that it be brought to a place – מעשר טעון הבאת מקום: Second tithe is eaten by its owner, but only within the walls of Jerusalem (Rambam *Sefer Zera'im, Hilkhot Ma'aser Sheni* 2:1).

First fruits require that they be brought to a place – בכורים טעונים הבאת מקום: First fruits must be brought to the Temple, and therefore this mitzva can be observed only when the Temple is standing (Rambam *Sefer Zera'im, Hilkhot Bikkurim* 2:1, 3:5).

Second tithe requires a declaration – מעשר טעון וידוי: It is a positive mitzva to make a declaration before God after one has separated all the agricultural gifts from the produce of his land (Rambam *Sefer Zera'im, Hilkhot Ma'aser Sheni* 11:1).

First fruits require a declaration – בכורים טעונים וידוי: It is a positive mitzva to make a declaration in the Temple when one brings the first fruits there (Rambam *Sefer Zera'im, Hilkhot Bikkurim* 3:10).

Second tithe is forbidden to an acute mourner – מעשר אסור לאונן: If one eats second tithe in Jerusalem while in acute mourning by Torah law, he has transgressed a Torah prohibition and is liable to receive lashes. If he eats it outside the city, or even inside but when he is an acute mourner by rabbinic law, he receives lashes for rebelliousness that are administered by rabbinic decree (Rambam *Sefer Zera'im, Hilkhot Ma'aser Sheni* 3:5).

First fruits are prohibited to an acute mourner – בכורים אסורים לאונן: An acute mourner may not eat first fruits, in accordance with the opinion of the Rabbis (Rambam *Sefer Zera'im, Hilkhot Bikkurim* 3:5).

Second tithe and first fruits require eradication – מעשר ובכורים בביעור: If one has left in his possession second-tithe fruit, fourth-year produce, or first fruits, he is obligated to remove them from his house and throw them into the sea or burn them (Rambam *Sefer Zera'im, Hilkhot Ma'aser Sheni* 11:8).

It is prohibited to burn second tithe in a state of ritual impurity – אסור לבערם בטומאה: Second tithe that has become ritually impure may not be used even for lighting a lamp (Rambam *Sefer Zera'im, Hilkhot Ma'aser Sheni* 3:2).

וְאוֹכְלָן בְּטוּמְאַת עַצְמָן לוֹקֶה, מַה שֶּׁאֵין כֵּן בִּתְרוּמָה – לָא קָתָנֵי, אַלְמָא: תָּנֵי וְשַׁיֵּיר.

and one who eats them when they themselves, the second tithe and first fruits, **are ritually impure**[H] **is flogged,** even though he himself is ritually pure, **which is not** the case **with** regard to ***teruma***; and these differences the *tanna* **does not teach. Apparently,** the *tanna* of the mishna **taught** certain differences between the cases **and omitted** others. Therefore, the omission of the *halakha* governing an uncircumcised man does not prove that it is permitted for him to eat second tithe.

״וַאֲסוּרִין לְאוֹנֵן וְרַבִּי שִׁמְעוֹן מַתִּיר״, מְנָא לְהוּ? דִּכְתִיב ״לֹא תוּכַל לֶאֱכוֹל בִּשְׁעָרֶיךָ מַעְשַׂר דְּגָנְךָ וְתִירֹשְׁךָ וְיִצְהָרֶךָ״ וגו׳ ״וּתְרוּמַת יָדֶךָ״ וַאֲמַר מָר: ״תְּרוּמַת יָדֶךָ״ אֵלּוּ בִּכּוּרִים, וְאִיתְקַשׁ בִּכּוּרִים לְמַעֲשֵׂר: מַה מַּעֲשֵׂר אָסוּר לְאוֹנֵן, אַף בִּכּוּרִים אָסוּר לְאוֹנֵן.

§ Having cited the mishna, the Gemara proceeds to discuss it. It was taught in the *baraita* that second tithe and first fruits **are forbidden to an acute mourner; and Rabbi Shimon permits** an acute mourner to partake of first fruits. The Gemara asks: **From where do** the Rabbis derive that first fruits are forbidden to one who is in acute mourning? **As it is written: "You may not eat within your gates the tithe of your grain, or of your wine, or of your oil… nor the offering of your hand"** (Deuteronomy 12:17), **and the Master said: "The offering [*teruma*] of your hand," these are the first fruits. And first fruits are juxtaposed** in this verse **to** second **tithe:**[N] **Just as the** second **tithe is forbidden to an acute mourner, so too, first fruits** are **forbidden to an acute mourner.**[H]

וְרַבִּי שִׁמְעוֹן: ״תְּרוּמָה״ קָרֵינְהוּ רַחֲמָנָא, מַה תְּרוּמָה מוּתֶּרֶת לְאוֹנֵן, אַף בִּכּוּרִים מוּתָּר לְאוֹנֵן.

And Rabbi Shimon counters that since **the Merciful One calls** first fruits ***"teruma,"*** the *halakha* governing them is similar to that which governs *teruma*: **Just as *teruma* is permitted to an acute mourner,**[H] **so too, first fruits** are **permitted to an acute mourner.**

״וְחַיָּיבִין בְּבִיעוּר, וְרַבִּי שִׁמְעוֹן פּוֹטֵר״ – מָר מַקִּישׁ, וּמָר לָא מַקִּישׁ.

The *baraita* continues: **And** both second tithe and first fruits **require eradication** before Passover in the fourth and seventh years of the Sabbatical cycle; **and Rabbi Shimon exempts** first fruits from the obligation of eradication. **One Sage,** the Rabbis, **juxtaposes** first fruits to second tithe: Just as second tithe is subject to eradication, so too are first fruits. **And one Sage,** Rabbi Shimon, **does not juxtapose**[N] the two *halakhot* and derive one from the other.

״וְאָסוּר לְבַעֵר מֵהֶן בְּטוּמְאָה, וְאוֹכְלָן בְּטוּמְאַת עַצְמָן לוֹקֶה״ מְנָלַן? דְּתַנְיָא, רַבִּי שִׁמְעוֹן אוֹמֵר: ״לֹא בִעַרְתִּי מִמֶּנּוּ בְּטָמֵא״ – בֵּין שֶׁאֲנִי טָמֵא וְהוּא טָהוֹר, בֵּין שֶׁאֲנִי טָהוֹר וְהוּא טָמֵא.

It was stated above that **it is prohibited to burn** second tithe and first fruits even when they are **in** a state of **ritual impurity, and** that **one who eats them when they themselves,** the second tithe and first fruits, **are ritually impure is flogged,** even though he himself is ritually pure. **From where do we** derive these *halakhot*? **As it is taught** in a *baraita*: **Rabbi Shimon says:** The verse with regard to the confession of tithes states: **"I did not consume of it while impure"** (Deuteronomy 26:14), a general statement that means **whether I,** the one who ate it, was **ritually impure, and** the tithe **was ritually pure,** or **whether I was ritually pure and** the tithe **was ritually impure.** Regardless, the tithe may not be consumed through burning or eating in a state of impurity.

HALAKHA

Tithe that is itself ritually impure – מַעֲשֵׂר בְּטוּמְאַת עַצְמוֹ: One who eats second tithe in a state of ritual impurity is liable to receive lashes, whether he is impure and the tithe is pure or he is pure and the tithe is impure (Rambam *Sefer Zera'im, Hilkhot Ma'aser Sheni* 3:1).

First fruits for an acute mourner – בִּכּוּרִים לְאוֹנֵן: An acute mourner is prohibited from eating first fruits, in accordance with the unattributed view in the mishna, against the lone dissenting view of Rabbi Shimon (Rambam *Sefer Zera'im, Hilkhot Bikkurim* 3:5).

***Teruma* for an acute mourner – תְּרוּמָה לְאוֹנֵן:** It is permitted for an acute mourner to partake of *teruma* (Rambam *Sefer Tahara, Hilkhot Avot HaTuma* 12:15).

NOTES

And first fruits are juxtaposed to second tithe – וְאִתְקַשׁ בִּכּוּרִים לְמַעֲשֵׂר: Some ask: In accordance with the rule that there cannot be half an analogy, and therefore the inferences drawn by way of an analogy must be bilateral, why aren't the *halakhot* of first fruits likewise applied to tithes? The answer given is that the *halakhot* governing first fruits are derived primarily from *teruma*, as the Torah calls them "the offering [*teruma*] of your hand." Consequently, since several exclusions appear with regard to *teruma*, e.g., "And they shall die through it when they profane it" (Leviticus 22:9), the word "it" emphasizing that this punishment applies only to "it" and no other case, and since it says about ritual impurity: "Its impurity is upon it" (Numbers 19:13), the stringencies of tithe are applied to first fruits but the stringencies of first fruits are not in force for second tithe as well (*Tosefot Yeshanim*; Ritva).

And one Sage does not juxtapose – וּמָר לָא מַקִּישׁ: *Tosafot Yeshanim* elaborate on the point made by *Tosafot* that according to Rabbi Shimon first fruits are like *teruma* in all respects. The two differ only with respect to the *halakhot* governing first fruits that are explicitly stated in the Torah, but other *halakhot* of first fruits that do not apply to *teruma* are not derived by way of analogy or the like.

NOTES

And where one is warned against eating it – **וְהֵיכָא מוּזְהָר עַל אֲכִילָתוֹ**: The question has been raised: Why can't the verse that states: "And I did not consume of it while impure" (Deuteronomy 26:14), which is clearly referring to eating second tithe in a state of ritual impurity, be understood as a warning, i.e., a source for the prohibition? The Rosh explains that this is not stated in the form of a command but merely as part of a narrative account. Therefore, although it is evident from the declaration that eating in a state of impurity is prohibited, this verse cannot serve as a source for that prohibition.

HALAKHA

Burning *teruma* that became ritually impure – **בִּיעוּר תְּרוּמָה בְּטָמֵא**: *Teruma* is the property of priests, whether it is ritually pure or impure. If it is impure it must be burned, and the priest may derive benefit from it while it is burning. For example, he may light a lamp with ritually impure *teruma* oil (Rambam *Sefer Zera'im*, *Hilkhot Terumot* 2:14).

וְהֵיכָא מוּזְהָר עַל אֲכִילָתוֹ אֵינִי יוֹדֵעַ. טוּמְאַת הַגּוּף בְּהֶדְיָא כְּתִיב בֵּיהּ: "נֶפֶשׁ אֲשֶׁר תִּגַּע בּוֹ וְטָמְאָה עַד הָעָרֶב וְלֹא יֹאכַל מִן הַקֳּדָשִׁים כִּי אִם רָחַץ בְּשָׂרוֹ בַּמָּיִם"!

The *tanna* adds: **And where one is** actually **warned against eating** second tithe[N] in a state of impurity, this **I do not know.** Although it is obvious from the verse that this is prohibited, the source for the prohibition is unclear. The Gemara is puzzled by this last statement: The prohibition against eating second tithe when one is in a state of **ritual impurity of the body is explicitly written,** as it is stated with regard to the ritual impurity imparted by a creeping animal: **"The soul that touches it shall be impure until the evening, and he shall not eat from the holy things unless he has washed his flesh in water"** (Leviticus 22:6). This is referring to second tithe, as will be explained later (74b).

הָכִי קָמִיבַּעְיָא לֵיהּ: טוּמְאַת עַצְמוֹ מִנַּיִן? תַּלְמוּד לוֹמַר "לֹא תוּכַל לֶאֱכוֹל בִּשְׁעָרֶיךָ מַעְשַׂר דְּגָנְךָ" וּלְהַלָּן הוּא אוֹמֵר "בִּשְׁעָרֶיךָ תֹּאכְלֶנּוּ הַטָּמֵא וְהַטָּהוֹר יַחְדָּו כַּצְּבִי וְכָאַיָּל", וְתָנָא דְּבֵי רַבִּי יִשְׁמָעֵאל: אֲפִילּוּ טָמֵא וְטָהוֹר אוֹכְלִין עַל שׁוּלְחָן אֶחָד בִּקְעָרָה אַחַת – וְאֵינָן חוֹשְׁשִׁין. וְקָאָמַר רַחֲמָנָא: הַהוּא דְּאָמְרִי לָךְ הָתָם "בִּשְׁעָרֶיךָ תֹּאכְלֶנּוּ" – הָכָא לָא תֵּיכוּל.

The Gemara explains: Rather, **this is** the **dilemma he is raising: From where** is it derived that one may not eat it when the tithe **itself** is in a state of **ritual impurity? The verse states: "You may not eat within your gates the tithe of your grain"** (Deuteronomy 12:17), **and later it states** with regard to offerings that have been disqualified: **"You shall eat it within your gates, the impure and the pure alike, as the gazelle and as the hart"** (Deuteronomy 15:22). **And** a Sage **of the school of Rabbi Yishmael taught: Even a ritually impure and a ritually pure** person **may eat** together **on one table** and **out of one bowl without concern. And the Merciful One states: That which I said to you there,** with regard to disqualified offerings: **"You shall eat it within your gates,"** means regardless of whether it is the individual or the meat that is impure; but **here,** with regard to second tithe, **you may not eat** it in that state. From here it is derived that one may not eat second tithe when the tithe itself is ritually impure.

"מַה שֶּׁאֵין כֵּן בִּתְרוּמָה", מְנָא לָן? אָמַר רַבִּי אַבָּהוּ אָמַר רַבִּי יוֹחָנָן: דְּאָמַר קְרָא "לֹא בִעַרְתִּי מִמֶּנּוּ בְּטָמֵא", "מִמֶּנּוּ" אִי אַתָּה מַבְעִיר, אֲבָל אַתָּה מַבְעִיר שֶׁמֶן שֶׁל תְּרוּמָה שֶׁנִּטְמָא.

It was stated above that one is prohibited from burning second tithe and first fruits even when they are ritually impure, **which is not** the case **with** regard to ***teruma.*** The Gemara asks: **From where do we** derive that this *halakha* does not apply to *teruma*? **Rabbi Abbahu said** that **Rabbi Yoḥanan said: As the verse** with regard to the declaration of tithes **states: "I did not consume of it while impure"** (Deuteronomy 26:14), and the words "of it" teach that **of it,** i.e., tithe, **you may not burn** when it is impure, **but you may burn** and derive benefit from **the oil of *teruma* that has become ritually impure.**[H]

וְאֵימָא: "מִמֶּנּוּ" אִי אַתָּה מַבְעִיר, אֲבָל אַתָּה מַבְעִיר שֶׁמֶן שֶׁל קֹדֶשׁ שֶׁנִּטְמָא! לָאו קַל וָחוֹמֶר הוּא?! וּמַה מַּעֲשֵׂר הַקַּל אָמְרָה תוֹרָה "לֹא בִעַרְתִּי מִמֶּנּוּ בְּטָמֵא", קֹדֶשׁ חָמוּר לֹא כָּל שֶׁכֵּן?!

The Gemara asks: **But say** perhaps as follows: **Of it you may not burn, but you may burn** and derive benefit from **consecrated oil that became ritually impure.** The Gemara refutes this suggestion: That possibility is unacceptable. Is it **not an *a fortiori*** inference? **If** with regard to **the tithe, which is lenient, the Torah said: "I did not burn of it while impure,"** then with regard to **consecrated** oil, **which is more stringent,** is it **not all the more so** prohibited to burn them while ritually impure?

אִי הָכִי תְּרוּמָה נַמִי קַל וָחוֹמֶר הוּא! הָא כְּתִיב "מִמֶּנּוּ".

The Gemara retorts: **If so,** then with regard to ***teruma* as well,** say that **it is an *a fortiori*** inference, as *teruma* is certainly more sacred than tithes. If it is prohibited to benefit from second tithe while it is burning, all the more so would it be prohibited to benefit from *teruma* while it is burning. The Gemara answers: **Isn't it written "of it"?** From there it is derived that there is an item excluded from the prohibition against burning in a state of ritual impurity.

וּמָה רָאִיתָ? מִסְתַּבְּרָא: קֹדֶשׁ לָא מְמַעֵיטְנָא, שֶׁכֵּן פנקעכ"ס:

The Gemara asks: **And what did you see** that led you to conclude that "of it" comes to exclude *teruma*? Perhaps it comes to exclude consecrated items. The Gemara replies: **It is reasonable** that **I do not exclude consecrated items** from the prohibition against benefiting from their burning, as with regard to consecrated items there are many stringent elements. Their Hebrew acronym is ***peh, nun, kuf, ayin, kaf, samekh,*** which is a mnemonic for the following stringencies that apply to consecrated items and not to *teruma*:

פִּגּוּל, נוֹתָר, קׇרְבָּן, מְעִילָה, כָּרֵת, וְאָסוּר לְאוֹנֵן.

***Piggul*:** If, during one of the rites involved in the sacrifice of an offering, i.e., slaughter, receiving the blood, bringing it to the altar, or sprinkling it on the altar, the priest or the one bringing the offering entertains the thought of eating the offering at a time that is unfit for eating, the offering is thereby invalidated.[H] ***Notar*:** Meat of an offering that remained beyond its allotted time may not be eaten and must be burned.[H] **Offering [*korban*]:** It is an offering to God. **Misuse** of consecrated objects **[*me'ila*]:** One who unwittingly derives benefit from consecrated items is required to bring a guilt-offering for misuse of consecrated objects.[H] ***Karet*:** The punishment of one who eats consecrated items while ritually impure is *karet*.[H] **Forbidden to an acute mourner [*asur le'onen*]:** An acute mourner is prohibited from eating consecrated items.[H] None of these *halakhot* apply to *teruma*. Therefore, consecrated items are more stringent than *teruma*, and accordingly they are not excluded from the prohibition against deriving benefit while ritually impure.

אַדְּרַבָּה, תְּרוּמָה לָא מְמַעֵיטְנָא, שֶׁכֵּן מחפ״ז: מִיתָה, וְחוֹמֶשׁ, וְאֵין לָהּ פִּדְיוֹן, וַאֲסוּרָה לְזָרִים!

The Gemara rejects this argument. **On the contrary, it is *teruma* that I would not exclude** from the prohibition, **as** with regard to *teruma* there are many stringent elements, represented by the acronym ***mem, ḥet, peh, zayin***, which is a mnemonic for the following: **Death [*mita*]:** One who is prohibited from eating *teruma* but ate it intentionally is liable to the punishment of death at the hand of Heaven.[H] **One-fifth [*ḥomesh*]:**[H] A non-priest, to whom *teruma* is forbidden, who unwittingly ate *teruma* is obligated to pay its value to the priest plus one-fifth of the sum. **And** *teruma* **does not have** the possibility of **redemption [*pidyon*]:** Once it is sanctified, *teruma* may not be redeemed and rendered non-sacred. **And it is forbidden to non-priests [*zarim*].**[HN] These stringencies do not apply to consecrated items.

הָנָךְ נְפִישָׁן. וְאִיבָּעֵית אֵימָא: כָּרֵת עֲדִיפָא.

The Gemara answers: **Those** stringencies that apply to consecrated items **are** more **numerous** than those that apply to *teruma*. Therefore, it is appropriate to be more stringent with consecrated items and exclude impure *teruma* from the prohibition against deriving benefit from it while it is burned. **And if you wish, say** instead a different reason, without counting the number of stringencies: Consecrated items are more stringent because one who eats them while ritually impure is liable to receive ***karet***, which **is more severe** than death at the hand of Heaven, the punishment in the case of *teruma*.

״וְאוֹכְלָן בְּטוּמְאַת עַצְמָן לוֹקֶה, מַה שֶּׁאֵין כֵּן בִּתְרוּמָה״. מִילְקָא הוּא דְּלָא לָקֵי הָא אִיסּוּרָא אִיכָּא, מְנָלַן? אָמַר קְרָא ״בִּשְׁעָרֶיךָ תֹּאכְלֶנּוּ״ לְזֶה וְלֹא לְאַחֵר וְלָאו הַבָּא מִכְּלַל עֲשֵׂה – עֲשֵׂה.

It was further stated above that **one who eats** second tithe and first fruits **when they themselves,** the second tithe and first fruits, **are ritually impure is flogged, which is not** the case **with** regard to ***teruma***. The Gemara infers from this that **it is lashes that he does not receive** when he eats *teruma* that is ritually impure; **however,** the transgression of **a prohibition is** involved. **From where do we** derive that this is prohibited? **The verse** referring to offerings that have been disqualified **states: "You shall eat it within your gates"** (Deuteronomy 15:22).[N] The word "it" indicates that it is only **this,** disqualified offerings, that may be eaten in a state of impurity, **but not another** type of consecrated food. This is a prohibition that is derived by inference from a positive mitzva, i.e., it is not stated in the Torah in the form of a prohibition. **And** there is a principle that **a prohibition that stems from a positive mitzva** is classified as **a positive mitzva,** for which no lashes are administered.[H]

אָמַר רַב אַשִׁי: מֵרֵישָׁא נַמִּי שָׁמְעַתְּ מִינַּהּ דְּתָנָא וְשַׁיֵּיר, מִדְּלָא קָתָנֵי:

The Gemara demonstrated earlier that no proof can be adduced from the mishna cited by Rav Sheshet, as the *tanna* of that mishna taught only some of the differences between second tithe and *teruma*. **Rav Ashi said: From the first part** of the mishna **as well, you** can **conclude that he taught** certain differences **and omitted** others, **from** the fact that **he does not teach** the following additional difference:

HALAKHA

***Piggul* – פִּגּוּל:** If, while performing one of the sacrificial rites connected to an offering, a priest had the intention of performing a different rite not at its proper time, or of eating or burning the offering not at its proper time, this thought invalidates the offering and renders it *piggul*, an offering disqualified by improper intention (Rambam *Sefer Avoda, Hilkhot Pesulei HaMukdashin* 13:1).

***Notar* – נוֹתָר:** If an offering was sacrificed in the proper manner, but its meat was left over after the fixed time for its consumption, the leftover meat is called *notar* and may not be eaten (Rambam *Sefer Avoda, Hilkhot Pesulei HaMukdashin* 13:3).

Misuse of consecrated objects – מְעִילָה: An ordinary person may not derive benefit from consecrated property. Whoever unwittingly derives such benefit to the value of a *peruta*, whether the property had been consecrated for the maintenance of the Temple or for the altar, is required to bring a guilt-offering for misuse of consecrated property (Rambam *Sefer Avoda, Hilkhot Me'ila* 1:1).

***Karet* – כָּרֵת:** One who was ritually impure with a severe level of impurity and ate an olive-bulk of sacrificial meat is liable to receive *karet* (Rambam *Sefer Avoda, Hilkhot Pesulei HaMukdashin* 18:13).

Sacrificial food is prohibited to an acute mourner – אָסוּר לְאוֹנֵן: An acute mourner may not eat sacrificial food (Rambam *Sefer Tahara, Hilkhot Avot HaTuma* 12:15).

Death for *teruma* – מִיתָה בִּתְרוּמָה: One who is ritually impure and ate pure *teruma* is liable to the penalty of death at the hand of Heaven (Rambam *Sefer Zera'im, Hilkhot Terumot* 7:1).

One-fifth – חוֹמֶשׁ: A non-priest who unwittingly ate *teruma* must repay its value plus one-fifth of the sum (Rambam *Sefer Zera'im, Hilkhot Terumot* 10:1).

Forbidden to non-priests – אֲסוּרָה לְזָרִים: It is prohibited for non-priests to partake of any kind of *teruma* (Rambam *Sefer Zera'im, Hilkhot Terumot* 6:5).

Eating impure *teruma* – אוֹכֵל תְּרוּמָה טְמֵאָה: If a pure priest ate ritually impure *teruma*, he has transgressed a prohibition, but he is not liable to be flogged. This is because the prohibition stems from a positive mitzva, and a prohibition that is derived by inference from a positive mitzva has the status of a positive mitzva, for which no lashes are administered (Rambam *Sefer Zera'im, Hilkhot Terumot* 7:3).

NOTES

And it is forbidden to non-priests – וַאֲסוּרָה לְזָרִים: *Tosafot* maintain that the statement that *teruma* is punishable by death does not refer to its consumption in a state of impurity but to its being prohibited to non-priests. The problem with this interpretation is that the statement that it is forbidden to non-priests is rendered redundant. *Tosafot Yeshanim* explain, based on the Jerusalem Talmud, that this is referring to the prohibition that applies to half of a legal measure.

From where do we derive this; the verse states…"Within your gates" – מְנָלַן אָמַר קְרָא בִּשְׁעָרֶיךָ: The Rambam cites a different verse as the source for this *halakha*, as it is stated with regard to a priest: "And afterward he may eat from the holy things" (Leviticus 22:7), which indicates that he may eat *teruma* only after his purification.

וְנוֹהֲגִין בִּשְׁאָר שְׁנֵי שָׁבוּעַ, וְאֵין לָהֶם פִּדְיוֹן, מַה שֶּׁאֵין כֵּן בְּמַעֲשֵׂר, שְׁמַע מִינָּהּ.

Teruma and first fruits **apply in all the years of the seven-year** Sabbatical cycle, including the third and the sixth years, **and they do not have** the possibility of **redemption,** as once they are sanctified they may not be redeemed and rendered non-sacred. **This is not** the case **with** regard to **second tithe,** which applies only in the first, second, fourth, and fifth years of the cycle and which can be redeemed. The Gemara concludes: **Learn from here** that the *tanna* did not list all of the differences between second tithe and *teruma*.

תָּא שְׁמַע: נִשְׁתַּיְּירוּ בּוֹ צִיצִין הַמְעַכְּבִין אֶת הַמִּילָה – הֲרֵי זֶה אֵינוֹ אוֹכֵל לֹא בִּתְרוּמָה, וְלֹא בְּפֶסַח, וְלֹא בְּקָדָשִׁים, וְלֹא בְּמַעֲשֵׂר. מַאי לָאו, מַעְשַׂר דָּגָן? לָא, מַעְשַׂר בְּהֵמָה.

The Gemara resumes its discussion of whether or not an uncircumcised man is prohibited from eating second tithe. **Come and hear** a proof with regard to this question from the following *baraita*: If **shreds** of flesh **that invalidate the circumcision** remain after the foreskin was removed, **one may not eat *teruma*, nor the Paschal lamb, nor sacrificial food, nor tithe. What, is it not** referring to **tithe of produce,** and so the dilemma is resolved? The Gemara refutes this suggestion: **No,** the tithe mentioned in this *baraita* is **animal tithe.**[NB] The *baraita* teaches that the meat of the animal tithe was forbidden to one who is uncircumcised.

מַעְשַׂר בְּהֵמָה הַיְינוּ קָדָשִׁים! וְלִיטַעֲמִיךְ, מִי לָא תְּנַן פֶּסַח וְקָתָנֵי קָדָשִׁים?

The Gemara expresses surprise: **Animal tithe is** the same as **sacrificial food,** as it too is an offering the meat of which is eaten by the animal's owner; why would the *tanna* single it out? The Gemara counters: **And according to your reasoning** that the *baraita* would not have singled out specific offerings, **didn't we learn** in the *baraita* that an uncircumcised man may not eat the **Paschal lamb, and** yet **it** also **teaches** that the same *halakha* applies to **sacrificial food?**

בִּשְׁלָמָא פֶּסַח וְקָדָשִׁים צְרִיכִי, דְּאִי תָּנָא פֶּסַח – מִשּׁוּם דַּעֲרֵלוּת בְּפֶסַח כְּתִיבָא, אֲבָל קָדָשִׁים – אֵימָא לָא. וְאִי תָּנָא קָדָשִׁים – הֲוָה אָמִינָא: מַאי קָדָשִׁים – פֶּסַח. אֶלָּא, מַעְשַׂר בְּהֵמָה לָמָּה לִי?

The Gemara rejects this argument: **Granted,** it is **necessary** to mention both **the Paschal lamb and sacrificial food. As, if** the *baraita* had **taught** only the *halakha* in the case of **the Paschal lamb,** one might have said that an uncircumcised man may not eat the Paschal lamb **because** the disqualification resulting from **lack of circumcision is written** explicitly **with regard to the Paschal lamb, but** with regard to other **sacrificial food,** concerning which the Bible says nothing about circumcision, one might **say** that there is **no** such prohibition. **And** conversely, **if** the *baraita* had **taught** only the *halakha* with respect to **sacrificial food, I would say: What** is meant here by **sacrificial food?** This is referring specifically to **the Paschal lamb,** concerning which the prohibition with regard to an uncircumcised man is stated explicitly, but other sacrificial food is permitted to him. **But why do I need animal tithe** to be mentioned at all? It is no different than any other sacrificial food. In that case, the tithe mentioned in the *baraita* is referring to second tithe.

אֶלָּא – מַעֲשֵׂר רִאשׁוֹן, וְרַבִּי מֵאִיר הִיא, דְּאָמַר: מַעֲשֵׂר רִאשׁוֹן אָסוּר לְזָרִים.

The Gemara suggests a different refutation of this proof: **Rather,** the tithe mentioned in the *baraita* is referring to **first tithe,** the one-tenth of the produce that is given to the Levites, **and** the *baraita* **is** in accordance with the opinion of **Rabbi Meir, who said** that **first tithe is forbidden to common** Israelites. Since first tithe is forbidden to an ordinary Israelite, it may similarly be forbidden to an uncircumcised man. However, there is no proof from here that second tithe is forbidden to one who is uncircumcised, as second tithe is permitted even to ordinary Israelites.

תָּא שְׁמַע, מִדְּתָנֵי רַבִּי חִיָּיא בַּר רַב מִדִּפְתִּי: עָרֵל אָסוּר בִּשְׁתֵּי מַעַשְׂרוֹת. מַאי לָאו, אֶחָד מַעְשַׂר דָּגָן וְאֶחָד מַעְשַׂר בְּהֵמָה! הָכָא נַמִי מַעֲשֵׂר רִאשׁוֹן, וְרַבִּי מֵאִיר.

The Gemara suggests: **Come and hear** a different proof **from** that which **Rabbi Ḥiyya bar Rav of Difti taught** in the following *baraita*: **An uncircumcised** man **is prohibited** from eating **of two** different **tithes. What, is it not** that **one** is the **tithe of produce and one is animal tithe?** The Gemara refutes this argument: **Here, too,** the *baraita* is referring to **first tithe, and** the *baraita* is in accordance with the opinion of **Rabbi Meir.**

NOTES

Animal tithe – מַעְשַׂר בְּהֵמָה: Animal tithe is a unique offering in several respects. It is not a gift offering; rather, it is selected by releasing all the newborn sheep and cattle of a calendar year one by one from an enclosure and designating every tenth animal as tithe. The owner brings this offering to Jerusalem, and after its blood has been sprinkled with a single sprinkling, he himself may eat it. These leniencies give the animal tithe a unique status, which is why it is listed separately and not included along with the other offerings.

BACKGROUND

Animal tithe – מַעְשַׂר בְּהֵמָה: On three occasions each year, the owner of a herd of kosher animals was required to gather all the animals born during the preceding period into an enclosure and release them one by one. These animals were passed "under the shepherd's rod" (Leviticus 27:32), and every tenth animal was marked with red paint to indicate that it was consecrated. These animals are called animal tithe. If the animal was fit to be sacrificed, the it was brought to the Temple and sacrificed in a manner similar to that of a peace-offering. Its blood was sprinkled on the altar, and its meat was eaten by its owner, but not by the priests. The details of the *halakhot* of animal tithe are elucidated in tractate *Bekhorot*.

תָּא שְׁמַע: אוֹנֵן אָסוּר בְּמַעֲשֵׂר, וּמוּתָּר בִּתְרוּמָה וּבְפָרָה. טְבוּל יוֹם אָסוּר בִּתְרוּמָה, וּמוּתָּר בְּפָרָה וּבְמַעֲשֵׂר. מְחוּסַּר כִּפּוּרִים אָסוּר בְּפָרָה, וּמוּתָּר בִּתְרוּמָה וּבְמַעֲשֵׂר. וְאִם אִיתָא – נִיתְנֵי: עָרֵל אָסוּר בִּתְרוּמָה וּמוּתָּר בְּפָרָה וּבְמַעֲשֵׂר!

Come and **hear** a proof from yet another *baraita*: **It is prohibited for an acute mourner** to eat second **tithe, but** it is **permitted** for him to eat *teruma* **and** to participate in the preparation of the red **heifer. It is prohibited for one who immersed himself that day** but does not become completely purified until nightfall to eat *teruma*, **but** it is **permitted** for him to participate in the preparation of the red **heifer and** to eat second **tithe. It is prohibited for** one who **lacks atonement**, e.g., a *zav* or leper who immersed at the conclusion of his period of impurity but has not yet brought an offering for his atonement, to participate in the preparation of the red **heifer, but** it is **permitted** for him to eat *teruma* **and** second **tithe. And if it is so** that an uncircumcised man may eat second tithe, **let** the *baraita* also **teach: It is prohibited for an uncircumcised** man to eat *teruma*, **but** it is **permitted** for him to participate in the preparation of the red **heifer and** to eat second **tithe.** The fact that the *baraita* omits this ruling proves that an uncircumcised man is in fact prohibited from eating second tithe.

הַאי תַּנָּא דְּבֵי רַבִּי עֲקִיבָא הִיא, דִּמְרַבֵּי לֵיהּ לְעָרֵל כְּטָמֵא. דְּתַנְיָא, רַבִּי עֲקִיבָא אוֹמֵר: ״אִישׁ אִישׁ״ – לְרַבּוֹת אֶת הֶעָרֵל.

The Gemara rejects this argument: No proof can be adduced from here, as **this** *baraita* was **taught** by a *tanna* **from the school of Rabbi Akiva, who includes an uncircumcised** man in the same *halakha* **as** that which governs one who is **ritually impure. As it is taught** in a *baraita*, **Rabbi Akiva says:** The words "any man" in the verse "**Any man** from the seed of Aaron who is a leper or a *zav* shall not eat of the holy things until he be pure" (Leviticus 22:4) come **to include** one who is **uncircumcised;** he, too, is prohibited from partaking of consecrated food or participating in the preparation of the red heifer.

וּמַאן תַּנָּא דִּפְלִיג עֲלֵיהּ דְּרַבִּי עֲקִיבָא – תַּנָּא דְּרַבִּי יוֹסֵף הַבַּבְלִי הִיא. דְּתַנְיָא: שְׂרֵפַת אוֹנֵן וּמְחוּסַּר כִּפּוּרִים – כְּשֵׁרָה, רַבִּי יוֹסֵף הַבַּבְלִי אוֹמֵר: אוֹנֵן – כְּשֵׁרָה, מְחוּסַּר כִּפּוּרִים – פְּסוּלָה.

With regard to the issue itself, the Gemara inquires: **And who** is the *tanna* **who disagrees**[N] **with Rabbi Akiva? It is the** *tanna* who disagrees with **Rabbi Yosef the Babylonian. As it is taught** in a *baraita*: **The burning** of the red heifer **by an acute mourner or by** one who **lacks atonement is valid.**[H] **Rabbi Yosef the Babylonian says:** If the burning is performed by **an acute mourner,** it is **valid;** but if it is performed by one who **lacks atonement,** it is **invalid.** The anonymous first *tanna* clearly disagrees with Rabbi Akiva, as the previous *baraita*, which was attributed to Rabbi Akiva, states that one who lacks atonement is prohibited from participating in the preparation of the red heifer. It may be presumed that this *tanna* disagrees with Rabbi Akiva with respect to one who is uncircumcised as well.

וְאַף רַבִּי יִצְחָק סָבַר: עָרֵל אָסוּר בְּמַעֲשֵׂר, דְּאָמַר רַבִּי יִצְחָק: מִנַּיִן לְעָרֵל שֶׁאָסוּר בְּמַעֲשֵׂר – נֶאֱמַר ״מִמֶּנּוּ״ בְּמַעֲשֵׂר וְנֶאֱמַר ״מִמֶּנּוּ״ בְּפֶסַח, מַה ״מִמֶּנּוּ״ הָאָמוּר בְּפֶסַח – עָרֵל אָסוּר בּוֹ, אַף ״מִמֶּנּוּ״ הָאָמוּר בְּמַעֲשֵׂר – עָרֵל אָסוּר בּוֹ.

The Gemara further comments on this issue. **And Rabbi Yitzḥak, too, maintains** that **an uncircumcised** man is **prohibited from** eating second **tithe, as Rabbi Yitzḥak said: From where** is it derived that **an uncircumcised** man **is prohibited from** eating second **tithe? It is stated:** "And I did not consume **of it** while impure" (Deuteronomy 26:14) **with regard to** second **tithe, and it is stated:** "Do not eat **of it** raw" (Exodus 12:9) **with regard to the Paschal lamb. Just as** in the case of **the Paschal lamb,** with regard to which **"of it" is stated, an uncircumcised** man **is prohibited from** eating **it, so too,** in the case of second **tithe,** with regard to which **"of it"** is **stated, an uncircumcised** man **is prohibited from** eating **it.**

מוּפְנֵי, דְּאִי לָא מוּפְנֵי אִיכָּא לְמִיפְרַךְ: מַה לְּפֶסַח שֶׁכֵּן חַיָּיבִין עָלָיו מִשּׁוּם פִּיגּוּל וְנוֹתָר וְטָמֵא, לָאֵיי, אַפְנוּיֵי מוּפְנֵי.

With regard to this verbal analogy, the Gemara comments: It must be that this phrase "of it" **is available,** i.e., it is superfluous in its own context and therefore available for the purpose of establishing a verbal analogy. **As, if it is not available,** the verbal analogy **can be refuted** logically, as it is possible to say: **What** is unique **to the Paschal lamb?** It is **that one is liable** to receive *karet* **for** eating **it due to** it being ***piggul*** **or *notar*,** or due to him being **ritually impure.** It could therefore be argued that it is owing to the Paschal lamb's special sanctity and severity that an uncircumcised man may not partake of it. But from where is it derived that an uncircumcised man may not eat second tithe? The Gemara concludes: This is **not so,** as the phrase "of it" **is** indeed **available** for establishing the verbal analogy.

NOTES

Who is the *tanna* who disagrees – מַאן תַּנָּא דִּפְלִיג: Rashi explains that the Gemara is asking about the *tanna* who disagrees with Rabbi Akiva with regard to an uncircumcised man. *Tosafot* point out several difficulties with this interpretation, as according to the text of the Gemara here, there is no proof that Rabbi Yosef the Babylonian and the *tanna* who disagrees with him refer at all to an uncircumcised man. The whole proof is roundabout and somewhat vague. For this reason, most early authorities prefer a different interpretation, first suggested by Rabbeinu Ḥananel: The Gemara is inquiring as to the identity of the *tanna* who disagrees with Rabbi Akiva with regard to the red heifer. According to this opinion, the discussion is straightforward and the proof is clear (Ramban; Rashba).

HALAKHA

The burning of the red heifer by an acute mourner or by one who lacks atonement – שְׂרֵפַת אוֹנֵן וּמְחוּסַּר כִּפּוּרִים: If a red heifer was burned by an acute mourner or one who is lacking atonement, it is valid, in accordance with the unattributed opinion in the *baraita* and against the dissenting view of the single *tanna* (Rambam *Sefer Tahara*, *Hilkhot Para Aduma* 4:14).

מַאי מוּפְנֵי? אֲמַר רָבָא אָמַר רַבִּי יִצְחָק: תְּלָתָא "מִמֶּנּוּ" כְּתִיבִי בְּפֶסַח, חַד לְגוּפֵיהּ, וְחַד לִגְזֵירָה שָׁוָה, וְחַד,

The Gemara asks: **Which** of the phrases "of it" is not needed in its own context and **is** therefore **available** for establishing a verbal analogy? **Rava said** that **Rabbi Yitzḥak said: "Of it" is written three** times **with** regard to **the Paschal lamb:** "Do not eat of it raw… And you shall not leave any of it until morning, and that which remains of it until the morning you shall burn with fire" (Exodus 12:9–10). The three instances of "of it" are expounded as follows: **One for itself,** to teach that the prohibition relates to the Paschal lamb; **and one for the verbal analogy; and one for** another purpose.

לְמַאן דְּאָמַר: בָּא הַכָּתוּב לִיתֵּן לָךְ עֲשֵׂה אַחַר לֹא תַעֲשֶׂה, אַיְּידֵי דִּכְתִיב נוֹתָר, כְּתִיב נַמִי "מִמֶּנּוּ". וּלְמַאן דְּאָמַר לִיתֵּן לוֹ בֹּקֶר שֵׁנִי לִשְׂרֵיפָתוֹ, אַיְּידֵי דִּכְתִיב "עַד בֹּקֶר" – כְּתִיב נַמִי "מִמֶּנּוּ",

According to the one who says that **the verse comes to provide you with a positive** mitzva to burn that which is left over **after** it has taught **the prohibition** against leaving it over until the morning, to teach that one is not flogged for violating the prohibition, because any prohibition that can be rectified by the performance of a positive mitzva does not carry a punishment of lashes; **since "that which remains [*notar*]" is written, "of it" is also written. And according to the one who says** that the verse comes **to provide him with the second morning for burning,** i.e., to teach that the leftover meat of the Paschal lamb is not burned on the following morning, which is a Festival, but rather on the following morning, the first of the intermediate days of the Festival; **since "until morning" is written, "of it" is also written.**

תְּלָתָא "מִמֶּנּוּ" כְּתִיבִי בְּמַעֲשֵׂר, חַד לְגוּפֵיהּ, וְחַד לְדְרַבִּי אַבָּהוּ אָמַר רַבִּי יוֹחָנָן, וְחַד לְדְרֵישׁ לָקִישׁ.

Similarly, **"of it" is written three** times **with** regard to second **tithe:** "I did not eat of it in my mourning, and I did not consume of it while impure, and I did not give of it for the dead" (Deuteronomy 26:14). The three instances of "of it" are expounded as follows: **One for itself; and one for** that which **Rabbi Abbahu said** that **Rabbi Yoḥanan** said, that the verse comes to permit a priest to burn impure *teruma* oil and derive benefit from its light; **and one for** the following teaching of **Reish Lakish.**

דַּאֲמַר רֵישׁ לָקִישׁ אָמַר רַבִּי סַמְיָא: מִנַּיִן לְמַעֲשֵׂר שֵׁנִי שֶׁנִּטְמָא שֶׁמּוּתָּר לְסוּכוֹ – שֶׁנֶּאֱמַר "וְלֹא נָתַתִּי מִמֶּנּוּ לְמֵת", לְמֵת הוּא דְּלָא נָתַתִּי – הָא לְחַי דּוּמְיָא דְּמֵת – נָתַתִּי, אֵיזֶה דָּבָר שֶׁשָּׁוֶה בַּחַיִּים וּבַמֵּתִים – הֱוֵי אוֹמֵר: זוֹ סִיכָה.

As Reish Lakish said that **Rabbi Samya said: From where** is it derived that if the **second tithe became ritually impure, it is permitted for one to anoint** one's body **with it? As it is stated: "Nor did I give of it for the dead."** It is **for the dead that I did not give** of it, **but for the living** in a manner **similar** to the way it is given for **the dead, I gave** of it. Now, **what usage** of tithe **is the same for the living and the dead? You must say it is anointing.**

מַתְקִיף לָהּ מָר זוּטְרָא: וְאֵימָא לִיקַּח לוֹ אָרוֹן וְתַכְרִיכִים? אֲמַר רַב הוּנָא בְּרֵיהּ דְּרַב יְהוֹשֻׁעַ: "מִמֶּנּוּ" – מִגּוּפוֹ. רַב אַשִׁי אֲמַר: "לֹא נָתַתִּי" דּוּמְיָא דְּ"לֹא אָכַלְתִּי", מָה לְהַלָּן מִגּוּפוֹ – אַף כָּאן מִגּוּפוֹ.

Mar Zutra strongly objects to this: But say that the verse is referring not to anointing but to **purchasing a coffin**[N] **and shrouds for** a one who is deceased with money received in exchange for the second tithe; this is prohibited, but buying clothing and the like for one who is living is permitted. **Rav Huna, son of Rav Yehoshua, said: "Of it"** indicates benefit derived **from** the tithe **itself** and not from the money acquired in exchange for the tithe. **Rav Ashi said** a different answer: **"I did not give"** must be **similar to "I did not eat"; just as there,** eating is **from** the tithe **itself, so too here,** giving is **from** the tithe **itself.** In any event, the three instances of "of it" written with regard to second tithe are required for different expositions.

וְאַכַּתִּי, מוּפְנֶה מִצַּד אֶחָד הוּא? הָנִיחָא לְמַאן דְּאָמַר לְמֵדִין וְאֵין מְשִׁיבִין, אֶלָּא לְמַאן דְּאָמַר לְמֵדִין וּמְשִׁיבִין – מַאי אִיכָּא לְמֵימַר?

The Gemara asks: **And** yet there is **still** a difficulty, as the verbal analogy **is available** only **from one side,** since only the verse with regard to the Paschal lamb is superfluous in its own context. Granted, **this works out well according to the one who says** that **one can derive from** a verbal analogy that is available only from one side **and one cannot refute it** logically, even if there are valid counterarguments. **But according to the one who said** that **one can derive from** such an analogy and **one can** also **refute it**[N] logically, if there are grounds to distinguish between the two cases, **what can be said?** As explained above, the analogy between the Paschal lamb and second tithe can be refuted.

NOTES

But say it is referring to purchasing a coffin – וְאֵימָא לִיקַּח לוֹ אָרוֹן: *Tosafot* and other early authorities claim that this is merely a theoretical alternative, not an accepted conclusion for *halakha*. However, it is in fact permitted according to *halakha* to purchase clothes for the living from the money of impure tithe, as it is prohibited only to use it for the dead.

But according to the one who said that one can derive from it and one can also refute it – אֶלָּא לְמַאן דְּאָמַר לְמֵדִין וּמְשִׁיבִין: The commentaries note that the Gemara could simply have said that Rabbi Yitzḥak agrees with the opinion that one can derive from such an analogy and one cannot refute it, in which case there would be no need to prove that the phrase "from it" with respect to *teruma* is free for an analogy, but it wanted to establish his approach as consistent with all opinions.

הַךְ דְּרַבִּי אַבָּהוּ מִדְּרַב נַחְמָן אָמַר רַבָּה בַּר אֲבוּהּ נָפְקָא, דְּאָמַר רַב נַחְמָן אָמַר רַבָּה בַּר אֲבוּהּ: מַאי דִּכְתִיב: ״וַאֲנִי הִנֵּה נָתַתִּי לְךָ אֶת מִשְׁמֶרֶת תְּרוּמֹתָי״ בִּשְׁתֵּי תְּרוּמוֹת הַכָּתוּב מְדַבֵּר, אַחַת תְּרוּמָה טְהוֹרָה וְאַחַת תְּרוּמָה טְמֵאָה, וְאָמַר רַחֲמָנָא: ״לְךָ״ שֶׁלְּךָ תְּהֵא, לְהַסָּקָה תַּחַת תַּבְשִׁילְךָ.

The Gemara answers: **This** *halakha* **of Rabbi Abbahu** with regard to the burning of impure *teruma* oil **is derived from what Rav Naḥman said** that **Rabba bar Avuh** said. **As Rav Naḥman said** that **Rabba bar Avuh said: What is** the meaning of that **which is written: "And I, behold, I have given you the charge of My** *terumot*" (Numbers 18:8)? From the amplification of the plural "My *terumot*," it is derived that **the verse is speaking of two** *terumot*, **one** *teruma* **that is ritually pure and one** *teruma* **that is ritually impure. And the Merciful One states:** "I have given **you**," i.e., **it shall be yours,** and you may derive benefit from it. Since there is a stringent prohibition against eating impure *teruma*, the benefit that is permitted is **to burn it beneath your cooked dish.** As the allowance to benefit from the burning of impure *teruma* is derived from here, the phrase "of it" is available on both sides.

וְכָל הַטְּמֵאִים כו׳. מְנָא הָנֵי מִילֵּי? אָמַר רַבִּי יוֹחָנָן מִשּׁוּם רַבִּי יִשְׁמָעֵאל: אָמַר קְרָא ״אִישׁ אִישׁ מִזֶּרַע אַהֲרֹן וְהוּא צָרוּעַ אוֹ זָב״ וגו׳ אֵי זֶהוּ דָּבָר שֶׁשָּׁוֶה

§ It is taught in the mishna that **all** those **who are ritually impure** with any type of ritual impurity may not eat *teruma*. The Gemara asks: **From where are these matters** derived? **Rabbi Yoḥanan said in the name of Rabbi Yishmael: The verse states: "Any man from the seed of Aaron who is a leper or a** *zav* shall not eat of the holy things until he be pure" (Leviticus 22:4). Now, **what matter is the same**

Perek **VIII**
Daf **74** Amud **b**

בְּזַרְעוֹ שֶׁל אַהֲרֹן – הֱוֵי אוֹמֵר זוֹ תְּרוּמָה. וְאֵימָא בְּחָזֶה וָשׁוֹק! אֵינָהּ בְּחוֹזֶרֶת.

for all the **seed of Aaron,** both sons and daughters? **You must say it is** *teruma*. The Gemara raises a difficulty: **But say** that perhaps the verse is referring to **the breast and thigh** of a peace-offering, which also may be eaten by all the seed of Aaron, both male and female? The Gemara answers: The breast and thigh are not permitted to males and females in equal manner, as they **are not** permitted **to** the daughter of a priest **who returns**[H] to the home of her father. If the daughter of a priest marries a non-priest, it is prohibited for her to partake of *teruma* or sacrificial food. If she is widowed or divorced and has no living descendants by her non-priest husband, it is once again permitted for her to eat *teruma*, but she may not partake of the breast and thigh of the offerings.

תְּרוּמָה נַמִי אֵינָהּ בַּחֲלָלָה! חֲלָלָה לָאו זַרְעוֹ דְּאַהֲרֹן הִיא.

The Gemara asks: If so, the same may be said about *teruma* **as well,** as it is **not** permitted **to a** *ḥalala*,[NH] a woman who is disqualified from marrying a priest, even though she is the daughter of a priest. The Gemara answers: **A** *ḥalala* **is not** considered **the seed of Aaron.**

וּמִמַּאי דְּהַאי ״עַד אֲשֶׁר יִטְהָר״ עַד דְּאִיכָּא הֶעֱרֵב שֶׁמֶשׁ? אֵימָא: עַד דְּמַיְיתֵי כַּפָּרָה!

The Gemara challenges the *halakha* recorded in the *baraita* that one who lacks atonement may eat *teruma*. **And from where** do you know **that this** verse: "Any man from the seed of Aaron who is a leper or a *zav* shall not eat of the holy things **until he be pure,"** means that he may not eat of the holy things **until sunset? Say** that perhaps it means that he may not eat of them **until he brings** his **atonement** offering and is entirely pure.

HALAKHA

They are not permitted to one who returns – אֵינָהּ בְּחוֹזֶרֶת: If the daughter of a priest married a non-priest, and he died or divorced her and she has no living descendants from him, she may once again eat *teruma*, but she may not eat the breast and thigh of peace-offerings (Rambam *Sefer Zera'im, Hilkhot Terumot* 6:9).

Teruma…is not permitted to a *ḥalala* – תְּרוּמָה...אֵינָהּ בַּחֲלָלָה: If the daughter of a priest had relations with a man who is forbidden to her, she is disqualified from marrying a priest and may never again eat *teruma* (Rambam *Sefer Zera'im, Hilkhot Terumot* 6:7).

NOTES

It is not permitted to a *ḥalala* – אֵינָהּ בַּחֲלָלָה: The Ritva notes that the Gemara here is not asking about only a *ḥalala* in the strict sense, i.e., the daughter of a union between a priest and a woman who is forbidden to him, but also about the daughter of a priest who had relations with a man who is forbidden to her. The Gemara answers that in all such cases the woman is no longer considered the seed of Aaron, and therefore she is prohibited from partaking of *teruma*.

לָא סָלְקָא דַּעְתָּךְ, דְּתָנָא דְּבֵי רַבִּי יִשְׁמָעֵאל: בְּזָב בַּעַל שְׁתֵּי רְאִיּוֹת וּבִמְצוֹרָע מוּסְגָּר הַכָּתוּב מְדַבֵּר, דּוּמְיָא דִּטְמֵא נֶפֶשׁ, מַה טְּמֵא נֶפֶשׁ – דְּלָאו בַּר כַּפָּרָה הוּא, הָנֵי נַמִּי – דְּלָאו בְּנֵי כַּפָּרָה נִינְהוּ.

The Gemara answers: **This cannot enter your mind, as a *tanna* of the school of Rabbi Yishmael taught that the verse is speaking of a *zav* who** experienced only **two sightings**[N] of an emission, **and of a quarantined leper,**[N] i.e., a suspected leper who has not yet been declared conclusively ritually impure by a priest. Both of these individuals are ritually impure, but they need not bring an offering as part of the purification process. When understood in this way, the leper and *zav* are **similar to** one who touches any object that is **impure** with ritual impurity imparted by **a corpse,** mentioned later in the verse: **Just as** one who touches anything that is **impure** with ritual impurity imparted by **a corpse does not require an atonement** offering for his impurity, **these too,** the *zav* and leper referred to in this verse, **do not require an atonement** offering; rather, they achieve complete purification at sunset.

וְאֵימָא: הָנֵי מִילֵּי – דְּלָאו בַּר כַּפָּרָה, אֲבָל דְּבַר כַּפָּרָה – עַד דְּמַיְיתֵי כַּפָּרָה!

The Gemara raises a question: **But say** that **this** *halakha* **that** sunset alone suffices to permit the eating of *teruma* **applies only** to one **who does not require** an **atonement** offering but merely has to wait until sunset to achieve complete purification. **However,** with regard to **one who does require** an **atonement** offering, perhaps he may not eat *teruma* **until he brings** his **atonement** offering.

וְתוּ: הָא דִּתְנַן: טָבַל וְעָלָה – אוֹכֵל בְּמַעֲשֵׂר, הֶעֱרִיב שִׁמְשׁוֹ – אוֹכֵל בִּתְרוּמָה, הֵבִיא כַּפָּרָה – אוֹכֵל בְּקָדָשִׁים, מְנָא לַן?

And furthermore, the Gemara raises a question with regard to **that which we learned** in a mishna (*Nega'im* 14:3): When the period of ritual impurity of a *zav* or a leper has been completed and he **immersed** during the day **and emerged, he may** immediately **partake of** second **tithe;**[H] once **the sun has set for him,** he may **partake of *teruma*;**[H] once he has **brought his atonement** offering, he may **eat sacrificial food.**[H] **From where do we** derive these different *halakhot*?[N]

אֲמַר רָבָא אֲמַר רַב חִסְדָּא: תְּלָתָא קְרָאֵי כְּתִיבִי; כְּתִיב "וְלֹא יֹאכַל מִן הַקֳּדָשִׁים כִּי אִם רָחַץ בְּשָׂרוֹ בַּמָּיִם", הָא רָחַץ – טָהוֹר. וּכְתִיב "וּבָא הַשֶּׁמֶשׁ וְטָהֵר וְאַחַר יֹאכַל מִן הַקֳּדָשִׁים", וּכְתִיב "וְכִפֶּר עָלֶיהָ הַכֹּהֵן וְטָהֵרָה". הָא כֵּיצַד? כָּאן לְמַעֲשֵׂר, כָּאן לִתְרוּמָה, כָּאן לְקָדָשִׁים.

Rava said that **Rav Ḥisda said: Three verses are written** with regard to purity for eating sacred food. **It is written: "And he shall not eat of the holy things, unless he has bathed his flesh in water"** (Leviticus 22:6); **but if he has bathed,** i.e., immersed, he is immediately **pure** and may partake of sacred food. **And it is written: "And when the sun has set, he shall be pure, and afterward he may eat from the holy things"** (Leviticus 22:7), which indicates that he must wait until sunset. **And it is further written: "And the priest shall make atonement for her, and she shall be pure"** (Leviticus 12:8), which indicates that following childbirth a woman is not completely pure until she has brought her offering. **How so?** How can the apparent discrepancy between these three verses be resolved? **Here,** in the first verse, it is referring **to** second **tithe; there,** in the second verse, it is referring **to *teruma*;** and **here,** in the third verse, it is referring **to sacrificial food.**

וְאֵיפוֹךְ אֲנָא! מִסְתַּבְּרָא, תְּרוּמָה עֲדִיפָא שֶׁכֵּן מחפ"ז.

The Gemara asks: **But I can reverse** this construct and apply the more stringent condition to tithe. The Gemara answers: **It is reasonable** to say that ***teruma*** **is** subject to the **more stringent** condition, **as it is** already subject to many stringent elements represented by the acronym ***mem, ḥet, peh, zayin,***[N] which is a mnemonic for the following: One who is prohibited from eating *teruma* but ate it intentionally is liable to the punishment of death [*mita*] at the hand of Heaven; a non-priest who unwittingly ate *teruma* is obligated to pay its value to the priest plus one-fifth [*ḥomesh*] of the sum; *teruma* does not have the possibility of redemption [*pidyon*]; and it is prohibited to non-priests [*zarim*]. These stringencies do not apply to second tithe.

NOTES

A *zav* who experienced two sightings – זָב בַּעַל שְׁתֵּי רְאִיּוֹת: It is learned by tradition that a man has the status of a full-fledged *zav* only if he experiences three gonorrheal emissions, which are termed sightings. After the first sighting he is not considered a *zav* at all but simply as one who experienced a seminal emission. Following his second sighting he is a *zav* with regard to ritual impurity, but if he does not experience a third emission he need not bring an offering to achieve purification.

A quarantined leper – מְצוֹרָע מוּסְגָּר: The impurity of a leper has two stages. When one first discovers a spot he suspects might be leprous, he must go to a priest, who quarantines him for seven days to see if the plague advances. Sometimes he is quarantined for a further seven days. Only when it becomes clear that he suffers from a full manifestation of leprosy, i.e., if it spreads, is he declared a confirmed leper. However, there is no difference between these two stages with regard to their impurity; the main difference between them is that a confirmed leper must bring special offerings of atonement upon his purification.

From where do we derive these different *halakhot* – מְנָא לַן: *Otzar HaShitot* raises the difficulty that Rava's answer seems to resolve only the second question, but not the first that perhaps sunset alone does not suffice to permit the eating of *teruma* in a case where an atonement offering is required. The Meiri, however, already hinted that once it is learned by tradition that this verse is dealing with a *zav* and leper who are not obligated to bring offerings, a principle can be derived from here that in order to eat *teruma*, only immersion is required. Were this not the case, the Torah would have had to state that those who are obligated to bring offerings must bring them before they can partake of *teruma*.

As it is subject to *mem, ḥet, peh, zayin* – שֶׁכֵּן מחפ"ז: The Ramban points out that there are other stringencies in connection with *teruma*, e.g., it requires the washing of hands and it is nullified only in a mixture of one hundred to one. He suggests several answers to the question why these are not mentioned here. First, these stringencies are rabbinic in origin. In addition, second tithe is not nullified by a simple majority either, as it is in the category of things that are only temporarily prohibited. Furthermore, even if the Gemara had mentioned these two *halakhot*, there would be merely an equal number of stringencies, and therefore the Gemara would still have had to answer that the punishment of death is a greater stringency.

HALAKHA

Once he immersed and emerged, he may partake of second tithe – טָבַל וְעָלָה אוֹכֵל בְּמַעֲשֵׂר: After one who was ritually impure has immersed, he need not wait for sunset but may eat second tithe immediately (Rambam *Sefer Zera'im, Hilkhot Ma'aser Sheni* 3:4).

Once the sun has set for him, he may partake of *teruma* – הֶעֱרִיב שִׁמְשׁוֹ אוֹכֵל בִּתְרוּמָה: One who was ritually impure and has immersed may not eat *teruma* until the sun has set and three stars have emerged (Rambam *Sefer Zera'im, Hilkhot Terumot* 7:2).

Once he has brought his atonement offering, he may eat sacrificial food – הֵבִיא כַּפָּרָה אוֹכֵל בְּקָדָשִׁים: Those who must bring an offering to complete their purification process, i.e., a *zav*, a *zava*, a woman after childbirth, and a leper, even if they have immersed and waited until sunset, may not partake of sacrificial food until they have brought their atonement offerings (Rambam *Sefer Korbanot, Hilkhot Meḥusrei Kappara* 1:1).

אַדְּרַבָּה, מַעֲשֵׂר עֲדִיפָא שֶׁכֵּן הד"ס ט"ב!

The Gemara counters: **On the contrary,** second **tithe** should be governed by the **more stringent** condition, **as it has** the stringencies represented by the acronym ***heh, dalet, samekh, tet, beit,***[N] which is a mnemonic for the following: Second tithe must be brought [*hava'a*] to Jerusalem; it requires that a declaration [*viddui*] be made on the last day of Passover in the fourth and seventh year of the Sabbatical cycle, stating that one's agricultural obligations with regard to tithes have been properly fulfilled; it is prohibited [*asur*] to be eaten by one in acute mourning; it may not be burned in a state of impurity [*tuma*]; and it must be removed [*biur*] from one's house before Passover in the fourth and seventh years of the Sabbatical cycle, if one failed to do so beforehand.

אֲפִילּוּ הָכִי, מִיתָה עֲדִיפָא.

The Gemara responds: **Even so,** the punishment of **death is a greater** stringency, and therefore it is appropriate that *teruma* should be subject to the additional stringency of waiting until sunset.

רָבָא אֲמַר: בְּלָא מִיתָה עֲדִיפָא נַמִי לָא מָצֵית אָמְרַתְּ, אָמַר קְרָא "נֶפֶשׁ", אֵיזֶהוּ דָּבָר שֶׁשָּׁוֶה בְּכׇל נֶפֶשׁ הֱוֵי אוֹמֵר זֶה מַעֲשֵׂר.

Rava said: Even **without** the rationale that the punishment of **death is a greater** stringency, **you still could not say** that the first verse that speaks only of immersion is referring to *teruma*. As **the verse states** in the continuation: "The **soul** that touches it" (Leviticus 22:6). Now, **what matter is the same for every soul? You must say it is tithe,** as *teruma* may be eaten only by priests.

וְאַכַּתִּי, הָנֵי מִילֵּי הֵיכָא דְּלָאו בַּר כַּפָּרָה, אֲבָל הֵיכָא דְּבַר כַּפָּרָה – עַד דְּמַיְיתֵי כַּפָּרָה!

The Gemara raises a difficulty with the mishna: **But still,** say that **this** *halakha* **that** sunset alone is enough for the eating of *teruma* **applies only** to one **who does not require** an **atonement** offering but merely has to wait until sunset when he is completely purified. **However,** with regard to **one who does require** an **atonement** offering, such as a confirmed leper, perhaps he may not eat *teruma* **until he brings** his **atonement** offering.

אָמַר אַבָּיֵי: תְּרֵי קְרָאֵי כְּתִיבִי בְּיוֹלֶדֶת: כְּתִיב "עַד מְלֹאת יְמֵי טׇהֳרָהּ", כֵּיוָן שֶׁמָּלְאוּ יָמֶיהָ – טְהוֹרָה, וּכְתִיב "וְכִפֶּר עָלֶיהָ הַכֹּהֵן וְטָהֵרָה", הָא כֵּיצַד? כָּאן לִתְרוּמָה, כָּאן – לְקָדָשִׁים.

Abaye said: Two verses are written with regard to a woman after childbirth: It is written: "She shall touch no hallowed thing, nor come into the Sanctuary, **until the days of her purification are completed**" (Leviticus 12:4), which suggests that **once her days are completed** and the sun has set on the last day, **she is** completely **pure** and requires nothing more. **And** elsewhere **it is written: "And the priest shall make atonement for her, and she shall be pure"** (Leviticus 12:8), which indicates that following childbirth a woman is not completely pure until she has brought her offerings. **How so? Here,** in the first verse, it is referring **to *teruma*; there,** in the second verse, it is referring **to sacrificial food.** A woman following childbirth falls into the category of one who lacks atonement, but nevertheless the verse teaches that if she has immersed, she may eat *teruma* after sunset. The same is true of a confirmed leper and all others who lack atonement.

וְאֵיפוֹךְ אֲנָא! מִסְתַּבְּרָא, קֹדֶשׁ חָמוּר, שֶׁכֵּן פנקעכ"ס.

The Gemara asks: **But I can reverse** this construct and apply the more stringent condition to *teruma*. The Gemara answers: **It is reasonable** to say that **sacrificial food is** subject to the **more stringent** condition, as it is already subject to many stringent elements represented by the acronym, ***peh, nun, kuf, ayin, kaf, samekh,*** which is a mnemonic for the following stringencies that apply to sacrificial food and not to *teruma*: An offering is disqualified by improper intention during one of the rites involved in its sacrifice with regard to the time it will be eaten [*piggul*]; meat of an offering that remained beyond its allotted time [*notar*] may not be eaten and must be burned; it is an offering [*korban*] to God; one who unwittingly derives benefit from sacrificial food is required to bring a guilt-offering for misuse of consecrated items [*me'ila*]; the punishment of one who eats sacrificial food while ritually impure is excision [*karet*]; sacrificial food is prohibited [*asur*] to an acute mourner.

אַדְּרַבָּה, תְּרוּמָה חֲמוּרָה, שֶׁכֵּן מחפ"ז! הָנָךְ נְפִישָׁן.

The Gemara challenges this argument: **On the contrary,** ***teruma*** should be subject to the **more stringent** condition, **as,** with regard to *teruma,* there are many stringent elements represented by the acronym ***mem, ḥet, peh, zayin.*** The Gemara answers: **Those** stringencies that apply to sacrificial food **are** more **numerous** than those that apply to *teruma*.

NOTES

As it has *heh, dalet, samekh, tet, beit* – שֶׁכֵּן הד"ס ט"ב: The Ramban understands that the *tet* of this mnemonic means that one who eats tithe in a state of impurity [*tuma*] is flogged. He is therefore puzzled as to why the Gemara does not also mention the *halakha* that it is prohibited to burn tithe in a state of impurity. He answers that it was unnecessary, as even without this *halakha* second tithe has more stringencies than *teruma*. Sensing this difficulty, Rashi explains that the *tet* alludes to both of the above *halakhot*.

רָבָא אֲמַר: בְּלֹא הָנָךְ נְפִישָׁן לָא מָצֵית אָמְרַתְּ, אָמַר קְרָא "וְכִפֶּר עָלֶיהָ הַכֹּהֵן וְטָהֵרָה" מִכְּלָל שֶׁהִיא טְמֵאָה. וְאִי סָלְקָא דַּעְתָּךְ בְּקָדָשִׁים – אִיקְרֵי כָּאן "וְהַבָּשָׂר אֲשֶׁר יִגַּע בְּכָל טָמֵא לֹא יֵאָכֵל". אֶלָּא שְׁמַע מִינָּהּ בִּתְרוּמָה.

Rava said: Even **without** the rationale that **those** stringencies that apply to sacrificial food **are** more **numerous, you still could not say** that the verse that renders a woman pure at sunset refers to sacrificial food, as **the verse states: "And the priest shall make atonement for her, and she shall be pure,"** which indicates **by inference that she** remains **ritually impure** to some degree until she has sacrificed her offerings. **And if it enters your mind** that she may eat **sacrificial food** immediately after sunset, you should **apply here** what is stated in a different verse: **"And the flesh that touches anything impure shall not be eaten"** (Leviticus 7:19), which indicates that one who is impure with any type of ritual impurity is prohibited from eating sacrificial food. **Rather, learn from this** that the verse is referring to *teruma*.

מַתְקִיף לָהּ רַב שֵׁישָׁא בְּרֵיהּ דְּרַב אִידִי: וּמִי מָצֵית אָמְרַתְּ תְּרוּמָה כְּתִיבָא הָכָא? וְהָתַנְיָא: "דַּבֵּר אֶל בְּנֵי יִשְׂרָאֵל", אֵין לִי אֶלָּא בְּנֵי יִשְׂרָאֵל, גִּיּוֹרֶת וְשִׁפְחָה מְשׁוּחְרֶרֶת מִנַּיִן – תַּלְמוּד לוֹמַר "אִשָּׁה". וְאִי סָלְקָא דַּעְתָּךְ בִּתְרוּמָה – גִּיּוֹרֶת וְשִׁפְחָה בְּנוֹת מֵיכַל תְּרוּמָה נִינְהוּ?!

Rav Sheisha, son of Rav Idi, strongly objects to this argument: **And how can you say** that a *halakha* governing *teruma* **is written here,** in the verse: "Until the days of her purification are completed" (Leviticus 12:4)? **Isn't it taught** in a *baraita*: The section dealing with a woman following childbirth opens with the verse: **"Speak to the children of Israel,** saying: If a woman delivers and bears a male, then she shall be unclean seven days; as in the days of the impurity of her menstrual affliction shall she be unclean" (Leviticus 12:2). From this verse **I have** derived **only** that **the children of Israel** are included in this *halakha*; **from where** do I derive that **a convert and an emancipated maidservant** are also included? Therefore, **the verse states: "A woman,"** which includes other women.[H] **And if it enters your mind** that the verse is speaking **of** *teruma*, **are a convert and a maidservant eligible to eat** *teruma*? It is prohibited for them to marry priests, so there can be no possibility of their eating *teruma*.

אֲמַר רָבָא: וְלָא?!

Rava said: And is the verse **not** referring to *teruma* as well?

HALAKHA

A woman following childbirth who is a convert or an emancipated maidservant – יוֹלֶדֶת שֶׁהִיא גִּיּוֹרֶת אוֹ שִׁפְחָה: If one had intercourse with a woman who gave birth to a male child within the last seven days or to a female child within the last fourteen days, whether she was an ordinary Jew, a convert, or an emancipated maidservant, he is liable to receive *karet* (Rambam *Sefer Kedusha, Hilkhot Issurei Bia* 4:2).

Perek **VIII**
Daf **75** Amud **a**

וְהָכְתִיב "בְּכָל קֹדֶשׁ לֹא תִגָּע" לְרַבּוֹת הַתְּרוּמָה! אֶלָּא: קְרָא מִילֵּי מִילֵּי קָא חָשֵׁיב.

But isn't it written in that same section dealing with a woman after childbirth: **"She shall touch no hallowed thing,** nor come into the Sanctuary, until the days of her purification are completed" (Leviticus 12:4), which comes **to include** ***teruma*****?**[H] **Rather, the Torah considers several** distinct **matters** separately, and not all the verses refer to *teruma*.

וּתְלָתָא קְרָאֵי בִּתְרוּמָה לָמָּה לִי? צְרִיכִי, דְּאִי מֵ"עַד אֲשֶׁר יִטְהָר" לָא הֲוָה יָדַעְנָא בְּמַאי, כְּתַב רַחֲמָנָא "וּבָא הַשֶּׁמֶשׁ וְטָהֵר".

The Gemara asks: **And why do I** need **three verses with regard to** ***teruma*****?** The Gemara answers: **They are** all **necessary, as, had** *teruma* been derived solely from the verse: "He shall not eat of the holy things **until he be pure"** (Leviticus 22:4), **I would not have known by what** means ritual purity is achieved, whether by immersion alone or in some other way. Therefore, **the Merciful One writes: "And when the sun has set he shall be pure,** and afterward he may eat from the holy things" (Leviticus 22:7), to teach that he must also wait for sunset.

וְאִי כְּתַב רַחֲמָנָא "וּבָא הַשֶּׁמֶשׁ" – הָנֵי מִילֵּי דְּלָאו בַּר כַּפָּרָה, אֲבָל דְּבַר כַּפָּרָה – אֵימָא עַד דְּמַיְיתֵי כַּפָּרָה, כְּתַב רַחֲמָנָא "עַד מְלֹאת".

And had the Merciful One written only: **"And when the sun has set,"** I might have said that **this applies** only **to one who does not require** an **atonement** offering, **but** as for one **who requires** an **atonement** offering, one might **say** that he may not eat *teruma* **until he brings** his **atonement** offering. Therefore, **the Merciful One writes:** "She shall touch no hallowed thing, nor come into the Sanctuary, **until the days of her purification are completed"** (Leviticus 12:4), which indicates that she may eat *teruma* as soon as her days of purification are completed, and she need not wait until after she has brought her atonement offering.

HALAKHA

No hallowed thing, to include ***teruma*** **– בְּכָל קֹדֶשׁ...לְרַבּוֹת הַתְּרוּמָה:** During her period of purity, it is permitted for a woman after childbirth to eat second tithe. However, it is prohibited for her to eat *teruma*, which she disqualifies, as does one who was ritually impure who immersed on that day (Rambam *Sefer Tahara, Hilkhot Metamei Mishkav UMoshav* 5:4).

וְאִי כָּתַב רַחֲמָנָא "עַד מְלֹאת" הֲוָה אָמֵינָא: אֲפִילּוּ בְּלֹא טְבִילָה, כָּתַב רַחֲמָנָא "עַד אֲשֶׁר יִטְהָר".

And had the Merciful One written only: "**Until** the days of her purification **are completed**,"[N] **I would say** that upon the completion of the purification period she is immediately purified **even without immersion.** Therefore, **the Merciful One writes: "Until he be pure."**

וּלְהַךְ תַּנָּא דִּפְלִיג עֲלֵיהּ דְּתַנָּא דְּבֵי רַבִּי יִשְׁמָעֵאל, דְּאָמַר: בְּזָב בַּעַל שָׁלֹשׁ רְאִיּוֹת וּבִמְצוֹרָע מוּחְלָט הַכָּתוּב מְדַבֵּר, וְהַאי "עַד אֲשֶׁר יִטְהָר" עַד דְּמַיְיתֵי כַּפָּרָה – תְּרֵי קְרָאֵי בְּקָדָשִׁים לָמָּה לִי?

The Gemara asks: **And according to that** ***tanna*** **who disagrees with the** ***tanna*** **of the school of Rabbi Yishmael and says** that **the verse** "Any man from the seed of Aaron who is a leper or a *zav* shall not eat of the holy things until he be pure" (Leviticus 22:4) **is speaking of a** ***zav*** who already experienced **three sightings** of an emission, **and of a confirmed leper,** both of whom must bring an offering as part of their purification process; **and,** this being the case, **that** phrase "**until he be pure**" must mean **until he brings** his **atonement** offering; then **why do I need two verses with regard to sacrificial food,** this verse and the verse with regard to a woman after childbirth: "And the priest shall make atonement for her, and she shall be pure" (Leviticus 12:8), to teach us that sacrificial food may not be eaten until after the atonement offering has been brought?

צְרִיכִי; דְּאִי כָּתַב רַחֲמָנָא בְּיוֹלֶדֶת – מִשּׁוּם דִּמְרוּבָּה טוּמְאָתָהּ, אֲבָל בְּזָב – אֵימָא לָא. וְאִי כָּתַב רַחֲמָנָא בְּזָב – דְּלָא הוּתַּר מִכְּלָלוֹ, אֲבָל יוֹלֶדֶת אֵימָא לָא – צְרִיכָא.

The Gemara answers: **They are** both **necessary, as had the Merciful One written** this *halakha* only **with regard to a woman after childbirth,** one might have said that it applies only to her **because her** period of ritual **impurity is so long,** as she may not return to eating *teruma* or sacrificial food for either forty days, in the case of a male child, or eighty days, in the case of a female. **But with regard to a** ***zav,*** **say** that this is **not** the case. **And had the Merciful One written** this *halakha* only **with regard to a** ***zav,*** one might have said that it applies only to him, **as no exemption is** ever **made from its general prohibition** and he is always impure. **But** as for **a woman after childbirth,** who is permitted to her husband for thirty-three or sixty-six days of that period, **say** that this is **not** the case.[N] Both verses **are** therefore **necessary.**

"בַּמַּיִם יוּבָא וְטָמֵא עַד הָעֶרֶב" לָמָּה לִי? אָמַר רַבִּי זֵירָא: לִנְגִיעָה.

The Gemara asks: As for the verse stated with regard to a vessel that contracted ritual impurity through contact with a creeping animal: **"It must be put into water, and it shall be impure until the evening;** then shall it be pure" (Leviticus 11:32), **why do I** need it? **Rabbi Zeira said:** It is necessary in order to teach about **touching.** An impure vessel, even after it has been immersed, still imparts ritual impurity to the *teruma* that it touches until nightfall. The same applies to an impure individual who has already undergone immersion; not only is it prohibited for him to eat *teruma,* but also he renders it impure if he touches it.

דְּתַנְיָא: "וְטָמֵא", יָכוֹל לַכֹּל – תַּלְמוּד לוֹמַר "וְטָהֵר", אִי "וְטָהֵר" יָכוֹל לַכֹּל – תַּלְמוּד לוֹמַר "וְטָמֵא". הָא כֵּיצַד? כָּאן – לְמַעֲשֵׂר, כָּאן – לִתְרוּמָה.

As it is taught in a *baraita*: Had the verse stated only: "It must be put into water, **and it shall be impure** until the evening," one **might** have thought that it remains ritually impure until the evening **in all regards. Therefore, the verse states: "Then shall it be pure,"** indicating that it is pure following immersion, even before sunset. And **had** it stated only: **"Then shall it be pure,"** one **might** have thought that it is pure following immersion **in all** regards. **Therefore, the verse states: "And it shall be impure** until the evening." **How so;** how can the apparent contradiction between the two parts of the verse be resolved? **Here,** the verse is referring **to** second **tithe,** for which immersion alone suffices; and **there** it is referring **to** ***teruma,*** for which sunset is required.

וְאֵיפוֹךְ אֲנָא! מִסְתַּבְּרָא, כִּי הֵיכִי דַּחֲמִירָא אֲכִילָה דִּתְרוּמָה מֵאֲכִילָה דְּמַעֲשֵׂר הָכִי נַמִי חֲמִירָא נְגִיעָה דִּתְרוּמָה מִנְּגִיעָה דְּמַעֲשֵׂר.

The Gemara asks: **But I can reverse**[N] this construct and say that the greater stringency should be applied to second tithe. The Gemara answers: **It is reasonable** to say that *teruma* is subject to the greater stringency; **just as the eating of** ***teruma*** **is** subject to **greater stringency than the eating of** second **tithe, so too, the touching of** ***teruma*** should be subject to **greater stringency than the touching of** second **tithe.**

NOTES

And had the Merciful One written: Until the days of her purification are completed – וְאִי כָּתַב רַחֲמָנָא עַד מְלֹאת: The early authorities ask: The Torah could have written only "Until the days of her purification are completed" (Leviticus 12:4), and the verse "And when the sun has set" (Leviticus 22:7) would not have been necessary. The Ramban and the Rashba answer that the *halakhot* governing a woman after childbirth are stringent in certain aspects, e.g., concerning the duration of her impurity, as stated by the Gemara here, and lenient in other ways, as she is permitted to her husband for an extended period of time. Consequently, nothing can be derived from her case with regard to others who lack atonement.

But for a woman after childbirth, say that this is not the case – אֲבָל יוֹלֶדֶת אֵימָא לָא: The early authorities point out that this opinion, that a special allowance is made with regard to a woman after childbirth, is that of Rav, who maintains that the blood of childbirth during the woman's days of purity is related to menstrual blood, and so a special allowance is necessary. However, according to the opinion that there is no link between the two types of blood, the reason that she is permitted to her husband during her days of purity is because the blood she sees during that period comes from a source of purity, whereas her own status renders her prohibited from partaking of sacrificial food. The *Arukh LaNer* asserts that it can be said that a special allowance is made here without recourse to this dispute, as it is a simple fact that during her first days of impurity a woman after childbirth is prohibited both from partaking of sacrificial food and from engaging in relations with her husband, but later she is permitted to him. Therefore, an allowance is made with regard to her general prohibition.

But I can reverse – וְאֵיפוֹךְ אֲנָא: This is puzzling: How could it be prohibited to touch something but permitted to eat it, as one must come into contact with the tithe when he eats it? The Ra'avad and others suggest a case where one can eat something without coming into contact with it, e.g., where he shoves the food down deep into his throat by means of a utensil that is not susceptible to impurity.

וְאִיבָּעֵית אֵימָא: נְגִיעָה דִּתְרוּמָה מֵהָכָא נָפְקָא: ״בְּכׇל קֹדֶשׁ לֹא תִגָּע״ – אַזְהָרָה לְאוֹכֵל, אוֹ אֵינוֹ אֶלָּא לְנוֹגֵעַ?

And if you wish, say that the prohibition with regard to the **touching of** *teruma* **is derived from here: "She shall touch no hallowed thing,** nor come into the Sanctuary, until the days of her purification are completed" (Leviticus 12:4); this is **a warning with respect to one who eats** *teruma* after having immersed but before sunset.[H] **Or,** perhaps, **it is nothing other than** a warning **with respect to one who touches** *teruma* before sunset, as is implied by the plain reading of the verse?

תַּלְמוּד לוֹמַר ״בְּכׇל קֹדֶשׁ לֹא תִגָּע וְאֶל הַמִּקְדָּשׁ לֹא תָבֹא״ – מַקִּישׁ קֹדֶשׁ לְמִקְדָּשׁ, מָה מִקְדָּשׁ – דָּבָר שֶׁיֵּשׁ בּוֹ נְטִילַת נְשָׁמָה, אַף קֹדֶשׁ – דָּבָר שֶׁיֵּשׁ בּוֹ נְטִילַת נְשָׁמָה, וּבִנְגִיעָה נְטִילַת נְשָׁמָה לֵיכָּא.

Therefore, **the verse states: "She shall touch no hallowed thing, nor come into the Sanctuary,** until the days of her purification are completed" (Leviticus 12:4), thereby **juxtaposing consecrated** food **to the Sanctuary. Just as** the prohibition against entering **the Sanctuary is a matter that involves the taking of life,** as one who enters the Sanctuary while impure is liable to receive *karet*, **so too,** the prohibition against touching **consecrated** food must be **a matter that involves the taking of life,** e.g., eating *teruma* in a state of ritual impurity; **but** the prohibition against **touching** *teruma* in a state of impurity **does not involve the taking of life,** as there is no punishment of *karet* for mere touching.

וְהַאי דְּאַפְקֵיהּ בִּלְשׁוֹן נְגִיעָה – הָכִי קָאָמַר: נְגִיעָה כַּאֲכִילָה.

And as for the fact **that** the verse **expressed** this *halakha* **in terms of touching, this is what** it **is saying:** The *halakha* governing **touching is like** that of **eating,** as they are both prohibited to an impure person, even after immersion, until sunset. But the verse is actually speaking of the prohibition against eating *teruma* in a state of impurity.

״פְּצוּעַ דַּכָּא״ וכו׳. מַאן תְּנָא מִשְׁתַּמֶּרֶת לְבִיאָה פְּסוּלָה דְּאוֹרָיְיתָא אָכְלָה? אָמַר רַבִּי אֶלְעָזָר: בְּמַחְלוֹקֶת שְׁנוּיָה, וְרַבִּי אֶלְעָזָר וְרַבִּי שִׁמְעוֹן הִיא.

§ It is taught in the mishna that the wife of a priest with **crushed testicles** or a severed penis may eat *teruma* on his account, provided that they have not engaged in sexual relations since his injury. The Gemara asks: **Who is the** *tanna* **who taught** with regard to a woman **awaiting intercourse that would disqualify** her from marrying into the priesthood **by Torah** law, as in this case, where the woman would become disqualified from marrying into the priesthood if she had relations with her injured husband, that such a woman **may eat** *teruma*? **Rabbi Elazar said:** This *halakha* **is subject to dispute, and it is** taught in the mishna in accordance with the opinion of **Rabbi Elazar and Rabbi Shimon,** who similarly stated that a widow betrothed to a High Priest may eat *teruma* on his account, provided that he has not engaged in sexual relations with her.

רַבִּי יוֹחָנָן אָמַר: אֲפִילּוּ תֵּימָא רַבִּי מֵאִיר, שָׁאנֵי הָכָא שֶׁכְּבָר אָכְלָה.

Rabbi Yoḥanan said: The mishna can be understood **even** if **you say** that it is in accordance with the opinion of **Rabbi Meir,** who maintains that a widow betrothed to a High Priest may not eat *teruma* on his account, as **it is different here, as she** had **already eaten**[N] *teruma* on her husband's account before his injury. Since she has done nothing to disqualify herself, she retains her presumptive status as one for whom it is permitted to eat *teruma*.

וְרַבִּי אֶלְעָזָר: שֶׁכְּבָר אָכְלָה לָא אָמְרִינַן, דְּאִי לָא תֵּימָא הָכִי, בַּת יִשְׂרָאֵל שֶׁנִּשֵּׂאת לְכֹהֵן וּמֵת בַּעְלָהּ – תֹּאכַל, שֶׁכְּבָר אָכְלָה.

And how does **Rabbi Elazar** counter this argument? He maintains that **we do not say that** since **she** had already **eaten** *teruma* on her husband's account she continues to do so, **as, if you do not say** that **this** argument must be rejected, then it **should** be permitted for **an Israelite woman who married a priest and her husband died** without children to continue **eating** *teruma* on his account, **as she** had **already eaten** *teruma* because of him during his lifetime. However, such a conclusion is clearly incorrect. This *halakha* indicates that the fact that she had already eaten *teruma* is irrelevant.

וְרַבִּי יוֹחָנָן: הָתָם – פָּקַע קִנְיָינֵיהּ, הָכָא – לָא פָּקַע קִנְיָינֵיהּ.

And Rabbi Yoḥanan holds that the two cases are not comparable, as **there,** where the husband died, **his acquisition** of his wife **has lapsed,** i.e., they are no longer married, and therefore she cannot continue to eat *teruma* on his account, whereas **here,** where his genitals were injured, **his acquisition has not lapsed.** While sexual relations between them are forbidden, their marriage remains intact.

HALAKHA

One who has immersed himself during that day – טְבוּל יוֹם בִּתְרוּמָה: If a ritually impure person who immersed on that day touches *teruma* food or drink, he has disqualified it, as he is considered impure with second-degree ritual impurity. He thereby renders the *teruma* impure with third-degree ritual impurity, so that it is impure but does not further transmit ritual impurity (Rambam *Sefer Tahara, Hilkhot Avot HaTuma* 10:3).

NOTES

As she had already eaten – שֶׁכְּבָר אָכְלָה: This dispute is also mentioned in the Jerusalem Talmud, where Rabbi Yoḥanan states that the woman retains her presumptive status as one for whom it is permitted to eat *teruma* because her husband did not perform a subsequent act of acquisition, i.e., betrothal, that would disqualify her.

"אֵיזֶהוּ פְּצוּעַ". תָּנוּ רַבָּנַן: אֵיזֶהוּ פְּצוּעַ דַּכָּא – כׇּל שֶׁנִּפְצְעוּ בֵּיצִים שֶׁלּוֹ, וַאֲפִילּוּ אַחַת מֵהֶן. וַאֲפִילּוּ נִיקְּבוּ, וַאֲפִילּוּ נִמּוֹקוּ, וַאֲפִילּוּ חָסְרוּ. אָמַר רַבִּי יִשְׁמָעֵאל בְּנוֹ שֶׁל רַבִּי יוֹחָנָן בֶּן בְּרוֹקָה, שָׁמַעְתִּי מִפִּי חֲכָמִים בְּכֶרֶם בְּיַבְנֶה: כׇּל שֶׁאֵין לוֹ אֶלָּא בֵּיצָה אַחַת – אֵינוֹ אֶלָּא סְרִיס חַמָּה, וְכָשֵׁר.

§ It is taught in the mishna: **Who is deemed a man with crushed** testicles? **The Sages taught** in a *baraita*: **Who is deemed a man with crushed testicles?**[H] It is **anyone whose testicles have been wounded, even** if only **one of them.** Furthermore, a man is considered to have crushed testicles not only if they have been wounded, but **even** if they have been **punctured, or** have **decayed** as the result of an injury, **or are** partly **deficient** for some other reason. **Rabbi Yishmael, son of Rabbi Yoḥanan ben Beroka,**[N] **said: I heard from the Sages in the vineyard in Yavne**[B] that **anyone who has only one testicle**[B] **is nothing other** than **a eunuch by natural causes, and he is fit.**

סְרִיס חַמָּה סָלְקָא דַּעְתָּךְ?! אֶלָּא: הֲרֵי הוּא כִּסְרִיס חַמָּה, וְכָשֵׁר.

The Gemara is puzzled by the wording of this last teaching: **Can it enter your mind** that he is **a eunuch by natural causes,**[N] i.e., from birth? That designation refers to one who was born without testicles, whereas the reference here is to one who lost a testicle as the result of an injury. **Rather,** say that **he resembles a eunuch by natural causes, and he is fit.**

וְנִיקָּב לָא מוֹלִיד? וְהָא הַהוּא גַּבְרָא דִּסְלִיק לְדִיקְלָא

The Gemara asks: As for one whose testicles **were punctured, is he incapable of having children,** so that he should have the status of one whose testicles were crushed? **Wasn't** there an incident where **a certain man was climbing up a palm tree,**

BACKGROUND

The vineyard in Yavne – כֶּרֶם בְּיַבְנֶה: The great yeshiva in Yavne, which served as a meeting place of the Sages and the seat of the *Nasi* after the destruction of the Second Temple, is commonly referred to as *kerem beYavne* or the vineyard in Yavne. According to the Jerusalem Talmud (*Berakhot* 4:1) the place was called a vineyard because the students would sit in rows, evoking the rows of grapevines in a vineyard. Since the majority of that generation's leading Sages were gathered there, their decisions were decisive in safeguarding the continued existence of the Jewish people. The place is held in high esteem, and the *halakhot* taught in this vineyard [*matnita dekarma*] have special authority.

Anyone who has only one testicle – כׇּל שֶׁאֵין לוֹ אֶלָּא בֵּיצָה אַחַת: From a medical standpoint, a man who has only one testicle, whether from birth or due to the removal of or damage to the second testicle, can still be fertile and father children, provided that his condition is not the result of general underdevelopment.

HALAKHA

Who is a man with crushed testicles – אֵיזֶהוּ פְּצוּעַ דַּכָּא: If even one of a man's testicles has been removed, damaged, or crushed, or is deficient or punctured, he is defined as a man with crushed testicles. Some authorities are lenient in accordance with the opinion of Rabbi Yishmael, son of Rabbi Yoḥanan ben Beroka, and rule that if only the left testicle was removed in a whole state, the man is fit. Although this ruling is in accordance with many authorities (*Tosafot*), according to the Rema this opinion should not be followed (Rambam *Sefer Kedusha, Hilkhot Issurei Bia* 16:3; *Shulḥan Arukh, Even HaEzer* 5:7).

NOTES

The opinion of Rabbi Yishmael, son of Rabbi Yoḥanan ben Beroka – שִׁיטַת רַבִּי יִשְׁמָעֵאל בְּרַבִּי יוֹחָנָן בֶּן בְּרוֹקָה: The early authorities discuss the opinion of Rabbi Yishmael, son of Rabbi Yoḥanan ben Beroka, and arrive at different conclusions. According to the Rid, Rabbi Yishmael disagrees with the first *tanna* entirely, as he maintains that a man is disqualified only if both of his testicles are crushed, but the injury or deficiency of a single testicle does not impair his status. The Ra'avad and Rabbeinu Tam claim that even Rabbi Yishmael agrees that one who is injured in one testicle is disqualified, but he contends that the ruling with regard to one whose testicle has been entirely removed is more lenient. They cite a proof for this opinion from the *halakha* of a defective spleen: The *halakha* is that a perforated spleen renders an animal a *tereifa*, but if the organ is missing entirely, it is kosher. According to this opinion, Rabbi Yishmael maintains that a man with a single testicle is fit. By contrast, the Rif and Rambam maintain that Rabbi Yishmael does not in fact disagree with the first *tanna* at all, as his statement refers to one whose testicle was removed not by way of an injury but at the hand of Heaven, i.e., by natural causes. A man of this kind is not disqualified.

This dispute among the early authorities is further complicated by the Jerusalem Talmud. The Ra'avad maintains that the Jerusalem Talmud proves that this case is that of the removal of a testicle, as the Gemara there differentiates between the right and left testicle (see HALAKHA and *Yam shel Shlomo*). Those who disagree argue that the Jerusalem Talmud demonstrates that this case is that of one who was injured at the hand of Heaven. They claim additional proof from the fact that the Gemara later joins Rabbi Yishmael's opinion to that of Shmuel, who states that all of these blemishes render one disqualified only if inflicted by man. Another point of discussion is the contention stated in the Jerusalem Talmud that according to Rabbi Yishmael, son of Rabbi Yoḥanan, a man with only one testicle cannot father children, and yet he is still fit to enter into the congregation. On this point it has been noted that generally, a man with a single testicle can father children; see the early and later authorities in this regard, in particular the Ritva.

Can it enter your mind that he is a eunuch by natural causes [*seris ḥamma*] – סְרִיס חַמָּה סָלְקָא דַּעְתָּךְ: The Rid and the Meiri explain this as follows: A *seris ḥamma* is a man with a physical abnormality that prevents him from having children, whereas this individual merely suffers from a blemish in his testicles.

וְחַרְזֵיהּ סִילְוָא בְּבֵיצִים, וּנְפַק מִינֵּיהּ כְּחוּט דְּמוּגְלָא, וְאוֹלֵיד. הָא שָׁלַח שְׁמוּאֵל לְקַמֵּיהּ דְּרַב, וַאֲמַר לֵיהּ: צֵא וְחַזֵּר עַל בָּנָיו מֵאַיִן הֵם.

and a thorn [*silva*][L] from the tree **punctured him in the testicles,**[B] and semen **resembling a thread of pus issued from him,** as the thorn had perforated his testicle, **and** yet **he** later **had children.** The Gemara answers: **Didn't Shmuel send** this case **before Rav, who said to him:** Go out and **inquire about his children where they come from,** as he doubted that this man could father children, and therefore his wife must have committed adultery.

אָמַר רַב יְהוּדָה אָמַר שְׁמוּאֵל: פְּצוּעַ דַּכָּא בִּידֵי שָׁמַיִם כָּשֵׁר. אֲמַר רָבָא: הַיְינוּ דְּקָרֵינַן "פְּצוּעַ" וְלָא קָרֵינַן "הַפָּצוּעַ".

Rav Yehuda said that **Shmuel said: A man wounded with crushed** testicles **at the hand of Heaven,**[H] e.g., from birth or as the result of an illness, **is fit** to marry a woman who was born Jewish. **Rava said: This is** the reason **that we read** in the Torah: **"A man wounded** with crushed testicles,"[N] **and we do not read: The man wounded** with crushed testicles. In the Hebrew text, the latter phrase: The man wounded, can be understood to include one whose testicles have always been crushed, whereas "a man wounded" indicates that he was wounded, i.e., his disability is the result of injury.

בְּמַתְנִיתָא תָּנָא: נֶאֱמַר "לֹא יָבֹא פְּצוּעַ" וְנֶאֱמַר "לֹא יָבֹא מַמְזֵר" מַה לְּהַלָּן בִּידֵי אָדָם – אַף כָּאן בִּידֵי אָדָם.

A similar idea **was taught in a *baraita*. It is stated: "A man wounded** [*petzua*] with crushed testicles [*dakka*] or a severed [*kerut*] penis **shall not enter** into the congregation of the Lord" (Deuteronomy 23:2), **and it is stated** in the very next verse: **"A *mamzer* shall not enter**[N] into the congregation of the Lord" (Deuteronomy 23:3). **Just as there,** with regard to a *mamzer*, his blemish was created **at the hands of man,** i.e., by his parents who sinned, **so too, here,** with regard to one with crushed testicles, the verse must be speaking about one whose mutilation was **at the hands of man.**

אָמַר רָבָא: פָּצוּעַ בְּכוּלָּן, דַּךְ בְּכוּלָּן, כָּרוּת בְּכוּלָּן. פָּצוּעַ בְּכוּלָּן – בֵּין שֶׁנִּפְצַע הַגִּיד, בֵּין שֶׁנִּפְצְעוּ בֵּיצִים, בֵּין שֶׁנִּפְצְעוּ חוּטֵי בֵּיצִים. דַּךְ בְּכוּלָּן – בֵּין שֶׁנִּידַּךְ הַגִּיד, בֵּין שֶׁנִּידְּכוּ בֵּיצִים, בֵּין שֶׁנִּידְּכוּ חוּטֵי בֵּיצִים. כָּרוּת [בְּכוּלָּן] – בֵּין שֶׁנִּכְרַת הַגִּיד, בֵּין שֶׁנִּכְרְתוּ בֵּיצִים, בֵּין שֶׁנִּכְרְתוּ חוּטֵי בֵּיצִים.

Rava said: The verse dealing with injured genitals speaks of three types of injury: Wounded [*petzua*], crushed [*dakka*], and severed [*kerut*]. **Wounded** applies **to all of them;**[HN] **crushed** applies **to all of them;** and **severed** applies **to all of them,** as will immediately be explained. **Wounded** applies **to all of them, whether the member was wounded, or the testicles were wounded, or the spermatic cords**[B] **were wounded.** Similarly, **crushed** applies **to all of them, whether the member was crushed, or the testicles were crushed, or the spermatic cords were crushed.** And **severed** also applies **to all of them, whether the member was severed, or the testicles were severed, or the spermatic cords were severed.**

LANGUAGE

Thorn [*silva*] – סִילְוָא: The meaning of this word is like the Arabic سلاء, *sullā'*, the thorn of a palm tree. These are the small leaves found on palm fronds that become hard and thorny over time and whose stabs can be very painful. The term seems to parallel the word *sol* found in the Mishna, and it may also be related to the word *silon* appearing in the Bible (Ezekiel 2:6, 28:24), which also refers to a prickly thorn.

BACKGROUND

A thorn punctured him in the testicles – חַרְזֵיהּ סִילְוָא בְּבֵיצִים: The mere fact that a testicle was pierced does not necessarily lead to infertility, but only if the wound did not cause an infection. An infected wound would likely cause irreversible damage. The emission of what the Gemara terms a thread of pus might have served as proof of an infected wound. Furthermore, palm fronds are coated with a substance that by itself can cause an allergic reaction.

Spermatic cords of the testicles – חוּטֵי בֵּיצִים: While it is possible to explain this as referring to the thin vessels in the testicles themselves, the context indicates that it refers to the vas deferens, the spermatic artery, as well as other nerves and blood vessels that connect the testicles to the penis.

HALAKHA

A man wounded with crushed testicles at the hand of Heaven – פְּצוּעַ דַּכָּא בִּידֵי שָׁמַיִם: The categories of a man with crushed testicles and a man with a severed penis refer to disabilities caused by man, whether by intentional injury or by accident. However, if the disability was caused at the hand of Heaven, e.g., it is congenital or the result of illness, one is fit (Rambam). Rashi and the Rosh maintain that if the disability was caused by illness, it is regarded as caused by man, and only one who is born with this condition is considered impaired at the hand of Heaven (Rambam *Sefer Kedusha, Hilkhot Issurei Bia* 16:9; *Shulḥan Arukh, Even HaEzer* 5:10).

Wounded applies to all of them – פָּצוּעַ בְּכוּלָּן: These blemishes of wounding, crushing, severing, and perforation disqualify the injured party whether they involve the penis, the testicles, or the spermatic cords, in accordance with the opinion of Rava (Rambam *Sefer Kedusha, Hilkhot Issurei Bia* 16:3; *Shulḥan Arukh, Even HaEzer* 5:2).

NOTES

This is the reason that we read: A man wounded with crushed testicles [*petzua*] – הַיְינוּ דְּקָרֵינַן פְּצוּעַ: Rashi indicates that the difference here is between: The man with crushed testicles [*hapatzua*], a formulation that would include any man suffering from that blemish, no matter its source, and: A man with crushed testicles [*petzua*], which refers specifically to the victim of an injury. The *Yam shel Shlomo* and others wonder why the Rosh asserts that Rashi disagrees with the Rambam with regard to one whose blemish was caused by an illness. Rabbeinu Ḥananel has a different version of the text in which the distinction is between the words *petzua* and *petzia*. He understands that *petzua* is a passive form referring to one who was injured by others, whereas *petzia* is an adjective that can be applied to anyone suffering from this blemish.

And it is stated: A *mamzer* shall not enter – וְנֶאֱמַר לֹא יָבֹא מַמְזֵר: In the Babylonian Talmud the only opinion cited is that one who was wounded at the hand of Heaven is not disqualified, but in the Jerusalem Talmud a dispute in this regard is mentioned, as there is an opinion that even one injured at the hand of Heaven is unfit. There, too, the Gemara derives a proof from the case of a *mamzer* that this disqualification must be the result of human action. Some, however, see this as a proof supporting the contrary opinion: Since the actual creation of a *mamzer* is in the hand of Heaven, here too the case must be that of a congenital defect.

Wounded applies to all of them – פָּצוּעַ בְּכוּלָּן: If the same *halakha* applies to both testicles and penis, whether they were crushed or severed, why does the Torah choose the particular formulation: "A man wounded with crushed testicles or a severed penis" (Deuteronomy 23:2)? It may be suggested that this formulation is used because it is more likely for the penis to be severed and for the testicles to be crushed.

אֲמַר לֵיהּ הַהוּא מֵרַבָּנַן לְרָבָא: מִמַּאי דְּהַאי פְּצוּעַ דַּכָּא בְּאוֹתוֹ מָקוֹם? אֵימָא מֵרֹאשׁוֹ! אֲמַר לֵיהּ: מִדְּלָא מָנָה בֵּיהּ דּוֹרוֹת, שְׁמַע מִינָּהּ – בְּאוֹתוֹ מָקוֹם.

§ **One of the Sages said to Rava: From where** is it derived **that this** phrase "*petzua dakka*," literally meaning wounded by crushing, is referring to a man who suffered an injury **in that place,**[N] i.e., his genitals? **Say** that perhaps it is referring to one who was injured **on his head. Rava said to him: From** the fact that the verse **does not mention** the number of **generations** of his descendants that may not enter into the congregation, as do the verses with regard to a *mamzer* or an Ammonite or Moabite, **learn from this** that it is referring to a man who suffered an injury **in that place.** The blemish is evidently one that prevents him from having children, and therefore he has no generations of descendants.

וְדִלְמָא הַאי דְּלָא מָנָה בּוֹ דּוֹרוֹת – דְּאִיהוּ הוּא דְּאָסוּר, בְּרֵיהּ וּבַר בְּרֵיהּ – כָּשֵׁר?

The Gemara asks: **But perhaps** the fact **that** the Torah **does not mention** the number of **generations** of his descendants that may not enter into the congregation is due to a halakhic reason rather than a biological one, i.e. **that** only **he is prohibited** from entering into the congregation, whereas **his son and his son's son are fit** to do so?

דּוּמְיָא דִּכְרוּת שָׁפְכָה, מַה כְּרוּת שָׁפְכָה בְּאוֹתוֹ מָקוֹם – אַף הַאי נַמִי בְּאוֹתוֹ מָקוֹם.

The Gemara explains that the identity of a *petzua dakka* is derived in a different way: The case of a *petzua dakka* is **similar to** that of **one whose penis has been severed,** mentioned immediately afterward: **Just as one whose penis has been severed** suffered an injury **in that place, so too, this** man was injured **in that place.**

וּכְרוּת שָׁפְכָה גּוּפֵיהּ, מִמַּאי דִּבְאוֹתוֹ מָקוֹם הוּא? אֵימָא מִשִּׂפְתֵיהּ! "שָׁפְכָה" כְּתִיב, בְּמָקוֹם שֶׁשּׁוֹפֵךְ.

The Gemara asks: As for the **one whose penis has been severed** [*kerut shofkha*] **himself, from where** is it derived that the phrase *kerut shofkha*, literally meaning severed emission, is referring to a man who suffered an injury **in that place,** i.e., his genitals? **Say** that perhaps it is referring to one who was injured **to his lips,** from where spittle is discharged. The Gemara answers: **It is written** "*shofkha*," which indicates that the injury was **in a place that pours out** [*shofekh*], whereas spittle is spat out.

וְאֵימָא מֵחוֹטְמוֹ! מִי כְּתִיב "בִּשְׁפוֹךְ" "כְּרוּת שָׁפְכָה" כְּתִיב, מִי שֶׁעַל יְדֵי כְּרִיתָה שׁוֹפֵךְ, שֶׁלֹּא עַל יְדֵי כְּרִיתָה אֵינוֹ שׁוֹפֵךְ, אֶלָּא מְקַלֵּחַ, לְאַפּוֹקֵי הַאי דְּאִידִי וְאִידִי שׁוֹפֵךְ הוּא.

The Gemara asks further: **But say** that perhaps it is referring to one who suffered an injury **to his nose.** The Gemara answers: **Is it written *bishpokh*,** which would indicate a place from which there is a discharge even if nothing was severed? Rather, **it is written "*kerut shofkha*,"** implying **something that pours out as a result of** an organ **having been severed. But in the absence of** an organ **having been severed,** the semen **does not pour out; rather, it is ejected out.** This comes **to exclude this** possibility of the nose, **as whether** it is in **this** state **or that** state, i.e., severed or not, the mucus **pours out.**

בְּמַתְנִיתָא תָּנָא: נֶאֱמַר "לֹא יָבֹא פְּצוּעַ דַּכָּא" וְנֶאֱמַר "לֹא יָבֹא מַמְזֵר" מַה לְּהַלָּן בְּאוֹתוֹ מָקוֹם – אַף כָּאן בְּאוֹתוֹ מָקוֹם.

With regard to this issue, **it was taught in a *baraita*** as follows: **It is stated: "A man wounded with crushed testicles shall not enter** into the congregation," **and it is stated: "A *mamzer* shall not enter** into the congregation." **Just as there,** the blemish of a *mamzer* comes **from that place,** through sexual misconduct, **so too, here,** a man with crushed testicles is one who suffered an injury **in that place** that is connected to cohabitation.

נִיקַּב לְמַטָּה מֵעֲטָרָה, שֶׁכְּנֶגְדּוֹ לְמַעְלָה מֵעֲטָרָה, סָבַר רַבִּי חִיָּיא בַּר אַבָּא לְאַכְשׁוּרֵי. אֲמַר לֵיהּ רַבִּי אַסִּי: הָכִי אֲמַר רַבִּי יְהוֹשֻׁעַ בֶּן לֵוִי: עֲטָרָה כׇּל שֶׁהִיא מְעַכֶּבֶת.

§ The Gemara considers the following case: If a man's member **was punctured** from one side **below the corona,** i.e., at the corona itself, and the puncture ended **on the opposite** side **above the corona** which is nearer the body,[H] **Rabbi Ḥiyya bar Abba thought to render him fit** for marriage on the grounds that on one side the puncture was below the corona. **Rabbi Asi said to him: This is what Rabbi Yehoshua ben Levi said:** A puncture in **the corona of any size impedes** the man's fitness, even if one end of the puncture is below the corona, as any puncture in the corona affects his fertility.

"וְאִם נִשְׁתַּיֵּיר מֵעֲטָרָה" כּוּ'. יָתֵיב רָבִינָא וְקָמִיבַּעְיָא לֵיהּ: מְלֹא הַחוּט שֶׁאָמְרוּ – עַל פְּנֵי כּוּלָּהּ אוֹ עַל פְּנֵי רוּבָּהּ? אֲמַר לֵיהּ רָבָא תּוֹסְפָאָה לְרָבִינָא: מְלֹא הַחוּט עַל פְּנֵי רוּבָּהּ, וּכְלַפֵּי רֵישָׁא.

It is taught in the mishna that **if there remains** a portion **of the corona,** even as much as a hairsbreadth, he is still fit. **Ravina sat and raised the** following **dilemma:** This **hairsbreadth of which they spoke,**[H] must it surround **the entire** member **or** only **a majority of it? Rava Tosfa'a said to Ravina: A hairsbreadth** of the corona must surround **a majority** of the member, **and toward its head,** that is, in the portion closer to the body.

NOTES

From where is it derived that this…is referring to an injury in that place – מִמַּאי דְּהַאי...בְּאוֹתוֹ מָקוֹם: This question is also raised in the Jerusalem Talmud, where it is inferred from the juxtaposition of the two injuries that these blemishes are located in close proximity on the body. The Gemara there suggests that the verse might be referring to a wound in the eye, as it is near the nostril, which also emits liquid, and thus a wound in that area can be called *kerut shofkha*, literally meaning severed emission. The Gemara rejects this suggestion with the argument that the word *dakka* also means low, and no part of a sitting male is lower than the testicles.

HALAKHA

Punctured opposite the corona – נִיקַּב כְּנֶגֶד עֲטָרָה: If a man's penis is punctured from one side at the corona, and the puncture ended on the other side above the corona, he is unfit to enter the congregation, as the entire corona must be intact. This is in accordance with the opinion of Rabbi Yehoshua ben Levi (Rambam *Sefer Kedusha, Hilkhot Issurei Bia* 16:5; *Shulḥan Arukh, Even HaEzer* 5:5).

The hairsbreadth of which they spoke – מְלֹא הַחוּט שֶׁאָמְרוּ: If one suffered an injury such that the head of penis was severed, leaving only a hairsbreadth of the corona all the way round the member, he is fit. This is the Rambam's ruling, in accordance with his reading of the Gemara, which omits the words: Toward its head. The Rosh and Rabbeinu Yeruḥam had a version that reads: A hairsbreadth over all of it, and toward its head. According to this opinion, he is fit to enter into the congregation only if the entire circumference of the corona is covered by skin on the side closer to the body. The *Tur* accepts the version of the text cited here and therefore rules that if most of the corona is covered on the side toward the body, he is fit. The Rosh's opinion is accepted as *halakha* (*Baḥ*; Rambam *Sefer Kedusha, Hilkhot Issurei Bia* 16:4; *Shulḥan Arukh, Even HaEzer* 5:2).

NOTES

Like a quill – כְּקוּלְמוֹס: In the Jerusalem Talmud a distinction is drawn between a cut from below, like an actual quill, where the man remains fit, and an incision from above, like an upside-down quill, which disqualifies him. The *Yam shel Shlomo* rules accordingly.

To mislead Mareimar – לְשַׁבּוּשֵׁי לְמָרֵימָר: The word mislead is rather surprising in this context, and there are several different versions of the text. The Ritva explains that after stating his novel *halakha* that a man is fit no matter how he was cut, Ravina did not want Mareimar to raise any difficulties, and he therefore distracted him with a different question.

LANGUAGE

Quill [*kulmus*] – קוּלְמוֹס: This word derives from the Greek κάλαμος, *kalamos*, meaning a reed, especially one that is fashioned into a writing utensil.

אָמַר רַב הוּנָא: כְּקוּלְמוֹס כְּשֵׁרָה, כְּמַרְזֵב – פְּסוּלָה. הַאי – שָׁלֵיט בָּהּ אֲוִירָא, וְהַאי – לָא שָׁלֵיט בָּהּ אֲוִירָא. וְרַב חִסְדָּא אֲמַר: כְּמַרְזֵב – כְּשֵׁרָה, כְּקוּלְמוֹס – פְּסוּלָה, הַאי – גָּרֵיד, וְהַאי – לָא גָּרֵיד.

Rav Huna said: If a man's member was cut **like a quill [*kulmus*]**,[NL] which is sharp on all sides, he is **fit;** but if it was cut **like a gutter,**[B] which is partly open, he is **unfit.** He explains: In **this** case, where it was cut like a gutter, he is unfit because **the air penetrates** and this interferes with the proper flow of his semen; **whereas in that** case, where it was cut like a quill, he remains fit because **the air does not penetrate** and the semen is unaffected. **And Rav Ḥisda said** the reverse: If a man's member was cut **like a gutter, he is fit;** but if it was cut **like a quill,** he is **unfit.** This is because in **this** case, where it was cut like a gutter, the member **rubs** against the woman's sexual organ and becomes aroused, **whereas in that** case, where it was cut like a quill, it **does not rub** against it, as it is too thin and insubstantial.

אֲמַר רָבָא: כְּוָותֵיהּ דְּרַב הוּנָא מִסְתַּבְּרָא, הַאי – לָא שָׁלֵיט בָּהּ אֲוִירָא, וְהַאי – שָׁלֵיט בָּהּ אֲוִירָא. אִי מִשּׁוּם גְּרִידוּתָא – מִידֵּי דַּהֲוָה אַבַּרְזָא דְּחָבִיתָא.

Rava said: It stands to reason in accordance with the opinion of **Rav Huna,** that in **this** case **the air penetrates, whereas** in **that** case **the air does not penetrate. With respect to the rubbing,** this is **just as it is in** the case of **a stopper of a barrel.**[B] Although one end of the stopper tapers to a sharp point, the stopper nevertheless closes the hole when it is jammed inside and its other end makes contact with the sides of the hole. Here, too, sufficient contact and friction can be created by the upper end of the man's member.

אֲמַר לֵיהּ רָבִינָא לְמָרֵימָר, הָכִי אֲמַר מָר זוּטְרָא מִשְּׁמֵיהּ דְּרַב פַּפָּא: הִלְכְתָא, בֵּין כְּקוּלְמוֹס בֵּין כְּמַרְזֵב – כְּשֵׁרָה. מִיהוּ, מִיבַּעְיָא לֵיהּ: לְמַטָּה מֵעֲטָרָה אוֹ לְמַעְלָה? פְּשִׁיטָא דִּלְמַעְלָה מֵעֲטָרָה, דְּאִי סָלְקָא דַּעְתָּךְ לְמַטָּה מֵעֲטָרָה – אֲפִילּוּ נִכְרַת הַגִּיד נַמִי! וְרָבִינָא: לְשַׁבּוּשֵׁי לְמָרֵימָר הוּא דְּבָעֵי.

Ravina said to Mareimar that **Mar Zutra said in the name of Rav Pappa as follows: The *halakha*** is that **whether** the man's member was cut **like a quill or like a gutter,**[H] he is **fit. However, he raised a dilemma** as to whether this is referring to a cut **below the corona,** i.e., on the corona itself, **or above** it, on that part of the penis that is closer to the body. The Gemara answers: It **is obvious** that this is referring **to** a cut **above the corona, as, if it enters your mind** that it is referring **to below the corona,** i.e., on the corona itself, this would be difficult because **even** if the end of **the member was** completely **severed,** he would **also** be fit, provided that a hairsbreadth of the corona remained. The Gemara adds: **And Ravina** asked this question only because **he wanted to mislead Mereimar**[N] and test his understanding of the issue.

הַהוּא עוּבְדָּא דַּהֲוָה בְּמָתָא מְחַסְיָא, שַׁפְיֵיהּ מָר בַּר רַב אַשִׁי כְּקוּלְמוֹס וְאַכְשְׁרֵיהּ. הַהוּא עוּבְדָּא דַּהֲוָה בְּפוּמְבְּדִיתָא אִיסְתַּתֵּים גּוּבְתָּא דְּשִׁכְבַת זֶרַע וְאַפֵּיק בִּמְקוֹם קְטַנִּים, סָבַר רַב בֵּיבָי בַּר אַבַּיֵי לְאַכְשׁוּרֵי, אֲמַר רַב פַּפִּי: מִשּׁוּם דְּאָתוּ

The Gemara relates: **A certain incident** actually **occurred in** the town of **Mata Meḥasya,** where a man's member was cut like a gutter. **Mar bar Rav Ashi cut** back the flesh on all sides until it was **like a quill and** thereby **rendered him fit** to enter into the congregation. **A certain incident occurred in Pumbedita,** where **the seminal duct** of a certain man **became blocked,**[B] **and he emitted** semen **through the urinary duct. Rav Beivai bar Abaye thought to render him fit,** as his genitals were neither crushed nor severed. **Rav Pappi said: Because you come**

BACKGROUND

Like a quill…like a gutter – כְּקוּלְמוֹס...כְּמַרְזֵב: Running along both sides of the penis are blood vessels that enable an erection, and on the inside is the urethra. As long as at least one of the blood vessels is whole and there is no damage to the urethra, a man is capable of fathering children. Damage to the penis, e.g., being cut like a quill or a gutter, might make sexual contact difficult but does not necessarily cause infertility.

Stopper of a barrel – בַּרְזָא דְּחָבִיתָא: Ceramic wine barrels had openings at their tops that were closed up by means of a stopper. In order to pour a large quantity of wine at once, the stopper was removed and the wine poured out. However, if one's intention was to pour only small amounts of wine from time to time, especially in the case of large barrels, a special craftsman would bore a hole near the bottom of the barrel that would be plugged with a conical-shaped piece of wood wrapped in rags.

The seminal duct became blocked, etc. – אִסְתַּתֵּים גּוּבְתָּא וכו׳: Both semen and urine exit the body through the urethra, but there is a special mechanism of nerves and muscles that closes the urethra to urine during ejaculation. It is possible for this mechanism to malfunction due to injury or disease. In that case, the sperm might not exit normally but instead enter the bladder through the urethra and later exit the body in the urine. A man suffering from this problem would be incapable of having children through normal intercourse.

HALAKHA

Like a quill or like a gutter – כְּקוּלְמוֹס וּכְמַרְזֵב: If a man's member was cut above the corona, sloping downward like a quill, he is fit. If it was cut like a gutter, the inner portion having been removed and only the outer layer remaining intact, Rashi and the Rosh disqualify him in accordance with the opinion of Rav Huna, following the practical ruling of Mar bar Rav Ashi. According to the Rambam one is fit even if his member was cut like a gutter, as he rules in accordance with the opinion of Mar Zutra and understands that the incident of Mar bar Rav Ashi involved a different type of injury, not similar to a gutter (Rambam *Sefer Kedusha*, *Hilkhot Issurei Bia* 16:4 and *Kesef Mishne* there; *Shulḥan Arukh*, *Even HaEzer* 5:3).

מִמּוּלָאֵי אָמְרִיתוּ מִילֵּי מוּלַיְיתָא? בִּמְקוֹמָהּ – מְבַשְּׁלָה, שֶׁלֹּא בִּמְקוֹמָהּ – לָא מְבַשְּׁלָה.

from truncated [*mimula'ei*] **people,**[N] as Rav Beivai's family traced their lineage to the house of Eli, all of whose descendants were destined to be short-lived (see I Samuel 2:31), **you speak truncated** [*mulayata*] and unsound **matters.** When the semen passes through **its** proper **place, it fertilizes;**[H] but if it does **not** pass through **its** proper **place, it does not fertilize.** Since he cannot father children, he is like one whose testicles have been crushed, and therefore he may not enter into the congregation.

אָמַר רַב יְהוּדָה אָמַר שְׁמוּאֵל: נִיקַּב וְנִסְתַּם, כָּל שֶׁאִילּוּ נִקְרֵי וְנִקְרַע פָּסוּל, וְאִי לָאו כָּשֵׁר. הָוֵי בָּהּ רָבָא: הֵיכָא? אִילֵימָא לְמַטָּה מֵעֲטָרָה – אֲפִילּוּ נִכְרַת נַמִי, אֶלָּא בַּעֲטָרָה עַצְמָהּ. אִיתְּמַר נַמִי, אֲמַר רַב מָרִי בַּר מָר אֲמַר מָר עוּקְבָא אֲמַר שְׁמוּאֵל: נִיקַּב בַּעֲטָרָה עַצְמָהּ וְנִסְתַּם, כָּל שֶׁאִילּוּ נִקְרֵי וְנִקְרַע – פָּסוּל, וְאִי לָאו – כָּשֵׁר.

Rav Yehuda said that **Shmuel said:** If a man's member **had been punctured and it** later healed and the hole **closed** up with flesh, in **any** case **where,** if **he would emit semen, it would tear** open again, he is **unfit** to enter into the congregation; **but if not,** he is **fit. Rava discussed** this ruling and raised a question: **Where** is this perforation? **If we say** it is **below the corona,** at the end of the man's member, why should this perforation render him unfit? **Even if** the member **was** entirely **severed,** he would **also** be fit. **Rather,** the hole is **in the corona itself,** that is, at the point where the corona meets the rest of the member.[H] **It was also stated** explicitly that this is the case, as **Rav Mari bar Mar said** that **Mar Ukva said** that **Shmuel said:** If a man's member **had been punctured in the corona itself, and it** later healed and the hole **closed** up with flesh, in **any** case **where** if **he would emit semen it would tear** open again, he is **unfit; but if not,** he is **fit.**

שְׁלַח לֵיהּ רָבָא בְּרֵיהּ דְּרַבָּה לְרַב יוֹסֵף: יְלַמְּדֵנוּ רַבֵּינוּ, הֵיכִי עָבְדִינַן? אֲמַר לֵיהּ: מַיְיתִינַן נַהֲמָא חֲמִימָא דִּשְׂעָרֵי, וּמַנְחִינַן לֵיהּ אַבֵּי פוּקְרֵי, וּמִקְּרֵי, וְחָזֵינַן לֵיהּ.

With regard to this issue, **Rava, son of Rabba, sent** the following question **to Rav Yosef: Let our teacher teach us, what** should **we do** to verify whether or not the perforation was adequately closed? Rav Yosef **said to him: We bring warm barley bread and place it upon his anus** [*bei pukrei*],[L] **and** owing to the heat **he emits semen, and we observe** what happens and see whether or not the perforation remains closed.

אֲמַר אַבַּיֵי: אַטּוּ כּוּלֵּי עָלְמָא יַעֲקֹב אָבִינוּ הֲוַאי, דִּכְתִיב בֵּיהּ ״כֹּחִי וְרֵאשִׁית אוֹנִי״ שֶׁלֹּא רָאָה קֶרִי מִיָּמָיו?

Abaye said: Is that to say that **everyone is like our Patriarch Jacob, with regard to whom it is written:** "Reuben, you are my firstborn, **my might and the first fruits of my strength**" (Genesis 49:3), implying **that** Jacob **never experienced an emission of semen**[N] **in all his days,** so that his eldest son Reuben was conceived from his first drop of seed, i.e., "the first fruits of my strength." The implication is that there is certainly no need for such measures in order to bring a man to ejaculate.

אֶלָּא אֲמַר אַבַּיֵי: מְעַבְּרִינַן קַמֵּיהּ בִּגְדֵי צִבְעוֹנִין. אֲמַר רָבָא: אַטּוּ כּוּלֵּי עָלְמָא בַּרְזִילַי הַגִּלְעָדִי הוּא? אֶלָּא, מְחַוַּורְתָּא כִּדְשָׁנִין מֵעִיקָּרָא.

Rather, Abaye said that a different method is used: **We pass before him colorful garments** of a woman, and thereby bring him to arousal, so that he will experience an emission. **Rava said: Is that to say** that **everyone is like Barzilai the Gileadite,** traditionally known for his licentious character? Not all men are brought to excitement when they merely see such clothes. **Rather,** the Gemara rejects this proposal and states that **it is clear as we initially answered,** that we follow the former procedure even though not all men require it.

תָּנוּ רַבָּנַן: נִיקַּב – פָּסוּל, מִפְּנֵי שֶׁהוּא שׁוֹתֵת. נִסְתַּם – כָּשֵׁר, מִפְּנֵי שֶׁהוּא מוֹלִיד. וְזֶהוּ פְּסוּל שֶׁחוֹזֵר לְהֶכְשֵׁירוֹ. זֶהוּ – לְמַעוּטֵי מַאי? לְמַעוּטֵי קְרוּם שֶׁעָלָה מֵחֲמַת מַכָּה בָּרֵיאָה, דְּאֵינוֹ קְרוּם.

The Sages taught in a *baraita*: If a man's member **was punctured,** he is **unfit** to enter into the congregation of Israel **because** his semen **is discharged gently** and does not fertilize; if the perforation later **closed**[B] up with flesh, he is **fit, because** now **he can father** children. **And this is** an instance of one who is **unfit who returns to his** previous state of **fitness.** The Gemara asks: **What** does the word **this** come **to exclude?** The Gemara explains that it comes **to exclude** a case involving an entirely different matter, that of **a membrane that formed on the lung** of an animal **in the wake of a wound, which is not** considered a proper **membrane,** as it is likely to rupture. If a puncture in the lung became covered with such a membrane the animal does not regain its former kosher status.

NOTES

Because you come from truncated [*mimula'ei*] people – מִשּׁוּם דְּאָתוּ מִמּוּלָאֵי: The meaning of this expression, which appears in several places with regard to Rav Beivai bar Abaye, is not entirely clear. Rashi explains that *mula'ei* means wretched [*umlalim*], or cut off, as Rav Beivai descended from the house of Eli, whose descendants were condemned to premature death (see I Samuel 2:33). A slightly different interpretation is attributed to Rabbeinu Ḥananel (cited in *Tosafot*), who asserts that Rav Beivai's family came from the village of Mamla, whose residents were descendants of Eli. An alternative opinion is that *mula'ei* means important people who speak in a superior manner. In other words, since he comes from a distinguished family, Rav Beivai permits himself to speak haughtily, without examining his words carefully (*Arukh*).

He never experienced an emission of semen – שֶׁלֹּא רָאָה קֶרִי: *Tosafot* understand that Reuben was born from the very first drop of semen that issued from Jacob's body. Rabbi Avraham min HaHar cites various proofs from the Bible that this was not necessarily the case. Rather, what this means here is that Jacob did not experience a nocturnal emission before marriage, and that Reuben was the product of his first relationship with Leah.

HALAKHA

In its place it fertilizes – בִּמְקוֹמָהּ מְבַשְּׁלָה: If one's seminal tract becomes obstructed, and semen emerges from his urinary tract, he is disqualified from entering the congregation, in accordance with the opinion of Rav Pappi (Rambam *Sefer Kedusha, Hilkhot Issurei Bia* 16:6; *Shulḥan Arukh, Even HaEzer* 5:6).

If it had been punctured and it closed up – נִיקַּב וְנִסְתַּם: If one's member was punctured below the corona, i.e., at the end of the member, he is fit. If it was perforated on the corona itself, i.e., at the point where the corona meets the rest of the member, and semen emerges from this hole, he is disqualified. If the hole subsequently seals up he regains his fit status, in accordance with the opinion of Shmuel (Rambam *Sefer Kedusha, Hilkhot Issurei Bia* 16:5; *Shulḥan Arukh, Even HaEzer* 5:4).

LANGUAGE

Anus [*bei pukrei*] – בֵּי פּוּקְרֵי: This word may mean the house or housing of the hole. Some explain *pukrei* as an abbreviation of two words, *pok re'i*, which means the place from where excrement exits.

BACKGROUND

Punctured and closed – נִיקַּב וְנִסְתַּם: A puncture in the penis that reaches the urethra may cause the sperm to exit in the wrong place and thereby render fertilization impossible. However, if such a puncture were sealed without having caused any permanent internal damage, the penis could return to its former functioning state.

BACKGROUND

We bring an ant – מַיְיתִינַן שׁוּמְשְׁנָא: Using ants to heal wounds was widespread in different parts of the world, principally in central and east Africa. The ants would hold on to the sides of the wound when they were joined together, essentially serving the same purpose as modern stitches. The advantage of using ants was that it allowed one to avoid the insertion of metal needles into the body that could cause infection, enlarge the wound, and even worsen the injury. The species generally used for this was the army ant of the genus Dorylus, also known as driver ants. After the ant bites the skin its body is severed from its head, which is left behind to hold the wound closed.

Driver ant, with its large mandibles

LANGUAGE

Ant [*shumshena*] – שׁוּמְשְׁנָא: The *Arukh* has a version of the text that reads *shushmena*, but other texts read *shumshemana*. There are parallels for both readings in Aramaic and Arabic, and all of them mean ant, or a particular species of ant.

Cause inflammation [*zareif*] – זָרֵיף: Some understand this term here in its Aramaic sense as meaning to create a wound or a crack.

שָׁלַח לֵיהּ רַב אִידִי בַּר אָבִין לְאַבַּיֵי: הֵיכִי עָבְדִינַן? מַיְיתִינַן שְׂעַרְתָּא, וּמְסָרְטִינַן לֵיהּ, וּמַיְיתִינַן תַּרְבָּא וְשָׁיְיפִינַן, וּמַיְיתִינַן שׁוּמְשְׁנָא גַּמְלָא וּמְנַכְתִינַן לֵיהּ, וּפָסְקִינַן לֵיהּ לְרֵישֵׁיהּ. וְדַוְקָא שְׂעַרְתָּא, אֲבָל פַּרְזְלָא – מִזְרַף זָרֵיף. וְהָנֵי מִילֵּי – קָטָן, אֲבָל גָּדוֹל – מִיקְפּוּלֵי מִיקְפַל.

With regard to this issue, **Rav Idi bar Avin sent** the following question **to Abaye: What** should **we do** to expedite the healing of such a perforation? Abaye answered: **We bring** a sharp-edged grain **of barley and lacerate** the area around the hole with it. **We** then **bring fat and rub it** on the spot, **and** afterward **we bring a large ant** [***shumshena***][BL] **and let it bite** inside the hole. This leads to bleeding and the formation of a scab, which eventually heals as new flesh grows there. **We** also **cut off** the ant's **head** so that it should remain in place until the wound is fully healed. The Gemara comments: **And** this procedure must be done **specifically** with a grain of **barley, but** an **iron** tool would **cause inflammation** [***zareif***].[L] The Gemara adds: **And this applies only** to **a small** perforation,[N] **but a large one will** eventually **peel** off and reopen.

אֲמַר רַבָּה בַּר רַב הוּנָא: הַמַּטִּיל מַיִם מִשְּׁתֵּי מְקוֹמוֹת – פָּסוּל. אֲמַר רָבָא: לֵית הִלְכְתָא לָא כִּבְרָא וְלָא כְּאַבָּא. בְּרָא – הָא דַּאֲמָרַן, אַבָּא – דַּאֲמַר רַב הוּנָא: נָשִׁים הַמְסוֹלְלוֹת זוֹ בָּזוֹ פְּסוּלוֹת לִכְהוּנָּה.

Rabba bar Rav Huna said: One who passes water from two places, so that he appears to have a hole or some other blemish in his member, is **unfit** to enter into the congregation of Israel, as is a man with crushed testicles. **Rava said:** With regard to these matters, the ***halakha* is in accordance neither with** the opinion of **the son nor with** that of **the father. The son,** this refers to **that** opinion of Rabba bar Rav Huna, **which we** just **stated.** As for the ruling of **the father,** this is referring to that which **Rav Huna said: Women who rub against one another**[NH] motivated by sexual desire **are unfit to** marry into **the priesthood,** as such conduct renders a woman a *zona*, whom a priest is prohibited from marrying. It was about this that Rava said that the *halakha* is not in accordance with Rav Huna's opinion.

וַאֲפִילּוּ לְרַבִּי אֶלְעָזָר דְּאָמַר פָּנוּי הַבָּא עַל הַפְּנוּיָה שֶׁלֹּא לְשֵׁם אִישׁוּת עֲשָׂאָהּ זוֹנָה, הָנֵי מִילֵּי אִישׁ, אֲבָל אִשָּׁה – פְּרִיצוּתָא בְּעָלְמָא.

And even according to the opinion of **Rabbi Elazar, who said that an unmarried man who has intercourse with an unmarried woman not for the sake of marriage renders her a *zona*,** a woman who has had sexual relations with a man forbidden to her by the Torah, **this applies only to** intercourse with **a man, but** lewd behavior with another **woman is mere licentiousness** that does not render her a *zona*, and therefore she is still permitted to marry into the priesthood.

NOTES

And this applies only to a small perforation – וְהָנֵי מִילֵּי קָטָן: Most commentaries explain that a small perforation means one that has been fully sealed, whereas a large perforation refers to one that has not been properly closed. The wording of the *She'iltot deRav Aḥai Gaon* indicates that he understood small and large as referring respectively to a minor and an adult: Since a minor does not emit semen his perforation is more likely to become completely sealed.

Women who rub against one another – נָשִׁים הַמְסוֹלְלוֹת: According to Rashi, the question is whether a woman who engages in such behavior is considered a *zona* and therefore disqualified. The Ritva maintains that in the absence of intercourse the issue does not arise. Rather, the question here is whether such women are fit for a High Priest: If they lost their virginity in this manner, are they treated like a woman whose hymen was torn as the result of an injury or like one who engaged in intercourse? See the Ritva for his explanation of the continuation of the passage in the Gemara, as he claims that Rabbi Elazar's view was cited not as a proof with regard to the matter itself, but in order to demonstrate that even Rabbi Elazar, who is stringent with regard to cohabitation, does not render one unfit if there was no act of intercourse.

HALAKHA

Women who rub against one another – נָשִׁים הַמְסוֹלְלוֹת: Women who rub against one another motivated by sexual desire transgress the prohibition against following the conduct of Egypt, and it is appropriate for them to receive lashes for rebelliousness administered by rabbinic decree. Men must take precautions to prevent their wives from engaging in such behavior. However, such conduct does not render a woman forbidden to her husband, nor does it disqualify her from marrying into the priesthood (Rambam *Sefer Kedusha*, *Hilkhot Issurei Bia* 21:8; *Shulḥan Arukh*, *Even HaEzer* 20:2).

מתני׳ פְּצוּעַ דַּכָּא וּכְרוּת שָׁפְכָה מוּתָּרִין בְּגִיּוֹרֶת וּמְשׁוּחְרֶרֶת, וְאֵינָן אֲסוּרִין אֶלָּא מִלָּבֹא בַּקָּהָל, שֶׁנֶּאֱמַר ״לֹא יָבֹא פְצוּעַ דַּכָּא וּכְרוּת שָׁפְכָה בִּקְהַל ה׳״.

MISHNA **A man with crushed testicles** or with other wounds to his genitals **and one whose penis has been severed are permitted** to marry a female **convert or an emancipated** maidservant, **and they are prohibited only from entering into the congregation** and marrying a woman who was born Jewish,[H] **as it is stated: "A man wounded with crushed testicles or a severed penis shall not enter into the congregation of the Lord"** (Deuteronomy 23:2).

גמ׳ בָּעוּ מִינֵּיהּ מֵרַב שֵׁשֶׁת: פְּצוּעַ דַּכָּא כֹּהֵן, מַהוּ בְּגִיּוֹרֶת וּמְשׁוּחְרֶרֶת? בִּקְדוּשָּׁתֵיהּ קָאֵי, וַאֲסִיר, אוֹ דִלְמָא לָאו בִּקְדוּשָּׁתֵיהּ קָאֵי, וְשָׁרֵי?

GEMARA **They raised a dilemma before Rav Sheshet: What is** the *halakha* governing **a priest with crushed testicles**[NH] **with respect to** a female **convert or an emancipated** maidservant? The Gemara clarifies the two sides of this dilemma: Does **he retain his** state of **sanctity** like any other priest **and is** therefore **prohibited** from marrying either one of these women, **or perhaps he does not retain his** state of **sanctity and** therefore **is permitted** to marry a convert, like an ordinary Israelite with crushed testicles?

אָמַר לְהוּ רַב שֵׁשֶׁת: תְּנֵיתוּהָ, פְּצוּעַ דַּכָּא יִשְׂרָאֵל מוּתָּר בִּנְתִינָה. וְאִי סָלְקָא דַּעְתָּךְ בִּקְדוּשָּׁתֵיהּ קָאֵי – אִיקְּרֵי כָּאן ״לֹא תִתְחַתֵּן בָּם״!

Rav Sheshet said to them: You already **learned** the answer to **this** question in the following *baraita*: **It is permitted for an** ordinary **Israelite with crushed testicles** to marry **a Gibeonite woman.**[NH] **Now, if it enters your mind** that he **retains his sanctity** as a Jew, one should **apply here** the prohibition stated with regard to Canaanites: **"You shall not marry them"** (Deuteronomy 7:3). Apparently, then, one whose testicles have been crushed loses his former sanctity, and the same should apply to a priest.

אֲמַר רָבָא: אַטּוּ הָתָם מִשּׁוּם קְדוּשָּׁה וְלָאו קְדוּשָּׁה הוּא? דִּלְמָא מוֹלִיד בֵּן וְאָזֵיל פָּלַח לַעֲבוֹדָה זָרָה, וְהָנֵי מִילֵּי – בְּגוֹיוּתָן, כִּי מִגַּיְּירִי – בְּיִשְׂרָאֵל שָׁרוּ, וְרַבָּנַן הוּא דִּגְזַרוּ בְּהוּ, וְכִי גָּזְרוּ בְּהוּ רַבָּנַן – בְּהָנָךְ דִּבְנֵי אוֹלוּדֵי, אֲבָל הַאי דְּלָאו בַּר אוֹלוּדֵי לָא גָּזְרוּ בֵּיהּ רַבָּנַן.

Rava said: This is no proof, as **is that to say** that the prohibition **there** against marrying Canaanites **is due to sanctity or lack of sanctity?** Rather, the reason for the prohibition is that **perhaps one will father a child** from his Canaanite wife **and** that child **will** later **go** off and engage in **idolatrous worship. Now, this** concern **applies only when** they are still **gentiles,** but **when** they **convert,** as did the Gibeonites, they are **permitted to Jews. And it is the Sages who decreed** that Gibeonites are forbidden like *mamzerim* even after their conversion. **And when the Sages decreed** that one may not marry them, the decree was limited **to those who are capable of having children, but** with regard to **this one,** a man with crushed testicles **who is incapable of having children, the Sages did not issue a decree.**

NOTES

A priest with crushed testicles – **פְּצוּעַ דַּכָּא כֹּהֵן**: This problem is also addressed in the Jerusalem Talmud, which cites a dispute with regard to this very issue. It appears that according to the opinion that a priest with crushed testicles is forbidden to women who are unfit for the priesthood, an ordinary Israelite with crushed testicles is forbidden to a *mamzeret*. The Gemara there differentiates between physical disqualifications and other types of marriage disqualifications. Those who are forbidden in marriage for other reasons are permitted to all disqualified women, but those with physical disabilities are not. This opinion is similar to that of the Rambam, who maintains that a man with crushed testicles is permitted only to those who are disqualified due to uncertainty, e.g., a child whose father's identity is not known, or a foundling, and to those who are forbidden by rabbinic decree, e.g., a Gibeonite woman. However, he may not marry a woman who is prohibited by Torah law to enter into the congregation. Others claim that in this regard there is no difference between women forbidden by the Sages and those forbidden by the Torah. Rather, all disqualified women are permitted to a man with crushed testicles. According to this opinion, a priest whose testicles have been crushed lacks the sanctity of the priesthood altogether, to the extent that he is not even barred from contracting ritual impurity imparted by a corpse.

The prohibition against marrying Gibeonites – **אִיסּוּר נְתִינִים**: According to the Rambam and others, gentiles from the seven Canaanite nations who converted are in principle permitted to marry Jews, as the biblical prohibition stated in their regard applies only while they are gentiles. However, owing to ancient decrees of Moses, Joshua, and David, each with its own degree of severity, members of these nations are disqualified from entering into the congregation. On the other hand, many authorities maintain that the biblical prohibition against marrying them applies specifically after they have converted, which means they are forbidden by Torah law, like all others disqualified from entering into the congregation (see Ritva).

HALAKHA

A man with crushed testicles is prohibited from entering into the congregation – **פְּצוּעַ דַּכָּא אָסוּר בַּקָּהָל**: It is prohibited for a man with crushed testicles or a severed penis to marry a woman who was born Jewish, but it is permitted for him to marry a convert or an emancipated maidservant (Rambam *Sefer Kedusha, Hilkhot Issurei Bia* 16:1; *Shulḥan Arukh, Even HaEzer* 5:1).

A priest with crushed testicles – **פְּצוּעַ דַּכָּא כֹּהֵן**: It is permitted for a priest with crushed testicles to marry a convert or an emancipated maidservant, in accordance with the opinion of Rav Sheshet and the second version of Rava's opinion (see Beit Shmuel; Rambam *Sefer Kedusha, Hilkhot Issurei Bia* 16:1; *Shulḥan Arukh, Even HaEzer* 5:1).

It is permitted for a man with crushed testicles to marry a Gibeonite woman – **פְּצוּעַ דַּכָּא מוּתָּר בִּנְתִינָה**: It is permitted for a man with crushed testicles to marry a Gibeonite woman or a woman of uncertain lineage, e.g., one whose father's identity is not known, or a foundling, or the like, in accordance with the *baraita* (Rambam *Sefer Kedusha, Hilkhot Issurei Bia* 16:1–2; *Shulḥan Arukh, Even HaEzer* 5:1).

אלא מעתה, ממזר דבר אולודי – הכי נמי דאסיר? והא תנן: ממזרים ונתינים מותרים לבא זה בזה! אלא: כי גזור רבנן – בכשרים, בפסולים לא גזור רבנן.

The Gemara raises an objection against Rava: **However, if that is so,** then with regard to a ***mamzer*****, who is capable of having children, so too** one would say **that he is prohibited** from marrying a Gibeonite. **But didn't we learn** otherwise in a mishna (*Kiddushin* 69a): ***Mamzerim* and Gibeonites are permitted**[N] **to marry one another.**[H] **Rather,** retract this explanation and replace it with the following: **When the Sages decreed** that one may not marry a Gibeonite, they limited their decree **to** those who are **fit,** so as to prevent them from mingling with Gibeonites; but **with regard to** those who are **unfit** to enter into the congregation, **the Sages did not issue a decree.**

הדר אמר רבא: לאו מילתא היא, בגויותן לית להו חתנות, נתגיירו – אית להו חתנות.

Rava then reconsidered and **said** that what he had previously argued, that the prohibition against marrying them applies only when they are gentiles, **is not correct.** The prohibition cannot be referring to gentiles, as **when they are gentiles there can be no** valid **marriage with them**[H] at all. It is only after **they have converted** that **there can be** valid **marriage with them,** and therefore the prohibition against entering into marriage with them applies. Nevertheless, it is permitted for a man with crushed testicles to marry a Gibeonite woman.

מתיב רב יוסף: "ויתחתן שלמה את בת פרעה מלך מצרים"! גיורי גיירה. והא לא קבלו גרים לא בימי דוד ולא בימי שלמה! מידי הוא טעמא – אלא לשולחן מלכים,

Rav Yosef raised an objection from the verse that states: **"And Solomon married the daughter of Pharaoh, king of Egypt"** (1 Kings 3:1), which indicates that there can, in fact, be valid marriage even with gentiles. The Gemara answers: Before Solomon took Pharaoh's daughter as his wife, **he converted her.** The Gemara asks: **But isn't** it so that **they did not accept converts, neither in the days of David**[H] **nor in the days of Solomon?** The Gemara answers: **But isn't the reason** that they did not accept converts during those periods **only** due **to** concern that the converts were not acting for the sake of Heaven but in fact desired the power of **the table of kings,** David and Solomon?

NOTES

Mamzerim and Gibeonites are permitted – ממזרים ונתינים מותרים: Why is this teaching necessary? It is permitted for a *mamzer* to marry any woman who is disqualified from the congregation; what, then, is special about a Gibeonite woman? The *Ḥazon Ish* suggests that since he is certainly prohibited from marrying a Gibeonite woman before she converts, as he retains the sanctity of a Jew even though he is disqualified from entering the congregation, one might have thought that the Sages decreed that he may not marry her even after her conversion.

HALAKHA

Mamzerim and Gibeonites are permitted to marry one another – ממזרים ונתינים מותרים לבא זה בזה: It is permitted for *mamzerim* and Gibeonites to marry each other. The child born from such a union has the status of a *mamzer* (Rambam *Sefer Kedusha, Hilkhot Issurei Bia* 15:33).

When they are gentiles there can be no valid marriage with them – בגויותן לית להו חתנות: By Torah law, a convert from one of the seven Canaanite nations may enter the congregation. It is known, however, that of them only the Gibeonites converted, and that Joshua decreed that they may not marry Israelites. The Ramban, Rashba, and *Tur* maintain that Gibeonites are forbidden by Torah law (Rambam *Sefer Kedusha, Hilkhot Issurei Bia* 12:22).

They did not accept converts in the days of David, etc. – לא קבלו גרים בימי דוד וכו׳: During the reigns of David and Solomon the courts did not accept converts out of concern that the prospective converts were driven by impure motives. As for those who converted in the presence of ordinary people, the High Court was skeptical about their conversions. They did not reject these individuals, in case they were proper converts, but neither did they draw converts near until they observed their behavior over the course of time (Rambam *Sefer Kedusha, Hilkhot Issurei Bia* 13:15).

Perek **VIII**
Daf **76** Amud **b**

הא לא צריכא ליה.

But **this one,** Pharaoh's daughter, **did not require such** things, as she herself was the daughter of royalty, and therefore there would have been no reason to doubt the sincerity of her conversion.

[ותיפוק ליה] דהא מצרית ראשונה היא! וכי תימא: הנך אזלי לעלמא והני אחריני נינהו –

The Gemara asks: **But let him derive** that Pharaoh's daughter was forbidden to Solomon for a different reason, **as she** was **a first-**generation **Egyptian** convert. Even if she converted, she would still have been an Egyptian convert of the first generation, and as such neither she nor her children would have been permitted to marry a Jew by birth (Deuteronomy 23:8–9). **And if you would say** that **those** whom the Torah rendered forbidden have already **left** Egypt and are now living elsewhere **in the world,**[N] **and those** currently living in Egypt **are others,** there is a difficulty.

NOTES

Those have left and are living elsewhere in the world – הנך אזלי לעלמא: Rashi explains that all of the Egyptians forbidden by Torah law drowned in the Red Sea. Other early authorities are puzzled by his opinion, as it appears that only some of the Egyptian military drowned, not the entire population. The Ritva suggests that perhaps Rashi means that after the Egyptians were reduced in number as a result of the plagues they suffered in Egypt and at the Red Sea, many members of other nations entered their country and intermingled with them. The Rashba and most commentaries understand the passage in its plain sense: Over the years other nations came to Egypt while the original Egyptians departed for other lands.

וְהָא תַּנְיָא, אָמַר רַבִּי יְהוּדָה: מִנְיָמִין גֵּר מִצְרִי הָיָה לִי חָבֵר מִתַּלְמִידֵי רַבִּי עֲקִיבָא, אָמַר: אֲנִי מִצְרִי רִאשׁוֹן, וְנָשָׂאתִי מִצְרִית רִאשׁוֹנָה. אַשִּׂיא לִבְנִי מִצְרִית שְׁנִיָּה, כְּדֵי שֶׁיְּהֵא בֶּן בְּנִי רָאוּי לָבֹא בַּקָּהָל.

As, isn't it taught in a *baraita* that **Rabbi Yehuda said: Minyamin,**[L] **an Egyptian convert,**[N] **was a friend of mine from among the students of Rabbi Akiva, and he said:** After I converted I was a **first**-generation **Egyptian** convert, **and** so **I married** another **first**-generation **Egyptian** convert. **I will marry off my son,** who is a second-generation Egyptian convert, **to** another **second**-generation **Egyptian** convert, **so that my grandson will be fit to enter into the congregation.** This indicates that first- and second-generation converts of Egyptian extraction were prohibited from entering into the congregation even during the period of the Mishna.

אֲמַר רַב פַּפָּא: אֲנַן מִשְּׁלֹמֹה לֵיקוּ וְנֵתִיב? שְׁלֹמֹה לָא נְסֵיב מִידֵּי דִּכְתִיב בֵּיהּ "מִן הַגּוֹיִם אֲשֶׁר אָמַר ה' אֶל בְּנֵי יִשְׂרָאֵל לֹא תָבֹאוּ בָהֶם וְהֵם לֹא יָבֹאוּ בָכֶם אָכֵן יַטּוּ אֶת לְבַבְכֶם אַחֲרֵי אֱלֹהֵיהֶם בָּהֶם דָּבַק שְׁלֹמֹה לְאַהֲבָה". אֶלָּא קַשְׁיָא "וַיִּתְחַתֵּן"!

Rav Pappa said: Shall we stand up and raise an objection from Solomon? Solomon did not marry anyone, as it is written in his regard: "Of the nations concerning which the Lord said to the children of Israel, You shall not go among them, neither shall they come among you; for surely they will turn away your heart after their gods; Solomon cleaved to these in love" (I Kings 11:2). Solomon cleaved to these women in love, but was not legally married to them. As Solomon had other forbidden wives, the case of Pharaoh's daughter presents no special difficulty. In fact, none of these marriages were valid at all. **But the phrase "and Solomon married"** (I Kings 3:1) that appears in connection with Pharaoh's daughter **is difficult,**[N] as it indicates that this marriage was in fact valid.

מִתּוֹךְ אַהֲבָה יְתֵירָה שֶׁאֲהֵבָהּ מַעֲלֶה עָלָיו הַכָּתוּב כְּאִילּוּ נִתְחַתֵּן בָּהּ.

The Gemara answers: **Due to the extraordinary love that he had for her, the verse relates to him as if he had married her** through a legally valid marriage, even though this was not the case.

אֲמַר לֵיהּ רָבִינָא לְרַב אַשִׁי: וְהָא אֲנַן תְּנַן פְּצוּעַ דַּכָּא וּכְרוּת שָׁפְכָה – מוּתָּרִים בְּגִיּוֹרֶת וּמְשׁוּחְרֶרֶת, הָא בִּנְתִינָה אֲסִירִי!

Ravina said to Rav Ashi: But didn't we learn in the mishna that **a man with crushed testicles and one whose penis has been severed are permitted to** marry a female **convert and an emancipated** maidservant? That indicates that it is only these women whom they are permitted to marry, **but they are prohibited from** marrying **a Gibeonite woman.** This appears to contradict the *baraita* that permits a man with crushed testicles to marry a Gibeonite.

אֲמַר לֵיהּ: וְלִיטַעֲמִיךְ, אֵימָא סֵיפָא: וְאֵינָן אֲסוּרִין אֶלָּא מִלָּבֹא בַּקָּהָל הָא בִּנְתִינָה – שָׁרוּ. אֶלָּא, מֵהָא לֵיכָּא לְמִשְׁמַע מִינָּהּ.

Rav Ashi **said to** Ravina: **And according to your** line of **reasoning, say the latter clause** of the mishna as follows: **And they are prohibited only from entering into the congregation,** and infer just the opposite, that it is only a woman who was born Jewish whom they are prohibited from marrying, **but they are permitted to** marry **a Gibeonite woman,** as she is not part of the congregation of the Lord. **Rather, no** inference is **to be learned from this** mishna, as the possible inferences are contradictory, and one must therefore rely on the *halakha* that was expressly taught.

מתני׳ עַמּוֹנִי וּמוֹאָבִי אֲסוּרִים, וְאִיסּוּרָן אִיסּוּר עוֹלָם, אֲבָל נְקֵבוֹתֵיהֶם מוּתָּרוֹת מִיָּד.

MISHNA **Ammonite and Moabite** converts **are prohibited** from entering into the congregation and marrying a woman who was born Jewish, **and their prohibition is eternal,** for all generations. **However, their female** counterparts, even the convert herself, **are permitted immediately.**[H]

מִצְרִי וַאֲדוֹמִי אֵינָם אֲסוּרִים אֶלָּא עַד שְׁלֹשָׁה דוֹרוֹת, אֶחָד זְכָרִים וְאֶחָד נְקֵבוֹת. רַבִּי שִׁמְעוֹן מַתִּיר אֶת הַנְּקֵבוֹת מִיָּד. אָמַר רַבִּי שִׁמְעוֹן: קַל וָחוֹמֶר הַדְּבָרִים: וּמָה אִם בְּמָקוֹם שֶׁאָסַר אֶת הַזְּכָרִים אִיסּוּר עוֹלָם – הִתִּיר אֶת הַנְּקֵבוֹת מִיָּד, מָקוֹם שֶׁלֹּא אָסַר אֶת הַזְּכָרִים אֶלָּא עַד שְׁלֹשָׁה דוֹרוֹת – אֵינוֹ דִּין שֶׁנַּתִּיר אֶת הַנְּקֵבוֹת מִיָּד?

Egyptian and Edomite converts **are prohibited** from entering into the congregation **only for three generations, both males and females.**[H] **Rabbi Shimon renders permitted** Egyptian and Edomite **females immediately. Rabbi Shimon said: The matter** may be derived by way of an *a fortiori* inference: **If in a place where** the Torah rendered **prohibited the males with an eternal prohibition,** i.e., Ammonites and Moabites, it **rendered permitted the females immediately,** then **in a place where it rendered prohibited the males for only three generations,** i.e., Egyptians and Edomites, **is it not right that we should render permitted the females immediately?**

LANGUAGE

Minyamin – מִנְיָמִין: This name appears already in the Bible (II Chronicles 31:15). However, as it was used in the time of the Mishna and later, both in this form and in Aramaic, Manyumei, the name seems to be a variant of the name Binyamin, with the *beit* being replaced by a *mem*, a phenomenon found in several first names over the generations.

NOTES

Minyamin, an Egyptian convert – מִנְיָמִין גֵּר מִצְרִי: Many commentaries, from *Tosafot* to the later authorities, deal with the issue of Egyptian converts nowadays. The Gemara here indicates that Egyptians remain forbidden. This is the case even though the Sages ruled elsewhere in regard to other nations, such as Ammon and Moab, that Sennacherib came and mixed up the nations and therefore the present inhabitants of those lands are not the descendants of those who were living there in the time of Moses. This question is clearly the subject of a tannaitic dispute. Conflicting sources are also recorded in the *Tosefta*. According to one source, Egyptians are still forbidden, either because Sennacherib and Nebuchadnezzar did not mix up the entire country and only exiled a minority of its residents, or because there is an explicit guarantee in the Bible, with reference to time and place, that God will restore them to their land (see Ramban, Rashba, and Rabbeinu Tam's *Sefer HaYashar*). On the other hand, the Rambam and many others maintain that all the nations were mingled together. Therefore, nowadays all of the special prohibitions applying to specific nations are no longer in force (see Meiri).

But "and he married" is difficult – אֶלָּא קַשְׁיָא וַיִּתְחַתֵּן: The early authorities understand Rashi's presentation and resolution of the problem as follows: Since she was an Egyptian convert, how can their relationship be described as marriage? Some object that although the marriage is forbidden, it is nevertheless valid. Consequently, they explain that if the previous claim that Solomon only "cleaved in love" to his foreign wives is accepted, and there was no marriage at all, why does the verse use the phrase "and he married"? (Ramban; Rashba).

HALAKHA

The prohibition proscribing an Ammonite and Moabite – אִיסּוּר עַמּוֹנִי וּמוֹאָבִי: It is prohibited for male Ammonite and Moabite converts to enter into the congregation for all generations. However, female Ammonites and Moabites who converted are permitted. Nowadays, it is permitted for even male Ammonite and Moabite converts to marry Jewish women, as the ancient Ammonites and Moabites have become intermingled with other nations (Rambam *Sefer Kedusha, Hilkhot Issurei Bia* 12:18; *Shulḥan Arukh, Even HaEzer* 4:2, 7).

An Egyptian and an Edomite – מִצְרִי וַאֲדוֹמִי: It is prohibited for Egyptian and Edomite converts to enter into the congregation until the third generation. This prohibition applies to both males and females, in accordance with the unattributed view in the mishna. Nowadays Edomites are permitted, as the ancient Edomites have become intermingled with other nations. As for Egyptian converts, some authorities (Rosh) rule that they are forbidden, whereas others (Rambam; *Baḥ*) permit them, based on the assumption that the ancient Egyptians have also become intermingled with other nations (Rambam *Sefer Kedusha, Hilkhot Issurei Bia* 12:19; *Shulḥan Arukh, Even HaEzer* 4:3, 7).

אמרו לו: אם הלכה – נקבל, ואם לדין – יש תשובה, אמר להם: לא כי, הלכה אני אומר.

Rabbi Shimon's colleagues **said to him: If** you are reporting a *halakha* that you received from your teachers, **we will accept** it from you. **But if** you merely wish to prove your case with an *a fortiori* **inference** based on your own reasoning, **there is a refutation** of your argument. Rabbi Shimon **said to them:** That is **not so.** I disagree with your claim that the *a fortiori* inference can be refuted, but in any case **I am stating a** ***halakha*** handed down to me by my teachers.

גמ׳ מנא הני מילי? אמר רבי יוחנן: דאמר קרא ״וכראות שאול את דוד יוצא לקראת הפלשתי אמר אל אבנר שר הצבא בן מי זה הנער, אבנר, ויאמר אבנר חי נפשך המלך אם ידעתי״. ולא ידע ליה? והכתיב ״ויאהבהו מאד ויהי לו נושא כלים״! אלא: אאבוה קא משאיל.

GEMARA The Gemara asks: **From where are these matters** derived that female Ammonites and Moabites are permitted immediately? **Rabbi Yoḥanan said: As the verse states: "And when Saul saw David go forth against the Philistine, he said to Abner, the captain of the host: Abner, whose son is this youth? And Abner said: As your soul lives, O king, I cannot tell"** (I Samuel 17:55). This verse is puzzling: **Did** Saul really **not recognize him? But isn't it** previously **written:** "And David came to Saul, and stood before him; **and he loved him greatly; and he became his armor-bearer"** (I Samuel 16:21)? **Rather,** it must be that **he was asking about** David's **father.**

ואביו לא ידע ליה? והכתיב ״והאיש בימי שאול זקן בא באנשים״. ואמר רב ואיתימא רבי אבא: זה ישי אבי דוד שנכנס באוכלוסא ויצא באוכלוסא!

The Gemara is still puzzled by this verse: **And did** Saul **not recognize** David's **father? But isn't it written** with regard to Jesse, David's father: **"And the man in the days of Saul was old, and came among men"** (I Samuel 17:12), **and Rav, and some say Rabbi Abba, said: This** is referring to **Jesse, father of David, who** always **entered with multitudes** [*ukhlusa*][L] **and left with multitudes.** As he was clearly a man of importance, everyone must have known who he was.

הכי קאמר שאול: אי מפרץ אתי, אי מזרח אתי? אי מפרץ אתי – מלכא הוי, שהמלך פורץ לעשות דרך ואין ממחין בידו, אי מזרח אתי – חשיבא בעלמא הוי.

Rather, **this is** what **Saul was saying,** in his attempt to clarify David's lineage: **Does he come from** the descendants of **Perez, or does he come from** the descendants of **Zerah?**[B] What is the significance of this question? **If he comes from Perez he will be king, as a king may breach** [*poretz*] **a way**[H] for himself **and no one can stop him.** And **if he comes from Zerah he will be merely a man of importance,** but not a king.

מאי טעמא אמר ליה שאל עליה? דכתיב ״וילבש שאול את דוד מדיו״ – כמדתו, וכתיב ביה בשאול ״משכמו ומעלה גבוה מכל העם״. אמר ליה דואג האדומי: עד שאתה משאיל עליו אם הגון הוא למלכות אם לאו, שאל עליו אם ראוי לבא בקהל אם לאו. מאי טעמא – דקאתי מרות המואביה.

The Gemara continues with its explanation: **For what reason did** Saul **say to** Abner that he should **inquire about** David? **As it is written: "And Saul clad David**[N] **with his apparel** [***maddav***]**"** (I Samuel 17:38), which indicates that the clothes were **of** David's **size** [***kemiddato***]. **And it is written with regard to Saul: "From his shoulders and upward he was higher than any of the people"** (I Samuel 9:2). Upon seeing that his clothes fit David, Saul began to fear that it might be David who was destined for the throne, and he therefore inquired into his background. At that point, **Doeg the Edomite said to** Saul: **Before you inquire as to whether or not he is fit for kingship, inquire as to whether or not he is even fit to enter into the congregation. What is the reason** for such doubts? It is **that** he **descends from Ruth the Moabite,** and Moabites are permanently barred from entering the congregation.

אמר ליה אבנר: תנינא, ״עמוני״ ולא עמונית ״מואבי״ ולא מואבית. אלא מעתה ״ממזר״ ולא ממזרת! ״ממזר״ כתיב, מום זר.

Abner said to him: We already **learned** that there is no room for such concern. As the verse states: "An Ammonite or a Moabite shall not enter into the congregation of the Lord" (Deuteronomy 23:4), teaching that **an Ammonite** man is barred from entering into the congregation, **but not an Ammonite woman;** and similarly, **a Moabite** man is barred from entering into the congregation, **but not a Moabite woman.** Doeg said to him: **However, if that is so,** say that the verse that renders it prohibited for a *mamzer* to enter the congregation renders prohibited only a male ***mamzer***, **but not a female** ***mamzer***. Abner replied: **It is written: "A** ***mamzer***,**"**[N] which should be understood not as a noun but as an adjective, denoting **a strange blemish** [***mum zar***], one who is defective due to a forbidden relationship, and this applies to males and females alike.

LANGUAGE

Multitudes [*ukhlusa*] – **אוכלוסא**: This word derives from the Greek ὄχλος, *okhlos*, meaning throng or large crowd of followers.

BACKGROUND

Does he come from Perez or does he come from Zerah – **אי מפרץ אתי אי מזרח אתי**: Perez and Zerah were twin brothers who were born to Tamar following her liaison with Judah (see Genesis, chapter 38). According to Jacob's blessings to his children (Genesis 48:8–12), the Jewish people's monarchy was destined to be established from the descendants of Judah, and they therefore posed a threat to Saul's continued rule.

HALAKHA

A king may breach a way – **המלך פורץ לעשות דרך**: A king may breach a fence to make a road for himself, and none may object. The road may be made as wide as is necessary. The king need not divert its course due to an individual's field or vineyard; rather, he may proceed in a straight line in order to wage his war (Rambam *Sefer Shofetim, Hilkhot Melakhim* 5:3).

NOTES

And Saul clad David – **וילבש שאול את דוד**: Saul knew that he was clearly taller than everyone else. Why, then, did he even attempt to dress David in his own apparel? The *Yefe Toar* answers that although he did not expect his clothes to fit David, he wished to perform a symbolic act in order to honor him and strengthen his resolve.

It is written: A *mamzer* – **ממזר כתיב**: The *Ba'al Halakhot Gedolot* explains that had the verse said *mamzir*, one might have interpreted it as referring specifically to males, but the word "*mamzer*" signifies an impairment of some sort that can apply to both males and females. As the *She'iltot deRav Aḥai Gaon* says, it is as though the verse said *mimzar*, or, in the words of Rabbeinu Avraham min HaHar: One who has this blemish [*mum*] is an alien [*zar*].

״מִצְרִי״ וְלֹא מִצְרִית! שָׁאנֵי הָכָא דִּמְפָרֵשׁ טַעֲמָא דִּקְרָא: ״עַל אֲשֶׁר לֹא קִדְּמוּ אֶתְכֶם בַּלֶּחֶם וּבַמַּיִם״ – דַּרְכּוֹ שֶׁל אִישׁ לְקַדֵּם, וְלֹא דַּרְכָּהּ שֶׁל אִשָּׁה לְקַדֵּם. הָיָה לָהֶם לְקַדֵּם אֲנָשִׁים לִקְרַאת אֲנָשִׁים וְנָשִׁים לִקְרַאת נָשִׁים! אִישְׁתִּיק.

Doeg retorted: If so, say that it is prohibited for only **an Egyptian** man to enter into the congregation, **but not an Egyptian woman.** Abner answered: **Here it is different, as the reason for** the prohibition recorded in this **verse** with regard to Ammonites **is explicit: "Because they did not meet you with bread and with water** on the way, when you came forth out of Egypt" (Deuteronomy 23:5). Since **it is the way of a man** to go forth **to meet** guests **but it is not the way of a woman** to go forth, females were not included in this prohibition. Doeg countered: Still, **the men should have gone** forth **to meet the men, and the women to meet the women.** Abner **was silent,** as he did not know how to respond to this objection.

מִיָּד: ״וַיֹּאמֶר הַמֶּלֶךְ שְׁאַל אַתָּה בֶּן מִי זֶה הָעָלֶם״. הָתָם קָרֵי לֵיהּ ״נַעַר״, הָכָא קָרֵי לֵיהּ ״עֶלֶם״, הָכִי קָא אָמַר לֵיהּ: הֲלָכָה נִתְעַלְּמָה מִמְּךָ, צֵא וּשְׁאַל בְּבֵית הַמִּדְרָשׁ, שָׁאַל, אָמְרוּ לֵיהּ: ״עַמּוֹנִי״ וְלֹא עַמּוֹנִית, ״מוֹאָבִי״ וְלֹא מוֹאָבִית.

Immediately: "And the king said, inquire you whose son is this lad" (I Samuel 17:56). The Gemara comments: **There,** in the previous verse, Saul **calls him youth** [*na'ar*], and **here he calls him lad** [*elem*]. This change in the wording hints at the following discussion. Saul **said to** Doeg **as follows:** The *halakha* **is hidden** [*nitalma*] **from you,** and you are ignorant of the law. **Go and inquire** about the matter **in the study hall. He** went to the study hall and **asked. They said to him:** The *halakha* is: **An Ammonite** man is forbidden, **but not an Ammonite woman; a Moabite** man is forbidden, **but not a Moabite woman.**

Perek **VIII**
Daf **77** Amud **a**

אַקְשֵׁי לְהוּ דּוֹאֵג כָּל הָנֵי קוּשְׁיָיתָא, אִישְׁתִּיקוּ, בָּעֵי לְאַכְרוֹזֵי עֲלֵיהּ, מִיָּד ״וַעֲמָשָׂא בֶן אִישׁ וּשְׁמוֹ יִתְרָא הַיִּשְׂרְאֵלִי אֲשֶׁר בָּא אֶל אֲבִיגַל בַּת נָחָשׁ״, וּכְתִיב ״יֶתֶר הַיִּשְׁמְעֵאלִי״ אָמַר רָבָא: מְלַמֵּד שֶׁחָגַר חַרְבּוֹ כְּיִשְׁמָעֵאל וְאָמַר: כָּל מִי שֶׁאֵינוֹ שׁוֹמֵעַ הֲלָכָה זוֹ – יִדָּקֵר בַּחֶרֶב, כָּךְ מְקוּבְּלַנִי מִבֵּית דִּינוֹ שֶׁל שְׁמוּאֵל הָרָמָתִי: ״עַמּוֹנִי״ וְלֹא עַמּוֹנִית, ״מוֹאָבִי״ וְלֹא מוֹאָבִית.

Doeg raised before them all those objections from the others who are disqualified from entering into the congregation, and **they were silent,** not knowing how to respond. Doeg then **wanted to proclaim** that David was disqualified from entering into the congregation. He was **immediately** answered. Here it says: **"Now Amasa was the son of a man, whose name was Jithra the Israelite, that went into Abigal the daughter of Nahash"** (II Samuel 17:25), **and** yet elsewhere **it is written** that Amasa's father was named **"Jether the Ishmaelite"** (I Chronicles 2:17). **Rava said:** This **teaches that he girded his sword like Ishmael,**[N] i.e., like an Arab, **and said: Whoever does not accept this *halakha*** and act accordingly **shall be stabbed with the sword. This** is the tradition that **I received from the court of Samuel from Rama: An Ammonite** man is prohibited from entering into the congregation, **but not an Ammonite woman; a Moabite** man is prohibited from entering into the congregation, **but not a Moabite woman.**

וּמִי מְהֵימָן? וְהָאָמַר רַבִּי אַבָּא אָמַר רַב: כָּל תַּלְמִיד חָכָם שֶׁמּוֹרֶה הֲלָכָה וּבָא, אִם קוֹדֶם מַעֲשֶׂה אֲמָרָהּ – שׁוֹמְעִין לוֹ, וְאִם לָאו – אֵין שׁוֹמְעִין לוֹ! שָׁאנֵי הָכָא, דְּהָא שְׁמוּאֵל וּבֵית דִּינוֹ קַיָּים.

The Gemara asks about this incident: **And is he trusted** to offer such testimony? **But didn't Rabbi Abba say** that **Rav said:** With regard to **every Torah scholar who issues a halakhic ruling**[N] based on a tradition he claims to have received from his teacher, and that ruling has practical ramifications for himself as well, **if he stated** the ruling already **before the incident,** i.e., before it had a bearing on his own case, **one listens to him; but if not,** if he reported the tradition only after it was personally relevant to him, **one does not listen to him,**[H] as he is an interested party. Since Amasa was the son of Jesse's daughter Abigail, as stated in the aforementioned verse in Chronicles, the matter certainly affected his own status. The Gemara answers: **Here it is different, as Samuel** and the other members **of his court were still living,**[N] and the truth of Amasa's report could be easily verified.

NOTES

He girded his sword like Ishmael – חָגַר חַרְבּוֹ כְּיִשְׁמָעֵאל: The Maharsha raises the following difficulty, citing the *Yefe Toar*: Why is girding a sword connected here to Ishmael? After all, the sword was traditionally associated with Esau. Several answers have been suggested (see Riaf). According to one suggestion, Ishmael is mentioned here because it says about him: "His hand will be against all, and the hand of all against him" (Genesis 16:12), and Amasa maintained his opinion in opposition to all his peers (*Iyyun Ya'akov*). The *Arukh LaNer* explains that the reference is to Ishmael, son of Nethaniah, who girded his sword and killed Gedaliah (see Jeremiah 40–41).

With regard to the incident itself, while it is generally prohibited to bring weapons into the study hall, there were times when this rule was disregarded in order to affirm and establish a particular *halakha* (see *Gilyonei HaShas*).

Every Torah scholar who issues a halakhic ruling – כָּל תַּלְמִיד חָכָם שֶׁמּוֹרֶה הֲלָכָה: Rabbeinu Tam explains that this does not refer to all scholars who issue practical rulings but only to those who are personally involved, as their testimony might be compromised. Most early authorities accept this opinion, as it is stated in the Jerusalem Talmud in tractate *Sanhedrin* that the reference is in fact to a case of this kind. However, some commentaries maintain that any novel ruling in a practical case is suspect because the scholar in question is personally involved, as he seeks to verify his own ruling. Rabbeinu Avraham min HaHar attributes this interpretation to Rashi (see Meiri).

Samuel and his court were still living – שְׁמוּאֵל וּבֵית דִּינוֹ קַיָּים: According to Rashi, there is no concern that one might be lying about a matter that can easily be verified. The Ritva states that one does not suspect a Torah scholar of outright falsehood; the only concern is that in his attempt to establish his own opinion, he might report a ruling that he thinks he heard from his teacher when he did not actually do so. However, when his teacher is still alive, it is assumed that his report will be precise.

HALAKHA

A scholar who issues a halakhic ruling – חָכָם הַמּוֹרֶה הֲלָכָה: With regard to a scholar who issues a halakhic ruling that has practical ramifications for himself, if he had already stated the *halakha* before the personal incident arose, his ruling is accepted; but if not, the ruling is not accepted (*Shulḥan Arukh, Yoreh De'a* 242:36, and in the comment of Rema).

NOTES

The king's daughter is all glorious within – **כָּל כְּבוּדָּה בַּת מֶלֶךְ פְּנִימָה**: The Maharshal, in his *Yam shel Shlomo*, explains that this verse does not refer to Ammonite or Moabite women, as they certainly are not considered modest; rather, it is speaking of Jewish women. The idea is that since Jewish women stay in their homes, their gentile counterparts cannot greet them with bread and water.

An Ammonite man but not an Ammonite woman – **עַמּוֹנִי וְלֹא עַמּוֹנִית**: *Tosafot* raise the following difficulty: Why doesn't Rabbi Yehuda likewise expound: An Egyptian man and not an Egyptian woman? *Tosafot Yeshanim* and the Ramban explain that with respect to Egyptian converts, Rabbi Yehuda relies on the phrase "that are born to them" (Deuteronomy 23:9), which makes the issue dependent on birth, a matter that applies equally to males and females.

Because they did not meet you – **עַל דְּבַר אֲשֶׁר לֹא קִדְּמוּ אֶתְכֶם**: The details of this exposition involve many difficulties. The Rashba raises the point that the verse "Because they did not meet you" refers only to Ammonites, whereas David's case concerned Moabites. He answers that since the Bible deals with the two nations together, they must be treated the same way. The Ramban, in his Commentary on the Torah, asks the following question: It is stated explicitly: "You shall sell me food for money… as the Moabites, who dwell in Ar, did to me" (Deuteronomy 2:28–29); doesn't this indicate that the Moabites did ultimately provide them with food and water? One suggestion is that only a few Moabites, i.e., the residents of Ar and certain others, acted in this manner (see Meiri). The clearest answer is offered in the Jerusalem Talmud: With regard to the Moabites the verse states that the reason they are barred from entering into the congregation is "because they hired Balaam" (Deuteronomy 23:5), and it is certainly not the way of women to be involved in such a transaction.

You have loosened my bands – **פִּתַּחְתָּ לְמוֹסֵרָי**: The Riaf states that this exposition refers to the beginning of the verse, which states: "I am Your servant, the son of Your maidservant; You have loosened my bands [*moserai*]." Ruth calls herself "your maidservant Ruth" (Ruth 3:9), and this verse refers to the prohibitions [*issurim*] relating to her.

מִכָּל מָקוֹם קַשְׁיָא! הָכָא תַּרְגְּמוּ: ״כָּל כְּבוּדָּה בַּת מֶלֶךְ פְּנִימָה״, בְּמַעְרְבָא אָמְרִי, וְאִיתֵימָא רַבִּי יִצְחָק: אָמַר קְרָא ״וַיֹּאמְרוּ אֵלָיו אַיֵּה שָׂרָה אִשְׁתֶּךָ״ וגו׳.

The Gemara asks: **In any case,** the unanswered question raised by Doeg is **difficult.** The Gemara answers: **Here,** in Babylonia, **they explained** the matter based on the verse: **"The king's daughter is all glorious within"** (Psalms 45:14),[N] which indicates that it is unbefitting for a woman to venture outside at all, and therefore the Ammonite women would not have been expected to go forth to meet the Jewish women. **In the West,** Eretz Yisrael, **they say, and some say** it was **Rabbi Yitzḥak** who said: **The verse states: "And they said to him: Where is Sarah your wife?** And he said: Behold, in the tent" (Genesis 18:9), which teaches that it is praiseworthy for a woman to remain inside her home.

כְּתַנָּאֵי ״עַמּוֹנִי״ וְלֹא עַמּוֹנִית, ״מוֹאָבִי״ וְלֹא מוֹאָבִית, דִּבְרֵי רַבִּי יְהוּדָה, רַבִּי שִׁמְעוֹן אוֹמֵר: ״עַל דְּבַר אֲשֶׁר לֹא קִדְּמוּ אֶתְכֶם בַּלֶּחֶם וּבַמַּיִם״ – דַּרְכּוֹ שֶׁל אִישׁ לְקַדֵּם וכו׳.

The Gemara comments that this disagreement with regard to the source of the *halakha* that it is permitted for an Ammonite or Moabite woman to enter into the congregation is **like the** following dispute between *tanna'im*: The verse states: "An Ammonite or a Moabite" (Deuteronomy 23:4); **an Ammonite** man is barred from entering into the congregation, **but not an Ammonite woman,**[N] and similarly, **a Moabite** man is barred from entering into the congregation, **but not a Moabite woman.** This is **the statement of Rabbi Yehuda,** who derives the *halakha* from the masculine form of these two terms. **Rabbi Shimon says:** The verse states: **"Because they did not meet you[N] with bread and with water** on the way" (Deuteronomy 23:5). Since **it is the way of a man,** but not the way of a woman, to go forth **to meet** guests, females were not included in the prohibition.

דָּרַשׁ רָבָא: מַאי דִּכְתִיב ״פִּתַּחְתָּ לְמוֹסֵרָי״ אָמַר דָּוִד לִפְנֵי הַקָּדוֹשׁ בָּרוּךְ הוּא: רִבּוֹנוֹ שֶׁל עוֹלָם, שְׁנֵי מוֹסֵרוֹת שֶׁהָיוּ עָלַי פִּתַּחְתָּם, רוּת הַמּוֹאֲבִיָּה וְנַעֲמָה הָעַמּוֹנִית.

With regard to the same issue, **Rava taught: What is** the meaning of that **which is written: "You have loosened my bands"** (Psalms 116:16)?[N] **David said before the Holy One, Blessed be He: Master of the Universe, You have loosened the two bands that were on me,** on account of which I and my entire family might have been disqualified, i.e., **Ruth the Moabite woman and Na'ama the Ammonite woman.** Owing to the allowance granted to Moabite and Ammonite women, we are permitted to enter the congregation.

דָּרַשׁ רָבָא: מַאי דִּכְתִיב ״רַבּוֹת עָשִׂיתָ אַתָּה ה׳ אֱלֹהַי נִפְלְאוֹתֶיךָ וּמַחְשְׁבוֹתֶיךָ אֵלֵינוּ״, ״אֵלַי״ לֹא נֶאֱמַר אֶלָּא ״אֵלֵינוּ״, מְלַמֵּד שֶׁהָיָה רְחַבְעָם יוֹשֵׁב בְּחֵיקוֹ שֶׁל דָּוִד, אָמַר לוֹ: עָלַי וְעָלֶיךָ נֶאֶמְרוּ שְׁתֵּי מִקְרָאוֹת הַלָּלוּ.

Rava further **taught: What is** the meaning of that **which is written: "Many things have You done, O Lord my God, Your wonders and Your thoughts are upon us"** (Psalms 40:6)? **Upon me is not stated, but** rather **"upon us,"** which **teaches that Rehoboam,** son of Solomon and grandson of David, was **sitting on the lap of David,** who **said to him: These two verses were stated about me and about you,** as Rehoboam's mother was Na'ama the Ammonite.

דָּרַשׁ רָבָא: מַאי דִּכְתִיב ״אָז אָמַרְתִּי הִנֵּה בָאתִי בִּמְגִלַּת סֵפֶר כָּתוּב עָלָי״, אָמַר דָּוִד: אֲנִי אָמַרְתִּי עַתָּה בָּאתִי, וְלֹא יָדַעְתִּי שֶׁבִּמְגִלַּת סֵפֶר כָּתוּב עָלַי. הָתָם כְּתִיב ״הַנִּמְצָאוֹת״ הָכָא כְּתִיב ״מָצָאתִי דָּוִד עַבְדִּי בְּשֶׁמֶן קָדְשִׁי מְשַׁחְתִּיו״.

With regard to the same issue, **Rava** also **taught: What is** the meaning of that **which is written: "Then I said: Behold, I have come; in the scroll of a book it is written about me"** (Psalms 40:8)? **David said:** I had **said** that **I have come** only **now;** my life was created only recently, at the time of my birth. **But I did not know that it was** already **written about me in the scroll of a book,** that an ancient text already hints at my existence. **There,** with regard to the daughters of Lot, **it is written:** "And your two daughters **that are found** here" (Genesis 19:15), and **here,** with regard to David, **it is written: "I have found David, My servant; I have anointed him with My holy oil"** (Psalms 89:21). The lost article that was found among the daughters of Lot, the mothers of Ammon and Moab, is David and his royal house.

אָמַר עוּלָּא אָמַר רַבִּי יוֹחָנָן: בַּת גֵּר עַמּוֹנִי כְּשֵׁרָה לִכְהוּנָּה. אֲמַר לֵיהּ רָבָא בַּר עוּלָּא לְעוּלָּא: כְּמַאן? אִי כְּרַבִּי יְהוּדָה – הָא אָמַר: בַּת גֵּר זָכָר כְּבַת חָלָל זָכָר. וְאִי כְּרַבִּי יוֹסֵי – פְּשִׁיטָא, הָא אָמַר: אַף גֵּר שֶׁנָּשָׂא גִּיּוֹרֶת בִּתּוֹ כְּשֵׁרָה לִכְהוּנָּה!

Ulla said that **Rabbi Yoḥanan said: The daughter of an Ammonite convert is fit** not only to marry an ordinary Israelite, but even **to** marry into **the priesthood. Rava bar Ulla said to Ulla: In accordance with whose** opinion did you state this *halakha*? **If** it is **in accordance with** the opinion of **Rabbi Yehuda, didn't he say** that **the daughter of a male convert is like the daughter of a male *ḥalal*,** one rendered unfit for the priesthood, which means that the daughter of any convert should be disqualified from the priesthood? **And if** you spoke **in accordance with** the opinion of **Rabbi Yosei, it is obvious** that this is the case, **as he said** that **even if a male convert marries a female convert, his daughter is fit to** marry into **the priesthood.**

וְכִי תֵּימָא: בְּהָנָךְ דִּרְאוּיִן לָבֹא בַּקָּהָל, אֲבָל הַאי דְּאֵין רָאוּי לָבֹא בַּקָּהָל – לָא, מְנָא לֵיהּ?

And if you would say that Rabbi Yosei spoke only **of those** converts **who are fit to enter into the congregation, but** with regard to **this one,** an Ammonite convert, **who is not fit to enter into the congregation,** his daughter is **not** fit to marry a priest, there is a difficulty: **From where** does **he** derive this distinction?

דְּיָלֵיף מִכֹּהֵן גָּדוֹל בְּאַלְמָנָה. מַה לְּכֹהֵן גָּדוֹל בְּאַלְמָנָה שֶׁכֵּן בִּיאָתוֹ בַּעֲבֵירָה.

The Gemara answers: **He derives** this **from** the case of **a High Priest** who married **a widow,** a woman whom he is prohibited from marrying. Just as his daughter is disqualified from marrying into the priesthood, so too is the daughter of an Ammonite convert disqualified from marrying into the priesthood. However, an objection may be raised: **What** comparison can be made to **a High Priest** who married **a widow,** which is a stringent prohibition, **as his intercourse involves a transgression?** Can one say the same with regard to the daughter of an Ammonite convert, who could be born from a permitted relationship, e.g., from a male Ammonite convert who married a female Ammonite convert?

חָלָל יוֹכִיחַ, מַה לְּחָלָל – שֶׁכֵּן יְצִירָתוֹ בַּעֲבֵירָה,

The Gemara answers: **Let** the case of **a *ḥalal* prove** that this is not relevant, as his intercourse does not involve a transgression and yet his children are also *ḥalalim*, who are prohibited from marrying into the priesthood. However, another objection may be raised: **What** comparison can be made to **a *ḥalal*,** seeing **that his** essential **formation involved a transgression,** and therefore it is understandable that his disqualification extends to his offspring. Can one say the same with regard to the daughter of an Ammonite convert who was not the product of a forbidden union?

כֹּהֵן גָּדוֹל יוֹכִיחַ, וְחָזַר הַדִּין,

The Gemara answers: **Let** the case of **a High Priest** who marries a widow **prove** that this is not relevant, as he was not the product of a forbidden union but nevertheless his daughter is disqualified from marrying into the priesthood. **And the derivation has reverted** to its starting point,[N] and the discussion can go back and forth.

לֹא רְאִי זֶה כִּרְאִי זֶה, וְלֹא רְאִי זֶה כִּרְאִי זֶה, הַצַּד הַשָּׁוֶה שֶׁבָּהֶן: שֶׁאֵינוֹ בְּרוֹב קָהָל, וּבִתּוֹ פְּסוּלָה – אַף כָּאן, שֶׁאֵינוֹ בְּרוֹב קָהָל וּבִתּוֹ פְּסוּלָה.

At this point, however, the *halakha* can be derived from a combination of the two sources: **The aspect of this** case, that of a High Priest, **is not like the aspect of that** case, that of a *ḥalal*, **and the aspect of that** case **is not like the aspect of this** case; **their common denominator is that he is not included in the majority of the congregation,** i.e., the man is governed by a *halakha* that differs from that of most Jews. The High Priest's intercourse with a widow involves a transgression, and the *ḥalal* is the product of a forbidden union. **And** in each case, the man's **daughter is disqualified** from marrying into the priesthood. **So too,** an Ammonite convert **is not included in the majority of the congregation,** as it is prohibited for him to enter the congregation of Israel, **and** so **his daughter is** also **disqualified** from marrying into the priesthood.

מַה לְּהַצַּד הַשָּׁוֶה שֶׁבָּהֶן שֶׁכֵּן יֵשׁ בָּהֶן צַד עֲבֵירָה –

The Gemara objects: **What** is **the common denominator** between the case of the High Priest and that of the *ḥalal* that prevents one from utilizing it as a paradigm for other cases? Both of those cases **include an aspect of transgression;** the High Priest engaged in a forbidden act of intercourse, and the *ḥalal* is the product of a forbidden union. Perhaps that is the reason that the daughter in each of these cases is prohibited from marrying into the priesthood. In the case of the Ammonite convert, however, there is no transgression.

דִּלְמָא וַדַּאי בְּעַמּוֹנִי שֶׁנָּשָׂא בַּת יִשְׂרָאֵל קָאָמְרַתְּ, אַף עַל גַּב דְּבִיאָתוֹ בַּעֲבֵירָה – בִּתּוֹ כְּשֵׁרָה? אָמַר לֵיהּ: אִין,

The Gemara answers: **Perhaps you spoke of an Ammonite** convert **who married the daughter of a Jew,** and Rabbi Yoḥanan wished to teach that **although his intercourse involves a transgression,** as it is prohibited for him to enter into the congregation, **his daughter is** nevertheless **fit** to marry into the priesthood. Ulla **said to him: Yes,** this was Rabbi Yoḥanan's teaching.

NOTES

The derivation has reverted to its starting point – חָזַר הַדִּין: This style of argumentation is often utilized when the Gemara tries to derive a *halakha* by means of analogy [*binyan av*]. If it cannot be proven from one case, as the comparison between the two *halakhot* is subject to refutation, the Gemara will cite a second case to which the previous difficulty does not apply. When a different problem is discovered in the second case, the discussion reverts back to the first case, which does not involve the present difficulty. Therefore, as the argument goes back and forth between these two proofs, the Gemara combines them in order to find their common denominator, a shared aspect from which one can derive the *halakha* that can be applied to other cases.

HALAKHA

The daughter of an Ammonite convert in forbidden marriage with a woman of Jewish birth – בת גר עמוני: If an Ammonite convert or a second-generation Egyptian convert married a woman of Jewish birth, the daughter is fit to marry even into the priesthood, in accordance with Rabbi Yoḥanan's ruling cited by Ravin (Rambam *Sefer Kedusha*, *Hilkhot Issurei Bia* 19:13).

דכי אתא רבין אמר רבי יוחנן: בת גר עמוני ובת מצרי שני, רבי יוחנן אמר: כשרה, וריש לקיש אמר: פסולה. ריש לקיש אמר פסולה, דיליף לה מכהן גדול באלמנה. רבי יוחנן אמר כשרה,

As, when Ravin came from Eretz Yisrael to Babylonia, he said that **Rabbi Yoḥanan said:** With regard to **the daughter of an Ammonite convert** who is the offspring of his forbidden marriage with a woman of Jewish birth,[H] **and** similarly, with regard to **the daughter of a second-generation Egyptian** convert from his forbidden marriage with a woman of Jewish birth, **Rabbi Yoḥanan said** that she is **fit** to marry into the priesthood, **whereas Reish Lakish said** that she is **disqualified** from marrying a priest. **Reish Lakish said** she is **disqualified, as he derives from** the *halakha* governing **a High Priest** who married **a widow** that the daughter of any forbidden union is disqualified from the priesthood. **Rabbi Yoḥanan said** she is **fit,**

Perek **VIII**
Daf **77** Amud **b**

NOTES

An established [*mikanna*] female convert – גיורת מכנה: The early authorities disagree with regard to the meaning of this term. According to Rashi, it is similar to *mimekhona*, meaning a convert who comes from well-established lineage, from converts whose marriage did not involve a transgression. The *Arukh* explains that *mikana* means from her *ken*, her base. In other words, one whose base, i.e., her mother, was also a convert (see *Gilyonei HaShas*).

And according to this version – ולהך לישנא: The Rashba is puzzled by this passage, as the question and answer with regard to the daughter of a second-generation Egyptian convert is relevant only according to the first version, not the second. He maintains that the Gemara could have made this point briefly, but preferred to do so at length in the form of a discussion. In sum, the question applies only according to the first version.

דתני רבי זכאי קמיה דרבי יוחנן: "כי אם בתולה מעמיו יקח אשה" – להביא גיורת מכנה שהיא כשרה לכהונה. ואמר ליה: אני שונה "עמיו" "מעמיו" – להביא בתולה הבאה משני עממין, ואת אמרת גיורת מכנה ותו לא?

as Rabbi Zakkai taught the following *baraita* **before Rabbi Yoḥanan:** That which is stated with regard to a High Priest: **"But a virgin of his own people shall he take to wife"** (Leviticus 21:14), comes **to include an established female convert,**[N] one who was a convert from birth, i.e., who was born to a father and mother who converted after their marriage but prior to her birth, and this indicates **that she is fit** to marry **into the priesthood. And** Rabbi Yoḥanan **said to him: I teach** that the words **"his own people"** and the more inclusive phrase **"of his own people"** come **to include a virgin who comes from two peoples,** from a union of converts hailing from two different peoples, **and you say** only **an established female convert and no more?**

מאי שני עממין? אילימא עמוני שנשא עמונית, ומאי משני עממין, דזכרים אסורין ונקבות מותרות – היינו גיורת מכנה! אלא בעמוני שנשא בת ישראל.

The Gemara asks: **What** are these **two peoples? If we say** this is referring to **an Ammonite** man **who married an Ammonite woman, and what** is the meaning of **"from two peoples,"** that they are legally considered like two separate peoples, as their **males are prohibited** from entering into the congregation, **whereas** their **females are permitted** to do so, there is a difficulty. In that case, **this is** the same as **an established female convert,** as the daughter of such a union is a proper convert in all regards. **Rather,** it must refer **to an Ammonite** man **who married the daughter of a Jew,** as they belong to two separate peoples.

ואיכא דאמרי, אמר ליה: אני שונה "עמיו" "מעמיו" – להביא בתולה הבאה משני עממין, ומעם שיש בו שני עממין ואת אמרת גיורת מכנה ותו לא?

And there are those **who say** an alternative version of this discussion. Rabbi Yoḥanan **said to** Rabbi Zakkai: **I teach** that the words **"his own people"** and the more inclusive phrase **"from his own people"** come **to include a virgin who comes from two peoples,** i.e., whose mother was Jewish from birth and whose father was a convert, **and** that convert is **from a people that** itself **consists of two peoples,** i.e., an Ammonite or a Moabite, who hail from peoples whose males are prohibited from entering into the congregation, while it is permitted for their females to do so, **and you say** only **an established female convert and no more?**

ולהך לישנא, בת מצרי שני דכשרה לכהונה מנא ליה? וכי תימא דיליף מעמוני שנשא בת ישראל – מה לעמוני שנשא בת ישראל שכן נקבות מותרות!

The Gemara asks: **And according to this** second **version,**[N] **from where** does Rabbi Yoḥanan derive that **the daughter of a second**-generation **Egyptian** convert who had entered into a forbidden marriage with a woman of Jewish birth **is fit** to marry **into the priesthood,** as with respect to Egyptian converts, there is no difference between males and females? **And if you would say that he derives** this **from** the case of **an Ammonite** convert **who married** the **daughter of a Jew,** the following difficulty arises: **What** comparison can be made to **an Ammonite** convert **who married** the **daughter of a Jew** and had a daughter, who is permitted to enter the congregation although she is an Ammonite, **as female** Ammonite converts **are** entirely **permitted?** Perhaps for this reason it is permitted for the daughter to marry into the priesthood as well. Can one say the same with regard to the daughter of a second-generation Egyptian convert who had entered into a forbidden marriage with a woman of Jewish birth, when it is prohibited for female Egyptian converts, like their male counterparts, to enter into the congregation until the third generation?

מִצְרִי שֵׁנִי שֶׁנָּשָׂא מִצְרִית שְׁנִיָּה יוֹכִיחַ.

The Gemara responds: **Let** the case of **a second**-generation **male Egyptian** convert **who married a second**-generation **female Egyptian** convert **prove** that this is not relevant, as it is permitted for their daughter, a third-generation Egyptian convert, to enter the congregation, even though she belongs to the Egyptian people, whose female converts are prohibited in the same manner as their male converts.

מַה לְמִצְרִי שֵׁנִי שֶׁנָּשָׂא מִצְרִית שְׁנִיָּה – שֶׁכֵּן אֵין בִּיאָתוֹ בַּעֲבֵירָה!

The Gemara refutes this proof: **What** comparison can be made to a **second**-generation **male Egyptian** convert **who married a second**-generation **female Egyptian** convert, seeing **that his intercourse does not involve a transgression,** as it is permitted for him to marry her? Can one say the same with regard to a second-generation Egyptian convert who entered into a forbidden marriage with the daughter of a Jew?

עַמּוֹנִי שֶׁנָּשָׂא בַּת יִשְׂרָאֵל יוֹכִיחַ, וְחָזַר הַדִּין וכו׳.

This leads back to the first proof: **Let an Ammonite** man **who married the daughter of a Jew prove** that this is not irrelevant, as they too entered into a forbidden union, and yet it is permitted for the daughter of that marriage to marry into the priesthood. **And the derivation has reverted** to its starting point, and the discussion can go back and forth. The two cases differ in their particular aspects, but their common denominator is that it is permitted for the daughter to marry into the priesthood. So too, it is permitted for the daughter of a second-generation Egyptian convert who married a woman who was born Jewish to marry into the priesthood.

אֲמַר רַב יוֹסֵף: הַיְינוּ דְּשַׁמְעֲנָא לֵיהּ לְרַב יְהוּדָה דַּאֲמַר "עַמּוֹ" "מֵעַמָּיו" וְלָא יָדַעֲנָא מַאי קָאָמַר.

Rav Yosef said: This is what I heard Rav Yehuda say in his lecture about the phrases **"his own people"** and **"from his own people," and** at the time **I did not know what he was saying.** Now I understand that he was saying that it is permitted for the daughter of an Ammonite convert who married a Jewish woman to marry into the priesthood, as taught by Rabbi Yoḥanan.

כִּי אֲתָא רַב שְׁמוּאֵל בַּר יְהוּדָה אֲמַר, הָכִי תָּנָא קַמֵּיהּ: אִשָּׁה עַמּוֹנִית כְּשֵׁרָה, בְּנָהּ מֵעַמּוֹנִי פָּסוּל, וּבִתָּהּ מֵעַמּוֹנִי כְּשֵׁרָה, בַּמֶּה דְּבָרִים אֲמוּרִים – בְּעַמּוֹנִי וְעַמּוֹנִית שֶׁנִּתְגַּיְּירוּ, אֲבָל בִּתָּהּ מֵעַמּוֹנִי – פְּסוּלָה.

When Rav Shmuel bar Yehuda came from Eretz Yisrael to Babylonia, **he said that** Rabbi Zakkai **taught before** Rabbi Yoḥanan **as follows: An Ammonite woman is fit, her son from an Ammonite is unfit, and her daughter from an Ammonite is fit. In what** case **is this statement said?** It is said **with regard to an Ammonite** man **and an Ammonite woman who converted, but her daughter from an Ammonite** who did not convert **is unfit.**

אֲמַר לֵיהּ: פּוֹק תְּנֵי לְבָרָא. מַאי דְּאָמְרַתְּ אִשָּׁה עַמּוֹנִית כְּשֵׁרָה – עַמּוֹנִי וְלֹא עַמּוֹנִית, בְּנָהּ מֵעַמּוֹנִי פָּסוּל, דְּהָא עַמּוֹנִי הוּא,

Rabbi Yoḥanan **said to him: Go out** and **teach it outside,**[N] i.e., this *baraita* is not in accordance with the accepted *halakha*, and therefore it should not be made part of the regular learning in the study hall. **What you said,** that **an Ammonite woman is fit,** is well known and need not be taught because it is just another way of saying that **a male Ammonite** is barred from entering the congregation **but not a female Ammonite.** As for the teaching that **her son from an Ammonite is unfit,** this too is unnecessary, **as he is an Ammonite.**

וּבִתָּהּ מֵעַמּוֹנִי כְּשֵׁרָה, לְמַאי? אִילֵימָא לָבֹא בַּקָּהָל – הָשְׁתָּא אִמָּהּ כְּשֵׁרָה, הִיא מִיבַּעְיָא? אֶלָּא לִכְהוּנָּה.

But that which you said: **Her daughter from an Ammonite is fit, with regard to what** issue did you teach this? **If we say** that she is fit **to enter into the congregation,** this too is redundant: **Now** that it was taught that even **her mother is fit** to enter the congregation, is it **necessary** to say that **she** herself, the daughter, is fit to do so? **Rather,** you must mean to say that she is fit to marry **into the priesthood.**

בַּמֶּה דְּבָרִים אֲמוּרִים – בְּעַמּוֹנִי וְעַמּוֹנִית שֶׁנִּתְגַּיְּירוּ, אֲבָל בִּתָּהּ מֵעַמּוֹנִי – פְּסוּלָה. מַאי בִּתָּהּ מֵעַמּוֹנִי? אִילֵימָא עַמּוֹנִי שֶׁנָּשָׂא עַמּוֹנִית – הַיְינוּ גִּיּוֹרֶת מִכַּנָּה. אֶלָּא, עַמּוֹנִי שֶׁנָּשָׂא בַּת יִשְׂרָאֵל. אֲמַר לֵיהּ: פּוֹק תְּנֵי לְבָרָא.

The *baraita* continues: **In what case is this statement said?** It is said **with regard to an Ammonite** man **and an Ammonite woman who converted, but her daughter from an Ammonite** man **is unfit. What** is meant here by **her daughter from an Ammonite? If we say** it means **an Ammonite** man **who married an Ammonite woman,** and they converted prior to the birth of their daughter, **this is an established female convert,** who was previously declared fit to marry into the priesthood. **Rather,** it must mean **an Ammonite** convert **who** unlawfully **married the daughter of a Jew,** and according to what is stated here, their daughter is unfit to marry a priest. Rabbi Yoḥanan, however, ruled that such a woman is fit, and therefore **he said to** Rabbi Zakkai: **Go out** and **teach** it **outside,** as this *baraita* is unreliable.

NOTES

Go out and teach it outside – פּוֹק תְּנֵי לְבָרָא: This expression indicates that a *baraita* quoted in the study hall is viewed by the Sage as insufficiently established, either because it contains an internal contradiction or due to its unclear wording. Such a *baraita* is unsuitable for discussion in the study hall. Even if the scholar teaching the *baraita* knows that it represents a tradition, the text must be clarified properly before it is presented for debate.

NOTES

What refutation – מַאי תְּשׁוּבָה: In the Rambam's Commentary on the Mishna, a simple answer is provided to Rabbi Shimon's argument: There is a difference between the prohibitions governing Egyptians and Edomites and those relating to Ammonites and Moabites. In the case of Egyptians and Edomites the Torah does not provide a reason for their prohibition, and therefore there are no grounds for supposing that the *halakha* of females differs in any way from that of males. This is not the case with regard to Ammonites and Moabites. The later authorities point out that the fact that the Gemara does not suggest this answer poses no difficulty, as the mishna does not specify the response Rabbi Shimon received, and therefore it is possible that the Rabbis had recourse to several arguments, not all of which are cited by the Gemara.

I am stating a *halakha* – הֲלָכָה אֲנִי אוֹמֵר: This does not mean that if it is a tradition the Rabbis would accept Rabbi Shimon's opinion as the actual *halakha*, as they did not rescind their view even after he affirmed that he had learned it by tradition. Rather, they meant that if it is a tradition, they will allow it to remain unchallenged while they will preserve their own traditional teachings (Rabbi Yehuda al-Madari).

״מִצְרִי וַאֲדוֹמִי אֵינָן אֲסוּרִין״ וכו׳. מַאי תְּשׁוּבָה?

It is taught in the mishna that **Egyptian and Edomite** converts **are prohibited** from entering into the congregation **only** for three generations, both males and females, while Rabbi Shimon permits females immediately based on the following *a fortiori* inference. If regarding Ammonites and Moabites, where the Torah prohibited the males with an eternal prohibition, it permitted the females immediately, then regarding Egyptians and Edomites, where it prohibited the males for only three generations, the females should certainly be permitted immediately. Rabbi Shimon's colleagues informed him that there is a refutation of his argument. The Gemara asks: **What is this refutation**[N] mentioned by the mishna?

אֲמַר רַבָּה בַּר בַּר חָנָה אָמַר רַבִּי יוֹחָנָן: מִשּׁוּם דְּאִיכָּא לְמֵימַר: עֲרָיוֹת יוֹכִיחוּ, שֶׁלֹּא אָסַר בָּהֶן אֶלָּא עַד שְׁלֹשָׁה דּוֹרוֹת, אֶחָד זְכָרִים וְאֶחָד נְקֵבוֹת.

Rabba bar bar Ḥana said that **Rabbi Yoḥanan said:** It is **because it may be said** that **those with whom relations are forbidden,** i.e., incestuous relationships, **prove** that the above-mentioned factor is irrelevant, **as** the Torah **prohibits them only for** up to **three generations,** i.e., up to his granddaughter, and yet it prohibits **both males and females,** i.e., the daughter of his son and the daughter of his daughter.

מַה לַעֲרָיוֹת שֶׁכֵּן כָּרֵת. מַמְזֵר יוֹכִיחַ.

The Gemara rejects this proof: **What** comparison can be made to **those with whom relations are forbidden,** which involve stringent prohibitions, **as** they entail the punishment of ***karet*?** The Gemara answers: **Let** the prohibition with regard to **a *mamzer* prove** that this is not relevant, as its violation does not involve the punishment of *karet* and yet it applies equally to males and females.

מַה לְּמַמְזֵר שֶׁכֵּן אֵינוֹ רָאוּי לָבֹא בַּקָּהָל לְעוֹלָם, עֲרָיוֹת יוֹכִיחוּ. וְחָזַר הַדִּין,

The Gemara rejects this argument: **What** comparison can be made to **a *mamzer*,** seeing that he is governed by the stringency **that he is forever unfit to enter into the congregation** for all generations? The Gemara counters: **Let those with whom relations are forbidden prove** that this is not relevant, as the Torah prohibits them only for up to three generations. **And the derivation has reverted** to its starting point, and the discussion can go back and forth.

לֹא רְאִי זֶה כִּרְאִי זֶה וְלֹא רְאִי זֶה כִּרְאִי זֶה, הַצַּד הַשָּׁוֶה שֶׁבָּהֶן: שֶׁאֲסוּרִין, וְאֶחָד זְכָרִים וְאֶחָד נְקֵבוֹת, אַף אֲנִי אָבִיא מִצְרִי וּמִצְרִית שֶׁיִּהְיוּ אֲסוּרִין, אֶחָד זְכָרִים וְאֶחָד נְקֵבוֹת.

However, the *halakha* with regard to an Egyptian can be derived from a combination of the two sources. **The aspect of this** case, that of incestuous relationships, **is not like the aspect of that** case, that of a *mamzer*, **and the aspect of that** case **is not like the aspect of this** case; **their common denominator is that their prohibition** applies to **both males and females. I will also bring** the additional *halakha* of **a male Egyptian** convert **and a female Egyptian** convert **that they are forbidden, both males and females.**

מַה לְּהַצַּד הַשָּׁוֶה שֶׁבָּהֶן שֶׁכֵּן יֵשׁ בָּהֶן צַד כָּרֵת.

The Gemara objects: **What** is unique about **the common denominator** between the cases of incestuous relationships and a *mamzer* that prevents utilizing it as a paradigm for other cases? Both **include an aspect of *karet*,** either with respect to the act of incestuous intercourse itself or with respect to the conception of the *mamzer*, as a *mamzer* is the offspring of a union punishable by *karet*. However, the prohibition concerning an Egyptian, which does not include an aspect of *karet*, may apply only to males, but not females.

וְרַבָּנַן: מֵחָלָל, דְּחַיָּיבֵי עֲשֵׂה וּכְרַבִּי אֱלִיעֶזֶר בֶּן יַעֲקֹב.

And the Rabbis, who reject Rabbi Shimon's proof, derive the prohibition applying to female Egyptians **from** the *halakha* governing **a *ḥalal*,** one rendered unfit for the priesthood. A *ḥalal* is the child of a union for which the parties involved are **liable** to receive punishment **for** the transgression of **a positive mitzva,** e.g., the child of a High Priest and a woman who was not a virgin when he married her, and this status applies to males and females alike. **And** this is **in accordance with** the opinion of **Rabbi Eliezer ben Ya'akov,** who ruled that the child of such a relationship is a *ḥalal*.

וּמַאי ״לֹא כִּי״? הָכִי קָאָמַר לְהוּ: לְדִידִי – לָא סְבִירָא לִי דְּרַבִּי אֱלִיעֶזֶר בֶּן יַעֲקֹב, לְדִידְכוּ דִּסְבִירָא לְכוּ כְּרַבִּי אֱלִיעֶזֶר בֶּן יַעֲקֹב – הֲלָכָה אֲנִי אוֹמֵר.

The Gemara asks: **And what** did Rabbi Shimon mean when he responded: **Not so?** The Gemara explains that **this is what he said to them: According to my own** opinion, **I do not hold in accordance with** the opinion of **Rabbi Eliezer ben Ya'akov,** and therefore your refutation is not valid for me. But even **according to you, who do maintain in accordance with** the opinion of **Rabbi Eliezer ben Ya'akov, I am** nevertheless **stating a *halakha***[N] handed down to me by my teachers that female Egyptians and Edomites are permitted.

תַּנְיָא, אָמַר לָהֶן רַבִּי שִׁמְעוֹן: הֲלָכָה אֲנִי אוֹמֵר. וְעוֹד: מִקְרָא מְסַיְּיעֵנִי: ״בָּנִים״ וְלֹא בָּנוֹת.

It is taught in a *baraita* that **Rabbi Shimon said to them: I am stating** a traditional ***halakha*****, and furthermore a verse supports me,** as the verse with regard to Edomites and Egyptians states: "The **sons** of the third generation that are born to them may enter to them, the congregation of the Lord" (Deuteronomy 23:9), teaching that the prohibition applies to their sons, **but not** to their **daughters.**[N]

תָּנוּ רַבָּנַן: ״בָּנִים״ וְלֹא בָּנוֹת, דִּבְרֵי רַבִּי שִׁמְעוֹן. אָמַר רַבִּי יְהוּדָה: הֲרֵי הוּא אוֹמֵר ״בָּנִים אֲשֶׁר יִוָּלְדוּ לָהֶם דּוֹר שְׁלִישִׁי״ – הַכָּתוּב תְּלָאָן בְּלֵידָה.

The Sages taught a *baraita* that further clarifies the matter: The prohibition with regard to Egyptians and Edomites applies only to their **sons, but not** to their **daughters;** this is **the statement of Rabbi Shimon. Rabbi Yehuda said:** The verse **states: "The sons of the third generation that are born to them** may enter to them, the congregation of the Lord," and the phrase "born to them" indicates that **the verse made their** prohibition **dependent on birth,** with regard to which there is no difference between males and females.

אָמַר רַבִּי יוֹחָנָן: אִי לָאו דַּאֲמַר רַבִּי יְהוּדָה הַכָּתוּב תְּלָאָן בְּלֵידָה – לֹא מָצָא יָדָיו וְרַגְלָיו בְּבֵית הַמִּדְרָשׁ. כֵּיוָן דַּאֲמַר מָר ״קְהַל גֵּרִים אִיקְּרֵי קָהָל״ –

Rabbi Yoḥanan says: Had Rabbi Yehuda not said that **the verse made their** prohibition **dependent on birth,** so that females are also included in the prohibition, **he would not have found his hands and feet in the study hall,** i.e., he would have been caught in a self-contradiction. Why? **Since the Master said** that according to Rabbi Yehuda **a congregation of converts is** also **called a congregation** of the Lord,[H]

NOTES

Sons but not daughters – בָּנִים וְלֹא בָּנוֹת: The Ritva points out that based on this verse one could just as easily claim that sons should be permitted after three generations, while daughters are disqualified forever. He explains that since the verse speaks of the prohibition proscribing Egyptian and Edomite males, and it limits the prohibition to three generations, the implication is that whoever is not in this category is permitted outright. The *Arukh LaNer* answers that there is no reason to render females forbidden for any longer than males, as any justification for a permanent ban would apply more to sons than to daughters.

HALAKHA

A congregation of converts – קְהַל גֵּרִים: A congregation of converts is not called a congregation of the Lord. Therefore, all those for whom it is prohibited to enter into the congregation, e.g., *mamzerim*, are permitted to female converts, and similarly, converts and emancipated slaves are permitted to *mamzerot*, in accordance with the opinion of Rabbi Yosei and against that of Rabbi Yehuda (*Shulḥan Arukh, Even HaEzer* 4:22).

Perek **VIII**
Daf **78** Amud **a**

מִצְרִי שֵׁנִי בְּמַאי יִטְהָר? דִּלְמָא דְּאִי עָבַר וְנָסֵיב. ״דְּאִי״ לָא כְּתִיב קְרָא,

how could a second-generation **Egyptian** convert ever **achieve purity,**[N] so that it is permitted for his offspring, the third generation, to enter into the congregation? He may marry neither a Jew nor a female Egyptian convert. The Gemara answers: **Perhaps** it means **that if he transgressed and married** a convert or a Jewish woman, his seed will be purified. The Gemara rejects this suggestion: A case of: **That if, is not written** in the **verse.** In other words, the Bible does not speak of situations that can arise only through the commission of a transgression.

הֲרֵי מַמְזֵר, דְּאִי, וּכְתָבֵיהּ קְרָא! דְּאִי לְאִיסּוּרָא – כָּתַב, דְּאִי לְהֶיתֵּירָא – לָא כָּתַב.

The Gemara asks: But **isn't** there the *halakha* of **a *mamzer*,** which is a case of **that if,** as a *mamzer* is the child of a forbidden union, **and** yet **the verse writes it?** The Gemara answers: A case of **that if** that results in a **prohibition,** the Torah **writes,** but a case of **that if** that leads **to an allowance,** the Torah **does not write.** The Torah teaches the *halakha* of a *mamzer*, whose very existence is the result of his parents having engaged in forbidden relations, in order to render it prohibited for him to enter into the congregation. However, it would not teach the *halakha* of a second-generation Egyptian convert who transgressed and married a woman who was forbidden to him, in order to permit his offspring to enter into the congregation.

הֲרֵי מַחֲזִיר גְּרוּשָׁתוֹ, דְּאִי לְהֶיתֵּירָא, וּכְתָבֵיהּ! הָתָם מִשּׁוּם עִיקַּר אִיסּוּרָא הוּא דִּכְתָבֵיהּ.

The Gemara raises an objection: But **isn't** there the *halakha* governing **one who remarries his divorcée** after she had been married to another man? This is a case of **that if** that leads **to an allowance, and** yet the Torah **writes it.** The words "It is an abomination before the Lord" (Deuteronomy 24:4) stated with regard to this case teach that although the woman herself is forbidden to her first husband, if she nevertheless remarried him, their children are fit to enter into the congregation. The Gemara answers: **There,** the Torah **writes** that case **due to the basic prohibition,** i.e., that a man may not remarry his divorced wife after she has been married to another man, and the allowance with regard to their children is learned incidentally.

NOTES

How could a second-generation Egyptian achieve purity – מִצְרִי שֵׁנִי בְּמַאי יִטְהָר: Many early authorities proposed various ways by which a second-generation Egyptian convert can achieve purity without entering into the congregation, even according to Rabbi Yehuda (see *Tosafot*, Ramban, Rashba, and Meiri). Some later authorities suggest that he may marry a *mamzeret* after ten generations, in accordance with the opinion of Reish Lakish, or that he may marry without a betrothal, or by means of levirate marriage (see *Arukh LaNer*). In the Jerusalem Talmud it is stated that according to Rabbi Yehuda he may purify his seed by marrying an emancipated maidservant, who is not part of the congregation of converts, and therefore he is permitted to her, and their children will be fit from both sides.

NOTES

Why is it stated: "Sons" – לָמָּה נֶאֱמַר בָּנִים: Even Rabbi Shimon, who expounds this word to exclude daughters, would agree that this is not the primary source of that *halakha*, as he merely cites the verse in support of a *halakha* that he derives by way of an *a fortiori* inference (*Otzar HaShitot*).

HALAKHA

From them you should count – מֵהֶם מְנֵה: Egyptian and Edomite converts, both males and females, are disqualified from entering into the congregation until the third generation. Consequently, it is prohibited for the son of an Egyptian convert to enter into the congregation, but it is permitted for his grandson to do so (Rambam *Sefer Kedusha, Hilkhot Issurei Bia* 12:19; *Shulḥan Arukh, Even HaEzer* 4:3).

Follow their disqualification – הַלֵּךְ אַחַר פְּסוּלָן: If a convert who is disqualified from entering into the congregation unlawfully married a Jew, the status of the child born to them follows the unfit parent (Rambam *Sefer Kedusha, Hilkhot Issurei Bia* 12:19; *Shulḥan Arukh, Even HaEzer* 4:6).

A pregnant Egyptian woman who converted – מִצְרִית מְעוּבֶּרֶת שֶׁנִּתְגַּיְּירָה: If a pregnant Egyptian woman converted, the child born to her is considered a second-generation Egyptian convert (Rambam *Sefer Kedusha, Hilkhot Issurei Bia* 12:20; *Shulḥan Arukh, Even HaEzer* 4:4).

תָּנוּ רַבָּנַן: אִם נֶאֱמַר בָּנִים – לָמָּה נֶאֱמַר דּוֹרוֹת, וְאִם נֶאֱמַר דּוֹרוֹת לָמָּה נֶאֱמַר בָּנִים? אִם נֶאֱמַר בָּנִים וְלֹא נֶאֱמַר דּוֹרוֹת הָיִיתִי אוֹמֵר: בֵּן רִאשׁוֹן וְשֵׁנִי – אָסוּר, שְׁלִישִׁי – מוּתָּר, לְכָךְ נֶאֱמַר דּוֹרוֹת.

The Sages taught in a *baraita*: The verse states with respect to Egyptian and Edomite converts that "the sons of the third generation that are born to them may enter to them, the congregation of the Lord" (Deuteronomy 23:9). **If it is stated "sons" why is it** also **stated "generation," and if it is stated "generation" why is it** also **stated "sons"?**[N] One of these terms seems superfluous. The *baraita* explains: **If it** had **stated** only **"sons" and not stated "generation," I would say** that the prohibition depends on the number of the son, meaning that the **first and second sons** of an Egyptian convert are **forbidden,** whereas the **third** is **permitted. Therefore, it is stated "generation"** to indicate that the prohibition depends not on the number of the son but on his generation.

וְאִם נֶאֱמַר דּוֹרוֹת וְלֹא נֶאֱמַר בָּנִים הָיִיתִי אוֹמֵר: לְאוֹתָן הָעוֹמְדִים עַל הַר סִינַי, לְכָךְ נֶאֱמַר בָּנִים.

And conversely, **if** it had **stated** only **"generation" and not stated "sons," I would say** that the generations are counted from **those standing on Mount Sinai,** so that any Egyptian born after three generations have passed from the time of the giving of the Torah would be permitted. **Therefore, it is stated "sons"** to indicate that certain sons are prohibited in later generations as well.

"לָהֶם" – מֵהֶם מְנֵה, "לָהֶם" – הַלֵּךְ אַחַר פְּסוּלָן.

The verse states: "The sons of the third generation that are born to them may enter to them, the congregation of the Lord." The Sages expounded each of the two instances of the words "to them": The first mention of **"to them"** teaches that **from them** you should **count.**[H] The count of generations begins with the converts themselves, as they are considered the first generation, and therefore their grandchildren are permitted. The second mention of **"to them"** teaches that you should **follow their disqualification.**[H] If a male Egyptian convert married a Jewish woman, or if a female Egyptian convert married a Jewish man, the *halakha* with regard to the offspring born to them is that although one of the parents is not disqualified from entering into marriage, the status of the child follows the unfit parent, who disqualifies his or her offspring until the third generation.

וְאִיצְטְרִיךְ לְמִיכְתַּב "לָהֶם" וְאִיצְטְרִיךְ לְמִיכְתַּב "אֲשֶׁר יִוָּלְדוּ". דְּאִי כָּתַב רַחֲמָנָא "אֲשֶׁר יִוָּלְדוּ" הֲוָה אָמִינָא: מִבְּנֵיהֶם מְנֵה, כְּתַב רַחֲמָנָא "לָהֶם". וְאִי כָּתַב רַחֲמָנָא "לָהֶם" – הֲוָה אָמִינָא: מִצְרִית מְעוּבֶּרֶת שֶׁנִּתְגַּיְּירָה הִיא וּבְנָהּ – חַד, כְּתַב רַחֲמָנָא "אֲשֶׁר יִוָּלְדוּ".

The Gemara comments: **And it is necessary to write "to them," and it is** also **necessary to write "that are born." As, if the Merciful One had written** only **"that are born," I would say** that one should **count** the generations **from** the converts' **sons.** Therefore, **the Merciful One writes "to them"** to teach that the converts themselves are counted as the first generation. **And if the Merciful One had written** only **"to them," I would say** that in the case of **a pregnant Egyptian** woman **who converted,**[H] **she and her child,** i.e., the fetus, are considered **one** generation, as the fetus is deemed to be a part of its mother. Therefore, **the Merciful One writes "that are born,"** to indicate that each birth marks a new generation, and accordingly the fetus is regarded as a second-generation Egyptian convert.

וְאִיצְטְרִיךְ לְמִיכְתַּב "לָהֶם" הָכָא, וְאִיצְטְרִיךְ לְמִיכְתַּב "לוֹ" גַּבֵּי מַמְזֵר.

The verse concerning a *mamzer* states: "A *mamzer* shall not enter into the congregation of the Lord; even to the tenth generation shall none of his [*lo*] enter into the congregation of the Lord" (Deuteronomy 23:3). **And it is necessary to write "to them" here,** with regard to an Egyptian convert, to teach that the child's status follows the disqualified parent in his case, **and it is** also **necessary to write "to him [*lo*]" with regard to a *mamzer*,** to teach that a similar *halakha* applies to a *mamzer*. In the translation of the verse, *lo* is translated as: Of his, i.e., of his ilk. However, *lo* can also be translated as: To him.

דְּאִי כָּתַב רַחֲמָנָא הָכָא – מִשּׁוּם דְּבָא מִטִּיפָּה פְּסוּלָה, אֲבָל מַמְזֵר דְּבָא מִטִּיפָּה כְּשֵׁרָה – אֵימָא לָא.

Lo is written with regard to both the Egyptian and the *mamzer*, **as, if the Merciful One had written** it only **here,** with regard to an Egyptian, one might have said that only in this case does the child's status follow the disqualified parent, **because** the Egyptian **comes from an unfit drop** of semen, that of a gentile. **But** as for **a *mamzer*, who comes from a fit drop** of semen, as his parents were proper Jews despite their grave sin, one might say that there is **no** room for such stringency. Therefore, the Torah teaches that the same *halakha* applies to a *mamzer*.

וְאִי כְּתַב רַחֲמָנָא גַּבֵּי מַמְזֵר – מִשּׁוּם דְּאֵין רָאוּי לָבֹא בַּקָּהָל לְעוֹלָם, אֲבָל הָכָא – אֵימָא לָא, צְרִיכָא.

And conversely, **if the Merciful One had written** this stringent *halakha* only **with regard to a *mamzer*,** one might have said that this is because **he is forever unfit to enter into the congregation, but here,** with regard to an Egyptian convert, I might **say** that this is **not** the case. Therefore, both verses are **necessary.**

אָמַר רַבָּה בַּר בַּר חָנָה אָמַר רַבִּי יוֹחָנָן: מִצְרִי שֵׁנִי שֶׁנָּשָׂא מִצְרִית רִאשׁוֹנָה – בְּנָהּ שְׁלִישִׁי הֲוֵאי. אַלְמָא קָסָבַר: בָּתַר דִּידֵיהּ שָׁדֵינַן לֵיהּ,

Rabba bar bar Ḥana said that **Rabbi Yoḥanan said:** If a **second**-generation male **Egyptian** convert **married a first**-generation female **Egyptian** convert, **her child is** considered **a third**-generation convert[N] for whom it is permitted to enter the congregation. The Gemara comments: **Apparently** Rabbi Yoḥanan **maintains** that **we assign** the child **to him,** the father, and not to the mother.

מְתִיב רַב יוֹסֵף: רַבִּי טַרְפוֹן אוֹמֵר: יְכוֹלִין מַמְזֵרִים לִיטָּהֵר, כֵּיצַד? מַמְזֵר נָשָׂא שִׁפְחָה – הַוָּלָד עֶבֶד, שִׁחְרְרוֹ – נִמְצָא בֶּן חוֹרִין. אַלְמָא בָּתַר דִּידָהּ שָׁדֵינַן לֵיהּ! שָׁאנֵי הָתָם, דְּאָמַר קְרָא ״הָאִשָּׁה וִילָדֶיהָ תִּהְיֶה לַאדֹנֶיהָ״.

Rav Yosef raised an objection from the following mishna (*Kiddushin* 69a): **Rabbi Tarfon says:** ***Mamzerim* can purify themselves**[H] over the course of the generations. **How so?** If a ***mamzer* married** his non-Jewish **maidservant, the child** born to them is **a slave.** If the slave's master, the *mamzer* who owns the maidservant, subsequently **freed** the child, **he becomes a free man** and is fit to enter into the congregation. **Apparently we assign** the child **to her,** the mother, and not to the father, as the child is deemed a slave rather than a *mamzer*. The Gemara answers: **It is different there,** in the case of the slave, **as the verse states: "The wife and her children shall be her master's"** (Exodus 21:4). The words "her children" indicate that the children born to a non-Jewish maidservant are assigned to her.

מְתִיב רָבָא, אָמַר רַבִּי יְהוּדָה: מִנְיָמִין גֵּר מִצְרִי הָיָה לִי חָבֵר מִתַּלְמִידֵי רַבִּי עֲקִיבָא, וְאָמַר: אֲנִי מִצְרִי רִאשׁוֹן, וְנָשָׂאתִי מִצְרִית רִאשׁוֹנָה, אַשִּׂיא לִבְנִי מִצְרִית שְׁנִיָּה כְּדֵי שֶׁיְּהֵא בֶּן בְּנִי רָאוּי לָבֹא בַּקָּהָל. וְאִי סָלְקָא דַּעְתָּךְ בָּתְרֵיהּ דִּידֵיהּ שָׁדֵינַן לֵיהּ – אֲפִילּוּ רִאשׁוֹנָה נַמִי! הָא אֲמַר לֵיהּ רַבִּי יוֹחָנָן לְתַנָּא: תְּנֵי רִאשׁוֹנָה.

Rava raised an objection from a previously mentioned *baraita*: **Rabbi Yehuda said: Minyamin, an Egyptian convert, was a friend of mine from among the students of Rabbi Akiva, and he said:** Following my conversion **I was a first-generation Egyptian** convert, **and so I married** another **first-generation Egyptian** convert.[N] **I will marry off my son,** who is a second-generation Egyptian convert, **to** another **second**-generation **Egyptian** convert, **so that my grandson will be fit to enter into the congregation. Now, if it enters your mind** to say that **we assign** the child **to** the father, **even** if he marries off his son to a **first**-generation Egyptian convert his grandson should be permitted. The Gemara answers: **Didn't Rabbi Yoḥanan** already **say to the *tanna*** reciting the *baraita*: You should **teach** that Minyamin sought to marry off his son to **a first**-generation Egyptian convert.[N]

כִּי אֲתָא רַב דִּימִי אָמַר רַבִּי יוֹחָנָן: מִצְרִי שֵׁנִי שֶׁנָּשָׂא מִצְרִית רִאשׁוֹנָה – בְּנָהּ שֵׁנִי הֲוֵאי. אַלְמָא: בָּתַר אִימֵּיהּ שָׁדֵינַן לֵיהּ.

When Rav Dimi came from Eretz Yisrael to Babylonia, **he said** that **Rabbi Yoḥanan said** just the opposite: If a **second**-generation male **Egyptian** convert **married a first**-generation female **Egyptian** convert,[H] **her son is** considered **a second**-generation convert who is prohibited from entering the congregation. **Apparently,** Rabbi Yoḥanan maintains that **we assign** the child **to the mother** and not to the father.

אֲמַר לֵיהּ אַבָּיֵי: אֶלָּא הָא דְּאָמַר רַבִּי יוֹחָנָן: הִפְרִישׁ חַטָּאת מְעוּבֶּרֶת וְיָלְדָה, רָצָה – מִתְכַּפֵּר בָּהּ, רָצָה – מִתְכַּפֵּר בִּוְלָדָהּ.

Abaye said to him: But what, then, will you say about **that which Rabbi Yoḥanan said:** If **one set aside a pregnant** animal as a **sin-offering,**[H] and the animal later **gave birth** to a female, if **he wishes he may gain atonement with** the mother **itself,** in which case the young is left to graze until it develops a blemish that renders it unfit for sacrifice, whereupon it is sold and the proceeds are used for a gift offering; and if **he wishes he may gain atonement with** the animal's **young,** and the mother is left to graze until it develops a blemish.

HALAKHA

Mamzerim can purify themselves – יְכוֹלִין מַמְזֵרִים לִיטָּהֵר: If a *mamzer* had intercourse with a gentile woman, the child born to them is a gentile. If the child subsequently converts, he is a full-fledged Jew. Similarly, if a *mamzer* had intercourse with a maidservant, their child is a slave, and if he is subsequently set free, he is a Jew. Therefore, a *mamzer* may marry a maidservant *ab initio*, in order to allow their children to enter the congregation once the children have been released. The *halakha* follows the opinion of Rabbi Tarfon, as the Gemara in *Kiddushin* rules in accordance with his opinion, against the other Sages who disagree with him (Rambam *Sefer Kedusha, Hilkhot Issurei Bia* 15:4; *Shulḥan Arukh, Even HaEzer* 4:20).

A second-generation male Egyptian convert married a first-generation female Egyptian convert – מִצְרִי שֵׁנִי שֶׁנָּשָׂא מִצְרִית רִאשׁוֹנָה: If a second-generation male Egyptian convert married a first-generation female Egyptian convert, their child is a second-generation Egyptian convert, in accordance with the latter version of Rabbi Yoḥanan's statement. The early authorities disagree about the rationale of this ruling and about the connection between this *halakha* and the subsequent ones. Therefore, they disagree about whether the mother's status always determines that of the child, so that the child of a first-generation male Egyptian convert and a second-generation female Egyptian convert is a third-generation convert (Ramban; *Tur*), or whether even this child is regarded as a second-generation convert, as only one whose parents are both second-generation converts is considered a third-generation Egyptian, as the Rambam rules (Rambam *Sefer Kedusha, Hilkhot Issurei Bia* 12:20; *Shulḥan Arukh, Even HaEzer* 4:6).

One who set aside a pregnant animal as a sin-offering – הִפְרִישׁ חַטָּאת מְעוּבֶּרֶת: If one set aside a pregnant animal as a sin-offering and it gave birth to a female, it is as though he had separated two sin-offerings as a guarantee (Rambam *Sefer Avoda, Hilkhot Pesulei HaMukdashin* 4:6).

NOTES

Her child is a third-generation convert – בְּנָהּ שְׁלִישִׁי הֲוֵאי: The early authorities explain that this does not contradict the teaching that the child's status is determined by the parent with the greater disqualification, as that principle applies only to a marriage that involves a transgression. If the marriage itself is permitted, the child's status follows that of the father. The Gemara therefore raises a difficulty from the statement of Rabbi Tarfon, whose example of the marriage of a *mamzer* and a maidservant constitutes a transgression, and even so the child's status is not affected by the parent's disqualification (Rashba).

And I married another first-generation Egyptian convert – וְנָשָׂאתִי מִצְרִית רִאשׁוֹנָה: See HALAKHA for the dispute among the halakhic authorities concerning the *halakha* in practice, whether the child's status is determined based on the mother, the father, or the more impaired partner. The Ramban maintains that the mother's status determines that of the child in all cases, but this gives rise to a difficulty: Why did Minyamin marry a first-generation Egyptian? Had he married a second-generation convert, it would have already been permitted for his own son to enter into the congregation. One answer is that Minyamin was essentially saying that he made a mistake when he married a first-generation Egyptian, but that he would take care not to repeat that error with his son.

Teach a first-generation convert – תְּנֵי רִאשׁוֹנָה: This is precisely the Jerusalem Talmud's version of the text. The Gemara there also quotes the continuation of the *baraita* that records the dissenting view of Rabbi Akiva that the third-generation Egyptian who is permitted is one who comes from three generations of Jews on both sides of his family.

HALAKHA

One who sets aside two sin-offerings as a guarantee – הַמַּפְרִישׁ שְׁתֵּי חַטָּאוֹת לְאַחֲרָיוּת: If one set aside two sin-offerings for the same sin, as a guarantee in case one of the animals becomes unavailable for sacrifice, he may sacrifice either animal as he chooses. The other must be left to graze until it develops a blemish, after which it may be redeemed and the money used for gift offerings (Rambam *Sefer Avoda, Hilkhot Pesulei HaMukdashin* 4:5).

The young of a sin-offering – וְלַד חַטָּאת: If an animal that had been set aside for a sin-offering subsequently conceived and gave birth, the offspring goes to its death (Rambam *Sefer Avoda, Hilkhot Pesulei HaMukdashin* 4:1).

A pregnant gentile woman who converted – גּוֹיָה מְעוּבֶּרֶת שֶׁנִּתְגַּיְּירָה: If a pregnant gentile woman converted, her child does not require immersion. If the court that converted her did not know that she was pregnant, there is uncertainty as to whether her immersion counts for the fetus as well (Rambam *Sefer Kedusha, Hilkhot Issurei Bia* 13:7; *Shulḥan Arukh, Yoreh De'a* 268:6).

Interposition with regard to immersion – חֲצִיצָה בִּטְבִילָה: Nothing may interpose between the object or individual requiring immersion and the water. If an interposition is present, the immersion is invalid. By Torah law, a substance is considered an interposition only if it covers the majority of one's body and is a substance that he is ordinarily particular to remove. However, by rabbinic law, even if one is not particular about the substance but it covers the majority of his body, or if it does not cover the majority of his body but he is particular about removing it, it is considered an interposition that disqualifies the immersion.

As for the immersion of a *nidda*, in practice women are stringent to remove all interpositions of any kind (Rambam *Sefer Tahara, Hilkhot Mikvaot* 1:12; *Shulḥan Arukh, Yoreh De'a* 198:1).

NOTES

A fetus is the thigh of its mother – עוּבָּר יֶרֶךְ אִמּוֹ הוּא: The later authorities raise a basic question: What is the connection between these two issues? There seems to be no reason that one's lineage should be affected by the ruling on whether or not a fetus is considered part of its mother. One answer is that this is a special case, as the question is not one of disqualification, with regard to which the status of both the father and the mother determines that of the child, but rather of the number of generations. If a fetus is part of its mother, the generations are counted only through her, but if it is considered a separate creature from the time of its conception, the generations can include the father's side as well (*Keren Ora*).

Man of great skull – קַרְקַפָּנָא: The *Arukh* cites two interpretations of this term, either a man with a large skull (see Rabbeinu Ḥananel), or a great and important man, as explained by Rashi on *Eruvin* 22b. With regard to the issue itself, *Tosafot* explain that Rabba, Abaye's teacher or head, figuratively speaking, studied Torah with Rabbi Yoḥanan in Eretz Yisrael. However, there is no clear proof for this in the Talmud, and chroniclers of the generations maintain that Rabba was never in Eretz Yisrael. If so, Rav Dimi was merely using a picturesque manner of speech (see Maharit).

אִי אָמְרַתְּ בִּשְׁלָמָא עוּבָּר לָאו יֶרֶךְ אִמּוֹ הוּא – הֲוָה לֵיהּ כְּמַפְרִישׁ שְׁתֵּי חַטָּאוֹת לְאַחֲרָיוּת, וְאָמַר רַב אוֹשַׁעְיָא: הִפְרִישׁ שְׁתֵּי חַטָּאוֹת לְאַחֲרָיוּת – מִתְכַּפֵּר בְּאַחַת מֵהֶן, וְהַשְּׁנִיָּה תִּרְעֶה.

Granted, if you say that **a fetus is not** considered **the thigh,** i.e., a part, **of its mother** but rather a separate creature, despite the fact that it is still attached to her, then an individual in this situation **is like one who sets aside two sin-offerings as a guarantee,**[H] i.e., one who, owing to his concern that his sin-offering might become lost, sets aside two animals from the outset with the intention of using whichever one he chooses. **And Rav Oshaya said** with regard to such a case: If **one set aside two sin-offerings as a guarantee,** so that if one is lost he may gain atonement with the other, **he gains atonement with one of them, and the second is left to graze** until it develops a blemish and can be redeemed.

אֶלָּא אִי אָמְרַתְּ עוּבָּר יֶרֶךְ אִמּוֹ הוּא – הֲוָה לֵיהּ וְלַד חַטָּאת, וּוְלַד חַטָּאת לְמִיתָה אָזֵיל!

But if you say that **a fetus is** considered **the thigh of its mother**[N] and is regarded as part of her, **it is the young of a sin-offering, and the young of a sin-offering goes to** its **death.**[H] Such an animal is not left to graze. Rather, it is put into isolation and caused to die, as it has been sanctified as a sin-offering through its mother but cannot be sacrificed on the altar and used to gain atonement. In summary, it would appear that Rabbi Yoḥanan himself maintains that a fetus is not considered a part of its mother. Why, then, in the case of the Egyptian convert is the child assigned to the mother and not to the father?

אִישְׁתִּיק. אָמַר לֵיהּ: דִּלְמָא שָׁאנֵי הָתָם, דִּכְתִיב: ״אֲשֶׁר יִוָּלְדוּ״ – הַכָּתוּב תְּלָאוֹ בְּלֵידָה? אָמַר לֵיהּ: קַרְקַפָּנָא, חֲזֵיתֵיהּ לְרֵישָׁךְ בֵּינֵי עַמּוּדֵי כִּי אֲמַר רַבִּי יוֹחָנָן לְהָא שְׁמַעְתָּא,

Rav Dimi **was silent,** momentarily unable to find an answer. Abaye **said to him: Perhaps it is different there,** with regard to Egyptian converts, **as it is written** with regard to them: "The sons of the third generation **that are born to them** may enter to them, the congregation of the Lord" (Deuteronomy 23:9), indicating that **the verse made** their prohibition **dependent on birth,** and therefore the child of Egyptian converts is assigned to the mother. Rav Dimi **said to him:** Man of great **skull,**[N] i.e., man of distinction, **I saw your head between the pillars**[B] of the study hall **when Rabbi Yoḥanan taught this *halakha*.** In other words, you grasped the meaning as though you were actually present in the study hall and heard the statement from Rabbi Yoḥanan himself.

טַעֲמָא דִּכְתִיב ״אֲשֶׁר יִוָּלְדוּ״, הָא בְּעָלְמָא – בָּתַר אֲבוּהּ שָׁדֵינַן לֵיהּ, אֶלָּא הָא דְּאָמַר רָבָא: גּוֹיָה מְעוּבֶּרֶת שֶׁנִּתְגַּיְּירָה – בְּנָהּ אֵין צָרִיךְ טְבִילָה. אַמַּאי אֵין צָרִיךְ טְבִילָה?

The Gemara draws an inference: **The reason** that the child is assigned to its Egyptian mother is **that it is written: "That are born** to them." **But generally,** with regard to others for whom it is prohibited to enter into the congregation, **we assign** the child **to the father.** The Gemara asks: **But** what about **that which Rava said:** If **a pregnant gentile** woman **converted,** then **her son,** who was a fetus at the time of the conversion, **does not require immersion**[H] after he is born. But if the child is not assigned to its mother, **why should he not require immersion?**

וְכִי תֵּימָא מִשּׁוּם דְּרַבִּי יִצְחָק, דְּאָמַר רַבִּי יִצְחָק: דְּבַר תּוֹרָה, רוּבּוֹ וּמַקְפִּיד עָלָיו חוֹצֵץ, רוּבּוֹ שֶׁאֵינוֹ מַקְפִּיד עָלָיו אֵינוֹ חוֹצֵץ,

And if you would say that this is **because of** a statement of **Rabbi Yitzḥak,** there is still a difficulty. **As Rabbi Yitzḥak said: By Torah law,** if some substance is found on a person's body during immersion, and it covers **the majority of his body, and he is particular** and wants the substance removed, only then **is it** considered **an interposition** that invalidates immersion in a ritual bath. If, however, the substance covers **the majority of his** body, but **he is not particular about** that substance, **it is not** considered **an interposition.**[H] Accordingly, it may be argued that although the fetus is covered by its mother, since it is not particular about this necessary covering, the fetus itself is regarded as having undergone valid immersion.

BACKGROUND

Between the pillars – בֵּינֵי עַמּוּדֵי: Both from written sources and from the archaeological excavations conducted at the site, it seems that the synagogue and the study hall in Tiberias, where Rabbi Yoḥanan lived, were built in the form of a basilica, a building whose roof rests on a row of pillars. Consequently, Rav Dimi's expression: Between the pillars, is essentially describing the structure of this study hall.

Floor of ancient synagogue in Tiberias with remains of pillars

וְהָא אָמַר רַב כָּהֲנָא: לֹא שָׁנוּ אֶלָּא רוּבּוֹ, אֲבָל כּוּלּוֹ – חוֹצֵץ! שָׁאנֵי עוּבָּר דְּהַיְינוּ רְבִיתֵיהּ.

However, this is difficult, as **didn't Rav Kahana say** that **they taught** this *halakha* that if one is not particular about the substance it is not considered an interposition **only** when the substance covers just **a majority of his** body; **but** if it covers **all of it, it is** considered **an interposition** by Torah law, even if he is not particular about it. The Gemara answers: **A fetus is different, as this is its** natural manner of **growth.**[N] Its mother's womb cannot be considered an interposition, as it is the fetus' natural place of development, and therefore the fetus itself is regarded as having undergone immersion.

כִּי אֲתָא רָבִינָא אָמַר רַבִּי יוֹחָנָן: בָּאוּמּוֹת – הַלֵּךְ אַחַר הַזָּכָר, נִתְגַּיְּירוּ – הַלֵּךְ אַחַר פָּגוּם שֶׁבִּשְׁנֵיהֶם. ״בָּאוּמּוֹת הַלֵּךְ אַחַר הַזָּכָר״ – כִּדְתַנְיָא: מִנַּיִן לְאֶחָד מִן הָאוּמּוֹת שֶׁבָּא עַל הַכְּנַעֲנִית וְהוֹלִיד בֵּן, שֶׁאַתָּה רַשַּׁאי לִקְנוֹתוֹ בְּעֶבֶד – שֶׁנֶּאֱמַר ״וְגַם מִבְּנֵי הַתּוֹשָׁבִים הַגָּרִים עִמָּכֶם מֵהֶם תִּקְנוּ״.

When Ravina came from Eretz Yisrael to Babylonia, he said that **Rabbi Yoḥanan said:** With respect to lineage, **among the** other **nations** of the world, i.e., while they are still gentiles, **follow the male,**[H] but if they married after **they converted, follow the** more **flawed** in lineage **of the two.** The Gemara explains: **Among the nations, follow the male, as it is taught** in a *baraita*: **From where** is it derived **that** if **one from the** other **nations**[N] **had relations with a Canaanite** woman[H] **and had a son** from her, **you are permitted to purchase him as a slave,** and he is not considered a Canaanite who may not be allowed to remain in Eretz Yisrael? **As it is stated: "And also from the children of the strangers that dwell among you, of them may you buy,** and of their families that are with you, which they have begotten in your land; and they may be your possession" (Leviticus 25:45).

יָכוֹל אֲפִילּוּ אֶחָד מִן הַכְּנַעֲנִים שֶׁבָּא עַל אַחַת מִן הָאוּמּוֹת וְהוֹלִיד בֵּן שֶׁאַתָּה רַשַּׁאי לִקְנוֹתוֹ בְּעֶבֶד – תַּלְמוּד לוֹמַר ״אֲשֶׁר הוֹלִידוּ בְּאַרְצְכֶם״ – מִן הַנּוֹלָדִים בְּאַרְצְכֶם, וְלֹא מִן הַגָּרִים בְּאַרְצְכֶם.

One **might** have thought that **even** if **one from the Canaanite** nations **had relations with** a woman **from** one of **the** other **nations and had a son** from her, **you are permitted to purchase him as a slave.** Therefore, **the** same **verse states: "Which they have begotten in your land,"** which indicates that slaves may be bought only **from those begotten in your land,** i.e., from those whose father was a non-Canaanite and whose mother was a Canaanite. It is the way of women to remain in their own land, and so a child born in Eretz Yisrael was certainly born to a Canaanite mother. **But** slaves may **not** be bought **from those dwelling in your land.** If a child is born to a Canaanite man and a non-Canaanite woman outside of Eretz Yisrael, and that offspring later returns to dwell in Eretz Yisrael, the offspring may not be acquired as a slave, because his lineage follows his father. He is regarded as a Canaanite, who may not be allowed to remain in Eretz Yisrael.

NOTES

This is its growth – **הַיְינוּ רְבִיתֵיהּ**: An interposition involves an object or substance that serves as a barrier between the item or individual requiring immersion and the water. As stated above, for a substance to be considered an interposition, the one involved must be particular about it and desire its removal. However, in the case discussed here, not only is the fetus not particular about the interposition, i.e., its mother's body, but it actually wants it to be there, as it cannot survive without it. A further relevant point is that since this is the natural manner of growth of the fetus, the mother's body cannot be viewed as an interposition at all. Therefore, in light of the vital connection between a fetus and its mother's body, even if the fetus is not regarded as part of its mother, her body cannot be regarded as an interposition.

From where is it derived that if one from the other nations – **מִנַּיִן לְאֶחָד מִן הָאוּמּוֹת**: Rashi and the Rambam disagree with regard to the basic meaning of this passage. According to Rashi the question concerns the Canaanite who is the object of the mitzva: "You shall not let any soul live" (Deuteronomy 20:16). Does the mother or the father determine the child's status in this regard? The Rambam, as explained by the *Maggid Mishne*, maintains that the question pertains to a child born to a Canaanite slave or maidservant belonging to a Jew. Is such a child considered a Canaanite slave? According to this opinion, if the mother is a maidservant the child's status is based on hers, but if it is the father who is a slave, since a slave has no lineage, the offspring's status is based on the mother, and if she is from one of the other nations, her child is considered free.

HALAKHA

Among the other nations, follow the male – **בָּאוּמּוֹת הַלֵּךְ אַחַר הַזָּכָר**: If a male Ammonite married a female Egyptian, their child is an Ammonite. If the male is Egyptian and the female an Ammonite, the child is an Egyptian, as with respect to gentiles the child's status is determined by the male, as stated by Ravina (*Shulḥan Arukh, Even HaEzer* 4:7).

One from the other nations had relations with a Canaanite woman – **אֶחָד מִן הָאוּמּוֹת שֶׁבָּא עַל הַכְּנַעֲנִית**: If a gentile had relations with a Canaanite maidservant belonging to a Jew, a child resulting from this union would be a Canaanite slave. However, if a Canaanite slave had relations with a gentile woman, a child from this union would not be a slave, as his status is determined by his mother's lineage (Rambam *Sefer Kinyan, Hilkhot Avadim* 9:3 and *Kesef Mishne* and *Leḥem Mishne* there).

"נִתְגַּיְּירוּ, הַלֵּךְ אַחַר פָּגוּם שֶׁבִּשְׁנֵיהֶם". בְּמַאי? אִילֵּימָא בְּמִצְרִי שֶׁנָּשָׂא עַמּוֹנִית – מַאי פָּגוּם שֶׁבִּשְׁנֵיהֶם אִית בָּהּ? עַמּוֹנִי וְלֹא עַמּוֹנִית! אֶלָּא בְּעַמּוֹנִי שֶׁנָּשָׂא מִצְרִית, אִי זָכָר הָוֵי – שַׁדְיֵיהּ בָּתַר עַמּוֹנִי, אִי נְקֵבָה הָוֵי – שַׁדְיָיהּ בָּתַר מִצְרִית.

It was taught above in the name of Rabbi Yoḥanan that if they married after **they converted, follow the more flawed**[H] in lineage **of the two.** The Gemara asks: **To what** circumstances is this referring? **If we say** it is referring to **a male Egyptian** convert **who married a female Ammonite** convert, **what** is the meaning of: More **flawed** in lineage **of the two,** in **this** case? The *halakha* is that **an Ammonite** man is barred from entering into the congregation, **but not an Ammonite woman,** and so she is not flawed at all. **Rather,** it must be referring **to a male Ammonite** convert **who married a female Egyptian** convert. If the child **is male, assign him to** his **Ammonite** father, so that he is permanently barred from entering the congregation. **If it is a female, assign her to** her **Egyptian** mother, so that she is treated like a second-generation Egyptian convert.

מתני׳ מַמְזֵרִין וּנְתִינִין אֲסוּרִין, וְאִיסּוּרָן אִיסּוּר עוֹלָם, אֶחָד זְכָרִים וְאֶחָד נְקֵבוֹת.

MISHNA ***Mamzerim*** **and** the **Gibeonites**[H] who converted to Judaism in the days of Joshua **are prohibited** from entering into the congregation and marrying a woman who was born Jewish. **Their prohibition is eternal,** for all generations, and it applies to **both males and females.**

גמ׳ אָמַר רֵישׁ לָקִישׁ: מַמְזֶרֶת, לְאַחַר עֲשָׂרָה דּוֹרוֹת מוּתֶּרֶת. יָלֵיף עֲשִׂירִי עֲשִׂירִי מֵעַמּוֹנִי וּמוֹאָבִי, מַה לְּהַלָּן נְקֵבוֹת מוּתָּרוֹת – אַף כָּאן נְקֵבוֹת מוּתָּרוֹת.

GEMARA **Reish Lakish said: A** ***mamzeret,*** a female *mamzer,* **is permitted after ten generations.**[N] Why? He **derived** this *halakha* by way of a verbal analogy between the word **"tenth"** stated in relation **to an Ammonite and a Moabite** in the verse "An Ammonite or a Moabite shall not enter into the congregation of the Lord; even to the tenth generation shall none of them enter into the congregation of the Lord forever" (Deuteronomy 23:4), and the word **"tenth"** stated in relation to a *mamzer* in the verse "A *mamzer* shall not enter into the congregation of the Lord; even to the tenth generation shall none of his enter into the congregation of the Lord" (Deuteronomy 23:3) He explained the analogy as follows: **Just as below,** with regard to an Ammonite and a Moabite, **females are permitted, so too here,** with regard to a *mamzer,* **females are permitted.**

אִי, מַה לְּהַלָּן מִיָּד אַף כָּאן מִיָּד! כִּי אַהֲנֵי גְּזֵירָה שָׁוָה – מֵעֲשִׂירִי וְאֵילָךְ.

The Gemara raises a difficulty: **Or** perhaps one should say that **just as below,** with regard to an Ammonite and a Moabite, their females are permitted **immediately, so too here,** a *mamzeret* is permitted **immediately.** The Gemara answers: **The verbal analogy is effective** only **from** the **tenth** generation **and onward.**

וְהָאֲנַן תְּנַן: מַמְזֵרִים וּנְתִינִין אֲסוּרִין וְאִיסּוּרָן אִיסּוּר עוֹלָם, אֶחָד זְכָרִים וְאֶחָד נְקֵבוֹת! לָא קַשְׁיָא, הָא – כְּמַאן דְּאָמַר דּוֹן מִינָּהּ וּמִינָּהּ,

The Gemara raises another difficulty: **But didn't we learn** in the mishna that ***mamzerim*** **and Gibeonites are prohibited, and their prohibition is eternal** for all generations, and it applies to **both males and females?** The Gemara answers: This is **not difficult** for Reish Lakish, as he understands that there is a dispute in this regard: **This** opinion, that of Reish Lakish, is **in accordance with** the *tanna* **who said** that the application of a verbal analogy is extended by way of the principle: **Infer from it, and again from it.**[N] In other words, after deducing case B from case A, all of the characteristics of case A are applied to case B. In the case discussed here, although the verbal analogy comes primarily to render a *mamzer* permanently forbidden, it is extended and understood to mean that a *mamzeret* is permitted after ten generations.

HALAKHA

If they converted, follow the more flawed – נִתְגַּיְּירוּ, הַלֵּךְ אַחַר הַפָּגוּם: The status of a child of converts from different nations is determined based on the more impaired of his two parents, as explained in the Gemara. Consequently, if a male Ammonite convert and a female Egyptian convert have a son, he is an Ammonite, whereas their daughter is considered an Egyptian.

If a convert from any of the nations has relations with a gentile woman, some say that their child is assigned to the mother, while others maintain that its status is determined by the more impaired of the two (Rambam *Sefer Kedusha, Hilkhot Issurei Bia* 12:20; *Shulḥan Arukh, Even HaEzer* 4:7, and in the comment of Rema).

Mamzerim **and Gibeonites – מַמְזֵרִים וּנְתִינִים:** *Mamzerim* and Gibeonites, both males and females, are permanently prohibited from entering into the congregation, against the opinion of Reish Lakish (Rambam *Sefer Kedusha, Hilkhot Issurei Bia* 15:21; *Shulḥan Arukh, Even HaEzer* 4:1).

NOTES

A *mamzeret*…after ten generations – מַמְזֶרֶת לְאַחַר עֲשָׂרָה דּוֹרוֹת: In the Jerusalem Talmud Reish Lakish's opinion is attributed to a *tanna*. The Gemara here indicates likewise, as it does not reject Reish Lakish's opinion although it contradicts the mishna.

Infer from it, and again from it – דּוֹן מִינָּהּ וּמִינָּהּ: Expositions based on verbal analogies raise many difficulties. Some of these difficulties stem from the fact that this mode of exegesis is not derived from logical reasoning but is a kind of biblical decree by which, in accordance with special indications and traditions, two verses and the *halakhot* derived from them are combined. It is an established principle that there cannot be half a verbal analogy, and so the inferences drawn with it must be bilateral, but there is disagreement as to the extent of the comparison between the different issues. Are they equated in all regards, based on the principle of: Infer from it, and again from it, i.e., in addition to the *halakha* for which the verbal analogy was initially applied, one may proceed to derive other *halakhot* as well? Or perhaps the comparison extends to only one particular matter, based on the principle of: Infer from it, and leave it in its place, which means that the association between the two topics pertains only to the specific issue with regard to which there is a tradition.

הָא כְּמַאן דְּאָמַר דּוּן מִינָּהּ וְאוֹקֵי בְּאַתְרָא.

That other opinion, i.e., the mishna, is **in accordance with the** *tanna* **who said** that the application of a verbal analogy is limited, according to the principle: **Infer from it, and** then **leave it in its place.** That is to say, after the main provision of case A is applied to case B, case B is recognized as having its own character and specific rules that apply to it. Accordingly, in the case discussed here, the verbal analogy teaches one specific *halakha* that a *mamzer* is prohibited permanently, but nothing else.

שָׁאֲלוּ אֶת רַבִּי אֱלִיעֶזֶר: מַמְזֶרֶת לְאַחַר עֲשָׂרָה דָּרֵי מַהוּ? אָמַר לָהֶם: מִי יִתֵּן לִי דּוֹר שְׁלִישִׁי וַאֲטַהֲרֶנּוּ. אַלְמָא קָסָבַר מַמְזֵרָא לָא חַיֵּי, וְכֵן אָמַר רַב הוּנָא: מַמְזֵרָא לָא חַיֵּי,

The Gemara relates that the students **asked Rabbi Eliezer:** With regard to **a** *mamzeret* **after ten generations, what is the** *halakha*? **He said to them: Who will give me a third-generation** *mamzer* so that **I will declare him pure?** The Gemara comments: **Apparently he maintains** that **a** *mamzer* **does not survive.**[N] *Mamzerim* perish at the hand of Heaven, and therefore this question is not a practical one. **And similarly, Rav Huna said** that **a** *mamzer* **does not survive.**

וְהָא אֲנַן תְּנַן: מַמְזֵרִין אֲסוּרִין וְאִיסּוּרָן אִיסּוּר עוֹלָם! אָמַר רַבִּי זֵירָא: לְדִידִי מְפָרְשָׁא לִי מִינֵּיהּ דְּרַב יְהוּדָה: דִּידִיעַ – חַיֵּי, דְּלָא יְדִיעַ – לָא חַיֵּי. דִּידִיעַ וְלָא יְדִיעַ – עַד תְּלָתָא דָּרֵי חַיֵּי, טְפֵי לָא חַיֵּי.

The Gemara raises a difficulty: **But didn't we learn** in the mishna that *mamzerim* **are prohibited** from entering into the congregation, **and their prohibition is eternal** for all generations? How is this possible if they do not even live long enough to produce three generations? **Rabbi Zeira said:** This matter **was explained to me by Rav Yehuda** himself: One **who is known** to be a *mamzer* will **survive,** as there is no concern that there will be any mingling of his seed. On the other hand, one **who is not known** as a *mamzer* will **not survive,** as he will die at the hand of Heaven so that there will be no mingling of his seed. As for one **who is known and not known,** i.e., one who is under suspicion, but it is unclear whether or not he is actually a *mamzer*, his descendants will **survive for three generations,** but **more** than this they will **not survive.**

הַהוּא דַּהֲוֵי בְּשִׁבְבוּתֵיהּ דְּרַבִּי אַמִי, אַכְרֵיז עֲלֵיהּ דְּמַמְזֵרָא הֲוָה. בָּכֵי וְאָזֵיל. אֲמַר לֵיהּ: חַיִּים נָתַתִּי לְךָ.

It is related that **a certain person** lived **in Rabbi Ami's neighborhood,** and following an investigation Rabbi Ami **declared him to be a** *mamzer*. The man **went about weeping** until Rabbi Ami **said to him:** You should not be upset, as now **I have given you life.** As explained above, once one is publicly known as a *mamzer*, he and his descendants may survive.

אָמַר רַב חָנָא בַּר אַדָּא: נְתִינִים – דָּוִד גָּזַר עֲלֵיהֶם, שֶׁנֶּאֱמַר ״וַיִּקְרָא הַמֶּלֶךְ לַגִּבְעֹנִים וַיֹּאמֶר אֲלֵיהֶם וְהַגִּבְעֹנִים לֹא מִבְּנֵי יִשְׂרָאֵל הֵמָּה״ וגו׳.

§ **Rav Ḥana bar Adda said:** As for the **Gibeonites,**[H] it was King **David** who **decreed that they** may not enter into the congregation, **as it is stated: "And the king called the Gibeonites and said to them. Now the Gibeonites are not of the children of Israel,** but of the remnant of the Amorites" (II Samuel 21:2). This verse indicates that it was David who ruled that they are not part of the Jewish people and that they are barred from the congregation even though they converted.

מַאי טַעְמָא גָּזַר עֲלַיְיהוּ – דִּכְתִיב ״וַיְהִי רָעָב בִּימֵי דָוִד שָׁלֹשׁ שָׁנִים שָׁנָה אַחַר שָׁנָה״. שָׁנָה רִאשׁוֹנָה אָמַר לָהֶם: שֶׁמָּא עוֹבְדֵי עֲבוֹדָה זָרָה יֵשׁ בָּכֶם דִּכְתִיב ״וַעֲבַדְתֶּם אֱלֹהִים אֲחֵרִים וְהִשְׁתַּחֲוִיתֶם לָהֶם...וְעָצַר אֶת הַשָּׁמַיִם וְלֹא יִהְיֶה מָטָר״ וגו׳ – בָּדְקוּ וְלֹא מָצְאוּ.

The Gemara asks: **What is the reason** that David **decreed** that they may not enter into the congregation? In order to answer this question, the Gemara recounts all the relevant background events. **As it is written: "And there was a famine in the days of David three years, year after year"** (II Samuel 21:1). In the **first year** David **said to the** Jewish people: **Perhaps there are idol worshippers among you,** this being a sin that can lead to drought, **as it is written:** "Take heed to yourselves, lest your heart be deceived, and you turn aside, **and serve other gods, and worship them;** and the anger of the Lord be kindled against you, **and He shut up the heaven, so that there shall be no rain,** and the ground shall not yield her fruit" (Deuteronomy 11:16–17). **They examined** the matter **but did not find**[N] sinners of this kind.

שְׁנִיָּה אָמַר לָהֶם: שֶׁמָּא עוֹבְרֵי עֲבֵירָה יֵשׁ בָּכֶם, דִּכְתִיב ״וַיִּמָּנְעוּ רְבִבִים וּמַלְקוֹשׁ לוֹא הָיָה וּמֵצַח אִשָּׁה זוֹנָה הָיָה לָךְ״ וגו׳ – בָּדְקוּ וְלֹא מָצְאוּ.

In the **second** year of the drought David **said to them: Perhaps there are transgressors** in sexual matters **among you,** as this too can lead to drought, **as it is written: "Therefore the showers have been withheld, and there has been no latter rain; yet you had a harlot's forehead,** you refused to be ashamed" (Jeremiah 3:3), which indicates that licentious behavior can lead to a cessation of rainfall. Again **they examined** the matter, **but did not find** sinners of this kind either.

NOTES

A ***mamzer*** **does not survive – מַמְזֵרָא לָא חַיֵּי:** In the Jerusalem Talmud this is explained slightly differently and in greater detail. Rav Huna states there that a *mamzer* cannot survive for longer than thirty days. As for the possibility of generations of *mamzerim*, it is mentioned there in the name of Rav Ḥanina that once every sixty or seventy years a plague strikes the world that wipes out, among others, the *mamzerim* among the Jews.

They examined but did not find – בָּדְקוּ וְלֹא מָצְאוּ: The later authorities explain that they first thought that the drought was precisely the type that is a divine punishment for particular sins, and therefore there was no cause to inquire through the *Urim VeTummim*. However, once they realized it was not the result of a widespread sin among the people David concluded that it must be caused by a sin of the king, as he represents the entire nation. In fact, although David was not directly responsible for the sins, both in the case of Nob, the city of priests, and in the case of Saul's eulogy, he was ultimately the indirect cause for these events (see Riaf and *Iyyun Ya'akov*).

HALAKHA

The prohibition with regard to Gibeonites – אִיסּוּר הַנְּתִינִים: According to the Rambam, by Torah law it is not prohibited for a convert from one of the seven Canaanite nations to enter into the congregation. Rather, it was Joshua who issued a decree against the Gibeonites, and therefore the prohibition with regard to them is rabbinic. This is also the opinion of Rashi and the Razah. Others (Ramban; Rashba; *Tur*) maintain that first-generation Gibeonites are forbidden by Torah law, whereas their descendants are forbidden by decree of the Sages (Rambam *Sefer Kedusha*, *Hilkhot Issurei Bia* 12:22).

BACKGROUND

He killed Nob, the city of priests – מִתּוֹךְ שֶׁהָרַג נוֹב עִיר הַכֹּהֲנִים: While David was fleeing from King Saul, who perceived him as a threat to his monarchy, Ahimelech, the priest in the city of Nob, offered him bread and Goliath's sword, believing him to be on a secret mission in the service of the king. Doeg the Edomite reported this to King Saul, who then ordered the destruction of the city (see I Samuel, chapters 21–22).

שְׁלִישִׁית אָמַר לָהֶם: שֶׁמָּא פּוֹסְקֵי צְדָקָה בָּרַבִּים יֵשׁ בָּכֶם וְאֵין נוֹתְנִין, דִּכְתִיב "נְשִׂיאִים וְרוּחַ וְגֶשֶׁם אָיִן אִישׁ מִתְהַלֵּל בְּמַתַּת שָׁקֶר" – בָּדְקוּ וְלֹא מָצְאוּ.

In the **third** year **he said to them: Perhaps there are among you those who pledge** money **to charity in public, but do not** actually **give** any charity. **As it is written: "As vapors and wind without rain, so is he that boasts himself of a false gift"** (Proverbs 25:14), teaching that one who falsely boasts of making a gift prevents the rain from falling. Once again **they examined** the matter, **but could not find** such sinners.

אָמַר: אֵין הַדָּבָר תָּלוּי אֶלָּא בִּי, מִיָּד – "וַיְבַקֵּשׁ דָּוִד אֶת פְּנֵי ה'" מַאי הִיא? אָמַר רֵישׁ לָקִישׁ: שֶׁשָּׁאַל בָּאוּרִים וְתוּמִּים.

Having unsuccessfully searched the Jewish people for sins that cause drought, David **said: The matter depends on nothing other than myself. Immediately** it is stated: **"And David sought the presence of the Lord"** (II Samuel 21:1). The Gemara asks: **What is this?** How did David seek God? **Reish Lakish said: He inquired through the *Urim VeTummim*,** the stones embedded in the High Priest's breastplate, which served as a means of communicating with God.

מַאי מַשְׁמַע? אָמַר רַבִּי אֶלְעָזָר: אָתְיָא "פְּנֵי" "פְּנֵי", כְּתִיב הָכָא "וַיְבַקֵּשׁ דָּוִד אֶת פְּנֵי ה'" וּכְתִיב הָתָם "וְשָׁאַל לוֹ בְּמִשְׁפַּט הָאוּרִים לִפְנֵי ה'".

The Gemara asks: **From where** may it **be inferred** that David's seeking was by way of the *Urim VeTummim*? **Rabbi Elazar said:** This is **derived** by way of a verbal analogy between the word **"presence" used** here and the word **"presence"** used elsewhere. **It is written here: "And David sought the presence of the Lord," and it is written there:** "And he shall stand before Eleazar the priest, **who shall inquire for him by the judgment of the *Urim* in the presence of the Lord"** (Numbers 27:21). Consequently, the "presence of the Lord" sought by David must have involved the *Urim VeTummim*.

"וַיֹּאמֶר ה' אֶל שָׁאוּל וְאֶל בֵּית הַדָּמִים עַל אֲשֶׁר הֵמִית הַגִּבְעוֹנִים". "אֶל שָׁאוּל" – שֶׁלֹּא נִסְפַּד כַּהֲלָכָה, "וְאֶל בֵּית הַדָּמִים" – "עַל אֲשֶׁר הֵמִית הַגִּבְעוֹנִים". וְכִי הֵיכָן מָצִינוּ בְּשָׁאוּל שֶׁהֵמִית הַגִּבְעוֹנִים? אֶלָּא, מִתּוֹךְ שֶׁהָרַג נוֹב עִיר הַכֹּהֲנִים שֶׁהָיוּ מַסְפִּיקִין לָהֶם מַיִם וּמָזוֹן – מַעֲלֶה עָלָיו הַכָּתוּב כְּאִילּוּ הֲרָגָן.

The verse continues: **"And the Lord said: It is for Saul, and for his bloody house, because he put to death the Gibeonites"** (II Samuel 21:1). The Gemara explains: **"For Saul"** means that the Jewish people were punished **because he was not eulogized properly.**[N] **"And for his bloody house"** is **"because he put to death the Gibeonites."** The Gemara is puzzled by this explanation: **Now, where do we find that Saul put to death the Gibeonites?** The Gemara clarifies: **Rather, because he killed**[N] the people of **Nob, the city of priests,**[B] **who would provide** the Gibeonites **with water and food** in exchange for their services, **the verse ascribes to him as if he** himself had **killed them.**

קָא תָּבַע אֶל שָׁאוּל שֶׁלֹּא נִסְפַּד כַּהֲלָכָה וְקָא תָּבַע עַל אֲשֶׁר הֵמִית הַגִּבְעוֹנִים?! אִין, דַּאֲמַר רֵישׁ לָקִישׁ: מַאי דִּכְתִיב "בַּקְּשׁוּ אֶת ה' כָּל עַנְוֵי אָרֶץ אֲשֶׁר מִשְׁפָּטוֹ פָּעָלוּ", בַּאֲשֶׁר מִשְׁפָּטוֹ – שָׁם פָּעֳלוֹ,

The Gemara questions this understanding: On one hand, God **demands** retribution **because Saul was not eulogized properly, while** on the other hand, **He demands** retribution **because** Saul himself **put to death the Gibeonites.** The Gemara answers: **Yes,** this is how it should be. **As Reish Lakish said: What is** the meaning of that **which is written: "Seek the Lord, all the humble of the earth, that have executed [*pa'alu*] His justice"** (Zephaniah 2:3)? **Where** mention is made of the **justice** to be carried out against a person, **his** good **deeds [*pa'alo*]** should be mentioned **there** as well.

אֲמַר דָּוִד: שָׁאוּל נְפַקוּ לְהוּ

David said: With regard to the eulogy for **Saul, there have** already **passed**

NOTES

Saul, because he was not eulogized properly – שָׁאוּל שֶׁלֹּא נִסְפַּד כַּהֲלָכָה: The Maharatz Ḥayyut points out that Saul is the only king for whom a great and lengthy eulogy is recorded, delivered by David himself (see II Samuel, chapter I). Rather, the Gemara means that Saul was not eulogized properly because David's eulogy, due to its very length and poetic style, was that of one private individual for another private individual; it was inappropriate for a king of Israel.

The later authorities note that although the verse does not mention the lack of honor paid to Saul, this misconduct can be inferred from the fact that David later brought the bones of Saul and his sons and buried them in a dignified manner in their ancestral graves.

Rather because he killed – אֶלָּא מִתּוֹךְ שֶׁהָרַג: In the Jerusalem Talmud in tractate *Kiddushin* it is stated that Saul did in fact kill seven Gibeonites in the course of his destruction of Nob, which is why they asked for seven of his own sons in return. The Maharsha suggests that it was the Gibeonites who had provided the priests with food and water and that they were upset now that they were deprived of this sacred service.

As for the entire people being held responsible for the sin committed by Saul, the Riaf explains that since all of the Jewish people swore to safeguard the Gibeonites' lives and welfare, any suffering of the Gibeonites was a desecration of God's name. Therefore, the restitution to them was also exaggerated in order to sanctify the name of God.

תריסר ירחי שתא, ולא דרכיה למספדיה.

the **twelve months of the year**[N] of mourning, i.e., several years have elapsed since the twelve-month mourning period for Saul, **and it is not the** proper **way to eulogize** after such a long time.[H]

נתינים ניקרינהו ונפייסינהו, ״ויקרא המלך לגבעונים ויאמר אליהם מה אעשה לכם ובמה אכפר וברכו את נחלת ה׳. ויאמרו לו הגבעונים אין לנו כסף וזהב עם שאול ועם ביתו ואין לנו איש וגו׳ יתן לנו שבעה אנשים מבניו והוקענום לה׳״ וגו׳. מיפייס, ולא פייסינהו.

As for the **Gibeonites, let us call them and appease them.** Consequently, the verse states: **"And the king called the Gibeonites and said to them…What shall I do for you, and with what shall I make atonement that you may bless the inheritance of the Lord? And the Gibeonites said to him: It is not a matter of silver or gold between us and Saul or his house; neither is it for us** to put any man to death in Israel… **Let seven men of his sons be delivered to us, and we will hang them up to the Lord…"** (II Samuel 21:1–6). He tried to **appease them** in other ways, **but they would not be appeased.**

אמר: שלשה סימנים יש באומה זו: הרחמנים, והביישנין, וגומלי חסדים. רחמנים – דכתיב ״ונתן לך רחמים ורחמך והרבך״. ביישנין – דכתיב ״בעבור תהיה יראתו על פניכם״. גומלי חסדים – דכתיב ״למען אשר יצוה את בניו ואת ביתו״ וגו׳. כל שיש בו שלשה סימנים הללו ראוי להדבק באומה זו.

David **said: There are three distinguishing marks**[N] **of this nation,** the Jewish people.[H] They are **merciful,** they are **shamefaced, and they perform acts of kindness.**

They are **merciful, as it is written: "And He will give you mercy, and have mercy upon you and multiply you"** (Deuteronomy 13:18); not only will God have mercy upon you, but He will bestow the attribute of mercy upon you.

They are **shamefaced, as it is written: "And that His fear shall be upon your faces"** (Exodus 20:17), and the fear that is on one's face is his shame.

They perform acts of kindness, as it is written: "For I have known him, **to the end that he may command his children and his household** after him, that they may keep the way of the Lord, to practice righteousness and justice" (Genesis 18:19), i.e., to perform acts of kindness.

Whoever has these three distinguishing marks is fit to cleave to this nation. Those who lack these qualities, however, are unfit to be part of the Jewish people. When David saw the cruelty of the Gibeonites, he decreed that they may never enter into the congregation of Israel.

״ויקח המלך את שני בני רצפה בת איה אשר ילדה לשאול את ארמני ואת מפבשת ואת חמשת בני מיכל בת שאול אשר ילדה לעדריאל בן ברזילי המחלתי״. מאי שנא הני? אמר רב הונא: העבירום לפני ארון, כל שארון קולטו – למיתה, כל שאין ארון קולטו – לחיים.

The Gemara continues with its understanding of the incident: **"And the king took the two sons of Rizpah, daughter of Aiah, whom she bore unto Saul, Armoni and Mephibosheth, and the five sons of Michal, daughter of Saul, whom she bore to Adriel the son of Barzillai the Meholathite"** (II Samuel 21:8). The Gemara asks: **What is different** about **these** sons that David chose them from among all the descendants of Saul? **Rav Huna said: He passed** all of Saul's descendants **before the Ark**[N] of the Covenant. **Whoever was held back by the Ark,**[N] so that he could not move on, was condemned **to death; whoever was not held back by the Ark** was set apart **for life.**

מתיב רב חנא בר קטינא: ״ויחמל המלך על מפבשת בן יהונתן בן שאול״! שלא העבירו.

Rav Ḥana bar Ketina raised an objection: The verse states: **"And the king had pity on Mephibosheth, son of Jonathan, son of Saul,** because of the Lord's oath that was between them, between David and Jonathan, son of Saul" (II Samuel 21:7). If the seven men were condemned by the Ark, how did the king's pity affect their sentence? The Gemara answers: It means **that he did not pass** Mephibosheth before the Ark at all, so that he would not be in danger of being held back at all.

וכי משוא פנים יש בדבר? אלא: שהעבירו וקלטו, ובקש עליו רחמים ופלטו. ואכתי, משוא פנים יש בדבר? אלא שבקש רחמים שלא יקלטנו הארון.

The Gemara questions this behavior: May **favoritism** be shown **in this matter?** Once the decision was placed in the hand of Heaven, how could David have intervened in matters of life and death and not pass Mephibosheth before the Ark? **Rather,** what happened was **that** David **passed** Mephibosheth before the Ark **and** the Ark **held him back, but** David immediately **asked for mercy on his behalf, and** the Ark **released him.** The Gemara asks: But the difficulty **still** remains: May **favoritism** be shown **in this matter?** Once the Ark condemned Mephibosheth to death, how could David have intervened so that another would have to die in his place? **Rather,** David **asked for mercy**[N] on his behalf, **that the Ark should not hold him back** and performed no other action.

NOTES

Twelve months of the year – תריסר ירחי שתא: The later authorities suggest various reasons for this *halakha*. It seems that a period of twelve months was fixed as the maximum period of mourning, because one's sorrow for the dead diminishes with time. If a eulogy is delivered after this time, it will not increase mourning and distress, and it is improper to deliver a eulogy if the level of grief will remain unaffected.

Three distinguishing marks – שלשה סימנים: In the Jerusalem Talmud in tractate *Kiddushin* and elsewhere, it is stated about these traits: Three good gifts were given to the Jewish people. The Maharsha likewise explains that these characteristics are not inherent qualities of the Jewish people but rather gifts that God gave to those who stood at Sinai, so that they can fulfill the mitzvot properly.

He passed them before the Ark – העבירום לפני ארון: In the Jerusalem Talmud it is stated that he passed them before the altar, and anyone who was held back by the altar was set apart for life, while the others were condemned to death. The *Yefe Mareh* explains that there is no dispute between the Babylonian and Jerusalem Talmuds, as it is known that those who draw too near to the Ark are sentenced to death, and therefore being held back by the Ark is a sign of death, whereas the altar serves as a refuge for those whose lives are in danger.

Whoever was held back by the Ark – כל שארון קולטו: The Ritva writes that God certainly does not treat people unjustly, and presumably these individuals deserved to die for their sins at the hand of God. They were not supposed to have been tried by an earthly court, but their sentence was changed due to the Jewish people's desecration of God's name.

Rather, he asked for mercy – אלא שבקש רחמים: The later authorities point out that this does not appear to resolve the problem of favoritism. The *Iyyun Ya'akov* explains that the question referred to actions performed openly, since if one was initially held back by the Ark and subsequently released, it would appear as though justice had not been served. However, no one would have observed anything untoward if the Ark did not hold him back due to a private prayer of David.

HALAKHA

A eulogy after twelve months – הספד לאחר שנים עשר חדש: Eulogies for the dead are not delivered after twelve months have passed. Similarly, if word of a scholar's death arrived twelve months after the fact, he is not eulogized (*Shulḥan Arukh, Yoreh De'a* 394:2).

There are three signs of the Jewish people – שלשה סימנים יש בישראל: If one is brazen or cruel, hates others, and does not act kindly toward them, he is suspected to be a Gibeonite, as the characteristic marks of the Jewish people are that they are shamefaced, merciful, and perform acts of kindness (Rambam *Sefer Kedusha, Hilkhot Issurei Bia* 12:24, 19:17; *Shulḥan Arukh, Even HaEzer* 2:2).

וְהָא כְּתִיב "לֹא יוּמְתוּ אָבוֹת עַל בָּנִים" וגו'! אָמַר רַבִּי חִיָּיא בַּר אַבָּא אָמַר רַבִּי יוֹחָנָן: מוּטָב שֶׁתֵּעָקֵר אוֹת אַחַת מִן הַתּוֹרָה, וְאַל יִתְחַלֵּל שֵׁם שָׁמַיִם בְּפַרְהֶסְיָא.

The Gemara raises a difficulty with regard to the story as related by the Bible: **But isn't it written: "The fathers shall not be put to death for the children;** neither shall the children be put to death for the fathers" (Deuteronomy 24:16)? As Saul's sons had not sinned, why were they put to death? **Rabbi Ḥiyya bar Abba said** that **Rabbi Yoḥanan said:** It is **better that one letter** and one mitzva **be uprooted**[NH] **from the Torah** in this manner and thereby the **name of Heaven not be desecrated in public** [*parhesya*].[L] The killing of the Gibeonites by the Jewish people constituted a desecration of God's name. In order to repair the damage, David acquiesced to the Gibeonites' demands, even though they contradicted Torah law.

"וַתִּקַּח רִצְפָּה בַת אַיָּה אֶת הַשַּׂק וַתַּטֵּהוּ לָהּ אֶל הַצּוּר מִתְּחִלַּת קָצִיר עַד נִתַּךְ מַיִם עֲלֵיהֶם מִן הַשָּׁמַיִם וְלֹא נָתְנָה עוֹף הַשָּׁמַיִם לָנוּחַ עֲלֵיהֶם יוֹמָם וְחַיַּת הַשָּׂדֶה לָיְלָה". וְהָא כְּתִיב "לֹא תָלִין נִבְלָתוֹ עַל הָעֵץ"!

The Gemara continues with its analysis of the incident. The verse states: **"And Rizpah, daughter of Aiah, took sackcloth and spread it for her upon the rock, from the beginning of harvest until water was poured upon them from heaven; and she allowed neither the birds of the air to rest on them by day, nor the beasts of the field by night"** (II Samuel 21:10). The Gemara raises a difficulty: How could they have left Saul's executed sons unburied all that time? **Isn't it written: "His body shall not remain all night upon the tree;** but you shall surely bury him the same day" (Deuteronomy 21:23)?

אָמַר רַבִּי יוֹחָנָן מִשּׁוּם רַבִּי שִׁמְעוֹן בֶּן יְהוֹצָדָק: מוּטָב שֶׁתֵּעָקֵר אוֹת אַחַת מִן הַתּוֹרָה וְיִתְקַדֵּשׁ שֵׁם שָׁמַיִם בְּפַרְהֶסְיָא. שֶׁהָיוּ עוֹבְרִים וְשָׁבִים אוֹמְרִים: מַה טִּיבָן שֶׁל אֵלּוּ? הַלָּלוּ בְּנֵי מְלָכִים הֵם. וּמֶה עָשׂוּ? פָּשְׁטוּ יְדֵיהֶם בְּגֵרִים גְּרוּרִים. אָמְרוּ: אֵין לְךָ אוּמָּה שֶׁרְאוּיָה לְהִדָּבֵק בָּהּ כְּזוֹ. וּמַה בְּנֵי מְלָכִים כָּךְ, בְּנֵי הֶדְיוֹטוֹת עַל אַחַת כַּמָּה וְכַמָּה! וּמַה גֵּרִים גְּרוּרִים כָּךְ, יִשְׂרָאֵל עַל אַחַת כַּמָּה וְכַמָּה!

Rabbi Yoḥanan said in the name of Rabbi Shimon ben Yehotzadak: It is **better that one letter be uprooted from the Torah and** thereby **the name of Heaven be sanctified**[N] **in public.** How so? **As the** gentile **passersby would say: What is the nature of these** people who have been left hanging here for so long? They were told that **these are sons of kings. And what did they do** to deserve such a fate? **They had laid their hands upon** and caused harm to **calculating converts** who had converted for personal gain and were never permitted to enter into the congregation. Those passersby **said: There is no nation as worthy of cleaving to it as this one. If the sons of kings** who harmed converts are treated **in this** manner, **all the more so** would **the sons of ordinary people** [*hedyotot*][L] be. **And if calculating converts** are related to **in this way, all the more so** would this apply to members of **the Jewish people** themselves.

מִיָּד נִתּוֹסְפוּ עַל יִשְׂרָאֵל מֵאָה וַחֲמִשִּׁים אֶלֶף, שֶׁנֶּאֱמַר "וַיְהִי לִשְׁלֹמֹה שִׁבְעִים אֶלֶף נֹשֵׂא סַבָּל וּשְׁמֹנִים אֶלֶף חֹצֵב בָּהָר". וְדִלְמָא יִשְׂרָאֵל הָווּ! לָא סָלְקָא דַּעְתָּךְ, דִּכְתִיב "וּמִבְּנֵי יִשְׂרָאֵל לֹא נָתַן שְׁלֹמֹה עָבֶד".

Immediately, one hundred and fifty thousand converts **joined the Jewish people,**[N] **as it is stated: "And Solomon had seventy thousand that bore burdens and eighty thousand that were hewers in the mountains"** (I Kings 5:29), all of whom were converts. The Gemara asks: **But perhaps** these carriers and hewers **were Jews?** The Gemara answers: **This cannot enter your mind, as it is written: "But of the children of Israel Solomon made no slaves"** (I Kings 9:22).

וְדִלְמָא דּוֹגְזַר בְּעָלְמָא! אֶלָּא מֵהָכָא: "וַיִּסְפֹּר שְׁלֹמֹה כָּל הָאֲנָשִׁים הַגֵּרִים אֲשֶׁר בְּאֶרֶץ יִשְׂרָאֵל [וגו'] וַיִּמָּצְאוּ מֵאָה וַחֲמִשִּׁים אֶלֶף [וגו'] וַיַּעַשׂ מֵהֶם שִׁבְעִים אֶלֶף (נוֹשֵׂא) סַבָּל וּשְׁמוֹנִים אֶלֶף חוֹצֵב בָּהָר".

The Gemara raises another difficulty: **But** from where may it be inferred that these men were slaves? **Perhaps** they were **merely** workers **employed** [*dogzar*][L] in the ranks of public service, in which case they could have been born Jews and not converts. **Rather,** the matter is derived from **here: "And Solomon counted all the converted men that were in Eretz Yisrael…and they were found to be one hundred and fifty thousand…and he made seventy thousand of them to bear burdens, and eighty thousand to be hewers in the mountains"** (II Chronicles 2:16–17). It is apparent from here that these carriers and hewers were in fact converts. These large numbers of converts had been influenced by the sanctification of God's name in the wake of the punishment meted out to the descendants of Saul.

NOTES

It is better that one letter be uprooted – מוּטָב שֶׁתֵּעָקֵר אוֹת אַחַת: Certain early authorities (Ritva) and later authorities attempt to explain that this refers literally to a single letter, but their interpretations are somewhat far-fetched. Nearly all commentaries conclude that this does not mean one letter but an entire verse.

And the name of Heaven be sanctified – וְיִתְקַדֵּשׁ שֵׁם שָׁמַיִם: In the Jerusalem Talmud it is stated that from here it is understood that the gain from the sanctification of God's name is greater than the loss caused by its desecration. This is derived from the fact that the very reason that the dead may not be left hanging overnight is that it is considered a desecration of God's name, as explained in tractate *Sanhedrin* and elsewhere, and yet the sanctification of His name caused by doing so in this case is deemed greater than the desecration involved.

Immediately…they joined the Jewish people – מִיָּד נִתּוֹסְפוּ עַל יִשְׂרָאֵל: Although the Sages said that converts were not accepted in the days of David and Solomon, this refers exclusively to conversion in authorized courts, whereas these gentiles were converted in the presence of ordinary people (Rashba).

HALAKHA

It is better that one letter be uprooted – מוּטָב שֶׁתֵּעָקֵר אוֹת אַחַת: The court has the authority to temporarily uproot a positive or negative mitzva in order to restore the public to the proper observance of religion or prevent the masses from erring in some matter (Rambam *Sefer Shofetim, Hilkhot Mamrim* 2:4).

LANGUAGE

Public [*parhesya*] – פַּרְהֶסְיָא: From the Greek παρρησία, *parēsia*, meaning a matter stated openly and without restraint. In mishnaic Hebrew, it describes an act performed in the open with no attempt made to conceal it.

Ordinary people [*hedyotot*] – הֶדְיוֹטוֹת: From the Greek ἰδιώτης, *idiotēs*. Both in Greek and in the language of the Sages the term carries a variety of associated meanings. Here it is used in its fundamental sense, denoting an ordinary citizen with no official appointment.

Employed [*dogzar*] – דּוֹגְזַר: The correct reading of this word, which is preserved in medieval records, is *rogzar*. The term comes from the Middle Persian rōz, meaning day, and the agent gār, giving the approximate literal meaning: Day laborer.

וּנְתִינִים, דָּוִד גָּזַר עֲלֵיהֶם? מֹשֶׁה גָּזַר עֲלֵיהֶם, דִּכְתִיב ״מֵחוֹטֵב עֵצֶיךָ עַד שׁוֹאֵב מֵימֶיךָ״! מֹשֶׁה גָּזַר לְהַהוּא דָּרָא, דָּוִד גָּזַר לְכוּלֵּי דָּרֵי.

The Gemara returns to the main issue under discussion. As for **the Gibeonites,** was it **David** who **issued a decree against them** that they may not enter the congregation? Wasn't it **Moses** who **issued a decree against them, as it is written: "From the hewer of your wood to the drawer of your water"** (Deuteronomy 29:10), which indicates that there was a distinct class of wood hewers and water drawers already in the time of Moses. This class must have been composed of insincere converts who constituted a separate group unto themselves, apart from the rest of the Jewish people. The Gemara answers: **Moses issued a decree** only **with regard to that generation** that they must remain separate, whereas **David decreed for all generations.**

וְאַכַּתִּי יְהוֹשֻׁעַ גָּזַר עֲלַיְיהוּ דִּכְתִיב ״וַיִּתְּנֵם יְהוֹשֻׁעַ בַּיּוֹם הַהוּא חוֹטְבֵי עֵצִים וְשׁוֹאֲבֵי מַיִם לָעֵדָה וּלְמִזְבַּח ה׳״! יְהוֹשֻׁעַ גָּזַר בִּזְמַן שֶׁבֵּית הַמִּקְדָּשׁ קַיָּים, דָּוִד גָּזַר בִּזְמַן שֶׁאֵין בֵּית הַמִּקְדָּשׁ קַיָּים.

The Gemara raises another difficulty: **But still,** it was **Joshua** who **issued a decree against** the Gibeonites, **as it is written: "And Joshua made them that day hewers of wood and drawers of water, for the congregation and for the altar of the Lord"** (Joshua 9:27). The Gemara answers: **Joshua issued a decree**[H] **for the period when the Temple is standing,** as indicated by the phrase "for the altar of the Lord," whereas **David issued a decree** even **for the period when the Temple is not standing.**

HALAKHA

Joshua issued a decree – יְהוֹשֻׁעַ גָּזַר: By Torah law it is not prohibited for a convert from one of the seven Canaanite nations to enter into the congregation; it was Joshua who permanently barred both males and females from doing so. However, his decree applied only during the time when the Temple was standing. King David extended the decree to apply even to the period when the Temple was not standing (Rambam *Sefer Kedusha, Hilkhot Issurei Bia* 12:22–23).

Perek **VIII**
Daf **79** Amud **b**

בִּימֵי רַבִּי בִּקְּשׁוּ לְהַתִּיר נְתִינִים אָמַר לָהֶם רַבִּי: חֶלְקֵנוּ נַתִּיר, חֵלֶק מִזְבֵּחַ מִי יַתִּיר?

It is related that **in the days of Rabbi** Yehuda HaNasi the Sages **sought to permit the Gibeonites**[N] and treat them like Jews in all regards, thereby allowing them to enter into the congregation. **Rabbi** Yehuda HaNasi **said to them:** Even if **we permit our share** and say that the court nullifies the Jewish people's right to enslave the Gibeonites, and so they should be treated like emancipated slaves, **who can permit the altar's share?** Do they not belong to the Temple and the altar as well?

וּפְלִיגָא דְּרַבִּי חִיָּיא בַּר אַבָּא דְּאָמַר רַבִּי חִיָּיא בַּר אַבָּא אָמַר רַבִּי יוֹחָנָן: חֵלֶק עֵדָה – לְעוֹלָם אָסוּר, חֵלֶק מִזְבֵּחַ, בִּזְמַן שֶׁבֵּית הַמִּקְדָּשׁ קַיָּים – אָסוּר, אֵין בֵּית הַמִּקְדָּשׁ קַיָּים – שָׁרֵי.

The Gemara comments: **And** Rabbi Yehuda HaNasi **disagrees with** the teaching of **Rabbi Ḥiyya bar Abba. As Rabbi Ḥiyya bar Abba said** that **Rabbi Yoḥanan said: The share** in the enslavement of the Gibeonites that belongs **to the congregation** of Israel **is forbidden forever** and can never be permitted. However, with regard to **the share** belonging **to the altar, when the Temple is standing** it is **forbidden,** but when **the Temple is not standing** it is **permitted.**

NOTES

They sought to permit the Gibeonites – בִּקְּשׁוּ לְהַתִּיר נְתִינִים: The early authorities discuss this matter at length, as it concerns the prohibition with regard to the Gibeonites in general concerning whether they are prohibited by Torah law or by rabbinic law, or whether only the first generation was prohibited by Torah law. According to the opinion that this is a rabbinic prohibition, the meaning of the Gemara is straightforward, as it discusses whether it was subsequently permitted for Gibeonites to enter into the congregation. If the prohibition applies by Torah law, it is possible that the Gemara here is referring only to their enslavement, not to their eligibility for marriage (see *Sefer HaYashar*). The early authorities point out that at least according to the Jerusalem Talmud, the subject under discussion is clearly their eligibility to marry Jews.

In any event, the enslavement of the Gibeonites to the altar and to the congregation is either a sign of their prohibition, according to the opinion that they are forbidden by Torah law, or a way of accentuating their different status, according to the opinion that they are forbidden by rabbinic law. Although they are not full-fledged slaves, as all agree that they are not bodily enslaved, their subjugation rendered them quasi slaves. Due to this, it was suggested that Rabbi Yehuda HaNasi's court, or Rabbi Eliezer's court according to the Jerusalem Talmud, could seek to permit a matter that had been prohibited by a greater court, which is ordinarily impossible. They could do this because they wished to release the Gibeonites from their subjugation, based on the principle that property declared ownerless by the court is ownerless. This procedure would automatically have rendered it permitted for the Gibeonites to enter into the congregation (see the Ramban, Rosh, and Rashba).

מתני׳ אָמַר רַבִּי יְהוֹשֻׁעַ: שָׁמַעְתִּי שֶׁהַסָּרִיס חוֹלֵץ וְחוֹלְצִין לְאִשְׁתּוֹ, וְהַסָּרִיס לֹא חוֹלֵץ וְלֹא חוֹלְצִין לְאִשְׁתּוֹ, וְאֵין לִי לְפָרֵשׁ.

MISHNA Rabbi Yehoshua said: I heard two rulings from my teachers. One ruling is that a eunuch performs *ḥalitza* with his *yevama*, and his brothers perform *ḥalitza* with his wife, and the other ruling is that a eunuch does not perform *ḥalitza* with his *yevama*, and his brothers do not perform *ḥalitza* with his wife. And I cannot explain[N] these two rulings, as I do not remember the circumstances to which each ruling applies.

אָמַר רַבִּי עֲקִיבָא: אֲנִי אֲפָרֵשׁ: סְרִיס אָדָם – חוֹלֵץ וְחוֹלְצִין לְאִשְׁתּוֹ, מִפְּנֵי שֶׁהָיְתָה לוֹ שְׁעַת הַכּוֹשֶׁר סְרִיס חַמָּה לֹא חוֹלֵץ וְלֹא חוֹלְצִין לְאִשְׁתּוֹ מִפְּנֵי שֶׁלֹּא הָיְתָה לוֹ שְׁעַת הַכּוֹשֶׁר.

Rabbi Akiva said: I will explain. A eunuch caused **by man,** i.e., one who became emasculated after birth, **performs *ḥalitza***[H] with his *yevama* **and** his brothers **perform *ḥalitza* with his wife, because he had an hour of fitness,** a time when he was fertile. On the other hand, **a eunuch by natural causes,** i.e., who was entirely lacking in sexual capacity from birth, **does not perform *ḥalitza***[H] with his *yevama* **and** his brothers **do not perform *ḥalitza* with his wife, because he did not have an hour of fitness,** as he never had the potential to father children.

רַבִּי אֱלִיעֶזֶר אוֹמֵר: לֹא כִּי, אֶלָּא: סְרִיס חַמָּה – חוֹלֵץ וְחוֹלְצִין לְאִשְׁתּוֹ, מִפְּנֵי שֶׁיֵּשׁ לוֹ רְפוּאָה. סְרִיס אָדָם – לֹא חוֹלֵץ וְלֹא חוֹלְצִין לְאִשְׁתּוֹ, מִפְּנֵי שֶׁאֵין לוֹ רְפוּאָה.

Rabbi Eliezer says: No; rather, the opposite is the case: **A eunuch by natural causes performs *ḥalitza*** with his *yevama* **and** his brothers **perform *ḥalitza* with his wife because he can be cured,**[B] whereas **a eunuch** caused **by man does not perform *ḥalitza*** with his *yevama* **and** his brothers **do not perform *ḥalitza* with his wife because he cannot be cured.**

הֵעִיד רַבִּי יְהוֹשֻׁעַ בֶּן בְּתֵירָא עַל בֶּן מְגוּסַת שֶׁהָיָה בִּירוּשָׁלַיִם סְרִיס אָדָם, וְיִבְּמוּ אֶת אִשְׁתּוֹ, לְקַיֵּים דִּבְרֵי רַבִּי עֲקִיבָא.

Rabbi Yehoshua ben Beteira testified about a man named **ben Megusat, who** lived **in Jerusalem** and **was a eunuch** caused **by man,** that his brothers nevertheless **entered into levirate marriage with his wife,** in order **to fulfill** and confirm **the statement of Rabbi Akiva.**

הַסָּרִיס לֹא חוֹלֵץ וְלֹא מְיַיבֵּם, וְכֵן אַיְילוֹנִית לֹא חוֹלֶצֶת וְלֹא מִתְיַיבֶּמֶת.

A sexually underdeveloped man does not perform *ḥalitza* or enter into levirate marriage with his *yevama*. **And similarly,** a **sexually underdeveloped woman** [*aylonit*],[L] who is incapable of bearing children, **does not perform *ḥalitza* or enter into levirate marriage** with her *yavam*.

הַסָּרִיס שֶׁחָלַץ לִיבִמְתּוֹ – לֹא פְּסָלָהּ, בְּעָלָהּ – פְּסָלָהּ, מִפְּנֵי שֶׁהִיא בְּעִילַת זְנוּת. וְכֵן אַיְילוֹנִית שֶׁחָלְצוּ לָהּ אַחִין – לֹא פְּסָלוּהָ, בְּעָלוּהָ – פְּסָלוּהָ, מִפְּנֵי שֶׁבְּעִילָתָהּ בְּעִילַת זְנוּת.

If **a sexually underdeveloped man performed *ḥalitza* with his *yevama*, he has not** thereby **disqualified her**[H] from marrying into the priesthood, as his *ḥalitza* is invalid. However, if **he had intercourse with her, he has disqualified her.**[H] This is **because it is** considered **licentious sexual intercourse,** since such intercourse does not fulfill the mitzva of levirate marriage and is therefore categorized as forbidden relations with one's sister-in-law. **And similarly,** with regard to **a sexually underdeveloped woman,** if one of **the brothers performed *ḥalitza*** with her he **has not** thereby **disqualified her** from marrying into the priesthood. However, if he **had intercourse with her,** he **has disqualified her because the intercourse is** considered **licentious sexual intercourse.**

גמ׳ מִכְּדֵי שָׁמְעִינַן לְרַבִּי עֲקִיבָא דְּאָמַר חַיָּיבֵי לָאוִין כְּחַיָּיבֵי כָּרֵיתוֹת דָּמוּ – וְחַיָּיבֵי כָּרֵיתוֹת לָאו בְּנֵי חֲלִיצָה וְיִיבּוּם נִינְהוּ!

GEMARA Now, we learned that **Rabbi Akiva said: Those liable** for violating **a prohibition are like those liable** to receive ***karet*** with regard to the validity of their marriage and all its ramifications, **and those liable to** receive ***karet*** **are not eligible** to perform ***ḥalitza*** **or levirate marriage.** A eunuch caused by man has the status of a man with crushed testicles, and is therefore prohibited by a standard negative mitzva from marrying a Jewish woman. If he violated the prohibition and married her, his marriage is invalid according to Rabbi Akiva, just as if he had married a woman who is forbidden to him by a prohibition punishable by *karet*. Why, then, should his *ḥalitza* be valid?

NOTES

And I cannot explain – וְאֵין לִי לְפָרֵשׁ: Rabbi Yehoshua's uncertainty, which concerns the very point about which Rabbi Akiva and Rabbi Eliezer disagree, is connected to a fundamental problem with regard to levirate marriage. On one hand it seems that the purpose of levirate marriage is to have children in the deceased brother's name, but on the other hand, even if the *yevama* and the *yavam* are each capable of becoming parents, they do not have the power to determine whether and when this duty will actually be fulfilled. Consequently, the only cases that can be discussed are those in which the possibility of having children exists. As a result, a sexually underdeveloped woman who is incapable of bearing children is excluded from the obligation of levirate marriage. The same dilemma arises with regard to the case of a eunuch: Does inclusion in the mitzva depend on one's ability to have children in the future or on the mere fact that at some point one had been able to become a father?

HALAKHA

A eunuch caused by man performs *ḥalitza* – סְרִיס אָדָם חוֹלֵץ: If a eunuch had once been fertile and died without fathering children, his brother may perform *ḥalitza* or levirate marriage with his widow. If his brother died without children, the eunuch may perform *ḥalitza* with his *yevama* but may not enter into levirate marriage, as it is prohibited for him to enter into the congregation. The *halakha* is in accordance with the opinion of Rabbi Akiva, based on the testimony given by Rabbi Yehoshua ben Beteira (Rambam *Sefer Nashim, Hilkhot Yibbum* 6:4; *Shulḥan Arukh, Even HaEzer* 172:3).

A eunuch by natural causes does not perform *ḥalitza* – סְרִיס חַמָּה לֹא חוֹלֵץ: A male who was entirely lacking in sexual capacity from birth and a sexually underdeveloped woman are not included in the mitzvot of *ḥalitza* and levirate marriage (Rambam *Sefer Nashim, Hilkhot Yibbum* 6:2; *Shulḥan Arukh, Even HaEzer* 172:1).

If a sexually underdeveloped man performed *ḥalitza*… he has not disqualified her – הַסָּרִיס שֶׁחָלַץ...לֹא פְּסָלָהּ: If a sexually underdeveloped man performed *ḥalitza* with his *yevama*, or if his brother performed *ḥalitza* with his widow, and similarly, if a sexually underdeveloped woman performed *ḥalitza*, these women have not been disqualified from marrying into the priesthood, as the *ḥalitza* is of no consequence (Rambam *Sefer Nashim, Hilkhot Yibbum* 6:2; *Shulḥan Arukh, Even HaEzer* 172:1).

If a eunuch had intercourse with a woman, he has disqualified her – סָרִיס שֶׁבָּא עַל אִשָּׁה פְּסָלָהּ: If a eunuch had intercourse with any woman, he has disqualified her from marrying into the priesthood. If she was the daughter of a priest, she is barred from eating *teruma* (Rambam *Sefer Kedusha, Hilkhot Issurei Bia* 18:3).

LANGUAGE

A sexually underdeveloped woman [*aylonit*] – אַיְילוֹנִית: The source of the word, as stated in the Gemara (*Ketubot* 11b), is the Hebrew term for a male sheep, *eyal*. A male sheep, called *dikhra*, meaning male in Aramaic, is a symbol of masculinity. A sexually underdeveloped woman is a masculine woman, so to speak, as she is incapable of giving birth.

BACKGROUND

A defect that can be cured – לִיקּוּי שֶׁיֵּשׁ לוֹ רְפוּאָה: As will be explained on 80b, a eunuch by natural causes is one who suffers from defective sexual development, whether due to a hereditary condition or one that stems from a glandular dysfunction. Sometimes a glandular defect can be cured, either spontaneously or through supplement of various hormones. Although there is no definite knowledge on this matter, it is possible that in the past this condition was treated by ingesting natural substances containing hormones, or by means of herbal remedies that strengthened glandular function in general.

אֲמַר רַבִּי אַמִי: הָכָא בְּמַאי עָסְקִינַן – כְּגוֹן שֶׁנָּשָׂא אָחִיו גִּיּוֹרֶת. וְרַבִּי עֲקִיבָא סָבַר לָהּ כְּרַבִּי יוֹסֵי, דַּאֲמַר: קְהַל גֵּרִים לָא אִקְרִי קָהָל.

Rabbi Ami said: With what are we dealing here? We are dealing with a case **where** the eunuch's **brother** had **married a convert,**[H] **and Rabbi Akiva holds in accordance with** the opinion of **Rabbi Yosei,** who **said** that the **congregation of converts is not called a congregation** of the Lord. Consequently, it is permitted even for those for whom it is prohibited to enter into the congregation, e.g., a eunuch, to marry converts.

אִי הָכִי יַבּוּמֵי נַמִי מְיַיבֵּם! אִין הָכִי נַמִי וְאַיְּידֵי דַּאֲמַר רַבִּי יְהוֹשֻׁעַ חוֹלֵץ אֲמַר אִיהוּ נַמִי חוֹלֵץ.

The Gemara raises a difficulty: **If so,** the eunuch should also be able to **perform levirate marriage** with the convert. The Gemara answers: **Yes, it is indeed so, but since Rabbi Yehoshua said** that a eunuch **performs *ḥalitza*** with his *yevama*, Rabbi Akiva **as well said** that **he performs *ḥalitza*** with her, while in fact he may enter into levirate marriage with her if he so chooses.

דַּיְקָא נַמִי, דְּקָתָנֵי: הֵעִיד רַבִּי יְהוֹשֻׁעַ בֶּן בְּתֵירָא עַל בֶּן מְגוּסַת שֶׁהָיָה בִּירוּשָׁלַיִם סְרִיס אָדָם, וְיִבְּמוּ אֶת אִשְׁתּוֹ, לְקַיֵּים דִּבְרֵי רַבִּי עֲקִיבָא. שְׁמַע מִינָּהּ.

The Gemara adds: The language of the mishna **is also precise** in this regard, **as it teaches: Rabbi Yehoshua ben Beteira testified about** a man named **ben Megusat, who** lived **in Jerusalem** and **was a eunuch** caused **by man,** that his brothers **entered into levirate marriage with his wife, to fulfill the statement of Rabbi Akiva.** This indicates that according to Rabbi Akiva, not only *ḥalitza* but even levirate marriage is permitted. The Gemara concludes: **Learn from this** that this is the correct understanding of the mishna.

מְתִיב רַבָּה: פְּצוּעַ דַּכָּא, וּכְרוּת שָׁפְכָה, סְרִיס אָדָם, וְהַזָּקֵן – אוֹ חוֹלְצִין אוֹ מְיַיבְּמִין. כֵּיצַד? מֵתוּ וְלָהֶם נָשִׁים, וְלָהֶם אַחִין, וְעָמְדוּ אַחִין וְעָשׂוּ מַאֲמָר בִּנְשׁוֹתֵיהֶן וְנָתְנוּ גֵּט אוֹ שֶׁחָלְצוּ – מַה שֶּׁעָשׂוּ עָשׂוּ, וְאִם בָּעֲלוּ – קָנוּ.

Rabba raised an objection from the following *baraita*: **A man with crushed testicles, and one whose penis has been severed,** and a **eunuch** caused **by man, and an elderly** man[N] who is no longer capable of fathering children, may **either perform *ḥalitza* or enter into levirate marriage.** The *baraita* clarifies the matter: **How so?** If these men **died and they had wives and they** also **had brothers, and the brothers proceeded to perform levirate betrothal with their wives, or gave them a bill of divorce, or performed *ḥalitza*** with them, **what they did is done,** i.e., it is a valid act. **And if** the brothers **had intercourse** with the wives, **they acquired** them in levirate marriage, like any other *yevama*.[H]

מֵתוּ אַחִין וְעָמְדוּ הֵן וְעָשׂוּ מַאֲמָר בִּנְשׁוֹתֵיהֶן וְנָתְנוּ גֵּט אוֹ חָלְצוּ – מַה שֶּׁעָשׂוּ עָשׂוּ, וְאִם בָּעֲלוּ – קָנוּ, וְאָסוּר לְקַיְּימָן, מִשּׁוּם שֶׁנֶּאֱמַר ״לֹא יָבֹא פְצוּעַ דַּכָּא וּכְרוּת שָׁפְכָה בִּקְהַל ה׳״. אַלְמָא בְּקָהָל עָסְקִינַן!

If **the brothers** of these sexually impaired men **died, and** the sexually impaired men **proceeded to perform levirate betrothal with their** brothers' **wives,** or **gave them a bill of divorce, or performed *ḥalitza*** with them, **what they did is done,** i.e., it is a valid act. **And if they had intercourse** with their brothers' wives **they acquired** them in levirate marriage, **but** they are **prohibited from maintaining them**[H] as their wives **because it is stated: "A man with crushed testicles or a severed penis shall not enter into the congregation of the Lord"** (Deuteronomy 23:2). **Apparently, we are dealing with** a case where the eunuch's brother had married a woman who is **in the congregation** of the Lord, i.e., a Jew from birth who is governed by this prohibition, and not a convert.

אֶלָּא אָמַר רַבָּה: כְּגוֹן שֶׁנָּפְלָה לוֹ וּלְבַסּוֹף נִפְצַע.

Rather, Rabba said that the case here is one **where** one's brother died and his *yevama* **happened before him** for levirate marriage, **and he was injured** only **afterward.** Since the mitzva of levirate marriage had initially applied to him, he performs *ḥalitza* with her.

אֲמַר לֵיהּ אַבַּיֵי: וְלֵיתֵי אִיסּוּר פְּצוּעַ וְנִידְחֵי עֲשֵׂה דְּיִיבּוּם! מִי לָא תְּנַן, רַבָּן גַּמְלִיאֵל אוֹמֵר: אִם מֵיאֲנָה – מֵיאֲנָה,

Abaye said to him: If so, **let the prohibition** applying to a man with **crushed** testicles **come and override** the **positive** mitzva **of levirate marriage. Didn't we learn** in a mishna (109a) as follows: With regard to a case of two brothers who were married to two sisters, one of whom was a minor married off by her brothers in a marriage valid only by rabbinic decree, and the brother who was married to the adult sister passed away, **Rabban Gamliel says: If** the minor sister **refuses** her husband, declaring that she does not desire the marriage, **she has refused him.** Since the marriage is valid only by rabbinic decree, the girl may terminate it before she reaches the age of twelve by declaring that she does not wish to remain in the marriage, and no bill of divorce is required. In such a case the marriage is nullified retroactively, and so her former husband, the *yavam*, may perform levirate marriage with her sister.

HALAKHA

Where his brother married a convert – כְּגוֹן שֶׁנָּשָׂא אָחִיו גִּיּוֹרֶת: If a man married a convert and died childless, and he had a brother who was a eunuch, it is permitted for the latter to perform levirate marriage with his *yevama*, in accordance with the opinion of Rabbi Yosei that the congregation of converts is not called a congregation (*Shulḥan Arukh, Even HaEzer* 172:3, and in the comment of Rema).

Forbidden to the husband and permitted to the *yavam* – אֲסוּרָה לַבַּעַל וּמוּתֶּרֶת לַיָּבָם: If a woman was forbidden to her husband by a positive or negative mitzva or a rabbinic prohibition, but she is permitted to his brother, and her husband died without children, she may enter into levirate marriage (Rambam *Sefer Nashim, Hilkhot Yibbum* 6:4; *Shulḥan Arukh, Even HaEzer* 174:2).

But they are prohibited from maintaining them – וְאָסוּר לְקַיְּימָן: If a woman is forbidden to her *yavam* by a positive or negative mitzva or a rabbinic prohibition, she must undergo *ḥalitza* and may not enter into levirate marriage. If the *yavam* transgressed and had intercourse with her, he acquired her as his wife and exempted her rival wife from levirate marriage and *ḥalitza*, but he must divorce her (Rambam *Sefer Nashim, Hilkhot Yibbum* 6:2; *Shulḥan Arukh, Even HaEzer* 173:3, 174:1).

NOTES

And an elderly man – וְהַזָּקֵן: The early authorities note that an elderly man does not belong to this category in all respects, as the *tanna* is stressing that although he cannot have children in practice, since he was inherently capable of fathering children he is obligated in levirate marriage. Consequently, the prohibition stated here against maintaining the woman as his wife does not apply to an old man, as he is not classified as one with crushed testicles. Some commentaries distinguish between an elderly man who is no longer capable of the act of intercourse, and one who can perform the act but cannot have children (see Meiri, Rambam, and *Maggid Mishne*).

וְאִם לָאו – תַּמְתִּין עַד שֶׁתַּגְדִּיל, וְתֵיצֵא הַלֵּזוּ מִשּׁוּם אֲחוֹת אִשָּׁה. אַלְמָא: אָתֵי אִיסּוּר אֲחוֹת אִשָּׁה וְדָחֵי, הָכָא נַמִי נֵיתֵי אִיסּוּר פָּצוּעַ וְנִידְחֵי!

The mishna continues: **But if** she does **not** refuse him, the minor **must wait** and her husband must not have relations with her **until she reaches adulthood** and their marriage is valid by Torah law, since in the meantime she is forbidden to him as the sister of a woman awaiting levirate marriage with him. At that point, when the minor reaches adulthood, **this one,** the adult sister, **goes out** free from the *yavam* without levirate marriage or *ḥalitza* **as** his **wife's sister. Apparently, the prohibition** with regard to **a wife's sister comes and overrides** the mitzva of levirate marriage that had previously been in effect. **Here too,** then, **let the prohibition** applying to a man with **crushed** testicles **come and override** the positive mitzva of levirate marriage.

אֶלָּא אֲמַר רַב יוֹסֵף: הַאי תַּנָּא – הַךְ תַּנָּא דְּבֵי רַבִּי עֲקִיבָא הִיא, דַּאֲמַר: מְחַיָּיבֵי לָאוִין דִּשְׁאֵר הָוֵי מַמְזֵר, מְחַיָּיבֵי לָאוִין גְּרֵידֵי – לָא הָוֵי מַמְזֵר.

Rather, Rav Yosef said: This *tanna* of our mishna **is the** *tanna* of **the school of Rabbi Akiva, who said** that only the child born of a union between those who **are liable for** violating **prohibitions involving incestuous relationships is a** ***mamzer***, but the child born of a union between people who **are liable for** violating **ordinary prohibitions is not a** ***mamzer***. The prohibition applying to a man with crushed testicles falls into the latter category, and therefore his marriage is valid and he may perform *ḥalitza*.

אִיקְּרֵי כָּאן ״לְהָקִים לְאָחִיו שֵׁם״ וְהָא לָאו בַּר הָכִי הוּא!

The Gemara asks: Why does the mitzva of levirate marriage apply at all to a eunuch? **Read here** the verse with regard to levirate marriage: **"To establish a name for his brother** in Israel" (Deuteronomy 25:7), **and this one is no** longer **capable of this,** even if previously he had an hour of fitness when he was fertile earlier in his life.

אֲמַר רָבָא: אִם כֵּן אֵין לְךָ אִשָּׁה שֶׁכְּשֵׁרָה לְיַבֵּם שֶׁלֹּא נַעֲשָׂה בַּעֲלָהּ סְרִיס חַמָּה שָׁעָה אַחַת קוֹדֶם לְמִיתָתוֹ.

Rava said: If it is **so** that anyone who cannot presently father children is exempt from levirate marriage even if he had previously been capable of doing so, **there is no instance of a woman who is fit for the** ***yavam***, as even if **her husband** died of natural causes it is impossible that he **did not become** like **a eunuch by natural causes an hour before his death.** He had certainly lost his fertility before dying, and therefore he has the status of a eunuch, which means that the mitzva of levirate marriage should not apply in his case at all. Rather, it must be that a man who had previously been capable of fathering children is considered fit for the purposes of levirate marriage.

לְרַבִּי אֱלִיעֶזֶר פֵּירוּקָא דְּרָבָא פִּירְכָא הִיא!

The Gemara comments: **According to** the opinion of **Rabbi Eliezer** in the mishna that a eunuch caused by man does not perform *ḥalitza* and his marriage is invalid even though he had an hour of fitness when he was fertile, **Rava's answer,** his proof from the fact that all men on their deathbeds lack sexual capacity, **is** undoubtedly **a refutation.**

הָתָם כְּחִישׁוּתָא דְּאַתְחִילָה בֵּיהּ.

The Gemara answers: Rabbi Eliezer maintains that a man who is about to die cannot be compared to a eunuch, as **there,** he can no longer father children due to **the** general **weakness that begins** to take over his body as death approaches, which prevents him from engaging in relations with a woman, but his basic ability to father children remains unimpaired.

הֵיכִי דָּמֵי סְרִיס חַמָּה? אָמַר רַב יִצְחָק בַּר יוֹסֵף אָמַר רַבִּי יוֹחָנָן: כָּל

The Gemara raises a practical question: **What are the circumstances of a eunuch by natural causes?**[N] **Rav Yitzḥak bar Yosef said that Rabbi Yoḥanan said: Anyone**

NOTES

What are the circumstances of a eunuch by natural causes – הֵיכִי דָּמֵי סְרִיס חַמָּה: The Ritva and the Meiri claim that this question is not referring to the basic definition of a man entirely lacking in sexual capacity, but only to the case mentioned in the mishna here. This is because this category includes two different types: A man regarding whom there is no external indication that he is incapable of fathering children, and a eunuch by natural causes.

שֶׁלֹּא רָאָה שָׁעָה אַחַת בְּכַשְׁרוּתוֹ. מְנָא יָדְעִינַן? אָמַר אַבָּיֵי: כָּל הַמַּטִּיל מַיִם וְאֵינוֹ עוֹשֶׂה כִּיפָּה.

who never saw a single hour of life **in** a state of **fitness,** as he was born infertile. The Gemara asks: **How do we know** that one was born this way and was never capable of having children? **Abaye said: Anyone who passes water and does not form an arch** with his urine, but rather his urine dribbles out downward, never had sexual capacity.

מִמַּאי הָוֵאי? דְּאָפְיָה אִימֵּיהּ בְּטִיהֲרָא וְשָׁתְיָא שִׁיכְרָא מַרְקָא. אָמַר רַב יוֹסֵף: הַיְינוּ דִּשְׁמַעְנָא לְאַמֵי דְּאָמַר ״כָּל שֶׁמִּמְּעֵי אִמּוֹ לָקוּי״ וְלָא יָדַעְנָא מַאי נִיהוּ.

Incidentally, the Gemara inquires: **From what** does this defect arise? What is its cause? The Gemara answers: It results from **his mother baking** bread **at noon and drinking strong beer** [*shikhra marka*][L] while pregnant. The excessive heating of the mother's body causes her child to be born with defective reproductive organs. **Rav Yosef said: This is** the meaning of that **which I heard** Rabbi **Ami say: Anyone who is impaired from his mother's womb,**[N] **and** at the time **I did not know what** he was referring to. Now I understand that he was speaking about a man who was infertile from birth.

וְלֵיחוּשׁ שֶׁמָּא הַבְרִיא בֵּינְתַיִם? כֵּיוָן דִּתְחִלָּתוֹ וְסוֹפוֹ לָקוּי – לָא חָיְישִׁינַן.

The Gemara asks: **Let us be concerned that perhaps he was cured** for some period **in the meantime,** without our having known about it, in which case he would have had an hour of fitness at some point. The Gemara answers: **Since** both **his beginning and his end are impaired,** i.e., he was born with a defect and he presently suffers from the same condition, **we are not concerned** about such a possibility.

מְתִיב רַב מָרִי, רַבִּי חֲנִינָא בֶּן אַנְטִיגְנוֹס אוֹמֵר: בּוֹדְקִין אוֹתוֹ שָׁלֹשׁ פְּעָמִים בְּתוֹךְ שְׁמוֹנִים יוֹם!

Rav Mari raised an objection from the following mishna (*Bekhorot* 38b): **Rabbi Ḥanina ben Antigonus says: One examines** a firstborn animal that developed a blemish in its eye **three times within eighty days**[H] to see whether the defect is permanent. This shows that no presumptions are made in such a case; rather, there is concern that the animal may have been cured in the meantime, even if it had the defect at the beginning and at the end of the period.

לְחַד אֲבָר חָיְישִׁינַן, לְכוּלֵּיהּ גּוּפָא לָא חָיְישִׁינַן.

The Gemara answers: **With respect to** a blemish affecting **a single organ,** e.g., an eye, **we are concerned** that the blemish might have passed and then later redeveloped, but **with regard to** a defect affecting **the entire body, we are not concerned** about such a possibility. A eunuch is not impaired in a single organ; rather, he has a defect that affects his entire body. Consequently, there is no concern that, though he was born with the defect and presently suffers from it, he might have regained his potency for some time in the middle.

״רַבִּי אֱלִיעֶזֶר אוֹמֵר לֹא כִּי״ וכו׳. וּרְמִינְהוּ: בֶּן עֶשְׂרִים שָׁנָה וְלֹא הֵבִיא שְׁתֵּי שְׂעָרוֹת – יָבִיאוּ רְאָיָה שֶׁהוּא בֶּן עֶשְׂרִים, וְהוּא הַסָּרִיס, לֹא חוֹלֵץ וְלֹא מְיַיבֵּם. בַּת עֶשְׂרִים וְלֹא הֵבִיאָה שְׁתֵּי שְׂעָרוֹת – יָבִיאוּ רְאָיָה שֶׁהִיא בַּת עֶשְׂרִים, וְהִיא הָאַיְילוֹנִית, לֹא חוֹלֶצֶת וְלֹא מִתְיַיבֶּמֶת, דִּבְרֵי בֵּית הִלֵּל. וּבֵית שַׁמַּאי אוֹמְרִים: זֶה וָזֶה בְּנֵי שְׁמֹנֶה עֶשְׂרֵה.

§ It is taught in the mishna that **Rabbi Eliezer says: No; rather,** a eunuch by natural causes performs *ḥalitza*, whereas a eunuch caused by man does not perform *ḥalitza*. The Gemara **raises a contradiction** from the following mishna (*Nidda* 47b): If a **twenty-year-old** man **has not grown two** pubic **hairs,** a sign of sexual maturity, the relatives of the widow who wish to exempt her from *ḥalitza* and levirate marriage **must bring proof that he is twenty years old, and he,** having been established as **a sexually underdeveloped man, does not perform *ḥalitza***[N] **or levirate marriage** with his *yevama*. If **a twenty-year-old** woman **has not grown two** pubic **hairs,** the relatives of her deceased husband's brother **must bring proof that she is twenty years old, and she,** having been established as **a sexually underdeveloped woman, does not perform *ḥalitza* or enter into levirate marriage** with her *yavam*.[H] This is **the statement of Beit Hillel. And Beit Shammai say:** With regard to both **this and that,** males and females, the relevant age is **eighteen years old,** not twenty.[B]

LANGUAGE

Strong beer [*shikhra marka*] – שִׁיכְרָא מַרְקָא: The early authorities are divided as to whether this term denotes a strong alcoholic beverage, a mixed alcoholic beverage (Rashi), or an alcoholic beverage that is fermenting (*Arukh*). They further discuss the etymology of the word, some asserting that it comes from the Latin meracum, meaning unmixed wine, and others claiming that it is derived from the Hebrew root *m-r-k*, meaning clear or pure.

NOTES

Anyone who is impaired from his mother's womb – כָּל שֶׁמִּמְּעֵי אִמּוֹ לָקוּי: This definition is not entirely precise, as it leaves unanswered a question raised in the Jerusalem Talmud: What about a child who was a eunuch caused by man while still in his mother's womb? It is concluded in the Jerusalem Talmud that the *halakha* is stringent in that case, as both possible stringencies are applied: The stringency of one who is a eunuch caused by man, i.e., that he may not enter into the congregation, and the stringencies of a naturally infertile man, i.e., that he is ineligible for both *ḥalitza* and levirate marriage.

And he, as a sexually underdeveloped man, does not perform *ḥalitza* – וְהוּא הַסָּרִיס לֹא חוֹלֵץ: In the Jerusalem Talmud it is stated that the mishna's distinction between a eunuch caused by man and a eunuch by natural causes is merely the opinion of the Sages mentioned there. However, according to others, both types of eunuchs may neither perform *ḥalitza* nor enter into levirate marriage.

HALAKHA

The examination of a firstborn – בְּדִיקַת בְּכוֹר: One of the blemishes that disqualify a firstborn animal is permanent blindness, which is established after the animal has been observed for eighty days and remained unable to see. The animal must be examined on three occasions: On the twenty-seventh day from when the problem was first detected, on the fifty-fourth day, and on the eightieth day, in accordance with the opinion of Rabbi Ḥanina ben Antigonus (Rambam *Sefer Avoda, Hilkhot Issurei Mizbe'aḥ* 2:12).

A twenty-year-old who has not grown two pubic hairs – בֶּן עֶשְׂרִים וְלֹא הֵבִיא שְׁתֵּי שְׂעָרוֹת: A male or a female who has not grown two pubic hairs is considered a minor. If a male or female reaches the age of twenty and shows signs of sexual underdevelopment, he or she is considered a sexually underdeveloped man or a sexually underdeveloped woman, respectively, even if he or she later grows two hairs. This ruling is in accordance with the opinion of Beit Hillel in the mishna.

The Rema, based on the Rivash, says that nowadays there are no experts in the examination of eunuchs, and therefore even if a male showed signs of sexual underdevelopment, he is considered as one whose status as a eunuch is in doubt (Rambam *Sefer Nashim, Hilkhot Ishut* 2:4; *Shulḥan Arukh, Even HaEzer* 155:12, 172:6).

BACKGROUND

An eighteen year old, a twenty year old – בֶּן שְׁמוֹנָה עֶשְׂרֵה, בֶּן עֶשְׂרִים: The medical phenomenon of late adolescence, both in males and in females, is caused by a low level of secretion of the appropriate sex hormones, which prevents secondary sexual characteristics such as pubic hair from developing at the usual time.

Sometimes this delay is only temporary. In such cases, several years later the level of glandular secretion rises to the normal level, and the boy or girl reaches full maturity. However, if this does not occur before a certain age, which based on modern medical knowledge is nineteen, then by the twentieth year normal sexual development is no longer possible, and a fixed state of eunuchism sets in.

רַבִּי אֱלִיעֶזֶר אוֹמֵר: הַזָּכָר כְּדִבְרֵי בֵּית הִלֵּל, וּנְקֵבָה כְּדִבְרֵי בֵּית שַׁמַּאי, מִפְּנֵי שֶׁהָאִשָּׁה מְמַהֶרֶת לָבֹא לִפְנֵי הָאִישׁ.

The mishna continues: **Rabbi Eliezer says** that for **a male** the *halakha* is **in accordance with the statement of Beit Hillel, and** for **a female** the *halakha* is **in accordance with the statement of Beit Shammai, because a woman reaches** maturity **more quickly than** does **a man,** and therefore, if she fails to develop the signs of maturity by the age of eighteen it is assumed that she is a sexually underdeveloped woman. In any case, it is clear from this mishna that even Rabbi Eliezer agrees that one who lacks sexual capacity from birth may neither perform *ḥalitza* nor enter into levirate marriage.

אָמַר רָמִי בַּר דִּיקוּלֵי אָמַר שְׁמוּאֵל: חָזַר בּוֹ רַבִּי אֱלִיעֶזֶר. אִיבַּעְיָא לְהוּ: מֵהֵי הֲדַר בֵּיהּ? תָּא שְׁמַע, דְּתַנְיָא: רַבִּי אֱלִיעֶזֶר אוֹמֵר: סְרִיס חַמָּה חוֹלֵץ וְחוֹלְצִין לְאִשְׁתּוֹ, שֶׁכֵּן בְּמִינָן מִתְרַפְּאִין בַּאֲלֶכְּסַנְדְּרִיָּא שֶׁל מִצְרַיִם.

Rami bar Dikulei said that **Shmuel said: Rabbi Eliezer retracted his** opinion. **A dilemma was raised before** the Sages: **Which** statement **did he retract?** Did he retract what he said here in the mishna, that a eunuch by natural causes performs *ḥalitza* with his *yevama* and his brothers perform *ḥalitza* with his wife? Alternatively, perhaps the mishna here reflects his final view, after he retracted what he said in the other mishna. The Gemara suggests: **Come** and **hear** a resolution to this question, **as it is taught** in a *baraita* that **Rabbi Eliezer says: A eunuch by natural causes performs *ḥalitza*** with his *yevama* **and** his brothers **perform *ḥalitza* with his wife, as such type** of men **are cured in Alexandria of Egypt.**[B] This additional source and its reasoning suggest that Rabbi Eliezer did not retract what he said in the mishna here. Rather, he retracted his statement with regard to the dispute between Beit Hillel and Beit Shammai in the other mishna.

רַבִּי אֶלְעָזָר אוֹמֵר: לְעוֹלָם לָא הֲדַר בֵּיהּ, וְכִי תְּנַן הַהִיא – לְעוֹנָשִׁין.

Rabbi Elazar says: Actually, he did not retract anything at all. **And when we learned** Rabbi Eliezer's ruling in **that** mishna with regard to the age of a sexually underdeveloped individual, that ruling was stated **with regard to punishments,** i.e., the age at which such an individual is considered an adult so that he is liable to receive punishment, and not with regard to *ḥalitza* or levirate marriage.

אִיתְּמַר: אָכַל חֵלֶב, מִבֶּן שְׁתֵּים עֶשְׂרֵה [וְיוֹם אֶחָד] עַד בֶּן שְׁמוֹנֶה עֶשְׂרֵה, וְנוֹלְדוּ בּוֹ סִימָנֵי סָרִיס, וּלְאַחַר מִכָּאן הֵבִיא שְׁתֵּי שְׂעָרוֹת. רַב אָמַר: נַעֲשָׂה סָרִיס לְמַפְרֵעַ, וּשְׁמוּאֵל אָמַר: קָטָן הָיָה בְּאוֹתָהּ שָׁעָה.

And **it was stated** that the *amora'im* disagreed on this issue: With regard to one who **ate** forbidden **fats** or performed any other transgression for which one is liable to receive lashes or *karet*, when he was **between the age of twelve years**[N] **and one day and the age of eighteen years, and he developed the signs of one who was a eunuch** by natural causes, as explained below, **and afterward he grew two** pubic **hairs, Rav said:** He is **retroactively considered a eunuch** by natural causes.[H] In other words, these hairs are not viewed as a sign of maturity. Rather, he lacked sexual capacity from the outset, which means he became an adult at the standard age of thirteen and is held liable for his actions from that point in time. **And Shmuel said:** No, **he was a minor at the time** he committed his offense, as the two hairs are a sign of his maturity, albeit delayed.

מַתְקִיף לָהּ רַב יוֹסֵף: לְרַב, אַיְלוֹנִית לְרַבִּי מֵאִיר יְהֵא לָהּ קְנָס!

Rav Yosef strongly objects to this: If so, **according to Rav, a sexually underdeveloped woman according to Rabbi Meir should be entitled to the fine** paid by a rapist. Rabbi Meir maintains that a rapist is liable to be fined only if he raped a young woman between the ages of twelve and twelve and a half, but not if he raped a minor. And furthermore, a sexually underdeveloped woman is not entitled to the fine because she is considered a minor, as she never showed the signs of maturity. But according to Rav she should retroactively be viewed as an adult and would therefore be entitled to the fine.

אֲמַר לֵיהּ אַבַּיֵּי: מִקַּטְנוּתָהּ יָצְתָה לְבֶגֶר.

Abaye said to him: A sexually underdeveloped woman **passes** directly **from minority to** full **adulthood.**[N] In other words, she is first considered a minor and then immediately an adult, without passing through the intermediate stage of young womanhood, and an adult woman is not entitled to the rapist's fine.

BACKGROUND

Alexandria of Egypt – אֲלֶכְּסַנְדְּרִיָּא שֶׁל מִצְרַיִם: Since there were other cities named Alexandria, such as the one in Syria, known as Alexandretta, the Sages sometimes referred to the Egyptian city as Alexandria of Egypt.

Alexandria, the capital of Egypt during the Ptolemaic dynasty and under the Romans, was the world's leading cultural and scientific center and remained so for many generations. Alexandria hosted a great medical center in which many experiments were conducted, and its physicians were famous and praised the world over. The Sages of the Talmud were familiar with the doctors of Alexandria and held them in high esteem, often lauding their medical successes.

Location of Alexandria

NOTES

One who ate forbidden fats between the age of twelve years – אָכַל חֵלֶב, מִבֶּן שְׁתֵּים עֶשְׂרֵה: Rashi explains that although this teaching is stated in the masculine, it is in fact referring to females, which is why the decisive age is twelve years and one day, and not thirteen. The Ramban suggests that this is not necessarily the case and that it might be referring to both males and females. This is because there is an opinion that a certain period of time before puberty is also considered part of adulthood. The Rashba and others reject the Ramban's opinion, arguing that despite the slight linguistic difficulty, it is nevertheless preferable to establish Rav's opinion in accordance with the opinion that has been accepted as the *halakha*, and consequently, they accept Rashi's interpretation. Some of the later authorities point out that similar discrepancies, where the Gemara is not particular about gender-based details, are found elsewhere as well.

Passes from minority to adulthood – מִקַּטְנוּתָהּ יָצְתָה לְבֶגֶר: With regard to a minor girl, and to a certain extent in the case of a stubborn and rebellious son as well, there is a period of time between minority, which ends with the appearance of two pubic hairs, and full maturity, marked by an abundance of hair around the sexual organs. This period is called young womanhood or youth. Special *halakhot* apply only to this period, which lasts for roughly six months. However, since the period of young womanhood depends on the signs of maturity, this period never applies to a sexually underdeveloped woman at all.

HALAKHA

He is retroactively considered a eunuch by natural causes – נַעֲשָׂה סָרִיס לְמַפְרֵעַ: The same *halakha* applies to a sexually underdeveloped woman. Therefore, any girl who has not grown two pubic hairs and has not given birth is regarded as a minor and may refuse her husband. However, once she reaches the age of twenty and displays the signs of a sexually underdeveloped woman, she is considered an adult retroactively from the age of twelve years and one day (Rema), as the *halakha* is ruled in accordance with the opinion of Rav, against that of Shmuel, in matters of ritual law (*Shulḥan Arukh, Even HaEzer* 155:12).

אָמַר לֵיהּ: כׇּל כִּי הָנֵי מִילֵּי מַעַלְיָיתָא יִתְאָמְרוּ מִשְּׁמַאי. דְּתַנְיָא: אֵין הַסָּרִיס נִידּוֹן כְּבֵן סוֹרֵר וּמוֹרֶה, לְפִי שֶׁאֵין בֵּן סוֹרֵר וּמוֹרֶה נִידּוֹן אֶלָּא בַּחֲתִימַת זָקָן הַתַּחְתּוֹן; וְאֵין אַיְלוֹנִית נִידּוֹנֶית כְּנַעֲרָה הַמְאוֹרָסָה, שֶׁמִּקְּטַנּוּתָהּ יָצְתָה לְבֶגֶר.

Greatly impressed with this answer, Rav Yosef **said to** Abaye: Would that **all such excellent matters**[N] **be stated in my name. As it is taught** in a *baraita*: **A sexually underdeveloped man is not judged as a stubborn and rebellious son,**[HB] **as a boy is judged as a stubborn and rebellious son only when** he has **the mark of** his **lower beard,** i.e., when his pubic hair begins to grow in. At that point he has reached the age of maturity but is not yet a fully developed man, a stage that parallels young womanhood for women. A sexually underdeveloped man never passes through this intermediate stage between minority and full adulthood. **And** similarly, **a sexually underdeveloped woman** who was betrothed and raped **is not judged** in accordance with the laws governing **a betrothed young woman** (see Deuteronomy 22:23–27), **as she passes** directly **from minority to** full **adulthood** without the intermediate stage of young womanhood.[H] Therefore, the *baraita* fully corroborates Abaye's view.

אָמַר רַבִּי אַבָּהוּ: סִימָנֵי סָרִיס וְאַיְלוֹנִית וּבֶן שְׁמוֹנָה אֵין עוֹשִׂין בָּהֶן מַעֲשֶׂה עַד שֶׁיְּהוּ בְּנֵי עֶשְׂרִים.

Rabbi Abbahu said: If one has **the signs of a sexually underdeveloped man;** or the signs of **a sexually underdeveloped woman;**[H] **or** the signs of a child **born during the eighth** month[N] of pregnancy, whose survival is uncertain; **no action is taken in their regard,** i.e., the sexually underdeveloped male or female is not treated as an adult and the child born during the eighth month is not deemed viable, **until they are twenty** years old.

וּבֶן שְׁמוֹנָה מִי קָחָיֵי? וְהָתַנְיָא: בֶּן שְׁמוֹנָה – הֲרֵי הוּא כְּאֶבֶן, וְאָסוּר לְטַלְטְלוֹ, אֲבָל אִמּוֹ שׁוֹחָה עָלָיו וּמְנִיקָתוֹ

The Gemara asks: **Can a** child **born during the eighth** month[H] of pregnancy **survive? But isn't it taught in a** *baraita*: A child **born during the eighth** month **is like a stone** with regard to the *halakhot* of set-aside [*muktze*] on Shabbat, and therefore **it is prohibited to move him** on Shabbat, as it may be presumed that he is not viable at all. **However, his mother may bend over him and nurse him,**

HALAKHA

A stubborn and rebellious son – בֵּן סוֹרֵר וּמוֹרֶה: A boy can be judged as a stubborn and rebellious son only if he transgresses after he has reached the age of thirteen years and a day and has grown two pubic hairs, but before his member is entirely surrounded with hair. Before that he is a minor, and afterward he is an adult and therefore can no longer be judged as a stubborn and rebellious son (Rambam *Sefer Shofetim, Hilkhot Mamrim* 7:5).

A sexually underdeveloped woman passes into adulthood – אַיְלוֹנִית יָצְתָה לְבֶגֶר: A sexually underdeveloped woman does not go through the stage of young womanhood. Rather, she is considered an adult as soon as she is no longer a minor (Rambam *Sefer Nashim, Hilkhot Ishut* 2:5).

The signs of a sexually underdeveloped man or a sexually underdeveloped woman – סִימָנֵי סָרִיס וְאַיְלוֹנִית: If a young woman reaches the age of twelve years and one day without growing two pubic hairs, even if she shows the signs of a sexually underdeveloped woman, she is considered a minor until she turns twenty. The same applies to a thirteen-year-old boy who has not grown two pubic hairs and demonstrates the signs of a sexually underdeveloped man. The *halakha* is in accordance with the opinion of Rabbi Abbahu (Rambam *Sefer Nashim, Hilkhot Ishut* 2:3, 11; *Shulḥan Arukh, Even HaEzer* 155:12; 172:6).

Born during the eighth month – בֶּן שְׁמוֹנָה: If a baby was born during the eighth month, or if a doubt exists as to whether he was born during the seventh or during the eighth month, and his hair and nails are not fully developed, he may not be moved on Shabbat. However, his mother may bend over him and nurse him if she suffers due to her milk.

Some later authorities (*Mishna Berura*), based on *Tosafot* on *Shabbat* 135a, maintain that nowadays no one has sufficient expertise with regard to the matter, and therefore all babies may be moved, as they are all considered as possibly having been born during the ninth month (Rambam *Sefer Zemanim, Hilkhot Sabbath* 25:6; *Shulḥan Arukh, Oraḥ Ḥayyim* 330:8).

NOTES

All such excellent matters – כׇּל כִּי הָנֵי מִילֵּי מַעַלְיָיתָא: The standard version of the text appears incomplete. According to the Ritva's version, Abaye said to Rav Yosef: They say in your name that a sexually underdeveloped woman passes directly from minority to full adulthood. This version is convincing, as it is well known that Rav Yosef became ill and forgot much of his learning, and his disciple Abaye had to remind him of matters, including teachings that Rav Yosef himself had taught. Rav Yosef's reply also fits in well with this version.

The signs of a…child born during the eighth month – סִימָנֵי...בֶּן שְׁמוֹנָה: There are many explanations with regard to Rabbi Abbahu's statement about a baby born during the eighth month. According to Rashi, this *halakha* is similar to the previous two: He is not removed from the category of a possible stillborn until the age of twenty. However, other early authorities are puzzled by the logic of such a *halakha*. If this child, who was suspected of not being viable, grows up and reaches adulthood, it is clear that he is not stillborn. Why, then, should uncertainty remain for so many years (see Ramban and Rashba)? Rabbeinu Ḥananel and the *ge'onim*, as well as the Ra'avad, understand that owing to the child's unusual weakness, even if he grows two hairs at the proper time, he is not considered an adult until he reaches the age of twenty.

The Ramban cites an opinion that Rabbi Abbahu's statement with regard to a baby born during the eighth month is totally unrelated to the teachings concerning sexually underdeveloped people. He merely means to say that also in the case of a child born during the eighth month, no immediate action is taken. Rather, one waits until the matter is clarified, in accordance with either the requirements of Rabban Shimon ben Gamliel or those of Rabbi Yehuda HaNasi. The Ramban himself accepts the following explanation: If a boy born during the eighth month fails to grow two hairs at the age of thirteen, even if he shows signs of sexual incapacity he is not treated as a eunuch until he is twenty, as he might be a late developer due to his weak constitution. He adduces support for his opinion from the Jerusalem Talmud (see Razah and *Keren Ora*).

BACKGROUND

A stubborn and rebellious son – בֵּן סוֹרֵר וּמוֹרֶה: The Torah (Deuteronomy 21:18–21) and the Mishna (*Sanhedrin,* chapter 8) describe the punishment administered to a son between the ages of thirteen and thirteen and three months who steals money from his parents to eat a gluttonous meal of meat and wine in the company of worthless men. If his parents bring him to court for this act, he is exhorted to desist and is punished with lashes. If he repeats the same misdeed and is again brought to court by his parents within this same three-month period, he is liable to receive the death penalty. Nevertheless, the halakhic limitations surrounding such a case are so severe that some of the Sages said that the execution of a stubborn and rebellious son never actually took place.

מִפְּנֵי הַסַּכָּנָה. הָכָא בְּמַאי עָסְקִינַן – כְּשֶׁגָּמְרוּ סִימָנָיו. דְּתַנְיָא: אֵיזֶהוּ בֶּן שְׁמוֹנָה – כָּל שֶׁלֹּא כָּלוּ לוֹ חֳדָשָׁיו. רַבִּי אוֹמֵר: סִימָנִין מוֹכִיחִין עָלָיו: שְׂעָרוֹ וְצִפָּרְנָיו שֶׁלֹּא גָּמְרוּ. טַעֲמָא – דְּלָא גָּמְרוּ, הָא גָּמְרוּ – אָמְרִינַן: הַאי בַּר שִׁבְעָה הוּא, וְאִישְׁתַּהוּיֵי הוּא דְּאִישְׁתַּהֵי,

due to the danger,[N] both to the baby, who might in fact be viable, as well as to the mother, who might suffer fatal complications if she has to retain all her milk. The Gemara answers: **With what are we dealing here?** We are dealing with a case **where his signs** of viability **are fully developed,** and he has the appearance of a viable child. **As it is taught** in a *baraita*: **Who is a baby born during the eighth** month? It is **anyone whose months** of gestation **have not been completed,** i.e., a baby that was born prematurely. **Rabbi** Yehuda HaNasi **says:** The **signs** that **prove**[HB] that the child falls into this category are that **his hair and nails are not** fully **developed. Now, the reason is that they are not** fully **developed; but** if his hair and nails **are** fully **developed, we say** that **this** fetus was fit to be **born after seven** months **but** for some reason **was delayed** in its mother's womb.

אֶלָּא הָא דַּעֲבַד רָבָא תּוֹסְפָאָה עוּבְדָא בְּאִשָּׁה שֶׁהָלַךְ בַּעֲלָהּ לִמְדִינַת הַיָּם, וְאִישְׁתַּהֵי עַד תְּרֵיסַר יַרְחֵי שַׁתָּא, וְאַכְשְׁרֵיהּ, כְּמַאן – כְּרַבִּי דַּאֲמַר מִשְׁתַּהֵא.

But if so, with regard to **the action taken by Rava Tosfa'a concerning a woman whose husband went overseas**[H] **and** her baby was **delayed** in her womb **for the twelve months of the year**[B] following her husband's departure, **and** Rava Tosfa'a **rendered** the child **fit,** arguing that the husband is presumed to be the father and the child is not a *mamzer*, **according to whose** opinion did he issue this ruling? It must have been **in accordance with** the opinion of **Rabbi** Yehuda HaNasi, **who says** that a baby **can be delayed** for an extended period of time in its mother's womb even after it is fully developed and ready to be born. But how could Rava Tosfa'a have ruled in accordance with the minority opinion of Rabbi Yehuda HaNasi, against the majority opinion of his colleagues?

כֵּיוָן דְּאִיכָּא רַבָּן שִׁמְעוֹן בֶּן גַּמְלִיאֵל, דַּאֲמַר מִשְׁתַּהֵי – כְּרַבִּים עֲבַד. דְּתַנְיָא, רַבָּן שִׁמְעוֹן בֶּן גַּמְלִיאֵל אוֹמֵר: כָּל שֶׁשָּׁהָה שְׁלֹשִׁים יוֹם בְּאָדָם אֵינוֹ נֵפֶל.

The Gemara answers: **Since there is** also **Rabban Shimon ben Gamliel,**[N] **who says** that a baby **can be delayed** in its mother's womb, Rava Tosfa'a in fact **acted in accordance with the majority,** as Rabbi Yehuda HaNasi's opinion is not that of a lone dissenting scholar. **As it is taught** in a *baraita* that **Rabban Shimon ben Gamliel says: Any human** child **who stays** alive **for thirty days**[H] **is not a stillborn.** Even if the child was not carried for a full nine months, once he has survived for thirty days he is no longer treated like an infant whose viability is in doubt. The reason is that he is presumed to be a child that was fit to be born after seven months but for some reason was delayed in its mother's womb and not born immediately upon reaching full development.

HALAKHA

The signs prove – סִימָנִין מוֹכִיחִין עָלָיו: A boy born during his mother's eighth month of pregnancy may not be circumcised on Shabbat unless his hair and nails are fully developed, in accordance with the opinion of Rabbi Yehuda HaNasi and Rabban Shimon ben Gamliel, and following the opinion of Rava Tosfa'a (Rambam *Sefer Ahava, Hilkhot Mila* 1:13; *Shulḥan Arukh, Yoreh De'a* 266:11).

A woman whose husband went overseas – אִשָּׁה שֶׁהָלַךְ בַּעֲלָהּ לִמְדִינַת הַיָּם: If a woman whose husband is overseas gives birth a full twelve months after his departure, the child is a *mamzer*. The *Halakhot Gedolot* maintains that he is not a definite *mamzer*, as the husband might have returned secretly (*Be'er HaGola*; see *Perisha* and *Taz*). A child born within twelve months of the husband's departure is considered fit, in accordance with the opinion of Rava Tosfa'a (Rambam *Sefer Kedusha*, *Hilkhot Issurei Bia* 15:19; *Shulḥan Arukh, Even HaEzer* 4:14).

Any…child who stays alive for thirty days – כָּל שֶׁשָּׁהָה שְׁלֹשִׁים יוֹם: If a man died, leaving a pregnant wife, and she bore a live child, she is exempt from levirate marriage. By rabbinic law the baby does not exempt the mother unless it is known that the baby was carried to full term. If there is no proof in this regard, a child that survives thirty days exempts his mother and her rival wives from *ḥalitza* and levirate marriage, even if he dies afterward (*Shulḥan Arukh, Even HaEzer* 156:4).

BACKGROUND

The signs prove – סִימָנִין מוֹכִיחִין עָלָיו: Fetal development is not uniform. Some fetuses develop so quickly that in the seventh month they already have fully developed bodies. Similarly, there are fetuses that develop more slowly. One measure of development is the growth of fingernails past the fingertips. Another measure is the growth of hair such as eyelashes and eyebrows.

Delayed for the twelve months of the year – אִישְׁתַּהֵי עַד תְּרֵיסַר יַרְחֵי שַׁתָּא: In general it is very difficult to determine the precise length of a pregnancy, both due to the uncertainty as to when it began and because for various reasons one cannot rely on the testimony of the woman involved. Nevertheless, it is clear that many women, approximately 10 percent of all childbearing women, give birth significantly later than after the usual nine months. Though rare, doctors allow for the possibility of a pregnancy continuing for forty-eight weeks, i.e., around eleven months, and there are extremely rare cases of pregnancies lasting even longer than this.

Though the courts in certain countries have officially recognized pregnancies as having continued for even longer than eleven months, their rulings are not based on reliable scientific evidence.

NOTES

Due to the danger – מִפְּנֵי הַסַּכָּנָה: According to Rashi, this refers both to the danger posed to the mother due to excess milk, as well as the danger to the baby. Some early authorities (Meiri; Rabbi Avraham min HaHar) maintain that the Gemara is speaking only of the danger to the mother, as Rashi himself explains in tractate *Shabbat*, since if the child was thought to be potentially viable it would be treated as an invalid, not as a stone.

Rabbi Yehuda HaNasi and Rabban Shimon ben Gamliel – רַבִּי וְרַבָּן שִׁמְעוֹן בֶּן גַּמְלִיאֵל: The early authorities (see *Tosafot*) discuss Rabban Shimon ben Gamliel's opinion and compare it to that of Rabbi Yehuda HaNasi, as well as to the opinion of the Rabbis who disagree with them both. Most early authorities distinguish between the opinions of Rabbi Yehuda HaNasi and Rabban Shimon ben Gamliel. According to Rabbi Yehuda HaNasi, the physical signs are the decisive factor; a child that lacks these signs is not removed from the category of a possible stillborn for an extended period of time, which according to some is twenty years. According to Rabban Shimon ben Gamliel, on the other hand, even if the child's hair and nails are incompletely formed, once he has survived for thirty days he is no longer classified as stillborn. See the comments of *Tosafot*, the Ramban, and the Rashba with regard to the relationship between this issue and the *halakha* that is in accordance with Rabbi Abbahu. According to a different approach, even Rabban Shimon ben Gamliel agrees that a baby who does not show the proper physical signs is not considered fully viable. Therefore, in a case where he was definitely born in the eighth month and did not develop these signs, if he survives thirty days he is no longer treated as a possible stillborn, but he is not seen as viable in all regards until he reaches the age of twenty. According to this approach there is no contradiction between ruling in accordance with the opinion of Rabban Shimon ben Gamliel and ruling in accordance with the opinion of Rabbi Abbahu (*Tosefot Ḥad MiKamma'ei*; Meiri).

תָּנוּ רַבָּנַן: אֵיזֶהוּ סְרִיס חַמָּה – כָּל שֶׁהוּא בֶּן עֶשְׂרִים וְלֹא הֵבִיא שְׁתֵּי שְׂעָרוֹת, וַאֲפִילּוּ הֵבִיא לְאַחַר מִכָּאן הֲרֵי הוּא כְּסָרִיס לְכָל דְּבָרָיו. וְאֵלּוּ הֵן סִימָנָיו: כָּל שֶׁאֵין לוֹ זָקָן, וּשְׂעָרוֹ לָקוּי, וּבְשָׂרוֹ מַחֲלִיק. רַבָּן שִׁמְעוֹן בֶּן גַּמְלִיאֵל אוֹמֵר מִשּׁוּם רַבִּי יְהוּדָה בֶּן יָאִיר: כָּל שֶׁאֵין מֵימָיו מַעֲלִין רְתִיחוֹת.

§ **The Sages taught: Who is considered a eunuch by natural causes?**[B] It is **anyone who is twenty years old and has not** yet **grown two** pubic **hairs.**[H] **And even if he grows** pubic hairs **afterward, he is** still considered **a eunuch** by natural causes with regard to **all his matters. And his signs are as follows: Whoever does not have a beard, and his hair is defective,** unlike that of ordinary individuals, **and his skin is smooth,** i.e., hairless. **Rabban Shimon ben Gamliel says in the name of Rabbi Yehuda ben Ya'ir:** It is **anyone whose urine does not raise foam.**

וְיֵשׁ אוֹמְרִים: כָּל הַמַּטִּיל מַיִם וְאֵין עוֹשֶׂה כִּיפָּה. וְיֵשׁ אוֹמְרִים: כָּל שֶׁשִּׁכְבַת זַרְעוֹ דּוֹחָה. וְיֵשׁ אוֹמְרִים: כָּל שֶׁאֵין מֵימֵי רַגְלָיו מַחְמִיצִין. אֲחֵרִים אוֹמְרִים: כָּל שֶׁרוֹחֵץ בִּימוֹת הַגְּשָׁמִים וְאֵין בְּשָׂרוֹ מַעֲלֶה הֶבֶל. רַבִּי שִׁמְעוֹן בֶּן אֶלְעָזָר אוֹמֵר: כָּל שֶׁקּוֹלוֹ לָקוּי, וְאֵין נִיכָּר בֵּין אִישׁ לְאִשָּׁה.

And some say: It is **anyone who urinates without forming an arch. And some say:** It is **anyone whose semen dissipates**[N] and fails to congeal in the proper manner. **And some say: Anyone whose urine does not ferment. Others say:** It is **anyone who bathes in the rainy season and his flesh does not give off steam. Rabbi Shimon ben Elazar says:** It is **anyone whose voice is defective, so that it is not evident** from it **whether** he **is a man or a woman.**[H]

וְאֵיזוֹ הִיא אַיְלוֹנִית? כָּל שֶׁהִיא בַּת עֶשְׂרִים וְלֹא הֵבִיאָה שְׁתֵּי שְׂעָרוֹת. וַאֲפִילּוּ הֵבִיאָה לְאַחַר מִכָּאן – הֲרֵי הִיא כְּאַיְלוֹנִית לְכָל דְּבָרֶיהָ. וְאֵלּוּ הֵן סִימָנֶיהָ: כָּל שֶׁאֵין לָהּ דַּדִּים, וּמִתְקַשָּׁה בִּשְׁעַת תַּשְׁמִישׁ. רַבָּן שִׁמְעוֹן בֶּן גַּמְלִיאֵל אוֹמֵר: כָּל שֶׁאֵין לָהּ שִׁיפּוּלֵי מֵעַיִם כְּנָשִׁים. רַבִּי שִׁמְעוֹן בֶּן אֶלְעָזָר אוֹמֵר: כָּל שֶׁקּוֹלָהּ עָבֶה, וְאֵינָהּ נִיכֶּרֶת בֵּין אִשָּׁה לְאִישׁ.

And who is a sexually underdeveloped woman [*aylonit*]**?**[B] It **is anyone who is twenty years old and has not** yet **grown two** pubic **hairs.**[H] **And even if she grows** pubic hairs **afterward, she is** still considered **a sexually underdeveloped woman** with regard to **all her matters. And her signs are as follows:** A sexually underdeveloped woman is **anyone who does not have breasts and experiences pain during intercourse. Rabban Shimon ben Gamliel says:** It is **anyone whose lower abdomen is not** formed **like** that of other **women,** as she lacks the cushion of flesh that is usually situated above a woman's genitals. **Rabbi Shimon ben Elazar says: It is anyone whose voice is deep, so that it is not evident** from it **whether** she **is a woman or a man.**[H]

אִיתְּמַר, סִימָנֵי סָרִיס, רַב הוּנָא אָמַר: עַד שֶׁיְּהוּ כּוּלָּם. רַבִּי יוֹחָנָן אָמַר: אֲפִילּוּ בְּאֶחָד מֵהֶן. הֵיכָא דְּהֵבִיא שְׁתֵּי שְׂעָרוֹת בַּזָּקָן – כּוּלֵּי עָלְמָא לָא פְּלִיגִי דְּעַד שֶׁיְּהוּ כּוּלָּן, כִּי פְּלִיגִי – בְּשֶׁלֹּא הֵבִיא.

It was stated that *amora'im* disagreed over the **signs of a eunuch. Rav Huna said** that one is not categorized as a eunuch **unless all** these signs **are present;**[HN] **Rabbi Yoḥanan said:** He is categorized as such **even** if only **one of them** is present. The Gemara comments: In a case **when he has grown two hairs in** his **beard, everyone agrees that** he is not considered sexually impotent **unless all** the signs **are present. When they disagree,** it is with regard to a case **when he has not grown** two hairs.

HALAKHA

A eunuch by natural causes – סְרִיס חַמָּה: A boy who has reached the age of thirteen and has not grown two pubic hairs is considered a minor until he is twenty, even if he shows the signs of a eunuch from birth. According to the Rambam the relevant age is twenty years less thirty days, while Ra'avad maintains that it is nineteen and thirty days (Rambam *Sefer Nashim, Hilkhot Ishut* 2:11).

The signs of a eunuch by natural causes – סִימָנֵי סְרִיס חַמָּה: The signs of a eunuch by natural causes are as follows: The first sign is that he lacks a beard; this is understood in several ways. The other signs of a eunuch are: His hair is defective and unlike that of others; his skin is smooth; he urinates without forming an arch; his semen dissipates; his urine does not ferment; when he bathes in the winter his skin does not give off steam; and his voice is defective, so that it is unclear whether he is a man or a woman. The Vilna Gaon, based on the Rambam and the *Tur*, adds that his urine does not raise foam (Rambam *Sefer Nashim, Hilkhot Ishut* 2:13; *Shulḥan Arukh, Even HaEzer* 172:5).

And has not yet grown two pubic hairs – וְלֹא הֵבִיאָה שְׁתֵּי שְׂעָרוֹת: A girl who has not grown two pubic hairs at the proper time remains a minor until her twentieth year, even if she already demonstrates the signs of a sexually underdeveloped woman. If she reaches the age of twenty and shows signs of sexual underdevelopment, she is from that time on regarded as an adult (Rambam *Sefer Nashim, Hilkhot Ishut* 2:4; *Shulḥan Arukh, Even HaEzer* 155:12; 172:6).

The signs of a sexually underdeveloped woman – סִימָנֵי אַיְילוֹנִית: The signs of a sexually underdeveloped woman are as follows: She lacks breasts; she experiences pain during intercourse; her lower abdomen is not formed like that of other women; she has a deep voice, so that it is unclear whether she is a man or a woman. It appears that all these signs are required (*Kesef Mishne*). Some (Rema, based on *Tur*) rule that one of these signs is sufficient for her to be deemed a sexually underdeveloped woman (Rambam *Sefer Nashim, Hilkhot Ishut* 2:6; *Shulḥan Arukh, Even HaEzer* 172:4).

Unless all these signs are present – עַד שֶׁיְּהוּ כּוּלָּם: One who has grown two hairs in his beard is not considered lacking in sexual capacity unless he displays all the other signs of this. However, if he lacks two hairs, he is regarded as a eunuch, even if only one other sign is present, in accordance with the opinion of Rabbi Yoḥanan. Some (*Beit Shmuel*, based on *Tosafot* and Ra'avad) claim that the absence of two hairs is a definitive sign of sexual impotence, even if none of the other signs are present (*Shulḥan Arukh, Even HaEzer* 172:5, and in the comment of Rema).

BACKGROUND

The signs of a eunuch by natural causes [*seris ḥamma*] – סִימָנֵי סְרִיס חַמָּה: The term *seris ḥamma* seems to describe different kinds of defects. Consequently, the signs of a eunuch mentioned here might not necessarily all be present in one individual, as they might be associated with different kinds of defects. In one kind of eunuchism, hypogonadotropic hypogonadism, the hormones that cause production of testosterone and sperm are low. In such cases the physique and the voice may be feminized, and there is also a decreased amount of pubic and facial hair. There are various possible causes for this phenomenon, most of which are genetic. Another cause of eunuchism is hypergonadotrophic hypogonadism, where the testicles are unable to respond to the hormones sent to them and thus do not produce adequate amounts of testosterone and sperm. The most common condition causing this is Klinefelter syndrome, characterized by the presence of an extra female chromosome and resulting in a genetic makeup of XXY. In addition to the outward signs, eunuchism may be accompanied by various health problems, including obesity, excess fat in the blood, and diabetes, among others. Apparently the accompanying signs mentioned here, such as those involving urination (see 80a), are linked to these illnesses.

A sexually underdeveloped woman [*aylonit*] – אַיילוֹנִית: From the description provided here, it seems that *aylonit* is a general term for a woman with a basic defect in her reproductive system. From a medical standpoint there are several conditions that would fall into this category. Some of the descriptions of a sexually underdeveloped woman found here are typical of an enzymatic birth defect, which ultimately may cause several hormonal issues. One of these is an oversecretion of male hormones. This causes various changes in the woman's external sex organs and a general resemblance to a male, which the Gemara describes as follows: It is not evident whether she is a woman or a man. On the other hand, a sexually underdeveloped woman can also be a woman who suffers from Turner syndrome, due to a missing X chromosome. These woman have non-functioning ovaries and no menstrual cycle, and often possess high waist-to-hip ratios. They may also have a short stature, low hairline, low-set ears, and webbed necks, as well as cognitive defects.

NOTES

Whose semen dissipates [*doḥa*] – שֶׁשִּׁכְבַת זַרְעוֹ דּוֹחָה: Some commentaries read *diha*, meaning that the color of his semen differs from that of other men.

Unless all these signs are present – עַד שֶׁיְּהוּ כּוּלָּם: According to the opinion that all these signs must be present, the various Sages do not disagree with each other; rather, they are adding to one another's observations. In other words, they are all describing the same physical state, each one stressing a particular detail that he feels is important and easy to determine. With regard to a sexually underdeveloped woman, some commentaries maintain that since there is no disagreement on the matter, one sign is enough (*Yam shel Shlomo*), while other argue the opposite: Since there is no single prominent sign, she must show all the listed signs in order to be considered sexually underdeveloped (see HALAKHA).

אֶלָּא הָא דַּאֲמַר לְהוּ רַבָּה בַּר אֲבוּהּ לְרַבָּנַן: עַיְּינוּ בֵּיהּ בְּרַב נַחְמָן, אִי בְּשָׂרוֹ מַעֲלֶה הֶבֶל – אֵיתִיב לֵיהּ בְּרַת – כְּמַאן, כְּרַב הוּנָא?! לָא, רַב נַחְמָן סִיכֵּי דִּיקְנָא הֲוָיא לֵיהּ.

The Gemara asks: **But** if so, with regard to **that which Rabba bar Avuh said to the Sages: Examine Rav Naḥman** when he bathes and **if his flesh gives off steam I will give him** my **daughter** for a wife, **in accordance with whose** opinion did he issue these instructions? Is it not **in accordance with** the opinion of **Rav Huna,** who maintains that all the signs must be present, as presumably he could see that Rav Naḥman did not have a beard? The Gemara answers: **No, Rav Naḥman had wisps of a beard,** and therefore Rabba bar Avuh wanted to know whether he displayed the other signs of sexual incapacity.

״הַסָּרִיס לֹא חוֹלֵץ וְלֹא מְיַיבֵּם וְכֵן אַיְלוֹנִית״ וכו׳, קָתָנֵי סָרִיס דּוּמְיָא דְּאַיְלוֹנִית, מָה אַיְלוֹנִית בִּידֵי שָׁמַיִם – אַף סָרִיס בִּידֵי שָׁמַיִם, וּסְתָמָא כְּרַבִּי עֲקִיבָא, דְּאָמַר: בִּידֵי אָדָם – אִין, בִּידֵי שָׁמַיִם – לָא.

§ It is taught in the mishna that **a sexually underdeveloped man does not perform *ḥalitza* or enter into levirate marriage** with his *yevama*, **and similarly, a sexually underdeveloped woman** does not perform *ḥalitza* or enter into levirate marriage with her *yavam*. The Gemara comments that the *tanna* **teaches** the case of **a sexually underdeveloped man similarly to** that of **a sexually underdeveloped woman,** from which it can be inferred: **Just as** in the case of a **sexually underdeveloped woman,** her disability is **by the hand of Heaven, so too,** in the case of **a sexually underdeveloped man,** his disability must be **by the hand of Heaven. And** this **unattributed** view in the mishna is **in accordance with** the opinion of **Rabbi Akiva, who said:** With regard to one whose incapacity was brought about **by the hands of man, yes,** he is considered like any other man and performs *ḥalitza*, whereas one who suffers his condition **by the hand of Heaven** does **not** do so.

״הַסָּרִיס שֶׁחָלַץ לִיבִמְתּוֹ לֹא פְּסָלָהּ״ כו׳. טַעְמָא דִּבְעָלָהּ הוּא, הָא אַחֵר – לָא.

§ It is further taught in the mishna that if **a eunuch performed *ḥalitza* with his *yevama*, he has not** thereby **disqualified her** from marrying into the priesthood, but if he had intercourse with her, he has disqualified her. The Gemara infers from this wording that **the reason** for her disqualification **is that he,** the *yavam*, **had intercourse with her,** as she had intercourse with her *yavam* outside the framework of permitted levirate marriage. **But** if **a different** individual had relations with her she would **not** be disqualified.

Perek **VIII**
Daf **81** Amud **a**

לֵימָא תֶּיהֱוֵי תְּיוּבְתָּא דְּרַב הַמְנוּנָא, דְּאָמַר: שׁוֹמֶרֶת יָבָם שֶׁזִּינְּתָה פְּסוּלָה לִיבָמָהּ! לָא, הוּא הַדִּין אֲפִילּוּ לְאַחֵר נַמִי, וְאַיְּידֵי דְּתָנָא רֵישָׁא בְּדִידֵיהּ תָּנָא נַמִי סֵיפָא בְּדִידֵיהּ.

Shall we say that this **is a conclusive refutation**[N] of the opinion of **Rav Hamnuna, who said: A widow waiting for her *yavam*, who engaged in an act of licentious relations,**[H] **is disqualified from** entering into levirate marriage with **her *yavam*,** like an ordinary married woman who committed adultery? The Gemara rejects this argument: **No,** this presents no difficulty for Rav Hamnuna, as it is possible that **the same is true even** in a case where she had relations **with a different** man, that she **too** would be disqualified from marrying into the priesthood. **But since** the *tanna* **taught the first clause with regard to** the *yavam* **himself, he also taught the latter clause with regard to** the *yavam* **himself,** even though the same *halakha* applies if she cohabitated with another.

HALAKHA

A widow waiting for her *yavam* who engaged in an act of licentious relations – שׁוֹמֶרֶת יָבָם שֶׁזִּינְּתָה: If a woman waiting for her *yavam* to enter into levirate marriage with her had intercourse with another man, she is not forbidden to her *yavam* if he is an ordinary Israelite, against the opinion of Rav Hamnuna. According to the Rema, she is prohibited to the other man in any event, as a penalty (*Shulḥan Arukh, Even HaEzer* 159:3).

NOTES

Shall we say that this is a conclusive refutation – לֵימָא תֶּיהֱוֵי תְּיוּבְתָּא: The phrase shall we say generally indicates that the proposed suggestion or difficulty will ultimately be dismissed by the Gemara. In this case, however, the *halakha* is not ruled in accordance with Rav Hamnuna's opinion, and it is therefore unclear why the Gemara goes to such lengths to explain the mishna in accordance with his opinion. While it is true that the Gemara occasionally defends an entirely rejected view, it is uncommon. The Ritva asserts that there is a reason for this inquiry, as the ruling of the mishna is in accordance with the opinion of Rabbi Akiva, and Rav Hamnuna's opinion must be accepted in order to reach Rabbi Akiva's conclusion. This is because it may be argued that a woman awaiting levirate marriage who married or had relations with another man before *ḥalitza* has transgressed a prohibition. According to Rabbi Akiva, who equates those who have transgressed standard negative prohibitions with those liable to receive *karet* with regard to the validity of their marriage, she is considered a harlot even in that case. However, ultimately, the *halakha* is not ruled in accordance with the opinion of Rabbi Akiva. Therefore, a woman awaiting levirate marriage is not considered like a married or a betrothed woman, and having relations with another man does not disqualify her from marrying her *yavam*.

"וְכֵן אַיְילוֹנִית שֶׁחָלְצוּ לָהּ אַחִין" כו׳, טַעֲמָא דִּבְעָלוּהָ, הָא לָא בְּעָלוּהָ לָא, כְּמַאן – דְּלָא כְּרַבִּי יְהוּדָה, דְּאִי רַבִּי יְהוּדָה – הָאָמַר: אַיְילוֹנִית זוֹנָה הִיא.

It is taught in the mishna: **And similarly,** with regard to **a sexually underdeveloped woman,** if one of **the brothers performed *ḥalitza* with her** he has not disqualified her, but if he engaged in intercourse with her he has disqualified her. The Gemara infers from this wording that **the reason** for her disqualification **is that he had intercourse with her; but if he did not have intercourse with her** she is **not** disqualified. **According to whose** opinion was this clause of the mishna taught? One must say that it was **not** taught **in accordance with** the opinion of **Rabbi Yehuda. As, if** one would claim that this teaching is in accordance with the opinion of **Rabbi Yehuda, didn't he say** that **a sexually underdeveloped woman is** considered like **a woman who has had sexual relations with a man forbidden to her by the Torah** [***zona***], and so she is in any case disqualified from marrying into the priesthood?[H]

מתני׳ סְרִיס חַמָּה כֹּהֵן שֶׁנָּשָׂא בַּת יִשְׂרָאֵל מַאֲכִילָהּ בִּתְרוּמָה. רַבִּי יוֹסֵי וְרַבִּי שִׁמְעוֹן אוֹמְרִים: אַנְדְּרוֹגִינוֹס כֹּהֵן שֶׁנָּשָׂא בַּת יִשְׂרָאֵל מַאֲכִילָהּ בִּתְרוּמָה.

MISHNA If **a priest who is a eunuch by natural causes married an Israelite woman,** he **enables her to eat**[H] ***teruma*. Rabbi Yosei and Rabbi Shimon say:** If **a priest who is a hermaphrodite,** possessing both male and female genitals, **married an Israelite woman,** he **enables her to eat *teruma*.**

רַבִּי יְהוּדָה אוֹמֵר: טוּמְטוּם שֶׁנִּקְרַע וְנִמְצָא זָכָר לֹא יַחֲלוֹץ, מִפְּנֵי שֶׁהוּא כִּסְרִיס. אַנְדְּרוֹגִינוֹס נוֹשֵׂא, אֲבָל לֹא נִישָּׂא. רַבִּי אֱלִיעֶזֶר אוֹמֵר: אַנְדְּרוֹגִינוֹס חַיָּיבִין עָלָיו סְקִילָה כְּזָכָר.

Rabbi Yehuda says: If **a *tumtum*,** whose external sexual organs are indeterminate, **was torn** open so that his genitals were exposed, **and he was found** to be **a male,** he **must not perform *ḥalitza*,**[H] **because he is** treated **like a eunuch. A hermaphrodite may marry** a woman **but he may not be married**[H] by a man, as he is considered a man. **Rabbi Eliezer says:** If one had intercourse with **a hermaphrodite, he is liable to** receive the punishment of **stoning on his account as if** he had had relations with **a male.**

גמ׳ פְּשִׁיטָא! מַהוּ דְּתֵימָא: מוֹלִיד – מַאֲכִיל, שֶׁאֵינוֹ מוֹלִיד – אֵינוֹ מַאֲכִיל, קָא מַשְׁמַע לָן.

GEMARA The Gemara questions the mishna's teaching concerning a priest who was sexually impotent from birth: This **is obvious;** why should such a priest not enable his wife to partake of *teruma*? The Gemara answers: This *halakha* is necessary **lest you say** that since the verse states: "And such as are born in his house, they eat of his bread" (Leviticus 22:11), the allowance to eat *teruma* depends on the priest's capacity to father children, i.e., that only **one who can father** children **enables** his wife **to eat**[N] *teruma*, but **one who cannot father** children **does not enable** his wife **to eat** *teruma*. Therefore, the *tanna* **teaches us** that the priest's capacity to have children is irrelevant.

HALAKHA

A sexually underdeveloped woman marrying a priest – **אַיְילוֹנִית לְכֹהֵן:** It is permitted for a sexually underdeveloped woman to marry a priest, as she is not forbidden to him as a harlot. This ruling is in accordance with the opinion of the Rabbis who disagree with Rabbi Yehuda (Rambam *Sefer Kedusha, Hilkhot Issurei Bia* 18:3).

A eunuch by natural causes…enables her to eat – **סְרִיס חַמָּה מַאֲכִיל:** If a priest who was sexually incapacitated from birth married an Israelite woman, he enables her to eat *teruma* (Rambam *Sefer Zera'im, Hilkhot Terumot* 7:14).

A *tumtum* with regard to *ḥalitza* and levirate marriage – **טוּמְטוּם בַּחֲלִיצָה וְיִבּוּם:** A *tumtum* may perform *ḥalitza* but not levirate marriage, as his status as a man is in doubt. If he was torn open so that his genitals were exposed, and he was found to be a male, he may either perform *ḥalitza* or enter into levirate marriage, as the Gemara later (83b) indicates that the Rabbis disagree with Rabbi Yehuda, and the *halakha* is in accordance with their opinion. Others (*Be'er HaGola*) maintain that he, too, is considered of doubtful status, and the ruling is stringent, as nowhere is it stated explicitly that the Rabbis disagree with Rabbi Yehuda (*Shulḥan Arukh, Even HaEzer* 172:9).

A hermaphrodite may marry, but he may not be married – **אַנְדְּרוֹגִינוֹס נוֹשֵׂא אֲבָל לֹא נִישָּׂא:** It is permitted for a hermaphrodite to marry a woman. He is likewise considered a male to the extent that if a man had relations with him, he is liable to be stoned, in accordance with the opinion of Rabbi Eliezer and Rabbi Yehuda (Rambam *Sefer Kedusha, Hilkhot Issurei Bia* 1:15).

NOTES

One who can father children enables his wife to eat – **מוֹלִיד מַאֲכִיל:** Rashi and other early authorities explain that this suggestion is based on the verse "And such as are born in his house, they eat of his bread" (Leviticus 22:11). Regardless of the fact that the verse refers to slaves and not children, Rashi still cites it as proof. The underlying idea is that if a man, by his very nature, is incapable of fathering children, his marriage is considered incomplete. Therefore, a woman who is married to a sexually impotent priest is not fully acquired by him, and consequently he does not enable her to eat *teruma*.

"רַבִּי יוֹסֵי וְרַבִּי שִׁמְעוֹן אוֹמְרִים אַנְדְּרוֹגִינוֹס".
אָמַר רֵישׁ לָקִישׁ: מַאֲכִילָהּ בִּתְרוּמָה, וְאֵין מַאֲכִילָהּ בְּחָזֶה וָשׁוֹק. רַבִּי יוֹחָנָן אוֹמֵר: אַף מַאֲכִילָהּ בְּחָזֶה וָשׁוֹק. וּלְרֵישׁ לָקִישׁ, מַאי שְׁנָא חָזֶה וָשׁוֹק, דְּאוֹרַיְיתָא – תְּרוּמָה נַמִי דְּאוֹרַיְיתָא!

It is taught in the mishna that **Rabbi Yosei and Rabbi Shimon say:** If a priest who is **a hermaphrodite**[H] married an Israelite woman, he enables her to eat *teruma*. **Reish Lakish said: He enables her to eat *teruma*, but he does not enable her to eat the breast and thigh** of peace-offerings. **Rabbi Yoḥanan says: He even enables her to eat the breast and thigh**[N] of peace-offerings. The Gemara asks: **And according to Reish Lakish, what is different** about **the breast and thigh** of peace-offerings? If you say it is that they are **by Torah** law, ***teruma* is also by Torah** law. Why, then, is it permitted for her to eat *teruma*, but not the breast and thigh of peace-offerings?

הָכָא בְּמַאי עָסְקִינַן – בִּתְרוּמָה בַּזְּמַן הַזֶּה, דְּרַבָּנַן. אֲבָל בִּזְמַן שֶׁבֵּית הַמִּקְדָּשׁ קַיָּים מַאי – לָא, אַדְּתָנֵי: אֵין מַאֲכִילָהּ בְּחָזֶה וָשׁוֹק, לִיפְלוֹג וְלִיתְנֵי בְּדִידָהּ: בַּמֶּה דְּבָרִים אֲמוּרִים בִּתְרוּמָה דְּרַבָּנַן, אֲבָל בִּתְרוּמָה דְּאוֹרַיְיתָא לָא!

The Gemara answers: **With what are we dealing here?** We are dealing **with *teruma* in the present,**[HN] after the destruction of the Temple, when *teruma* is in effect only **by rabbinic** law. The Gemara asks: **But when the Temple is standing, what** is the *halakha*? He does **not** enable his wife to eat *teruma*. But if so, there is a difficulty. **Instead of teaching** that **he does not enable her to eat the breast and thigh** of peace-offerings, **let him distinguish and teach** it **within** the case of *teruma* **itself** as follows: **In what case is this statement said?** It is said **with regard to *teruma*** that is in effect only **by rabbinic** law, **but with regard to *teruma*** that is in effect **by Torah** law this ruling does **not** apply.

הָכִי נַמִי קָאָמַר: כְּשֶׁהוּא מַאֲכִילָהּ – מַאֲכִילָהּ בִּתְרוּמָה בַּזְּמַן הַזֶּה, דְּרַבָּנַן, וְאֵין מַאֲכִילָהּ בִּזְמַן חָזֶה וָשׁוֹק, וַאֲפִילּוּ בִּתְרוּמָה דְּרַבָּנַן, דִּלְמָא אָתֵי לְאוֹכְלָהּ בִּתְרוּמָה דְּאוֹרַיְיתָא.

The Gemara answers: **That is also what he is saying.** In other words, this is actually what Reish Lakish means, as his statement should be understood as follows: **When he enables her to eat, he enables her to eat *teruma* in the present,** when *teruma* is in effect only **by rabbinic** law, **but he does not enable her to eat** *teruma* **at a time** that **the breast and thigh** are given to the priests, i.e., when the Temple is standing, not **even *teruma*** that is in effect only **by rabbinic** law. This is due to the concern that **perhaps he will bring her to eat *teruma*** that is in effect **by Torah** law.

HALAKHA

A priest who is a hermaphrodite – אַנְדְּרוֹגִינוֹס כֹּהֵן: Since a hermaphrodite has both male and female sexual organs, he constitutes a category of his own. If he is a priest, he does not enable his wife to eat *teruma*, in accordance with the conclusion of the Gemara on 83a. The Rema rules that he has the status of a male, in accordance with the mishna (Rambam *Sefer Zera'im*, *Hilkhot Terumot* 7:14; *Shulḥan Arukh*, *Even HaEzer* 44:5).

***Teruma* in the present – תְּרוּמָה בַּזְּמַן הַזֶּה:** The obligation to set aside *terumot* and tithes nowadays is not by Torah law but rather by rabbinic decree, even in locales that were settled by those who returned to Eretz Yisrael from Babylonia, in accordance with the opinion of Rabbi Yoḥanan in explanation of the Rabbis (Vilna Gaon; *Shulḥan Arukh*, *Yoreh De'a* 331:2).

NOTES

He even enables her to eat the breast and thigh – אַף מַאֲכִילָהּ בְּחָזֶה וָשׁוֹק: The discussion in the Jerusalem Talmud, which also cites this dispute but with the opinions reversed, concerns the breast and thigh themselves. According to one opinion, the ruling is lenient due to an *a fortiori* inference. The reasoning is that had the Jews not sinned with the Golden Calf they would all have been fit to eat the breast and thigh, but owing to that sin, the right to partake of the priestly gifts was awarded exclusively to the descendants of Aaron. *Teruma*, in contrast, was from the very outset a gift to the descendants of Aaron. For this reason, one for whom it is permitted to partake of *teruma* may certainly share in the breast and thigh.

***Teruma* in the present – תְּרוּמָה בַּזְּמַן הַזֶּה:** The issue of *teruma* in the present time is already disputed by the *tanna'im*. In various forms this disagreement is taken up by the *amora'im* and early authorities. Some maintain that the opinion that *teruma* nowadays applies by rabbinic law is based on the assumption that by Torah law the sanctity of Eretz Yisrael has lapsed but the Sages ruled that mitzvot dependent on the Land must still be observed. However, even according to this opinion, the Gemara's wording: At a time that the breast and thigh are given to the priests, is imprecise, as the sanctity of Eretz Yisrael with regard to *terumot* and tithes is tied not to the existence of the Temple but to the fact that the majority of Jews are living in Eretz Yisrael. Accordingly, this opinion, as explained by the Rambam, maintains that even during the time of the Second Temple, *terumot* and tithes were not practiced by Torah law; rather, the people accepted upon themselves the obligation to give *teruma* (see Nehemiah, chapter 9).

וְרַבִּי יוֹחָנָן אָמַר: אַף מַאֲכִילָהּ בְּחָזֶה וָשׁוֹק. אָמַר לֵיהּ רַבִּי יוֹחָנָן לְרֵישׁ לָקִישׁ: מִי סָבְרַתְּ תְּרוּמָה בַּזְּמַן הַזֶּה דְּרַבָּנַן? אָמַר לֵיהּ: אִין, שֶׁאֲנִי שׁוֹנֶה: עִיגּוּל בַּעִיגּוּלִים עוֹלֶה.

However, **Rabbi Yoḥanan** disagrees and **says** that **he even enables her to eat the breast and thigh** of peace-offerings. With respect to this dispute, **Rabbi Yoḥanan said to Reish Lakish:** Since you distinguish between *teruma* and the breast and thigh, **do you maintain** that *teruma* **in the present** is mandated only **by rabbinic** law? **He said to him: Yes,** and the proof is **that I teach** that **a cake**[B] of dried figs that became intermingled **with** other **cakes**[NH] **is nullified.**[N] If a cake of *teruma* figs became intermingled with one hundred ordinary cakes, the cake is nullified and it is not necessary to treat them all as *teruma*. If the cake, which is a food of importance in its own right, is nullified, this must be because the *teruma* is only by rabbinic law.

אֲמַר לֵיהּ: וַהֲלֹא אֲנִי שׁוֹנֶה: חֲתִיכָה בַּחֲתִיכוֹת עוֹלָה. מִי סָבְרַתְּ ״כָּל שֶׁדַּרְכּוֹ לִימָּנוֹת״ שָׁנִינוּ? ״אֶת שֶׁדַּרְכּוֹ לִימָּנוֹת״ שָׁנִינוּ.

Rabbi Yoḥanan **said to him: But don't I teach** that even **a piece** of a sin-offering that became intermingled **with** other **pieces** of meat **is nullified,** as I maintain that the *halakha* of nullification applies even to Torah prohibitions? **Do you maintain** that **we learned** that **any** object **that it is usual to count,** i.e., any object that is even occasionally sold by unit, rather than by weight or measure, is considered to be important and therefore cannot be nullified? This is not so, as in fact **we learned** that only **that which it is usual to count,** i.e., an object that is always sold by unit and in no other manner, is considered to be important and is therefore not subject to nullification; and cakes of dried figs are not always sold by unit.

מַאי הִיא? דִּתְנַן: מִי שֶׁהָיוּ לוֹ חֲבִילֵי תִּלְתָּן שֶׁל כִּלְאֵי הַכֶּרֶם – יִדָּלְקוּ. נִתְעָרְבוּ בַּאֲחֵרוֹת

The Gemara asks: **What is** this *halakha* to which Rabbi Yoḥanan alludes? **As we learned** in a mishna (*Orla* 3:6–7): In the case of **one who had bundles of clover,**[B] a type of legume, **of** a forbidden mixture of **food crops in a vineyard,**[H] i.e., clover plants that grew in a vineyard, these bundles **must be burned,** as it is prohibited for one to derive benefit from a forbidden mixture of food crops in a vineyard. If the forbidden bundles **became intermingled with others** that are permitted,

BACKGROUND

Cake [*iggul*] – **עִיגּוּל**: During the talmudic period figs were preserved in various ways. One method involved drying them after they were harvested and then pressing them into round vessels. A cake of this kind was therefore called an *iggul*, literally meaning round. After these cakes were removed from these vessels the figs formed the shape of a flat cylinder. These cakes of figs were usually of uniform size and shape, and were often sold wholesale rather than individually.

Clover – **תִּלְתָּן**: *Tiltan* has been identified with the clover-like plant fenugreek, which is Latin for Greek hay, or *Trigonella foenum-graecum*, a plant of the Fabaceae family. It is less than 1 m tall and has white flowers and hollow, hairy, light green leaves that are clustered in sets of three. It produces thin pods, which measure up to 15 cm and contain flat seeds of up to 5 mm in length. Fenugreek is usually cultivated for its seeds, which can be eaten or used in the preparation of many different spices. Its young branches are also used as a spice after they are cooked. In many countries fenugreek is also used as animal fodder and fertilizer.

Fenugreek leaves, seeds, and pods

NOTES

A cake of dried figs with other cakes – **עִיגּוּל בַּעִיגּוּלִים**: Some early authorities raise a difficulty here: It is possible that the reason a cake of *teruma* is nullified by other cakes is that the *teruma* of fruit applies by rabbinic law, as opposed to Torah-mandated *teruma*, which is limited to the produce specified by the Torah, i.e., grain, wine, and oil. If so, this case has no bearing on the status of *teruma* nowadays. Consequently, they explain that this must follow the view that the *teruma* of fruit is by Torah law, or, as the Ra'avad explains, that the *teruma* of the fruit of the seven species of Eretz Yisrael is mandated by the Torah. Otherwise, one could say that if the *teruma* of fruit is by Torah law, *teruma* nowadays is not by Torah law, and even if the *halakhot* of *teruma* do apply nowadays by Torah law, the *teruma* of fruit applies by rabbinic law. Either way, there is no proof from here with regard to the *halakhot* of *teruma* in general (see Ritva and Meiri).

Nullified [*oleh*] – **עוֹלֶה**: Rabbi Avraham min HaHar explains that the word *oleh*, which literally means raised, is used here instead of the more usual term *batel*, meaning nullified, because even if the *halakhot* of *teruma* do not apply to the mixture, as it need not be eaten exclusively by priests in a state of ritual purity, the monetary aspect of the obligation is not negated, and the owner must give a priest the value of the nullified *teruma* cake.

HALAKHA

A cake of dried figs with other cakes – **עִיגּוּל בַּעִיגּוּלִים**: If a cake of *teruma* figs became intermingled with ordinary cakes and it cannot be identified, the cake is nullified in a mixture of one hundred parts of non-*teruma* to one part *teruma* (Rambam *Sefer Zera'im*, *Hilkhot Terumot* 14:2).

Bundles of clover of food crops in a vineyard – **חֲבִילֵי תִּלְתָּן שֶׁל כִּלְאֵי הַכֶּרֶם**: It is prohibited to sow seeds or vegetables near vines, or to plant a vine alongside grain or vegetables. If one did so, it is prohibited to derive benefit from the seeds, vegetables, or grapes, and they must all be burned (*Shulḥan Arukh*, *Yoreh De'a* 296:3).

כּוּלָּן יִדָּלְקוּ, דִּבְרֵי רַבִּי מֵאִיר. וַחֲכָמִים אוֹמְרִים: יַעֲלוּ בְּאֶחָד וּמָאתַיִם, שֶׁהָיָה רַבִּי מֵאִיר אוֹמֵר: כׇּל שֶׁדַּרְכּוֹ לִימָּנוֹת מְקַדֵּשׁ, וַחֲכָמִים אוֹמְרִים: אֵינוֹ מְקַדֵּשׁ אֶלָּא שִׁשָּׁה דְּבָרִים בִּלְבַד. רַבִּי עֲקִיבָא אוֹמֵר שִׁבְעָה.

they must all be burned; this is **the statement of Rabbi Meir. And the Rabbis say: They are nullified in** a mixture of **one** part forbidden food **to two hundred**[H] parts permitted food. **As Rabbi Meir would say: Any** object **that it is usual to count renders** a mixture **prohibited.** In other words, objects that are counted and sold by the unit, rather than by weight or estimation, are considered of special importance, and so they cannot be nullified by any majority and therefore must be burned. **But the Rabbis say: Only six objects**[N] are important enough that they cannot be nullified and therefore **render** their mixtures **forbidden. Rabbi Akiva says:** There are **seven** such objects.

אֵלּוּ הֵן: אֱגוֹזֵי פֶרֶךְ, וְרִמּוֹנֵי בָדָן, וְחָבִיּוֹת סְתוּמוֹת, וְחִלְפֵי תְרָדִין, וְקוֹלְסֵי כְרוּב, וּדְלַעַת יְוָנִית. וְרַבִּי עֲקִיבָא מוֹסִיף אַף כִּכָּרוֹת שֶׁל בַּעַל הַבַּיִת. הָרְאוּיִן לְעׇרְלָה – עׇרְלָה, לְכִלְאֵי הַכֶּרֶם – כִּלְאֵי הַכֶּרֶם.

They are as follows: **Perekh nuts,**[H] high-quality nuts from a place called Perekh; **Badan**[B] **pomegranates,** pomegranates from a place called Badan; **sealed barrels**[N] of wine; **shoots of beet;**[B] **cabbage stalks; and Greek gourd. Rabbi Akiva adds,** as his seventh item, **a homeowner's loaves.**[N] Different prohibitions apply to these seven items: **Those that are fit for** the prohibition of ***orla***, fruit that grows in the first three years after a tree has been planted, i.e., the nuts and pomegranates, render the entire mixture ***orla***. **Those that are fit** for the prohibition proscribing a mixture of **food crops in a vineyard,** i.e., the beets, cabbage, and gourd, render the entire mixture a mixture of **food crops in a vineyard.**

רַבִּי יוֹחָנָן סָבַר: ״אֵת שֶׁדַּרְכּוֹ לִימָּנוֹת״ שָׁנִינוּ, וְרֵישׁ לָקִישׁ סָבַר: ״כׇּל שֶׁדַּרְכּוֹ לִימָּנוֹת״ שָׁנִינוּ.

And it was stated that *amora'im* disagreed about the precise wording of this mishna: **Rabbi Yoḥanan holds** that **we learned: That which it is usual to count,** i.e., Rabbi Meir's stringent ruling is limited to objects that are sold exclusively by unit. **And Reish Lakish holds** that **we learned: Any** object **that it is usual to count,** i.e., even items that are only sometimes sold by unit are considered important and cannot be nullified.

BACKGROUND

Badan – בָּדָן: Badan is identified today with Ḥirvat Parva in the Badan valley, a few kilometers northwest of Shechem.

Shoots of beet [*ḥilfei teradin*] – חִלְפֵי תְרָדִין: The vegetable mentioned here is chard, *Beta vulgaris cicla*, a subspecies of the beet plant. Chard is an annual garden vegetable from the Chenopodiaceae family. Its large, fleshy leaves, 15–30 cm long, are eaten only after being cooked, and their flavor is similar to that of spinach. Today the leaves also serve as chicken feed. The *ge'onim* explain that the *ḥilfei teradin* mentioned in the Talmud are *tzela'ot hateradim*, spinach ribs. Some say that this is a special type of spinach with unique leaves.

Chard

HALAKHA

Nullified in a mixture of one to two hundred – יַעֲלוּ בְּאֶחָד וּמָאתַיִם: If a bundle of vegetables that are forbidden as a mixture of crops in a vineyard became intermingled with two hundred permitted bundles, or if a fruit that is forbidden as *orla* became intermingled with two hundred pieces of permitted fruit, the entire mixture is permitted. The *halakha* is ruled in accordance with the opinion of the Rabbis, against the sole dissenting opinion of Rabbi Meir (Rambam *Sefer Kedusha*, *Hilkhot Ma'akhalot Assurot* 16:8).

Perekh nuts, etc. – אֱגוֹזֵי פֶרֶךְ וכו׳: If an object of importance that is forbidden became intermingled with permitted objects, it is not nullified even in a mixture of one to one thousand. This category consists of seven items: Perekh nuts, Badan pomegranates, sealed barrels of wine, shoots of beet, cabbage stalks, Greek gourd, and a homeowner's loaves. Though this is presented here as Rabbi Akiva's view, the subsequent unattributed mishna follows his opinion (Vilna Gaon). Similarly, animals are considered to be significant and therefore cannot be nullified. Other items can be nullified, each in accordance with the relevant prohibition.

Some authorities maintain that any item that is always counted and only sold by the unit cannot be nullified, and this is the accepted custom. This is the opinion of the Rema, based on *Tosafot* and others, in accordance with Rabbi Yoḥanan. The fact that the *amora'im* disagree in accordance with the opinion of Rabbi Meir indicates that the *halakha* follows his opinion. Some (*Sefer HaTeruma*; see Vilna Gaon) rule that even objects occasionally sold by number cannot be nullified (Rambam *Sefer Kedusha*, *Hilkhot Ma'akhalot Assurot* 16:9; *Shulḥan Arukh*, *Yoreh De'a* 110:1).

NOTES

Only six objects – שִׁשָּׁה דְּבָרִים בִּלְבַד: The Rabbis maintain that it is not enough for an object to be of some importance for it to be immune to nullification. Rather, it must be of special significance, like the six items enumerated here. The Rambam writes that the listing of these six items was appropriate for their time and place, but the same applies to anything of equal importance. This opinion helps resolve the difficulties raised by *Tosafot* and the Rashba that there are also other items that cannot be nullified.

Sealed barrels – חָבִיּוֹת סְתוּמוֹת: *Tosafot* in tractate *Zevaḥim* claim that this term includes barrels filled with oil. The Meiri, on the other hand, maintains that sealed barrels refers exclusively to barrels of wine, as only with respect to wine is there a difference between barrels that are sealed and thereby protected from going sour and barrels that are not sealed.

A homeowner's loaves – כִּכָּרוֹת שֶׁל בַּעַל הַבַּיִת: Most commentaries, including *Tosafot*, explain that bakers' loaves are less important than a homeowner's loaves because they are smaller. Others maintain that bakers' loaves are not prepared with great care, unlike those made by a homeowner (*Tiferet Yisrael*). The Meiri suggests a somewhat different interpretation: Since baker's loaves are made to be sold, they are of no significance individually, whereas those of a homeowner are each prepared and handled separately.

מַאי חֲתִיכָה? דְּתַנְיָא: חֲתִיכָה שֶׁל חַטָּאת טְמֵאָה שֶׁנִּתְעָרְבָה בְּמֵאָה חֲתִיכוֹת שֶׁל חַטָּאוֹת טְהוֹרוֹת, וְכֵן פְּרוּסָה שֶׁל לֶחֶם הַפָּנִים טְמֵאָה שֶׁנִּתְעָרְבָה בְּמֵאָה פְּרוּסוֹת שֶׁל לֶחֶם הַפָּנִים טְהוֹרוֹת – תַּעֲלֶה. רַבִּי יְהוּדָה אוֹמֵר: לֹא תַּעֲלֶה.

The Gemara further explains: **What is the case of a piece,** referred to by Rabbi Yoḥanan? **As it is taught in a** *baraita*: **If a piece of a ritually impure sin-offering became intermingled**[H] **with one hundred pieces of ritually pure sin-offerings, and similarly, if a slice of ritually impure shewbread became intermingled with one hundred slices of ritually pure showbread,** the impure piece of a sin-offering or slice of shewbread **is nullified** in its respective mixture.[N] **Rabbi Yehuda says: It is not nullified.**

אֲבָל חֲתִיכָה שֶׁל חַטָּאת טְהוֹרָה שֶׁנִּתְעָרְבָה בְּמֵאָה חֲתִיכוֹת שֶׁל חוּלִּין טְהוֹרוֹת, וְכֵן פְּרוּסָה שֶׁל לֶחֶם הַפָּנִים טְהוֹרָה שֶׁנִּתְעָרְבָה בְּמֵאָה פְּרוּסוֹת שֶׁל חוּלִּין טְהוֹרוֹת – דִּבְרֵי הַכֹּל לֹא תַּעֲלֶה.

However, if a piece of a ritually pure sin-offering became intermingled[H] **with one hundred pieces of ritually pure non-sacred** meat, **and similarly, if a slice of ritually pure shewbread became intermingled with one hundred slices of ritually pure non-sacred bread, everyone agrees that** the pure piece of sin-offering or slice of shewbread **is not nullified** in its respective mixture.

קָתָנֵי מִיהַת רֵישָׁא תַּעֲלֶה! אָמַר רַבִּי חִיָּיא בְּרֵיהּ דְּרַב הוּנָא: בְּנִימּוֹחָה.

The Gemara asks: **In any event, the first clause** of this *baraita* **teaches**[N] that a piece of ritually impure sin-offering **can be nullified.** This poses a difficulty with respect to the opinion of Reish Lakish, as such a piece of meat is an item that is sometimes counted and considered important in its own right, and it is forbidden by Torah law, but nevertheless it can still be nullified. **Rabbi Ḥiyya, son of Rav Huna, said:** This *baraita* is referring not to a whole piece of meat but **to one that had been crushed**[N] and broken into small parts. Once it is no longer a whole piece, it loses its importance and can be nullified.

אִי הָכִי מַאי טַעְמָא דְּרַבִּי יְהוּדָה?

The Gemara asks: **If** it is **so** that the piece has been crushed, **what is the reason for Rabbi Yehuda's** opinion that the piece is not nullified?

HALAKHA

If a piece of a ritually impure sin-offering became intermingled – חֲתִיכָה שֶׁל חַטָּאת טְמֵאָה שֶׁנִּתְעָרְבָה: If a piece of a ritually impure sin-offering became intermingled with one hundred pieces of ritually pure sin-offerings, or if a slice of ritually impure shewbread became intermingled with one hundred slices of ritually pure shewbread, the impure piece or slice is nullified in its respective mixture, in accordance with the opinion of the Rabbis (Rambam *Sefer Avoda, Hilkhot Pesulei HaMukdashin* 6:23).

If a piece of a ritually pure sin-offering became intermingled – חֲתִיכָה שֶׁל חַטָּאת טְהוֹרָה שֶׁנִּתְעָרְבָה: If a piece of a ritually pure sin-offering became intermingled with one hundred pieces of ritually pure non-sacred meat, or if a slice of ritually pure shewbread became intermingled with one hundred slices of ritually pure, non-sacred bread, the impure piece or slice is not nullified, and the entire mixture must be eaten by priests (Rambam *Sefer Avoda, Hilkhot Pesulei HaMukdashin* 6:24).

NOTES

A piece of a ritually impure sin-offering is nullified – חֲתִיכַת חַטָּאת טְמֵאָה תַּעֲלֶה: The commentaries raise a question with regard to this *halakha* that a piece of such a sin-offering is nullified in a mixture of one hundred to one. Even if this piece is not an item that is invariably counted, there would appear to be another reason why it cannot be nullified, i.e., the principle of: A piece fit to be served. The principle is that a piece that is fit to be served to guests is significant in its own right and cannot be nullified. The Rashba discusses at length the various solutions offered to this problem. He suggests that a piece that is fit to be served to guests that became intermingled with non-sacred food is not nullified, because were it nullified, it could later be served to guests. But in the case of such a piece that became intermingled with sacrificial meat, since it could not be served to guests even after nullification, as it may be eaten only by priests, it is not considered a piece fit to be served. The Ritva rejects this explanation in favor of the Ra'ah's suggestion that this refers to an uncooked piece of meat that is not fit to be served, or alternatively, that any item that is forbidden not in and of itself but only due to some external factor, e.g., impurity, is not subject to the *halakha* with regard to a piece that is fit to be served.

In any event the first clause teaches – קָתָנֵי מִיהַת רֵישָׁא: According to most commentaries, this difficulty concludes Rabbi Yoḥanan's proof from this *baraita* with regard to nullification, an objection raised against the opinion of Reish Lakish. The Razah maintains that the difficulty posed here relates to the opinions of both Rabbi Yoḥanan and Reish Lakish, as this piece is an item that is usually counted. According to his opinion, some of the subsequent answers are in accordance with Rabbi Yoḥanan's opinion while others follow that of Reish Lakish. The Ramban rejects this explanation and proves that the difficulty applies only to the opinion of Reish Lakish.

One that had been crushed – נִימּוֹחָה: Most commentaries maintain that while the first clause of the *baraita* is referring to a crushed piece of meat, the latter clause applies to a whole piece as well. The Rashba claims that according to this answer the entire *baraita* is dealing with a crushed piece. How this dispute is understood depends to a certain extent on how the rest of the discussion is understood, according to the various opinions.

Perek **VIII**
Daf **82** Amud **a**

רַבִּי יְהוּדָה לְטַעְמֵיהּ, דְּאָמַר: מִין בְּמִינוֹ לָא בָּטֵיל.

The Gemara answers: **Rabbi Yehuda** conforms **to his** standard line of **reasoning, as he stated** a principle that if a particular **type** of food is mixed **with** food of **its own type, it cannot be nullified**[N] under any circumstances.

אֲבָל לֹא נִימּוֹחַ מַאי, לֹא תַּעֲלֶה – אַדְּתָנֵי: אֲבָל חֲתִיכָה שֶׁל חַטָּאת טְהוֹרָה שֶׁנִּתְעָרְבָה בְּמֵאָה חֲתִיכוֹת שֶׁל חוּלִּין טְהוֹרוֹת לֹא תַּעֲלֶה – נִיפְלוֹג וְנִיתְנֵי בְּדִידָהּ: בַּמֶּה דְּבָרִים אֲמוּרִים בְּשֶׁנִּימּוֹחָה, אֲבָל לֹא נִימּוֹחָה – לֹא תַּעֲלֶה!

The Gemara asks further: **But** had the piece of meat **not** been **crushed, what** would the *halakha* be? Presumably, it would **not** be **nullified.** If so, there is a difficulty, as **instead of teaching** a case involving non-sacred meat in the second half of the *baraita*, as follows: **However, if a piece of a ritually pure sin-offering became intermingled with one hundred pieces of ritually pure non-sacred** meat, the impure piece of a sin-offering **is not nullified; let the** *tanna* **distinguish and teach** it **in** the case involving only sacred meat, as follows: **In what** case **is this statement said?** It is in a case **where** the piece of meat **has been crushed** and broken into small parts, **but** if it **has not been crushed,** it is **not nullified.**

NOTES

A type mixed with its own type cannot be nullified – מִין בְּמִינוֹ לָא בָּטֵיל: The reason that the ruling is more stringent with regard to an item that became intermingled with its own type than with one that became mixed with a different type is that in the latter case the nullification is apparent, as the appearance and taste of the forbidden item have become imperceptible in the mixture. However, if an item became intermingled with its own type, it cannot be said that the unique essence of the prohibition has been canceled in the permitted substance.

טְהוֹרוֹת בִּטְהוֹרוֹת עָדִיף לֵיהּ.

The Gemara answers: Even so, the *tanna* **prefers** to address the case of an intermingling of **ritually pure** items **with** other **ritually pure** items and thereby teach a novel *halakha*, notwithstanding the fact that he could have made a distinction within the case of a ritually impure piece itself.

וְלְרֵישׁ לָקִישׁ, מַאי שְׁנָא רֵישָׁא וּמַאי שְׁנָא סֵיפָא? אָמַר רַב שֵׁישָׁא בְּרֵיהּ דְּרַב אִידִי: רֵישָׁא בְּטוּמְאַת מַשְׁקִין דְּרַבָּנַן, סֵיפָא דְּאוֹרַיְיתָא.

The Gemara asks: **And according to Reish Lakish,** who establishes the *baraita* as referring to a piece of meat that has been crushed, **what is different**[N] in **the first clause** of the *baraita* **and what is different in the latter clause?** Why is nullification possible in the case of impure pieces, but not in the case of pure ones? **Rav Sheisha, son of Rav Idi, said: The first clause** is dealing with a piece of a sin-offering that contracted **ritual impurity due to liquids,**[N] which is imparted **by rabbinic** law. Since the sacred food contracted impurity that is only rabbinic in origin, it may be nullified rather than allowed to go to waste. **The latter clause,** on the other hand, deals with sacred food that became intermingled with ordinary non-sacred food. The sacred food is forbidden to non-priests **by Torah** law, and therefore it is not nullified.

אֲבָל טוּמְאַת שֶׁרֶץ מַאי, לֹא תַּעֲלֶה.

The Gemara asks: **But** had the piece of meat mentioned in the first clause of the *baraita* contracted **ritual impurity through** contact with **a creeping animal,** which is imparted by Torah law, **what** would the *halakha* be? Presumably, it would **not** be **nullified.**

אַדְּתָנֵי סֵיפָא: אֲבָל חֲתִיכָה שֶׁל חַטָּאת טְהוֹרָה שֶׁנִּתְעָרְבָה בְּמֵאָה חֲתִיכוֹת שֶׁל חוּלִּין טְהוֹרוֹת לֹא תַּעֲלֶה – נִיפְלוֹג וְלִיתְנֵי בְּדִידָהּ: בַּמֶּה דְּבָרִים אֲמוּרִים בְּטוּמְאַת מַשְׁקִין, אֲבָל בְּטוּמְאַת שֶׁרֶץ לֹא! טְהוֹרָה בִּטְהוֹרוֹת עָדִיף לֵיהּ.

If so, there is a difficulty, as **instead of teaching** a case involving non-sacred meat in the **latter clause** of the *baraita*, as follows: **However, if a piece of a ritually pure sin-offering became intermingled with one hundred pieces of ritually pure non-sacred** meat, the impure piece of a sin-offering **is not nullified; let** the *tanna* **distinguish and teach** it **in** the case involving only sacred meat, as follows: **In what** case **is this statement said?** It is said in a case **where** the piece of meat contracted **ritual impurity due to liquids, but where** it contracted **ritual impurity through a creeping animal** it is **not** nullified. The Gemara answers: Even so, the *tanna* **prefers** to address the novel case of an intermingling of **ritually pure** items **with** other **ritually pure** items.

רַבָּה אָמַר: רֵישָׁא – אִיסּוּר לָאו, סֵיפָא – אִיסּוּר כָּרֵת.

Rabba said that an alternative explanation may be suggested for the difference between the two clauses of the *baraita*: In **the first clause** of the *baraita*, which deals with the intermingling of impure sacred meat with pure sacred meat, there is concern about the violation of **a standard prohibition,** i.e., the prohibition against eating impure sacred meat; therefore, the piece of meat is nullified. In **the latter clause** of the *baraita*, which deals with the intermingling of sacred meat and non-sacred meat, there is concern about the violation of **a prohibition** that bears the punishment **of *karet*,** which bars a non-priest from eating pure sacrificial food; therefore, the piece of meat is not nullified.

וְהָא רַבָּה הוּא דְּאָמַר: כָּל בִּדְאוֹרַיְיתָא – לָא שְׁנָא אִיסּוּר לָאו וְלָא שְׁנָא אִיסּוּר כָּרֵת! קַשְׁיָא.

The Gemara asks: **But wasn't it Rabba** himself **who said:** With regard to the nullification of **any** item forbidden **by Torah** law that became intermingled with a permitted substance, there is **no difference between** that which is forbidden due to a **standard prohibition** and that which is forbidden due to **a prohibition** that entails the punishment **of *karet*.** The Gemara concludes: This is **difficult** for Rabba.

רַב אַשִׁי אָמַר: סֵיפָא – מִשּׁוּם דְּהָוֵי לֵיהּ דָּבָר שֶׁיֵּשׁ לוֹ מַתִּירִין, וְכָל דָּבָר שֶׁיֵּשׁ לוֹ מַתִּירִין – אֲפִילּוּ בְּאֶלֶף לָא בָּטֵיל.

Rav Ashi said yet another explanation: In **the latter clause,** where ritually pure sacred meat became intermingled with ritually pure non-sacred meat, the sacred meat does not become nullified **because it is an object whose prohibition is temporary.**[H] The piece of sacred meat is not absolutely forbidden, as it is permitted for a priest to eat it. **And** the *halakha* is that **any object whose prohibition is temporary cannot be nullified,** no matter how great the amount of permitted substance, **even in** a mixture of one to **one thousand.**

NOTES

And according to Reish Lakish, what is different – וְלְרֵישׁ לָקִישׁ מַאי שְׁנָא: There are many different versions of the text here, each of which presents its own set of difficulties. See Rashi, who goes to great lengths to explain why this difficulty applies only to Reish Lakish and not to Rabbi Yoḥanan. The Rashba explains this version in accordance with his general approach: Rabbi Yoḥanan maintains that this is not a case of: That which is counted; rather, the question of nullification concerns the issue of a piece fit to be served. The difference between a piece intermingled with pure sacred food and a piece mixed with non-sacred food is that in the former case the mixture is not fit to be served to guests, as the entire mixture must be given to priests. Other early authorities cite the following version, citing the *ge'onim*: And according to Rabbi Yoḥanan, what is different between the first clause, etc. According to this version, Reish Lakish does differentiate between the first and latter clauses of the *baraita*, as a crushed piece is nullified whereas a piece that has not been crushed is not nullified. But according to Rabbi Yoḥanan, since both cases involve whole pieces, the question is: What is the reason for the difference in the *halakha* (see Rashba and Ritva)? Rabbi Avraham min HaHar cites a reading that omits any mention of either Rabbi Yoḥanan or Reish Lakish, which means the question applies equally to both.

The first clause is dealing with ritual impurity due to liquids, etc. – רֵישָׁא בְּטוּמְאַת מַשְׁקִין וכו׳: The early authorities cite Rabbeinu Ḥananel's version, which omits the phrases: The first clause, and: The latter clause. According to this version, the entire *baraita* is referring to the impurity of liquids. Rabbi Yehuda maintains that the ritual impurity of liquids is by Torah law and therefore cannot be nullified, whereas the Rabbis contend that such impurity is merely rabbinic. This version also resolves the question raised by the *Arukh LaNer* as to why the Gemara uses the example of the impurity of liquids rather than that of some other type of ritual impurity that everyone agrees is of rabbinic origin.

HALAKHA

An object whose prohibition is temporary – דָּבָר שֶׁיֵּשׁ לוֹ מַתִּירִים: If a temporarily prohibited object, or one that can be permitted in some manner, became intermingled with permitted items, it is not nullified even in a mixture of one to one thousand, whether it is whole or crushed. This applies only if it became intermingled with its own type, but if it fell into a different type it is nullified in a mixture of one to sixty, like any other prohibited item (Rambam *Sefer Kedusha, Hilkhot Ma'akhalot Assurot* 15:6, 12; *Shulḥan Arukh, Yoreh De'a* 102:1).

LANGUAGE

Mistake [*beduta*] – **בְּדוּתָא**: The word *beduta* comes from the root *b-d-h*, meaning false. This word is used by the Sages to reject an unfounded tradition or *halakha*. It essentially means that the statement in question was never made by the Sage to whom it is attributed. Some read: *Baruta*, outside, meaning that the matter is unworthy of being included and discussed in the study hall.

וְהָא דְּרַב אַשִׁי בְּדוּתָא הִיא. לְמַאן? אִי לְכֹהֵן – מִישְׁרָא שָׁרֵי, אִי לְיִשְׂרָאֵל – לְעוֹלָם אָסוּר. אֶלָּא הָא דְּרַב אַשִׁי בְּדוּתָא הִיא.

The Gemara comments: **Now, that** teaching ascribed **to Rav Ashi** is certainly **a mistake** [*beduta*],[L] as the application of this principle to the case at hand can easily be shown to be erroneous. With regard **to whom** is the prohibition temporary? **If** one would say that it is **for a priest,** the sacred meat **was** always **permitted** to him, even before it became intermingled, as a priest may eat both sacred and non-sacred food, and therefore it was never a forbidden mixture with respect to him. And **if** one would say that it is **for an Israelite,** the meat will **always** be **forbidden** to him. **Rather, that** teaching attributed **to Rav Ashi is** clearly **a mistake.**

וְסָבַר רַבִּי יוֹחָנָן תְּרוּמָה בִּזְמַן הַזֶּה דְּאוֹרָיְיתָא? וְהָתַנְיָא: שְׁתֵּי קוּפּוֹת, אַחַת שֶׁל חוּלִּין וְאַחַת שֶׁל תְּרוּמָה, וְלִפְנֵיהֶם שְׁתֵּי סְאִין, אַחַת שֶׁל חוּלִּין וְאַחַת שֶׁל תְּרוּמָה, וְנָפְלוּ אֵלּוּ בְּתוֹךְ אֵלּוּ – הֲרֵי אֵלּוּ מוּתָּרִים, שֶׁאֲנִי אוֹמֵר: תְּרוּמָה לְתוֹךְ תְּרוּמָה נָפְלָה, וְחוּלִּין בְּתוֹךְ חוּלִּין נָפְלוּ.

The Gemara raises a question with regard to Rabbi Yoḥanan's opinion: **And does Rabbi Yoḥanan maintain that** ***teruma*** **in the present** applies **by Torah** law? **But isn't it taught** in a *baraita*: There were **two** large **baskets, one** filled with **non-sacred** produce **and** the other **one** filled with ***teruma*****, and before them** were **two** one-*se'a* vessels, **one** filled with **non-sacred** produce **and** the other **one** filled with ***teruma*****. And these,** the contents of each of the *se'a* vessels, **fell into those,** each of the baskets. It is possible that the *teruma* fell into the non-sacred produce, and it is prohibited for non-priests to eat a mixture of *teruma* and non-sacred produce. Nevertheless, the produce found in the basket containing the non-sacred produce **is permitted, as I say**[N] that **the** ***teruma*** **fell into the** ***teruma*** **and the non-sacred** produce **fell into the non-sacred** produce.[H]

וְאָמַר רֵישׁ לָקִישׁ: וְהוּא שֶׁרַבּוּ חוּלִּין עַל הַתְּרוּמָה. וְרַבִּי יוֹחָנָן אָמַר: אַף עַל פִּי שֶׁלֹּא רַבּוּ חוּלִּין עַל הַתְּרוּמָה.

And Reish Lakish said that **this** is only the case **if the non-sacred** produce in the basket **was greater**[N] in quantity **than the** ***teruma*** in the one-*se'a* vessel, so that even if the *teruma* fell into the non-sacred produce, it is nullified. **And Rabbi Yoḥanan said:** The mixture is permitted **even if the non-sacred** produce **was not greater** in quantity **than the** ***teruma*****,** as one may rely on the assumption that each type of produce fell into its own type.

בִּשְׁלָמָא לְרֵישׁ לָקִישׁ – קָסָבַר: בִּדְרַבָּנַן נָמֵי רִבּוּיָא הוּא דְּבָעֵינַן. אֶלָּא לְרַבִּי יוֹחָנָן, קַשְׁיָא!

Granted, according to Reish Lakish, who maintains that *teruma* nowadays applies by rabbinic law, this is logical, as **he maintains** that even **with regard to** *teruma* that is in effect only **by rabbinic** law, **we also require** the permitted portion of the mixture to be **greater** in quantity so that it can nullify the forbidden part. **But according to Rabbi Yoḥanan,** it is **difficult** because if he maintains that even nowadays *teruma* is mandated by Torah law, how can one disregard the concern and permit the mixture based merely on the assumption that the events occurred in a way that preserves the produce in its permitted state?

הָא מַנִּי – רַבָּנַן הִיא,

The Gemara answers that Rabbi Yoḥanan can say: In accordance with **whose** opinion **is this** *baraita* taught? **It is** in accordance with the opinion of **the Rabbis,** who maintain that *teruma* nowadays is in effect only by rabbinic law.

NOTES

As I say – שֶׁאֲנִי אוֹמֵר: The argument of: As I say, is applied in situations when an uncertainty exists as to whether there was ever an intermingling of forbidden and permitted substances, and so there is room to assume that there was never a mixture containing a forbidden substance. The rationale is based on the internal logic of the idea of an established presumption [*ḥazaka*]. Since the food had a prior presumption of fitness, proof is required to undermine this presumption (see *Tosafot*). Usually, the Gemara seeks to buttress this rationale with another justification.

If it was greater – וְהוּא שֶׁרַבּוּ: By Torah law, even a bare majority of a permitted substance nullifies a forbidden substance. This principle may be combined with the argument of: As I say. If the permitted part was not larger in quantity, there is an equal chance that the mixture is forbidden in such a manner that it is not nullified by Torah law (Rashba).

HALAKHA

Two baskets and two *se'a* – שְׁתֵּי קוּפּוֹת וּשְׁתֵּי סְאִין: If there were two baskets, one filled with non-sacred produce and the other with *teruma*, and before them were two one-*se'a* containers, one filled with non-sacred produce and the other with *teruma*, and the contents of each container fell into a different basket, it is assumed that the non-sacred produce fell into the basket of non-sacred produce and the *teruma* into the *teruma*, even if the non-sacred produce is not greater in quantity than the *teruma*, in accordance with the opinion of Rabbi Yoḥanan (Rambam *Sefer Zera'im*, *Hilkhot Terumot* 13:14; *Shulḥan Arukh*, *Yoreh De'a* 111:1).

וַאֲנָא דַּאֲמַרִי כְּרַבִּי יוֹסֵי,

But I, Rabbi Yoḥanan, **said** what I said **in accordance with** the opinion of **Rabbi Yosei** that a priest who is a hermaphrodite enables his wife to eat *teruma*, and Rabbi Yosei himself maintains that even nowadays the *halakha* of *teruma* is in effect by Torah law. Accordingly, I argued that a hermaphrodite enables his wife to eat not only *teruma*, but even the breast and thigh of peace-offerings.

דְּתַנְיָא בְּסֵדֶר עוֹלָם ״אֲשֶׁר יָרְשׁוּ אֲבוֹתֶיךָ וִירִשְׁתָּהּ״ – יְרוּשָּׁה רִאשׁוֹנָה וּשְׁנִיָּה יֵשׁ לָהֶן, וּשְׁלִישִׁית אֵין לָהֶן.

As it is taught in a *baraita* in the anthology called ***Seder Olam***,[B] with regard to a verse that speaks of the Jewish people's return to Eretz Yisrael following their exile: "And the Lord your God will bring you into the land **that your fathers inherited, and you shall inherit it**" (Deuteronomy 30:5). These two expressions of inheritance teach that **they had a first inheritance** of Eretz Yisrael in the days of Joshua **and a second** inheritance[N] at the time of the return from the Babylonian exile. That is to say, since the sanctity of the land had lapsed when the First Temple was destroyed and the Jewish people exiled to Babylonia, a second sanctification was necessary when they returned to their land. **But they will not have a third** inheritance. In other words, it will never be necessary to sanctify the land for a third time, as the second sanctification was permanent.

וְאָמַר רַבִּי יוֹחָנָן: מַאן תְּנָא סֵדֶר עוֹלָם – רַבִּי יוֹסֵי.

And Rabbi Yoḥanan said: Who is the *tanna* who **taught *Seder Olam***? It is **Rabbi Yosei.** Since Rabbi Yosei maintains that the second sanctification of Eretz Yisrael never lapsed even after the destruction of the Second Temple, he also holds that *teruma* nowadays is in effect by Torah law.

BACKGROUND

Seder Olam – סֵדֶר עוֹלָם: *Seder Olam* is a book that deals with the chronology of biblical times and continues its chronological outline until the destruction of the Second Temple. Woven into its thirty chapters are various *halakhot* and *aggadot*. The work is based on verses and ancient traditions. The Gemara here and elsewhere states that the *tanna* who taught *Seder Olam* is Rabbi Yosei.

The book is also called *Seder Olam Rabba* in order to distinguish it from a similar book composed in a later period, called *Seder Olam Zuta*. *Seder Olam* has been published over the generations in several editions, some with various commentaries.

NOTES

The first and second sanctifications – קְדוּשָּׁה רִאשׁוֹנָה וּשְׁנִיָּה: The nature of the sanctity of Eretz Yisrael in the aftermath of the destruction of the Temple, or, according to certain opinions, following the fall of the kingdom of Israel, is a subject of dispute among the *tanna'im* and *amora'im*. The early authorities likewise differ over the *halakha* in this regard, without reaching a consensus.

The sanctity of the land impacts a variety of *halakhot*. It is clear that the essential sanctity of Eretz Yisrael as the chosen land is permanent, in that sanctity can rest only on this land. The issue is whether further conditions are necessary for this sanctity to be halakhically relevant. The additional condition might be the existence of the Temple, the presence of a majority of the world's Jews in the land, or an independent Jewish government. According to many authorities the sanctity of the land for the Sabbatical Year ceased with the cessation of the observance of the Jubilee Year, after the exile from Samaria, which means that even during the Second Temple period the Sabbatical Year was kept only by rabbinic law. The main dispute apparently concerns the status of *terumot* and tithes. The Rambam maintains that even in this regard the sanctity of the land was rabbinic from the beginning of the Second Temple period, and all the more so after its destruction. However, the Ra'avad and others assert that the land is sacred by Torah law from the time of the second inheritance (see *Yam shel Shlomo*). There is also a difference between these *halakhot* and those which govern *ḥalla*, the fruit that grows in the first three years after a tree has been planted [*orla*], and the prohibition of diverse kinds.

וסבר רבי יוחנן בדרבנן לא בעינן רבויא? והא תנן: מקוה שיש בו ארבעים סאה מכוונות, נתן סאה ונטל סאה כשר, ואמר רבי יהודה בר שילא אמר רבי אסי אמר רבי יוחנן: עד רובו.

The Gemara raises another objection to Rabbi Yoḥanan's opinion: **But does Rabbi Yoḥanan maintain that with regard to** a mixture containing an item that is forbidden **by rabbinic law, we do not require** the permitted portion of the mixture to be **greater** in quantity so that it can nullify the prohibited part? **Didn't we learn** otherwise in a mishna (*Mikvaot* 7:2): With regard to **a ritual bath**[N] **that contains exactly forty *se'a***[BH] of water, the minimal measure of a fit ritual bath, and **one added** to it a ***se'a*** of liquid other than water, **and** then **removed** from it **a *se'a***[N] of the mixture, the ritual bath remains **fit**, as the liquid that was added was nullified in the forty *se'a* of water, so that when one *se'a* of the mixture was removed there still remained the requisite forty *se'a* of fit water. **And Rabbi Yehuda bar Sheila said** that **Rabbi Asi said** that **Rabbi Yoḥanan said** that this *halakha* applies **up to the greater part**[N] of the ritual bath.

מאי לאו – דנשתייר רובו? לא, דלא נשקול רובו.

The Gemara clarifies the opinion of Rabbi Yoḥanan: **What, is it not that its greater part must remain,** i.e., that most of the original forty *se'a* of water must remain in the ritual bath? In other words, up to nineteen *se'a* of other liquids may be added to the ritual bath, with an equal quantity of the mixture then removed from it, and these other liquids are nullified by the ritual bath water. But if twenty *se'a* are removed, so that fit water no longer constitutes the majority, the ritual bath is no longer fit for use. Since certain liquids are unfit for a ritual bath only by rabbinic law, this shows that even with respect to rabbinic prohibitions the permitted portion of a mixture must be greater in quantity, so that it can nullify the prohibited part. The Gemara refutes this proof: **No,** it means **that its greater part must not be removed,** but if the water and other liquids are present in equal proportion, the ritual bath remains fit.

ואיבעית אימא: שאני הכא, דאיכא למימר "שאני אומר".

And if you wish, say an alternative explanation of Rabbi Yoḥanan's opinion: **It is different here,** with regard to the case of two baskets, one of which contains *teruma,* **since it may be said: As I say** that the *teruma* fell into the *teruma* and the non-sacred produce fell into the non-sacred produce, it is therefore assumed that that is what actually took place, and therefore the permitted portion need not be the greater part of the mixture.

תנן: "אנדרוגינוס נושא"! תני: "אם נשא".

§ **We learned** in the mishna: **A hermaphrodite may marry** a woman. This formulation indicates that he may do so *ab initio,* as he is considered a full-fledged male. Accordingly, a hermaphrodite who is a priest should enable his wife to eat the breast and thigh of peace-offerings, as is maintained by Rabbi Yoḥanan, and against the opinion of Reish Lakish. The Gemara rejects this argument and suggests that the text be emended: **Teach** in the mishna: **If he married.** That is to say, if he married a woman, the marriage is valid and a bill of divorce is required, as it is possible that he is a male. But even if he married, he does not enable his wife to eat *teruma,* as he may be a female.

והא "נושא" קתני! וליטעמיך, מאי "אבל לא נישא"? אלא מאי "נישא" דיעבד – "נושא" נמי דיעבד.

The Gemara raises a difficulty: **But doesn't** the mishna **teach** that **he may marry** a woman, which indicates that he may do so *ab initio*? The Gemara rejects this argument: **And according to your reasoning, what is** the meaning of the next clause: **But he may not be married** to a man? This teaching is certainly referring to a case after the fact, as, if he is a full-fledged male there would be no reason to say that he may not be married to a man *ab initio*. **Rather, what is** the meaning of: He may not **be married** to a man? It means that even **after the fact** the marriage is not valid. This being the case, when the mishna states that a hermaphrodite **may marry** a woman, it is **also** speaking **after the fact.**

אמרי: לא, "נושא" – לכתחלה משמע, "אבל לא נישא" – דיעבד נמי לא.

It may be **said** in response: **No;** the words: **May marry, indicate** that a hermaphrodite may marry a woman ***ab initio,*** whereas the words: **But he may not be married,** mean that his marriage to a man is **not** valid **even after the fact.** Accordingly, the difficulty raised against Reish Lakish remains.

NOTES

Didn't we learn: A ritual bath – והא תנן מקוה: Rashi and other commentaries explain the difficulty that this poses to Rabbi Yoḥanan's opinion on the basis of the assumption, at least in the first answer, that Rabbi Yoḥanan's ruling does not rest on the argument of: As I say. For they understand that he in fact permits all such mixtures since he does not require a majority of permitted substance for the nullification of a rabbinic prohibition. The Gemara questions this opinion based on the mishna in tractate *Mikvaot*, which indicates that a majority is needed even for prohibitions of rabbinic origin. This interpretation raises several problems from other issues with regard to the *halakhot* of nullification of rabbinic prohibitions, which are discussed at length by the early authorities (see Ramban's *Kuntres Aḥaron* and Rashba). The Ritva explains that the difficulty is based on the argument of: As I say, as one can also say in the case of the ritual bath that the *se'a* he removed is the same one that he added. According to this opinion, the second answer is that in the case of the baskets it might in fact be the exact same *se'a*, whereas with regard to a ritual bath the waters intermingle and therefore he cannot possibly take out the very same liquid he added.

Added a *se'a* and removed a *se'a* – נתן סאה ונטל סאה: According to Rashi and *Tosafot* this is referring to liquid other than water, but which does not have a particular coloring, such as fruit juice. The Rambam, Ra'avad, and others contend that this *halakha* applies solely to drawn water, which only invalidates the ritual bath according to rabbinic law. It is possible that the Meiri maintains that the mishna refers to both fruit juice and drawn water.

Up to the greater part – עד רובו: Many early authorities struggle to explain this clause in accordance with Rashi's opinion that the mishna is referring to fruit juice. The problem is that it is unanimously agreed that one cannot immerse in fruit juice, even by Torah law, which means this is not a rabbinic prohibition at all. The answer given is that by Torah law each drop of the liquid is nullified as it enters the mixture, and it is the Sages who decreed that it is not nullified (*Tosefot HaRosh*); alternatively, they declared the ritual bath unfit in this particular case because they wanted it to be noticeable that the water is the majority. The Ramban suggests that if the fruit juice leaves the color of the water unchanged, then it invalidates the fit water only by rabbinic law.

BACKGROUND

Forty *se'a* – ארבעים סאה: Forty *se'a* is the equivalent of eighty *hin* or 5,760 egg-bulks, which is the minimum quantity of water necessary for a ritual bath. The forty-*se'a* measure is the basis of all modern calculations of the various measures of volume. The Talmud states that the dimensions of a ritual bath must be three cubits by one cubit by one cubit, and that its volume must be forty *se'a*. Therefore, according to the calculation of Rabbi Ḥayyim Na'e, a ritual bath must contain 332 ℓ of water, and, according to the calculations of the Ḥazon Ish, 573 ℓ.

HALAKHA

A ritual bath that contains…forty *se'a*, etc. – מקוה שיש בו ארבעים סאה וכו׳: If a *se'a* of drawn water was added to a ritual bath that contained precisely forty *se'a* of fit water, and a *se'a* of the mixture was subsequently removed, even if this process is repeated many times the ritual bath remains fit, in accordance with the opinion of Rabbi Yoḥanan, who establishes the mishna as referring to drawn water. Some (*Shulḥan Arukh*) say that this is referring to a *se'a* of fruit juice or other liquids, rather than water (Rambam *Sefer Tahara, Hilkhot Mikvaot* 4:7; *Shulḥan Arukh, Yoreh De'a* 201:24).

וְהָא מִדְּקָתָנֵי סֵיפָא רַבִּי אֱלִיעֶזֶר אוֹמֵר: אַנְדְּרוֹגִינוֹס חַיָּיבִין עָלָיו סְקִילָה כְּזָכָר, מִכְּלָל דְּתַנָּא קַמָּא סַפּוּקֵי מְסַפְּקָא לֵיהּ!

The Gemara challenges this understanding: **But from** the fact **that** the mishna **teaches in the latter clause: Rabbi Eliezer says** that if a man had intercourse with **a hermaphrodite,** he **is liable to** receive the punishment of **stoning on his account as if** he had relations with **a male,** this proves **by inference that the first *tanna* is uncertain** as to whether or not a hermaphrodite is considered a full-fledged male, and this presents a difficulty to Rabbi Yoḥanan's opinion.

בֵּין לְמָר בֵּין לְמָר מִפְשַׁט פְּשִׁיטָא לֵיהּ, אִיכָּא בֵּינַיְיהוּ סְקִילָה מִשְּׁנֵי מְקוֹמוֹת: דְּמָר סָבַר חַיָּיבִין עָלָיו סְקִילָה מִשְּׁנֵי מְקוֹמוֹת, וּמָר סָבַר – כְּזָכָר.

The Gemara answers: No, it **is obvious both to this Master and to that Master** that a hermaphrodite is deemed a full-fledged male. The practical difference **between them** relates to the question of whether one is liable to receive the punishment of **stoning** for intercourse with him at only one place or **at two places. As one Sage,** the first *tanna*, **holds** that **one is liable to** be punished with **stoning on** a hermaphrodite's **account** for intercourse **at two places,** whether he penetrated him anally, in the manner of homosexual intercourse, or through his female organ. Since the hermaphrodite is deemed a male, one is liable to be punished with stoning for intercourse at either place. **And one Sage,** Rabbi Eliezer, **holds** that one is liable to be punished with stoning for relations with a hermaphrodite only if he penetrated him anally, **as if** he were **a male.**

אָמַר רַב:

Rav said:

Perek **VIII**
Daf **83** Amud **a**

לֵיתָא לְמַתְנִיתִין מִקַּמֵּי בָּרַיְיתָא. דְּתַנְיָא, רַבִּי יוֹסֵי אוֹמֵר: אַנְדְּרוֹגִינוֹס בְּרִיָּה בִּפְנֵי עַצְמָהּ הוּא, וְלֹא הִכְרִיעוּ בּוֹ חֲכָמִים אִם זָכָר אִם נְקֵבָה.

The mishna here, which states that according to Rabbi Yosei a priest who is a hermaphrodite enables his wife to eat *teruma*, **is not**[N] to be relied upon **in the presence of a *baraita*** that teaches otherwise. **As it is taught** in a *baraita* that **Rabbi Yosei says: A hermaphrodite is a creature unto himself,**[HBN] **and the Sages did not determine whether he is a male or a female.** He is consequently prohibited from marrying a woman, and if he does so he does not enable her to eat *teruma*.

HALAKHA

A hermaphrodite is a creature unto himself – אַנְדְּרוֹגִינוֹס בְּרִיָּה בִּפְנֵי עַצְמָהּ הוּא: If a *tumtum* or hermaphrodite betrothed a woman or was betrothed by a man, the validity of the betrothal is in doubt and therefore a bill of divorce is required owing to the uncertainty. The *halakha* is ruled in accordance with Rabbi Yosei's opinion as recorded in the *baraita*.

The Rema, based on Rashi, *Tosafot*, and the Rosh, maintains that a hermaphrodite is considered a definite male, as the ruling of the mishna is followed rather than that of the *baraita* (Rambam *Sefer Nashim, Hilkhot Ishut* 2:24; *Shulḥan Arukh, Even HaEzer* 44:5).

BACKGROUND

A hermaphrodite is a creature unto himself – אַנְדְּרוֹגִינוֹס בְּרִיָּה בִּפְנֵי עַצְמָהּ הוּא: Modern medicine distinguishes between two different kinds of hermaphrodite: The more common case of a pseudo-hermaphrodite, who only appears to be a hermaphrodite, and a true hermaphrodite. A true hermaphrodite has both male and female gonads, i.e., testicles and ovaries. A pseudo-hermaphrodite, however, has the gonads of a single gender, although he has the external sex organs of both genders.

Due to this dual identity a hermaphrodite cannot be regarded as male or female, unlike a *tumtum*, whose sexual identity remains concealed due to a developmental defect. For this reason, the Sages regarded a hermaphrodite as a third gender, a male-female, who does not belong to either sex.

NOTES

The mishna is not – לֵיתָא לְמַתְנִיתִין: The Gemara assumes that the *halakha* governing a hermaphrodite is part of the statement of Rabbi Yosei and Rabbi Shimon, although this is not obvious from the mishna itself, as Rabbi Yehuda's comments intervene. Rabbi Avraham min HaHar explains that since only Rabbi Yosei and Rabbi Shimon deal with a hermaphrodite in the mishna, it is clear that the last *halakha* is also theirs, despite the fact that the teaching of a different *tanna* is parenthetically inserted in the middle of their statement. In the Jerusalem Talmud, on the other hand, this *halakha* of a hermaphrodite is understood as a continuation of Rabbi Yehuda's statement. This opinion removes many of the difficulties arising from the Babylonian Talmud's understanding.

A creature unto himself – בְּרִיָּה בִּפְנֵי עַצְמָהּ: The early authorities note that the phrase: A creature unto himself, has more than one meaning. Subtle differences in the way this phrase should be understood lead to conflicting opinions with regard to the definition of a hermaphrodite. According to *Tosafot*, a hermaphrodite is called: A creature unto himself, because he remains in a permanent state of uncertainty that can never be clarified. The Rambam's ruling concerning a hermaphrodite indicates a similar understanding. In contrast, the Ramban, in his *Kuntres Aḥaron*, maintains that a hermaphrodite is literally a separate type of being, neither a male nor a female but a third gender. The early and later authorities include intermediate opinions that lie between these two extreme views. Some contend that a hermaphrodite is half male and half female, or else comprised of two elements, the status of each of them being in doubt. Other possibilities are also suggested (see *Einayim LaMishpat*).

אַדְּרַבָּה, לֵיתָא לְבָרַיְיתָא מִקַּמֵּי מַתְנִיתִין! מִדְּשַׁבְקֵיהּ רַבִּי יוֹסֵי לְבַר זוּגֵיהּ, שְׁמַע מִינָּהּ הֲדַר בֵּיהּ.

The Gemara asks: **On the contrary,** say that **the *baraita* is not** to be relied upon **in the presence of the mishna** here, as *baraitot* are generally considered less authoritative than *mishnayot.* The Gemara answers: **From** the fact **that Rabbi Yosei left his colleague,**[N] Rabbi Shimon, as the mishna's ruling is attributed to both Rabbi Yosei and Rabbi Shimon whereas the teaching of the *baraita* is reported only in the name of Rabbi Yosei, **learn from this** that Rabbi Yosei **retracted** his original opinion that he had maintained together with Rabbi Shimon and reached a different conclusion.

וּשְׁמוּאֵל אָמַר: לֵיתָא לְבָרַיְיתָא מִקַּמֵּי מַתְנִיתִין. אַדְּרַבָּה, לֵיתָא לְמַתְנִיתִין מִקַּמֵּי בָרַיְיתָא, דְּהָא שָׁמְעִינַן לֵיהּ לִשְׁמוּאֵל דְּחָיֵישׁ לִיחִידָאָה! הָנֵי מִילֵּי כִּי לָא מִתְעַקְּרָא מַתְנִיתִין, אֲבָל כִּי מִתְעַקְּרָא מַתְנִיתִין – לָא חָיֵישׁ.

And Shmuel said the reverse: **The *baraita* is not** to be relied upon **in the presence of the mishna** here. The Gemara asks: **On the contrary,** say that **the mishna** here **is not** to be relied upon **in the presence of the *baraita*, as we** have **heard that Shmuel takes into consideration** even **an individual** dissenting opinion appearing in a *baraita*. The Gemara answers: **This applies only when the mishna** itself is **not** thereby **uprooted,** as the *baraita* merely adds to it. **But when the mishna is uprooted** by a contrary statement taught in a *baraita*, **he does not take it into consideration.**

אָמְרִי בֵּי רַב מִשְּׁמֵיהּ דְּרַב: הֲלָכָה כְּרַבִּי יוֹסֵי בְּאַנְדְּרוֹגִינוֹס וּבְהַרְכָּבָה. וּשְׁמוּאֵל אָמַר: בְּקוֹשִׁי וּבְקִידּוּשׁ.

The Sages of **the school of Rav said in the name of Rav** that the ***halakha* is in accordance with** the opinion of **Rabbi Yosei,** both **with regard to** the *halakha* of **a hermaphrodite**[N] **and with regard to** the *halakha* of **grafting. And Shmuel says:** The *halakha* is in accordance with his opinion **with regard to** the laws of **protracted labor**[B] **and forfeiture.**

אַנְדְּרוֹגִינוֹס – הָא דַּאֲמָרַן, הַרְכָּבָה – דִּתְנַן: אֵין נוֹטְעִין, וְאֵין מַבְרִיכִין, וְאֵין מַרְכִּיבִין עֶרֶב שְׁבִיעִית פָּחוֹת מִשְּׁלֹשִׁים יוֹם לִפְנֵי רֹאשׁ הַשָּׁנָה. וְאִם נָטַע וְהִבְרִיךְ וְהִרְכִּיב – יַעֲקוֹר. רַבִּי יְהוּדָה אוֹמֵר: כׇּל הַרְכָּבָה שֶׁאֵינָהּ קוֹלֶטֶת בִּשְׁלֹשָׁה יָמִים – שׁוּב אֵינָהּ קוֹלֶטֶת. רַבִּי יוֹסֵי וְרַבִּי שִׁמְעוֹן אוֹמְרִים: שְׁתֵּי שַׁבָּתוֹת.

The Gemara clarifies: The *halakha* of **a hermaphrodite** is **that which we** just **said,** that he is considered a creature unto himself (Rabbeinu Ḥananel). The *halakha* of **grafting** is **as we learned** in a mishna (*Shevi'it* 2:6): **One may not plant,**[H] **or sink** the shoot of a vine into the ground, **or graft** a shoot onto a tree on the **eve of the Sabbatical Year less than thirty days before Rosh HaShana,** lest it take root in the seventh year. **And if he planted or sank or grafted, he must uproot** it. **Rabbi Yehuda says: Any graft that does not take root in three days will never take root,** and therefore it is prohibited to plant only for three days before the start of the Sabbatical Year. **Rabbi Yosei and Rabbi Shimon say** that it takes **two weeks** for a plant to take root.

BACKGROUND

Protracted labor – קוֹשִׁי: In addition to the bleeding that occurs during labor, one of the signs of imminent childbirth is a bloody discharge from the uterus. Usually this occurs the day before birth, but it can happen as early as a week or more beforehand.

It is also possible for the placenta to develop a hole. In such a case the woman might bleed well before the time she gives birth, at different stages of the development of the fetus. The disagreement in the Gemara here might relate to the classification of this phenomenon. Should it be seen as part of the natural birth process, in which case the blood would be associated with the labor, or is it a sui generis pathological phenomenon, which would mean that halakhically it would be considered blood of *ziva*?

HALAKHA

One may not plant, etc. – אֵין נוֹטְעִין וכו׳: Even nowadays it is prohibited to plant, sink, or graft trees shortly before the start of the Sabbatical Year. There must be sufficient time for the plant to take root and still leave thirty days before Rosh HaShana of the Sabbatical Year. The time for taking root is two weeks, in accordance with the opinion of Rabbi Yosei and Rabbi Shimon (Rambam *Sefer Zera'im, Hilkhot Shemitta* 3:11).

NOTES

From the fact that Rabbi Yosei left his colleague – מִדְּשַׁבְקֵיהּ רַבִּי יוֹסֵי לְבַר זוּגֵיהּ: The early authorities discuss the following question: Why couldn't one say just the opposite, i.e., that Rabbi Yosei changed his mind with regard to his lone dissenting opinion and accepted Rabbi Shimon's opinion? Several explanations have been suggested. One suggestion is that the Mishna, redacted by Rabbi Yehuda HaNasi, preceded the *Tosefta*, compiled by Rabbi Ḥiyya, and therefore the teaching of the *baraita* must be the later one (*Tosafot Yeshanim*; *Tosefot HaRosh*). Alternatively, the phrase: And the Sages did not determine, indicates that the scholars had already discussed this case, with some of them claiming that a conclusion can be reached. Therefore, when Rabbi Yosei disagrees with them, it can be assumed that his objection is referring to Rabbi Shimon's opinion as well (*Tosafot Yeshanim*). Furthermore, if the *baraita* came before the mishna it should also have mentioned Rabbi Shimon's dissenting view. Its omission of the latter indicates that the *baraita* seeks to dispute the mishna's earlier ruling (Ritva).

The *halakha* is in accordance with Rabbi Yosei with regard to a hermaphrodite – הֲלָכָה כְּרַבִּי יוֹסֵי בְּאַנְדְּרוֹגִינוֹס: The commentaries disagree about the meaning of Rav's statement, specifically with regard to whether he rules in accordance with Rabbi Yosei's opinion as stated in the mishna or the *baraita*. Most early authorities (Rabbeinu Ḥananel; Rif; Rid; Ritva) maintain that Rav accepts Rabbi Yosei's view in the *baraita*, as his statement is placed alongside the latter source. By contrast, Rashi, *Tosafot*, and Rabbi Yehuda al-Madari claim that Rav is referring to the mishna. Their proof is that his grouping of the *halakha* of a hermaphrodite with that of grafting shows that Rav does not come to rule in accordance with Rabbi Yosei in general, but only in rulings with regard to which Rabbi Yosei agrees with Rabbi Shimon, and so Rav must be referring to the mishna. The Ramban accepts Rabbeinu Ḥananel's opinion, but he combines the explanations and says that Rav was certainly speaking of those cases where Rabbi Yosei and Rabbi Shimon issued a combined ruling; however, the very fact that he states that the *halakha* is in accordance with Rabbi Yosei, and not in accordance with Rabbi Yosei and Rabbi Shimon, proves that he wishes to rule in accordance with Rabbi Yosei's sole dissenting opinion.

NOTES

Protracted labor – **קוֹשִׁי**: The following *halakhot* apply to the monthly cycle of a menstruating woman. Any blood that she sees during the first seven days from the start of the bleeding is considered menstrual blood, the *halakhot* of which are written explicitly in the Torah. This is followed by eleven days during which any bleeding she experiences is considered blood of *ziva*. If she sees blood on three consecutive days during that period she becomes a *zava*, whose *halakhot* differ from those of a menstruating woman. Although a woman does not typically experience bleeding during pregnancy, she continues counting this cycle as before, and if she experiences bleeding on a day on which she could have expected to see menstrual blood were she not pregnant, she has the status of a menstruating woman. If bleeding occurs on the other days of the cycle, she is a *zava*. However, she has the status of a *zava* only if the bleeding is spontaneous and not due to some external factor. Consequently, if the bleeding occurs near childbirth, during protracted labor, it is treated as the blood of childbirth, which does not impart ritual impurity. The question discussed here is: How long before childbirth does this *halakha* apply?

וְאָמַר רַב נַחְמָן אָמַר רַבָּה בַּר אֲבוּהּ: לְדִבְרֵי הָאוֹמֵר שְׁלֹשִׁים – צָרִיךְ שְׁלֹשִׁים וּשְׁלֹשִׁים, לְדִבְרֵי הָאוֹמֵר שְׁלֹשָׁה – צָרִיךְ שְׁלֹשָׁה וּשְׁלֹשִׁים, לְדִבְרֵי הָאוֹמֵר שְׁתֵּי שַׁבָּתוֹת – צָרִיךְ שְׁתֵּי שַׁבָּתוֹת וּשְׁלֹשִׁים.

And Rav Naḥman said that **Rabba bar Avuh said: According to** the first *tanna*, **who says thirty** days, he means that **thirty** days are **required** for the tree to take root **and** another **thirty** days are required for the addition to the Sabbatical Year, as the prohibitions of the Sabbatical Year apply already during the last thirty days of the sixth year. It is consequently prohibited to plant sixty days before Rosh HaShana. And similarly, **according to** Rabbi Yehuda, **who says three** days, he means that **three** days **are required** for the tree to take root **and** another **thirty** days are required for the addition to the Sabbatical Year. And so too, **according to** Rabbi Yosei and Rabbi Shimon, **who say two weeks,** they mean that **two weeks are required** for the tree to take root **and** another **thirty** days are required for the addition to the Sabbatical Year. Rav rules on this matter in accordance with the opinion of Rabbi Yosei.

וּשְׁמוּאֵל אָמַר: בְּקוֹשִׁי וְקִידּוּשׁ. קוֹשִׁי – דִּתְנַן:

And Shmuel said that the *halakha* is ruled in accordance with the opinion of Rabbi Yosei **with regard to protracted labor and proscription** as well. The Gemara explains: What is the case of **protracted labor?**[N] **As we learned** in a mishna (*Nidda* 36b): Ordinarily a woman who experiences a flow of blood on three consecutive days during a time of the month when she does not expect to experience menstrual bleeding is rendered ritually impure as a *zava*. However, if she experiences such bleeding while she is in protracted labor, the bleeding is attributed to her labor, and she is governed by the *halakhot* of a woman after childbirth.

כַּמָּה יְהֵא קִישּׁוּיָהּ? רַבִּי מֵאִיר אוֹמֵר: אוֹ אַרְבָּעִים אוֹ חֲמִשִּׁים יוֹם, רַבִּי יְהוּדָה אוֹמֵר: דַּיָּיהּ חָדְשָׁהּ, רַבִּי יוֹסֵי וְרַבִּי שִׁמְעוֹן: אוֹמְרִים אֵין קִישּׁוּי יוֹתֵר מִשְּׁתֵּי שַׁבָּתוֹת.

The *tanna'im* disagree about the question: **How long is** a woman's period of **protracted labor?**[H] For what period of time prior to her giving birth is the bleeding attributed to her labor? **Rabbi Meir says:** It is up to **forty or fifty days** before she delivers. **Rabbi Yehuda says: Her month suffices for her,** i.e., it is from the beginning of the month in which she gives birth. **Rabbi Yosei and Rabbi Shimon say: Protracted labor does not last for more than two weeks.** Shmuel rules in accordance with Rabbi Yosei in this case.

קִידּוּשׁ – דִּתְנַן: הַמְסַכֵּךְ גַּפְנוֹ עַל גַּבֵּי תְּבוּאָתוֹ שֶׁל חֲבֵרוֹ הֲרֵי זֶה קִדֵּשׁ, וְחַיָּיב בְּאַחֲרָיוּתוֹ, דִּבְרֵי רַבִּי מֵאִיר. רַבִּי יוֹסֵי וְרַבִּי שִׁמְעוֹן אוֹמְרִים:

What is this *halakha* of **proscription? As we learned** in a mishna (*Kilayim* 7:4): If **one causes his grapevine to overshadow the grain of another,**[H] **he has proscribed** it, rendering it forbidden as a food crop in a vineyard, **and he bears** financial **responsibility for it,** i.e., he must compensate the other individual for the loss of the produce that has been rendered forbidden. This is **the statement of Rabbi Meir. Rabbi Yosei and Rabbi Shimon say:**

HALAKHA

How long is her protracted labor – **כַּמָּה יְהֵא קִישּׁוּיָהּ**: Any bleeding experienced by a woman during labor is considered to be the result of her labor. If the bleeding occurs during the period of time in which she would ordinarily expect to menstruate, she is ritually impure as a menstruating woman; if it occurs at any other time, she is ritually pure. The period of protracted labor begins fourteen days before childbirth, provided that she gives birth to a viable child. Any bleeding that occurs beforehand is considered *ziva* blood and is impure. If she subsequently gives birth she is governed by the *halakhot* applying to a woman who gives birth while in a state of *ziva*, in accordance with the opinion of Rabbi Yosei and Rabbi Shimon, against that of Rabbi Meir (Rambam *Sefer Kedusha*, *Hilkhot Issurei Bia* 7:1).

One who causes his grapevine to overshadow the grain of another – **מְסַכֵּךְ גַּפְנוֹ עַל גַּבֵּי תְּבוּאַת חֲבֵרוֹ**: One cannot render produce forbidden as food crops in a vineyard if it does not belong to him. Therefore, if one causes his grapevine to overshadow the grain of another, the fruit of his vine is forbidden but the other individual's produce remains permitted, in accordance with the opinion of Rabbi Yosei and Rabbi Shimon. Although it would appear that Rav ruled against this opinion, and the *halakha* follows the opinion of Rav rather than Shmuel in matters of ritual law, since there is a dispute with regard to Rav's own teaching in this case Shmuel's clear ruling is followed. Furthermore, the Jerusalem Talmud indicates that even Rav agrees with Rabbi Yosei, and the mishna explicitly states that they ruled in practice in accordance with this opinion (Rambam *Sefer Zera'im*, *Hilkhot Kilayim* 5:8 and *Kesef Mishne* there; *Shulḥan Arukh*, *Yoreh De'a* 296:4).

אֵין אָדָם אוֹסֵר דָּבָר שֶׁאֵינוֹ שֶׁלּוֹ.

A person cannot render forbidden an item that is not his.[N] Since the grain does not belong to him, he cannot render it forbidden. According to Shmuel, the *halakha* is in accordance with Rabbi Yosei in this case as well.

אִיבַּעְיָא לְהוּ: בְּאַנְדְּרוֹגִינוֹס מַה לִּי אָמַר שְׁמוּאֵל? תָּא שְׁמַע, דַּאֲמַר שְׁמוּאֵל לְרַב עָנָן: לֵיתָא לְבָרַיְיתָא מִקַּמֵּי מַתְנִיתִין.

A dilemma was raised before the Sages: **As for a hermaphrodite, what did Shmuel say?**[N] It was stated in the name of Rav that the *halakha* is ruled in accordance with the opinion of Rabbi Yosei with regard to a hermaphrodite, but no ruling was attributed to Shmuel concerning this case. The Gemara suggests: **Come** and **hear, as Shmuel said to Rav Anan: The** ***baraita*** **is not** to be relied upon **in the presence of the mishna.** This indicates that Shmuel rejects Rabbi Yosei's opinion as stated in the *baraita* that a hermaphrodite is considered a creature unto himself.

הַרְכָּבָה מַה לִּי אָמַר שְׁמוּאֵל? תָּא שְׁמַע, דַּאֲמַר לֵיהּ שְׁמוּאֵל לְרַב עָנָן: תְּנֵי כְּמַאן דַּאֲמַר שְׁלֹשָׁה וּשְׁלֹשִׁים.

The Gemara asks further: Concerning **grafting, what did Shmuel say?** The Gemara suggests: **Come** and **hear, as Shmuel said to Rav Anan** that he should **teach in accordance with** the opinion of **the one who said** that it is prohibited to plant for **thirty-three** days before Rosh HaShana of the Sabbatical Year. Evidently, he ruled on this matter in accordance with the opinion of Rabbi Yehuda, and not that of Rabbi Yosei.

קוֹשִׁי מַה לִּי אָמַר רַב? תֵּיקוּ.

The Gemara continues to ask along these lines: With regard to the case of **protracted labor, what did Rav say?** Does he accept Rabbi Yosei's opinion, as does Shmuel? No resolution was found for this question, and the Gemara concludes that this dilemma **shall stand** unresolved.

קִידּוּשׁ מַה לִּי אָמַר רַב? אֲמַר רַב יוֹסֵף: תָּא שְׁמַע, דְּאָמַר רַב הוּנָא אָמַר רַב: אֵין הֲלָכָה כְּרַבִּי יוֹסֵי. אֲמַר לֵיהּ אַבַּיֵי: מַאי חֲזֵית דְּסָמְכַתְּ אַהָא, סְמוֹךְ אַהָא דַּאֲמַר רַב אַדָּא אֲמַר רַב הֲלָכָה כְּרַבִּי יוֹסֵי! אָמְרִי בֵּי רַב מַנּוּ – רַב הוּנָא, וְרַב הוּנָא אֲמַר: אֵין הֲלָכָה.

The Gemara further inquires: With regard to **proscription, what did Rav say? Rav Yosef said: Come** and **hear, as Rav Huna said** that **Rav said** that the ***halakha*** **is not in accordance with** the opinion of **Rabbi Yosei. Abaye said to him: What did you see that** led **you to rely on that** source? **Rely on this** source; **as Rav Adda said** that **Rav said** that the ***halakha*** **is** in fact **in accordance with** the opinion of **Rabbi Yosei.** There is, then, a tradition that Rav accepted Rabbi Yosei's view. The Gemara responds: When it is stated that the Sages of **the school of Rav said** a teaching, to **whom** is it referring? The reference is to **Rav Huna. And** it was **Rav Huna** who **said** that the ***halakha*** **is not** in accordance with the opinion of Rabbi Yosei. It may be presumed, then, that Rav Adda's version of Rav's ruling is in error, as preference is given to the report of Rav's preeminent disciple, Rav Huna.

״רַבִּי יְהוּדָה אוֹמֵר טוּמְטוּם״ וכו׳. אָמַר רַבִּי אַמִּי: מַאי עָבֵיד לֵיהּ רַבִּי יְהוּדָה לְטוּמְטוּם דְּבִירִי דְּאוֹתְבוּהּ אַבֵּי כּוּרְסֵיהּ וְאִיקְּרַע, וְאוֹלֵיד שִׁבְעָה בְּנִין? וְרַבִּי יְהוּדָה אָמַר לָךְ: חֲזֵר עַל בָּנָיו מֵאַיִן הֵם.

§ It is taught in the mishna that **Rabbi Yehuda says: If a** ***tumtum***, whose external sexual organs are indeterminate, was torn open so that his genitals were exposed, and he was found to be a male, he must not perform *ḥalitza* because he is treated like a eunuch. **Rabbi Ami said: What would Rabbi Yehuda do with the** ***tumtum*** living in the town of **Biri,**[B] **who was placed in a seat**[N] for an operation, **and** the tissue covering his genitals **was torn** open **and** he later **fathered seven children?** Evidently, a *tumtum* who was torn open is not necessarily sexually impotent. The Gemara answers that **Rabbi Yehuda** could have **said to you:** Go and **inquire about his children** and find out **from where they came.** He did not believe that they were fathered by this man but rather by someone else.

תַּנְיָא, רַבִּי יוֹסֵי בְּרַבִּי יְהוּדָה אוֹמֵר: טוּמְטוּם לֹא יַחֲלוֹץ, שֶׁמָּא יִקָּרַע וְנִמְצָא סְרִיס חַמָּה. אַטּוּ כׇּל דְּמִקְּרַע זָכָר הָוֵי? הָכִי קָאָמַר: שֶׁמָּא יִקָּרַע וְנִמְצָא נְקֵבָה, וַאֲפִילּוּ נִמְצָא זָכָר – שֶׁמָּא יִמָּצֵא סְרִיס חַמָּה.

It is taught in a *baraita*: **Rabbi Yosei, son of Rabbi Yehuda, says: A** ***tumtum*** **must not perform** ***ḥalitza***, as **perhaps he will be torn** open **and found** to be **a eunuch by natural causes.** The Gemara asks: Why did he formulate his teaching in this manner? **Is that to say** that **every** *tumtum* who is torn open is **a male?** It is certainly possible for a *tumtum* to be found to be a female. The Gemara explains: **This is what he said:** A *tumtum* must not perform *ḥalitza*, as **perhaps he will be torn** open **and found** to be **a female,** who certainly cannot perform *ḥalitza*, **and even if he is found** to be **a male, perhaps he will be found** to be **a eunuch by natural causes.**

NOTES

A person cannot render forbidden an item that is not his – אֵין אָדָם אוֹסֵר דָּבָר שֶׁאֵינוֹ שֶׁלּוֹ: *Tosafot* raise a basic question: Does it follow from this principle that even if one actively mingled his forbidden substance with someone else's permitted food that the mixture remains permitted? To answer this question, they explain that this principle applies only to cases in which one's thoughts and intentions are a determining factor. They attempt to prove that this is true of food crops in a vineyard as well. Continuing the line of thought of *Tosafot*, Rabbi Avraham min HaHar contends that there is a difference between a prohibition performed with the object itself, e.g., cooking meat with milk, and a case when the prohibition applies without any physical change occurring to the item, as in the case of food crops in a vineyard, where no change occurs to either the produce or the grapes. He further explains that this is connected to the amoraic dispute over whether or not one can render forbidden an item that does not belong to him if he performs an action that affects the object. *Tosafot Yeshanim* claim that food crops in a vineyard is a special case, as the verse states: "Your field" (Leviticus 19:19), implying that the prohibition takes effect only with respect to the owner of the field. This also appears to be the opinion of Rabbi Shimshon of Saens, who follows the Jerusalem Talmud and says that it is due to a biblical decree concerning food crops in a vineyard that one cannot render the produce forbidden if it is not in his possession (see *Kovetz He'arot*).

What did Shmuel say – מַה לִּי אָמַר שְׁמוּאֵל: Doesn't the very fact that Shmuel did not say the same as Rav prove that he disagrees with his ruling? One explanation is that the question is whether Shmuel's statement was originally issued as a response and in opposition to Rav, or if he was merely adding to Rav's words. It is likewise possible that Rav does not disagree with Shmuel, but he felt that in the cases mentioned by Shmuel there was no need to state that the *halakha* is ruled in accordance with the opinion of Rabbi Yosei and Rabbi Shimon, as theirs is the majority opinion (*Arukh LaNer*).

Who was placed in a seat – דְּאוֹתְבוּהּ אַבֵּי כּוּרְסֵיהּ: Rabbi Avraham min HaHar explains that this expression is a reference to marriage, as they sat him on the special chair prepared for a bridegroom. In other words, after it was decided that he would take a wife, he underwent the necessary operation.

BACKGROUND

The *tumtum* of Biri – טוּמְטוּם דְּבִירִי: This was one of uncertain gender who was torn open and discovered to be a man whose genitals were covered by a layer of skin. This is why it was permitted for him to marry a woman, as he was evidently a man, similar to a *tumtum* whose sexual organ is concealed but whose testicles are visible. The chances that such an individual, whose testicles were covered for many years, could eventually impregnate a woman are slim, as even if he could have intercourse with a woman his sperm cells would likely be incapable of fertilization. All the more so is this true of a full-fledged *tumtum*, who suffered a hormonal delay in the development of his sex organs over many years, as even if this situation were to change he would still be unable to father a child.

מַאי בֵּינַיְיהוּ? אֲמַר רָבָא: לִפְסוֹל בִּמְקוֹם אַחִין, וְלַחֲלוֹץ שֶׁלֹּא בִּמְקוֹם אַחִין, אִיכָּא בֵּינַיְיהוּ.

The Gemara asks: **What is** the practical halakhic difference **between** the opinions of Rabbi Yehuda and Rabbi Yosei? **Rava said: There is** a practical difference **between them** as to whether the *ḥalitza* performed by a *tumtum* **disqualifies** the brothers in a case **where there are** other **brothers** in addition to the *tumtum*. According to Rabbi Yehuda, a *tumtum* is regarded as definitely sexually impotent, and therefore his *ḥalitza* is of no consequence. Therefore, if the *tumtum* went ahead and performed *ḥalitza*, he has not disqualified the other brothers from performing levirate marriage. According to Rabbi Yosei, however, he is only doubtfully sexually impotent, and therefore he has disqualified the other brothers from performing levirate marriage. **And** there is also a difference between them as to whether the *tumtum* must **perform *ḥalitza* where there are no** other **brothers** besides him. According to Rabbi Yehuda he need not do so, whereas according to Rabbi Yosei he must perform *ḥalitza* owing to his uncertain status.

אָמַר רַב שְׁמוּאֵל בַּר יְהוּדָה אָמַר רַבִּי אַבָּא אֲחוּהּ דְּרַבִּי יְהוּדָה בַּר זַבְדִּי אָמַר רַב יְהוּדָה אָמַר רַב: אַנְדְּרוֹגִינוֹס חַיָּיבִין עָלָיו סְקִילָה מִשְּׁתֵּי מְקוֹמוֹת. מֵיתִיבִי, רַבִּי אֱלִיעֶזֶר אָמַר: אַנְדְּרוֹגִינוֹס חַיָּיבִין עָלָיו סְקִילָה כִּבְזָכָר, בַּמֶּה דְּבָרִים אֲמוּרִים בְּזַכְרוּת שֶׁלּוֹ, אֲבָל בְּנַקְבוּת שֶׁלּוֹ – פָּטוּר!

§ **Rav Shmuel bar Yehuda said** that **Rabbi Abba, brother of Rabbi Yehuda bar Zavdi, said** that **Rav Yehuda said** that **Rav said:** With regard to **a hermaphrodite, one is liable to** receive the punishment of **stoning on his account** for intercourse **at two places,** whether one penetrated him anally, in the manner of homosexual intercourse, or through his female organ. The Gemara **raises an objection** against this from the following teaching. **Rabbi Eliezer said:** If one had intercourse with **a hermaphrodite,** he **is liable to** be punished with **stoning on his account as if** he had relations **with a male.**[H] **In what** case **is this statement said?** It is if he had relations with him **through his male** organ, i.e., in the manner of homosexual intercourse, **but** if he engaged in intercourse with him **through his female** organ, he is **exempt.**

הוּא דְּאָמַר כִּי הַאי תַּנָּא, דְּתַנְיָא, רַבִּי סִימַאי אוֹמֵר: אַנְדְּרוֹגִינוֹס חַיָּיבִין עָלָיו סְקִילָה מִשְּׁתֵּי מְקוֹמוֹת. מַאי טַעְמָא דְּרַבִּי סִימַאי? אֲמַר רָבָא: בַּר הַמְדּוּרֵי אַסְבְּרָא לִי: ״וְאֶת זָכָר לֹא תִשְׁכַּב מִשְׁכְּבֵי אִשָּׁה״, אֵי זֶהוּ זָכָר שֶׁיֵּשׁ בּוֹ שְׁנֵי מִשְׁכָּבוֹת – הֱוֵי אוֹמֵר זֶה אַנְדְּרוֹגִינוֹס.

The Gemara answers that Rav **stated** his opinion **in accordance with** the opinion of **this *tanna*, as it is taught** in the following *baraita*: **Rabbi Simai says:** With regard to **a hermaphrodite, one is liable to** be punished with **stoning on his account** for intercourse **at two places.** The Gemara asks: **What is the reasoning of Rabbi Simai? Rava said:** The Sage **bar Hamedurei**[P] **explained** the matter **to me,** based on an allusion to this *halakha* found in the Bible. The verse states: **"And you shall not lie with a male as with a woman [*mishkevei isha*]"** (Leviticus 18:22). The phrase *mishkevei isha,* referring to lying with a woman, appears in the plural. Now, **what male has two** manners of **lying?**[N] **You must say** that **this** is referring to **a hermaphrodite,** and the plural form *mishkevei*, meaning: Lyings, indicates that there is liability for both manners of intercourse with him.

וְרַבָּנַן? אַף עַל גַּב דְּאִית בֵּיהּ שְׁנֵי מִשְׁכָּבוֹת, ״אֶת זָכָר״ כְּתִיב.

The Gemara asks: **And** how do **the Rabbis** who disagree with Rabbi Simai counter this argument? The Gemara explains: **Although he has two** manners of **lying, it is** nevertheless **written: "With a male,"** indicating that one is liable to be stoned on a hermaphrodite's account only if he had relations with him in the manner of a male.

וְרַבָּנַן, זָכָר גְּרֵידָא מְנָא לְהוּ? מֵ״אִשָּׁה״. בְּאִשָּׁה שֶׁלֹּא כְּדַרְכָּהּ מְנָא לְהוּ? מִ״וְאִשָּׁה״.

The Gemara asks: **And the Rabbis,** who explain this entire verse as referring to a hermaphrodite, **from where do they** derive that a man is prohibited from engaging in relations with **an ordinary male?** The Gemara answers: They derive it **from** the words **"a woman."** The Gemara asks further: And **from where do** the Rabbis derive that one is liable to be punished for engaging in intercourse with **a woman** who is forbidden to him even if he engaged in relations **in an unnatural manner,** i.e., anal intercourse? The Gemara responds: They derive it **from** the inclusive "and" in **"and...with a woman."**

אָמַר רַב שֵׁיזְבִי אָמַר רַב חִסְדָּא: לֹא לַכֹּל אָמַר רַבִּי אֱלִיעֶזֶר אַנְדְּרוֹגִינוֹס זָכָר מְעַלְּיָא הוּא, שֶׁאִם אַתָּה אוֹמֵר כֵּן – בְּמוּקְדָּשִׁין יִקְדַּשׁ.

§ **Rav Shezvi said** that **Rav Ḥisda said: Not in all** regards did **Rabbi Eliezer say** that **a hermaphrodite is a proper male. As, if you say so,** that a hermaphrodite is a proper male in every aspect, then **with regard to consecrated** animals an animal that is a hermaphrodite **should become sacred** if one consecrated it.

HALAKHA

One is liable on account of a hermaphrodite as if he had relations with a male – אַנְדְּרוֹגִינוֹס חַיָּיבִין עָלָיו כִּבְזָכָר: If a man had sexual relations with a hermaphrodite in the manner of homosexual intercourse, he is liable to be stoned. However, if he had intercourse with him by way of his female organ, he is exempt. The *halakha* follows the opinion of Rabbi Eliezer, in accordance with the Gemara's clarification that this is the opinion of the Rabbis, against that of Rabbi Simai (Rambam *Sefer Kedusha, Hilkhot Issurei Bia* 1:15).

PERSONALITIES

Bar Hamedurei – בַּר הַמְדּוּרֵי: This Sage, about whom almost nothing is known, was a disciple of Shmuel who transmitted *halakhot* in his master's name. He lived during the period of Rava as well, and Rava cites several teachings in his name, almost all of them introduced with the phrase: The Sage bar Hamedurei explained the matter to me.

The *Arukh* reads his name as bar Hamedudei, and he explains that Hamedudei means one who heats cauldrons [*dudei*], i.e., a cook. Based on this, it is possible that bar Hamedurei, who is never mentioned by any proper name or title, was an ordinary man who was never counted among the ranks of the Sages, but because he spent time in the presence of scholars, he heard words of Torah from their mouths and even merited to contribute of his own knowledge to their discussions.

NOTES

Two manners of lying – שְׁנֵי מִשְׁכָּבוֹת: Some early authorities maintain that the dispute is whether a hermaphrodite is a full-fledged male with an additional organ that does not affect his essential nature, or whether he merely resembles a male. Accordingly, the opinion that he is a full-fledged male renders one liable for two manners of lying with him, as even if he engaged in relations through his female organ he was still a male at the time of intercourse. The Rashba inquires as to why this view is not considered equivalent to Rabbi Yosei's opinion in the mishna, as he, too, claims that a hermaphrodite is a full-fledged male. He answers that Rabbi Yosei and Rabbi Shimon in the mishna do follow this opinion, but the Gemara wished to cite a proof from an explicit teaching to this effect.

It has been pointed out that the Rambam's ruling that a hermaphrodite is of doubtful status, but that nevertheless a man is liable to be stoned for sexual relations with him, is based on the assumption that a hermaphrodite is a unique being, whose prohibition to engage in homosexual intercourse is derived from the inclusive term: "And...a male [*ve'et zakhar*]" (Leviticus 18:22). The term "*et*" is understood as indicating one who is similar to, but not exactly the same as, a male. However, this does not mean that he is actually a male (see Rashba and Ritva).

וּמְנָלַן דְּלָא קָדַשׁ – דְּתָנוּ רַבָּנַן: הַנִּרְבָּע, וְהַמּוּקְצֶה, וְהַנֶּעֱבָד, וְהָאֶתְנָן, וּמְחִיר, וְטוּמְטוּם, וְאַנְדְּרוֹגִינוֹס מְטַמְּאִין בְּגָדִים אַבֵּית הַבְּלִיעָה.

And from where do we derive that it does not become sacred? As the Sages taught in a *baraita*: With regard to a bird **used for sexual relations** with a human being, **and one set aside**[H] for idolatrous purposes, **and one** that itself was **worshipped** as an idol, **and one** given as **payment** to a prostitute (see Deuteronomy 23:19), **and one** that was **the price of a dog** received in exchange for the sale of a dog (see Deuteronomy 23:19), **and** similarly, a bird that is a ***tumtum*** **or a hermaphrodite,** if one killed any of these birds by pinching their necks in the manner of an offering rather than by ritual slaughter, the birds **render** him and the **garments** he is wearing **ritually impure,** when the birds are eaten and come into contact **with his throat.**[HN] The reason is that pinching is valid only for sacrificial birds; any other bird that is killed by pinching is deemed an unslaughtered carcass. Since none of these birds are fit to be sacrificed, pinching their necks renders them unslaughtered carcasses, and the unslaughtered carcass of a clean bird imparts ritual impurity when it is eaten and reaches the individual's throat.

רַבִּי אֱלִיעֶזֶר אוֹמֵר: טוּמְטוּם וְאַנְדְּרוֹגִינוֹס אֵין מְטַמְּאִין בְּגָדִים אַבֵּית הַבְּלִיעָה. שֶׁהָיָה רַבִּי אֱלִיעֶזֶר אוֹמֵר: כָּל מָקוֹם שֶׁנֶּאֱמַר זָכָר וּנְקֵבָה – אַתָּה מוֹצִיא טוּמְטוּם וְאַנְדְּרוֹגִינוֹס מִבֵּינֵיהֶם, וְעוֹף, הוֹאִיל וְלֹא נֶאֱמַר בּוֹ זָכָר וּנְקֵבָה – אִי אַתָּה מוֹצִיא טוּמְטוּם וְאַנְדְּרוֹגִינוֹס מִבֵּינֵיהֶם.

Rabbi Eliezer says: If one pinched the neck of a bird that is a ***tumtum*** **or a hermaphrodite, it does not render** him and the **garments** he is wearing **ritually impure** when it is eaten and comes into contact **with his throat,** as the sanctity of an offering does in fact apply to it. **As Rabbi Eliezer would say: Wherever it is** explicitly **stated** in the Torah **"male"** and **"female," you are to remove a** ***tumtum*** **and a hermaphrodite from among them,** as their gender status is in doubt. This is true of animal offerings, with regard to which the Torah uses the terms male and female. In the case of a **bird**-offering, however, **since male and female are not stated with regard to it,** but instead the Torah simply mentions turtledoves and young pigeons, **you are not to remove a** ***tumtum*** **and a hermaphrodite from among them,** as they are fit for the altar. It is evident then that Rabbi Eliezer maintains that a hermaphrodite is not considered a proper male with respect to offerings.

אָמַר רַב נַחְמָן בַּר יִצְחָק: אַף אֲנַן נַמִּי תָּנֵינָא, רַבִּי אֱלִיעֶזֶר אוֹמֵר:

Rav Naḥman bar Yitzḥak said: We too learned this explicitly in a *baraita* that states: **Rabbi Eliezer says:**

Perek **VIII**
Daf **84** Amud **a**

הַכִּלְאַיִם וּטְרֵפָה, וְיוֹצֵא דוֹפֶן, טוּמְטוּם וְאַנְדְּרוֹגִינוֹס – לֹא קְדוֹשִׁין וְלֹא מְקַדְּשִׁין.

Forbidden crossbred livestock, an animal with a condition that will cause it to die within twelve months [***tereifa***],[H] **an animal delivered through the abdominal wall,**[B] **and an animal that is a** ***tumtum*** **or a hermaphrodite do not become sacred**[N] **and do not render** another animal **sacred** in their place.

HALAKHA

A bird used for sexual relations, and one set aside, etc. – הַנִּרְבָּע, וְהַמּוּקְצֶה וכו׳: A bird offering that was killed by pinching is not considered an unslaughtered carcass with respect to the *halakhot* of ritual impurity. This *halakha* applies only if the bird was fit for sacrifice, but if it was used for sexual relations with a human being, or set aside for idolatrous purposes, or was itself worshipped as an idol, or was given as payment to a prostitute, or was the price of a dog, or was a *tumtum* or a hermaphrodite, it is considered an unslaughtered carcass in all regards. Consequently, it renders one and the garments he is wearing ritually impure when it is eaten and comes into contact with one's throat. The *halakha* is ruled in accordance with the opinion of the Rabbis, against that of Rabbi Eliezer (Rambam *Sefer Avoda, Hilkhot Pesulei HaMukdashin* 7:1–4).

A *tumtum* and a hermaphrodite with regard to the offerings – טוּמְטוּם וְאַנְדְּרוֹגִינוֹס בְּקָדָשִׁים: An animal that is a *tumtum* or a hermaphrodite is considered to be blemished, so that the sanctity of the altar does not apply to it. Even a bird that is a *tumtum* or a hermaphrodite is unfit for the altar, as there is a doubt as to whether it is a male or a female. This is in accordance with the opinion of the Rabbis, against that of Rabbi Eliezer (Rambam *Sefer Avoda, Hilkhot Issurei Mizbe'aḥ* 3:3).

NOTES

They render garments ritually impure when they come into contact with his throat – מְטַמְּאִין בְּגָדִים אַבֵּית הַבְּלִיעָה: A special *halakha* applies to the carcass of a clean bird. Although it is impure, it does not impart ritual impurity via touching or carrying, as does the carcass of an animal, but only via eating. When a piece of the carcass enters one's esophagus, he contracts ritual impurity that affects not only himself but also the clothes he is wearing at the time.

BACKGROUND

Delivered through the abdominal wall – יוֹצֵא דוֹפֶן: An animal that was delivered through the abdominal wall is one that was not born naturally but by means of a caesarean section. The animal is called by this name because it was delivered through the abdominal wall of its mother. Various halakhic matters apply only in cases of natural birth, and animals delivered through the abdominal wall are governed by different *halakhot*.

HALAKHA

Forbidden crossbred livestock and a *tereifa*, etc. – הַכִּלְאַיִם וּטְרֵפָה וכו׳: If one attempted to substitute for an animal that had been designated as an offering a crossbred animal, an animal with a condition that will cause it to die within twelve months [*tereifa*], an animal delivered through the abdominal wall, or an animal that is a *tumtum* or a hermaphrodite, the substituted animal does not become sacred, and it is as though one had tried to transfer the sanctity of the offering to a camel or a donkey. The *halakha* follows the opinion of Rabbi Eliezer, in accordance with Shmuel's explanation (Rambam *Sefer Korbanot, Hilkhot Temura* 1:17).

NOTES

They do not become sacred – לֹא קְדוֹשִׁין: Why is it necessary to cite Shmuel's explanation that the phrase: They do not become sacred, is referring to substitution? Even if one would claim that: They do not become sacred, is referring to the initial consecration of an offering, this still proves that a hermaphrodite is not a male. The *Arukh LaNer* answers that were it not for Shmuel's statement, one might have said that a hermaphrodite does not become sacred because it is considered a male with a blemish. The Gemara therefore cites Shmuel's teaching that although a blemished animal becomes sacred through substitution, a hermaphrodite does not.

וְאָמַר שְׁמוּאֵל: לֹא קְדוֹשִׁין – בִּתְמוּרָה, וְלֹא מְקַדְּשִׁין – בְּעוֹשֶׂה תְּמוּרָה, שְׁמַע מִינָּהּ.

And Shmuel said: They do not become sacred by way of substitution,[N] i.e., if one had an animal that had been designated as an offering, and he wished to substitute one of these animals for it, the substituted animal does not become sacred. **And they** themselves **do not render** another animal **sacred when it is made a substitute**[N] for them. If one designated one of these animals as an offering and he wished to substitute another animal for it, it does not become sacred. The Gemara concludes: **Learn from this** that Rabbi Eliezer does not consider a hermaphrodite to be a proper male.

״רַבִּי אֱלִיעֶזֶר אוֹמֵר: חַיָּיבִין עָלָיו סְקִילָה כְּזָכָר״. תַּנְיָא, אָמַר רַבִּי: כְּשֶׁהָלַכְתִּי לִלְמוֹד תּוֹרָה אֵצֶל רַבִּי אֶלְעָזָר בֶּן שַׁמּוּעַ, חָבְרוּ עָלַי תַּלְמִידָיו כְּתַרְנְגוֹלִים שֶׁל בֵּית בּוּקְיָא, וְלֹא הִנִּיחוּנִי לִלְמוֹד אֶלָּא דָּבָר אֶחָד בְּמִשְׁנָתֵינוּ: רַבִּי אֱלִיעֶזֶר אוֹמֵר: אַנְדְּרוֹגִינוֹס חַיָּיבִין עָלָיו סְקִילָה כְּזָכָר.

It is taught in the mishna that **Rabbi Eliezer says:** If one had intercourse with **a hermaphrodite,** one **is liable to** be punished with **stoning on his account as if** one had relations with **a male. It is taught** on this matter in a *baraita* that **Rabbi** Yehuda HaNasi **says: When I went to learn Torah from Rabbi Elazar ben Shamua, his students joined** together **against me like the roosters of Beit Bukya,**[B] highly aggressive animals that do not allow other creatures to remain among them, **and they did not let me learn**[N] there. Therefore, I managed to learn **only one thing in our mishna,** which is that **Rabbi Eliezer says:** If one had intercourse with **a hermaphrodite,** one **is liable to** be punished with **stoning on his account as if** one had relations with **a male.**

הדרן עלך הערל

NOTES

Substitution – תְּמוּרָה: The *halakha* of substitution appears in Leviticus 27:10, and an entire tractate, *Temura*, deals with its details. The basic *halakha* of substitution is that while it is prohibited to replace a sanctified animal, i.e., one that has been consecrated as an offering, with another animal, and anyone who does so has transgressed a prohibition and is liable to be flogged, the animal designated as a substitute is nevertheless sanctified. However, the first animal still retains its own sanctity. Furthermore, although blemished animals cannot become sacred through initial consecration, they can become sacred through substitution. Nevertheless, a special biblical decree teaches that the animals listed in the Gemara do not become sacred through substitution.

And they do not render another animal sacred when it is made a substitute – וְלֹא מְקַדְּשִׁין בְּעוֹשֶׂה תְּמוּרָה: Rashi suggests several possibilities as to how these disqualified animals can become sanctified. The early authorities point out that one could simply say that they all became sacred as the offspring of offerings, but since not all Sages agree that the offspring of offerings are sanctified, it is preferable to find other explanations for their sanctification.

They did not let me learn – לֹא הִנִּיחוּנִי לִלְמוֹד: In the Jerusalem Talmud, where this incident is recounted as well, it is discussed whether the reason they prevented him from studying there was because they did not want him to reveal matters best kept secret or because they thought him unworthy to be a disciple of their teacher (see *Arukh LaNer*).

BACKGROUND

The roosters of Beit Bukya – תַּרְנְגוֹלִים שֶׁל בֵּית בּוּקְיָא: Roosters in general are aggressive birds, described by the Sages as fierce. A new rooster will encounter hostility from the local roosters whose turf it enters. Various other birds will also attack any stranger, even when the stranger is not of their own species. There are special breeds of roosters that are raised to act aggressively, such as fighting cocks. Apparently, the roosters of Beit Bukya were known for their especially aggressive nature.

One rooster attacking another

Summary of **Perek VIII**

This chapter dealt with subject matter that is unrelated to the central issues of tractate *Yevamot* and appears here merely to complete the discussion started in the previous chapter. Discussion of the *halakha* that an uncircumcised or ritually impure priest enables his wife and slaves to partake of *teruma*, although he himself is prohibited from doing so, led to a clarification of the source of the *halakha* that an uncircumcised man is disqualified from eating *teruma*. Incidental to the discussion concerning a man with crushed testicles, who may himself partake of *teruma* but does not enable his wife to do so, the Gemara clarified the details of the *halakhot* governing a man with crushed testicles. What is the nature of his injury? Is there a medical remedy that can influence his halakhic status?

As for the other cases of those disqualified from entering into marriage, the conclusion is reached that with regard to Ammonite and Moabite converts it is necessary to differentiate between males and females. Males, along with their male descendants, are permanently prohibited from entering into the congregation. Females, however, are permitted to do so even in the first generation. In the case of Egyptian and Edomite converts, on the other hand, male and female converts are equally prohibited from entering into the congregation, as are their direct descendants. However, the third-generation descendants are permitted. Those of *mamzer* status, as well as the Gibeonites, who by rabbinic decree have been given the same status, are prohibited from entering into the congregation forever, whether male or female.

A man with crushed testicles or a severed penis is prohibited from entering into the congregation. However, the mitzva of levirate marriage still applies to these men and their wives. Those who are incapable of having children due to illness or some flaw in their development, including a sexually underdeveloped male or a sexually underdeveloped female, are not prohibited from entering into marriage, although the mitzva of levirate marriage does not apply to them. However, owing to the absence of secondary sexual characteristics, e.g., pubic hair, the point at which they reach maturity is uncertain. The Gemara concluded that if their status is clearly identified, then they are considered to have reached adulthood at the age of twenty.

Since a hermaphrodite has male genitals, he is considered male and may marry a woman. He is also considered male with regard to sexual relations. As for a *tumtum*, since he is subject to an uncertainty that cannot be clarified, the *halakhot* of marriage do not apply to him at all.

Introduction to **Perek IX**

This chapter begins with a summary of the tractate's previous chapters, including a detailed review of all of the possible combinations of men and women whose either regular or levirate marriages are prohibited. Following this, the chapter turns to a matter that has not yet been discussed: Clarification of the rights of women in prohibited marriages.

In general, the property rights of a married woman depend on the circumstances of her marriage. During the time she is married, she is entitled to receive provisions for her sustenance from her husband, while he is entitled to the profits from usufruct properties that she brings into the marriage.

If the marriage is terminated as a result of the husband's death or a divorce, the woman is entitled to the main and additional sums specified in her marriage contract. The usufruct properties, which remained in her ownership even as her husband enjoyed the profits, now revert to her complete possession and control. Additionally, she retains possession of any articles of clothing that she brought into the marriage and wore.

If, however, the marriage is annulled retroactively because it is deemed to have been invalid, the woman is entitled to receive all the profits her husband accrued from use of her usufruct properties.

This chapter also deals with cases of marriage that, while prohibited by rabbinic or Torah law, are nevertheless deemed valid in the sense that they cannot be terminated without a bill of divorce. On this matter, a question arises: Is the woman bereft of rights in these cases of illegal marriage? Or perhaps, since she was in fact married, she retains some partial entitlements?

Similarly, this chapter summarizes the right of women married to priests to partake of *teruma* during their husbands' lifetimes and after their deaths, as well as the right of women married to Levites to partake of the tithes during their husbands' lives and after their deaths.

Perek **IX**
Daf **84** Amud **a**

מתני׳ יֵשׁ מוּתָּרוֹת לְבַעֲלֵיהֶן וַאֲסוּרוֹת לִיבְמֵיהֶן, מוּתָּרוֹת לִיבְמֵיהֶן וַאֲסוּרוֹת לְבַעֲלֵיהֶן, מוּתָּרוֹת לְאֵלּוּ וּלְאֵלּוּ, וַאֲסוּרוֹת לְאֵלּוּ וּלְאֵלּוּ.

MISHNA **There are** women **who are permitted to their husbands and forbidden to their** *yevamin*,[N] while others **are permitted to their** ***yevamin*** **and forbidden to their husbands.** Certain women **are permitted** both **to these and to those,** and others **are forbidden to** both **these and to those.**

וְאֵלּוּ מוּתָּרוֹת לְבַעֲלֵיהֶן וַאֲסוּרוֹת לִיבְמֵיהֶן: כֹּהֵן הֶדְיוֹט שֶׁנָּשָׂא אֶת הָאַלְמָנָה וְיֵשׁ לוֹ אָח כֹּהֵן גָּדוֹל; חָלָל שֶׁנָּשָׂא כְּשֵׁרָה וְיֵשׁ לוֹ אָח כָּשֵׁר;

The mishna elaborates: **And these are** cases of women who are **permitted to their husbands**[N] **and forbidden to their** ***yevamin***: In the case of **a common priest who married a widow, and he has a brother** who is **the High Priest,** the widow, who was permitted to her husband, is forbidden to her *yavam*, as it is prohibited for the High Priest to marry a widow. The same is true in the case of **a priest disqualified due to flawed lineage [*ḥalal*],** e.g., the son of a priest and a divorcée, **who married** a woman **fit** to marry a priest, **and he has a brother** who is a priest **fit** for service. That woman was permitted to marry the *ḥalal* but is forbidden to his brother. Having engaged in intercourse with the *ḥalal*, she is rendered a *ḥalala*, a woman disqualified from marrying a priest.

יִשְׂרָאֵל שֶׁנָּשָׂא בַּת יִשְׂרָאֵל וְיֵשׁ לוֹ אָח מַמְזֵר; מַמְזֵר שֶׁנָּשָׂא מַמְזֶרֶת וְיֵשׁ לוֹ אָח יִשְׂרָאֵל – מוּתָּרוֹת לְבַעֲלֵיהֶן וַאֲסוּרוֹת לִיבְמֵיהֶן.

Another example is the case of **an Israelite** of unflawed lineage **who married an Israelite woman** of similar lineage, **and he has a brother** who is **a son born from an incestuous or adulterous relationship [*mamzer*];** or **a** ***mamzer*** **who married a daughter born from an incestuous or adulterous relationship [*mamzeret*], and he has a brother** who is **an Israelite** of unflawed lineage. A *mamzer* is permitted to marry a *mamzeret*, but neither is permitted to a Jew of unflawed lineage. In each of these cases, these women **are permitted to their husbands and forbidden to their** ***yevamin.***

וְאֵלּוּ מוּתָּרוֹת לִיבְמֵיהֶן וַאֲסוּרוֹת לְבַעֲלֵיהֶן: כֹּהֵן גָּדוֹל שֶׁקִּידֵּשׁ אֶת הָאַלְמָנָה וְיֵשׁ לוֹ אָח כֹּהֵן הֶדְיוֹט; כָּשֵׁר שֶׁנָּשָׂא חֲלָלָה וְיֵשׁ לוֹ אָח חָלָל; יִשְׂרָאֵל שֶׁנָּשָׂא מַמְזֶרֶת וְיֵשׁ לוֹ אָח מַמְזֵר; מַמְזֵר שֶׁנָּשָׂא בַּת יִשְׂרָאֵל וְיֵשׁ לוֹ אָח יִשְׂרָאֵל – מוּתָּרוֹת לִיבְמֵיהֶן וַאֲסוּרוֹת לְבַעֲלֵיהֶן.

And these are cases of women who **are permitted to their** ***yevamin*** **and forbidden to their husbands:**[N] For example, there is the case of **a High Priest who betrothed a widow, and he has a brother** who **is a common priest,** whom she is permitted to marry. This is true only if the High Priest merely betrothed her. However, if he consummated the marriage, he rendered her a *ḥalala* forbidden to all priests, including her *yavam*. The additional cases are a priest **fit** for service **who married a** ***ḥalala*** **and he has a brother** who is **a** ***ḥalal***; **an Israelite** of unflawed lineage **who married a** ***mamzeret***, **and he has a brother** who is **a** ***mamzer***; and **a** ***mamzer*** **who married an Israelite woman** of unflawed lineage, **and he has a brother** who is, similarly, **an Israelite** of unflawed lineage. All of these women **are permitted to their** ***yevamin*** **and forbidden to their husbands.**[H]

וְאֵלּוּ אֲסוּרוֹת לְאֵלּוּ וּלְאֵלּוּ: כֹּהֵן גָּדוֹל שֶׁנָּשָׂא אֶת הָאַלְמָנָה וְיֵשׁ לוֹ אָח כֹּהֵן גָּדוֹל אוֹ כֹּהֵן הֶדְיוֹט; כָּשֵׁר שֶׁנָּשָׂא חֲלָלָה וְיֵשׁ לוֹ אָח כָּשֵׁר; יִשְׂרָאֵל שֶׁנָּשָׂא מַמְזֶרֶת וְיֵשׁ לוֹ אָח יִשְׂרָאֵל; מַמְזֵר שֶׁנָּשָׂא בַּת יִשְׂרָאֵל וְיֵשׁ לוֹ אָח מַמְזֵר – אֲסוּרוֹת לְאֵלּוּ וּלְאֵלּוּ. וּשְׁאָר כׇּל הַנָּשִׁים מוּתָּרוֹת לְבַעֲלֵיהֶן וְלִיבְמֵיהֶן.

And these are cases where women **are forbidden** both **to these and to those: A High Priest who married a widow, and he has a brother** who is **a High Priest or a common priest;** a priest **fit** for service **who married a** ***ḥalala***, **and he has a brother** who is a priest **fit** for service; **an Israelite** of unflawed lineage **who married a** ***mamzeret***, **and he has a brother** who is similarly an ordinary **Israelite,** or **a** ***mamzer*** **who married an Israelite woman** of unflawed lineage, **and he has a brother** who **is a** ***mamzer***. All of these women **are forbidden** both **to these and to those. And all other women**[N] **are permitted to their husbands and to their** ***yevamin***.

שְׁנִיּוֹת מִדִּבְרֵי סוֹפְרִים: שְׁנִיָּיה לַבַּעַל וְלֹא שְׁנִיָּיה לַיָּבָם – אֲסוּרָה לַבַּעַל וּמוּתֶּרֶת לַיָּבָם. שְׁנִיָּיה לַיָּבָם וְלֹא שְׁנִיָּיה לַבַּעַל – אֲסוּרָה לַיָּבָם וּמוּתֶּרֶת לַבַּעַל. שְׁנִיָּיה לָזֶה וְלָזֶה – אֲסוּרָה לָזֶה וְלָזֶה.

With regard to **secondary relatives,** who are forbidden **by rabbinic law,** if the woman is **a secondary relative to the husband but not a secondary relative to the** ***yavam***, she **is forbidden to the husband and permitted to the** ***yavam***. Conversely, if she is **a secondary relative to the** ***yavam*** **but not a secondary relative to the husband,** she **is forbidden to the** ***yavam*** **and permitted to the husband.** If she is **a secondary relative** both **to this** man **and to that** man, she **is forbidden to this** one **and to that** one.

NOTES

There are women who are permitted to their husbands and forbidden to their ***yevamin*** **– יֵשׁ מוּתָּרוֹת לְבַעֲלֵיהֶן וַאֲסוּרוֹת לִיבְמֵיהֶן:** *Tosafot* explain that this chapter presents a summary of the topic of forbidden and permitted *yevamot*. After this chapter, the tractate turns to other matters, which are connected to levirate marriage but not to the specific issue of permitted and forbidden *yevamot*. They further explain that there are certain novel elements in the mishna's statements with regard to those who are forbidden to their husbands but permitted to their *yevamin*. Furthermore, even if there is no novelty with regard to the *halakhot* of *yevamot*, the chapter does offer original *halakhot* with regard to the conditions of a marriage contract as well as the marriage contract itself.

And these are permitted to their husbands – וְאֵלּוּ מוּתָּרוֹת לְבַעֲלֵיהֶן: This mishna follows a format used elsewhere. It states a principle and then lists specific cases for each category. The specific cases are presented in the same order as the general categories. The *tanna* does not present those who are permitted both to their husbands and their *yevamin* in order, but rather states this *halakha* in shortened form at the end, because in all of the other cases he brings detailed examples, whereas the women who are permitted to both are mentioned in general terms (Ritva).

And these are permitted to their ***yevamin*** **and forbidden to their husbands – וְאֵלּוּ מוּתָּרוֹת לִיבְמֵיהֶן וַאֲסוּרוֹת לְבַעֲלֵיהֶן:** This ruling explains that although the marriage itself was improper, an obligation of levirate marriage exists nevertheless, and it is permitted for the *yevamin* to marry the women. This is true despite the fact that with regard to certain prohibitions the Gemara applies the following *a fortiori* inference: If she is forbidden to the man usually permitted to her, namely her husband, she is certainly also prohibited to her *yavam*, who as her husband's brother is ordinarily forbidden to her. Furthermore, although her marriage was never supposed to serve reproductive purposes, as her husband was obligated to divorce her, the mitzva to establish offspring for one's deceased brother still remains (Ritva; see *Nimmukei Yosef*).

And all other women – וּשְׁאָר כׇּל הַנָּשִׁים: In the Jerusalem Talmud, which is cited by several early authorities including the Rashba, it is pointed out that this statement is imprecise, as there are several other cases in which the woman is forbidden to the husband or *yavam* that are omitted by the mishna. The Gemara there infers a universal principle from this: Practical *halakha* cannot be derived from the generalizations of a mishna, as they are not always formulated precisely.

HALAKHA

Permitted to their ***yevamin*** **and forbidden to their husbands – מוּתָּרוֹת לִיבְמֵיהֶן וַאֲסוּרוֹת לְבַעֲלֵיהֶן:** In the case where a woman was forbidden to her husband by dint of a prohibition, a prohibition stated as a positive mitzva, or because they are secondary relatives forbidden to each other by rabbinic law, but she is permitted to her *yavam*, they may perform levirate marriage (Rambam *Sefer Nashim, Hilkhot Yibbum* 6:13; *Shulḥan Arukh, Even HaEzer* 174:2).

אֵין לָהּ לֹא כְּתוּבָּה, וְלֹא פֵּירוֹת, וְלֹא מְזוֹנוֹת, וְלֹא בְּלָאוֹת, וְהַוָּלָד כָּשֵׁר, וְכוֹפִין אוֹתוֹ לְהוֹצִיא.

Furthermore, if a man marries a woman forbidden to him as a secondary relative, **she does not have** the right to receive payment for her **marriage contract**[H] if divorced or widowed, **nor** is she entitled to payment from her husband for the **produce** of her property that he used, **nor** is she entitled to provisions for her **sustenance** from his estate, **nor** does she get back her **worn clothes** or other objects she brought with her to her marriage. **And** the lineage of **the offspring is unflawed, and** the court **forces him to divorce** her.[H]

אַלְמָנָה לְכֹהֵן גָּדוֹל, גְּרוּשָׁה וַחֲלוּצָה לְכֹהֵן הֶדְיוֹט, מַמְזֶרֶת וּנְתִינָה לְיִשְׂרָאֵל, בַּת יִשְׂרָאֵל לְנָתִין וּלְמַמְזֵר – יֵשׁ לָהֶן כְּתוּבָּה.

In contrast, **a widow** married **to a High Priest,**[H] **a divorcée or a *yevama* who performed *ḥalitza* [*ḥalutza*]** married **to a common priest, a *mamzeret* or a Gibeonite woman** married **to an Israelite** of unflawed lineage, and **an Israelite woman** of unflawed lineage married **to a Gibeonite or to a *mamzer*** all **have** the right to receive payment for their **marriage contract,** although it was prohibited for them to marry.

גמ׳ מַאי אִירְיָא דְּתָנֵי נָשָׂא, לִיתְנֵי קִידֵּשׁ!

GEMARA As an example of a woman who is permitted to her husband and forbidden to her *yavam*, the mishna cites the case of a widow married to a common priest whose brother was a High Priest. The Gemara asks: **Why does** the *tanna* **specifically teach** a case where the priest **married**[N] the widow? **Let him teach** that he **betrothed**[N] her, as even if she is widowed after betrothal she requires levirate marriage or *ḥalitza*.[B]

וְכִי תֵּימָא: טַעֲמָא דְּנָשָׂא, דַּהֲוָה לֵיהּ עֲשֵׂה וְלֹא תַעֲשֶׂה, אֲבָל קִידֵּשׁ אָתֵי עֲשֵׂה וְדוֹחֶה לֹא תַעֲשֶׂה – וְהָא כּוּלָּהּ פִּירְקִין עֲשֵׂה וְלֹא תַעֲשֶׂה הוּא, וְלָא אָתֵי עֲשֵׂה וְדָחֵי לֹא תַעֲשֶׂה!

And if you would say: The **reason** that the *tanna* cited the case where they **were married** is that in this case **there is a positive mitzva** that the High Priest marry a virgin **and** also **a prohibition** to marry a widow, and therefore she is forbidden to him. **However,** if **he betrothed** her, the **positive mitzva** of levirate marriage **comes and overrides** the **prohibition** against marrying a widow. To counter this argument, the *tanna* states: **But** that cannot be the case, as **the entire chapter**[N] discusses cases involving the **positive mitzva** of levirate marriage **and prohibitions,** and in all those cases, the **positive mitzva does not come and override the prohibition,** even in the absence of an additional positive mitzva.

מִשּׁוּם דְּקָבָעֵי לְמִיתְנֵי סֵיפָא: ״כֹּהֵן גָּדוֹל שֶׁנָּשָׂא אֶת הָאַלְמָנָה״ דַּוְקָא נָשָׂא – דְּשַׁוְיַיהּ חֲלָלָה, אֲבָל קִידֵּשׁ – שַׁרְיָא לֵיהּ, תָּנָא נַמִי רֵישָׁא ״נָשָׂא״.

The Gemara answers: The mishna could have cited a case where the priest betrothed the widow. Instead, the mishna cites a case where the priest married a widow, **due to** the fact **that** the *tanna* **wants to teach in the latter clause** of the mishna the case of a **High Priest who married a widow** who has a brother who is a common priest. That case is **specifically** if he **married** her, **because he** thereby **rendered her a *ḥalala*. However,** if he only **betrothed** her, **she is permitted** to his brother who is a common priest, as it is permitted for him to marry a widow. Therefore, the *tanna* **also taught** in the **first clause** the case where the priest **married** her.

HALAKHA

She does not have the right to receive payment for her marriage contract, etc. – **אֵין לָהּ לֹא כְּתוּבָּה וכו׳**: If a man marries a woman forbidden to him as a secondary relative, whether or not he was aware of this fact, she has no claim to the main sum of her marriage contract, meaning the primary commitment of two hundred dinars for a virgin or one hundred dinars for a bride who is not a virgin. She also has no claim to any of the additional stipulations in the marriage contract, clauses that obligate the husband to provide the wife with additional benefits in various circumstances. However, she does receive the additional sum of the marriage contract: a supplementary amount above the compulsory one hundred or two hundred dinars that the husband may have added voluntarily. She is not entitled to sustenance from her husband's estate, even after his death. Furthermore, as an additional disincentive, he does not have to pay for his consumption of the produce of her property during their marriage (Rambam *Sefer Nashim, Hilkhot Ishut* 24:2; *Shulḥan Arukh, Even HaEzer* 116:4).

And the court forces him to divorce her – **וְכוֹפִין אוֹתוֹ לְהוֹצִיא**: If a man married a woman forbidden to him, the court forces him to divorce her, even if she is prohibited only by rabbinic law, e.g., she is a secondary relative (Rambam *Sefer Nashim, Hilkhot Ishut* 24:2; *Shulḥan Arukh, Even HaEzer* 154:20).

A widow married to a High Priest, etc. – **אַלְמָנָה לְכֹהֵן גָּדוֹל וכו׳**: In the case of one who married a woman forbidden to him by a Torah prohibition, if he was aware of the prohibition at the time of marriage, she receives her basic marriage contract and his addition to it, as well as all the conditions of the marriage contract, and she is sustained from his property after his death.

If he did not know about the prohibited nature of the marriage, she does not receive her basic marriage contract or any of the conditions of the marriage contract, although she is entitled to the additional part. The Rambam rules that a woman who married a man forbidden to her by a positive mitzva is entitled to payment of her marriage contract, the additional sum, and her sustenance, as the transgression is a light one. He maintains that the mishna spoke only of prohibitions (Rambam *Sefer Nashim, Hilkhot Ishut* 24:4 and *Kesef Mishne* there; *Shulḥan Arukh, Even HaEzer* 116:1).

NOTES

Why does he specifically teach: Married – **מַאי אִירְיָא דְּתָנֵי נָשָׂא**: Many commentators, including Rashi, understand this question as referring to the first clause of the mishna. The Maharsha, in his second edition, asks why the same difficulty is not raised concerning all of the other cases in the mishna that state: Married, instead of: Betrothed. He answers that with regard to other prohibitions there is no practical halakhic difference whether he married or betrothed her, as the prohibition is created by the forbidden relationship. In the case of a High Priest, however, it does matter whether she is a virgin.

Let him teach that he betrothed – **לִיתְנֵי קִידֵּשׁ**: This and other related questions are posed by the Jerusalem Talmud as well. The primary answer given there is that the mishna's generalizations are not precise, and therefore nothing can be inferred from the omission of particular examples.

But the entire chapter – **וְהָא כּוּלָּהּ פִּירְקִין**: According to Rashi, this ruling is based on a biblical exposition. Rashba points out that the conclusion of the Gemara indicates otherwise, as stated by Rava: Although a positive mitzva does override a prohibition, the Sages decreed that they should not perform levirate marriage in this case, since only the first act of intercourse fulfills the mitzva of levirate marriage; and any additional cohabitation, which does not constitute a mitzva, is prohibited (*Peri Eshel*).

BACKGROUND

Betrothed and married – **קִידֵּשׁ וְנָשָׂא**: A Jewish wedding is divided into two distinct parts. Betrothal is the first stage of the marriage process. The bond created by betrothal is so strong that, after betrothal, the woman is forbidden to other men, and intercourse with another man is considered adulterous and is punishable by death. Consequently, a betrothed woman requires a divorce before she can marry another man. Nevertheless, at this stage the betrothed couple may not yet cohabit as man and wife, and most of the couple's mutual obligations do not yet apply.

The second stage of the marriage process follows the betrothal. Marriage is effected by having the bride and groom come under the wedding canopy, and this immediately confers both the privileges and the responsibilities associated with marriage upon the newlywed couple. After marriage, if one spouse dies, all the *halakhot* of mourning for a close relative apply to the surviving spouse. If a priest's wife dies, he is permitted to render himself ritually impure to bury her. All the monetary rights and obligations applying to married couples take effect after marriage.

Today, betrothal and marriage are performed in quick succession as part of a single ceremony, but in talmudic times there was usually a year-long gap between the two.

וְאַדְּתָנֵי מִשּׁוּם סֵיפָא – לִיתְנֵי מִשּׁוּם מְצִיעֲתָא: ״כֹּהֵן גָּדוֹל שֶׁקִּידֵּשׁ אֶת הָאַלְמָנָה וְיֵשׁ לוֹ אָח כֹּהֵן הֶדְיוֹט״! אֶלָּא מִשּׁוּם בַּת בּוּקְתָא. דְּקָבָעֵי לְמִיתְנֵי: ״חָלָל שֶׁנָּשָׂא כְּשֵׁרָה״, טַעֲמָא – דְּנָשָׂא, דְּשַׁוְיַיהּ חֲלָלָה. אֲבָל קִידֵּשׁ – שַׁרְיָא לֵיהּ, מִשּׁוּם הָכִי קָתָנֵי ״נָשָׂא״.

The Gemara asks: **But rather than teaching** a case where she was married in the first clause **due to the latter clause** of the mishna, **let him teach** a case where she was betrothed in the first clause **due to the middle clause,** which speaks of **a High Priest who betrothed a widow, and he has a brother** who is **a common priest.** The Gemara concludes: **Rather,** the reason the *tanna* taught the case where the priest married the widow is **due to** the *halakha* that is its **neighbor** [***bat bukta***],[L] i.e., due to the fact **that** in the adjacent case **he wants to teach** the case of **a *ḥalal* who married** a woman **fit** to marry a priest. There, the **reason** that the woman is forbidden to his brother is specifically that the *ḥalal* **married** her, **as he rendered her a *ḥalala*** by consummating the marriage. **However,** if the *ḥalal* merely **betrothed her, she is permitted to him. Due to that** reason, the *tanna* **teaches** the case where the priest **married** the widow.

וּמַאי אִירְיָא דְּקָתָנֵי ״אַלְמָנָה״, לִיתְנֵי ״בְּתוּלָה״!

The Gemara asks: **And why does** the *tanna* **specifically teach** the case of a common priest who married **a widow? Let him teach** that the priest married **a virgin.** Since in any case she becomes a widow upon his death, what difference is there whether she was previously a widow?

LANGUAGE

The *halakha* that is its neighbor [*bat bukta*] – בַּת בּוּקְתָא: *Bukta* or *bikta* is an Aramaic word, used in Hebrew as well, for a small house or a kind of shack. The source of the word is unclear and the Sages explained homiletically that it is an abbreviation of *bei akta*, a narrow house. Here the word is used metaphorically: Two things in the same shack is referring to a pair of adjacent items, i.e., objects that are linked based on spatial proximity.

Perek **IX**
Daf **84** Amud **b**

וְכִי תֵּימָא קָסָבַר הַאי תַּנָּא נִישּׂוּאִין הָרִאשׁוֹנִים מַפִּילִין – הֲרֵי חָלָל שֶׁנָּשָׂא כְּשֵׁרָה, וְלָא אָמְרִינַן נִישּׂוּאִין הָרִאשׁוֹנִים מַפִּילִין!

And if you would say that **this *tanna* holds** that it is her status at the time of **the first marriage** that determines her status when **she happens** before the *yavam*[N] for levirate marriage, and not her status at the time of her husband's death, and therefore if she had been a virgin when she married she would have been permitted to enter into levirate marriage with a High Priest, that cannot be so, as the mishna cites the case: **A *ḥalal* who married** a woman **fit** to marry a priest is permitted to her husband and forbidden to her *yavam*. **And** in that case, **we do not say** that **the first marriage** determines her status when **she happens** before him for levirate marriage, as the woman was fit to marry the brother when she married the *ḥalal* and was rendered a *ḥalala* only as a result of her marriage.

הָא וַדַּאי מִשּׁוּם סֵיפָא, מִשּׁוּם דְּקָבָעֵי לְמִיתְנָא סֵיפָא ״כֹּהֵן גָּדוֹל שֶׁנָּשָׂא אֶת הָאַלְמָנָה וְיֵשׁ לוֹ אָח כֹּהֵן גָּדוֹל אוֹ כֹּהֵן הֶדְיוֹט״, דַּוְקָא אַלְמָנָה, אֲבָל בְּתוּלָה חַזְיָא לֵיהּ, מִשּׁוּם הָכִי קָתָנֵי ״אַלְמָנָה״.

The Gemara answers: **That** fact, that the mishna cited a case where the priest married a widow, is **certainly due to the latter clause** of the mishna, i.e., **due to** the fact **that** the *tanna* **wants to teach** in **the latter clause: A High Priest who married a widow, and he has a brother** who is the **High Priest or a common priest.** In the case where the *yavam* is a common priest, the widow is forbidden to him **specifically** if the High Priest married **a widow,** as by consummating the marriage he rendered her a *ḥalala*. **However,** had she been **a virgin** when the High Priest married her, he would not render her a *ḥalala*, and when the High Priest dies **she** would be **fit for** his brother. It is **due to that** reason that the *tanna* **teaches** the case of **a widow** in the first clause as well.

מַתְקִיף לַהּ רַב פַּפָּא: אִם אִיתָא לְהָא דְּכִי אֲתָא רַב דִּימִי אָמַר רַבִּי יוֹחָנָן: מִצְרִי שֵׁנִי שֶׁנָּשָׂא מִצְרִית רִאשׁוֹנָה – בְּנָהּ שֵׁנִי הָוֵי, לִתְנֵי נַמִּי:

§ **Rav Pappa objects to** the mishna: **If it is so,** that the *halakha* is in accordance with Rabbi Yoḥanan's opinion, **as when Rav Dimi came** from Eretz Yisrael he reported that **Rabbi Yoḥanan said** that in the case of **a second-generation Egyptian who married a first-generation Egyptian woman, her son is considered a** second-generation Egyptian, as the child's status in this matter is determined according to the mother, then **let** the *tanna* of the mishna **also teach** the following case:

NOTES

It is her status at the time of the first marriage that determines her status when she happens before the *yavam* – נִישּׂוּאִין הָרִאשׁוֹנִים מַפִּילִין: *Tosafot* and other early authorities are puzzled by this claim, as the suggestion that the status of the *yevama* is determined at the onset of her original marriage is always raised as a stringency, and not as a leniency as it is here. This should be especially true of the case brought as response, since the woman is rendered a *ḥalala* and is forbidden due to her marriage to the *ḥalal* (see Rashba). For this reason, some commentaries interpret this as a suggestion for the sake of argument, meaning, even if one were to suggest such a novel and unlikely application of the principle, this can be refuted (*Tosefot HaRosh*).

NOTES

And if they married in the reverse manner – וְאִי אִיפּוּךְ וּנְסוּב: In their discussion of this case, *Tosafot* claim that a third-generation Egyptian is always permitted to marry a second-generation Egyptian woman, as the congregation of converts is not considered part of the congregation into which Egyptians may not enter. The later authorities point out that Rashi does not agree with this opinion. Rambam also indicates otherwise, as he maintains that anyone who is permitted to enter the congregation and whose mother is a Jew no longer has the status of a convert in this regard (see *Yam shel Shlomo*).

מִצְרִי שֵׁנִי שֶׁנָּשָׂא שְׁתֵּי מִצְרִיּוֹת, אַחַת רִאשׁוֹנָה וְאַחַת שְׁנִיָּה, וְהָיוּ לוֹ בָּנִים מֵרִאשׁוֹנָה וּשְׁנִיָּה, אִי נְסוּב כִּי אוֹרְחַיְיהוּ – מוּתָּרוֹת לְבַעֲלֵיהֶן וַאֲסוּרוֹת לְיִבְמֵיהֶן,

With regard to **a second-generation Egyptian who married two Egyptian women, one** of whom was **a first-generation** Egyptian convert **and one** of whom was from the **second** generation, **and he had sons** from both **the first and second** women, **if** these two sons **married in their** proper **way,** meaning that the third-generation Egyptian married an ordinary Jewish woman, and the second-generation convert married another second-generation Egyptian, then it is also true of these women that **they are permitted to their husbands and forbidden to their *yevamin*.** The second-generation Egyptian is forbidden to his Jewish *yevama,* while the third-generation Egyptian is an ordinary Jew and therefore prohibited to marry his *yevama,* who is a second-generation Egyptian woman.

וְאִי אִיפּוּךְ וּנְסוּב – מוּתָּרוֹת לְיִבְמֵיהֶן וַאֲסוּרוֹת לְבַעֲלֵיהֶן, מוּתָּרוֹת לְאֵלּוּ וּלְאֵלּוּ – גִּיּוֹרוֹת, אֲסוּרוֹת לְאֵלּוּ וּלְאֵלּוּ – אַיְלוֹנִיּוֹת!

And if they married in the **reverse** manner,[N] i.e., the third-generation convert married a second-generation Egyptian woman, and the second-generation man married an ordinary Jewish woman, **they are permitted to their *yevamin* and forbidden to their husbands.** Similarly, **they are permitted** both **to these and to those** if these sons married **converts,** for an Egyptian convert is permitted to marry a convert of a different nationality. And there is also a case in which **they are forbidden to these and to those,** namely if they married **sexually underdeveloped women [*ayloniot*].** If an Egyptian married an *aylonit,* she is forbidden to him as a Jewish woman, and she is forbidden to his brother, a third-generation Egyptian convert who is permitted to marry a Jewish woman, because levirate marriage is prohibited with an *aylonit.* The fact that the mishna omits these cases appears to indicate that the *halakha* is not in accordance with Rabbi Yoḥanan.

תָּנָא וְשַׁיֵּיר. מַאי שַׁיֵּיר דְּהַאי שַׁיֵּיר? שַׁיֵּיר פְּצוּעַ דַּכָּא.

The Gemara answers: There is no proof from here with regard to the *halakha,* as the *tanna* of the mishna did not mention all possible examples. Rather, **he taught** certain cases **and omitted** others. The Gemara asks: **What** else **did he omit that he omitted this?** The *tanna* would not have omitted only one example. The Gemara answers: **He omitted** the case of a **man with crushed testicles** or with other wounds to his genitals. If the husband is such a man, the wife is forbidden to her husband and permitted to her *yavam.* If the *yavam* is such a man, the opposite is true.

אִי מִשּׁוּם פְּצוּעַ דַּכָּא – לָאו שִׁיּוּרָא, דְּהָא תָּנָא לֵיהּ חַיָּיבֵי לָאוִין!

The Gemara asks: **If** this mishna is determined to have taught certain cases and omitted others **due to** the omission of the case **of a man with crushed testicles** or other wounds to his genitals, this **is not an omission,** as in this mishna the *tanna* **taught** a principle that applies to all forbidden relationships for which one is **liable for** violating **a prohibition.** This category includes such a case, and therefore it was not omitted.

אַטּוּ חַיָּיבֵי לָאוִין מִי לָא קָתָנֵי וַהֲדַר תָּנֵי? וְהָא קָתָנֵי ״כֹּהֵן הֶדְיוֹט שֶׁנָּשָׂא אַלְמָנָה, וְחָלָל שֶׁנָּשָׂא כְּשֵׁרָה״!

The Gemara answers: **Is that to say** that with regard to those relationships for which one is **liable for** violating **a prohibition, he does not teach** a principle **and again teach** them in detail? But this is not the case. **He teaches** the case of **a common priest who married a widow** and he had a brother who was a high priest, **and** the case of **a *ḥalal* who married** a woman **fit** to marry a priest and he had a brother who was a priest fit for service, both of whom are forbidden as they are liable for violating a prohibition. Therefore, since the *tanna* did not specifically teach the case of the man with crushed testicles, this constitutes an omission.

הַהוּא אִיצְטְרִיכָא לֵיהּ לְאַשְׁמוּעִינַן כִּדְרַב יְהוּדָה אָמַר רַב, דְּאָמַר רַב יְהוּדָה אָמַר רַב: לֹא הוּזְהֲרוּ כְּשֵׁרוֹת לְהִנָּשֵׂא לִפְסוּלִין.

The Gemara responds: **That** clause of the mishna is not merely a specification of the previous general *halakha,* as **it was necessary for** the *tanna* to mention these cases individually in order **to teach us** another *halakha* **that Rav Yehuda said** that **Rav** said, **as Rav Yehuda said** that **Rav said:** It is **not prohibited** for daughters of priests who are **fit** to marry priests to **marry men** who are **disqualified** from the priesthood, although this marriage disqualifies them from subsequently marrying a priest.

וְהָא קָתָנֵי "חָלָל שֶׁנָּשָׂא כְּשֵׁרָה, וְיִשְׂרָאֵל שֶׁנָּשָׂא בַּת יִשְׂרָאֵל וְיֵשׁ לוֹ אָח מַמְזֵר"! הָא נַמִי לָא מִהֲדַר מִיתְנָא הִיא, דְּאַשְׁמוֹעִינַן לָאו שֶׁאֵין שָׁוֶה בַּכֹּל וְקָמַשְׁמַע לָן לָאו הַשָּׁוֶה בַּכֹּל.

The Gemara challenges that answer: **But** the mishna also **teaches** these cases: A ***ḥalal*** **who married** a woman **fit** to marry a priest; **and an Israelite** of unflawed lineage **who married an Israelite woman** of unflawed lineage, **and he has a brother** who is a ***mamzer***. These are specifications that do not teach additional *halakhot*. The Gemara answers: **This too is not** a case of the *tanna* **going back and teaching** additional examples of the same *halakha* without adding anything, **as he teaches us** something new through each of these two examples. The first example is referring to **a prohibition that is not equally applicable to all,** such as one concerning priests, and the second example is referring to **a prohibition that is equally applicable to all,** such as one involving a *mamzer*.

הָא קָתָנֵי יִשְׂרָאֵל שֶׁנָּשָׂא מַמְזֶרֶת וְיֵשׁ לוֹ אָח יִשְׂרָאֵל, (וּמַמְזֵר שֶׁנָּשָׂא מַמְזֶרֶת וְיֵשׁ לוֹ אָח יִשְׂרָאֵל!) אֶלָּא לָאו שְׁמַע מִינַּהּ תָּנָא וְשַׁיַּיר, שְׁמַע מִינַּהּ.

The Gemara further challenges the answer: **But** the mishna also **teaches** the case of **an Israelite** of unflawed lineage **who married a *mamzeret* and who has a brother** who **is an Israelite** of similar lineage, **and** the example of **a *mamzer* who married a *mamzeret* and he has a brother** who **is an Israelite** of unflawed lineage. Consequently, the *tanna* does in fact teach the same *halakha* several times with regard to a prohibition that is equally applicable to all. **Rather, isn't it** correct to **conclude from it** that **he taught and omitted** certain cases and did not list all possible examples? The Gemara concludes: **Indeed, conclude from it** that this is the case, and therefore there is no proof from here that the *halakha* is not in accordance with Rabbi Yoḥanan.

גּוּפָא, אָמַר רַב יְהוּדָה אָמַר רַב: לֹא הוּזְהֲרוּ כְּשֵׁרוֹת לְהִנָּשֵׂא לִפְסוּלִין. לֵימָא מְסַיֵּיעַ לֵיהּ: "חָלָל שֶׁנָּשָׂא כְּשֵׁרָה". מַאי לָאו: כֹּהֶנֶת [הָרְאוּיָה לוֹ], וּמַאי "כְּשֵׁרָה", כְּשֵׁרָה לִכְהוּנָּה?

§ The Gemara returns to a statement cited incidentally above, in order to discuss **the matter itself: Rav Yehuda said** that **Rav said:** It is **not prohibited** for daughters of priests who are **fit** to marry priests to **marry** men who are **disqualified** from the priesthood,[NH] although this marriage would disqualify them from subsequently marrying a priest, and they may do so even *ab initio*. The Gemara suggests: **Let us say that** the following statement of the mishna **supports his** opinion: **A *ḥalal* who married** a woman who is **fit,** and he has a brother who is a priest fit for service, this woman is permitted to her husband and forbidden to her *yavam*. **What, is it not** referring to **a priestess,** i.e., a priest's daughter, **who is appropriate to** marry **him? And what is** the meaning of: **Fit?** This means that **she is fit for the priesthood,**[N] and yet the mishna says she is permitted to her husband, the *ḥalal*.

לָא, יִשְׂרְאֵלִית, וּמַאי "כְּשֵׁרָה" – כְּשֵׁרָה לַקָּהָל.

The Gemara rejects this suggestion: **No,** it is possible that the mishna is speaking of **an Israelite woman. And what is** the meaning of: **Fit?** It means that **she is fit to** enter **the congregation** of the Jewish people, through marriage. According to this explanation, there is no proof from the mishna about daughters of priests.

אִי הָכִי, יֵשׁ לוֹ אָח כָּשֵׁר נַמִי – כָּשֵׁר לַקָּהָל, מִכְּלָל דְּהוּא פָּסוּל לַקָּהָל?! אֶלָּא לָאו – כֹּהֵן, וּמִדְּהוּא כֹּהֵן – הִיא כֹּהֶנֶת! מִידֵּי אִירְיָא? הָא כִּדְאִיתָא וְהָא כִּדְאִיתָא.

The Gemara raises a difficulty: **If so,** consider the phrase: A *ḥalal* who married a woman fit to marry a priest, and **he has a brother** who **is** also **fit.** Consistency demands that here **too** it means that the brother **is fit to** enter **the congregation.** Can it not therefore be deduced **by inference that he,** the deceased *ḥalal*, was **unfit to** enter **the congregation?** But such an inference would be an error, as a *ḥalal* is disqualified only from the priesthood. **Rather, is it not** referring to a **priest, and from the fact that he** must **be a priest, she** too must be **a priestess?** The Gemara rejects this claim: **Are the cases comparable? This** case, of the *ḥalal*, is **as it is,** i.e., he is fit for the priesthood. **And that** case, of the woman, is **as it is,** i.e., she is fit to enter the congregation.

מְתִיב רָבִין בַּר נַחְמָן "לֹא יִקָּחוּ" "לֹא יִקָּחוּ" – מְלַמֵּד שֶׁהָאִשָּׁה מוּזְהֶרֶת עַל יְדֵי הָאִישׁ!

Ravin bar Naḥman raised an objection against Rav's ruling from the following *baraita*: The verse states about priests: **"They may not take** a woman who is a harlot [*zona*], or profaned [*ḥalala*]" (Leviticus 21:7). The same verse says: **"They** also **may not take** a woman divorced from her husband." This repetition of "they may not take" **teaches us that the woman is** also **prohibited by means of** the prohibition addressed to **the man.** Therefore, we can conclude that there is a prohibition for a daughter of a priest to marry a *ḥalal*.

NOTES

It is not prohibited for daughters of priests who are fit to marry priests to marry men who are disqualified from the priesthood – לֹא הוּזְהֲרוּ כְּשֵׁרוֹת לְהִנָּשֵׂא לִפְסוּלִין: Another proof of this principle is that the Torah forbids a *ḥalala* to a priest but does not prohibit a *ḥalal* from entering the congregation of priests by marrying a priest's daughter. This indicates that the daughter of a priest may marry a *ḥalal* (Ritva, citing Ra'avad). Some explain that since the sanctity of the priesthood is not transferred to the daughter of a priest, as her children from an Israelite are not priests, the Torah was not particular about her marriage to a *ḥalal*. The marriage is permitted, although by marrying her he disqualifies her permanently from eating *teruma*, as in any case her children will be Israelites and not priests (*She'iltot*).

Fit for the priesthood – כְּשֵׁרָה לִכְהוּנָּה: Rashi explains that although it is not prohibited for a priest to marry an Israelite, nevertheless, there is a special virtue in the marriage of a priest to the daughter of another priest. For many generations, it was the custom of priests to marry daughters of priests.

HALAKHA

It is not prohibited for daughters of priests who are fit to marry priests to marry men who are disqualified from the priesthood – לֹא הוּזְהֲרוּ כְּשֵׁרוֹת לְהִנָּשֵׂא לִפְסוּלִין: A daughter of a priest is permitted to marry a *ḥalal*, a convert, or an emancipated slave, as it is not prohibited for daughters of priests who are fit to marry priests to marry those disqualified from the priesthood, as stated by Rav (Rambam *Sefer Kedusha, Hilkhot Issurei Bia* 19:11; *Shulḥan Arukh, Even HaEzer* 7:22).

NOTES

And is this derived from here – וְהָא מֵהָכָא נָפְקָא: Ramban asks: Even without the proof from the verses, there is another reason why it is prohibited for a woman to marry a man to whom she is forbidden, as there is a general prohibition: "You shall not put a stumbling block before the blind" (Leviticus 19:14), which means that it is prohibited to assist another person in the performance of a transgression. He answers that a marriage of this sort would constitute a violation of the general prohibition, but the Gemara is inquiring into whether there is also a specific prohibition with regard to these marriages. Other early authorities add that the prohibition: "You shall not put a stumbling block before the blind" is stated in general terms, and therefore lashes are not administered for it. Consequently, the Gemara sought a source for her liability to receive lashes for this transgression.

HALAKHA

The verse equates a woman to a man – הִשְׁוָה הַכָּתוּב אִשָּׁה לְאִישׁ: There is no difference between men and women with regard to punishments: If he is liable to lashes, she is too; and if he is exempt, so is she. The sole exception is the case of a designated maidservant, i.e., a woman who is half free and half slave and betrothed to a Hebrew slave. In this case, the woman is liable to receive lashes, but the man is required to bring a guilt-offering (Rambam *Sefer Kedusha, Hilkhot Issurei Bia* 17:5).

אָמַר רָבָא: כָּל הֵיכָא דְּהוּא מוּזְהָר – הִיא מוּזְהֶרֶת, וְכָל הֵיכָא דְּהוּא לָא מוּזְהָר – הִיא לָא מִזְדַּהֲרָא.

Rava said: Ravin bar Naḥman's objection is not valid. All that the *baraita* teaches is that **anywhere that a prohibition** of sexual intercourse applies to **him,** i.e., to a man, the same **prohibition** applies to **her,** his female partner. **And anywhere that a prohibition does not** apply to **him, the prohibition does not** apply to **her** either. It does not, however, indicate that since it is prohibited for a priest to marry a *ḥalala* it is also prohibited for the daughter of a priest to marry a *ḥalal*.

וְהָא מֵהָכָא נָפְקָא: מִדְּרַב יְהוּדָה אָמַר רַב נָפְקָא! דְּאָמַר רַב יְהוּדָה אָמַר רַב, וְכֵן תָּנָא דְּבֵי רַבִּי יִשְׁמָעֵאל: "אִישׁ אוֹ אִשָּׁה כִּי יַעֲשׂוּ מִכָּל חַטֹּאת הָאָדָם" – הִשְׁוָה הַכָּתוּב אִשָּׁה לְאִישׁ לְכָל עוֹנָשִׁין שֶׁבַּתּוֹרָה!

The Gemara asks with regard to the *baraita* itself: **And is this** matter **derived from here?**[N] **It is derived from** a different statement that **Rav Yehuda said that Rav said, as Rav Yehuda said** that **Rav said, and the school of Rabbi Yishmael similarly taught:** The verse states: "**When a man or woman** shall **commit any sin** that **people** commit" (Numbers 5:6). **The verse** here **equates a woman to a man**[H] **with regard to all punishments of the Torah.** Consequently, the *halakhot* of forbidden marriages apply equally to women and to men. Why then do we need to learn the same thing from the repetition of "they may not take"?

אִי מֵהַהִיא הֲוָה אָמֵינָא: לָאו הַשָּׁוֶה בַּכֹּל, אֲבָל לָאו שֶׁאֵינוֹ שָׁוֶה בַּכֹּל – לָא.

The Gemara answers: **If** it was derived only **from that** verse, **I would say** that this principle is true of **a prohibition that is equally** applicable **to all, but** with regard to **a prohibition that is not equally** applicable **to all,** such as the prohibitions pertaining to priests, this is **not** the case. Since these prohibitions only apply to priests, we might have thought that they do not extend to women. The verse therefore teaches that the prohibition applies to women in the same manner as men.

Perek **IX**
Daf **85** Amud **a**

HALAKHA

The sons of Aaron and not the daughters of Aaron – בְּנֵי אַהֲרֹן וְלֹא בְּנוֹת אַהֲרֹן: Only priests fit for service, including blemished ones, are included in the prohibition against contracting ritual impurity from a corpse. This prohibition does not apply to daughters of priests (Rambam *Sefer Shofetim, Hilkhot Evel* 2:6; *Shulḥan Arukh, Yoreh De'a* 373:2).

וַהֲרֵי טוּמְאָה, דְּלָאו שֶׁאֵין שָׁוֶה בַּכֹּל, וְטַעְמָא דִּכְתַב רַחֲמָנָא "בְּנֵי אַהֲרֹן" וְלֹא בְּנוֹת אַהֲרֹן, הָא לָאו הָכִי – הֲוָה אָמֵינָא: נָשִׁים חַיָּיבוֹת. מַאי טַעְמָא – לָאו מִשּׁוּם דְּרַב יְהוּדָה אָמַר רַב?

The Gemara asks: **But** there is the prohibition for priests to contract **ritual impurity** from a corpse, **which is a prohibition that is not equally** applicable **to all,** as only priests are bound by this prohibition, **and the reason** that this command applies only to male priests is **that the Merciful One writes:** "Speak to the priests **the sons of Aaron,** and say to them: None shall defile himself" (Leviticus 21:1), from which it is inferred: **The sons of Aaron and not the daughters of Aaron.**[H] **Therefore,** were it **not** for **this** specific derivation, **I would say** that **women** from priestly families **are** also **obligated** to avoid becoming ritually impure. **What is the reason** for this? Is it **not due to** the principle that **Rav Yehuda said** that **Rav** said, that women are equated to men with regard to all punishments in the Torah, including those that are not equally applicable to all?

לָא, דְּגָמְרִינַן מִ"לֹּא יִקָּחוּ".

The Gemara rejects this proof: **No,** that initial assumption, that the daughters of priests might be obligated to avoid ritual impurity, is not due to the *halakha* that Rav Yehuda said that Rav said, but rather it is something that **we learn** through tradition **from** the words **"they may not take."** This phrase teaches that women are included in the marital prohibitions of the priesthood, and we might therefore have thought that they are included in all *halakhot* pertaining to priests.

איכא דאמרי: קיחה איצטריכא ליה, סלקא דעתך אמינא: ליגמר מטומאה, קמשמע לן.

There are those who say a different version of this answer:[N] With regard to that verse about **taking, it was necessary for him** to mention this explicitly, for **it might enter your mind to say: We should learn** this *halakha* **from** the prohibition of **impurity** and conclude that just as only male descendants of Aaron are prohibited from contracting **ritual impurity,** the restrictions of marriage also apply only to men. The verse therefore **teaches us,** with the words "they may not take," that this is not the case.

רב פפא ורב הונא בריה דרב יהושע איקלעו להינצבו, לאתריה דרב אידי בר אבין. בעו מיניהו: הוזהרו כשרות להנשא לפסולין או לא?

The Gemara relates: **Rav Pappa and Rav Huna, son of Rav Yehoshua, arrived at** the town of **Hintzevu, to the place of** Rav **Idi bar Avin.**[P] The townspeople **asked them:** Is it **prohibited** for daughters of priests who are **fit** to marry priests to **marry** men **disqualified** from the priesthood **or not?**

אמר להו רב פפא: תניתוה, עשרה יוחסין עלו מבבל: כהנים, לוים, וישראלים, חללים, גרים, וחרורים, וממזרים, נתינים, שתוקי, ואסופי; כהנים, לוים, ישראלים, מותרין לבא זה בזה. לוים, ישראלים, חללים, גרים, חרורים – מותרין לבא זה בזה; גירי, חרורי, וממזרי, נתיני, שתוקי, ואסופי – מותרים לבא זה בזה, ואילו כהנות לחלל – לא קתני.

Rav Pappa said to them: You learned it in a mishna (*Kiddushin* 69a): People of **ten** types of **lineages ascended from Babylonia: Priests, Levites, and Israelites, *halalim*, converts, and freed** slaves, **and *mamzerim*, Gibeonites, children of unknown paternity [*shetukim*], and foundlings.** With regard to **Priests, Levites,** and **Israelites,**[H] they **are permitted to marry** into **one another's** families; **Levites, Israelites, *halalim*,**[H] **converts,** and **freed** slaves **are permitted to marry** into **one another's** families; **converts, freed** slaves, **and *mamzerim*,**[H] **Gibeonites, *shetukim*, and foundlings are permitted to marry** into **one another's** families; **whereas** the *tanna* **does not teach** that **priestesses,** i.e., daughters of priests, are permitted **to** marry **a *halal*.** This must mean they are forbidden to them.

אמר ליה רב הונא בריה דרב יהושע: כל היכא דהני נסבי מהני והני נסבי מהני – קתני. כהן, כיון דאילו בעי למינסב חללה אסירא ליה – לא קתני. אתו לקמיה דרב אידי בר אבין, אמר להו: דרדקי, הכי אמר רב יהודה אמר רב: לא הוזהרו כשרות לינשא לפסולים.

Rav Huna, son of Rav Yehoshua, said to him: There is no proof from here, for **he teaches** the *halakha* **anywhere that these** men **may marry those** women, **and** there is also a parallel case where **these** women **may marry those** men. With regard to the case of **a priest,** however, **since if he wants to marry a *halala* this is prohibited** to him, the *tanna* **does not teach** this *halakha*. Consequently, there is no proof from this mishna that daughters of priests who are fit to marry priests are warned against marrying men disqualified from the priesthood. **They came before Rav Idi bar Avin** and told him about the question and their debate about the matter. **He said to them: Children, this** is what **Rav Yehuda said** that **Rav said:** Daughters of priests who are **fit** to marry priests **are not warned against marrying** men **disqualified** from the priesthood.

NOTES

There are those who say a different version of this answer – איכא דאמרי: The difference between these two versions is whether a distinction should be assumed between men and women with regard to a prohibition that does not apply equally to all. According to the first version, since the prohibition does not apply equally to all Jews, it cannot be assumed to apply equally to men and women. The need to negate the idea that daughters of priests are obligated to avoid impurity is simply because one might have drawn an analogy to priestly marriage *halakhot*. According to the second version, the *halakha* that Rav Yehuda said that Rav said could be seen as referring to all prohibitions. The *baraita* needed the exposition from the words "they may not take" to teach that a *halala* is prohibited from marrying a priest only to negate an alternative theory that could have been suggested (Ritva).

PERSONALITIES

Rav Idi bar Avin – רב אידי בר אבין: Rav Idi bar Avin was an *amora* from the third and fourth generations of Babylonian *amora'im*.

It is related that his father, Rav Avin Naggara, was meticulous concerning the lighting of Sabbath candles, and Rav Huna told him that he would merit sons who were Torah scholars. Indeed, he fathered Rav Ḥiyya bar Avin and Rav Idi bar Avin.

Rav Idi bar Avin was a disciple of Rav Ḥisda, but he transmits traditions in the name of various Sages from the second generation of Babylonian *amora'im*. He was one of the greatest *amora'im* of his generation, and he is found engaged in halakhic discourse primarily with Abaye. Rav Idi was the leader of his town, where he apparently ran a private yeshiva.

He lived an exceptionally long life. Rav Huna, son of Rav Yehoshua, and Rav Pappa were among the disciples who learned Torah from him. In his old age, he called these disciples his *dardekai*, children.

Very little is known of the events of his life, besides the fact that he had two sons who were Sages in the next generation.

HALAKHA

Priests, Levites, Israelites – כהנים, לוים, ישראלים: Priests, Levites, and Israelites are permitted to marry into each other's families. The lineage of the offspring follows that of the father (Rambam *Sefer Kedusha*, *Hilkhot Issurei Bia* 19:15; *Shulḥan Arukh*, *Even HaEzer* 8:1).

Levites, Israelites, *halalim* – לוים, ישראלים, חללים: Levites, Israelites, *halalim*, converts, and freed slaves are permitted to marry into each other's families. If a male convert or freed slave married a Levite or Israelite woman, the offspring is an Israelite. If a male Israelite, Levite or *halal* married a female convert or freed slave, their offspring's lineage follows that of the father (Rambam *Sefer Kedusha*, *Hilkhot Issurei Bia* 19:16; *Shulḥan Arukh*, *Even HaEzer* 8:2–3).

Converts, freed slaves, and *mamzerim* – גירי, חרורי, וממזרי: In the case of a *shetuki* and a foundling, there is uncertainty as to whether or not they are *mamzerim*. Therefore, they may not marry even other *shetukim*, nor may they marry a Jew of unflawed lineage or a *mamzeret*; but they may marry converts and Gibeonites, and their offspring similarly have the status of an uncertain *mamzer*, in accordance with the opinion of Rabbi Elazar in tractate *Kiddushin*. Definite *mamzerim* are permitted to marry converts, freed slaves, and Gibeonites, and their offspring are *mamzerim*. Converts and freed slaves may marry each other, and their children are fit to enter the congregation (Rambam *Sefer Kedusha*, *Hilkhot Issurei Bia* 15:33).

״שְׁנִיּוֹת מִדִּבְרֵי סוֹפְרִים״ וכו׳. בָּעוּ מִינֵּיהּ בְּנֵי בִּירִי מֵרַב שֵׁשֶׁת: שְׁנִיָּה לַבַּעַל וְלֹא שְׁנִיָּה לַיָּבָם, יֵשׁ לָהּ כְּתוּבָּה מִיָּבָם אוֹ לֹא? כֵּיוָן דְּאָמַר מָר כְּתוּבָּתָהּ עַל נִכְסֵי בַּעְלָהּ הָרִאשׁוֹן – לֵית לָהּ,

§ We learned in the mishna that **secondary** forbidden **relatives,** whose status is established **by rabbinic law,** are sometimes forbidden to the husband and sometimes to the *yavam*. **The residents of** the town of **Biri inquired of Rav Sheshet:** Is a woman who is a **secondary** forbidden **relative of the husband but not a secondary** forbidden **relative of the *yavam***[HN] entitled to **a marriage contract**[B] **from the *yavam* or not?** The Gemara clarifies the sides of the dilemma: Perhaps, **since the Master said** that in a levirate marriage, the payment of **her marriage contract is** due **from the property of her first husband,** and this woman, who was a secondary relative of her first husband, does not receive a marriage contract from him, **she** consequently **does not have** the right to one from the *yavam* either.

אוֹ דִּלְמָא: כֵּיוָן דְּאִילּוּ לֵית לָהּ מֵרִאשׁוֹן תַּקִּינוּ לָהּ רַבָּנַן מִשֵּׁנִי – אִית לָהּ?

Or perhaps, since there is a principle in levirate marriage **that if she does not have** a marriage contract **from the first** husband, e.g., he died without leaving behind any property, **the Sages instituted** a marriage contract **for her from the second** one, we should say that **she has** a marriage contract from the *yavam*?

אֲמַר לְהוּ רַב שֵׁשֶׁת: תְּנֵיתוּהָ, כְּתוּבָּתָהּ עַל נִכְסֵי בַּעְלָהּ הָרִאשׁוֹן, וְאִם הָיְתָה שְׁנִיָּה לַבַּעַל – אֲפִילּוּ מִיָּבָם אֵין לָהּ.

Rav Sheshet said to them: You learned it in a *baraita*: Payment of **her marriage contract is** due **from the property of her first husband, and if she was a secondary** forbidden **relative of the husband, she does not have** one **even from the *yavam*.** This *baraita* clearly answers the question.

מִכְּלָל דְּאִיכָּא דְּאִית לָהּ מִיָּבָם? חַסּוֹרֵי מִיחַסְּרָא וְהָכִי קָתָנֵי: כְּתוּבָּתָהּ עַל נִכְסֵי בַּעְלָהּ הָרִאשׁוֹן, וְאִי לֵית לָהּ מֵרִאשׁוֹן – תַּקִּינוּ לָהּ מִשֵּׁנִי, וְאִם הָיְתָה שְׁנִיָּה לַבַּעַל – אֲפִילּוּ מִיָּבָם אֵין לָהּ.

The Gemara asks: Can it be concluded **by inference** from the *baraita* **that there is** a case of a woman in a levirate marriage **who does have** a marriage contract **from the *yavam*?**[N] The Gemara answers: The *baraita* **is incomplete**[B] **and this is** what **it is teaching:** Payment of **her marriage contract is** due **from the property of her first husband, and if she does not have** anything **from the first husband** because he died without property, **they instituted** a marriage contract **for her from the second** one. **And if she was a secondary** forbidden **relative of the husband, she does not have** one **even from the *yavam*.**

בְּעָא מִינֵּיהּ רַבִּי אֶלְעָזָר מֵרַבִּי יוֹחָנָן: אַלְמָנָה לְכֹהֵן גָּדוֹל, גְּרוּשָׁה וַחֲלוּצָה לְכֹהֵן הֶדְיוֹט – יֵשׁ לָהֶן מְזוֹנוֹת אוֹ אֵין לָהֶן מְזוֹנוֹת? הֵיכִי דָּמֵי, אִילֵּימָא דְּיָתְבָה תּוּתֵיהּ – בַּ״עֲמוֹד וְהוֹצֵא״ קָאֵי, מְזוֹנוֹת אִית לָהּ?! לָא צְרִיכָא שֶׁהָלַךְ הוּא לִמְדִינַת הַיָּם, וְלָוְתָה וְאָכְלָה, מַאי?

Rabbi Elazar inquired of Rabbi Yoḥanan: Do women in cases like **a widow** married **to a High Priest** and **a divorcée or a *ḥalutza*** married **to a common priest have** rights to payment for their **sustenance** from their husbands, **or do they not have** a right to **sustenance?** The Gemara asks: **What are the circumstances** of the case under discussion? **If we say that** she **is dwelling under his** roof, he **stands in** a position where he is obligated to **arise and divorce**[N] her. In such a situation, does **she have** a right to **sustenance?** It is obvious that she does not. The Gemara clarifies: **No,** it is **necessary** to ask this question with regard to a case **where he went overseas** and therefore is not present to divorce her, **and** in the meantime **she borrowed** money for her sustenance **and ate. What is** the *halakha* is in that case?

HALAKHA

A secondary relative of the husband but not a secondary relative of the *yavam* – שְׁנִיָּה לַבַּעַל וְלֹא שְׁנִיָּה לַיָּבָם: If a *yevama* did not previously have a marriage contract from her husband because she was forbidden to him, but she was permitted to the *yavam* and married him, she is not entitled to a marriage contract from the *yavam*, as stated by Rav Sheshet. The Rema claims that although she has no rights to a marriage contract, he may not continue to cohabit with her unless he grants her one (*Maggid Mishne*, citing Ramban and Rashba); but the *Baḥ* maintains that he is permitted to do so even without a marriage contract (Rambam *Sefer Nashim, Hilkhot Yibbum* 2:17; *Shulḥan Arukh, Even HaEzer* 168:9).

BACKGROUND

Marriage contract – כְּתוּבָּה: This is a legal document given by a husband to his wife upon their marriage, stating his obligations toward her during and after their marriage. The contract includes a lien on the husband's estate, the minimum amount being two hundred dinars for a virgin bride and one hundred dinars for other brides, payable if she is divorced or widowed. The general guidelines for a marriage contract are provided by the Talmud. Its particular provisions, however, are often based on local custom. In addition, the marriage contract may include individual stipulations agreed to by the husband and wife. The marriage contract gives the marriage halakhic legitimacy. Without one, the couple's relationship is considered licentious.

The *baraita* is incomplete – חַסּוֹרֵי מִיחַסְּרָא: This method of explanation is often found in the Gemara. Generally, it does not suggest an actual emendation of the text of the mishna or *baraita*. The addition introduced by the Gemara is a necessary elaboration upon that which is written in the mishna, which is insufficiently clear in its current form. The addition provides the necessary clarification.

NOTES

A secondary relative of the husband but not a secondary relative of the *yavam* – שְׁנִיָּה לַבַּעַל וְלֹא שְׁנִיָּה לַיָּבָם: In the Jerusalem Talmud, this inquiry is extended to ask whether a woman who is fit to marry the husband but is forbidden to the *yavam* as a secondary relative is entitled to a marriage contract, and it leaves this issue unresolved. It appears that according to the Gemara here, this question does not arise at all, for since the husband was obligated to pay her the marriage contract, she does not forfeit this right just because she happened before a *yavam* for levirate marriage (Ramban; Rashba).

There is dispute among the commentaries and authorities in the case of a woman who was forbidden to her husband as a secondary relative, and her *yavam* consummated the levirate marriage with her. Some claim that although the *yavam* is not obligated to pay her marriage contract if they get divorced, nevertheless, the Sages forbade a woman to remain with her husband without a marriage contract, and therefore he must provide her with one. Others contend that since this woman is not entitled to a marriage contract at all, the Sages did not require one in this case.

Can it be concluded by inference that there is a woman who does have a marriage contract from the *yavam* – מִכְּלָל דְּאִיכָּא דְּאִית לָהּ מִיָּבָם: Rav Sheshet's proof from the *baraita* is clear enough, but the Gemara sought to undermine the *baraita* as a reliable source, since its wording is somewhat unclear. It was therefore necessary to resolve the difficulty in order to strengthen the proof (Ritva).

He stands in a position where he is obligated to arise and divorce her – בַּעֲמוֹד וְהוֹצֵא קָאֵי: This case is presumably referring to a wife who comes to court to claim sustenance from her husband. The court is obligated to separate the couple, and therefore she would certainly not receive her sustenance. The Rashba points out that if her husband chose to provide her with food he cannot demand repayment from her, and consequently the Gemara has to establish the case as referring to a woman demanding future sustenance.

מְזוֹנֵי תְּנַאי כְּתוּבָּה נִינְהוּ, מִדְּאִית לָהּ כְּתוּבָּה – אִית לָהּ מְזוֹנֵי, אוֹ דִּלְמָא: כְּתוּבָּה דִּלְמִשְׁקַל וּמֵיפַּק – אִית לָהּ, מְזוֹנֵי דִּלְמָא תִּיעַכַּב גַּבֵּיהּ – לֵית לָהּ? אָמַר לֵיהּ: לֵית לָהּ.

Is it correct to say that **sustenance is a stipulation in the marriage contract, and since she has a marriage contract she** also **has** a right to **sustenance,** and therefore the husband must pay her debt? **Or perhaps** there is a difference between the cases: Concerning **a marriage contract, which** gives her motivation to **take** the money **and leave** him, **she has** rights to it, as the Sages wanted to motivate her to seek divorce and end the prohibited marriage. However, with regard to **sustenance,** we are worried that if he provides for her sustenance, **perhaps she might tarry with him,** as she would have no reason to rush the divorce, and consequently **she does not have** rights to it. **He said to him: She does not have** a right to sustenance.

וְהָתַנְיָא: יֵשׁ לָהּ! כִּי תַּנְיָא הַהִיא – לְאַחַר מִיתָה.

The Gemara raises a difficulty: **But isn't it taught** in a *baraita* that **she does have**[N] a right to sustenance? The Gemara answers: **When that** *baraita* **is taught,** it is referring to sustenance she receives **after** his **death.** At that point, she is no longer in violation of a prohibition, while the obligation to sustain her remains intact.

אִית דְּאָמַר, אָמַר לֵיהּ: תַּנְיָא יֵשׁ לָהּ. הָא בַּ״עֲמוֹד וְהוֹצֵא״ קָאֵי! וְאֶלָּא הָתַנְיָא יֵשׁ לָהּ! כִּי תַּנְיָא הַהִיא – לְאַחַר מִיתָה.

Some say a different version of the discussion, which is that **he said to him:** It **is taught** in a *baraita* that **she has** a right to sustenance. He replied: He **stands in** a position where he is obligated to **arise and divorce** her. He should not be required to provide for her sustenance. He again asked: **But isn't it taught** in a *baraita* that **she has** a right to sustenance? He responded: **When that** *baraita* **is taught** it is referring to the period **after** his **death.**

תָּנוּ רַבָּנַן: אַלְמָנָה לְכֹהֵן גָּדוֹל, גְּרוּשָׁה וַחֲלוּצָה לְכֹהֵן הֶדְיוֹט – יֵשׁ לָהּ כְּתוּבָּה, פֵּירוֹת, מְזוֹנוֹת, בְּלָאוֹת, וְהִיא פְּסוּלָה וּוְלָדָהּ פָּסוּל, וְכוֹפִין אוֹתוֹ לְהוֹצִיא. שְׁנִיּוֹת מִדִּבְרֵי סוֹפְרִים – אֵין לָהּ כְּתוּבָּה, לֹא פֵּירוֹת, לֹא מְזוֹנוֹת וְלֹא בְּלָאוֹת, וְהִיא כְּשֵׁירָה וּוְלָדָהּ כָּשֵׁר, וְכוֹפִין אוֹתוֹ לְהוֹצִיא.

The Sages taught: A widow married **to a High Priest,** or **a divorcée or a *ḥalutza*** married **to a common priest**[H] **has** the right to receive payment for her **marriage contract;** and for the **produce of** her property that her husband used; and **sustenance;** and she gets back her **worn clothes** and other objects she brought to the marriage; **and she is disqualified** as a *ḥalala* from marrying a priest; **and her offspring is disqualified**[H] from the priesthood as a *ḥalal;* **and** the court **forces him to divorce** her.[H] A woman who is **a secondary relative** prohibited **by rabbinic law has neither a marriage contract; nor** payment for the **produce** of her property;[N] **nor sustenance; nor** does she get back her **worn clothes;**[N] **and she is fit** to marry a priest **and her offspring is fit**[H] for the priesthood; **and** the court **forces him to divorce** her.

אָמַר רַבִּי שִׁמְעוֹן בֶּן אֶלְעָזָר: מִפְּנֵי מָה אָמְרוּ: אַלְמָנָה לְכֹהֵן גָּדוֹל יֵשׁ לָהּ כְּתוּבָּה – מִפְּנֵי שֶׁהוּא פָּסוּל וְהִיא פְּסוּלָה, וְכָל מָקוֹם שֶׁהוּא פָּסוּל וְהִיא פְּסוּלָה

Rabbi Shimon ben Elazar said: For what reason did they **say** that **a widow** married **to a High Priest has a marriage contract? Because he is disqualified** from the priesthood by his marriage to her, as a priest who marries a woman forbidden to him is barred from the Temple service until he divorces her and agrees not to remarry her, **and she is** rendered a *ḥalala* and **disqualified**[N] from the priesthood by intercourse with him, **and any place where he is disqualified and she is disqualified,**

NOTES

But isn't it taught in a *baraita* that she does have – וְהָתַנְיָא יֵשׁ לָהּ: The Rashba writes that this difficulty was not stated by Rabbi Elazar, for had he been aware of the problem he would not have inquired of Rabbi Yoḥanan. The Ritva disagrees, maintaining that it is possible that Rabbi Elazar was familiar with the *baraita* but was unsure of its meaning. He therefore brought his dilemma before Rabbi Yoḥanan, and after hearing his answer raised a difficulty from the *baraita.*

Nor payment for the produce of her property – לֹא פֵּירוֹת: The literal translation of the phrase is: She does not have produce. This is somewhat problematic, as the Gemara is referring to the produce of the wife's own property, and therefore the issue would appear to be whether the husband has the right to the produce. Rashi and other earlier authorities maintain that the question is whether she has the right to demand repayment for the produce he consumed during the marriage. Another explanation, suggested in the Jerusalem Talmud, is that during the marriage she does not get produce from the property, since her husband is entitled to benefit from it. *Tosafot* contend that the term produce in this context means the rights extended to the wife in exchange for the husband's access to the produce of her property. In other words, this is referring to the rabbinic enactment that the husband receives the produce of her property in exchange for his obligation to redeem her if she is captured.

Worn clothes – בְּלָאוֹת: Rashi maintains that a woman whose marriage was in violation of a rabbinic prohibition has no rights to her actual worn clothing or other used objects, even if the objects themselves remain intact. *Tosafot* claim that if the items are still in existence, she certainly receives them. The dispute concerns only her right to the value of objects that have worn out completely. The Rif and the Rambam distinguish between the guaranteed property she brought to the marriage, for which she receives compensation even if they are entirely worn out, and the usufruct property, with regard to which her entitlement extends only to the objects themselves.

He is disqualified and she is disqualified – הוּא פָּסוּל וְהִיא פְּסוּלָה: This is the reading accepted by Rashi, who explains that the husband is temporarily disqualified from the Temple service, as long as he remains married to a woman forbidden to him. An alternative version of the text, cited by *Tosafot*, Meiri, and others, reads: He is fit and she is disqualified. According to this version, the husband cannot be called disqualified, as he reverts to a state of being fit for Temple service after divorcing her. However, she is permanently barred from the priesthood. Rabbeinu Ḥananel accepts Rashi's reading, but explains that the pronoun, he, is referring to their child. Rashba also prefers this explanation.

HALAKHA

A widow married to a High Priest, or a divorcée or a *ḥalutza* married to a common priest – אַלְמָנָה לְכֹהֵן גָּדוֹל, גְּרוּשָׁה וַחֲלוּצָה לְכֹהֵן הֶדְיוֹט: If a man marries a woman forbidden to him by Torah law, e.g., a priest marries a divorcée, and he knew she was forbidden, she is entitled to the basic marriage contract and all the conditions of a marriage contract. However, she receives sustenance only after his death but not during his lifetime, and even if she borrowed money in order to eat he does not have to repay her debt, consistent with the opinion of Rabbi Yoḥanan (Rambam *Sefer Nashim, Hilkhot Ishut* 24:4; *Shulḥan Arukh, Even HaEzer* 116:1).

She is disqualified and her offspring is disqualified – הִיא פְּסוּלָה וּוְלָדָהּ פָּסוּל: In this case, a priest married a divorcée or a *zona*, i.e., a woman who has had sexual relations with a man forbidden to her by Torah law and with whom she cannot establish a marital bond; or a High Priest married a divorcée, a *zona*, a widow, or a non-virgin. In any of these situations, the woman is permanently rendered a *ḥalala* as a result of intercourse with the priest or the High Priest. Any child they have is a *ḥalal* (Rambam *Sefer Kedusha, Hilkhot Issurei Bia* 19:3; *Shulḥan Arukh, Even HaEzer* 7:12).

The court forces him to divorce her – כּוֹפִין אוֹתוֹ לְהוֹצִיא: If someone marries a woman forbidden to him, whether by Torah law or by rabbinic decree, he is forced to divorce her (Rambam *Sefer Nashim, Hilkhot Ishut* 24:4; *Shulḥan Arukh, Even HaEzer* 154:20).

She is fit and her offspring is fit – הִיא כְּשֵׁירָה וּוְלָדָהּ כָּשֵׁר: If a priest has intercourse with a woman who underwent *ḥalitza*, she and her children are disqualified from the priesthood by rabbinic law. If he married a woman forbidden to him as a secondary relative prohibited by rabbinic law, she and her children are fit for the priesthood (Rambam *Sefer Kedusha, Hilkhot Issurei Bia* 18:4; *Shulḥan Arukh, Even HaEzer* 7:19).

קָנְסוּ אוֹתוֹ כְּתוּבָּה. וּמִפְּנֵי מָה אָמְרוּ שְׁנִיּוֹת מִדִּבְרֵי סוֹפְרִים אֵין לָהֶן כְּתוּבָּה – מִפְּנֵי שֶׁהוּא כָּשֵׁר וְהִיא כְּשֵׁרָה, וְכָל מָקוֹם שֶׁהוּא כָּשֵׁר וְהִיא כְּשֵׁרָה קָנְסוּ אוֹתָהּ כְּתוּבָּה.

they penalized him through the **marriage contract.** In other words, the Sages did not exempt him from payment of the marriage contract in that case. Since he is disqualified from the priesthood until he divorces her, the marriage will not last, and they did not force her to forfeit her marriage contract. **And for what** reason did **they say** that women forbidden as **secondary relatives by rabbinic law do not have a marriage contract? Because he is fit** for the priesthood **and she is** similarly **fit,** the couple therefore sees no need to divorce, **and any place where he is fit and she is fit they penalized her** by exempting him from payment of the **marriage contract,** in order to speed up the divorce.

רַבִּי אוֹמֵר: הַלָּלוּ דִּבְרֵי תוֹרָה – וְדִבְרֵי תוֹרָה אֵין צְרִיכִין חִיזּוּק, וְהַלָּלוּ דִּבְרֵי סוֹפְרִים – וְדִבְרֵי סוֹפְרִים צְרִיכִין חִיזּוּק. דָּבָר אַחֵר: זֶה – הוּא מַרְגִּילָהּ, וְזוֹ – הִיא מַרְגִּילָתוֹ.

Rabbi Yehuda HaNasi **says** a different reason: **These** cases, a widow married to a High Priest and a divorcée married to a common priest, are prohibited by **Torah law,**[H] **and Torah law does not require strengthening** by means of additional enactments. **But those** secondary relatives are forbidden by **rabbinic law, and rabbinic law** does **require strengthening. Alternatively,** the Gemara presents a second explanation: In **this** case, when they are both disqualified, it is **he who encourages her** to live with him despite the deleterious effect the prohibition will have on her and her offspring. Therefore, they penalized him by making him pay the marriage contract. **But** in **that** case, when they both remain fit for the priesthood despite the prohibited nature of their marriage, it is **she** who **encourages him,**[N] and they consequently penalized her.

דָּבָר אַחֵר מַאן קָתָנֵי לָהּ? אִיכָּא דַּאֲמַר: רַבִּי שִׁמְעוֹן בֶּן אֶלְעָזָר קָתָנֵי לָהּ, וּמַה טַּעַם קָאָמַר: מַה טַּעַם אָמְרוּ הוּא פָּסוּל וְהִיא פְּסוּלָה קָנְסוּ אוֹתוֹ כְּתוּבָּה – מִפְּנֵי שֶׁהוּא מַרְגִּילָהּ, וּמַה טַּעַם הוּא כָּשֵׁר וְהִיא כְּשֵׁרָה קָנְסוּ אוֹתָהּ כְּתוּבָּה – מִפְּנֵי שֶׁהִיא מַרְגִּילָתוֹ.

The Gemara asks: **Who teaches the alternative** explanation; whose opinion does it follow? **Some say** that **Rabbi Shimon ben Elazar teaches it and is saying: What is the reason?** In other words, the latter part of the *baraita* provides the rationale for the previous statement: **What is the reason** that **they said** that if **he is disqualified** from the priesthood **and she is** similarly **disqualified, they penalized him** through the **marriage contract?** It is **because** in such a case **he** primarily **encourages her** to violate the prohibition, as the main disqualification concerns her, so they penalize him for enticing her to sin. **And** for **what reason did they say** that when **he is fit and she is fit they penalized her** through the **marriage contract?** It is **because** in such a case **she encourages him,** since she is not disqualified and therefore may care less about the sin. The Sages therefore penalized her.

אִיכָּא דַּאֲמַר: רַבִּי קָתָנֵי לָהּ, וַחֲלוּצָה קָא קַשְׁיָא לֵיהּ: וְהָא חֲלוּצָה דְּרַבָּנַן וְאִית לָהּ כְּתוּבָּה! הֲדַר אֲמַר: כֵּיוָן דְּפָסֵיל לָהּ מִדְּרַבָּנַן, זֶה – הוּא מַרְגִּילָהּ, וְזוֹ – הִיא מַרְגִּילָתוֹ.

Conversely, **some say** that **Rabbi** Yehuda HaNasi is the one who **teaches it, and** the case of **a *ḥalutza*** poses **a difficulty** to his opinion,[N] as it seems to contradict his principle that rabbinic law requires strengthening: **A *ḥalutza*** is forbidden to a priest **by rabbinic** law, **and** yet **she does have a marriage contract.** In response, **he then said** an additional explanation: **Since he disqualifies her** from the priesthood **by rabbinic law,** in **this** case it is **he who encourages her, and** in **that** case of secondary relatives, when neither of them is disqualified, **she encourages him.**

מַאי אִיכָּא בֵּין רַבִּי לְרַבִּי שִׁמְעוֹן בֶּן אֶלְעָזָר? אָמַר רַב חִסְדָּא: מַמְזֶרֶת וּנְתִינָה לְיִשְׂרָאֵל אִיכָּא בֵּינַיְיהוּ.

The Gemara asks: Practically speaking, **what** difference **is there between** the explanations of **Rabbi** Yehuda HaNasi **and Rabbi Shimon ben Elazar?**[N] **Rav Ḥisda said: The** practical difference **between them** concerns the cases of **a *mamzeret* or a Gibeonite woman** married **to a Jew**[N] of unflawed lineage.

NOTES

She encourages him – **הִיא מַרְגִּילָתוֹ**: The early authorities explain that this entire discussion is based on an assumption that appears in many places in the Talmud, namely that a woman desires to be married more than a man does. Consequently, whenever a woman has no good reason to reject a marriage there is a presumption that she actively desires it. As a result, if the marriage involves a transgression that has no deleterious effects on the wife, the Sages penalized her with the forfeiture of her marriage contract (Rashba; Meiri).

The case of a *ḥalutza* poses a difficulty to his opinion – **חֲלוּצָה קָא קַשְׁיָא לֵיהּ**: Some early authorities maintain that according to the first version, the dispute between Rabbi Yehuda HaNasi and Rabbi Shimon ben Elazar concerns the rabbinic prohibition of a *ḥalutza* and the question of whether or not she receives her marriage contract. According to Rabbi Yehuda HaNasi, she does not receive it, whereas according to Rabbi Shimon ben Elazar, she does. The *Tur* claims that this is the opinion of the Rambam.

Others contend that even according to the first version, Rabbi Yehuda HaNasi agrees that a *ḥalutza* is entitled to a marriage contract, as the *halakha* in her case resembles the case of a divorcée, which is a Torah law, and therefore this *halakha* does not need strengthening (Rashba; Ritva). However, according to this opinion, the need for the justification: She encourages him, must be explained in the second version, which ascribes it to Rabbi Yehuda HaNasi. Some say that this is merely an additional point, so that we do not erroneously think that a *ḥalutza* does not get her marriage contract. Alternatively, it may be that this reason was also stated by Rabbi Shimon ben Elazar, and Rabbi Yehuda HaNasi simply agrees with him in this regard (see Ritva).

What difference is there between the explanations of Rabbi Yehuda HaNasi and Rabbi Shimon ben Elazar – **מַאי אִיכָּא בֵּין רַבִּי לְרַבִּי שִׁמְעוֹן בֶּן אֶלְעָזָר**: Many early authorities have a different version of the text that reads: What is the difference between them, referring to the two versions of the alternative explanation offered in the Gemara. The Ritva writes that there is in fact no substantial difference between the two versions, because according to the first interpretation Rabbi Yehuda HaNasi agrees that a *ḥalutza* receives a marriage contract. According to this, the two opinions differ in style alone.

A *mamzeret* or a Gibeonite woman married to a Jew – **מַמְזֶרֶת וּנְתִינָה לְיִשְׂרָאֵל**: *Tosafot Yeshanim* claim that even according to Rabbi Tarfon, the authority who holds that it is possible for the descendants of a *mamzeret* to enter into the congregation, the wife appears to gain nothing from this marriage, as the remedy of her son marrying a maidservant could be similarly achieved if she had married a *mamzer*. They offer several answers, one of which is that she nevertheless prefers to marry a Jew, so that her children will have at least one parent with unflawed lineage. Since neither she nor her offspring suffer from this marriage, it is assumed that it is she who encourages him.

HALAKHA

These are prohibited by Torah law – **הַלָּלוּ דִּבְרֵי תוֹרָה**: With regard to a secondary relative, the Sages did not distinguish between a husband who was aware of the problem and one who was not. In either case, the woman forfeits the basic part and the conditions of the marriage contract. This is because the Sages found it necessary to strengthen their decrees, as stated by Rabbi Yehuda HaNasi. According to the *Tur*, based on the Rif and the Rosh, the rationale: He encourages her, is accepted by Rabbi Yehuda HaNasi as well, in accordance with the second interpretation of the Gemara. Consequently, although a priest is prohibited by rabbinic law from marrying a *ḥalutza*, she is entitled to a marriage contract (Rambam *Sefer Nashim*, *Hilkhot Ishut* 24:4; *Tur*, *Even HaEzer* 116).

מַאן דְּאָמַר דְּאוֹרַיְיתָא הָא נַמִי דְּאוֹרַיְיתָא, מַאן דְּאָמַר מִפְּנֵי שֶׁהוּא מַרְגִּילָהּ, הָא הִיא מַרְגְּלָא לֵיהּ.

According to **the one who says** that the reason the marriage contract is not revoked from a widow who is married to the High Priest is because this relationship is prohibited **by Torah** law, which doesn't require strengthening, **this too is by Torah** law, and therefore she receives her marriage contract. But according to **the one who says** it is **because he encourages her,** in this case **she encourages him,** as the woman is disqualified regardless, and she wants to marry a Jew because there is a way for her descendants to be fit to enter the congregation: If her *mamzer* son marries a maidservant and has children, they will be slaves who can then be freed and enter the congregation.

וּלְרַבִּי אֱלִיעֶזֶר, דַּאֲמַר: הֲרֵי זֶה עֶבֶד וּמַמְזֵר, הָא לָא מַרְגְּלָא לֵיהּ וְלָא מִידֵּי! אֶלָּא אֲמַר רַב יוֹסֵף: מַחֲזִיר גְּרוּשָׁה מִשֶּׁנִּיסֵּת אִיכָּא בֵּינַיְיהוּ. מַאן דַּאֲמַר דְּאוֹרַיְיתָא – הָא נַמִי דְּאוֹרַיְיתָא, וּמַאן דַּאֲמַר מִפְּנֵי שֶׁהוּא מַרְגִּילָהּ – הָא הִיא מַרְגְּלָא לֵיהּ.

The Gemara asks: **But according to Rabbi Eliezer,**[N] **who said** in a mishna (*Kiddushin* 69a) that if a *mamzer* marries a maidservant and they have a child, their son is both **a slave and a *mamzer*,** since she has no hope of her descendants being fit to enter into the congregation, **she does not encourage him at all. Rather, Rav Yosef said: The** practical difference **between them is** with regard to one who **remarries his divorcée after she has married** another man.[B] According to **the one who says** that it depends on whether the prohibition is **by Torah** law, **this too is** prohibited **by Torah** law. **And** according to **the one who says** it is **because he encourages her,** in this case **she encourages him,** as she and her children are unaffected by this marriage.

וּלְרַבִּי עֲקִיבָא, דְּאָמַר יֵשׁ מַמְזֵר מֵחַיָּיבֵי לָאוִין, הָא לָא מַרְגְּלָא לֵיהּ וְלָא מִידֵּי! אֶלָּא, אֲמַר רַב פַּפָּא: בְּעוּלָה לְכֹהֵן גָּדוֹל אִיכָּא בֵּינַיְיהוּ. מַאן דַּאֲמַר דְּאוֹרַיְיתָא – הָא נַמִי דְּאוֹרַיְיתָא, וּמַאן דַּאֲמַר מִפְּנֵי שֶׁהוּא מַרְגִּילָהּ – הָא הִיא מַרְגְּלָא לֵיהּ.

The Gemara raises a difficulty: **But according to Rabbi Akiva, who said** that offspring **from** forbidden intercourse for which one **is liable** for violating **a prohibition is a *mamzer*, she does not encourage him at all,** because according to this opinion her children would be adversely affected by the marriage. **Rather, Rav Pappa said:** The practical difference **between them** involves **a non-virgin** married **to a High Priest.**[N] According to **the one who says** that it depends on whether the prohibition is **by Torah** law, **this too is** prohibited **by Torah** law. **And** according to **the one who says** it **is because he encourages her,** in this case **she encourages him,** as the marriage merely violates a positive mitzva, which does not disqualify her children.

וּלְרַבִּי אֱלִיעֶזֶר בֶּן יַעֲקֹב, דְּאָמַר: יֵשׁ חָלָל מֵחַיָּיבֵי עֲשֵׂה, הָא לָא מַרְגְּלָא לֵיהּ וְלָא מִידֵּי! אֶלָּא אֲמַר רַב אַשִׁי: מַחֲזִיר סָפֵק סוֹטָתוֹ אִיכָּא בֵּינַיְיהוּ.

The Gemara asks: **But according to Rabbi Eliezer ben Ya'akov, who said** that offspring conceived through intercourse with a priest **for which one is liable for** violating **a positive mitzva is a *ḥalal*, she does not encourage him at all. Rather, Rav Ashi said: The** practical difference **between them is** with regard to the case of one who **remarries his** wife when there is **an uncertainty** if she is **an adulteress.**[N] If a married woman was in seclusion with another man after her husband had become suspicious and had warned her concerning that man, and the husband did not subsequently bring her to be examined by the bitter waters as a *sota,* but rather continued to live with her, he has acted contrary to Torah law, as she is forbidden to him.

מַאן דְּאָמַר דְּאוֹרַיְיתָא – הָא נַמִי דְּאוֹרַיְיתָא, וּמַאן דְּאָמַר מִפְּנֵי שֶׁהוּא מַרְגִּילָהּ – הָא הִיא מַרְגְּלָא לֵיהּ. וּלְרַבִּי מַתְיָא בֶּן חָרָשׁ, דַּאֲמַר: אֲפִילּוּ הָלַךְ בַּעֲלָהּ לְהַשְׁקוֹתָהּ וּבָא עָלֶיהָ בַּדֶּרֶךְ – עֲשָׂאָהּ זוֹנָה, הָא לָא מַרְגְּלָא לֵיהּ וְלָא מִידֵּי? אֶלָּא, אֲמַר מָר בַּר רַב אַשִׁי: סוֹטָה וַדַּאי אִיכָּא בֵּינַיְיהוּ.

In this case, according to **the one who says** that it depends on whether the prohibition is **by Torah** law, **this too is** prohibited **by Torah** law. **And** according to **the one who says** it is **because he encourages her,** in this case **she encourages him,** as her children are not disqualified by such a relationship. The Gemara asks: **But according to Rabbi Matya ben Ḥarash, who said** that **even if her husband went to cause her to drink** the bitter waters **and had intercourse with her on the way, he has** thereby **rendered her a *zona*** and disqualified her from the priesthood, **she does not encourage him at all. Rather, Mar bar Rav Ashi said:** The practical difference **between them is** with regard to the case of a **definite adulteress.**[N] In such a case, all agree that their children are not *mamzerim,* despite the prohibition against their cohabitation. Consequently, she encourages him to sin.

NOTES

But according to Rabbi Eliezer, etc. – **וּלְרַבִּי אֱלִיעֶזֶר וכו׳**: The Ritva asks why we do not say that Rabbi Yehuda HaNasi and Rabbi Shimon ben Elazar in fact argue over whether the *halakha* is in accordance with Rabbi Tarfon or Rabbi Eliezer. *Arukh LaNer* addresses this point and suggests that the Gemara prefers to minimize disputes as much as possible, and since there is a way of saying that they do not argue, there is no need to create a dispute where one might not exist.

A non-virgin married to a High Priest – **בְּעוּלָה לְכֹהֵן גָּדוֹל**: The Ramban notes that even according to Rabbi Eliezer ben Ya'akov, the Gemara could have said that they argue over a High Priest who marries a woman who was a virgin until she engaged in relations with him, as everyone agrees that he does not disqualify her. The Ramban explains that the Gemara did not want to answer in a manner that depends on a dispute between *amora'im*. The Rashba maintains that it is unclear that this woman, i.e., a non-virgin who engaged in intercourse only with him, is forbidden by Torah law. It is possible that this is merely a rabbinic prohibition.

One who remarries his wife when there is an uncertainty if she is an adulteress – **מַחֲזִיר סָפֵק סוֹטָתוֹ**: The Ramban writes that this is not referring to one who divorced his wife and remarried her, but rather to one who separated from her out of fear that she was an adulteress and then changed his mind and had relations with her.

The practical difference between them is the case of a definite adulteress – **סוֹטָה וַדַּאי אִיכָּא בֵּינַיְיהוּ**: Following one reading of the text, Rabbeinu Ḥananel maintains that although the child is unflawed by Torah law, he is treated by rabbinic law as if he were a *mamzer*. The Ramban proves from this discussion that this cannot be the case. The Rashba agrees that Rabbeinu Ḥananel's second version, according to which their child is fit even for the priesthood, is more reasonable.

BACKGROUND

One who remarries his divorcée after she has married another man – **מַחֲזִיר גְּרוּשָׁה מִשֶּׁנִּיסֵּת**: According to the Torah (Deuteronomy 24:1–4), once a man has divorced his wife, he cannot remarry her if she has married someone else in the interim, even after she is widowed or divorced from her second husband. This *halakha* is mentioned by the prophet Jeremiah (Jeremiah 3:1) who uses it as a poetic contrast with the relationship between God and the Jewish people who can return to Him after atonement through exile (Radak).

HALAKHA

An Israelite woman…pregnant, etc. – בַּת יִשְׂרָאֵל...מְעוּבֶּרֶת וכו׳: An Israelite or Levite woman who is not married to a priest, but is pregnant from a priest, may not partake of *teruma*, despite the fact that she is carrying a priest's offspring. Similarly, if she is not married but merely betrothed to a priest, or if she is a widow awaiting her *yavam* who is a priest, she is prohibited from partaking of *teruma* (Rambam *Sefer Zera'im*, *Hilkhot Terumot* 8:2, 5).

מתני׳ בַּת יִשְׂרָאֵל מְאוֹרֶסֶת לְכֹהֵן, מְעוּבֶּרֶת מִכֹּהֵן, שׁוֹמֶרֶת יָבָם לְכֹהֵן, וְכֵן בַּת כֹּהֵן לְיִשְׂרָאֵל – לֹא תֹּאכַל בִּתְרוּמָה. בַּת יִשְׂרָאֵל מְאוֹרֶסֶת לְלֵוִי, מְעוּבֶּרֶת מִלֵּוִי, שׁוֹמֶרֶת יָבָם לְלֵוִי, וְכֵן בַּת לֵוִי לְיִשְׂרָאֵל – לֹא תֹּאכַל בְּמַעֲשֵׂר.

MISHNA If there is **an Israelite woman betrothed to a priest** or **pregnant from a priest,** and he died; and **a widow awaiting her *yavam*,** who is **a priest; and similarly,** the **daughter of a priest** who is betrothed, pregnant from, or is a widow waiting **for** her *yavam*, who is **an Israelite, she may not partake of *teruma*.**[H] If there is **an Israelite woman betrothed to a Levite or pregnant from a Levite; and a widow awaiting her *yavam*, who is a Levite; and similarly the daughter of a Levite** who is betrothed, pregnant from, or a widow waiting **for** her *yavam*, who is **an Israelite, she may not partake of tithes.**

בַּת לֵוִי מְאוֹרֶסֶת לְכֹהֵן, מְעוּבֶּרֶת מִכֹּהֵן, שׁוֹמֶרֶת יָבָם לְכֹהֵן, וְכֵן בַּת כֹּהֵן לְלֵוִי – לֹא תֹּאכַל לֹא בִּתְרוּמָה וְלֹא בְּמַעֲשֵׂר.

If there is a **daughter of a Levite betrothed to a priest** or **pregnant from a priest;** and **a widow awaiting her *yavam*, who is a priest; and similarly a daughter of a priest** who is betrothed **to** or pregnant from a Levite, or is a widow waiting for her *yavam*, who is **a Levite, she may partake of neither *teruma* nor tithes.** This follows the *halakha* that betrothal, pregnancy, and waiting for a *yavam* disqualify the daughter of a priest from eating *teruma*, but they do not enable an Israelite woman to partake of *teruma*.

גמ׳ וּתְהֵא זָרָה, זָרָה מִי לָא אָכְלָה בְּמַעֲשֵׂר?! אָמַר רַב נַחְמָן אָמַר שְׁמוּאֵל: הָא מַנִּי – רַבִּי מֵאִיר הִיא, דְּאָמַר: מַעֲשֵׂר רִאשׁוֹן אָסוּר לְזָרִים. דְּתַנְיָא:

GEMARA The mishna states that an Israelite woman betrothed to a Levite may not partake of tithes. The Gemara is puzzled by this ruling: **And let her** even **be** a complete **foreigner** who is not a Levite; **may a foreigner not partake of tithes?** In contradistinction to *teruma*, no special sanctity pertains to tithes; they are merely the possession of the Levite. What difference does it make, then, whether she is a Levite or not? **Rav Naḥman said** that **Shmuel said:** In accordance with **whose** opinion **is this** mishna? **It is** in accordance with the opinion of **Rabbi Meir, who said** that the **first tithe is forbidden to foreigners,** i.e., non-Levites, **as it is taught** in a *baraita*:

Perek **IX**
Daf **86** Amud **a**

HALAKHA

***Teruma* is for a priest** – תְּרוּמָה לְכֹהֵן: *Teruma* and *teruma* of the tithe may be eaten by adult and minor priests, both male and female, by their Canaanite slaves, and by their animals (Rambam *Sefer Zera'im*, *Hilkhot Terumot* 6:1).

The first tithe is for a Levite – מַעֲשֵׂר רִאשׁוֹן לְלֵוִי: The first tithe is given to Levites, both males and females. However, this tithe may also be eaten by Israelites, even in a state of impurity, as it has no sanctity (Rambam *Sefer Zera'im*, *Hilkhot Ma'asrot* 1:1–2).

תְּרוּמָה לְכֹהֵן וּמַעֲשֵׂר רִאשׁוֹן לְלֵוִי, דִּבְרֵי רַבִּי מֵאִיר. רַבִּי אֶלְעָזָר בֶּן עֲזַרְיָה מַתִּירוֹ לְכֹהֵן. מַתִּירוֹ – מִכְּלָל דְּאִיכָּא מַאן דְּאָסַר? אֶלָּא אֵימָא: נוֹתְנוֹ אַף לְכֹהֵן.

***Teruma* is for a priest**[H] and the **first tithe is for a Levite;**[H] this is **the statement of Rabbi Meir.**[N] **Rabbi Elazar ben Azarya permits** it, i.e., the first tithe, **to a priest,** as he too is from the tribe of Levi. The Gemara is puzzled by this last statement: It says: **Permits it.** Does this prove **by inference that there is one *tanna* that prohibits** a priest from partaking of tithes? But a priest is also a Levite and cannot be considered a foreigner. **Rather, say** that Rabbi Elazar ben Azarya meant that **one may give it even to a priest.** The tithe does not have to be handed to a Levite; one may choose to give it to a priest instead.

NOTES

The first tithe is for a Levite, this is the statement of Rabbi Meir – מַעֲשֵׂר רִאשׁוֹן לְלֵוִי, דִּבְרֵי רַבִּי מֵאִיר: This ruling of Rabbi Meir does not state explicitly that, in his opinion, foreigners are prohibited from partaking of the first tithe. Rashi attempts to prove this from Rabbi Elazar ben Azarya's response. However, *Tosafot* question this interpretation, as does the Rivan. The Ramban agrees with *Tosafot* and maintains that our knowledge of Rabbi Meir's opinion is not from the *baraita*, but rather from the tradition quoted by Rav Aḥa, son of Rabba, which is assumed to be in accordance with Rabbi Meir's opinion. It is based on this tradition that in several places the Talmud states as a generally accepted fact that Rabbi Meir is of the opinion that foreigners are prohibited from partaking of first tithe (Rashba; Ritva).

מַאי טַעְמָא דְּרַבִּי מֵאִיר? אֲמַר רַב אַחָא בְּרֵיהּ דְּרַבָּה מִשְּׁמֵיהּ דִּגְמָרָא: ״כִּי אֶת מַעְשַׂר בְּנֵי יִשְׂרָאֵל אֲשֶׁר יָרִימוּ לַה׳ תְּרוּמָה״, מַה תְּרוּמָה אֲסוּרָה לְזָרִים – אַף מַעֲשֵׂר רִאשׁוֹן אָסוּר לְזָרִים. אִי מַה תְּרוּמָה חַיָּיבִין עָלָיו מִיתָה וְחוֹמֶשׁ – אַף מַעֲשֵׂר חַיָּיבִין עָלָיו מִיתָה וְחוֹמֶשׁ?

The Gemara inquires: **What is the reason for Rabbi Meir's** opinion? **Rav Aḥa, son of Rabba, said in the name of tradition**[N] that the verse states: **"For the tithe of the children of Israel that they set apart as a *teruma* to the Lord,** I have given to the Levites for an inheritance" (Numbers 18:24). From the fact that this verse calls the tithe "*teruma*," we learn: **Just as *teruma* is forbidden to foreigners, so too is the first tithe forbidden to foreigners,** i.e., non-Levites. The Gemara asks: **If** so, is it true that **just as** with ***teruma***, a foreigner who eats it **is liable** to receive the punishment of **death** at the hand of Heaven **and** to pay the additional **fifth for it, so too,** with regard to **tithes,** a foreigner who eats it should be **liable for it** to receive the punishment of **death** at the hand of Heaven **and** to pay the additional **fifth?**

אָמַר קְרָא ״וּמֵתוּ בוֹ כִּי יְחַלְּלֻהוּ״ ״וְיָסַף חֲמִישִׁיתוֹ עָלָיו״, ״בּוֹ״ – וְלֹא בְּמַעֲשֵׂר, ״עָלָיו״ – וְלֹא עַל מַעֲשֵׂר. וְרַבָּנַן: מַה תְּרוּמָה טוֹבֶלֶת – אַף מַעֲשֵׂר רִאשׁוֹן נַמִי טוֹבֵל.

The Gemara answers that **the verse states: "They will die through it if they profane it"** (Leviticus 22:9), and a different verse states: **"Then he shall add the fifth part thereof unto it"** (Leviticus 22:14). A close reading of these verses shows that the Torah is emphasizing that the death penalty comes **through it,** *teruma*, **and not through tithes,** and that a fifth must be added **to it, but not to tithes.** The Gemara asks: **And the Rabbis,** who disagree with Rabbi Meir, how do they account for the comparison in the above verse? The Gemara answers: They would say it teaches that **just as** the requirement to separate ***teruma*** **produces** the status of forbidden **untithed produce,**[H] **so too** the requirement to separate the **first tithe also produces** the status of forbidden **untithed produce.**[H]

וְכִדְתַנְיָא, רַבִּי יוֹסֵי אוֹמֵר: יָכוֹל לֹא יְהֵא חַיָּיב אֶלָּא עַל טֶבֶל שֶׁלֹּא הוּרַם מִמֶּנּוּ כָּל עִיקָּר, הוּרַם מִמֶּנּוּ תְּרוּמָה גְּדוֹלָה וְלֹא הוּרַם מִמֶּנּוּ מַעֲשֵׂר רִאשׁוֹן, מַעֲשֵׂר רִאשׁוֹן וְלֹא מַעֲשֵׂר שֵׁנִי, וַאֲפִילּוּ מַעְשַׂר עָנִי – מִנַּיִן?

And this is **as it is taught** in a *baraita*: **Rabbi Yosei says:** One **might** have thought a person **should be liable only for untithed produce from which no** *terumot* or tithes **have been separated at all,** but if the **great *teruma* has been separated from it and the first tithe has not been separated from it;** or if the **first tithe** has been separated from it **and** the **second tithe has not; or even** if the **poor man's tithe,** which is merely given to the poor and has no sanctity, has not been separated, **from where** is it derived that such produce also has the status of untithed produce?

תַּלְמוּד לוֹמַר ״לֹא תוּכַל לֶאֱכוֹל בִּשְׁעָרֶיךָ״ וּלְהַלָּן הוּא אוֹמֵר ״וְאָכְלוּ בִשְׁעָרֶיךָ וְשָׂבֵעוּ״, מַה ״שְׁעָרֶיךָ״ הָאָמוּר לְהַלָּן מַעְשַׂר עָנִי, אַף ״שְׁעָרֶיךָ״ הָאָמוּר כָּאן מַעְשַׂר עָנִי, וְאָמַר רַחֲמָנָא ״לֹא תוּכַל״.

The verse states: "You may not eat within your gates[N] the tithe of your grain" (Deuteronomy 12:17), **and below,** with regard to the poor man's tithe, **it states: "That they may eat within your gates and be satisfied"** (Deuteronomy 26:12). **Just as "your gates" stated below** is referring to **the poor man's tithe, so too "your gates" stated here** is referring to **the poor man's tithe, and the Merciful One states** in the Torah **"you may not** eat," implying that it may be eaten only after separation.

וְאִי מֵהָתָם הֲוָה אָמִינָא לְלָאו, אֲבָל מִיתָה לֹא, קָא מַשְׁמַע לַן.

And if we had learned it only **from there, I would say** that it merely teaches **a prohibition** against partaking of untithed produce of this type, **but** the **death** penalty is **not** warranted. The comparison to *teruma* consequently **teaches us** that eating this type of untithed produce is also punishable by death at the hand of Heaven.

לִישָּׁנָא אַחֲרִינָא: מַעֲשֵׂר רִאשׁוֹן דְּטָבֵיל מִדְּרַבִּי יוֹסֵי נָפְקָא! אִי מֵהַהִיא – הֲוָה אָמִינָא: לְלָאו, אֲבָל מִיתָה לָא, קָא מַשְׁמַע לַן.

A different version of this discussion presents it in the form of a question: Isn't it the case that the *halakha* that failure to separate the **first tithe creates** the status of **untithed produce**[N] **is derived from** the *halakha* that **Rabbi Yosei** taught? If so, there is no need for the exposition of the verse referring to tithes as *teruma*. The Gemara answers: **If** the proof was **from that** source alone, **I would say** that it is only prohibited **by a prohibition but** the **death** penalty is **not** warranted. He therefore **teaches us** that all the stringencies of untithed produce are in force.

NOTES

In the name of tradition – מִשְּׁמֵיהּ דִּגְמָרָא: This expression, which appears in several places, means that the statement was not ascribed to a particular Sage. Rather, it was a tradition that each student received from his teacher, ultimately tracing back to Rabbi Meir himself (Ramban).

You may not eat within your gates – לֹא תוּכַל לֶאֱכוֹל בִּשְׁעָרֶיךָ: The verse states: "You may not eat within your gates the tithe of your grain, or of your wine, or of your oil" (Deuteronomy 12:17). It is understood as referring not to the first tithe itself, but to remaining tithes that have yet to be separated. In other words, one may not eat within his gates so long as the tithe of his grain has yet to be separated (see Ritva).

Failure to separate the first tithe creates the status of untithed produce – מַעֲשֵׂר רִאשׁוֹן דְּטָבֵיל: The question arises how it is that the *halakha* of the first tithe is derived from the *halakha* of the poor man's tithe? Admittedly, there is an *a fortiori* inference, but the principle is that we do not derive a prohibition by means of an *a fortiori* inference. According to *Tosafot Yeshanim*, this *halakha* relating to the first tithe is based on the *teruma* of the tithe contained within it. According to all opinions, the presence of this *teruma* creates the status of untithed produce, and therefore, as long as the first tithe has not been separated, it is considered untithed produce due to the *teruma* of the tithe.

HALAKHA

The requirement to separate *teruma* produces the status of forbidden untithed produce – תְּרוּמָה טוֹבֶלֶת: It is prohibited to partake of produce before the great *teruma* and *teruma* of the tithe have been separated from it. One who eats an olive-bulk of untithed produce is liable to be punished with death at the hand of Heaven (Rambam *Sefer Kedusha, Hilkhot Ma'akhalot Assurot* 10:19).

The requirement to separate the first tithe also produces the status of untithed produce – מַעֲשֵׂר רִאשׁוֹן נַמִי טוֹבֵל: One who eats an olive-bulk from which the great *teruma* and *teruma* of the tithe have been separated but from which the first tithe has not been separated or the poor man's tithe has yet to be set aside is liable to receive lashes for eating untithed produce. However, he is not liable to be punished with death at the hand of Heaven. Some maintain that one is liable even for eating produce from which the tithe has not been separated (Jerusalem Talmud; *Midrash Rabba*; Rambam *Sefer Kedusha, Hilkhot Ma'akhalot Assurot* 10:20).

בְּמַאי אוֹקִימְתָּא – כְּרַבִּי מֵאִיר, אֵימָא סֵיפָא: ״בַּת לֵוִי מְאוֹרֶסֶת לְכֹהֵן, וּבַת כֹּהֵן לְלֵוִי – לֹא תֹאכַל לֹא בִּתְרוּמָה וְלֹא בְּמַעֲשֵׂר״. הָכָא מַאי זָרוּת אִיכָּא? אֲמַר רַב שֵׁשֶׁת: מַאי ״אֵינָהּ אוֹכֶלֶת״ דְּקָתָנֵי – אֵינָהּ נוֹתֶנֶת רְשׁוּת לִתְרוֹם,

§ The Gemara asks: **In what** manner **did you establish** the mishna? **In accordance with** the opinion of **Rabbi Meir.** But if so, **say the latter clause:** The **daughter of a Levite betrothed to a priest** and the **daughter of a priest** betrothed **to a Levite may eat neither *teruma* nor tithe. Here, what foreignness is there**[N] that prohibits her from partaking of the tithe? Even according to the opinion that prohibits the first tithe to foreigners, this woman is a Levite on both sides. **Rav Sheshet said: What is** the meaning of: **She may not eat, that** the mishna **teaches?**[N] It means that **she may not give permission** to others **to separate** the *teruma* from the tithe. As long as she is merely betrothed to a Levite, she may not appoint a messenger to set aside the *teruma* from the tithe on behalf of the Levite, as she is not yet his wife.

מִכְּלָל דִּנְשׂוּאָה נוֹתֶנֶת רְשׁוּת? אִין, וְהָתַנְיָא: ״וַאֲכַלְתֶּם אוֹתוֹ בְּכָל מָקוֹם אַתֶּם וּבֵיתְכֶם״ – לִימֵּד עַל נְשׂוּאָה בַּת יִשְׂרָאֵל שֶׁנּוֹתֶנֶת רְשׁוּת לִתְרוֹם.

The Gemara asks: Is it to be concluded **by inference that a married** woman **may give permission** to separate *teruma* from the tithe? The Gemara answers: **Yes, and isn't it taught: "And you may eat it in any place, you and your households"** (Numbers 18:31)? This **teaches that an Israelite woman married** to a Levite **may give permission** to another **to separate** *teruma* from the Levite's tithe.

אַתָּה אוֹמֵר רְשׁוּת לִתְרוֹם, אוֹ אֵינוֹ אֶלָּא לֶאֱכוֹל? אָמַרְתָּ תְּרוּמָה חֲמוּרָה אוֹכֶלֶת, מַעֲשֵׂר הַקַּל – לֹא כׇּל שֶׁכֵּן?! אֶלָּא, לִימֵּד עַל נְשׂוּאָה בַּת יִשְׂרָאֵל שֶׁנּוֹתֶנֶת רְשׁוּת לִתְרוֹם.

The *baraita* continues to discuss this *halakha*: Do **you say** she may give **permission to separate** *teruma* from the tithe, **or** perhaps **it is only** referring **to eating? Say** in response: If an Israelite woman married to a priest **may partake of *teruma*,** which is **stringent,** is it **not all the more so** true for **tithe,** which is **lenient?** Consequently, there is no need to teach us this *halakha*. **Rather,** the verse **teaches that an Israelite woman married** to a Levite **may give permission** to another **to separate** *teruma* from the tithe.

מָר בְּרֵיהּ דְּרַבָּנָא אָמַר: לוֹמַר שֶׁאֵין חוֹלְקִין לָהּ מַעֲשֵׂר בְּבֵית הַגְּרָנוֹת. הָנִיחָא לְמַאן דְּאָמַר מִשּׁוּם יִיחוּד, אֶלָּא לְמַאן דְּאָמַר מִשּׁוּם גְּרוּשָׁה – גְּרוּשָׁה בַּת לֵוִי מִי לָא אָכְלָה בְּמַעֲשֵׂר?

Mar, son of Rabbana, said: The mishna is not teaching that the daughter of a Levite who was betrothed to a priest may not partake of tithe, but rather it is coming **to say that we do not distribute tithe to her in the granary.** The Gemara asks: **This works out well according to the one who says** that the reason for the decree against distributing *teruma* to a woman in the granary is **due to** the prohibition (*Yevamot* 100a) against a woman **being alone** with a strange man in the granary, which is a secluded place, as this concern applies equally to the case here. **But according to the one who says** that the Sages prohibited this practice **due to** concern that the woman might be **a divorcée,** who is no longer entitled to *teruma*, this concern should not apply to the **daughter of a Levite. Does she not partake of tithe** on her own account, even after she is divorced?

וְלִיטַעֲמִיךְ, גְּרוּשָׁה בַּת כֹּהֵן מִי לָא אָכְלָה בִּתְרוּמָה? אֶלָּא, גְּזֵירָה מִשּׁוּם גְּרוּשָׁה בַּת יִשְׂרָאֵל.

The Gemara refutes this argument: **And according to your reasoning** that rejects the explanation of Mar, son of Rabbana, with regard to the daughter of a Levite, **does a divorcée** who is the **daughter of a priest not partake of *teruma*?** Why should the daughter of a priest married to a priest not receive *teruma* in a granary? **Rather,** this is a rabbinic **decree** that was enacted primarily **due to** a priest's **divorcée** who is the **daughter of a non-priest,** as she may no longer partake of *teruma* after her divorce. They also applied this decree to the daughter of a priest divorced from a priest. For this reason, they also decreed against a Levite woman receiving a portion in the granary.

אִי הָכִי, מַאי אִירְיָא מְאוֹרֶסֶת? אֲפִילּוּ נְשׂוּאָה נַמִי! אַיְּידֵי דְּתָנָא רֵישָׁא מְאוֹרֶסֶת תָּנָא נַמִי סֵיפָא מְאוֹרֶסֶת.

The Gemara raises a difficulty: **If so, why specifically** one who was **betrothed; the same would hold true even** for **a married** woman **as well.** The Gemara answers: There is no difference between them in this regard, but **since the** *tanna* **taught** in the **first clause** of the mishna: **Betrothed, he also taught** in **the latter clause: Betrothed,** although the *halakha* in the latter clause does not apply exclusively to a betrothed woman.

תָּנוּ רַבָּנַן: תְּרוּמָה לְכֹהֵן וּמַעֲשֵׂר רִאשׁוֹן לְלֵוִי, דִּבְרֵי רַבִּי עֲקִיבָא. רַבִּי אֶלְעָזָר בֶּן עֲזַרְיָה אוֹמֵר:

§ **The Sages taught:** *Teruma* is given **to a priest, and the first tithe is** given only **to a Levite;** this is **the statement of Rabbi Akiva. Rabbi Elazar ben Azarya says:**

NOTES

What foreignness is there – מַאי זָרוּת אִיכָּא: This difficulty is also addressed in the Jerusalem Talmud, where a different answer is offered: The mishna follows the opinion that the first tithe is given only to Levites, not to priests. Consequently, the daughter of a Levite betrothed to a priest is no longer permitted to partake of tithes as a member of her father's household, but she has yet to be granted permission to partake of *teruma* from her husband's household.

The Ramban, without explicitly mentioning the Jerusalem Talmud, rejects this opinion, as he maintains that after Ezra's enactment everyone agrees that the first tithe may also be distributed to priests (see 86b). He explains that the mishna cannot be discussing the fundamental concept on the level of Torah law, as according to Torah law a betrothed woman is considered married, and consequently she would be able to partake of *teruma* as a married woman.

What is: She may not eat, that it teaches – מַאי אֵינָהּ אוֹכֶלֶת דְּקָתָנֵי: According to Rashi, Rav Sheshet's explanation refers to the entire mishna, not merely its last clause. *Tosafot* question this interpretation, because if it were correct the Gemara should have introduced his opinion with the expression: Rather, Rav Sheshet said, as it normally does in such a case. Consequently, they maintain that Rav Sheshet accepts the previous explanation of the first part of the mishna and differs only with regard to that specific clause. In his Commentary to the Mishna, the Rambam appears to adopt the same opinion. The Ritva, however, claims that the difficulty raised by *Tosafot* is not decisive, as it is occasionally found that the Gemara neglects to preface a new line of interpretation with the word: Rather. He contends that throughout the mishna the phrase: May not partake, means that since she does not have the authority to allow others to separate *teruma* from the tithe, she herself may not eat. The Meiri offers a similar interpretation.

לְכֹהֵן. לְכֹהֵן וְלֹא לְלֵוִי?! אֵימָא: אַף לְכֹהֵן. מַאי טַעְמָא דְּרַבִּי עֲקִיבָא – דִּכְתִיב ״וְאֶל הַלְוִיִּם תְּדַבֵּר וְאָמַרְתָּ אֲלֵיהֶם״, בַּלְוִיִּם קָא מִשְׁתָּעֵי קְרָא. וְאִידָּךְ – כִּדְרַבִּי יְהוֹשֻׁעַ בֶּן לֵוִי, דְּאָמַר רַבִּי יְהוֹשֻׁעַ בֶּן לֵוִי: בְּעֶשְׂרִים וְאַרְבָּעָה מְקוֹמוֹת נִקְרְאוּ כֹּהֲנִים ״לְוִיִּם״, וְזֶה אֶחָד מֵהֶם: ״וְהַכֹּהֲנִים הַלְוִיִּם בְּנֵי צָדוֹק״.

The first tithe is given **to a priest.** The Gemara is puzzled: **To a priest and not to a Levite?** But the Torah expressly states that the first tithe is for Levites. The Gemara answers: **Say** he means it can be given **also to a priest.** The Gemara clarifies: **What is the reason** for **Rabbi Akiva's** opinion? **As it is written: "You shall speak to the Levites, and you shall say to them"** (Numbers 18:26). Clearly, **the verse speaks of Levites,** not priests. **And the other** *tanna*, Rabbi Eliezer, maintains **in accordance with** the opinion **of Rabbi Yehoshua ben Levi, as Rabbi Yehoshua ben Levi said: In twenty-four places** in the Bible the **priests are called Levites. And this is one of those** verses: **"And the priests the Levites, the sons of Zadok"** (Ezekiel 44:15).

וְרַבִּי עֲקִיבָא: הָכָא לָא מָצֵית אָמְרַתְּ, דִּכְתִיב ״וַאֲכַלְתֶּם אוֹתוֹ בְּכָל מָקוֹם״ – מִי שֶׁיָּכוֹל לְאוֹכְלוֹ בְּכָל מָקוֹם, יָצָא כֹּהֵן שֶׁאֵין יָכוֹל לְאוֹכְלוֹ בְּבֵית הַקְּבָרוֹת. וְאִידָּךְ: כָּל הֵיכָא דְּבָעֵי, דְּלָא בָּעֵי חוֹמָה, וְאִי אָכֵיל לֵיהּ בְּטוּמְאַת הַגּוּף – לָא לָקֵי.

And Rabbi Akiva replies: **Here you cannot say** the verse is referring to priests, **as it is written: "And you may eat it in any place"** (Numbers 18:31), from which we learn that the tithe is given to **one who can eat it in any place.** This **excludes a priest, who cannot eat it in a cemetery,** as he is prohibited from entering such a place. Consequently, the verse cannot be referring to priests. **And the other** Sage, Rabbi Eliezer, how does he respond to this claim? He explains the verse as follows: He may eat it **anywhere that he wishes,** that is, in any city, **as it does not require** the **wall** of Jerusalem, like the second tithe. **And** we further learn from here that **if he eats it in** a state of **bodily impurity he is not flogged.** Consequently, we can say that tithe may be eaten by priests in any place.

הַהִיא גִּינְּתָא דַּהֲוָה שָׁקֵיל רַבִּי אֶלְעָזָר בֶּן עֲזַרְיָה מַעֲשֵׂר רִאשׁוֹן מִינָּהּ, אֲזַל רַבִּי עֲקִיבָא אַהַדְרֵיהּ לְפִתְחָא לְבֵי קִבְרֵי. אֲמַר: עֲקִיבָא בְּתַרְמִילוֹ וַאֲנָא חַיֵּי!

The Gemara relates: There was **a certain garden from which Rabbi Elazar ben Azarya,**[P] a priest, **would take the first tithe,** in accordance with his opinion that priests are also entitled to this tithe. **Rabbi Akiva went,** closed up the garden, and **changed its entrance** so that it would be facing **toward the cemetery,**[N] to prevent Rabbi Elazar ben Azarya from entering the garden. Rabbi Elazar **said** in the form of a lighthearted exaggeration: **Akiva,** a former shepherd, comes **with his satchel,**[NB] **but I have to live;** from where will I receive my livelihood if I cannot claim the first tithe? Rabbi Elazar was actually a very wealthy man and did not need the produce from this garden. However, his point was that Rabbi Akiva acted in order to stop him from receiving something that he felt was rightfully his.

אִיתְּמַר, מִפְּנֵי מָה קָנְסוּ לְוִיִּם בְּמַעֲשֵׂר? פְּלִיגִי בָּהּ רַבִּי יוֹנָתָן וְסָבַיָּא. חַד אָמַר: שֶׁלֹּא עָלוּ בִּימֵי עֶזְרָא, וְחַד אָמַר: כְּדֵי שֶׁיִּסְמְכוּ כֹּהֲנִים עָלָיו בִּימֵי טוּמְאָתָן.

§ **It was stated** that *amora'im* disagreed about the following question: **For what reason did** the Sages **penalize the Levites**[N] **with regard to** their **tithe,** by declaring that it may be given to priests as well? **Rabbi Yonatan and the Elders** who were with him **disagree** with regard to **this** matter. **One said** it was because **they did not ascend,** i.e., immigrate to the land of Israel, **in the days of Ezra. And one said** that it was not a penalty at all, but they gave the first tithe to the priests **so that they** could **rely on it during their days of impurity.** Because it is prohibited for priests to consume *teruma* while in a state of impurity, they would have had nothing to eat if they were dependent exclusively on *teruma*. It is permitted, however, to eat the tithe while impure.

PERSONALITIES

Rabbi Elazar ben Azarya – רַבִּי אֶלְעָזָר בֶּן עֲזַרְיָה: One of the most significant *tanna'im* in the generation following the destruction of the Temple, Rabbi Elazar ben Azarya descended from a family blessed with great wisdom, distinguished lineage, and wealth. His father, Azarya, was also a Torah scholar and an extremely wealthy man. Azarya supported his brother Shimon, one of the Sages, who is therefore referred to as Shimon, brother of Azarya. Rabbi Elazar ben Azarya was from a family of priests descended from Ezra the Scribe, and there are traditions that draw parallels between them.

NOTES

Changed its entrance so that it would be facing toward the cemetery – אַהַדְרֵיהּ לְפִתְחָא לְבֵי קִבְרֵי: The later authorities note that it was still possible to extract the *teruma* of the tithe while in a state of purity. For example, the *Iyyun Ya'akov* suggests that Rabbi Elazar could in fact have sent an agent to retrieve the tithe for him, but Rabbi Akiva was hinting that the very fact that a priest cannot eat in a cemetery is why the verse can be explained as referring only to Levites, not priests.

Akiva with his satchel – עֲקִיבָא בְּתַרְמִילוֹ: The Meiri explains the comment as follows: Even if Rabbi Akiva returns to his shepherd's satchel, I can survive without the tithe, as Rabbi Elazar ben Azarya was a wealthy man. According to the Maharsha, the satchel refers to Rabbi Akiva's position as charity collector. Rabbi Akiva wanted to give the tithe to the poor, as he thought the penalty was for the tithe to be transferred to paupers, to which Rabbi Elazar replied: But I have to live by this tradition, as Rabbi Elazar ben Azarya was a tenth-generation descendant of Ezra, and Ezra's decree was that the tithe may be given to priests.

For what reason did they penalize the Levites – מִפְּנֵי מָה קָנְסוּ לְוִיִּם: According to Rashi, there is no connection between this discussion and the dispute between Rabbi Akiva and Rabbi Elazar ben Azarya, as they disagreed over Torah law, whereas the Gemara deals with the situation after Ezra's enactment. However, the Ritva maintains that the two issues are related: Since Rabbi Akiva is of the opinion that according to Torah law tithe is given only to Levites, it is impossible for Ezra to deprive them of their rights entirely. Conversely, Rabbi Elazar ben Azarya rules that even by Torah law the first tithe may be given to priests, and therefore Ezra's decree can be understood to mean that only priests are entitled to receive this tithe. *Tosafot* offer a similar interpretation.

The Ritva adds that the question remains: According to Rabbi Akiva, who maintains that the first tithe belongs exclusively to Levites according to Torah law, how could Ezra transfer this right to the priests? He explains that since the first tithe has no sanctity and Levites have only a monetary right to this tithe, and since there is a general principle in *halakha* that a court has the authority to declare property ownerless, the Sages had the power to deprive them of their statutory rights. Consequently, the priests receive the tithe as representatives of the tribe of Levi. The *Mei Neftoaḥ* suggests that the dispute between Rabbi Akiva and Rabbi Elazar is whether the Sages have the right to not only declare property ownerless but also to transfer that ownership to another.

BACKGROUND

Satchel [*tarmil*] – תַּרְמִיל: A *tarmil* is a bag made out of leather. According to Rav Hai Gaon, it had a volume of five *kav*, equivalent to about 7 ℓ. The *tarmil* was used by people who would travel significant distances or who needed to take a significant amount of food with them, e.g., shepherds. The *tarmil* was sometimes associated with shepherds and also with converts, who may have immigrated from distant lands, and as such serves as a double hint to the origins of Rabbi Akiva, who was both a son of converts and a shepherd. Indeed, the Sage Asi ben Yehuda described him as a man who would gather everything he could find and afterward sort and arrange his collection. It is possible that this statement of Rabbi Elazar ben Azarya also hints at Rabbi Akiva's method of study, which involved collecting the opinions of various Sages and categorizing them. This was different from the method used by Rabbi Elazar himself, who apparently received his tradition principally from his forefathers.

בִּשְׁלָמָא לְמַאן דְּאָמַר שֶׁלֹּא עָלוּ – מִשּׁוּם הָכִי קְנָסִינְהוּ. אֶלָּא לְמַאן דְּאָמַר כְּדֵי שֶׁיִּסְמְכוּ עָלָיו כֹּהֲנִים בִּימֵי טוּמְאָתָן – מִשּׁוּם כֹּהֲנִים קָנְסִינְהוּ לַלְוִיִּם? אֶלָּא: כּוּלֵּי עָלְמָא קְנָסָא שֶׁלֹּא עָלוּ בִּימֵי עֶזְרָא, וְהָכָא בְּהָא קָמִיפַּלְגִי; מָר סָבַר: קְנָסָא לַעֲנִיִּים, וּמָר סָבַר: כֹּהֲנִים בִּימֵי טוּמְאָתָן עֲנִיִּים נִינְהוּ.

The Gemara asks: **Granted, according to the one who says** it was because **they did not ascend,** we can understand that **due to that** reason **they penalized** the Levites by forcing them to share their tithe with the priests. **But according to the one who says** it was done **so that the priests** could **rely on it during their days of impurity,** should we **penalize the Levites for** the benefit of **priests? Rather, everyone agrees** that it was **a penalty** for the fact **that they did not ascend in the days of Ezra,**[H] **and here they disagree about this:** One **Sage holds** that the **penalty** is that the tithe must be given **to the poor, and one Sage holds** that **priests are** classified as **poor in the days of their impurity.**

בִּשְׁלָמָא לְמַאן דְּאָמַר קְנָסָא לַעֲנִיִּים – מִשּׁוּם הָכִי אַהַדְרֵיהּ רַבִּי עֲקִיבָא לְפִתְחָא לְבֵי קִבְרֵי. אֶלָּא לְמַאן דְּאָמַר לְכֹהֲנִים – אַמַּאי אַהַדְרֵיהּ לְפִתְחָא לְבֵי קִבְרֵי? הָכִי קָאָמַר לֵיהּ: אִי דְּקָא אָתֵית בְּתוֹרַת קְנָסָא – אִית לָךְ, וְאִי קָא אָתֵית בְּתוֹרַת חֲלוּקָה – לֵית לָךְ.

The Gemara asks: **Granted, according to the one who says** that the **penalty** imposed on the Levites is that the tithe must be given **to the poor, due to that** reason **Rabbi Akiva changed** the garden **entrance** so that it would be facing **toward the cemetery,** as Rabbi Elazar ben Azarya was a wealthy man. **But according to the one who says** the tithe was given **to the priests, why did he change** the **entrance** so that it would be **toward the cemetery?** The Gemara answers: **This is what he said to him,** i.e., this is what he meant: **If you come** to receive the tithe **by virtue of** the **penalty** imposed on the Levites, **you may have it, but if you come by the standard** *halakha* **of distribution,**[N] demanding your share with the Levites, **you may not have** the tithe. If the owner of the garden chooses to give it to you, you may accept it, but you may not take it yourself.

וּמְנָא לָן דְּלָא סְלִיקוּ בִּימֵי עֶזְרָא – דִּכְתִיב "וָאֶקְבְּצֵם אֶל הַנָּהָר הַבָּא עַל אַהֲוָא וַנַּחֲנֶה שָׁם יָמִים שְׁלֹשָׁה וָאָבִינָה בָעָם וּבַכֹּהֲנִים וּמִבְּנֵי לֵוִי לֹא מָצָאתִי שָׁם". אָמַר רַב חִסְדָּא: בַּתְּחִלָּה לֹא הָיוּ מַעֲמִידִים שׁוֹטְרִים אֶלָּא מִן הַלְוִיִּם, שֶׁנֶּאֱמַר "וְשׁוֹטְרִים הַלְוִיִּם לִפְנֵיכֶם", עַכְשָׁיו אֵין מַעֲמִידִין שׁוֹטְרִים אֶלָּא מִיִּשְׂרָאֵל, שֶׁנֶּאֱמַר "וְשׁוֹטְרִים הָרַבִּים בְּרָאשֵׁיכֶם".

The Gemara asks with regard to the penalty imposed on Levites: **And from where do we derive that** the Levites **did not ascend in the days of Ezra? As it is written: "And I gathered them together to the river that runs to Ahava; and we encamped there for three days; and I viewed the people, and the priests, and found there none of the sons of Levi"** (Ezra 8:15). With regard to this, **Rav Ḥisda said: Initially they would establish officers** over the people **only from** among **the Levites, as it states: "And the officers, the Levites, before you"** (II Chronicles 19:11), but **now they establish officers only**[N] **from** among the **Israelites, as it is stated: And the officers of the many at your heads.**[N] This indicates that officers were appointed from: The many, meaning the largest group, ordinary Israelites.

מתני׳ בַּת יִשְׂרָאֵל שֶׁנִּיסֵּת לְכֹהֵן – תֹּאכַל בִּתְרוּמָה. מֵת וְלָהּ הֵימֶנּוּ בֵּן – תֹּאכַל בִּתְרוּמָה. נִיסֵּת לְלֵוִי תֹּאכַל בְּמַעֲשֵׂר. מֵת וְלָהּ הֵימֶנּוּ בֵּן תֹּאכַל בְּמַעֲשֵׂר. נִיסֵּת לְיִשְׂרָאֵל – לֹא תֹּאכַל לֹא בִּתְרוּמָה וְלֹא בְּמַעֲשֵׂר. מֵת וְלָהּ הֵימֶנּוּ בֵּן – לֹא תֹּאכַל לֹא בִּתְרוּמָה וְלֹא בְּמַעֲשֵׂר.

MISHNA **An Israelite woman married to a priest**[H] **may partake of *teruma*.** If the priest **died and she has a child from him,**[H] **she may** continue to **partake of *teruma*.** If she subsequently **married a Levite,** she may no longer partake of *teruma* but **she may partake of** the first **tithe** on his account. If he, too, **died and she had a child from him, she may** continue to **partake of tithe** on account of the child. If she then **married an Israelite,**[H] **she may partake of neither *teruma* nor tithe.** If her Israelite husband **died and she had a child from him, she** still **may partake of neither *teruma* nor tithe.**

מֵת בְּנָהּ מִיִּשְׂרָאֵל תֹּאכַל בְּמַעֲשֵׂר. מֵת בְּנָהּ מִלֵּוִי תֹּאכַל בִּתְרוּמָה. מֵת בְּנָהּ מִכֹּהֵן לֹא תֹּאכַל לֹא בִּתְרוּמָה וְלֹא בְּמַעֲשֵׂר.

If **her child from the Israelite** also **died,** while her son from the Levite remained alive, **she may partake of tithe** on account of the Levite's child. If **her child from the Levite died,** leaving her with a son from the priest, **she may** once again **partake of *teruma*. If her child from the priest died**[N] as well, **she may** no longer **partake of either *teruma* or tithe.**

NOTES

But if you come by the standard *halakha* of distribution – וְאִי קָא אָתֵית בְּתוֹרַת חֲלוּקָה: The Ritva explains that if Rabbi Elazar were to come demanding his share, he would be effectively misleading the owner of the produce, who would assume that he is fulfilling a Torah mitzva by giving it to a priest instead of a Levite.

The *Yam shel Shlomo* explains that Rabbi Elazar is permitted to take it in the form of a penalty, but he cannot claim it as his fair share, as he was wealthy enough not to require the tithe even during his days of impurity.

Now they establish…only – עַכְשָׁיו אֵין מַעֲמִידִין: Some commentaries understand that as part of the penalty imposed upon the Levites by Ezra, they would no longer receive any preference when officers were appointed (*Iyyun Ya'akov*; *Be'er Sheva*).

And the officers of the many at your heads – וְשׁוֹטְרִים הָרַבִּים בְּרָאשֵׁיכֶם: The early and later authorities note that this verse does not appear anywhere in the Bible. The early authorities add that the Talmud occasionally quotes an apparent verse that cannot be found in the Bible. The verse is sometimes from the book of Ben Sira. At other times it is paraphrased for its content. With regard to this particular verse, *Tosafot Yeshanim* suggest that it might be referring to the verse describing the appointment of officers and Elders over Israel: "Get you, from each one of your tribes, wise men, and understanding, and full of knowledge, and I will make them heads over you" (Deuteronomy 1:13).

If her child from the priest died, etc. – מֵת בְּנָהּ מִכֹּהֵן וכו׳: *Yam shel Shlomo* states that we can infer Rambam's ruling by reference to his ruling in the opposite situation: If an Israelite woman married an Israelite, had a child with him, was widowed, married a priest, had a child with him, and was widowed again, then she may partake of *teruma* on account of her child from the priest, despite the fact that she also has children from the Israelite. This opinion resolves the apparent contradiction between the first and latter clauses of the mishna. The Meiri concurs with this explanation.

HALAKHA

They did not ascend in the days of Ezra – שֶׁלֹּא עָלוּ בִּימֵי עֶזְרָא: On account of the Levites' failure to immigrate to the land of Israel with Ezra, he penalized the Levites of his time by declaring that the first tithe should be given to priests. The *Kesef Mishne* claims that after that period, each person had the right to give it to a Levite or to a priest, as he saw fit (Rambam *Sefer Zera'im*, *Hilkhot Ma'aser* 1:4).

An Israelite woman married to a priest – בַּת יִשְׂרָאֵל שֶׁנִּיסֵּת לְכֹהֵן: The daughter of an Israelite or Levite who is married to a priest may partake of *teruma*, even if she is younger than three years and one day old, and therefore has certainly not yet consummated her marriage (Rambam *Sefer Zera'im*, *Hilkhot Terumot* 6:3).

If he died and she has a child from him – מֵת וְלָהּ הֵימֶנּוּ בֵּן: An Israelite woman who has a child from a priest is permitted to partake of *teruma* on account of her child, whether her child is a son, a daughter, a person whose sexual organs are concealed, or an androgynous person. She may also partake of it on account of her child's child and so on, for all generations (Rambam *Sefer Zera'im*, *Hilkhot Terumot* 6:9).

If she then married an Israelite – נִיסֵּת לְיִשְׂרָאֵל: If an Israelite woman married a priest, had a child with him, was widowed, and then subsequently married an Israelite, she may not partake of *teruma*. In the event that her Israelite husband dies, if she has a child from him she may not partake of *teruma*, even if she has a child from the priest as well. However, if she has no children from the Israelite, or if her child from the Israelite died while her child from the priest remains alive, she may partake of *teruma* because of the priest's child (Rambam *Sefer Zera'im*, *Hilkhot Terumot* 6:13).

Perek **IX**
Daf **87** Amud **a**

בַּת כֹּהֵן שֶׁנִּיסֵּת לְיִשְׂרָאֵל לֹא תֹּאכַל בִּתְרוּמָה. מֵת, וְלָהּ הֵימֶנּוּ בֵּן, לֹא תֹּאכַל בִּתְרוּמָה. נִיסֵּת לְלֵוִי, תֹּאכַל בְּמַעֲשֵׂר. מֵת, וְלָהּ הֵימֶנּוּ בֵּן, תֹּאכַל בְּמַעֲשֵׂר. נִיסֵּת לְכֹהֵן, תֹּאכַל בִּתְרוּמָה. מֵת, וְלָהּ הֵימֶנּוּ בֵּן, תֹּאכַל בִּתְרוּמָה.

The **daughter of a priest married to an Israelite**[H] **may not partake of** ***teruma.*** If the Israelite **died and she** has **a son from him,**[H] **she may not partake of** ***teruma*** as long as that son is alive. If she subsequently **married a Levite she may partake of tithe.** If he **died, and she had a son from him, she may** still **partake of tithe.** If she subsequently **married a priest, she may partake of** ***teruma.***[H] If the priest **died and she had a son from him, she may partake of** ***teruma.***

מֵת בְּנָהּ מִכֹּהֵן, לֹא תֹּאכַל בִּתְרוּמָה. מֵת בְּנָהּ מִלֵּוִי, לֹא תֹּאכַל בְּמַעֲשֵׂר. מֵת בְּנָהּ מִיִּשְׂרָאֵל, חוֹזֶרֶת לְבֵית אָבִיהָ, וְעַל זוֹ נֶאֱמַר ״וְשָׁבָה אֶל בֵּית אָבִיהָ כִּנְעוּרֶיהָ מִלֶּחֶם אָבִיהָ תֹּאכֵל״.

If **her son from the priest** also **died, she may not partake of** ***teruma,*** but she may partake of tithe, as she has a son from a Levite. If **her son from the Levite died, she may no** longer **partake of tithe.** If **her son from the Israelite died, she returns to her father's house** and may once again partake of *teruma.* **And with regard to this** woman, it **is stated: "And she is returned unto her father's house, as in her youth; she may eat of her father's bread"** (Leviticus 22:13).

גמ׳ ״מֵת בְּנָהּ מִלֵּוִי תֹּאכַל בִּתְרוּמָה״, דְּהָדְרָא אָכְלָה מִשּׁוּם בְּנָהּ מְנָלַן? אָמַר רַבִּי אַבָּא אָמַר רַב: ״בַּת״ ״וּבַת״.

GEMARA We learned in the mishna: **If her son from the Levite died she may partake of** ***teruma.*** The Gemara asks: This *halakha* with regard to a woman previously married to a priest, who had a child from the priest and was then married to a Levite and separated from him, **that she once again may partake due to her son**[N] from the priest, **from where do we** derive it? **Rabbi Abba said** that **Rav said:** It states: "But if a priest's daughter be a widow, or divorced, and have no child, and is returned unto her father's house, as in her youth" (Leviticus 22:13). The verse could have stated: If a priest's **daughter.** Instead, it states: **"But** if a priest's **daughter,"**[N] with an extra word, represented by the single Hebrew letter *vav,* to include this case.

כְּמַאן – כְּרַבִּי עֲקִיבָא דְּדָרֵישׁ וָוֵי? אֲפִילּוּ תֵּימָא רַבָּנַן, כּוּלָּא ״וּבַת״ קְרָא יְתֵירָא הוּא.

The Gemara asks: **In accordance with** the opinion of **which** Sage is this exposition? Is it only **in accordance with Rabbi Akiva, who expounds** the additional letter *vav,* representing the word "and," as an inclusive term? The Gemara refutes this suggestion: It can be understood **even if you say** it is in accordance with **the Rabbis,** who do not usually derive *halakhot* from an additional *vav,* as in this case the **entire** phrase: **"But** if a priest's **daughter," is superfluous,** as the previous verse had already specified that we are dealing with "the daughter of a priest." Therefore, everyone agrees that in this context the additional letter in the text comes to include the additional case.

HALAKHA

The daughter of a priest married to an Israelite – בַּת כֹּהֵן שֶׁנִּיסֵּת לְיִשְׂרָאֵל: A non-priest is prohibited from partaking of *teruma.* The daughter of a priest who married a non-priest is considered like him and may not partake of *teruma* (Rambam *Sefer Zera'im, Hilkhot Terumot* 6:5).

If he died and she has a son from him – מֵת וְלָהּ הֵימֶנּוּ בֵּן: If the non-priest husband of a priest's daughter died, leaving her a son, she may not partake of *teruma* (Rambam *Sefer Zera'im, Hilkhot Terumot* 6:8, 13).

If she subsequently married a priest, she may partake of ***teruma*** **– נִיסֵּת לְכֹהֵן, תֹּאכַל בִּתְרוּמָה:** If the daughter of a priest was married to an Israelite, had a son from him, was widowed, and then subsequently married a priest, she may partake of *teruma.* If the priest died leaving her a son, she may still partake of *teruma.* If the priest's son subsequently dies, she is once again prohibited from partaking of *teruma* due to her son from the Israelite. If that son also dies, she goes back to partaking of *teruma* as the daughter of a priest, but she may not partake of the breast and the right hind leg (Rambam *Sefer Zera'im, Hilkhot Terumot* 6:18).

NOTES

That she once again may partake due to her son – דְּהָדְרָא אָכְלָה מִשּׁוּם בְּנָהּ: The Ra'avad asks: Before getting into the details of a woman's ability to return to eating *teruma* on account of her son, after the death of her second husband, there should be an inquiry as to the source for the basic *halakha* that a woman can partake of *teruma* if she has a son who is a priest. It is derived from the verse: "Those who are born in his house, they may eat [*yokhlu*] of his bread" (Leviticus 22:11), which is expounded to mean both *yokhlu,* they may eat, and *ya'akhilu,* they may feed. This means that the son of the priest enables his mother to eat of the bread as well.

It is, however, not obvious that this verse comes to teach the above *halakha,* as other *halakhot* have already been derived from that verse. The Ramban explains that the primary exposition is from the phrase: "They may eat of his bread." That clause is in fact entirely superfluous, as this is clearly the topic of the entire verse. Therefore, these redundant words teach that not only may such people themselves eat, but they may also feed others.

A priest's daughter, but a priest's daughter – בַּת, וּבַת: The Jerusalem Talmud offers an alternative derivation. The phrase "a priest's daughter" does not have to mean an actual daughter of a priest. Rather, it can be understood in a manner similar to the expression: "Daughter of Babylonia" (Psalms 137:8), which means a native of Babylonia or someone accustomed to its ways. Here too, "a priest's daughter" can refer to one who observes the practices of the priesthood, which includes the wife of a priest.

תָּנוּ רַבָּנַן: כְּשֶׁהִיא חוֹזֶרֶת – חוֹזֶרֶת לִתְרוּמָה, וְאֵינָהּ חוֹזֶרֶת לְחָזֶה וָשׁוֹק. אֲמַר רַב חִסְדָּא אֲמַר רָבִינָא בַּר שִׁילָא: מַאי קְרָא – "הִיא בִּתְרוּמַת הַקֳּדָשִׁים לֹא תֹאכֵל" – בַּמּוּרָם מִן הַקֳּדָשִׁים לֹא תֹּאכַל. רַב נַחְמָן אָמַר רַבָּה בַּר אֲבוּהּ: "מִלֶּחֶם" – וְלֹא כָּל לֶחֶם, פְּרָט לְחָזֶה וָשׁוֹק.

§ **The Sages taught:** With regard to the daughter of a priest, **when she returns** to her father's house after having been married to a non-priest and then separated from her husband, **she returns to** partaking of ***teruma*** **but she does not return to** partake of **the breast and right hind leg**[H] of peace-offerings. **Rav Ḥisda said** that **Ravina bar Sheila said: What is the verse** that teaches us this *halakha*? **"She may not eat of that which is set apart from the sacred things"** (Leviticus 22:12). This verse indicates: **From that which is separated from the sacred things,** i.e., offerings, and given to a priest, **she may not eat. Rav Naḥman** said that **Rabba bar Avuh said** that this *halakha* comes from a different source: We infer from the words "she may eat **of** her father's **bread**" (Leviticus 22:13), that she may **not** eat **all bread;** this comes to **exclude the breast and** right **hind leg.**

מַתְקִיף לַהּ רָמִי בַּר חָמָא: אֵימָא פְּרָט לַהֲפָרַת נְדָרִים! אָמַר רָבָא: כְּבָר פְּסָקָהּ תַּנָּא דְּבֵי רַבִּי יִשְׁמָעֵאל. דְּתָנָא דְּבֵי רַבִּי יִשְׁמָעֵאל: "וְנֵדֶר אַלְמָנָה וּגְרוּשָׁה... יָקוּם עָלֶיהָ" מַה תַּלְמוּד לוֹמַר? וַהֲלֹא מוּצָאָה מִכְּלַל אָב וּמוּצָאָה מִכְּלַל בַּעַל!

Rami bar Ḥama objects to this: But we can **say** that the verse comes to **exclude nullification of vows.**[N] The Torah would consequently be teaching us that even after she "is returned unto her father's house, as in her youth" (Leviticus 22:13), she does not return to her youth in all ways, as her father may not nullify her vows. **Rava said:** The connection between her and her father's house with regard to vows has **already been severed,** as taught by **the school of Rabbi Yishmael, as the school of Rabbi Yishmael taught: "But the vow of a widow, or of a divorcée… shall stand against her"** (Numbers 30:10). **What** is the meaning when **the verse states** this? **She was removed from the category** of one who is under the authority of her **father** when she married, **and she has** likewise **been removed from the category** of one who is under the authority of her **husband,** as she is no longer married to him.

אֶלָּא, הֲרֵי שֶׁמָּסַר הָאָב לִשְׁלוּחֵי הַבַּעַל, אוֹ שֶׁמָּסְרוּ שְׁלוּחֵי הָאָב לִשְׁלוּחֵי הַבַּעַל, וְנִתְאַרְמְלָה אוֹ נִתְגָּרְשָׁה בַּדֶּרֶךְ – הֵיאָךְ אֲנִי קוֹרֵא בָּהּ, בֵּית אָבִיהָ שֶׁל זוֹ אוֹ בֵּית בַּעְלָהּ שֶׁל זוֹ? אֶלָּא לוֹמַר לְךָ: כֵּיוָן שֶׁיָּצְאָה שָׁעָה אַחַת מֵרְשׁוּת הָאָב שׁוּב אֵינוֹ יָכוֹל לְהָפֵר.

Rather, the verse is referring to a case **where the father transferred** his daughter **to the husband's agents** for the purpose of marriage, and she consequently left her father's house. **Or,** it is referring to a case **where the father's agents transferred** her **to the husband's agents**[H] **and she was widowed or divorced on the way,** before she arrived at her husband's house. **How shall I consider her?** Is she in the **house of this one, her father, or** is she in the **house of that one, her husband? Rather,** this comes **to tell you: Since she has** entirely **left her father's jurisdiction** when she was transferred to the husband's agents, even if for just **one moment,** her father **is no longer able to nullify** her vows. We learn from here that a father cannot annul his daughter's vows after she has been married, and there is no need for an additional verse to teach this *halakha*.

רַב סָפְרָא אָמַר: "מִלֶּחֶם אָבִיהָ תֹּאכֵל" – לֶחֶם וְלֹא בָּשָׂר. רַב פַּפָּא אָמַר: "מִלֶּחֶם אָבִיהָ תֹּאכֵל" – לֶחֶם הַקָּנוּי לְאָבִיהָ, פְּרָט לְחָזֶה וָשׁוֹק דְּמִשֻּׁלְחַן גָּבוֹהַּ קָא זָכוּ.

Rav Safra said: The *halakha* that she does not return to her father's house with regard to the breast and the right hind leg is derived from the verse: **"From her father's bread she may eat,"** which indicates that she partakes of the **"bread"** of *teruma* **but not** of the **meat** of the breast and hind leg. **Rav Pappa said** a different interpretation: **"From her father's bread she may eat"** is referring to **bread owned by her father,** such as *teruma*, which is the property of the priest, which **excludes the breast and** right **hind leg, as** the priests **receive** their portion **from the table of** the **Most High.**[N] Unlike *teruma*, the breast and right hind leg do not belong to the priests. Rather, after the offering is sacrificed to God, they eat these portions but are not considered to own them.

HALAKHA

She does not return to partake of the breast and right hind leg – אֵינָהּ חוֹזֶרֶת לְחָזֶה וָשׁוֹק: The daughter of a priest who married an Israelite is permanently barred from eating the breast and the right hind leg, even if he divorced her or died without leaving her sons (Rambam *Sefer Zera'im, Hilkhot Terumot* 6:7).

Where the father's agents transferred her to the husband's agents – שֶׁמָּסַר הָאָב לִשְׁלוּחֵי הַבַּעַל: If a young daughter of a priest married, or if her father or his agents transferred her to the husband's agents for the purpose of marriage, and her husband died while she was still a young woman, she does not return to her father's jurisdiction and he may no longer nullify her vows (*Shulḥan Arukh, Yoreh De'a* 234:12).

NOTES

To exclude nullification of vows – פְּרָט לַהֲפָרַת נְדָרִים: The connection between this issue and the nullification of vows is not immediately apparent. The Ritva explains that the phrase "she may eat of her father's bread" indicates that she eats against her will. In other words, even if she vowed not to eat something, her father can nullify her vow. Some later authorities suggest that the resemblance between the verse referring to *teruma*: "And she is returned unto her father's house, as in her youth" (Leviticus 22:13) and the verse about vows: "Being in her youth, in her father's house" (Numbers 30:17) indicates a connection between the two cases.

As they receive their portion from the table of the Most High – דְּמִשֻּׁלְחַן גָּבוֹהַּ קָא זָכוּ: The later authorities point out that there are various opinions on this matter, as concerning other issues some Sages maintain that *teruma* is also viewed as something received from the table of the Most High. Nevertheless, it is clear that there is a difference between the two, as *teruma* is the priest's possession in all regards to use as he sees fits, whereas the breast and right hind leg are given to priests only for the purpose of eating, as their consumption of the offering is part of the service necessary for atonement.

וְרָבָא אָמַר: "וְאֵת חֲזֵה הַתְּנוּפָה וְאֵת שׁוֹק הַתְּרוּמָה תֹּאכְלוּ...אַתָּה וּבָנֶיךָ וּבְנוֹתֶיךָ אִתָּךְ" – בִּזְמַן שֶׁאִתָּךְ.

And Rava said: It states: **"And the breast of waving and the hind leg of heaving you shall eat…you, and your sons and your daughters with you"** (Leviticus 10:14). This indicates that daughters of priests may eat **at a time when** they are **"with you,"** but once they have left the priest's domain, e.g., by marrying an ordinary Israelite, they may no longer partake of these gifts even if they subsequently return to his household.

אֲמַר רַב אַדָּא בַּר אַהֲבָה: תָּנָא, כְּשֶׁהִיא חוֹזֶרֶת לְבֵית אָבִיהָ – חוֹזֶרֶת לִתְרוּמָה, וְאֵינָהּ חוֹזֶרֶת לְחָזֶה וָשׁוֹק. בִּשְׁבִיל בְּנָהּ – חוֹזֶרֶת אַף לְחָזֶה וָשׁוֹק.

Rav Adda bar Ahava said: It was **taught:** With regard to the daughter of a priest, **when she returns to her father's house,** after marrying and separating from her husband without a child, **she returns for** the purposes of eating ***teruma*, but she does not return for** the purposes of eating **the breast and** right **hind leg.** By contrast, if an Israelite woman ate **on account of her son** from a priest, if she later married an Israelite and he died, **she returns** to partake **even of the breast and** right **hind leg.**[H]

אֲזַל רַב מָרְדְּכַי אַמְרָהּ לִשְׁמַעְתָּא קַמֵּיהּ דְּרַב אַשִׁי. אֲמַר: מֵהֵיכָא קָא מְתַרְבְּיָא, מִ"וּבַת" – מִי עֲדִיפָא לָהּ מִינָּהּ? הָתָם כְּתִיבִי מִיעוּטֵי, הָכָא לָא כְּתִיבִי מִיעוּטֵי.

Rav Mordekhai went and **stated** this ***halakha* before Rav Ashi,** who **said** to him: **From where does** he **include** the case of a woman who partakes of *teruma* on account of her son? **From** the verse **"but** if a priest's **daughter"** (Leviticus 22:13). **Is** the Israelite woman **preferable to her,** the daughter of a priest herself, who does not return to eating the breast and hind leg? The Gemara answers: **There,** the Torah **writes exclusions,** as we learned above, which teach us that she does not return in all regards, whereas **here it does not write exclusions.** Consequently, although the *halakha* of a woman who has a son from a priest is itself derived from the case of the daughter of a priest returning to her father's house, she has more abilities than the latter.

"בַּת כֹּהֵן שֶׁנִּיסֵּת לְיִשְׂרָאֵל" וכו׳. תָּנוּ רַבָּנַן: "וְשָׁבָה אֶל בֵּית אָבִיהָ" – פְּרָט לְשׁוֹמֶרֶת יָבָם, "כִּנְעוּרֶיהָ" – פְּרָט לִמְעוּבֶּרֶת.

§ The Gemara returns to the mishna. The mishna taught: The **daughter of a priest married to an Israelite** may not partake of *teruma*. **The Sages taught: "And she is returned unto her father's house"** (Leviticus 22:13); this **excludes a widow awaiting her *yavam*,**[H] for she cannot go back to her father's house as long as she is still waiting for the *yavam* to perform levirate marriage. **"As in her youth"**; this **excludes a pregnant woman,**[H] as her pregnancy has changed her, and she is no longer as she was in her youth.

וַהֲלֹא דִּין הוּא: וּמַה בְּמָקוֹם שֶׁלֹּא עָשָׂה וָלָד מִן הָרִאשׁוֹן כְּוָלָד מִן הַשֵּׁנִי לְפוֹטְרָהּ מִן הַיִּבּוּם – עָשָׂה עוּבָּר כְּיָלוּד,

But could this **not** be derived through an ***a fortiori* inference,** without the need for a special exposition of a verse? **If in a place,** i.e., a case, **where** the Torah **did not make** the *halakha* pertaining to **a child from the first** husband **like** the *halakha* pertaining to **a child from the second** husband **to exempt her from levirate marriage;** this is the case of a woman who married a man, had a son with him, was widowed, remarried, and her second husband died childless. She requires levirate marriage despite the fact that she has a child, as the first husband's child is irrelevant with regard to her need for levirate marriage for the second husband. Despite this limitation, the Torah **made** the status of **a fetus like** that of a child who was **born,** as a pregnant woman does not perform levirate marriage.

HALAKHA

On account of her son from a priest, she returns to partake even of the breast and right hind leg – בִּשְׁבִיל בְּנָהּ חוֹזֶרֶת אַף לְחָזֶה וָשׁוֹק: If an Israelite woman married a priest, had a son with him, was widowed, remarried an Israelite, had a son with him, and was then widowed again, she may not partake of *teruma*. If her son from the Israelite died, she may once again partake of *teruma* on account of her son from the priest. She may also partake of the breast and right hind leg (Rambam *Sefer Zera'im*, *Hilkhot Terumot* 6:18, and *Kesef Mishne* there).

This excludes a widow awaiting her *yavam* – פְּרָט לְשׁוֹמֶרֶת יָבָם: The daughter of a priest who is waiting for an Israelite *yavam* may not partake of *teruma* (Rambam *Sefer Zera'im*, *Hilkhot Terumot* 8:5).

This excludes a pregnant woman – פְּרָט לִמְעוּבֶּרֶת: If the daughter of a priest was pregnant from an Israelite, she is prohibited from partaking of *teruma* on account of the fetus (Rambam *Sefer Zera'im*, *Hilkhot Terumot* 8:2).

מָקוֹם שֶׁעָשָׂה וָלָד מִן הָרִאשׁוֹן כְּוָלָד מִן הַשֵּׁנִי לְפוֹסְלָהּ מִן הַתְּרוּמָה – אֵינוֹ דִּין שֶׁנַּעֲשֶׂה עוּבָּר כְּיָלוּד?!

If this is so, then in **a place where** the Torah **did make** the *halakha* pertaining to **a child from the first** husband **like** the *halakha* pertaining to **a child from the second** husband **to disqualify her from *teruma*;** this is the case of a daughter of a priest who married an Israelite, had a son with him, was widowed, and afterward married another Israelite, who died childless. She may not partake of *teruma* on account of her son from the first husband. **Is it not,** therefore, **right that we should make a fetus like** a child who was **born** with regard to *teruma*, that would prevent her from returning to partake of *teruma* if she is pregnant? If this reasoning is correct, there is no need for the biblical exposition.

לֹא, מַה לִּי עָשָׂה עוּבָּר כְּיָלוּד, לְעִנְיַן יִיבּוּם, שֶׁהֲרֵי עָשָׂה מֵתִים כְּחַיִּים, נַעֲשֶׂה עוּבָּר כְּיָלוּד, לְעִנְיַן תְּרוּמָה, שֶׁלֹּא עָשָׂה מֵתִים כְּחַיִּים?! תַּלְמוּד לוֹמַר: ״כִּנְעוּרֶיהָ״ – פְּרָט לִמְעוּבֶּרֶת.

However, this proof can be refuted: **No, what I** should say is that the Torah **made a fetus like** a child who was **born with regard to levirate marriage, because** with regard to levirate marriage the Torah **made the dead like the living:** If the woman had a child at the time of her husband's death she is entirely exempt from levirate marriage, even if her son subsequently died. The deceased child is like a living one in the sense that he continues to exempt his mother from the requirement of levirate marriage. **Shall we** then **make a fetus like** a child who was **born with regard to *teruma*, where** the Torah **did not make the dead like the living?** In the case of *teruma*, as long as the daughter of a priest has a living son from her Israelite husband, she is disqualified from *teruma*, but if he dies she may partake of *teruma* again, as we do not consider him like a living son. Consequently, we cannot learn the *halakha* of *teruma* from levirate marriage with regard to the status of a fetus. Therefore, **the verse states "as in her youth"** to **exclude a pregnant woman.**

וְאִיצְטְרִיךְ לְמִכְתַּב מְעוּבֶּרֶת וְאִיצְטְרִיךְ לְמִכְתַּב ״וְזֶרַע אֵין לָהּ״, דְּאִי כָּתַב רַחֲמָנָא ״וְזֶרַע אֵין לָהּ״ – מֵעִיקָּרָא חַד גּוּפָא וְהָשְׁתָּא תְּרֵי גּוּפֵי, אֲבָל מְעוּבֶּרֶת, דְּמֵעִיקָּרָא חַד גּוּפָא וְהָשְׁתָּא חַד גּוּפָא – אֵימָא תֵּיכוֹל, צְרִיכָא. וְאִי כָּתַב רַחֲמָנָא מְעוּבֶּרֶת, דְּמֵעִיקָּרָא גּוּפָא

The Gemara comments: **And it was necessary to write** this verse that teaches the *halakha* of **a pregnant woman, and it was necessary** also **to write "and she have no child"** (Leviticus 22:13) **because had the Merciful One written** only: **"And she have no child,"** I would have said that **at the outset** she was only **one body** when she ate *teruma*, **and now,** upon her return, there are **two bodies,** and that is why she is no longer "as in her youth." **But a pregnant woman, who at the outset** was **one body and now** is still **one body,** one might **say** that **she may partake of** *teruma* until the birth of her son. Consequently, it is **necessary** for a verse to teach the *halakha*. **And** vice-versa, **had the Merciful One written** the *halakha* with regard to **a pregnant woman,** I might have said that this is true only of a pregnant woman **because at the outset** her **body**

Perek **IX**
Daf **87** Amud **b**

סְרִיקָא וְהָשְׁתָּא גּוּפָא מַלְיָא. אֲבָל ״זֶרַע אֵין לָהּ״, דְּמֵעִיקָּרָא גּוּפָא סְרִיקָא, וְהָשְׁתָּא גּוּפָא סְרִיקָא – אֵימָא לָא, צְרִיכָא.

was **empty, and now** her **body** is **full** with the child, and therefore she is no longer "as in her youth." **But** in a situation where **"she has no child," when at the outset** her **body** was **empty and now** her **body** is also **empty,** as she has given birth, you might **say** that she should **not** be disqualified. Therefore, it is **necessary** to write both verses.

(סימ״ן: אמר ליה לא נעש״ה מעשי״ה במית״ה נעש״ה ול״א נעש״ה בול״ד יב״ם ותרומ״ה יבו״ם ותרומ״ה. סימ״ן).

Parenthetically, the Gemara lists terms signifying the following discussions, to serve as **a mnemonic** device: **Said to him, we should not make, by death, we should make and not make, by a child,** ***yavam*** **and** ***teruma*****, levirate marriage and** ***teruma*****.** This list of terms, taken from the introductions or key phrases in each of the ensuing discussions, is the **mnemonic.**

אָמַר לֵיהּ רַב יְהוּדָה מִדְּאִסְקַרְתָּא לְרָבָא: לֹא נַעֲשֶׂה מֵתִים כְּחַיִּים לְעִנְיַן יִבּוּם מִקַּל וָחוֹמֶר: וּמַה בְּמָקוֹם שֶׁעָשָׂה וָלָד מִן הָרִאשׁוֹן כְּוָלָד מִן הַשֵּׁנִי לְפוֹסְלָהּ מִן הַתְּרוּמָה – לֹא עָשָׂה מֵתִים כְּחַיִּים, מָקוֹם שֶׁלֹּא עָשָׂה וָלָד מִן הָרִאשׁוֹן כְּוָלָד מִן הַשֵּׁנִי לְפוֹטְרָהּ מִן הַיִּבּוּם – אֵינוֹ דִּין שֶׁלֹּא נַעֲשֶׂה מֵתִים כְּחַיִּים?!

Rav Yehuda from De'iskarta[L] **said to Rava,** in continuation of the discussion of the *baraita*: Should **we not make the** *halakha* concerning **dead** children[N] **like the** *halakha* concerning **living** children **with regard to levirate marriage by an** ***a fortiori*** inference, and say: **And if in a place where** the Torah **made** the *halakha* with regard to **a child from the first** husband **like** the *halakha* with regard to **a child from the second** husband, **to disqualify her from** ***teruma***, for as long as she has a child who is not a priest she is prohibited from partaking of *teruma*, the Torah nevertheless **did not make dead** children **like living** ones; therefore, in **a place where** the Torah **did not make a child from the first** husband **like a child from the second to exempt her from levirate marriage, is it not right that we should not make the dead like the living?** Why, then, is a *yevama* exempt from levirate marriage if her late husband's only child dies?

תַּלְמוּד לוֹמַר ״דְּרָכֶיהָ דַרְכֵי נוֹעַם וְכָל נְתִיבוֹתֶיהָ שָׁלוֹם״.

The verse states: "Her ways are the ways of pleasantness,[N] **and all her paths are peace"** (Proverbs 3:17). In other words, since the ways of Torah are those of pleasantness, the Torah would not obligate a woman who has married in the meantime to subsequently perform *ḥalitza*, as this might demean her in her husband's eyes.

וְנַעֲשֶׂה מֵתִים כְּחַיִּים לְעִנְיַן תְּרוּמָה מִקַּל וָחוֹמֶר: וּמַה בְּמָקוֹם שֶׁלֹּא עָשָׂה וָלָד מִן הָרִאשׁוֹן כְּוָלָד מִן הַשֵּׁנִי לְפוֹטְרָהּ מִן הַיִּבּוּם – עָשָׂה מֵתִים כְּחַיִּים, מָקוֹם שֶׁעָשָׂה וָלָד מִן הָרִאשׁוֹן כְּוָלָד מִן הַשֵּׁנִי לְפוֹסְלָהּ מִן הַתְּרוּמָה – אֵינוֹ דִּין שֶׁנַּעֲשֶׂה מֵתִים כְּחַיִּים?! תַּלְמוּד לוֹמַר ״וְזֶרַע אֵין לָהּ״ – וְהָא אֵין לָהּ.

The Gemara inquires: **And let us make** the *halakha* with regard to **dead** children **like** the *halakha* with regard to **living** ones **with regard to** ***teruma***, **from an** ***a fortiori*** inference: **And if in a place where** the Torah **did not make a child from the first** husband **like a child from the second to exempt her from levirate marriage,** it nevertheless **made the living like the dead,** as a woman whose husband died and left a child is exempt from levirate marriage even if that child subsequently dies; then, in **a place where** the Torah **made a child from the first like a child from the second to disqualify her from** ***teruma***, **is it not right that we should make the living like the dead?** The Gemara responds: Therefore, **the verse states "and she have no child,** she is returned unto her father's house, as in her youth" (Leviticus 22:13), **and here she does not** currently **have** children.

וְנַעֲשֶׂה וָלָד מִן הָרִאשׁוֹן כְּוָלָד מִן הַשֵּׁנִי לְעִנְיַן יִבּוּם מִקַּל וָחוֹמֶר: וּמַה בְּמָקוֹם שֶׁלֹּא עָשָׂה מֵתִים כְּחַיִּים לְעִנְיַן תְּרוּמָה – עָשָׂה וָלָד מִן הָרִאשׁוֹן כְּוָלָד מִן הַשֵּׁנִי – מָקוֹם שֶׁעָשָׂה מֵתִים כְּחַיִּים לְעִנְיַן יִבּוּם אֵינוֹ דִּין שֶׁנַּעֲשֶׂה וָלָד מִן הָרִאשׁוֹן כְּוָלָד מִן הַשֵּׁנִי?! תַּלְמוּד לוֹמַר ״וּבֵן אֵין לוֹ״ – וְהָא אֵין לוֹ.

The Gemara further suggests: **And let us make** her **child from the first** husband **like** her **child from the second** one **with regard to levirate marriage,** again **from an** ***a fortiori*** inference: **And if in a place where** the Torah **did not make the living like the dead with regard to** ***teruma***, it still **made a child from the first** husband **like a child from the second,** then in **a place where it made the living like the dead, with regard to levirate marriage, is it not right that we should make a child from the first** husband **like a child from the second,** and thereby exempt her from levirate marriage? The Gemara answers: **The verse states** about levirate marriage: **"And he has no child"** (Deuteronomy 25:5), **and** in fact **he had none** at the time of his death.

וְלֹא נַעֲשֶׂה וָלָד מִן הָרִאשׁוֹן כְּוָלָד מִן הַשֵּׁנִי לִתְרוּמָה מִקַּל וָחוֹמֶר: מַה בְּמָקוֹם שֶׁעָשָׂה מֵתִים כְּחַיִּים לְפוֹטְרָהּ מִן הַיִּבּוּם לֹא עָשָׂה וָלָד מִן הָרִאשׁוֹן כְּוָלָד מִן הַשֵּׁנִי – מָקוֹם שֶׁלֹּא עָשָׂה מֵתִים כְּחַיִּים לְעִנְיַן תְּרוּמָה אֵינוֹ דִּין שֶׁלֹּא נַעֲשֶׂה וָלָד מִן הָרִאשׁוֹן כְּוָלָד מִן הַשֵּׁנִי?! תַּלְמוּד לוֹמַר ״אֵין לָהּ״ – וְהָא יֵשׁ לָהּ.

The Gemara offers another possibility: **And should we make a child from the first** husband **not like a child from the second** one **with regard to** ***teruma***, **from an** ***a fortiori*** inference: **If in a place where** the Torah **made the living like the dead to exempt her from levirate marriage,** it still **did not make a child from the first** husband **like a child from the second,** then in **a place where** the Torah **did not make the living like the dead, with regard to** ***teruma***, **is it not right that we should not make** the **child from the first** husband **like** the **child from the second?** The Gemara responds: Therefore, **the verse states:** "And she have no child," but in fact this woman **has** children.

הדרן עלך יש מותרות

LANGUAGE

De'iskarta – דְּאִסְקַרְתָּא: The name of this place is related to the Middle Persian word dastagird, meaning an inherited plot of land.

NOTES

Should we not make the ***halakha*** **concerning dead children – לֹא נַעֲשֶׂה מֵתִים:** *Arukh LaNer* points out that this line of inquiry is somewhat misleading, as there is an essential difference in the case of a child from the first husband with regard to *teruma* as opposed to levirate marriage. In the case of levirate marriage, there is no connection between the obligation itself and the woman's children, as everything depends on whether or not the deceased husband had children. By contrast, as far as *teruma* is concerned, the question is whether the woman herself has a non-priest child. To explain this, he argues that the comparison is suggested only as part of a comprehensive discussion of the question at hand that presents all possible permutations of the analysis.

Her ways are the ways of pleasantness – דְּרָכֶיהָ דַרְכֵי נוֹעַם: If the *halakha* were that whenever a deceased husband's children pass away, his surviving wife is obligated in levirate marriage, this would degrade her. Performing *ḥalitza* after she has remarried would seem to indicate retroactively that she was forbidden to her second husband until that point. Having every widow perform *ḥalitza* as a precautionary measure, in case her children pass away, is not a solution, as *ḥalitza* is entirely meaningless if no obligation of levirate marriage exists (Ritva).

With regard to the idea that "her ways are the ways of pleasantness," this does not mean that the *halakhot* of the Torah are always comfortable and pleasant, as there are aspects to levirate marriage that make life very difficult for the *yevama*. Rather, as explained by *Tosafot* on ב, the Torah did not distinguish between different women who are exempt from levirate marriage by allowing one to remain completely exempt while requiring the other to perform *ḥalitza* later. Consequently, "ways of pleasantness" is to be understood as equal and fair, without discrimination between different women.

Summary of **Perek IX**

There are four categories of women involved in prohibited ordinary or levirate marriages: Women who are permitted to both their husbands and their *yevamin*, women who are permitted to their husbands but not to their *yevamin* due to some prohibition with regard to marriage to one but not the other; women who are permitted to their *yevamin* but not to their husbands for the same reason; and women who are forbidden to both their husbands and their *yevamin* due to a prohibition that applies to both.

With regard to women's property rights, the conclusion is that in every case of forbidden marriage, the husband is forced to divorce his wife. In cases that stand in violation of Torah law, whereby the children are disqualified, the woman receives the sum specified in her marriage contract, while in cases where there is a violation of rabbinic law, the Sages imposed a penalty that denies all benefits to the wife, so as to hasten the divorce.

It was concluded that so long as the marriage is in effect, wives of priests and Levites may partake of *teruma* and tithes, respectively. However, after the husband's death, the principle is that the woman may continue to benefit from these gifts by virtue of her descendants from the priest or Levite, only as long as she has no subsequent offspring. Similarly, the daughter of a priest or a Levite who was married to an Israelite may again receive benefits from the gifts given to her father's household after her husband's death, provided she has no descendants from her non-priest or non-Levite husband.

Image **Credits**

All images are copyright © Koren Publishers Jerusalem Ltd., except:

p20 © Marie-Lan Nguyen; **p21** © Clara Amit, Yoram Lehman, Yael Yolovitch, Miki Koren, and Mariana Salzberger, courtesy of the Israel Antiquities Authority; **p46** © JMK; **p60** © Jason Picket; **p92** © Alekcey, www.shutterstock.com.

My Notes

My Notes

My Notes

My Notes

תלמוד בבלי

— מהדורת נאה —

יבמות חלק ה

Steinsaltz Center

KOREN

Please note that the number ranges that appear at the bottom of each daf of the Vilna pages indicate the corresponding pages of the Koren Talmud Bavli translation and commentary.

תלמוד בבלי

הוצאת קורן ירושלים

— מהדורת נאה —

מסכת יבמות
דף ע. עד דף פז:

COMMENTARY BY

Rabbi Adin Even-Israel
Steinsaltz

EDITOR-IN-CHIEF

Rabbi Dr Tzvi Hersh Weinreb

EXECUTIVE EDITOR

Rabbi Joshua Schreier

•

STEINSALTZ CENTER
KOREN PUBLISHERS JERUSALEM

הכי גרסינן: ה"ד אילימא דדרימא מניה ולא דרימא מעלמא צריכא למימר דתיכול אלא לאו דדרימא נמי מעלמא. לא ב"ש. דאי דרימא מניה ומעלמא, דמגרים דידיה שדרינן ליה. ומתני' בדלא דרימא כלל. מקמי הכי, לאו מניה ולאו מעלמא. הלכך אילטריך לאשמועינן דתאכל, דאמרינן מפני כיעור נתעברה. בני בנים הרי הן כבנים. כדפ' "הבא על יבמתו" (לעיל סב:). כמאן כר"ע. מתניתין דקתני גוי ועבד הבא על בת ישראל הולד ממזר. משום רבינו. רבי, ואע"ג דשמעינן דפליג אדר"ע בפ' ר"ג (לעיל מט.), דקאמר: אין דברים הללו אמורים אלא לדברי ר"ע, ולית ליה כר"ע, אפ"ה, בגוי ועבד מודה, כדקאמר בהחולץ (לעיל מה.): גוי "לא תתחתן", ועבד "לא תהיה קדשה". כותא. לאו כשמה, מתוך שהיא גרוע. ברא. לאו חשוב. כלומר, כהן גדול.

הדרן עלך אלמנה

אבל דרימא מניה, אע"ג דדרימא מעלמא, בתריה דידיה שדרינן ליה, אמר רבא: מנא אמינא לה, דקתני: ילדה — תאכל. היכי דמי? אילימא דדרימא מניה ולא דרימא מעלמא — צריכא למימר דתיכול?! אלא לאו — דדרימא נמי מעלמא, ושמע מינה, דלהאי איסורא ולהאי איסורא, בתריה דידיה שדרינן ליה, הכא דלהאי איסורא ולהאי היתירא — לא כל שכן?! א"ל אביי: לעולם אימא לך, כל היכא דדרימא מעלמא, אע"ג דדרימא מניה אמר רב הולד ממזר, ומתני' בדלא דרימא כלל. העבד פוסל משום ביאה כו'. מ"מ? אמר קרא "ואשה ילדיה תהיה וגו'". ממזר פוסל ומאכיל. ת"ר: "וזרע אין לה", אין לי אלא זרעה, זרע זרעה מנין? ת"ל "וזרע אין לה", מכל מקום. אין לי אלא זרע כשר, זרע פסול מנין? ת"ל "וזרע אין לה" — עיין עליה. והא אפיקתיה לזרע זרעה! זרע זרעה לא איצטריך קרא, בני בנים הרי הן כבנים, כי איצטריך קרא — לזרע פסול. א"ל ר"ל לרבי יוחנן: כמאן, כר"ע, דאמר: יש ממזר מחייבי לאוין? אפילו תימא רבנן, בעובד כוכבים ועבד מודו. דכי אתא רב דימי א"ר יצחק בר אבודימי משום רבינו: גוי ועבד הבא על בת ישראל — הולד ממזר. § בג' פעמים שפוסל. § ת"ר: חרש כפרת בן בתי כוא — שמאכילין בתרומה, ואיני כפרת בן בתי כרא — שפוסלין מן התרומה. §

הדרן עלך אלמנה

אבל דרימא מניה אע"ג דדרימא נמי מעלמא בתר דידיה שדרינן ליה. פי': דרימא מינים — שבא עליה בודאי, ודרימא מעלמא — היינו שם רע, דאי דרימא מינים נמי שם רע בעלמא — א"כ מאי מייתי רבא ממתני' דהתם בא עליה ודאי. משום הכי בתר דידיה שדרינן ליה.

הדרן עלך אלמנה

הערל וכל הטמאים לא יאכלו בתרומה, נשיהן ועבדיהן יאכלו בתרומה. פצוע דכא וכרות שפכה, הן ועבדיהן — יאכלו, ונשיהן — לא יאכלו, ואם לא *ידעה משנעשה פצוע דכא וכרות שפכה — הרי אלו יאכלו. ואי זהו פצוע דכא — כל שנפצעו הביצים שלו, ואפילו אחת מהן. וכרות שפכה — כל שנכרת הגיד. ואם נשתייר מעטרה אפי' כחוט השערה — כשר. § **גמ'** תניא, א"ר *אליעזר: מנין לערל שאין אוכל בתרומה — נאמר "תושב ושכיר" בפסח, ונאמר "תושב ושכיר" בתרומה, מה "תושב ושכיר" האמור בפסח ערל אסור בו, אף "תושב ושכיר" האמור בתרומה ערל אסור בו. *רבי עקיבא אומר: אינו צריך, הרי הוא אומר "איש איש" לרבות הערל. אמר מר: ר"א אומר נאמר "תושב ושכיר" בפסח ונאמר "תושב ושכיר" בתרומה, מה "תושב ושכיר" האמור בפסח ערל אסור בו, אף "תושב ושכיר" האמור בתרומה ערל אסור בו. מופנה, דאי לאו מופנה — איכא למיפרך: מה לפסח — שכן חייבין עליו משום פיגול ונותר וטמא. לאיי, אפנויי מופנה. הי מופנה? אי דתרומה — מצרך צריכי, דתניא: *"תושב" זה קנוי קנין עולם, "שכיר" זה קנוי קנין שנים. ויאמר "תושב" ואל יאמר "שכיר", ואני אומר: קנוי קנין עולם אינו אוכל, קנוי קנין שנים — לא כל שכן?! אילו כן, הייתי אומר: "תושב" זה קנוי קנין שנים, אבל קנוי קנין עולם אוכל — בא "שכיר" ולימד על תושב, שאף על פי שקנוי קנין עולם — אין אוכל. אלא דפסח מופני. האי "תושב ושכיר" דכתב רחמנא בפסח מאי ניהו? אי נימא תושב ושכיר ממש — משום דהוה ליה תושב ושכיר איפטר ליה מפסח?! והא קיימא לן גבי תרומה דלא אכיל, אלמא

שמות יב | ויקרא כב | שם

הערל. כהן (א) שמתו אחיו מחמת מילה. **נשיהם ועבדיהם יאכלו.** דהא משום ערלות וטומאה לא נפקי מכלל כהנים, אלא דאינהו גופייהו מיסרי באכילה. **נשיהם.** של פצוע דכא וכרות שפכה לא יאכלו דשוויוה חללה בביאתן, שהרי נבעלה לפסול לה. **ואם לא ידעה.** לא בא עליה אחרי כן, והיתה נשואה לו קודם לכן. **ואם נשתייר מעטרה.** שנכרת מעטרה ולהלן — כשר, דהתם בישרא בעלמא הוא ולא גיד, שאין גיד אלא מעטרה ולהלן לצד הגוף. **עטרה**(ב) שורת בשר המקפת במקום המילה בגובה, ושופע ויורד עד סופה. **גמ' תושב ושכיר בתרומה.** דכתיב "תושב כהן ושכיר לא יאכל קדש". **איש איש מזרע אהרן והוא צרוע או זב לרבות ערל.** כטמא אצל אכילת תרומה, דבהאי קרא תרומה כתיב, דכתיב (ויקרא כב) "ובא השמש וטהר ואחר יאכל מן הקדשים", והיינו תרומה, דסגי ליה בהערב שמש. **שכן חייבין עליו.** קרבן הפסח, אם אכלו פגול או נותר או בטומאת הגוף. דכולהו בכרת, דהא קדשים הוא. **קנוי קנין עולם.** עבד עברי הנרצע. וזה הכתוב ללמדך, שאין גופו קנוי לכהן זה שיאכילהו בתרומה ככנעני. **קנין שנים.** סתם עבד, שיוצא בשש שנים. **אילו כן.** דלא נאמר אלא תושב. **הייתי אומר** תושב זה קנוי קנין שנים. משום הכי אסור בתרומה, בא שכיר יתירא ולימד על כרחך דהאי קרא לנרצע אתא. וכיון דתרי כתיבי — מסתברא דתושב — זה המיושב אצלו לזמן מרובה, ושכיר — זה העומד לצאת. **אלא דפסח מופני.** האי שכיר ותושב דפסח, דכתיב "לא יאכלו בו". **מאי ניניהו אי נימא תושב ושכיר ממש.** קנוי קנין שנים, או נרצע. הכא

הערל. פי' בקונט': שמתו אחיו מחמת מילה. וכן נראה, דלא דמי לערלה שלא בזמנה דמיבעיא לן בגמ' (לקמן דף עא.) אי הויא ערלה. דהתם כיוצא בו לא הוי בר מילה בשום מקום. אבל אחר ח', אע"ג דאי אפשר לו למול מפני הסכנה — הוי ערל, כיון שהגיע הזמן. תדע, דלא פשיט ליה בגמ' מטומטום שאין אוכל בתרומה אערלה שלא בזמנה, אע"ג דאין חייב לקרוע ולמול, *כדמוכח בגמרא (שם:), דקאמר: זכריו דאיתנהו בשעת אכילה וליתנהו בשעת עשיה — משכחת לה בטומטום שנקרע הייני הייני ונמצא זכר, דלא קרינן ביה בשעת עשיה "המול לו כל זכר ואז יקרב לעשותו" דלא מיחייב לקרוע ולמול. ובפ"ק דחגיגה (דף ד.) נמי אמר: "זכורך" — להוציא טומטום ואנדרוגינוס, שפטור מן הראיה, ומוקי לה כשביציו מבחוץ. ובירושלמי מייתי ראיה ממתני' אאהזו תמה דממתינין לו למול ל' יום, דאסור בתרומה \ משמע דמתניתין איירי בערל שמתו אחיו מחמת מילה. ובהדיא מחלק בירושלמי בין ערלות שלא בזמנה ובין שהגיע זמנו למול אלא שסכנה היא לו. אלא שזה חולק על הש"ס שלנו: דהתם פשיטא ליה דערלות שלא בזמנה לא הויא ערלות, ואכיל בתרומה, ובש"ס שלנו בעיא היא בגמ' (דף עא.) ולא איפשיטא. **מה תושב ושכיר האמור בפסח.** וא"ת: באוכל תרומה בטומאת עצמה נילף בהאי ג"ש דלילקי, ולקמן (דף עג:) אמרינן דלית בה אלא עשה "בשעריך תאכלנו" — לזה ולא לאחר! וא"י: דהך ג"ש לא ניתנה אלא לענין פסול האדם האוכל, כגון ערל ואונן וכיוצא בו. אבל לענין פסול גופה, כגון טומאת עצמה — לא. אבל קשה: דאכתי נילף מבכורים שילקה עליה בטומאת עצמה, דכי היכי דילפינן (שם) בכורים מתרומה משום דתרומה קרינהו רחמנא — ה"נ נילף תרומה מבכורים, דהא ב"השעור והרוטב" (חולין קכ:) גמרינן תרומה מבכורים לענין דמשקין היוצאין מהן כמותן. **איש איש לרבות הערל.** תימה אמרינן בכל דוכתי (חגיגה דף ד:) דר"ע מרבה ערל כי טמא. ומ"מ אילטריך למכתב ערל בפסח, דאי לאו דכתיב בהדיא משום מקום שהוא כטמא — לא הוה מרבינן ליה מאיש איש, אע"ג דמילת זכריו ועבדיו מעכבתו בפסח. **מה לפסח שכן חייבין עליו משום פגול נותר וטמא.** יש ספרים דל"ג טמא, דבתרומה נמי איכא איסור טומאה. ואית דגרס ליה, משום דבפסח איכא כרת לאוכל בטומאת הגוף משא"כ בתרומה. ובקונטרס נמי פי' דחייבים עליו סטמא קאמר. והוא הדין דהוי מצי למיפרך מכל פנ"ק עכ"ס. אלמא

עין משפט נר מצוה

א ב מיי' פ"ז שם הל' י יב סמג לאוין רלח טור יו"ד שם:
ב ג מיי' שם הלכה יג:
ג ד מיי' פ"י מהל' איסורי ביאה הלכה ג סמג לאוין קיע טוש"ע אה"ע סימן ה סעיף ב:
ד ה מיי' פ"ז מהל' תרומות הלכה י טור יו"ד סימן שלא:
ה ו ז מיי' שם פ"ז הלכה ה:

תוספות ישנים

הדרן עלך אלמנה

פרק הערל. הערל וכל הטמאים לא יאכלו בתרומה פ"ה בכ"מ ערל שמתו אחיו מחמת מילה. ול"נ דא"כ אינה מטה למולו פי' למול א"ע לפי שהוא אנוס והוי כמו מילה שלא בזמנה וקשה דבגמ' בעי ערל קטן מהו לסוכו שמן של תרומה ערלות שלא בזמנה מעכבה או לא מעכבה ואמאי לא פשיט ממתני' דכיון דמיירי שמתו אחיו מחמת מילה א"כ נאנס הוא וכיון שנאנס ערלות שלא בזמנה הוא לכן פר"ת דערל ר"ל משומד לערלות: **פצוע** דכא נשיהם לא יאכלו. תימה אמאי פסלה בביאתו הא לאו זר מפיקרא הוא וי"ל משום דהוקש לממזר דאין הפיקש רק להורות מסיכן הוא פצוע דכא וי"ל כיון דנשתנה גופו חשיב כמו זר מעיקרא:

הגהות הב"ח

(א) רש"י ד"ה הערל כהן ערל שמתו: (ב) ד"ה ואם נשתייר וכו' עטרה (שורת בשר המקפת) תא"מ ונ"ב פ"א שורת בשר המוקפת וכו':

[מלבון והאלהים ידע את יוהו לבשו בראשית ד ועי' תוי"ט]

חגיגה ד: לקמן עב. עג.

ו א מיי' פ"ג מהלכות בכורים הלכה ה ופי"ב מהל' אבות הטומאה הלכה טו:

ז ב מיי' פ"א מהלכות מילה הלכה א סמג עשין כח טוש"ע י"ד סימן רסא:

ח ג מיי' פ"ה מהלכות קרבן פסח הלכה ה ופ"ט הלכה ט:

תורה אור

אלמא – לא קני ליה רביה, הכא נמי לא קני ליה רביה. אלא לאפנויי – ואכתי, מופנה מצד אחד הוא, ושמעינן ליה לר' *אליעזר דאמר: *מופנה מצד אחד למדין – ומשיבין! כיון דלגופיה לא צריך, שדי חד אלמד ושדי חד אמלמד והוה ליה גזירה שוה מופנה משני צדדין. אי מה פסח אונן אסור בו אף תרומה אונן אסור בה! א"ר יוסי בר חנינא: אמר קרא *("זר") °"וכל זר" *זרות אמרתי לך, אולא אנינות. אימא: ולא ערלות! הא כתיב °"תושב ושכיר", ומה ראית? מסתברא, ערלות הו"ל לרבויי שכן (מעשי"ם כרותי"ם בדב"ר העב"ד) מחוסר מעשה, ומעשה בגופו, בוענוש כרת, וישנו לפני הדבור, גומילת זכריו ועבדיו מעכבת. אדרבה, אנינות הוה ליה לרבויי, שכן: ישנה בכל שעה, ונוהגת באנשים ונשים, ואין בידו לתקן את עצמו! הנך נפישן. רבא אמר: בלא הנך נפישן נמי לא מצית אמרת, שבקינן ערלות דכתיב בגופיה דפסח וילפינן אנינות מפסח?! דפסח גופיה ממעשר גמרינן. אי מה פסח – מילת זכריו ועבדיו מעכבת, אף תרומה – מילת זכריו ועבדיו מעכבת! אמר קרא °"ומלתה אותו אז יאכל בו", *מילת זכריו ועבדיו מעכבת בו מלאכול בפסח, ואין מילת זכריו ועבדיו מעכבת בתרומה. אי הכי אימא: °"כל ערל לא יאכל בו", בו אינו אוכל, אבל אוכל הוא בתרומה! הא כתיב "תושב ושכיר". ומה ראית? מסתברא: ערלות דגופיה הוה ליה לרבויי, שכן מעשה בגופו, וענוש כרת. אדרבה, מילת זכריו ועבדיו הוה ליה לרבויי, שכן ישנה בכל שעה! הנך נפישן. ואב"א: בלא [הנך] נפישן נמי לא מצית אמרת, מי איכא מידי דערלות דגופיה לא מעכבא ביה, ערלות דאחריני מעכבא ביה?! השתא דאמרת "בו" לדרשה הוא דאתא, (א)°"כל בן נכר לא יאכל בו" למה לי? *"בו"

המרת

(ויקרא כב; שם; שמות יב; שם; שם)

הָכָא נַמִּי לָא קָנֵי. גּוּפֵיהּ לְרַבֵּיהּ, וְיִשְׂרָאֵל מְעַלְיָא הוּא, וְחַיָּיב בְּפֶסַח. וְשָׁמְעִינַן לֵיהּ לְר' אֱלִיעֶזֶר דְּאָמַר מוּפְנֶה מִצַּד אֶחָד לְמֵדִין. אִם אֵין לְהָשִׁיב. וְאִם יֵשׁ לְהָשִׁיב – מְשִׁיבִין. וְכָאן יֵשׁ תְּשׁוּבָה: מַה לְּפֶסַח – שֶׁכֵּן חַיָּיבִין עָלָיו כו', כִּדְלְעֵיל. וּלְקַמָּן בְּפֶרֶק "מִצְוַת חֲלִיצָה" (דף קד.) שָׁמְעִינַן לְרַבִּי אֱלִיעֶזֶר דְּאָמַר: מוּפְנֶה מִצַּד אֶחָד – לְמֵדִין וּמְשִׁיבִין. דְּקָתָנֵי: חֲלִיצָה בִּשְׂמֹאל פְּסוּלָה, וְר' אֱלִיעֶזֶר מַכְשִׁיר. וְאָמְרִינַן: מ"ט דְּתַנָּא קַמָּא – יָלֵיף 'רֶגֶל' 'רֶגֶל' מִמְּצוֹרָע דִּכְתִיב בֵּיהּ "עַל בֹּהֶן רַגְלוֹ הַיְמָנִית", וּקְרָא יְתֵירָא הוּא, דְּכֵיוָן דִּכְתִיב "עַל דַּם הָאָשָׁם", וּבְדַם הָאָשָׁם כְּתִיב בְּרֶגֶל יְמָנִית, ⊕וְלָא הֲוֵי בָּעֵי לְמֵיהֲדַר וּמִכְתְּבֵיהּ בַּשֶּׁמֶן, וְאָמְרִינַן בִּמְנָחוֹת בְּפ"ק (דף י.): מוּפְנֶה הוּא לְמִדְרְשֵׁיהּ, 'יָד' 'יָד' לִקְמִיצָה, 'רֶגֶל' 'רֶגֶל' לַחֲלִיצָה, 'אוֹזֶן' 'אוֹזֶן' לִרְצִיעָה. וְרַבִּי אֱלִיעֶזֶר מַכְשִׁיר חֲלִיצָה בִּשְׂמֹאל, דְּלָא גָּמַר מִמְּצוֹרָע, דְּאִיכָּא לְמִפְרַךְ: מַה לִּמְצוֹרָע שֶׁכֵּן טָעוּן עֵץ אֶרֶז וְאֵזוֹב וּשְׁנִי תוֹלַעַת. וּמַקְשִׁינַן הָתָם (ולקמן דף קד.): וְרַבִּי אֱלִיעֶזֶר לָא יָלֵיף 'רֶגֶל' 'רֶגֶל' מִמְּצוֹרָע? וְהַתַּנְיָא: מִנַּיִן לִרְצִיעָה שֶׁהִיא בְּיָמִין כו', וּמְשַׁנֵּינַן: 'אוֹזֶן' 'אוֹזֶן' – מוּפְנֶה, 'רֶגֶל' 'רֶגֶל' – לָא מוּפְנֶה. וְאַע"ג דְּג"ש מוּפְנֶה מִצַּד אֶחָד הוּא, דְּרֶגֶל דִּמְצוֹרָע מוּפְנֶה, הוֹאִיל וְרֶגֶל דַּחֲלִיצָה לָא מוּפְנֶה – פָּרְכִינַן. כֵּיוָן דִּלְגוּפֵיהּ לָא צְרִיךְ. לָא תּוֹשָׁב וְלָא שָׂכִיר, דְּלָא אֶפְשָׁר לְאוֹקְמִינְהוּ כִּפְשָׁטַיְיהוּ כְּלָל, הָוֵה לֵיהּ תְּרֵי קְרָאֵי יְתֵירֵי. שְׁדֵי חַד אַלָּמֵד וְחַד אַמְּלַמֵּד. וּמוּפְנֶה מִשְּׁנֵי לְדָדִים דִּבְרֵי הַכֹּל לְמֵדִין וְאֵין מְשִׁיבִין, אֲפִילּוּ יֵשׁ לְהָשִׁיב. מַה פֶּסַח אוֹנֵן כו'. דִּילְפִינַן (לקמן דף עג.) לְכוּלְּהוּ קֳדָשִׁים ק"ו מִמַּעֲשֵׂר. מעשים כרותים בדבר העבד. סִימָנָא הוּא, וּמְפָרֵשׁ לֵיהּ. וְעָנוּשׁ כָּרֵת. עַל הַמִּילָה. וּמִילַת זְכָרָיו וַעֲבָדָיו. אִם יֵשׁ לוֹ בֵּן רָאוּי לָמוּל, אוֹ עֶבֶד לָמוּל, אָסוּר הָאָב אוֹ הָאָדוֹן לֶאֱכוֹל בַּפֶּסַח אא"כ מָלוֹ, דִּכְתִיב (שמות יב) "הִמּוֹל לוֹ כָל זָכָר וְאָז יִקְרַב", וְגַבֵּי עֶבֶד כְּתִיב "וּמַלְתָּה אוֹתוֹ אָז יֹאכַל בּוֹ" (ג) הָאִישׁ בְּעָלָיו, דְּאִי מִשּׁוּם עֶבֶד – הָא כְּתַב "כָּל עָרֵל לֹא יֹאכַל בּוֹ". אַדְּרַבָּה אֲנִינוּת. פָּסַל טְפֵי מֵעֲרֵלוּת. דְּהָא אִית בֵּיהּ חוּמְרָא, שֶׁנּוֹהֵג כָּל שָׁעָה שֶׁמֵּת לוֹ מֵת. אֲבָל עֲרֵלוּת דְּגוּפֵיהּ, מִשֶּׁמָּל פַּעַם אַחַת – שׁוּב אֵינָהּ חוֹזֶרֶת עָלָיו. לָא מָצֵית אָמְרַתְּ. דְּנֵילַף תְּרוּמָה מִפֶּסַח לְעִנְיַן אֲנִינוּת, *וּמוֹקֵי קְרָא דְּמִיעוּטָא לַעֲרֵלוּת. שָׁבְקִינַן עֲרֵלוּת דִּכְתִיב בְּגוּפֵיהּ דְּפֶסַח. וְלָא מַגְמְרִינַן לָהּ (ג) *מִתְּרוּמָה בְּג"ש דְּתוֹשָׁב וְשָׂכִיר, וְיָלְפִינַן אֲנִינוּת כו'. מִמַּעֲשֵׂר גָּמַר. לְקַמָּן בְּפִרְקִין (דף עג.): ה"ג: מִסְתַּבְּרָא עֲרֵלוּת דְּגוּפֵיהּ הֲוָה לֵיהּ לְרַבּוּיֵי כו'.

הֲמָרַת

אלמא לא קני ליה רביה. והא דאמר בפ"ק דקידושין (דף טז. ושם) דעבד עברי גופו קנוי – היינו לענין שצריך גט שחרור ואין יוצא באמירה בעלמא. אבל לענין מצות – לא. והא דשרי בשפחה כנענית – היינו משום שצריך שיעבוד את רבו בין ביום בין בלילה, כדכתיב (דברים טו) "כי משנה שכר שכיר עבדך", דשכיר קרייה רחמנא. וא"ת: דמשמע דמטעמא דקני ליה רביה יש לו ליפטר, והלא עבד כנעני גופו חייב בפסח למ"ד (פסחים דף נא:) נשים בראשון חובה, ואפילו למאן דאמר (שם) רשות – מכל מקום שרי לאכול פסח, והכא כתיב לא יאכל בו! וי"ל: דאי הוה קני ליה רביה לא הוה אכיל אלא בהמנאת רבו, כעבד כנעני, ולא בהמנאת אחרים.

אלא לאפנויי. וא"ת: וכי בשביל לאפנויי כתב שקר? דכתב "לא יאכל בו" והם אוכלין! ואמר ר"י: דאיכא לאוקמי קרא בשכיר ותושב גוי. ומכל מקום לגופיה לא איצטריך, דלא עדיף מערל ובן נכר. ובהדיא דריש במכילתא הכי: תושב – זה גר תושב, שכיר – זה הגוי. א) *וא"ת: כיון דלגוי לא איצטריך, לכתוב "תושב ושכיר יאכל בו" ונוקמיה בישראל, ולאפנויי! ואמר רבינו יצחק: דאם כן הוה משמע גזירה שוה להקל, והוה דרשינן גזירה שוה להתיר אונן בפסח. והא דילפינן לקמן (דף עג.) דאונן אסור בפסח מגזירה שוה ד"ממנו" "ממנו" ממעשר – לא הוי דרשי הכי, אלא הוה מוקמינן לאסור ערל במעשר, כדלקמן (דף עד.).

שדי חד אלמד וחד אמלמד. והוי כאילו כתיב הכא תושב שלא לצורך, והכא שכיר שלא לצורך. ואע"ג דהכא תושב והכא שכיר – הויא שפיר ג"ש, כדתני דבי ר' ישמעאל (לעיל דף יז:) זו היא שיבה זו היא ביאה.

אי מה פסח אונן אסור בו. אר"י אע"פ דתנן בפ' "האשה" בפסחים (דף צא:) דאונן טובל ואוכל פסחו לערב, ומוקמינן ליה בגמרא כמ"ד אנינות לילה דרבנן, ולא העמידו דבריהם במקום כרת – הכא מצי למימר דאתיא אפי' אליבא דמ"ד אנינות לילה מדרבנן. דלא הוי דרבנן אלא כשמת ביום או נקבר ביום, למאן דאזיל בתר קבורה, דלא תפיס לילו עמו מדאורייתא. אבל אם מת בלילה – הוי אונן כמת ביום, דהיינו כיום מר. והא דפריך בפרק "טבול יום" (זבחים קא: ושם) וסבר רבי שמעון אנינות לילה דרבנן? והתניא: רבי שמעון אומר שלמים – כשהוא שלם הוא מביא, ולא כשהוא אונן, מנין לרבות תודה כו', מנין לרבות פסח כו'. קתני מיהא פסח! התם לא מצי לשנויי כשמת בלילה, דמשמע ליה דמרבי ליה לענין הבאה, דאין יכול להביא כשהוא אונן. ולהכי פריך כי הוי אונן בשעת הבאת פסח – יפסוק האנינות עד הלילה שהוא התחלת זמן אכילתו, ואמאי אסור להביא.

אף תרומה אונן אסור בה. בלא גזירה שוה הוה מצי למיפרך דליתסר אונן בתרומה, מדאיתקש תרומה לבכורים לקמן (דף עג:) ובכורים למעשר. ומיהו, בכמה מקומות יכול לומר וליטעמיך ולא קאמר.

שכן מעשים כרותים. הוה מצי למימר שכן נכרתו עליה י"ג בריתות.

הנך נפישן. בלא הנך נפישן נמי ה"מ למימר דכרת עדיפא ליה, כדלקמן (דף עג:).

דפסח גופיה ממעשר גמר. פירוש: בגזירה שוה ד"ממנו" "ממנו". וא"ת: ושאר כל הקדשים מנלן? דכל הקדשים אסורים לאונן, כדאמר בזבחים בפ' "טבול יום" (דף קא*.) מק"ו ממעשר, ואק"ו איכא למיפרך: מה למעשר – שכן טעון כסף צורה, דהכי פריך רבא גופיה בפ' בתרא דמכות (דף יז:) גבי הא דיליף מלקות באוכל תודה ושלמים חוץ לחומה בק"ו ממעשר? וי"ל: דשאר קדשים גמרינן מפסח בהיקשא ד"זאת התורה", דהתם איתקוש כל הקדשים, כדאמר בפ"ק דזבחים (דף ד:) ובמנחות בסוף "התודה" (דף פג:) ובההוא קרא כתיב נמי פסח, דדרשינן *"ביום צוותו" – זה בכור ומעשר ופסח. ואע"ג דבההוא קרא נמי כתיב "ולמילואים" שהם קדשי שעה, וקדשי שעה נאכלים באנינות, כדמוכח בפ' "טבול יום" (זבחים קא.) לאו בכל קדשי שעה קאמר דנאכלין באנינות, אלא בהנהו דאיירי בהו התם דוקא. והא דמשמע בפרק "איזהו מקומן" (שם דף נ.) דהוי פלוגתא בדבר הלמד בגזירה שוה אם חוזר ומלמד בהיקשא – היינו היכא דמלמד קודש, ואיכא למ"ד התם דוקא דכי הוו שניהם קודש דאין חוזר ומלמד, אבל הכא, דמעשר דגן חולין הוא – לכולי עלמא חוזר ומלמד בהיקש, כדאשכחן התם בהדיא שלמדנו לתודה שבאה מן המעשר מדאתקש לשלמים, ושלמים גופייהו גמרי "שם" "שם" ממעשר (שם).

אי מה פסח מילת זכריו ועבדיו מעכבתו כו'. תימה: דהא הך סוגיא כר' אליעזר, ור' אליעזר גופיה דריש במכילתא דמילת עבדיו אין מעכבת אדם מלאכול בפסח, ודריש "אז יאכל בו" – העבד! ואמר רבינו יצחק: דגמ' לפום רהיטא נקט כר' עקיבא, דדריש "אז יאכל בו" – האדון, ולר"א מ"זכריו" פריך.

בו אינו אוכל אבל אוכל הוא בתרומה. אבל מילת זכריו ועבדיו מעכבת בתרומה בג"ש ד"תושב ושכיר", ו"בו" דכתיב ביה – אתא למימר דאינה מעכבת במצה ומרור.

(**הכי** גרסינן "כל ערל לא יאכל בו למה לי". ולא גרסינן "תושב ושכיר", דהא אוקימנא קרא כו' לגזירה שוה, ועקרנא ליה מפשטיה לגמרי).

[טעות וכן לעיל סח: ולקמן עה. ליתא]

[ועי' היטיב תוספות כתובות לח: ד"ה מי אתיא]

תוספות ישנים

א) ועוי"ל אגב דכתיב בתרומה לא יאכל בו כתיב נמי בפסח לא יאכל בו. א"נ מכיון שהג"ש מלמדת איסור לומר דערל אסור בתרומה כתבה בלשון איסור ולהכי כתיב לא יאכל בו:

הגהות הב"ח

(א) גמ' השתא דאמרת בו לדרשה הוא דאתא כל ערל לא יאכל בו כל בן נכר לא יאכל בו למה לי כל ערל לא יאכל בו בו אינו אוכל אבל אוכל הוא במצה ומרור כל בן נכר לא יאכל בו בו המרת דת פוסלת ואין המרת דת פוסלת במעשר ואיצטריך למכתב ערל כנ"ל: (ב) רש"י ד"ה ומילת זכריו וכו' אז יאכל בו היינו בעליו: (ג) ד"ה שבקינן וכו' לה אתרומה בג"ש:

גליון הש"ס

רש"י ד"ה ושמעי' ליה כו' ולא הוי בעי למיהדר. עיין לקמן קד ע"א ברש"י ד"ה אוזן אוזן וכו' ובשבת דף קלא ע"א ד"ה מלד אחד ובקדושין דף טו ע"א ד"ה ונאמר להלן אוזן:

בס"א ליתו

מסורת הש"ס

[נ"ל אליעזר]

[לקמן עב. שבת סד. קלא. ב"ק כה: נדה כב:]

[לעיל סח: לקמן עה.]

פסחים נו.

שם

נ"ל ונוקים. יעב"ץ

[נ"ל לתרומה]

[ושם ד"ה ומה מעשר וכו' הגיהו בתימה]

[בזבחים ז:]

בו

הֲמָרַת דָּת פּוֹסֶלֶת. דְּאִם הֵמִיר דָּתוֹ וְנִתְנַכְּרוּ מַעֲשָׂיו לְאָבִיו שֶׁבַּשָּׁמַיִם, אֲמַר רַחֲמָנָא "לֹא יֹאכַל בּוֹ": ה"ג. כָּל עָרֵל לֹא יֹאכַל בּוֹ לָמָּה לִי. "בּוֹ" מַאי מְמַעֵט. וְלָא גָּרְסִינַן תּוֹשָׁב וְשָׂכִיר כְּלָל, דְּהָא אוֹקִימְנָא כּוּלֵּי קְרָא לִג"ש, וְעָקְרִינַן לֵיהּ מִפְּשָׁטֵיהּ לְגַמְרֵי. מִמֶּנּוּ. "אַל תֹּאכְלוּ מִמֶּנּוּ נָא", כֵּיוָן דְּאָמְרַתְּ "בּוֹ" לְמַעוֹטֵי, "מִמֶּנּוּ" נַמִי לְמַעוֹטֵי מַשְׁמַע. לְכִדְרַבָּה כו'. לְקַמָּן בְּפִרְקִין (דף עד.) תְּלָתָא "מִמֶּנּוּ" כְּתִיבִי בְּפֶסַח כו'. וְרַבִּי עֲקִיבָא, הַאי תּוֹשָׁב וְשָׂכִיר דְּפֶסַח מַאי עָבֵיד לֵיהּ. הָא לֵיכָּא לְאוֹקְמִי בְּעֶבֶד עִבְרִי כְּלָל. לְאִיתּוּיֵי עַרְבִי *וְגִבְעוֹנִי מָהוּל. שֶׁלֹּא יֹאכַל בְּפֶסַח. גִּבְעוֹנִי. שֵׁם אוּמָּה שֶׁמּוֹהֲלִין עַצְמָן. וְהָנֵי מוּלִין נִינְהוּ. בִּתְמִיָּה, וְל"ל לְמַעוֹטִינְהוּ? הָא עֲרֵלִים נִינְהוּ, וּמִכָּל עָרֵל מִימְעֲטִי! בְּעַרְלֵי יִשְׂרָאֵל. לְעִנְיַן נֶדֶר, מוּלִין נִינְהוּ, דְּהַלֵּךְ אַחַר לְשׁוֹן בְּנֵי אָדָם, וְיִשְׂרְאֵלִים לָא קָרֵי לְהוּ עֲרֵלִים וְאוּמּוֹת הָעוֹלָם לָא קָרֵי לְהוּ מוּלִין. וְקָטָן שֶׁנּוֹלַד מָהוּל. וְקָסָבַר ר"ע: קָטָן שֶׁנּוֹלַד מָהוּל צָרִיךְ לְהַטִּיף מִמֶּנּוּ דַּם בְּרִית. וְר"א. דְּלָא מְמַעֵט לְהוּ, אָזֵיל לְטַעְמֵיהּ, דְּאָמַר בְּ"הַחוֹלֵץ": גֵּר שֶׁמָּל וְלֹא טָבַל גֵּר מְעַלְיָא הוּא. וּבְקָטָן מָהוּל סְבִירָא לֵיהּ א"צ לְהַטִּיף מִמֶּנּוּ דַּם בְּרִית. קָטָן עָרֵל. תּוֹךְ שְׁמֹנָה. מַהוּ לְסוּכוֹ שֶׁמֶן שֶׁל תְּרוּמָה. דְּקַיְימָא לָן (שבת דף פו.) דְּסִיכָה כִּשְׁתִיָּה, דְּנָפְקָא לָן מִ"וַתָּבֹא כַמַּיִם בְּקִרְבּוֹ וְכַשֶּׁמֶן בְּעַצְמוֹתָיו". מְעַכְּבָא. מֵאֲכִילַת תְּרוּמָה. אֵין לִי. לְעַכֵּב בַּפֶּסַח אֶלָּא מִילַת זְכָרָיו שֶׁיֵּשׁ לוֹ בִּשְׁעַת עֲשִׂיָּה. דְּגַבֵּי מִילַת זְכָרָיו כְּתִיב (שמות יב) "וְאָז יִקְרַב לַעֲשׂוֹתוֹ" וְהַיְינוּ שְׁחִיטָה. וְגַבֵּי עֲבָדָיו כְּתִיב "אָז יֹאכַל בּוֹ", דַּאֲפִילּוּ לָא הֲוָה לֵיהּ עֶבֶד בִּשְׁעַת עֲשִׂיָּה וְהָיָה לוֹ בִּשְׁעַת אֲכִילָה – מְעַכְּבוֹ מִן אֲכִילַת פִּסְחוֹ. מִנַּיִן לִיתֵּן כו'. דְּגַבֵּי בָּנִים נַמִי, אִם רָאוּי לִימּוֹל בִּשְׁעַת אֲכִילָה וְלֹא הָיָה לוֹ בִּשְׁעַת עֲשִׂיָּה – מִנַּיִן שֶׁמְּעַכְּבוֹ מֵאֲכִילַת פִּסְחוֹ? תַּלְמוּד לוֹמַר אָז אָז. "אָז יִקְרַב לַעֲשׂוֹתוֹ", "אָז יֹאכַל בּוֹ". אֶלָּא זְכָרָיו. דִּמְרַבֵּינַן לְהוּ בִּשְׁעַת אֲכִילָה. אַלְמָא דְּלָא הֲווּ בִּשְׁעַת עֲשִׂיָּה. הֵיכִי דָּמֵי? לָאו דְּאִתְיְלוּד בֵּינֵי בֵּינֵי. אֶלָּא הָכָא כְּשֶׁחֲלָצַתּוּ חַמָּה. שֶׁהָיָה חוֹלֶה וְנִתְרַפֵּא, וְנִתְחַלְּלָה וְנִשְׁתַּלְּפָה מִמֶּנּוּ חַמָּה. וְנִיתּוּב לֵיהּ כָּל שִׁבְעָה. וְאִי בֵּינֵי וּבֵינֵי אִיתְפַּח, אַמַּאי מְעַכֵּב לֵיהּ מֵאֲכִילָה? אַכַּתִּי לָא מְטָא זִמְנֵיהּ, דְּתַנְיָא לְקַמָּן: יוֹם הַבְרָאָתוֹ כְּיוֹם הוֹלְדוֹ, דְּעַד ז' יוֹמֵי לָא מְהַלִּינַן לֵיהּ. דְּיָהֲבִינַן לֵיהּ. שֶׁכְּבָר נִתְרַפֵּא זֶה שְׁמוֹנָה יָמִים, וְחָל שְׁמִינִי שֶׁלּוֹ לִהְיוֹת עֶרֶב הַפֶּסַח. וְנִימְהֲלֵיהּ מִצַּפְרָא. וְכֵיוָן דְּמִצַּפְרָא בַּר מְהִילָא הוּא – אִשְׁתַּכַּח דִּמְעַכֵּב לֵיהּ מֵעֲשִׂיָּה, וְלָמָּה לִי קְרָא לְרַבּוּיֵי שְׁעַת אֲכִילָה? מֵעֵת

תורה אור

[א]מְשׁוּמָּדוּת פּוֹסֶלֶת, וְאֵין מְשׁוּמָּדוּת פּוֹסֶלֶת בְּמַעֲשֵׂר. "כָּל עָרֵל לֹא יֹאכַל בּוֹ" לָמָּה לִי? *"בּוֹ" [ב]אֵינוֹ אוֹכֵל, אֲבָל אוֹכֵל הוּא בְּמַצָּה וּמָרוֹר. *וְאִיצְטְרִיךְ* לְמִכְתַּב "עָרֵל", וְאִיצְטְרִיךְ לְמִכְתַּב "כָּל בֶּן נֵכָר". דְּאִי כָּתַב רַחֲמָנָא "עָרֵל" מִשּׁוּם דִּמְאִיס, אֲבָל בֶּן נֵכָר דְּלָא מְאִיס, אֵימָא לָא, וְאִי כָּתַב רַחֲמָנָא "כָּל בֶּן נֵכָר" מִשּׁוּם דְּאֵין לִבּוֹ לַשָּׁמַיִם, אֲבָל עָרֵל, דְּלִבּוֹ לַשָּׁמַיִם, אֵימָא לָא, צְרִיכָא. °"מִמֶּנּוּ" "מִמֶּנּוּ" לָמָּה לִי? *לְכִדְרַבָּה א"ר יִצְחָק. (שמות יב) אָמַר מָר, ר"ע אוֹמֵר: אֵינוֹ צָרִיךְ, הֲרֵי הוּא אוֹמֵר °"אִישׁ אִישׁ" לְרַבּוֹת אֶת הֶעָרֵל. (ויקרא כב) וְאֵימָא לְרַבּוֹת אֶת הָאוֹנֵן! א"ר יוֹסֵי בְּר' חֲנִינָא: אָמַר קְרָא °"וְכָל זָר" (שם) זָרוּת אָמַרְתִּי לְךָ וְלֹא אֲנִינוּת. אֵימָא: וְלֹא עֲרֵלוּת! הָא כְּתִיב "אִישׁ אִישׁ". וּמָה רָאִיתָ? מִסְתַּבְּרָא, עֲרֵלוּת הֲוָה לֵיהּ לְרַבּוּיֵי, שֶׁכֵּן מעשי"ם כרותי"ם בדב"ר העב"ד: מְחוּסַּר מַעֲשֶׂה, וּמַעֲשֶׂה בְּגוּפוֹ, וְעָנוּשׁ כָּרֵת, וְיֶשְׁנוֹ לִפְנֵי הַדִּבּוּר, וּמִילַת זְכָרָיו וַעֲבָדָיו מְעַכֶּבֶת. אַדְּרַבָּה, אֲנִינוּת הֲוָה לֵיהּ לְרַבּוּיֵי, שֶׁכֵּן יֶשְׁנָהּ בְּכָל שָׁעָה, וְנוֹהֶגֶת בַּאֲנָשִׁים וְנָשִׁים, וְאֵין בְּיָדוֹ לְתַקֵּן עַצְמוֹ. הָנָךְ נְפִישָׁן. רָבָא אָמַר: בְּלָא הָנָךְ נְפִישָׁן נַמִי לָא מָצֵית אָמְרַתְּ, אָמַר קְרָא "אִישׁ אִישׁ", אֵיזֶהוּ דָּבָר שֶׁיֶּשְׁנוֹ בְּאִישׁ וְאֵינוֹ בְּאִשָּׁה — הֱוֵי אוֹמֵר: זֶה עֲרֵלוּת. וְרַבִּי עֲקִיבָא, הַאי "תּוֹשָׁב וְשָׂכִיר" מַאי עָבֵיד לֵיהּ? אָמַר רַב שְׁמַעְיָא: לְאַתּוּיֵי עַרְבִי מָהוּל *וְגִבְעוֹנִי מָהוּל. וְהָנֵי מוּלִין נִינְהוּ?! וְהָא תְּנַן: *[ג]"קוֹנָם שֶׁאֲנִי נֶהֱנֶה לָעֲרֵלִים" מוּתָּר בְּעַרְלֵי יִשְׂרָאֵל, וְאָסוּר בְּמוּלֵי אוּמּוֹת הָעוֹלָם. [ד]"קוֹנָם שֶׁאֲנִי נֶהֱנֶה לַמּוּלִין" מוּתָּר בְּמוּלֵי אוּמּוֹת הָעוֹלָם, וְאָסוּר בְּעַרְלֵי יִשְׂרָאֵל. אֶלָּא, לְאַתּוּיֵי גֵּר שֶׁמָּל וְלֹא טָבַל, וְקָטָן שֶׁנּוֹלַד כְּשֶׁהוּא מָהוּל, *וְקָסָבַר: [ה]צָרִיךְ לְהַטִּיף מִמֶּנּוּ דַּם בְּרִית. וְר' אֱלִיעֶזֶר, לְטַעְמֵיהּ, דְּאָמַר: *גֵּר שֶׁמָּל וְלֹא טָבַל גֵּר מְעַלְיָא הוּא, וְקָסָבַר: קָטָן כְּשֶׁנּוֹלַד מָהוּל אֵין צָרִיךְ לְהַטִּיף מִמֶּנּוּ דַּם בְּרִית. וְר' אֱלִיעֶזֶר, הַאי "אִישׁ אִישׁ" מַאי עָבֵיד לֵיהּ? *דִּבְּרָה תּוֹרָה כִּלְשׁוֹן בְּנֵי אָדָם. בָּעֵי רַב חָמָא בַּר עוּקְבָא: קָטָן עָרֵל, מַהוּ לְסוּכוֹ בְּשֶׁמֶן שֶׁל תְּרוּמָה? עֲרֵלוּת שֶׁלֹּא בִּזְמַנָּהּ מְעַכְּבָא אוֹ לָא מְעַכְּבָא? א"ר זֵירָא, ת"ש: [ו]אֵין לִי אֶלָּא מִילַת זְכָרָיו בִּשְׁעַת עֲשִׂיָּה, וַעֲבָדָיו בִּשְׁעַת אֲכִילָה, מִנַּיִן לִיתֵּן אֶת הָאָמוּר שֶׁל זֶה בָּזֶה וְאֶת הָאָמוּר שֶׁל זֶה בָּזֶה — ת"ל °"אָז" "אָז" (שמות יב) לִגְזֵירָה שָׁוָה. בִּשְׁלָמָא עֲבָדָיו, מַשְׁכַּחַתְּ לָהּ דְּאִיתְנְהוּ בִּשְׁעַת אֲכִילָה וְלֵיתְנְהוּ בִּשְׁעַת עֲשִׂיָּה — כְּגוֹן דְּזַבְּנִינְהוּ בֵּינֵי בֵּינֵי. אֶלָּא זְכָרָיו דְּאִיתְנְהוּ בִּשְׁעַת אֲכִילָה וְלֵיתְנְהוּ בִּשְׁעַת עֲשִׂיָּה — הֵיכִי מַשְׁכַּחַתְּ לָהּ? לָאו דְּאִתְיְלוּד בֵּין עֲשִׂיָּה לַאֲכִילָה? ש"מ: עֲרֵלוּת שֶׁלֹּא בִּזְמַנָּהּ הָוְיָא עֲרֵלוּת. אֲמַר *רָבָא: [ז]וְתִסְבְּרָא? °"הִמּוֹל לוֹ כָל זָכָר" (שמות יב) אָמַר רַחֲמָנָא "וְאָז יִקְרַב לַעֲשׂוֹתוֹ", וְהַאי לָאו בַּר מְהִילָא הוּא! אֶלָּא, הָכָא בְּמַאי עָסְקִינַן — כְּגוֹן [ח]שֶׁחֲלָצַתּוּ חַמָּה. וְנִיתּוּב לֵיהּ כָּל שִׁבְעָה, *(דְּאָמַר שְׁמוּאֵל: [ט]חֲלָצַתּוּ חַמָּה נוֹתְנִין לוֹ כָּל שִׁבְעָה!) דִּיהָבִינַן לֵיהּ כָּל שִׁבְעָה. וְנִימְהֲלֵיהּ מִצַּפְרָא! [י]בָּעֵינַן מֵעֵת

פסחים כח: נו.
שם נו. זבחים כב: ס"א וגבעוני
פסחים נו. [לקמן עד. ע"ש]
ס"א וגבנוני
ע"ז כז. נדרים לא:
שבת קלה.
[לעיל מו.]
[ברכות לא: וש"נ]
שבת קלו. וכס"א כל זה איתו

בן משומדות פוסלת כו'. "בו" דכל ערל לא בעי למדרש הכי, דאין ערלות פוסלת במעשר, דלאומרא דרשינן ומוקמינן ליה לחייב במצה ומרור. ומ"בו" דבן נכר לא שייך למדרש הכי: בו אינו אוכל, אבל אוכל הוא במצה ומרור, דלאשמועינן דלא אסור במצה ומרור – לא איצטריך דאטו מצה ומרור קדושה אית בהו? ואי בעי למימר אבל חייב במצה ומרור – פשיטא הוא דחייב לעשות תשובה ולקיים כל המצות. ו"בו" דתושב ושכיר פי' בקונטרס דלא דריש מידי משום דאוקימנא (לעיל דף ע.) כולה קרא לגזירה שוה ועקרינן ליה מפשטיה לגמרי. ונראה שר"ל דאיידי דכתביה רחמנא בערל ובן נכר – כתביה נמי בתושב ושכיר. וכה"ג אמר לקמן (דף עד.) איידי דכתיב ו"הנותר" כתיב נמי "ממנו". ומיהו לא הוי ממש כי הכא, דהתם הוי כמו פרשה שנאמרה ונשנית בשביל דבר שנתחדש בה, ור"ת מפרש: ד"בו" דתושב ושכיר לגופיה, כדאמר לקמן (שם) גבי תלתא "ממנו" חד לגופיה. ואית ספרים דגרסי הכא: "בו" דערל ובן נכר בו אין אוכל, אבל אוכל במצה ומרור. ו"בו" דתושב ושכיר – בו משומדות פוסלת. וכן בכל הספרים בסוף "מי שהיה טמא" (פסחים דף נו. ושם), וכן משמע בפרק "כל שעה" (שם דף כח:) וב"ערבי פסחים" (שם דף קכ.) דמתרוייהו "בו" דערל ובן נכר דרשינן אבל אוכל במצה ומרור. ומיישב ר"י הגירסות, דשייך שפיר מ"בו" דבן נכר לידרוש אבל אוכל במצה ומרור, – לאשמועינן דחייב לאכול במצה ומרור אם עשה תשובה, אע"ג דבפסח אין אוכל – שהיה מומר בשעת עשיית פסח. ו"בו" דתושב ושכיר נמי שייך למדרש מיניה "בו" משומדות פוסלת, דבתושב ושכיר גוי איירי, כדפרישית לעיל.

ואין משומדות פוסלת במעשר. בסוף "מי שהיה טמא" (פסחים דף נו. ושם) גרסי' בכל הספרים: ואין משומדות פוסלת בתרומה. ושפיר ממעטינן תרוייהו מחד "בו" ד"בו" משמע: בו ולא בדברים אחרים. ואיצטריך למעוטי תרוייהו: תרומה – דלא נילף בגזירה שוה דתושב ושכיר, ומעשר – בגזירה שוה ד"ממנו" "ממנו"..

דאי כתב רחמנא ערל כו'. אע"ג דאיצטריך למכתב תרוייהו משום "בו" דאיצטריך למכתב בתרוייהו, (א)דהיה לכותבם בקראי דצריכי.

שאני נהנה כו'. לא גרס "שאיני", דאם כן – לא הוי נדר, דהיינו דבר שאין בו ממש, שאין אוסר על עצמו כלום. כמו "שאיני ישן" – דלא אמר כלום אי לא אמר "קונם עיני בשינה", כדאמר בריש "אלו מותרין" (נדרים טו.) אלא אומר ר"ת: דגרס "שאני נהנה" כלומר: מה שאני נהנה יהא עלי קונם. ומיהו, גרס שפיר "שאיני", דאין דרך התנא לדקדק בלשונו, כדאשכחן בפ' בתרא דנדרים (דף פא:) קונם שלא אתן תבן לפני בהמתך, ובשבועות בפ"ג (דף כ.) הרי עלי שלא אאכול בשר ושלא אשתה יין, דכהאי גוונא לא חל הנדר*. **והני** מולין נינהו והתנן קונם שאני נהנה. אין להקשות: היכי פריך מנדרים ללישנא דקרא, דבנדרים הלך אחר לשון בני אדם! דבסיפא דמתני' דהכא מפיק ליה מקרא, שנאמר "כי כל הגוים ערלים וכל בית ישראל ערלי לב". ואין להקשות מ"וכל ערל לא יאכל בו" – דההוא לא איצטריך אלא לישראל. ויש מקומות שהתנא לומד נדרים מלישנא דקרא, כגון הכא ובריש פסחים (דף ג.) גבי "הללוהו כל כוכבי אור" דקאמר הא קמשמע לן דאור כוכבים אור הוא, למאי נפקא מינה – לנודר, כדתנן: הנודר מן האור אסור באורן של כוכבים. והיינו דוקא היכא שאין הלשון ידוע מייתי שפיר ראיה מלישנא דקרא, אבל במקום שלשון בני אדם חלוק מלישנא דקרא – בנדרים הלך אחר לשון בני אדם, כדאמר בפרק "האומר משקלי" (ערכין יט:) דאורייתא – היד עד הפרק, בנדרים – הלך אחר לשון בני אדם.

ואיבעית

ט א מיי' פ"ט מהלכות קרבן פסח הלכה ז:
י ב מיי' שם הלכה ח:
יא ג מיי' פ"ט מהלכות נדרים הלכה כב טוש"ע י"ד סימן ריז סעיף מא:
יב ד מיי' שם טוש"ע שם סעיף מב:
[עי' תוספות פסחים קכ. ד"ה כל בן]
יג ה מיי' פ"א מהלכות מילה הלכה ז סמג עשין כח טוש"ע י"ד סימן רסח סעיף א וסי' רסג סעיף ד:
יד ו מיי' פ"ט מהלכות קרבן פסח הלכה ט:
טו ז מיי' פי"א מהל' תרומות הלכה ז:
טז ח מיי' פ"ט מהלכות קרבן פסח הלכה ט:
יז ט י מיי' פ"א מהלכות מילה הלכה טז סמג עשין כח טוש"ע י"ד סימן רסב סעי' ב:

הגהות הב"ח
(א) תום' ד"ה דאי וכו' בתרוייהו היה ליה לכותבם:

[נ"ל רבה ולקמן ע"ב אמר רבא כגון שהיו אביו ואמו כו' אבל הכא רבה הוא דמסיק כגון שחלצתו חמה]

[וע"ע תוס' ע"ז כז. ד"ה ה"ג קונם]

יח א מיי' פי"א מהלכות פרה אדומה הלכה ג סמג עשין רס:

מעת לעת. והתני *לודאה: יום הבראתו כיום הולדו, מאי לאו, מה יום הולדו לא בעינן מעת לעת אף יום הבראתו לא בעינן מעת לעת! לא, עדיף יום הבראתו מיום הולדו. דאילו יום הולדו לא בעינן מעת לעת, ואילו יום הבראתו – בעינן מעת לעת. רב פפא אמר: כגון דכאיב ליה עיניה לינוקא, ואיתפח ביני וביני. רבא אמר: כגון שהיו אביו ואמו חבושין בבית האסורין. רב כהנא בריה דרב נחמיה אמר: כגון טומטום, שנקרע ונמצא זכר ביני וביני. רב שרביא אמר: כגון שהוציא ראשו חוץ לפרוזדור. ומי חיי? *והתניא: *כיון שיצא לאויר העולם נפתח הסתום ונסתם הפתוח, שאלמלא כן אין יכול לחיות אפילו שעה אחת! הכא במאי עסקינן – כגון דזנתיה אישתא. אישתא דמאן? אילימא אישתא דידיה – אי הכי כל שבעה בעי, אלא דזנתיה אישתא דאימיה. ואיבעית אימא: ה"מ – היכא דלא מעוי, אבל היכא דמעוי – מחייא חיי. *אמר ר' יוחנן משום רבי בנאה: [א]ערל מקבל הזאה, שכן מצינו באבותינו שקבלו הזאה כשהן ערלים, שנאמר °"והעם עלו מן הירדן בעשור לחדש הראשון" (יהושע ד). בעשרה לא מהילי משום חולשא דאורחא, הזאה אימת עביד להו לאו כשהן ערלים?! ודלמא לא עבוד פסח כלל? לא ס"ד, דכתיב °"ויעשו את הפסח" (שם ה). מתקיף לה מר זוטרא: ודלמא פסח הבא בטומאה היה! א"ל רב אשי: תניא בהדיא, מלו וטבלו ועשו פסחיהן בטהרה. אמר רבה בר יצחק אמר רב: לא ניתנה פריעת מילה לאברהם אבינו, שנאמר: °"בעת ההיא אמר ה' אל יהושע עשה לך חרבות צרים וגו'" (שם). ודלמא הנך דלא מהול, דכתיב °"כי מלים היו כל העם היצאים וכל העם הילדים וגו'" (שם)? א"כ, מאי "שוב? אלא לאו – לפריעה, ומאי "שנית" לאקושי סוף מילה לתחלת מילה, מה תחלת מילה מעכבת, אף סוף מילה מעכבין בו. דתנן, *אלו הן ציצין המעכבין את המילה: בשר החופה את [רוב] העטרה, ואין אוכל בתרומה. *אמר רבינא, ואיתימא רב ירמיה בר אבא, אמר רב: *בשר החופה את רוב גובהה של עטרה. ובמדבר מאי טעמא לא מהול? איבעית אימא: משום חולשא דאורחא, ואיבעית

רש"י

מעת לעת. כגון שחללתו חמה אחר חלות היום זה ח' ימים. והתני לודאה. שם חכם. יום הבראתו כיום הולדו. צריך להמתין שמונה ימים. מאי לאו. הכי קאמר: מה יום הולדו לא בעינן מעת לעת, אף יום הבראה לא בעי מעת לעת. לא עדיף יום הבראתו כו'. והא דתנא לודאה יום הבראתו כיום הולדו – הא אתא לאשמועינן: שצריך להמתין עד יום שמיני. דכאיב ליה עיניה לינוקא ואיתפח. בין עשייה לאכילה, ואין נותנין שבעה ימים אלא למי שחללתו חמה. חבושין. בשעת עשייה, ומצות מילה מוטלת עליהם, ולא על אחרים, והם אינן יכולין לעשות את פסחן, ושחט שלוחן עליהם. ואשמעינן קרא, שאם יצאו בשעת אכילה מילת בנו מעכבתו. כגון שהוציא ולד ראשו חוץ לפרוזדור. וכבר עברו שבעה ימים, ומההיא שעתא הוה ליה ולד, דקיימא לן במסכת נדה (דף כט.): יצא ראשו – הרי הוא כילוד. והשתא, בין עשייה לאכילה יצא הגוף, דהויא ליה זמן מילה. והתניא. ב"המפלת" במסכת נדה: פיו סתום וטבורו פתוח, וכיון שיצא לאויר העולם – נפתח הסתום – פיו, ונסתם הפתוח – טבורו. אין יכול לחיות. משום דלא יניק. דזנתיה אישתא. החולי זן את החולה. אי נימא אישתא דידיה. שאחזתו חמה, וכשילא חללתו. כל שבעה בעי אמתוני. משילא, דהא אמרן: יום הבראתו כיום הולדו. מעוי. נועק, כמו עוי עוי ולא אשגחו ביה, בפרק בתרא דיומא (דף עז.). ערל. ישראל שנטמא במת – מקבל הזאה ליטהר מטומאתו, וכשימול אינו צריך לחזור ולהזות, ואוכל בקדשים, ולא אמרינן הזאת ערלות לא שמה הזאה. שכן מצינו באבותינו. בימי יהושע בפסח גלגל, שקבלו הזאה מטומאת מת כשהן ערלים. בעשרה לא מהול. אותן שהיו במדבר, שהיו ערלים. הזאה אימת עבוד. לטומאת מת שעליהן, שרוב צבור טמאי מת היו, שנטמאו באבותיהן. שכל יוצאי מצרים מתו במדבר, ואלו הן בניהם, כדכתיב (יהושע ה) "ואת בניהם הקים תחתם אותם מל יהושע". והיאך נטהרו לאכול פסחיהן, אם לא קבלו הזאת שלישי ושביעי כשהן ערלים? או כל אחד ואחד קבל הזאה לשלישי ושביעי שלו בעודו במדבר, או עכשיו הזו עליהן כולן יחד בעשור לחדש ובערב הפסח, והיו להן ד' ימים, כמשפט בין הזאה להזאה. דאם לא היו מזין עד יום אחד עשר לאחר מילה, נמצאת הזאה שניה מחוסרת זמן. ואית דמפרש להו הזאה – משום דכל הפורש מן הערלה כפורש מן הקבר. ולאו מילתא היא, דהא אמר רבי יוחנן בפרק "האשה" במסכת פסחים (דף צב.): לא שנו אלא ערל גוי, אבל ערל ישראל – דברי הכל טובל ואוכל מיד את פסחו לערב. ולשון ראשון שמעתי מפי(א) הזקן. א"כ מאי שוב. דמשמע זמנא אחריתי, אלא לאו ש"מ לפריעה. ומאי שנית. השתא דדרשת "שוב", "שנית" מאי תדרוש ביה? ל"א: מאי "שוב" ומאי "שנית", אלא לאו לפריעה. ולהאי לישנא גרסינן: ודלמא לאקושי סוף מילה כו' – ולאו לפריעה אתא אלא לעיכוב(ב). סוף מילה. ציצין שנשתיירו, שלא חתך כל הערלה. את רוב גובהה. אע"ג דאין רוב הקיפה.

רוש

תוספות

ואיבעית אימא הני מילי היכא דלא מעורה. פי': שהטבור אין מעורה לאמו. אבל מעורה – מחייא חיי ממה שאמו אוכלת.

ערל מקבל הזאה שכן מצינו כו'. תימה לר"י: מה ראיה צריך? למה לא יקבל הזאה? אפילו לרבי עקיבא דמרבה (לעיל דף ע.) לערל כי טמא – דהא טמא מקבל הזאה, כדאמר בפרק "דם חטאת" (זבחים דף צג.) מי חטאת שנטמאו – מטהרין, שהרי נדה מזין עליה והיא טהורה.

ודלמא פסח הבא בטומאה הוה. תימה: אם כן קרא למה ליה? דבפרק בתרא דזבחים (דף קיח.) דייק רבי שמעון דאף לבור לא הקריבו אלא פסחים וחובות הקבוע להם זמן, מדכתיב (יהושע ה) "ויעשו את הפסח בגלגל" למה לי קרא? אלא הא קמשמע לן: דחובה דהוי כעין פסח – קריב, דלאו כעין פסח – לא קריב. ורבנן; ההוא מיבעי ליה כדר' יוחנן משום רבי בנאה, דערל מקבל הזאה? ואמר רבינו יצחק: דעדיפא קמשני הכא, דתניא בהדיא שעשו פסחיהם בטהרה.

לא ניתנה פריעת מילה לאברהם אבינו. ומ"מ אברהם פרע מילתו, אע"ג דלא נצטווה, כדאמר בב"ר *(פ' (ס"ד) [מ"ז]) דאפי' עירוב תבשילין קיים. וא"ת: אם לא ניתנה פריעה עד יהושע – היכי גמרינן מיניה? הא כתיב (ויקרא כז) "אלה המצות" – שאין נביא רשאי לחדש דבר מעתה!* ויש לומר: דהלכה למשה מסיני הוה, ויהושע אסמכיה אקרא.

בקונטרס גרס אם כן מאי שוב. ומאי שנית בעיא באנפי נפשה היא, ומשני: לאקושי. ול"ג אלא לאקושי, ולא ודלמא. ור"ח מפרש דמאי שוב ומאי שנית – כולה חדא מילתא היא, וגרסינן ודלמא לאקושי כו'. ולהכי אתא ולא לפריעה. ולגי' זו לא משני במסקנא מידי אהך קושיא.

סוף מילה כו'. הק' הר' יצחק הלבן: דהכא דריש מ"שנית" ציצין המעכבין את המילה, והתם (לקמן דף עב.) דרשי "המול ימול" – לציצין כו'! ותירץ לו ר"ת: דהכא ציצין המעכבין את הפריעה קאמר, ולר"י נראה: דאע"ג דנצטווה אברהם על הציצין – דריש להו שפיר מקרא דיהושע. דהא כי פריך נמי דלמא הנך דלא מהול – אין שום חדוש בקרא דיהושע, אלא מה שכבר נצטווה תחלה. ואם תאמר: אם כן שוב נמי דאיירי בפריעה מצי למימר דנצטווה אברהם, והיכי מוכח מינה דלא ניתנה פריעה לאברהם! ויש לומר: דאין לנו לומר שנצטווה אלא מאי דכתיב ביה בהדיא, כגון ציצין, דדרשינן מ"המול ימול" דמשמע דלציצין אתא, ולא לפריעה. ד"המול ימול" משמע דבר המעכב גוף המילה. וה"ק: לא ניתנה פריעה לאברהם, כיון דלא כתיב בהדיא, אלא ליהושע.

מאי טעמא לא מהול. משמע דלא מהול כלל. ובפרקי דר' אליעזר (פ' כט) משמע שמלו, דקאמר: "מי מנה עפר יעקב" – ראה כל המדבר שהיה מלא מערלותיהן של ישראל, ובמגלת סתרים דרבינו נסים נמי משמע שמלו ולא פרעו, דכתב בהו: כל אותן ארבעים שנה שהיו ישראל במדבר לא היו פורעים מפני עינוי הדרך.

מאי טעמא לא מהול כו'. ואם תאמר: ואיך היו אוכלים קדשים, או אפילו בשר כלל, כיון שלא מלו? שלא הותר להם בשר תאוה אלא על ידי שלמים, וערל אסור בקדשים. ואפילו אם מלו ולא פרעו, כמו משמע בפרקי דרבי אליעזר ובמגלת סתרים, מ"מ, כיון דנצטוו על הפריעה ולא פרעו – כאילו לא מלו! דאי לאו הכי – היאך מדקדק דערל מקבל הזאה מאבותינו? וי"ל: דיוצאי מצרים מלו ופרעו, ואותם אכלו קדשים. אבל הילודים במדבר, שלא מלו – לא אכלו קדשים. אבל בבשר תאוה היו מותרים, שלא נאסרה להם, מאחר שאין יכולין לאכול קדשים. מידי דהוה אבכי ואיל, דהיכא דלא אפשר בהקרבה – שרי בשר תאוה, כדפירש בפ"ק דחולין (דף יז. ושם).

מסורת הש"ס

שבת קלז. | נדה ל: | [זבחים קיח.] | שבת קלז. לעיל מז: | צ"ל ואמר | [לעיל מז: שבת קלז.]

[בברייתא לא מצאתי אלא רבי שמלאי דריש הכי בנדה ל: וכבן מלת והתניא בעי תיקון ואולי צ"ל והאיתמר]

[וכן הוא להדיא בגמרא דילן יומא כח: קיים אברהם אבינו אפילו עירובי תבשילין]

[שבת קז.]

הגהות הב"ח

(א) רש"י ד"ה הזאה וכו' מפי מורי הזקן: (ב) ד"ה ל"א מאי וכו' אלא לעיכוב סוף מילה הס"ד ואח"כ מ"ה סוף מילה:

תוספות ישנים

לא עדיף יום הבראתו מיום הולדו והאי דקאמר יום הבראתו כיום הולדו היינו לענין לצריך להמתין שבעה: ערל מקבל הזאה פי' ערל שנטמא במת מקבל הזאה ואצטריך לר' עקיבא לאמר דמרבה ערל כטמא וסד"א דכיון דגם לאחר הזאה הוי ערל הוי לעולם כי טמא קודם הזאה: א"ב מאי שוב. ופריך תלמודא ומאי שנית ומשני לאקושי סוף מילה לתחלת מילה וכו'. י"מ א"כ מאי שוב ומאי שנית וגרסי ודלמא לאקושי סוף מילה לתחלת מילה ולא נהירא דא"כ תלמודא לא משני מידי מן הקושיא דקאמר ודלמא לאקושי לכן נראה כפי' קמא:

משום

וְאִיבָּעֵית אֵימָא: מִשּׁוּם דְּלָא נָשֵׁיב לְהוּ רוּחַ צְפוֹנִית. דְּתַנְיָא: כָּל אוֹתָן אַרְבָּעִים שָׁנָה שֶׁהָיוּ יִשְׂרָאֵל בַּמִּדְבָּר לֹא נָשְׁבָה לָהֶם רוּחַ צְפוֹנִית. מַאי טַעֲמָא? אִיבָּעֵית אֵימָא: מִשּׁוּם דִּנְזוּפִים הָווּ, וְאִי בָּעֵית אֵימָא: דְּלָא נִבְדּוּר עַנְנֵי כָבוֹד. א"ר פַּפָּא: הִלְכָּךְ, יוֹמָא דְּעֵיבָא וְיוֹמָא דְּשׁוּתָא — לָא מָהֲלִינַן בֵּיהּ, וְלָא *מְסוֹכְרִינַן בֵּיהּ. וְהָאִידָּנָא דְּדָשׁוּ בָּהּ רַבִּים — °"שׁוֹמֵר פְּתָאִים ה'". תהלים קטז § ת"ר: כָּל אוֹתָן אַרְבָּעִים שָׁנָה שֶׁהָיוּ יִשְׂרָאֵל בַּמִּדְבָּר לֹא הָיָה יוֹם שֶׁלֹּא נָשְׁבָה בּוֹ רוּחַ צְפוֹנִית בַּחֲצִי הַלַּיְלָה, שֶׁנֶּאֱ' °"וַיְהִי בַּחֲצִי הַלַּיְלָה וַה' הִכָּה כָל בְּכוֹר וגו'". שמות יב מַאי תַּלְמוּדָא? הָא קמ"ל *דְּעֵת רָצוֹן מִילְּתָא הִיא. א"ר הוּנָא: [א]דְּבַר תּוֹרָה מָשׁוּךְ אוֹכֵל בִּתְרוּמָה, וּמִדִּבְרֵיהֶם גָּזְרוּ עָלָיו, מִפְּנֵי שֶׁנִּרְאֶה כְּעָרֵל. מֵיתִיבֵי: *מָשׁוּךְ צָרִיךְ שֶׁיִּמּוֹל! [ב]מִדְּרַבָּנַן. *וּדְקָאָרֵי לַהּ מַאי קָאָרֵי לַהּ? הָא צָרִיךְ קָתָנֵי! קָטָעֵי בְּסֵיפָא: ר' יְהוּדָה אוֹמֵר: לֹא יִמּוֹל, מִפְּנֵי שֶׁסַּכָּנָה הִיא לוֹ. אָמְרוּ לוֹ: וַהֲלֹא הַרְבֵּה מָלוּ בִּימֵי בֶּן כּוֹזִיבָא וְהוֹלִידוּ בָּנִים וּבָנוֹת, שֶׁנֶּאֱמַר °"הִמּוֹל יִמּוֹל" אֲפִי' מֵאָה פְּעָמִים, בראשית יז שם וְאוֹמֵר °"אֶת בְּרִיתִי הֵפַר" לְרַבּוֹת אֶת הַמָּשׁוּךְ. מַאי "וְאוֹמֵר"? וְכִי תֵּימָא, הַאי "הִמּוֹל יִמּוֹל" לְרַבּוֹת צִיצִין הַמְעַכְּבִים אֶת הַמִּילָה, ת"ש: "אֶת בְּרִיתִי הֵפַר" לְרַבּוֹת אֶת הַמָּשׁוּךְ. הוּא סָבַר: מִדְּקָא נָסֵיב לָהּ תַּלְמוּדָא קְרָא דְּאוֹרַיְיתָא הִיא, וְלָא הִיא, מִדְּרַבָּנַן, וּקְרָא אַסְמַכְתָּא בְּעָלְמָא. מֵיתִיבֵי: *[ג]טוּמְטוּם אֵין אוֹכֵל בִּתְרוּמָה, נָשָׁיו [ד]וַעֲבָדָיו אוֹכְלִין. מָשׁוּךְ, [ה]וְנוֹלַד כְּשֶׁהוּא מָהוּל, הֲרֵי אֵלּוּ אוֹכְלִים. אַנְדְּרוֹגִינוֹס [ו]אוֹכֵל בִּתְרוּמָה [ז]וְאֵין אוֹכֵל בְּקָדָשִׁים, טוּמְטוּם אֵינוֹ אוֹכֵל לֹא בִּתְרוּמָה [ח]וְלֹא בְּקָדָשִׁים. קָתָנֵי מִיהַת: מָשׁוּךְ, וְנוֹלַד כְּשֶׁהוּא מָהוּל — הֲרֵי אֵלּוּ אוֹכְלִין, תְּיוּבְתָּא דְּרַב הוּנָא! תְּיוּבְתָּא. אָמַר מָר: טוּמְטוּם אֵינוֹ אוֹכֵל בִּתְרוּמָה, נָשָׁיו וַעֲבָדָיו אוֹכְלִים. נָשָׁיו לְטוּמְטוּם מְנָא לֵיהּ? אִילֵימָא דְּקָדֵישׁ, דְּתַנְיָא: *[ט]טוּמְטוּם שֶׁקִּידֵּשׁ קִדּוּשָׁיו קִדּוּשִׁין, נִתְקַדֵּשׁ קִדּוּשָׁיו קִדּוּשִׁין? אֵימַר דְּאָמַר — לְחוּמְרָא, לְקוּלָּא מִי אָמְרִינַן? סָפֵק אִשָּׁה הוּא, וְאֵין אִשָּׁה מְקַדֶּשֶׁת אִשָּׁה! אָמַר אַבַּיֵי: *כְּשֶׁבֵּיצָיו נִיכָּרוֹת מִבַּחוּץ. רָבָא אָמַר: מַאי נָשָׁיו — [י]אִמּוֹ. אִמּוֹ, פְּשִׁיטָא! מַהוּ דְּתֵימָא: מוֹלִיד מַאֲכִיל, שֶׁאֵין מוֹלִיד אֵינוֹ מַאֲכִיל, קמ"ל. ת"ש: טוּמְטוּם אֵינוֹ אוֹכֵל לֹא בִּתְרוּמָה וְלֹא בְּקָדָשִׁים. בִּשְׁלָמָא לְאַבַּיֵי — תָּנָא רֵישָׁא עָרֵל וַדַּאי, וְקָתָנֵי סֵיפָא סָפֵק עָרֵל. אֶלָּא לְרָבָא, טוּמְטוּם דְּסֵיפָא ל"ל? מַאי טוּמְטוּם — עָרֵל. הַשְׁתָּא סָפֵק עָרֵל לָא אָכֵיל, וַדַּאי עָרֵל אָכֵיל?! מַה טַּעַם קָאָמַר. מַה טַּעַם טוּמְטוּם אֵינוֹ אוֹכֵל בִּתְרוּמָה — מִפְּנֵי שֶׁסָּפֵק עָרֵל הוּא, וְעָרֵל אֵינוֹ אוֹכֵל לֹא בִּתְרוּמָה וְלֹא בְּקָדָשִׁים. לֵימָא כְּתַנָּאֵי: *מָשׁוּךְ, (וְנוֹלַד כְּשֶׁהוּא מָהוּל,) וְגֵר שֶׁנִּתְגַּיֵּיר כְּשֶׁהוּא מָהוּל, וְקָטָן שֶׁעָבַר זְמַנּוֹ, וּשְׁאָר כָּל הַנִּימּוֹלִים, לְאִיתּוּיֵי מִי שֶׁיֵּשׁ לוֹ שְׁתֵּי עָרְלוֹת — [כ]אֵינָן נִימּוֹלִין אֶלָּא בַּיּוֹם. רַבִּי אֶלְעָזָר בַּר שִׁמְעוֹן אוֹמֵר: בִּזְמַנּוֹ רס"ל מ"ז

אֵין

רש"י

רוּחַ צְפוֹנִית. נוֹחָה, לֹא חַמָּה וְלֹא צוֹנֶנֶת, וְחַמָּה זוֹרַחַת. לֹא נָשְׁבָה לָהֶם רוּחַ צְפוֹנִית. בַּיּוֹם, וְלֹא זָרְחָה חַמָּה עֲלֵיהֶם. אִיבָּעֵית אֵימָא מִשּׁוּם דִּנְזוּפִים הָיוּ. מִמַּעֲשֵׂה הָעֵגֶל, וְלֹא הָיוּ רְאוּיִין לְאוֹר נוֹגַהּ. וְאִיבָּעֵית אֵימָא. מִשּׁוּם הָכִי לֹא נָשְׁבָה, כִּי הֵיכִי דְּלָא נִיבַּדְרוּ עַנְנֵי כָבוֹד שֶׁהָיוּ מַקִּיפִין, וְלֹא הָיְתָה חַמָּה יְכוֹלָה לִיכָּנֵס. יוֹמָא דְּעֵיבָא. יוֹם הַמְעוּנָּן. יוֹמָא דְּשׁוּתָא. (א) שֶׁרוּחַ דְּרוֹמִית מְנַשֶּׁבֶת. וְהִיא קָשָׁה מִכָּל הָרוּחוֹת. עֵת רָצוֹן מִילְּתָא הִיא. וְכֵיוָן דַּחֲצוֹת הַלַּיְלָה עֵת רָצוֹן הֲוַאי לְמַכַּת בְּכוֹרוֹת — הֲוַאי נַמִּי עֵת רָצוֹן לְרוּחַ צְפוֹנִית. וְאֵין לְךָ יוֹם שֶׁרוּחַ צְפוֹנִית אֵין מְנַשֶּׁבֶת בּוֹ בַּחֲצִי הַלַּיְלָה וְזֶה הָיָה סִימָן לְדָוִד כִּנּוֹר תָּלוּי לוֹ לְמַעְלָה מִמִּטָּתוֹ וְנִקְבַּע כְּלַפֵּי צָפוֹן, כֵּיוָן שֶׁהִגִּיעַ חֲצוֹת לַיְלָה רוּחַ צְפוֹנִית מְנַשֶּׁבֶת בּוֹ וּמְנַגֵּן מֵאֵלָיו וְהוּא נֵעוֹר. וְהַאי דְּנָקַט הָכָא אַרְבָּעִים שָׁנָה — לוֹמַר לְךָ, שֶׁאֲפִילּוּ אוֹתָן מ' שָׁנָה דִּנְזוּפִים הָיוּ וְלֹא נָשְׁבָה לְהוּ בַּיָּמִים — נָשְׁבָה לְהוּ בַּחֲצוֹת לַיְלָה, מִשּׁוּם דְּעֵת רָצוֹן הוּא. מָשׁוּךְ. מָהוּל שֶׁנִּמְשְׁכָה עָרְלָתוֹ וְכִסְּתָה אֶת הָעֲטָרָה. הָא צָרִיךְ קָתָנֵי. מִדְּרַבָּנַן, מִדְּלָא קָתָנֵי: מָשׁוּךְ הֲרֵי זֶה עָרֵל. שֶׁסַּכָּנָה הִיא לוֹ. שֶׁמָּא יֵעָשֶׂה כְּרוּת שָׁפְכָה. בִּימֵי בֶּן כּוֹזִיבָא. שֶׁמְּשָׁכוּם גּוֹיִם בְּאוֹנֶס בְּכְרַךְ בֵּיתָר, וְגָבְרָה יַד בֶּן כּוֹזִיבָא וְנִלְחַם בָּהֶם וְנִלְכְּדוּ, וּמָלַךְ עַל יִשְׂרָאֵל שְׁתֵּי שָׁנִים וּמֶחֱצָה. וְחָזְרוּ וּמָלוּ בְּיָמָיו. הוּא סָבַר. הַהוּא דְּאוֹתִיב לְעֵיל לְרַב הוּנָא מֵרֵישָׁא, סָבַר: מִדְּנָסְבֵי לָהּ רַבָּנַן לִימּוּדָא לְמִילְּתַיְיהוּ מִדְּאוֹרַיְיתָא — אַלְמָא מִדְּאוֹרַיְיתָא הוּא: ה"ג. מֵיתִיבֵי טוּמְטוּם אֵינוֹ אוֹכֵל בִּתְרוּמָה כו'. וּבְסֵיפָא גָּרַס: קָתָנֵי מִיהָא מָשׁוּךְ תְּיוּבְתָּא דְּרַב הוּנָא תְּיוּבְתָּא. טוּמְטוּם אֵינוֹ אוֹכֵל בִּתְרוּמָה. שֶׁמָּא אִם הָיָה נִקְרָע יִמָּצֵא זָכָר, וַהֲרֵי הוּא עָרֵל. נָשָׁיו וַעֲבָדָיו. לְקַמָּן מְפָרֵשׁ נָשִׁים לְטוּמְטוּם מְנָא לֵיהּ. אַנְדְּרוֹגִינוֹס. מָהוּל, מוּתָּר לֶאֱכוֹל בִּתְרוּמָה מִמָּה נַפְשָׁךְ, בֵּין שֶׁהוּא אִישׁ בֵּין שֶׁהוּא אִשָּׁה, בֵּין שֶׁהוּא בְּרִיָּה בִּפְנֵי עַצְמָהּ — זַרְעוֹ שֶׁל כֹּהֵן הוּא. וְאֵין אוֹכֵל בְּקָדָשִׁים. בְּקָדְשֵׁי קָדָשִׁים קָמַיְירֵי, כְּגוֹן חַטָּאת וְאָשָׁם וּשְׁיָרֵי מְנָחוֹת, שֶׁאֵין נֶאֱכָלִין אֶלָּא לְזִכְרֵי כְהוּנָּה, וְזֶה סָפֵק אִשָּׁה הוּא. טוּמְטוּם אֵינוֹ אוֹכֵל. לְקַמָּן מְפָרֵשׁ אַמַּאי הֲדַר נָקַט לֵיהּ. קָתָנֵי מִיהַת מָשׁוּךְ אוֹכֵל. אַלְמָא לָא גְּזוּר עֲלֵיהּ. תְּיוּבְתָּא דְּרַב הוּנָא דְּאָמַר מִדִּבְרֵיהֶן גָּזְרוּ עָלָיו — תְּיוּבְתָּא. לִישָּׁנָא אַחֲרִינָא גָּרְסִי' (ב): [לֵימָא] מְסַיֵּיעַ לֵיהּ [לְרַב הוּנָא] טוּמְטוּם אֵינוֹ אוֹכֵל כו' וְהַאי אוֹכְלִין דְּמָשׁוּךְ וְנוֹלַד מָהוּל — מִדְּאוֹרַיְיתָא קָאָמַר, וְסִיַּיעְתָּא דְּרַב הוּנָא. וְזוֹ שָׁמַעְתִּי, וְהִיא נִרְאֵית עִיקָּר, מִדְּקָאָמְרִינַן לְקַמָּן לֵימָא כְּתַנָּאֵי כו', מַאי לָאו בְּהָא קָא מִיפַּלְגֵי דְּמַר סָבַר דְּאוֹרַיְיתָא וּמַר סָבַר דְּרַבָּנַן, אַלְמָא לֵיכָּא לְמַאן דְּמַכְשִׁיר לְגַמְרֵי. אִי נֵימָא דְּקָדֵישׁ. שֶׁקִּידֵּשׁ אִשָּׁה, וְשֶׁמָּא זָכָר הוּא וְקִדּוּשָׁיו קִדּוּשִׁין. דְּהָא תַּנְיָא: טוּמְטוּם שֶׁקִּידֵּשׁ — קִדּוּשָׁיו קִדּוּשִׁין מִסָּפֵק, וּצְרִיכָה גֵּט. נִתְקַדֵּשׁ קִדּוּשָׁיו קִדּוּשִׁין. וְנָפְקָא מִינַּהּ לְאִיתְסוּרֵי הַאי דְּקַדְּשֵׁיהּ בַּאֲחוֹתוֹ שֶׁל טוּמְטוּם וּבְאִמּוֹ, שֶׁמָּא אִשָּׁה הוּא. לְחוּמְרָא. דְּבָעֵינַן גֵּט מִינֵּיהּ. לְקוּלָּא מִי אָמְרִי'. דְּנִיחַזְקֵיהּ כְּזָכָר וַדַּאי, וְיַאֲכִיל בַּת יִשְׂרָאֵל בִּתְרוּמָה. מוֹלִיד מַאֲכִיל. אֶת אִמּוֹ בִּתְרוּמָה, דְּדָיְיקִינַן לַהּ "וִילִיד בֵּיתוֹ" (ויקרא כב) בְּרָאוּי לְהוֹלִיד, קָמַשְׁמַע לָן. מַאי טוּמְטוּם. דְּקָתָנֵי בְּסֵיפָא עָרֵל גָּמוּר. מַה טַּעַם קָאָמַר. סֵיפָא לְפָרוּשֵׁי רֵישָׁא אָתָא, וְהָכִי קָאָמַר: מַה טַּעַם טוּמְטוּם אֵין אוֹכֵל — מִפְּנֵי שֶׁהוּא סָפֵק עָרֵל, וְעָרֵל אֵין אוֹכֵל לֹא בִּתְרוּמָה וְלֹא בְּקָדָשִׁים. נֵימָא כְּתַנָּאֵי. מִילְּתָא דְּרַב הוּנָא תַּנָּאֵי הִיא, אִי הָוֵי מָשׁוּךְ דְּאוֹרַיְיתָא אוֹ דְּרַבָּנַן: (וְנוֹלַד כְּשֶׁהוּא מָהוּל. שֶׁצָּרִיךְ לְהַטִּיף מִמֶּנּוּ דַּם בְּרִית). רס"ל מ"ז וְגֵר שֶׁנִּתְגַּיֵּיר כְּשֶׁהוּא מָהוּל. כְּגוֹן עַרְבִי וְגִבְעוֹנִי שֶׁנִּתְגַּיְּירוּ, וְצָרִיךְ לְהַטִּיף מִמֶּנּוּ דַּם בְּרִית. שְׁתֵּי עָרְלוֹת. ב' עוֹרוֹת זוֹ עַל גַּבֵּי זוֹ* [ועי' רש"י שבת קלה]

מַר

תוספות

משום דלא נשיב להו רוח צפונית. בספרי אומר דבגונתן של ישראל סיפר הכתוב, שלא עשו אלא פסח אחד במ' שנה שהיו במדבר. שלא מלינו שעשו פסח אלא בשנה שניה. ותימה: וכי במזיד היו נמנעים? ואי משום מילת זכרים שהיו מעכבים, וחשיב גנות לפי שגרמו הם דבר זה, והא כיון דלא אפשר — לא היתה מעכבת, כדאמר לעיל (דף עא.) "המול לו" אמר רחמנא "ואז יקרב" וגו'. ואמר רבינו יצחק: דעשו פסחים, אבל לא עשו כתקנן אלא אחד*. **לא** נשבה להם רוח צפונית. פי': בפני עצמה. אבל אין לפרש דלא נשבה כלל, דהא אמר בסוף "כל הגט" (גיטין דף לא: ושם) ד' רוחות מנשבות בכל יום, ורוח צפונית מנשבת עם כולן, שאלמלא כן אין העולם מתקיים. **נזופין** היו. אמר רבינו יצחק: ממעשה מרגלים, ולא כמו שפירש בקונטרס ממעשה העגל, שהרי מחל להם הקב"ה ואמר להם "סלחתי", שאחר כך נעשה משכן והשרה שכינתו ביניהם. **דלא** ניבדור ענני כבוד. לא משום דתקיפה, דנוחה היא, וטובה לנחבלים. אלא שמפזרת העננים, והעת יפה, כדאמר (מגילה דף כח:) בעיא שמעתתא צילותא כיומא דאסתנא וכתיב נמי (איוב לז) "מצפון זהב יאתה", זהב — לשון אורה, כמו "המריקין זהב" (זכריה ד), וכן פירש מנחם, ואף לפי המדרש כן הוא, דדרשינן (ב"ב דף כה:) שמזלת הזהב, לפי שמפזרת את העננים והגשמים נעצרים והתבואה ביוקר, ולכן הזהב בזול. **ומדבריהם** גזרו עליהם. והא דאמר ב"נגמר הדין" (סנהדרין דף מד.) עכן משוך בערלתו היה, ומפיק ליה מקרא — אסמכתא בעלמא היא, והא דאמר בפרק קמא דשבועות (דף יג.) דמשוך ערלה נכרת — היינו שלא מל כלל. **מיתיבי** כו'. דמשוך אוכל בתרומה אע"ג דצריך שימול מדרבנן מפני שנראה כערל — לא אסרוהו בתרומה. ולפי הספרים דגרסי לימא מסייע ליה, צ"ל דמשמע ליה אוכל מן התורה, אבל מדרבנן — אסור, כדמוכח *[ברייתא], דקתני: צריך שימול. **מבחוץ** וא"ת: אכתי היאך מאכיל את אשתו? דכיון דאינו בן ביאה — לא הוי חופתו חופה, כמו פסותה מבת ג' לעיל בפרק "הבא על יבמתו" (דף נז:)! וי"ל: דכיון דראוי לקרוע — הוי בר חופה.

אין

עין משפט נר מצוה

יט א ב מיי' פ"ז מהל' תרומות הלכה י טוש"ע סימן שלא:
כ ג מיי' שם הלכה יא:
כא ד מיי' שם הלכה יב:
כב ה ו מיי' שם הלכה יא:
[ועי' תוס' קדושין לז: ד"ה הואיל]
כג ז ח מיי' פ"י מהלכות מעשה קרבן הלכה ט:
כד ט מיי' פ"ד מהלכות אישות הלכה יא סמג עשין מח טוש"ע אה"ע סימן מד סעיף ה:
כה י מיי' פ"ז מהלכות תרומות הלכה יב טוש"ע סימן שלא.
כו כ מיי' פ"א מהל' מילה הלכה ח סמג עשין כח טוש"ע י"ד סי' רסב סעיף א:

תוספות ישנים

השתא ספק ערל לא אכיל ודאי ערל מיבעיא. וא"ת ולימא דרישא מיירי בודאי ערל וסיפא מיירי טומטום ממש דהיינו ספק ערל וי"ל דא"א לומר דרישא בערל ודאי דא"כ לא הוה קרי ליה טומטום דא"ל דאגב סיפא נקטיה שאין דרך למתני רישא אגב סיפא אבל סיפא מצי לאוקומי בודאי ערל והאי דנקט טומטום אגב רישא נקטיה א) דמיירי בטומטום ממשנתא סיפא טומטום אע"ג דטומטום הוי ערל ודאי:

א) נראה דצ"ל דמיירי בטומטום סתמא נקט בסיפא נמי בטומטום אע"ג דטומטום היינו ערל וודאי.

כ"ה בדפו"י

מסורת הש"ס

[גירסת הערוך מסוברינן ועי' במס' ע"ז כט. תלת לסכורי]
[ברכות ח. תענית כב:]
[תוספתא דשבת פט"ז]
[ע' פרש"י בכתובות לו. ד"ה ודקארי]
[תוספתא פ"י]
[תוס' פי"א] בכורות מב:
[חגיגה ז.]
[תוס' דשבת פט"ז]

הגהות הב"ח

(א) רש"י ד"ה יומא דשותא יום שרוח: (ב) ד"ה קתני מיהת וכו' לישנא אחרינא גרסי' תניא דמסייעא ליה לרב הונא טומטום:

עין משפט נר מצוה

אין נימולין אלא ביום, שלא בזמנו — נימולין ביום ובלילה. מאי לאו בהא קמיפלגי, דמר סבר: משוך דאורייתא, ומר סבר: משוך דרבנן. ותסברא? קטן שעבר זמנו מי איכא למ"ד דרבנן?! אלא, דכולי עלמא: משוך דרבנן, וקטן שעבר זמנו דאורייתא, והכא בהא קמיפלגי, מר סבר: דרשינן "וביום", ומר סבר: לא דרשינן "וביום". כי הא דיתיב רבי יוחנן, וקדריש: נותר, בזמנו — אינו נשרף אלא ביום, שלא בזמנו — נשרף בין ביום בין בלילה, [א]ואיתיביה רבי אלעזר לרבי יוחנן: אין לי אלא נימול לשמיני שאין נימול אלא ביום, מנין לרבות לתשעה, לעשרה, לאחד עשר, לשנים עשר (מנין) — תלמוד לומר: "וביום". ואפילו למאן דלא *דריש וא"ו וא"ו וה"י דריש! אישתיק. בתר דנפק א"ל רבי יוחנן לר"ל: ראיתי לבן פדת שיושב ודורש כמשה מפי הגבורה. א"ל ר"ל: דידיה היא? מתניתא היא! היכא תנא ליה? בתורת כהנים. נפק, תנייה בתלתא יומי, וסברה בתלתא ירחי. אמר רבי אלעזר: [ב]ערל *שהזה — הזאתו כשרה, מידי דהוה אטבול יום, שאע"פ [ג]שאסור בתרומה [ד]כשר בפרה. מה לטבול יום — שכן [ה]מותר במעשר! אטו אנן לאכילה קאמרינן? אנן לנגיעה קאמרינן: ומה טבול יום שאסור בנגיעה דתרומה — מותר בפרה, ערל שמותר בנגיעה — אינו דין שמותר בפרה. תניא נמי הכי: ערל שהזה הזאתו כשרה. ומעשה היה והכשירו חכמים הזאתו. מיתיבי: *טומטום שקידש — קידושו פסול, מפני שהוא ספק ערל, וערל פסול לקדש. ואנדרוגינוס שקידש — קידושו כשר, רבי יהודה אומר: אף אנדרוגינוס שקידש — קידושיו פסולים, מפני שספק אשה, ואשה פסולה מלקדש. קתני מיהא: ערל וספק ערל פסול מלקדש! אמר רב יוסף: האי תנא — תנא דבי רבי עקיבא הוא, *דמרבי ליה לערל כטמא, דתניא: *ר"ע אומר: °"איש איש" — לרבות הערל. אמר רבא: הוה יתיבנא קמיה דרב יוסף, וקשיא לי: לא לישתמיט תנא וליתני "הערל והטמא" ולימא ר' עקיבא היא? ולא? והא קתני: *הערל והטמא פטורים מן הראיה! התם משום דמאיס. ואזדו לטעמייהו, דתניא: [ו]הכל *כשרים לקדש, חוץ מחרש שוטה וקטן, רבי יהודה מכשיר בקטן ופוסל באשה ובאנדרוגינוס. מאי טעמא דרבנן — דכתיב °"ולקחו לטמא מעפר שריפת החטאת" הנך דפסלי באסיפה — פסולין בקידוש, הנך דכשרין באסיפה — כשרים בקידוש. ורבי יהודה אמר לך: א"כ נימא (א) קרא "ולקח" מאי "ולקחו" דאפי' הנך דפסולין התם, כשרים הכא. אי הכי אשה נמי! "ונתן", ולא "ונתנה". ורבנן, אי כתיב "ולקח, ונתן" הוה אמינא שקיל חד ויהיב חד, [ז]כתב רחמנא "ולקחו". ואי כתב רחמנא "ולקחו ונתנו" — ה"א: דשקלי תרי ויהבי תרי, כתב רחמנא "ולקחו ונתן" דאפי' שקלי תרי ויהיב חד.

והזה

תורה אור

מר סבר דדרשינן וביום. וי"ו יתירא, דמצי למכתב "ביום השמיני ימול", וכתיב (ויקרא יב) "וביום" – לאיתויי מילה שלא בזמנה. ואע"ג דמשוך מהכא לא מיתרבי, דהא מדרבנן הוא, ובתר הכי תקון – כיון דקטן שעברה זמנו מתרבי, ואע"ג דשלא בזמנו הוא – האי נמי תקינוה רבנן כעין דאורייתא. ומר סבר לא דרשינן וביום. ולא גמרינן מיניה קטן שעברה זמנו, ונימול אפי' בלילה, וכ"ש משוך, דמדרבנן הוא. כי הא דתניא. בתיובתא דאותביה ר' אלעזר לרבי יוחנן, דקטן שעברה זמנו מ"וביום השמיני" איתרבי, דאינו נימול אלא ביום. נותר בזמנו. ביום שנעשה נותר אין נשרף אלא ביום דכתיב (ויקרא ז) "ביום השלישי". שלא בזמנו. ששהה שריפתו. לתשעה לעשרה לי"א לי"ב. כדקתני בפ' "ר' אליעזר" במסכת שבת (דף קלז.): נולד בין השמשות – נימול לתשעה, בין השמשות של ע"ש – נימול לעשרה, חל יו"ט לאחר השבת – נימול לי"א, שני יו"ט של ר"ה – נימול לי"ב. ואפילו למאן דלא דריש וי"ו. כגון ר' אלעזר ברבי שמעון, דאמר לעיל שלא בזמנו נימול אפילו בלילה. וי"ו וה"א. כגון "והנותר", איכא ו"ה יתירא. ראיתי לבן פדת. ראיתי את בן פדת שיושב ודורש את מקראות הללו כמשה מפי הגבורה – בלשון תנאים. רבי אלעזר בן פדת לאו תנא היה, ואמורא היה, תלמידו של רבי יוחנן, והוא רבי אלעזר סתם דמיירי בכל הש"ס בגמ'. ורבי אלעזר סתמא דמשנה וברייתא, הוא רבי אלעזר בן שמוע. תנייה. לתורת כהנים. טבול יום אסור בתרומה. לקמן בהאי פירקא (דף עד:) קראי דרשינן. ומותר להזאה. להזות על טמא מת, כדאמר לקמן בשמעתין: לימד על טבול יום שכשר בפרה. אנן באכילה קאמרינן. בתמיה, וכי אנן לאכילה דפרה אדומה קמרבינן ליה, דתיפרוך: תאמר בערל שאסור באכילת מעשר, לפיכך אסור בפרה? לנגיעה. בעלמא קשרינן ליה! ובנגיעה ליכא לאקשויי: תאמר בערל שאסור בנגיעת מעשר – דהא אפילו בנגיעת קדשים מותר, והכי דרשינן: ומה טבול יום שאסור בנגיעה דתרומה, כדגמרי' לקמן (דף עה.) מ"במים יובא וטמא עד הערב", והכא נגיעה היא, דבכלי משתעי קרא, וקאמר דבעי הערב שמש. מותר בהזאה. דפרה: ערל שמותר כו'. שקידש. שעירב אפר במים. אנדרוגינוס. מהול, שקידש – קידושו כשר, שאפי' אשה כשרה לקדש לרבנן. ולקמן ילפינן טעמייהו. רבי עקיבא. בריש פירקין (דף ע.). איש איש מזרע אהרן וגו'. מדרבי לערל גבי טמאים, שמע מינה דכי הדדי נינהו, ואפילו לנגיעה דתרומה אסור. לא לישתמיט. אם איתא דר' עקיבא לכל מילי ערל כטמא משוי ליה – לא לישתמיט תנא בעלמא דליתני לענין מגע טומאות הערל והטמא כי הדדי, ונימא ר"ע היא. מדלא אשכחן הכי(ב) – הכא משום חומרא דפרה היא, אבל לענין מגע תרומה – ערל מותר. דמאים. ליראות בעזרה. ואזדו לטעמייהו. ר' יהודה ורבנן, דאיפליגו לעיל באנדרוגינוס. הכל כשרים. כל הטהורים כשרין לקדש מי חטאת, אפי' אשה. אבל ערל וטמא – לא רבי. ולקחו לטמא. בתר אסיפת אפרה כתיב הך עבודה דקידוש, ואין עבודה מפסקת ביניהם. הנך דפסולים באסיפה פסולים לקידוש. והתם (יומא דף מג.) דרשינן "ואסף איש" – ולא קטן, "טהור" – להכשיר את האשה. וליכא למדרש איפכא, "איש" – ולא אשה, "טהור" – ואפי' קטן, דאמר בפרק "טרף בקלפי" (שם דף מג:): כל הפרשה כולה משמע מוציא מיד משמע,(ג) וע"כ סוגיא* דשמעתתא הכי איתא התם. אם כן. דההוא אסיפה נקט לגבי מקדש – לכתוב "ולקח לטמא", כי היכי דכתב באסיפה "ואסף", לשון יחיד. אפילו הנך דפסולין התם. כגון קטן. דשקיל חד. אפרא, ויהיב חד מים.

הטהור

אין נימול אלא ביום. הקשה הר"ר אפריס – דלמאי איצטריך פ"ק דקידושין (דף כט. ושם) "אותו" ולא אותה דאשה לא מחייבא למול את בנה, תיפוק לי דהוי מצות עשה שהזמן גרמא: ביום ולא בלילה, דמהאי טעמא פטרינן אשה מציצית? וי"ל: דלר' אלעזר ברבי שמעון איצטריך. והא דנימול לשמונה – לא חשיב זמן גרמא, כיון דמשמונה ואילך כל שעתא זמנו הוא*.

מר סבר דרשינן וביום. אע"ג דמדכתיב "ח' ימי"ם דרשינן (שבת דף קלב.) ולא לילות, "וביום" דרשינן (שם): אפילו בשבת – מ"מ שפיר דריש מוי"ו ד"וביום" לרבויי כל הני דאין נימולים אלא ביום..

שלא בזמנו נשרף בין ביום בין בלילה. וא"ת: הא (ד) דרשי' *ליתן בקר שני על שריפתו, וכיון דשלא בזמנו הוא – למה צריך להמתין עד הבקר? ישרפנו במוצאי יו"ט, דכבר נעשה נותר מקודם! ויש לומר: דכיון דלא אפשר לשורפו ביו"ט – קבע זמנו בבקר שני. שהזה כו'. איצטריך לאשמועינן דהזאה כשרה אע"ג דאסור בתרומה וקדשים כי טמא. שמותר בנגיעה דתרומה אינו דין שמותר בפרה. וא"ת: מחוסר כפרה יוכיח, שמותר בתרומה ואסור בפרה! וי"ל: דמה למחוסר כפרה – שכן אסור בנגיעת קדשים. ואיכא למיעבד ק"ו מתרוייהו: מה טבול יום שאסור בנגיעת תרומה וקדשים – מותר בפרה, ערל שמותר בנגיעת תרומה וקדשים כו', דתו ליכא מחוסר כפרה יוכיח. התם משום דמאיס. ואפי' רבנן מודו התם דפטור. ואם תאמר: בפ"ק דחגיגה (דף ד. ושם) למה לן "זכורך" למעוטי טומטום ואנדרוגינוס כשביליו מבחוץ? תיפוק לי דערל הוא, דפטור! וי"ל: דטומטום, כיון דלא אפשר למול – לא מאיס, ולא מיפטר מטעם ערל. א"נ, ה"פ: התם משום דמאיס, וחשיב התם לר' עקיבא ערל כי טמא. אבל לרבנן – לא. ולרבנן איצטריך "זכורך" למעוטי טומטום. חוץ מחש"ו. פי' הקונט' דדרשינן "ואסף איש" – ולא קטן. ואי אפשר לומר כן, דבפרק "טרף בקלפי" (יומא דף מג. ושם) דריש בהדיא: "איש" – להכשיר זר, "טהור" – להכשיר האשה, "והניח" – מי שיש בו דעת להניח, פרט לחש"ו. הנך דפסולים התם כשרים הכא. ומכשיר טפי בקטן, משום דאתי לכלל איש: דשקיל חד ויהיב חד. פי': אותו שנותן האפר בתוך מי חטאת – הוא עצמו יערב המים והאפר יחד. ונתן ולא ונתנה. קרא יתירא קדריש, ולא דריש מדכתב "ונתן" ולא ונתנה, שהרי כל התורה בלשון זכר נאמרה.

לימד

כז א מיי' פי"ט מהלכות פסולי המוקדשין הלכה ד ה:
כח ב מיי' פ"י מהלכות פרה אדומה הלכ' ו:
כט ג מיי' פ"ז מהלכות תרומות הלכה ב טוי"ד סימן שלה:
ל ד מיי' פ"א מהלכות פרה אדומה הלכה יג:
לא ה מיי' פ"ג מהלכות מעשר שני הלכה ד:
לב ו מיי' פ"ו מהלכות פרה אדומה הלכה ב סמג עשין רלב:
לג ז מיי' פ"י שם הלכה ו סמג עשין רלג:

[וע"ע תוס' מגילה כ. ד"ה דכתיב]

[שבת כד:]

הגהות הב"ח

(א) גמ' א"כ נימא בהאי קרא ולקח: (ב) רש"י ד"ה לא לישתמיט וכו' מדלא אשכחן הכי שמע מינה הכא משום: (ג) ד"ה הנך דפסולים וכו' מיד משמע וכולה סוגיא דפרשתא הכי איתא התם. נ"ב וע"ש בפרש"י דף מ"ג על איש טהור דכתיב גבי הזאה דצריך למדרש מעין היפוך הדרשה דכתוב הקודם כדי להיות משמע מוציא מיד משמע דאל"כ לישתוק מיניה ע"ש וה"ה הכא: (ד) תום' ד"ה שלא וכו' הא דדרשי':

מסורת הש"ס

[לעיל סח: וש"נ]

ערכין ג.

[תוספתא דפרה פ"ד]

חגיגה ד:
[לעיל ע. לקמן עד.]

[חגיגה שם]

שבת קלז. יומא מג. ערכין ג. פרה פ"ה מ"ד

דפרשתא רש"ל ס"א

ויקרא כב

במדבר יט

במדבר יט

תורה אור

"וְהִזָּה הַטָּהֹר עַל הַטָּמֵא", *טָהוֹר — מִכְּלָל שֶׁהוּא טָמֵא, [א]לִימֵּד עַל טְבוּל יוֹם שֶׁכָּשֵׁר בְּפָרָה. בָּעוּ מִינֵּיהּ מֵרַב שֵׁשֶׁת: עָרֵל מַהוּ בְּמַעֲשֵׂר? כִּי הֵיכִי דְּיָלֵיף פֶּסַח מִמַּעֲשֵׂר לְעִנְיַן אֲנִינוּת — [ב]יָלֵיף נַמִּי מַעֲשֵׂר מִפֶּסַח לְעִנְיַן עֲרֵלוּת, אוֹ דִּלְמָא: חָמוּר מִקַּל יָלֵיף, קַל מֵחָמוּר — לָא יָלֵיף? אֲמַר לְהוּ: תְּנֵיתוּהָ. *[ג]הַתְּרוּמָה וְהַבִּכּוּרִים חַיָּיבִים עֲלֵיהֶן מִיתָה וְחוֹמֶשׁ וַאֲסוּרִין לְזָרִים, וְהֵן נִכְסֵי כֹהֵן, וְעוֹלִין בְּאֶחָד וּמֵאָה, וּטְעוּנִין רְחִיצַת יָדַיִם וְהֶעֱרֵב שֶׁמֶשׁ, הֲרֵי אֵלּוּ בִּתְרוּמָה וּבְבִכּוּרִים, מַה שֶּׁאֵין כֵּן בְּמַעֲשֵׂר. וְאִם אִיתָא — נִיתְנֵי: עָרֵל אָסוּר בָּהֶן, מַה שֶּׁאֵין כֵּן בְּמַעֲשֵׂר! *תָּנָא וְשִׁיֵּיר! וּמַאי שִׁיֵּיר דְּהַאי שִׁיֵּיר? שִׁיֵּיר דְּקָא תָּנֵי סֵיפָא: *יֵשׁ בְּמַעֲשֵׂר וּבְבִכּוּרִים מַה שֶּׁאֵין כֵּן בִּתְרוּמָה: [ד]שֶׁהַמַּעֲשֵׂר [ה]וְהַבִּכּוּרִים טְעוּנִין הֲבָאַת מָקוֹם, [ו]וּטְעוּנִין וִידּוּי, *[ז]וְאָסוּר לְאוֹנֵן, וְרַבִּי שִׁמְעוֹן מַתִּיר. [ח]וְחַיָּיבִין בְּבִיעוּר, וְר"ש פּוֹטֵר. וְאִילּוּ [ט]אָסוּר לְבַעֵר מֵהֶן בְּטוּמְאָה וְאוֹכְלָן

הַטָּהוֹר. שֶׁטִּהַרְתִּי לְךָ כָּאן – מִכְּלָל שֶׁהוּא טָמֵא לְדָבָר אַחֵר, כְּגוֹן טְבוּל יוֹם שֶׁטָּמֵא לִתְרוּמָה. דְּאִי ס"ד טָהוֹר מַמָּשׁ – לִישְׁתּוֹק קְרָא מִינֵּיהּ, וַאֲנָא יָדַעְנָא דְּטָמֵא אָסוּר בְּפָרָה, דְּהָא חַטָּאת קָרְיֵיהּ רַחֲמָנָא. אֶלָּא מַאי טָהוֹר – טָהוֹר כָּל דְּהוּ. וְאַשְׁכַּחַן טְבוּל יוֹם דְּמִיקְּרֵי טָהוֹר, דִּכְתִיב (ויקרא יד) "וְרָחַץ בַּמַּיִם וְטָהֵר". אֲנִינוּת. גַּבֵּי מַעֲשֵׂר כְּתִיב, וְלֹא בְּפֶסַח, וּמִינֵּיהּ יָלְפִינַן. מִיתָה. טָמֵא הָאוֹכְלָהּ, כִּדְכְתִיב (שם כב) "וּמֵתוּ בוֹ כִּי יְחַלְּלֻהוּ". וּבִכּוּרִים כִּתְרוּמָה, דְּאָמַר מָר (מכות יז.) "וּתְרוּמַת יָדֶךָ" – אֵלּוּ הַבִּכּוּרִים. וְחוֹמֶשׁ. זָר הָאוֹכְלָן בְּשׁוֹגֵג, אֲבָל בְּמַעֲשֵׂר שֵׁנִי – לֹא, דְּהָא זָרִים אָכְלִי לֵיהּ, וְאֵין חוֹמֶשׁ אֶלָּא בְּפוֹדֶה אֶת מַעַשְׂרוֹ. וְהֵן (הן) נִכְסֵי כֹהֵן. לְקַדֵּשׁ בָּהֵן אֶת הָאִשָּׁה, וְלִיקַּח בָּהֵן עֲבָדִים וְקַרְקָעוֹת וּבְהֵמָה טְמֵאָה. אֲבָל מַעֲשֵׂר לֹא נִיתַּן אֶלָּא לַאֲכִילָה וּשְׁתִיָּה וְסִיכָה, וְאֵין אִשָּׁה מִתְקַדֶּשֶׁת בּוֹ. וּסְתָם מִשְׁנָה ר"מ, דְּאָמַר (ב"ק דף סט:): מַעֲשֵׂר מָמוֹן גָּבוֹהַּ הוּא. וְאע"ג דְּקוּלָּא הוּא לְגַבֵּי תְרוּמָה וּבִכּוּרִים – אפ"ה חָשֵׁיב לֵיהּ. וְהָכִי נַמִּי אָמְרִינַן בְּב"מ פ׳ "הַזָּהָב" (דף נג.) דְּקוּלָּא הוּא. בְּאֶחָד וּמֵאָה. אֲבָל מַעֲשֵׂר בָּטֵל בְּרוֹב וְלָא בָּעֵי אֶחָד וּמֵאָה. וּטְעוּנִין רְחִיצַת יָדַיִם. אֲפִילּוּ הֵן פֵּירוֹת, דִּסְתָם יָדַיִם שְׁנִיּוֹת הֵן מִדְּרַבָּנַן וּפוֹסְלוֹת אֶת הַתְּרוּמָה. אֲבָל מַעֲשֵׂר וְחוּלִּין קי"ל (חולין דף קו.): הַנּוֹטֵל יָדָיו לְפֵירוֹת ה"ז מִגַּסֵּי הָרוּחַ. וְהֶעֱרֵב שֶׁמֶשׁ. כִּדְיָלְפִינַן בְּהַאי פִּירְקָא (לקמן עד:): טְבוּל יוֹם מוּתָּר בְּמַעֲשֵׂר וְאָסוּר בִּתְרוּמָה. וְאִם אִיתָא. דְּקַל מֵחָמוּר לָא יָלֵיף, וּמוּתָּר עָרֵל בְּמַעֲשֵׂר. הֲבָאַת מָקוֹם. אֲבָל תְּרוּמָה נֶאֱכֶלֶת בַּגְּבוּלִין. וּטְעוּנִין וִידּוּי. "בִּעַרְתִּי הַקֹּדֶשׁ מִן הַבַּיִת" (דברים כו), "הִנֵּה הֵבֵאתִי אֶת רֵאשִׁית" בְּבִכּוּרִים. וַאֲסוּרִין לְאוֹנֵן. בִּכּוּרִים. וְר"ש מַתִּיר. בִּכּוּרִים לְאוֹנֵן, וּלְקַמָּן מְפָרֵשׁ טַעֲמַיְיהוּ. וְחַיָּיבִין בְּבִיעוּר. בִּכּוּרִים וּמַעֲשֵׂר שֵׁנִי בַּשָּׁנָה הַשְּׁלִישִׁית, שֶׁאִם שָׁהָה מַעַשְׂרוֹתָיו שָׁנָה רִאשׁוֹנָה וּשְׁנִיָּה – מוֹלִיכָן בַּשְּׁלִישִׁית לִירוּשָׁלַיִם וּמִתְוַדֶּה: בִּעַרְתִּי הַקֹּדֶשׁ מִן הַבַּיִת וכו׳, וְאִם לֹא הוֹלִיכָן – מִתְבַּעֲרִין בְּכָל מָקוֹם שֶׁהֵן. וְר"ש פּוֹטֵר. בְּבִכּוּרִים. וְאִילּוּ אָסוּר לְבַעֵר מֵהֶן בְּטוּמְאָה. לְת"ק דְּמַקִּישׁ בִּכּוּרִים לְמַעֲשֵׂר לְכָל מִילֵּי – ה"ל לְמִיתְנֵי: וְאָסוּר לְהַדְלִיק מֵהֶן אִם נִטְמְאוּ, דְּאֵין טוּמְאָתָן מַתִּירָתָן לְהַבְעָרָה. וְלָא אָמְרִי׳ אע"ג דְּלֹא נִיתַּן מַעֲשֵׂר אֶלָּא לַאֲכִילָה וּשְׁתִיָּה וְסִיכָה, כִּדְכְתִיב (שם יד) "וְאָכַלְתָּ" – הָנֵי מִילֵּי טָהוֹר, אֲבָל הֵיכָא דְּנִטְמָא, דְּלָא חֲזֵי לַאֲכִילָה, יַדְלִיק בּוֹ, אֶלָּא אָסוּר לְבַעֵר בְּטוּמְאָה, כִּדְכְתִיב (שם כו) "וְלֹא בִעַרְתִּי מִמֶּנּוּ בְּטָמֵא". משא"ב בִּתְרוּמָה. דְּטוּמְאָתָהּ מַתִּירָתָהּ בְּהַבְעָרָה, כִּדְיָלֵיף לְקַמָּן בִּשְׁמַעְתִּין. וְאוֹכְלָן

לימד על טבול יום שכשר בפרה. וא"ת: מהיכא תיסק אדעתיה לפסול? דאי משום דחטאת קרייה רחמנא – הא לא דמי הזאה לשאר עבודה, שהרי הזר כשר בהז? וי"ל: מדקפיד קרא אהנחה במקום טהור. וא"ת: והיכי ילפינן מהזאה להכשיר טבול יום בשאר עבודות דפרכינן מה להזאה שכן זר כשר בהז? וי"ל: דאפ"ה, כיון דעיקר טהרה בהזאה אתיא, ואכשר בה רחמנא טבול יום – כל שכן בשאר עבודות. וא"ת: ואימא לרבות מחוסר כפורים שהעריב שמשו, דלא מחסר אלא כפרה לחודה, אבל טבול יום לא! – ואמר ר"י: דמוקמא קרא בטומאה דכתיבא בהאי פרשה, כגון טומאת מת דלא שייך כפרה. והכי אמרינן בזבחים בפ"ב (דף יז: ושם) דמאן דמכשיר מחוסר כפרה קסבר טומאה דכל התורה כולה, דבכל טבול יום מכשיר, אפילו הוא מחוסר כפרה, ומאן דפסל קסבר: טומאה דאותה פרשה, היינו טבול יום דמת, [דלא בעי כפרה,] אבל דזב ומצורע ויולדת – אפי׳ העריב שמשו לא.. **קל** מחמור לא יליף. וא"ת: מאי מיבעיא (א) ליה? פשיטא, דהיכי נילף קל מחמור?! וי"ל: דמספקא להו הא דיליף פסח ממעשר: אי בג"ש ד"ממנו" יליף – ילפינן נמי מעשר מפסח, אע"ג דהוי קל מחמור, או בק"ו יליף ולא בג"ש. א) א"נ: מספקא ליה אי ג"ש מופנה או אינו מופנה. **ואסורים** לזרים. וא"ת: כיון דתנא דחייבין חומש, אמאי איצטריך תו למתני ואסורים לזרים? ואין לומר משום דבעי למתני משא"כ במעשר, דשרי לזרים – דהא במסכת חלה (פ"א מ"ט) קתני: *(התרומה והבכורים) חייבין עליהן מיתה וחומש ואסור לזרים, אע"ג דלא מסיים התם משא"כ במעשר! ותירץ בערוך, ערך טען, דאסור לזרים איצטריך לחצי שיעור, דאסור, למאן דאמר מדרבנן ולמ"ד מדאורייתא.ב) עוד פי׳ לשון אחר: ואסור לזרים – אפי׳ ע"י פדיון. ואין נראה פירוש זה. דאין להם פדיון אמרינן לקמן דשייר. **נכסי** כהן. בפרק "הזרוע והלחיים" (חולין קלא.) מפרש למה אמרו בכורים נכסי כהן – ליקח בהן עבדים וקרקעות ובהמה טמאה, משא"כ במעשר שני, כדתנן במסכת מעשר שני (פ"א מ"ז) ומייתי לה בקידושין בפ"ב (דף נו.) אין לוקחין בהמה טמאה עבדים וקרקעות ממעות מעשר שני. ולכאורה משמע דדוקא הני הוא דאסירי, אבל ליקח מהן מלבושין – שרי. וכן תנן במסכת מעשר שני (פ"ה משנה יב) ומייתינן לקמן (דף עד.): "לא נתתי ממנו למת" – ליקח לו ארון ותכריכין. משמע, הא לחי דומיא דמת – נתתי, דהיינו מלבושים, דהכי דייק לקמן גבי סיכה. וקשה: דבירושלמי אמר בהדיא "לא נתתי ממנו למת" – מה אנן קיימינן? אם להביא ארון ותכריכין – דבר זה אסור לחי ולמת, משמע דאסור לקנות מלבושים לחי! ובכמה מקומות תנן במסכת מעשר שני (פ"א מ"ז) דאסור לעשות שום סחורה במעשר, ולא ניתן אלא לאכילה ושתיה וסיכה! ואר"י: דמ"ל דהנהו משניות דאסרי – אתו כר"מ, דאמר (בקידושין דף נג:) ממון גבוה הוא והנך כר"י דשרי, דאמר (שם) ממון הדיוט הוא. והא דמשמע בפ"ב דקידושין (דף נד: ושם) דליכא אלא חד סתמא כרבי יהודה, אע"ג דההיא דשרי מלבושים אתיא כוותיה – מ"מ יש יותר סתמות כר"מ. עוד נראה לר"י, דהמשניות אינן חולקין זו על זו, ומן התורה לא אסירי אלא עבדים וקרקע ובהמה טמאה, אבל מלבושים – שרו ומדרבנן אסרו אפילו מלבושים. והא דדריש בירושלמי "לא נתתי למת" [אין] ליקח לו ארון ותכריכין – לחי נמי אסור – אסמכתא בעלמא היא. ואכילת בהמה דשריא במעשר שני בשעת דישה,* למ"ד ממון הדיוט הוא – נראה דבשלא בשעת דישה אסור מיהא מדרבנן, ולמ"ד ממון גבוה נראה דאסור מן התורה להאכיל לבהמה. **מה** שאין כן במעשר. תימה: כיון דלקמן (ע"ב) ילפינן בכורים ממעשר דאסורין לאונן מדאיתקוש למעשר שני, נילף נמי מעשר מביכורים שיתחייב מיתה האוכלו בטומאת הגוף? ולענין איסור זרות – ניחא, דבהדיא שריא רחמנא לזרים. וי"ל: דדרשינן "ומתו בו כי יחללוהו" (ויקרא כב) – בו ולא במעשר, כדדרשינן ב"יש מותרות" (לקמן פו. ושם): בו ולא במעשר ראשון. דאפילו לר"מ דאסר לזרים – לא מחייב מיתה. ודרשינן נמי ב"הנשרפין" (סנהדרין פד. ושם) בו ולא במעילה. והא דמעשר שני בטל ברוב היכא דאין לו מתירין, ולא ילפינן מבכורים דעולים באחד ומאה – משום דבכורים גופייהו בטלים ברוב מדאורייתא. והא דדרשינן בספרי מ"את מקדשו ממנו" – אסמכתא בעלמא היא, כדאמר ב"הניזקין" (גיטין דף נד: ושם) נפלו ונתפלעו, והא הכא דמדאורייתא בטלי ברובא כו׳, אלמא: ערלה וכלאי הכרם בטלים ברוב מדאורייתא. ועוד: בשילהי פירקין (לקמן פב.) גבי שאני אומר חולין לתוך חולין נפלו, דתלינן להקל כשרבו חולין על התרומה, משמע דבטל ברוב מדאורייתא. ומיהו קשה: דנילף בכורים ממעשר לענין דלא ליהוי נכסי כהן דהיינו לחומרא, ולא מתרומה לקולא. ואם מעשר גופיה הוי מדרבנן, הא דאין לוקחין בהמה טמאה ועבדים וקרקעות – הוה ניחא. אבל אי אפשר לומר כן, למאי דפרישית לעיל, דמדרבנן אפי׳ כל מילי נמי אסור. (אבל לענין ערל כי קאמר תנא ושייר – ק"ק: אמאי לא יליף מעשר מבכורים? ולמאי דפי׳ לעיל דאיכא למעוטי (ג)א"ש). וא"ת: והיכי קתני לענין רחילת ידים משא"כ במעשר, והתניא בפ"ב דחולין (ד׳ לג:) כל הטעון ביאת מים מדברי סופרים אסור בתרומה, ומותר בחולין ובמעשר, דברי ר"מ, וחכמים אוסרים במעשר? ואר"י: דהתם לאכילה, והכא לנגיעה. וא"ת: וליתני חלה, דבכורים ותרומה פטור מן החלה ומעשר חייב? וי"ל: דהא תנן במסכת חלה (פ"א מ"ג): מעשר שני והקדש שנפדו חייבים בחלה, נפדו – אין, לא נפדו – לא. **טעונין** הבאת מקום. אע"ג דתרומה נמי ילפא מבכורים, כדמוכח ב"העור והרוטב" (חולין קכ:) שמא לענין שתהא טעונה הבאת מקום אין ללמוד*. **וטעונין** וידוי. אע"ג דדרשינן בפ׳ בתרא דמ"ש (מ"י) "וגם נתתיו ללוי" – זו תרומה, אר"י: דלא היה מתודה על התרומה אלא אגב מעשר, אבל אם אבד המעשר – לא היה מתודה עליה בפני עצמה. **וחייבין** בביעור. פי׳ ריב"ן: דביעור מעשר לאו כביעור בכורים. דביעור מעשר בשנה ד׳, וביעור דבכורים לאחר החג. כדאמר במכות (ד׳ יח: ושם) הפריש בכורים קודם החג ועבר עליהן החג – ירקבו. ואין נראה לר"י, דאין זה ביעור. והתם טעמא דירקבו – לפי שנראו לקריאה ונדחו. וביעור דבכורים הוי כשל מעשר, דכי נתנן לכהן קודם החג, או הפרישן לאחר החג – יכול לשומרן עד שנה ד׳. וא"ת: תרומה נמי טעונה ביעור, כדתנן במסכת מעשר שני (פ"ה משנה ו), כיצד היה הביעור: תרומה ותרומת מעשר לבעלים? וי"ל: דתרומה א"צ ליה. רק ליתנה לכהן, והכהן יכול לשומרה כל זמן שירצה. אבל מעשר שני ובכורים – צריך לבערם מן העולם בכל מקום שהן. ור"ש דפטר בבכורים – היינו שאין הכהן צריך לבערם, אבל ישראל צריך ליתנם לכהן כתרומה. והכי תנן בפרק בתרא דמעשר שני: עי"ט של שנה רביעית ושל שביעית היה הביעור, כיצד היה ביעור? נותן תרומה ותרומת מעשר לבעליו, ומעשר ראשון לבעליו. אבל מעשר שני ובכורים – מתבערים בכל מקום שהן, ור"ש אומר: בכורים ניתנין לכהן כתרומה. ואוכלן

עין משפט נר מצוה

לד א מיי׳ פ"א מהלכות פרה אדומה הל׳ יג:
לה ב מיי׳ פ"ג מהלכות מעשר שני הלכה ד סמג לאוין רסב רסג:
לו ג מיי׳ פ"ג מהלכות בכורים הלכה ה ופ"ד הלכה יד:
לז ד מיי׳ פ"ב מהלכות מעשר שני הלכה א:
לח ה מיי׳ פ"ב מהלכ׳ בכורים הלכה א ופ"ג הלכה ה:
לט ו מיי׳ פי"א מהלכות מעשר שני הלכה א ופ"ג מהלכות בכורים הלכה י:
מ ז מיי׳ פ"ג מהלכות מעשר שני הלכה ה ופ"ג מהלכות בכורים הלכה ה:
מא ח מיי׳ פי"א מהלכות מעשר שני הלכה ח:
מב ט מיי׳ פ"ג מהלכות מעשר שני הלכה ב:

רש"ל

[נ"ל החלה והתרומה]

מסורת הש"ס

יומא מג: זבחים יז:

ב"מ נב: בכורים פ"ב מ"א חגיגה יח: [חלה פ"א מ"ט]

[סוכה נב. וש"נ]

בכורים פ"ב מ"ב

[פסחים לו: ושם איתא ואסורין לאונן]

הגהות הב"ח

(א) תוס׳ ד"ה קל וכו׳ מיבעיא להו פשיטא: (ב) ד"ה מה וכו׳ למעוטי מבו א"ש:

גליון הש"ס

גמ׳ משא"כ בתרומה. עי׳ מנחות טו ע"א תד"ה לחם:

רש"ל

[ב"מ נ.]

גליון

[ועי׳ תוספות מנחות טו. ד"ה לחם]

תוספות ישנים

כי היכי דיליף פסח ממעשר לענין אניגות. פירוש משום דילפינן ליה בק"ו ומה מעשר הקל אמרה תורה לא אכלתי באוני ממנו פסח חמור לכ"ש. ותימה מה למעשר שכן טעון כסף צורה וי"ל דילפינן לה ממעשר מג"ש דממנו ממנו וא"ת ושאר קדשים מנא לן דאסירי לאונן וי"ל דילפינן מפסח מזאת תורת וא"ת הלא למד מלמד הוא דפסח ילפינן ממעשר וי"ל כיון דמלמד קמא א) הוי חולין דמעשר לא הוי קדשים למדין וחוזרין ומלמדין: **א)** ולא נהירא לראב"י דהא איך היה מסופק אם מק"ו יליף הלא איכא פירכא כדפרישית מה למעשר שכן טעון כסף צורה אלא נראה דודאי ידע שפיר דילפינן פסח ממעשר לענין אניגות ממש אכן מספקא ליה אם הג"ש מופנית מכל צד וילפינן אף קל מחמור או אינה מופנית רק גבי מעשר. אכן אפרש לקמן בע"ה דפירכא דטעון כסף צורה לא מהניא מידי אלא לגבי אכילת חוץ לחומה אבל לגבי טומאה ואניגות לא שייכא מידי: **ב)** ואף למ"ד דחצי שיעור אסור מן התורה וא"כ אין חידוש לומר הכא דאסור בחצי שיעור דאפילו שאר איסורים שבתורה נמי. וי"ל דאצטריך דסד"א דהכא בתרומה כיון שאין זה איסור השוה בכל דהא שרי לכהנים ס"ד דלא מתסר לזרים חצי שיעור ולמ"ד חצי שיעור דרבנן ס"ד דהכא לא גזרו משום דאינו שוה בכל וי"מ וחייבין עליה מיתה לא מיירי בזר אלא בכהן האוכלה בטומאה: ונכסי כהן פ"ה לקדש

האשה משא"כ במעשר דממון גבוה לר׳ מאיר ואע"ג דהאי חומרא למעשר הוא מ"מ תנא את אשר [טוכג] בתרומה ובכורים דלא הוי במעשר ותימה דבפרק האיש מקדש דחיק לאשכוחי התם משנה דסבר למעשר שני ממון גבוה הוא ואמאי לא פסיק מהך מתני׳ וכ"ל והן נכסי כהן ליקח בהן בהמה טמאה עבדים וקרקעות משא"כ במעשר דלא ניתן רק לאכילה ולשתיה וסיכה ותימה דהא אמרינן לקמן לא נתתי ממנו למת ליקח לו ארון ותכריכים הא לחי דומיא דמת כגון חלוק ומכנסיים שרי וי"ל דמ"מ ליקח בהמה טמאה עבדים וקרקעות אסור. ולראב"י נראה דלא קשה מידי דהתם בטמא איירי וקאי אלא בערתי ממנו בטמא ור"ל ולא נתתי ממנו כשהיה טמא למת וכן פ"ה לקמן ב) למעשר דטהור ודאי דחזי לאכילה לא שרי רק לאכילה ולשתיה וסיכה: **ועולין** באחד ומאה. שאם נפלו תרומה ובכורים בק׳ ומאה בטלי משא"כ במעשר דמדאורייתא חד בתרי בטיל והאי עולין איתו ר"ל שמתבטל הסאה של תרומה שנפלה דודאי היא צריכה להרים כלמפרע בבכורות מפני גזל השבט וכאן לא שייך להאריך מזה: **וטעונין** רחילת ידים דידים שניות פוסלות את התרומה משא"כ במעשר דכל הנוטל ידיו לפירות ה"ז מגסי הרוח וא"ת והא אמרינן כל הטעון ביאת מים מדברי סופרים אסור בתרומה ומותר בחולין ובמעשר ורבי מאיר אומר אף במעשר וי"ל דהא דקאמר ר"מ אף במעשר היינו דוקא באכילת מעשר אבל הכא בנגיעה איירינן דידים שניות פוסלות תרומה במגע אבל לא מעשר: **וטעונים** וידוי משא"כ בתרומה לאינו טעונה וידוי והאי דקאמר דתרומה אינה טעונה וידוי היינו דוקא באפי נפשה אבל עם מעשר אגב גררא טעונה וידוי כדאמרי׳ וגם נתתיו ללוי לרבות את התרומה גדולה ותרומת מעשר א"נ ר"ל טעונים וידוי שוידוי מעכב במעשר ובכורים ואינו מעכב בתרומה דהכי משמע במסכת בכורים:

א) עי׳ בזבחים (דף כ׳) דלמ"ד דבתר למד אזלינן ס"ל באמת דדבר הלמד בגז"ש חוזר ומלמד בהיקש אפילו בקדשים וא"כ לר"ה ניחא ודו"ק: ב) נראה דצ"ל אבל מעשר שני טהור דחזי לאכילה ודאי לא שרי וכו׳.

עין משפט נר מצוה

מסורת הש"ס

וְאוֹכְלָן בְּטוּמְאַת עַצְמָן לוֹקֶה, מַה שֶּׁאֵין כֵּן בִּתְרוּמָה — לָא קָתָנֵי, אַלְמָא: תָּנֵי וְשַׁיֵּיר.§ (א) *"וַאֲסוּרִין לְאוֹנֵן וְר"ש מַתִּיר", מְנָא לְהוּ? דִּכְתִיב °"לֹא תוּכַל לֶאֱכוֹל בִּשְׁעָרֶיךָ מַעְשַׂר דְּגָנְךָ וְתִירֹשְׁךָ וְיִצְהָרֶךָ (ב) וגו' וּתְרוּמַת יָדֶךָ" *וְאָמַר מָר: "תְּרוּמַת יָדֶךָ" אֵלּוּ בִּכּוּרִים, וְאִיתַּקַּשׁ בִּכּוּרִים לְמַעֲשֵׂר: מַה מַּעֲשֵׂר אָסוּר לְאוֹנֵן, אַף בִּכּוּרִים [א]אָסוּר לְאוֹנֵן. וְר"ש: "תְּרוּמָה" קָרֵינְהוּ רַחֲמָנָא, מַה תְּרוּמָה [ב]מוּתֶּרֶת לְאוֹנֵן, אַף בִּכּוּרִים מוּתָּר לְאוֹנֵן. "וְחַיָּיבִין בְּבִיעוּר, וְר"ש פּוֹטֵר" — מָר מַקִּישׁ, וּמָר לָא מַקִּישׁ. "וְאָסוּר לְבַעֵר מֵהֶן בְּטוּמְאָה, וְאוֹכְלָן בְּטוּמְאַת עַצְמָן לוֹקֶה" מְנָלַן? דְּתַנְיָא, *ר' שִׁמְעוֹן אוֹמֵר: °"לֹא בִעַרְתִּי מִמֶּנּוּ בְּטָמֵא" — [ג]בֵּין שֶׁאֲנִי טָמֵא וְהוּא טָהוֹר, בֵּין שֶׁאֲנִי טָהוֹר וְהוּא טָמֵא. וְהֵיכָא מוּזְהָר עַל אֲכִילָתוֹ אֵינִי יוֹדֵעַ. טוּמְאַת הַגּוּף בְּהֶדְיָא כְּתִיב בֵּיהּ: °"נֶפֶשׁ אֲשֶׁר תִּגַּע בּוֹ וְטָמְאָה עַד הָעָרֶב וְלֹא יֹאכַל מִן הַקֳּדָשִׁים כִּי אִם רָחַץ בְּשָׂרוֹ בַּמָּיִם"! הָכִי קָמִיבַּעְיָא לֵיהּ: טוּמְאַת עַצְמוֹ מִנַּיִן? ת"ל "לֹא תוּכַל לֶאֱכוֹל בִּשְׁעָרֶיךָ מַעְשַׂר דְּגָנְךָ" וּלְהַלָּן הוּא אוֹמֵר °"בִּשְׁעָרֶיךָ תֹּאכְלֶנּוּ הַטָּמֵא וְהַטָּהוֹר יַחְדָּו כַּצְּבִי וְכָאַיָּל", וְתָנָא דְּבֵי רַבִּי יִשְׁמָעֵאל: אֲפִי' טָמֵא וְטָהוֹר אוֹכְלִין עַל שׁוּלְחָן אֶחָד בִּקְעָרָה אַחַת — וְאֵינָן חוֹשְׁשִׁין. וְקָאָמַר רַחֲמָנָא: הַהוּא דְּאָמְרִי לָךְ הָתָם "בִּשְׁעָרֶיךָ תֹּאכְלֶנּוּ" — הָכָא לָא תֵּיכוּל.§ "משא"כ בִּתְרוּמָה", מְנָא לָן? אָמַר ר' אַבָּהוּ א"ר יוֹחָנָן: דְּאָמַר קְרָא *"לֹא בִעַרְתִּי מִמֶּנּוּ בְּטָמֵא", "מִמֶּנּוּ" אִי אַתָּה מְבַעֵיר, [ד]אֲבָל אַתָּה מְבַעֵיר שֶׁמֶן שֶׁל תְּרוּמָה שֶׁנִּטְמָא. וְאֵימָא: "מִמֶּנּוּ" אִי אַתָּה מְבַעֵיר, אֲבָל אַתָּה מְבַעֵיר שֶׁמֶן שֶׁל קֹדֶשׁ שֶׁנִּטְמָא! לָאו קַל וָחוֹמֶר הוּא?! וּמַה מַּעֲשֵׂר הַקַּל אָמְרָה תּוֹרָה "לֹא בִעַרְתִּי מִמֶּנּוּ בְּטָמֵא", קֹדֶשׁ חָמוּר לֹא כ"ש?! אִי הָכִי תְּרוּמָה נַמִי ק"ו הוּא! הָא כְּתִיב "מִמֶּנּוּ" וּמָה רָאִיתָ? מִסְתַּבְּרָא: קֹדֶשׁ לָא מְמַעֲטִינָא, שֶׁכֵּן פנקעכ"ם: [ה]פִּגּוּל, [ו]נוֹתָר, קָרְבָּן, [ז]מְעִילָה, [ח]כָּרֵת, [ט]וְאָסוּר לְאוֹנֵן. אַדְּרַבָּה, תְּרוּמָה לָא מְמַעֲטִינָא, שֶׁכֵּן מחפ"ז: [י]מִיתָה, [כ]וְחוֹמֶשׁ, וְאֵין לָהּ פִּדְיוֹן, [ל]וַאֲסוּרָה לְזָרִים! הָנָךְ נְפִישָׁן. וְאִיבָּעֵית אֵימָא: כָּרֵת עֲדִיפָא.§ "וְאוֹכְלָן בְּטוּמְאַת עַצְמָן לוֹקֶה, מַה שֶּׁאֵין כֵּן בִּתְרוּמָה". מִילְקָא הוּא דְּלָא לָקֵי [מ]הָא אִיסּוּרָא אִיכָּא, מְנָלַן? אָמַר קְרָא "בִּשְׁעָרֶיךָ תֹּאכְלֶנּוּ" לָזֶה וְלֹא לְאַחֵר *[נ]וְלָאו הַבָּא מִכְּלַל עֲשֵׂה — עֲשֵׂה. אָמַר רַב אַשִׁי: מֵרֵישָׁא נַמִי שָׁמְעַתְּ מִינַּהּ דְּתָנָא וְשַׁיֵּיר, מִדְּלָא קָתָנֵי:

וְנוֹהֲגִין

(תורה אור: דברים יב; שם כו; ויקרא כב; דברים טו)

רש"י

וְאוֹכְלָן בְּטוּמְאַת עַצְמָן. שֶׁהַגּוּף טָהוֹר וְהֵם טְמֵאִים. לוֹקֶה. כִּדְיָלֵיף לְקַמָּן. מַה שֶּׁאֵין כֵּן בִּתְרוּמָה. דְּאֵינוֹ מוּזְהָר בָּהּ אֶלָּא בְּטוּמְאַת הַגּוּף, כִּדְכְתִיב (ויקרא כב) "בַּקֳּדָשִׁים לֹא יֹאכַל" וגו'. אֲבָל בְּטוּמְאַת עַצְמָהּ — לֹא מָלִינוּ אַזְהָרָה, אֶלָּא אִיסּוּר עֲשֵׂה הוּא דְּאַשְׁכְּחַן בֵּיהּ לְקַמָּן בִּשְׁמַעְתִּין. וּמִדְּלָא קָתָנֵי לֵיהּ שְׁמַע מִינַּהּ תָּנָא וְשַׁיֵּיר. וְאָמַר מָר. בְּמַסֶּכֶת מַכּוֹת (דף יז.). וּתְרוּמַת יָדֶךָ אֵלּוּ הַבִּכּוּרִים. דְּבָעֵי הֲבָאַת מָקוֹם, כִּדְכְתִיב (דברים כו) "וְשַׂמְתָּ בַטֶּנֶא וְהָלַכְתָּ". וְהָתָם אַשְׁמְעִי' עֲשֵׂה, וְהָכָא אַשְׁמְעִינַן אַזְהָרַת לָאו לְאוֹכְלָן בַּגְּבוּלִין. דְּאִילּוּ תְּרוּמָה מַמָּשׁ — קָדְשֵׁי הַגְּבוּל הִיא, וְלָא בָּעְיָא חוֹמָה. תְּרוּמָה מוּתֶּרֶת לְאוֹנֵן. כִּדְאָמַר בְּרֵישׁ פִּירְקִין (דף ע.): זָרוּת אָמַרְתִּי לָךְ וְלֹא אֲנִינוּת. מַר מַקִּישׁ. ת"ק מַקִּישׁ בִּכּוּרִים לְמַעֲשֵׂר, דִּכְתִיב בֵּיהּ (דברים כו) "בִּעַרְתִּי הַקֹּדֶשׁ". וְהֵיכָן מוּזְהָר עַל אֲכִילָה אֵינִי יוֹדֵעַ ת"ל לֹא תוּכַל כו'. וְהָכִי גָּרְסִינַן לְלִישָּׁנָא דְּבָרַיְיתָא בְּסִפְרֵי, גַּבֵּי הַאי קְרָא דְּ"לֹא תוּכַל". מִכְּלַל שֶׁנֶּאֱמַר "לֹא בִעַרְתִּי מִמֶּנּוּ בְּטָמֵא" — בֵּין שֶׁאֲנִי טָמֵא וְהוּא טָהוֹר, בֵּין שֶׁאֲנִי טָהוֹר וְהוּא טָמֵא, וְהֵיכָן מוּזְהָר עַל אֲכִילָה — אֵינִי יוֹדֵעַ, ת"ל "לֹא תוּכַל" כו'. וְהָכִי פֵּירוּשׁוֹ: מִכְּלַל שֶׁנֶּאֱמַר בְּוִידּוּי מַעֲשֵׂר "לֹא בִעַרְתִּי מִמֶּנּוּ בְּטָמֵא", דְּמַשְׁמַע בֵּין שֶׁאֲנִי טָמֵא כו' הוּא מִתְוַדֶּה שֶׁלֹּא בִּעֲרוֹ בָּאֵשׁ, וְלֹא הִדְלִיק בּוֹ אֶת הַנֵּר. וְכָל שֶׁכֵּן בְּטָהוֹר, דְּלֹא נִיתַּן אֶלָּא לַאֲכִילָה וּשְׁתִיָּה וְסִיכָה, וּמִמֵּילָא שָׁמְעִינַן, מִדְּלָא הוּצְרַךְ לְהִתְוַדּוֹת עַל הַטָּהוֹר — שְׁמַע מִינַּהּ הָכִי קָאָמַר: אֲפִילּוּ בִּשְׁעַת הַטּוּמְאָה, שֶׁלֹּא יָכוֹלְתִּי לְאוֹכְלוֹ — לֹא נְתַתִּיו לְהַדְלָקָה. אַלְמָא, אֵינוֹ נֶאֱכָל בְּטוּמְאָה, וְהֵיכָן מוּזְהָר עַל כָּךְ? אֵינִי יוֹדֵעַ. לָאו מְפוֹרָשׁ לְכָךְ נֶאֱמַר "לֹא תוּכַל". וְהַשְׁתָּא פָּרֵיךְ הַשַּׁ"ס, מִקַּמֵּי דְּלִיסְלִיק לְמִילְּתֵיהּ. טוּמְאַת הַגּוּף בְּהֶדְיָא כְּתִיבָא. וְאַמַּאי קָתָנֵי אֵינִי יוֹדֵעַ. לֹא יֹאכַל מִן הַקֳּדָשִׁים. וּמוֹקְמִינַן הַאי קְרָא בְּמַעֲשֵׂר לְקַמָּן בְּפִירְקִין (דף עד:) כִּדְכְתִיב "כִּי אִם רָחַץ בְּשָׂרוֹ בַּמָּיִם", וְלָא בָּעֵי הֶעֱרֵב שֶׁמֶשׁ, וּמְשַׁנֵּינַן: הָכִי קָמִיבַּעְיָא לֵיהּ לְתַנָּא: טוּמְאַת עַצְמוֹ מִנַּיִן ת"ל כו'. בִּשְׁעָרֶיךָ תֹּאכְלֶנּוּ. בִּפְסוּלֵי הַמּוּקְדָּשִׁין קָאֵי, לְאַחַר פִּדְיוֹנָן, שֶׁאוֹכְלָן זָר. הַהוּא. בִּשְׁעָרֶיךָ דְּהָתָם — דְּקַשְׁרֵי לֵיהּ לְטָהוֹר לְאוֹכְלוֹ אַחַר שֶׁנָּגַע טָמֵא בַּקְּעָרָה וְנִטְמְאָה, קָאָמֵינָא לָךְ: הָכָא — בְּמַעֲשֵׂר שֵׁנִי לֹא תֵּיכוּל. שֶׁמֶן קֹדֶשׁ. כְּגוֹן שֶׁהוּקְדַּשׁ לִמְנָחוֹת וְנִטְמָא. שֶׁכֵּן. מָלִינוּ חוּמְרוֹת בַּקּוֹדֶשׁ וְאֵין נוֹהֲגוֹת בִּתְרוּמָה. פִּגּוּל נוֹתָר. וְקָרוּי קָרְבָּן לַהֲבִיאוֹ לִפְנִים, וְיֵשׁ בּוֹ מְעִילָה לַנֶּהֱנֶה מִמֶּנּוּ בְּשׁוֹגֵג, וְכָרֵת לְאוֹכְלוֹ בְּטוּמְאַת הַגּוּף, וְאָסוּר לְאוֹנֵן. מחפ"ז. מִיתָה לְאוֹכְלוֹ בְּטוּמְאַת הַגּוּף, דִּכְתִיב (ויקרא כב) "וּמֵתוּ בוֹ כִּי יְחַלְּלוּהוּ". חוֹמֶשׁ. לְזָר הָאוֹכְלָהּ בְּשׁוֹגֵג לְעוֹלָם, וְאע"פ שֶׁמּוּתֶּרֶת לְכֹהֲנִים. אֲבָל קֹדֶשׁ, מִשָּׁעָה שֶׁיֵּשׁ לוֹ שְׁעַת הֶיתֵּר לְכֹהֲנִים — אֵין בּוֹ מְעִילָה וְלֹא חוֹמֶשׁ. וְאֵין לָהּ פִּדְיוֹן. לִתְרוּמָה. אֲבָל מָלִינוּ פִּדְיוֹן לְקֹדֶשׁ עַד שֶׁלֹּא קִידֵּשׁ בִּכְלִי. וּתְרוּמָה אֲסוּרָה לְזָרִים, אֲבָל קָדָשִׁים קַלִּים מוּתָּרִים לְזָרִים. הָא אִיסּוּרָא אִיכָּא. לֶאֱכוֹל תְּרוּמָה טְמֵאָה.

וְנוֹהֲגִין

תוספות

ואוכלן בטומאת עצמן. תימה לר"י: דאמאי לא לקי נמי בתרומה, דנילף מבכורים? ולעיל (דף ע. ד"ה "מה") כתבתי:

תרומת ידך אלו הבכורים. שנאמר בהן יד, "ולקח הכהן הטנא מידך". **ור"ש** תרומה קרינהו רחמנא. תימה לר"י: דפ' "אלו הן הלוקין" (מכות דף יז:) אמרינן, גבי הא דאר"ש: וכי מה בא זה ללמדנו, אם לאוכל בכורים חוץ לחומה – ק"ו ממעשר הקל? אמר רבא: מאי חומרא דבכורים ממעשר – שכן אסורים לזרים, אדרבה, מעשר חמור, שכן אסור לאונן! והשתא איסור אונן גופה, מ"ט לא ילפינן בכורים ק"ו ממעשר דמותר לזרים – משום דתרומה קרינהו רחמנא, כדאמר הכא, א"כ, מהאי טעמא גופה דתרומה קרינהו רחמנא לא נילף ממעשר לענין חוץ לחומה? וי"ל: כיון דמעשר ובכורים טעונים הבאת מקום ותרומה אינה טעונה הבאת מקום – שייך לדמות טפי בכורים למעשר לענין חוץ לחומה מלתרומה.

ומר לא מקיש. מטעם דתרומה קרינהו רחמנא. **והיכן** מוזהר על אכילתו כו'. תימא לר"י: דהכא משמע דמ"לא בערתי" לא נפקא לן אזהרה לאכילה, ובפ' "כל שעה" (פסחים דף כד.) אמרינן "והבשר אשר יגע בכל טמא לא יאכל" אם אינו ענין לגופו, דנפקא לן ממעשר הקל, דכתיב "לא בערתי ממנו בטמא"? וכ"ת אין מזהירין מן הדין – היקישא הוא, דכתב "לא תוכל לאכול בשעריך" וגו', משמע דאי מזהירין מן הדין – ידעינן שפיר לאו מ"לא בערתי". **טומאת** עצמן מנין ת"ל לא תוכל וגו'. אין להקשות: כיון שיש אזהרה לטומאת עצמן – למה לן אזהרה לאוכל בטומאת הגוף? דנפקא מינה דהיכא שתחב לו חבירו בבית הבליעה. אי נמי: בשלא הוכשר. אבל קשה: דמהאי קרא גופיה דנפקא לן טומאת עצמן תיפוק ליה טומאת הגוף, דההוא דאמר לך "בשעריך תאכלנו" – בין טומאת הגוף בין טומאת עצמן, הכא לא תוכל לאכול.

אסור לבער מהן בטומאה מה שאין כן בתרומה מנלן. וא"ת: מהיכי תיתי דתיתסר תרומה לבער ממנה בטומאה? ואין לומר משום דתרומה איקרי קדש, והוה ילפינן לה מקדש, או משום שהיא בשרפה כמוקדשין שנטמאו, ואע"ג דקדשים חמירי – הוה ילפינן תרומה מינייהו לאסור ליהנות ממנה בשעת שרפה, דגילוי מילתא הוא – דא"כ, מאי פריך ומה ראית ואימא "ממנו" למעוטי קדש. אבל תרומה יהא אסור, והשתא, מהיכא תיתי, כיון דקדש שרי? וי"ל: דהוה ילפינן תרומה מבכורים ומיהו, בכולה שמעתין לא ילפינן תרומה מבכורים! ואר"י: דמשום הכי קבעי תרומה מנלן, דהוה לן למילף מק"ו דמעשר כדקאמר בסמוך ולא שייך למיפרך מה למעשר שכן הדסט"ב – דלגבי טומאה מיהא מלינו שתרומה חמורה ממעשר. וליכא למפרך נמי מה למעשר שכן אוכלן בטומאת עצמן לוקה – דהיא גופה נילף בק"ו. ולפי המסקנא דשריא לבער תרומה בטומאתה – תו ליכא למילף לאוכל בטומאת עצמה.

שכן פנקעב"ם. מחוסר כפורים לא חשיב, משום דמהאי טעמא גופיה נפקא לן לקמן (דף עד:) אבל תימה: דליחשוב רביעי בקדש, וחיבת הקדש דמכשרת, וחוזרת לחזה ושוק, וכלי מצרף לקדש ולא לתרומה, ומומרת דפוסלת בקדש וכו', וטומאה עושה כיוצא בה לקדש ולא לתרומה, למ"ד בפרק קמא דפסחים (דף יז.) וישנו לפני הדבור, כגון פסח ותמיד, למ"ד (חגיגה דף ו.) עולה שהקריבו ישראל במדבר עולת תמיד הואי. **שכן** מחפ"ז. וא"ת: דמעיקרא אלימא ליה כרת ולבסוף אלימא ליה מיתה? וי"ל: דהשתא לאו מאוכל בטומאת הגוף פריך אלא מזר האוכלה, מה שאין כן בקדש, דבקדש יש שמותר לזרים כגון שלמים. ואפילו קדשים שאין נאכלים אלא לכהונה – ליכא מיתה בזר אלא אזהרה, ואפילו קדש דבר מעילה ליכא מיתה לרבנן, דאמרי: הזיד במעילה באזהרה.

אונן

תוספות ישנים

מקיש בכורים למעשר. וא"ת ואמאי לא מקשינן נמי מעשר לבכורים לחייב מיתה לאוכלו בטומאה וי"ל דכתיב גבי תרומה ומתו בו כי יחללוהו בו ולא במעשר ובכל הני דלעיל שיקשם בבכורים ולא במעשר נ"ל דסברת התלמוד כן הוא דלכל חומרות שיש בתרומה אקשינן בכורים מדכתיב תרומת ידך אלו בכורים ולחומרות דאתנהו במעשר מקשינן בכורים: **הא** דאמרי לך בשעריך תאכלנו הכא לא תאכל וא"ת א"כ למה לי קרא דנפש כי תגע לטומאת גופו הא מלא תוכל לאכול בשעריך נפקא דהא ר"ל דמה שהתרתי בשעריך תאכלנו הטמא והטהור הכא לא תוכל לאכול וי"ל דאיכא למימר דאגב דאשמעינן קרא דטבול יום שרי במעשר מובא השמש וטהר כתב רישיה דקרא לטומאת הגוף עוד מתרץ רבינו נתנאל דמלא תוכל לאכול בשעריך לא שמעינן טומאת הגוף דהא (דכ"ע) [בכולי דוכתי] לא שמעינן שום קרא דמיירי בטומאת הגוף דלא כתיב ביה עד אשר יטהר כדכתיב בקדשים לא יאכל עד אשר יטהר או כדכתיב אשר יקרב אל הקדשים וטומאתו עליו דמשמע בעוד שטומאתו עליו דמשמע דשייך ביה טהרה והיינו טומאת הגוף אבל הכא (לא) כתיב לא תוכל לאכול דמשמע לעולם לא תוכל וא"כ לא איירי בטומאת הגוף דהא מצי לאכול אחר טבילה. אבל בטומאת עצמו ניחא שפיר דלעולם לא מצי לאכול מן האוכלין שנטמאו דהא אין להם טהרה במקוה וא"ת ולמה לי קרא לאוכל קדשים בטומאת עצמו שהוא לוקה מדכתיב והבשר אשר יגע בכל טמא לא יאכל תיפוק לי מהכא דהא כתיב לא תוכל לאכול בשעריך וכתיב ובכורות בקרך וצאנך וי"ל דאיכא למימר א) דבשעריך לא קאי אלא אמעשר ואע"ג דבמכות חזינן חוץ לחומה הקדשים מהכא י"ל דוקא פשטיה דקרא (קאי) אכל דמפרש קאי אבל דרשא דהכא דקאמר הא דאמרינן לך התם בשעריך תאכלנו וכו' איכא למימר דלא אמרינן כן רק אמעשר דסמיך ליה. עי"ל דאיכא למימר דאצטריך קרא כשנטמאו בטבול יום דמהכא לא נפקא כיון דבכה"ג ליכא טומאה במעשר שהרי טבול יום מותר בו: **ומה** מעשר הקל וא"ת מה למעשר שכן טעון כסף צורה וי"ל דלא שייך למימר כן אלא גבי אכילתו בפנים אבל הכא לגבי טומאה איירינן לא שייך למפרך כן דודאי קדשים חמירי: **אדרבה** תרומה לא ממעיטנא שכן מחפ"ז וא"ת האי תנא מעיקרא אלימא ליה כרת ולבסוף אלימא ליה מיתה. וי"ל דר"ל מיתה בזר האוכלה במזיד משא"כ בקדש דליכא לזרים: **ואסורה** לזרים. ר"ל בחצי שיעור ומ"מ קאמר לקמן כרת עדיפא אע"ג דבכורים ליכא כרת מ"מ כיון דחמיר האוכל קדש בטומאה דלאית בה כרת ובתרומה ליכא רק מיתה חשבינן ליה לחמור:

א) נ"ל וי"ל דאיכא למימר דלא תוכל לאכול בשעריך לא קאי רק אמעשר ואף דבמכות ילפינן אזהרה לאוכל קדשים חוץ לחומה מהכא וכו'.

עין משפט נר מצוה

מג א מיי' פ"ג מהל' בכורים הלכה ה:

מד ב ג מיי' פי"ב מהלכות אבות הטומאה הל' טו ופ"ג מהל' מעשר שני הלכה א:

מה ד מיי' פ"ב מהל' תרומות הלכה יד ופי"א הלכה א טוש"ע י"ד סימן שלא סעיף יט:

מו ה מיי' פי"ג מהל' פסולי המוקדשין הלכה א:

מז ו מיי' שם הלכה ג:

מח ז מיי' פ"א מהלכות מעילה הלכה א:

מט ח מיי' פי"ח מהלכו' פסולי המוקדשין הלכה יג:

נ ט מיי' פ"ב מהלכות ביאת המקדש הל' ז ח ופי"ב מהל' אבות הטומאה הלכה טו:

נא י מיי' פ"ז מהל' תרומות הלכה א:

נב כ מיי' שם פ"ו הל' ו ופ"י הלכה א:

נג ל מיי' פ"ו שם הל' ה:

נד מ נ מיי' שם פ"ז הלכה ג:

מסורת הש"ס

[פסחים לו:]

גז"ש [מכות יז. חולין קכ: מעילה טו:]

מכות יט:

שבת כה.

[לעיל נב: וש"נ]

הגהות הב"ח

(א) גמ' תני ושייר אמר מר ואסורין לאונן: (ב) שם ותירושך ויצהרך ובכורות בקרך וגו' ותרומת ידך:

ונוהגין בשאר שני שבוע, ואין להם פדיון, מה שאין כן במעשר, ש"מ. ת"ש: נשתיירו בו ציצין המעכבין את המילה — הרי זה אינו אוכל לא בתרומה, ולא בפסח, ולא בקדשים, ולא במעשר. מאי לאו, מעשר דגן? לא, מעשר בהמה. — מעשר בהמה היינו קדשים! וליטעמיך, מי לא תנן פסח וקתני קדשים? בשלמא פסח וקדשים צריכי, דאי תנא פסח — משום דערלות בפסח כתיבא, אבל קדשים — אימא לא. ואי תנא קדשים — ה"א: מאי קדשים — פסח. אלא, מעשר בהמה למה לי? (א) אלא — מעשר ראשון, *ור' מאיר היא, דאמר: מעשר ראשון אסור לזרים. ת"ש, מדתני ר' חייא בר רב מדפתי: ערל אסור בשתי מעשרות. מאי לאו, אחד מעשר דגן ואחד מעשר בהמה! הכא נמי מעשר ראשון, ור' מאיר. ת"ש: אונן אסור במעשר, ומותר בתרומה ובפרה. טבול יום אסור בתרומה, ומותר בפרה ובמעשר. מחוסר כפורים אסור בפרה, ומותר בתרומה ובמעשר. ואם איתא — ניתני: ערל אסור בתרומה ומותר בפרה ובמעשר! האי תנא דבי רבי עקיבא היא, דמרבי ליה לערל כטמא. דתניא, *רבי עקיבא אומר: °"איש איש" — לרבות את הערל. ומאן תנא[א] דפליג עליה דרבי עקיבא — תנא דרבי יוסף הבבלי היא. דתניא: *[א] שרפת אונן ומחוסר כפורים — כשרה, רבי יוסף הבבלי אומר: אונן — כשרה, מחוסר כפורים — פסולה. ואף ר' יצחק סבר: ערל אסור במעשר, דא"ר יצחק: מנין לערל שאסור במעשר — נאמר "ממנו" במעשר ונאמר "ממנו" בפסח, מה "ממנו" האמור בפסח — ערל אסור בו, אף "ממנו" האמור במעשר — ערל אסור בו. מופני, דאי לא מופני איכא למיפרך: מה לפסח שכן חייבין עליו משום פיגול ונותר וטמא, לאיי, אפנויי מופני. מאי מופני? *אמר רבא א"ר יצחק: תלתא °"ממנו" כתיבי בפסח, חד לגופיה, וחד לגזירה שוה, וחד למאן דאמר: בא הכתוב ליתן לך עשה אחר לא תעשה, *איידי דכתיב נותר, כתיב נמי "ממנו". ולמאן דאמר ליתן לו בקר שני לשריפתו, איידי דכתיב "עד בקר" — כתיב נמי "ממנו", תלתא "ממנו" כתיבי במעשר, חד לגופיה, וחד לדרבי אבהו א"ר יוחנן, וחד לדריש לקיש. דאמר ריש לקיש א"ר סמיא: מנין למעשר שני שנטמא שמותר לסוכו — שנאמר °"ולא נתתי ממנו למת", למת הוא דלא נתתי — הא לחי דומיא דמת — נתתי, איזה דבר ששוה בחיים ובמתים — הוי אומר: זו סיכה. מתקיף לה מר זוטרא: *ואימא ליקח לו ארון ותכריכים? אמר רב הונא בריה דרב יהושע: "ממנו" — מגופו. רב אשי אמר: "לא נתתי" דומיא ד"לא אכלתי", מה להלן מגופו — אף כאן מגופו. ואכתי, מופנה מצד אחד הוא? הניחא למאן דאמר *למדין ואין משיבין, אלא למ"ד למדין ומשיבין — מאי איכא למימר? הך דרבי אבהו מדרב נחמן אמר רבה בר אבוה נפקא, *דאמר רב נחמן אמר רבה בר אבוה: מאי דכתיב: °"ואני הנה נתתי לך את משמרת תרומתי" *[ב] בשתי תרומות הכתוב מדבר, אחת תרומה טהורה ואחת תרומה טמאה, ואמר רחמנא: "לך" שלך תהא, להסקה תחת תבשילך.§ וכל הטמאים כו'.§ מנא הני מילי? א"ר יוחנן משום ר' ישמעאל: אמר קרא °"איש איש מזרע אהרן והוא צרוע או זב וגו'" *אי זהו דבר ששוה בזרעו

בזרעו

רש"י

ונוהגין. תרומה ובכורים, בשאר שני שבוע בכל שנות השמיטה, אבל מעשר שני אין נוהג בג' ובו'. ור' מאיר היא. דאמר בפרק "יש מותרות" (לקמן פה:): מעשר ראשון אסור לזרים, הלכך לענין ערלות נמי חמור. אונן מותר בפרה. דקדשי בדק הבית היא ולא קדשי מזבח, ומלינו טבול יום מותר בה, וכל שכן אונן. מחוסר כפרה. טומאה דבעיא קרבן, כל שלא הביא כפרתו — אסור בה, דמחוסר מעשה הוא, וכמי שטומאתו עליו דמי. וכל שכן טבול יום דילה, דאיכא תרתי, אבל טבול יום דטומאת מת ושרץ — מותר בה, דשמשא מעילא ערבא, ולאו מחוסר מעשה הוא. הלכך, כי כתיב "והזה הטהור על הטמא", טהור מכלל שהוא טמא — למישרי טבול יום אתא, ולא מחוסר כפורים. ואם איתא. דערל מותר במעשר, ליתני: וערל אסור בתרומה ומותר בפרה ובמעשר, כדאמר לעיל (דף עב:): ערל שהזה הזאתו כשרה. ומדלא תנייה — שמע מינה משום מעשר הוא דשבקיה. תנא דבי ר' עקיבא היא. דאסר ליה נמי בפרה, כדתני לעיל (שם): טומטום שקידש קידושו פסול, ואוקמינן כרבי עקיבא. ומאן תנא. דלעיל, דאכשר ערל בפרה ופליג עליה דרבי עקיבא, כדקתני לעיל (שם): ערל שהזה הזאתו כשרה: הכי גרסינן. תנא דיוסף הבבלי היא. ת"ק דיוסף הבבלי היא, דאמר: מחוסר כפורים כשר בפרה. והא מתניתא דאוקימנא כרבי עקיבא קתני מחוסר כפורים פסול בפרה, וכי היכי דפליג אמחוסר כפורים איכא למימר דאיהו פליג נמי עליה בערל לעיל: הכי גרסינן בתוספתא (דפרה פ"ג). שרפת אונן ומחוסר כפורים — כשרה, יוסף הבבלי אומר: אונן — כשרה, מחוסר כפורים — פסולה. דכיון דמחוסר מעשה הוא, עדיין טומאה עליו, ולא קרינא ביה טהור. תלתא ממנו כתיבי בפסח. "אל תאכלו ממנו נא" (שמות יב) "לא תותירו ממנו" "והנותר ממנו". ותלתא ממנו במעשר. "לא אכלתי" "ולא בערתי" "ולא נתתי" (דברים כו). בא הכתוב. "באש תשרופו" (שמות יב) ליתן עשה אחר ל"ת, לומר שאין לוקין עליו. בקר שני. דמצי למכתב "והנותר ממנו באש תשרופו", מאי "עד בקר"? הא כתיב ברישא דקרא "לא תותירו ממנו עד בקר"! אלא הכי קאמר: והנותר לבקר הראשון, שהוא יו"ט — המתן עד בקר שני, שהוא חול, ושורפו. ללמדך שאין שורפין קדשים ביו"ט. ותרווייהו ב"כיצד צולין" (פסחים דף פג:). לכדרבי אבהו. דאמר לעיל: למישרי הדלקה בשמן של תרומה שנטמאה. שמותר לסוכו. ואע"ג דקיימא לן (שבת דף פו.) דסיכה כשתיה והוה ליה כמאן דשתי ליה בטומאה. לא נתתי ממנו למת. לעיל מיניה כתיב "לא בערתי ממנו בטמא", וכתיב בתריה "ולא נתתי ממנו למת", כלומר: מן המעשר טמא לא נתתי ממנו למת. הא לחי דומיא דמת — נתתי. ואי זו נתינה משכחת במת — הוי אומר זו סיכה, ודייקינן: דכוותיה בחי שרי. ואימא. "לא נתתי ממנו למת" לא בסיכה קאמר, אלא כך הוא מתודה: לא קניתי ממנו ארון ותכריכים למת חליפו כשנטמא, דלא יכולתי לאוכלו, ולא שניתיו לדבר שאינו לאכילה, והוא צרכי המת, הא לחי דומיא דמת — נתתי, ואשמועינן דאף על גב דמעשר טהור לא יתן אלא לאכילה ושתיה וסיכה, אם נטמא — מותר לחללו לקנות ממנו חלוק. מופנה מצד אחד. דהכא דפסח מופנה לגזירה שוה, אבל דמעשר — כולהו תלתא אצרכת להו. הניחא למאן דאמר. פלוגתא דרבי ישמעאל ורבנן היא, ב"המפלת" במס' נדה (דף כב:). הך דרבי אבהו. דמפיק חד "ממנו" למישרי הדלקה בשמן תרומה שנטמאת, מדרב נחמן נפקא.

בזרעו

תוספות

אונן מותר בפרה. דלא גרע מטבול יום. ואע"ג דאונן אסור במעשר, וטבול יום מותר — היינו לאכילה, אבל לנגיעה תרווייהו שרי. הכי גרים בקונט' שרפת אונן ומחוסר כפורים כשרה. וגרים נמי: תנא דיוסף הבבלי היא. — ומדקדק: דמדפליג אתנא דלעיל במחוסר כפורים — הוא הדין בערל, דכשר. וקשה לר"י: דמה ענין זה אצל זה? דמשום דמכשר במחוסר כפורים (ב) לא יכשיר בערל?! ועוד: דלייתי מברייתא דלעיל, דמכשרא בהדיא ערל, או מדרבי אליעזר בריש פירקין, (דף ע.) דלא מרבה ערל כי טמא! ולספרים דגרסי הכא: שרפת ערל ומחוסר כפורים פסולה, יוסף הבבלי אומר: ערל — כשרה, מחוסר כפורים — פסולה, וגרסינן: יוסף הבבלי היא, — הוה ניחא דמייתי מהכא ולא מההיא דלעיל, דניחא ליה לאיתויי שם התנא דמכשר בדיא. אבל אמר ר"י: דאי אפשר לגרוס כן, דבפ"ב דזבחים (דף יז:) מוכח דיוסף הבבלי ורבנן פליגי במחוסר כפורים וגרסינן נמי: אונן במקום ערל. ואר"י: דאי הוה גרסינן כגירסת הקונט', והוה גרסינן כאן ובזבחים (דף יז:) ערל בהדי אונן — הוה ניחא. מה לפסח כו'. ה"מ למימר שכן (ג) פנקעכ"ס. חד לגופיה.[א] "אל תאכלו ממנו נא", דאי לא כתב "ממנו" ה"א דאמצות ומרורים (ד) דכתב לעיל קאי. מנין למעשר שני שנטמא שמותר לסוכו. דס"ד דאסור, משום שמבער בטומאה. ליקח לו ארון ותכריכים. אע"ג דבהדיא דרשי' ליה להכי במס' מעשר שני (פ"ה מי"ג), הכא (ה) פריך דלמה דוקא להכי הוא דאתא, אבל סיכה אסורה לפי שמבערו בטומאה. ומשני ד"ממנו" — מגופו, דמשמע נמי סיכה. תהא להסקה תחת תבשילך. אע"ג דבפרק "כל פסולי המוקדשים" (בכורות דף לד. ושם) מוקי לה בתרומה תלויה, דבעיא שימור — במסקנא לא קאי התם הכי. א"נ: התם דריש "משמרת", דלא קאי אטמאה, אבל "לך" — קאי אכולהו תרומות.

אינה

עין משפט נר מצוה

נה א מיי' פ"ד מהלכות פרה אדומה הל' יז:

נו ב מיי' פ"ב מהל' תרומות הלכה יד ופי"א הלכה א טוש"ע י"ד סימן שלא סעיף יט:

תוספות ישנים

תלתא ממנו כתיבי במעשר חד לגופיה למעט מעשר ראשון שמותר באנינות: ואימא ליקח לו ארון ותכריכין א"ל רב הונא בר יהושע ממנו מגופו ותימה דהאמת כך הוא דדרשינן במשניות לא נתתי ממנו למת ליקח לו ארון ותכריכין וי"ל דה"ק ואימא ליקח לו ארון ותכריכין דוקא. א"ל רב הונא ממנו כתיב ואפילו מגופו וכ"ש ליקח לו ארון ותכריכין לאסור: אחת תרומה טהורה ואחת תרומה טמאה. ותימה דהתם בפרק כל פסולי המוקדשין אמרינן אחת תרומה טהורה ואחת תרומה תלויה וי"ל דהא והא איתא התם דקאי גבי משמרת תרומותי דמיירי בשמירת תרומה קאמר אחת תרומה טהורה ואחת תרומה תלויה דליכא למימר דקאי אטמאה דהא לא שייך בטמאה שמור לשרפה אזלא. אבל הכא דר"ל דאמר רחמנא להסקה תחת תבשילך קא דריש אחת תרומה טהורה וטמאה יחד דאילו תלויה לאו מנותה בשרפה אלא תולין לא אוכלין ולא שורפין:

הגהות מהר"ב רנשבורג

א] תוס' ד"ה חד לגופיה וכו'. נ"ב עי' מנחות נח ע"ב תוס' ד"ה אין לוקין וכו' ודו"ק:

מסורת הש"ס

[לקמן פה: פו. כתובות כו.]

[לעיל ע. וש"נ]

זבחים יז:

ויקרא כב

[לעיל עה. ע"ש פסחים נו. ע"ש]

שמות יב

[לעיל נד: וש"נ]

[עי' תוס' ב"מ נג. ד"ה וכן נכסי ותוס' לעיל עג. ד"ה נכסי]

דברים כו

[לעיל ע: וש"נ]

במדבר יח

שבת כה. בכורות לד.

[שבת כו.]

ויקרא כב

מכות יד:

הגהות הב"ח

(א) גמ' בהמה למה לי (אלא) מעשר הז"מ. ונ"ב ס"א ולמאי מעשר כו': (ב) תוס' ד"ה הכי גרים וכו' במחוסר כפורים יכשיר כל"ל ותיבת לא נמחק: (ג) ד"ה מה וכו' שכן פנקעס"כ כל"ל ואות סמ"ך נמחק: (ד) ד"ה חד וכו' ומרורים דכתב לעיל קאי כל"ל ותיבת לא נמחק: (ה) ד"ה ליקח וכו' הכא הכי פריך:

הגהות הגר"א

[א] גמ' (דפליג עליה דר' עקיבא) תא"מ (וכמה דחקו בזה המפרשים):

תורה אור

בְּזַרְעוֹ שֶׁל אַהֲרֹן — הֱוֵי אוֹמֵר זוֹ תְּרוּמָה. — וְאֵימָא בְּחָזֶה וָשׁוֹק! אאֵינָהּ בְּחוֹזֶרֶת. תְּרוּמָה נַמִּי באֵינָהּ בַּחֲלָלָה! חֲלָלָה לָאו זַרְעוֹ דְּאַהֲרֹן הִיא. וּמִמַּאי דְּהַאי "עַד אֲשֶׁר יִטְהָר" עַד דְּאִיכָּא הֶעֱרֵב שֶׁמֶשׁ? אֵימָא: עַד דְּמַיְיתֵי כַּפָּרָה! לָא ס"ד, דְּתָנָא דְּבֵי ר' יִשְׁמָעֵאל: בְּזָב בַּעַל שְׁתֵּי רְאִיּוֹת וּבִמְצוֹרָע מוּסְגָּר הַכָּתוּב מְדַבֵּר, דּוּמְיָא דִּטְמֵא נֶפֶשׁ, מַה טְּמֵא נֶפֶשׁ — דְּלָאו בַּר כַּפָּרָה הוּא, הָנֵי נַמִּי — דְּלָאו בְּנֵי כַּפָּרָה נִינְהוּ. וְאֵימָא: הָנֵי מִילֵּי — דְּלָאו בַּר כַּפָּרָה, אֲבָל דְּבַר כַּפָּרָה — עַד דְּמַיְיתֵי כַּפָּרָה! וְתוּ: הָא דִּתְנַן: *גטָבַל וְעָלָה — אוֹכֵל בְּמַעֲשֵׂר, דהֶעֱרִיב שִׁמְשׁוֹ — אוֹכֵל בִּתְרוּמָה, ההֵבִיא כַּפָּרָה — אוֹכֵל בְּקָדָשִׁים, מְנָא לָן? אָמַר רָבָא אָמַר רַב חִסְדָּא: תְּלָתָא קְרָאֵי כְּתִיבֵי; כְּתִיב °"וְלֹא יֹאכַל מִן הַקֳּדָשִׁים כִּי אִם רָחַץ בְּשָׂרוֹ בַּמָּיִם", הָא רָחַץ — טָהוֹר. וּכְתִיב °"וּבָא הַשֶּׁמֶשׁ וְטָהֵר וְאַחַר יֹאכַל מִן הַקֳּדָשִׁים", וּכְתִיב °"וְכִפֶּר עָלֶיהָ הַכֹּהֵן וְטָהֵרָה". הָא כֵּיצַד? כָּאן לְמַעֲשֵׂר, כָּאן לִתְרוּמָה, כָּאן לְקָדָשִׁים. וְאֵיפוּךְ אֲנָא! מִסְתַּבְּרָא, תְּרוּמָה עֲדִיפָא שֶׁכֵּן מחפ"ז. אַדְּרַבָּה, מַעֲשֵׂר עֲדִיפָא שֶׁכֵּן הד"ם ט"ב! אֲפִי' הָכִי, מִיתָה עֲדִיפָא. רָבָא אָמַר: בְּלָא מִיתָה עֲדִיפָא נַמִּי לָא מָצֵית אָמְרַתְּ, אָמַר קְרָא "נֶפֶשׁ", אֵיזֶהוּ דָּבָר שֶׁשָּׁוֶה בְּכָל נֶפֶשׁ הֱוֵי אוֹמֵר זֶה מַעֲשֵׂר. וְאַכַּתִּי, הָנֵי מִילֵּי הֵיכָא דְּלָאו בַּר כַּפָּרָה, אֲבָל הֵיכָא דְּבַר כַּפָּרָה — עַד דְּמַיְיתֵי כַּפָּרָה! אָמַר אַבַּיֵי: תְּרֵי קְרָאֵי כְּתִיבֵי בְּיוֹלֶדֶת: כְּתִיב °"עַד מְלֹאת יְמֵי טָהֳרָהּ", כֵּיוָן שֶׁמָּלְאוּ יָמֶיהָ — טְהוֹרָה, וּכְתִיב "וְכִפֶּר עָלֶיהָ הַכֹּהֵן וְטָהֵרָה", הָא כֵּיצַד? כָּאן לִתְרוּמָה, כָּאן — לְקָדָשִׁים. וְאֵיפוּךְ אֲנָא! מִסְתַּבְּרָא, קֹדֶשׁ חָמוּר, שֶׁכֵּן פנקעכ"ס. אַדְּרַבָּה, תְּרוּמָה חֲמוּרָה, שֶׁכֵּן מחפ"ז! הָנָךְ נְפִישָׁן. רָבָא אָמַר: בְּלָא הָנָךְ נְפִישָׁן לָא מָצֵית אָמְרַתְּ, אָמַר קְרָא "וְכִפֶּר עָלֶיהָ הַכֹּהֵן וְטָהֵרָה" *מִכְּלָל שֶׁהִיא טְמֵאָה. וְאִי ס"ד בְּקָדָשִׁים — אִיקְּרֵי כָּאן °"וְהַבָּשָׂר אֲשֶׁר יִגַּע בְּכָל טָמֵא לֹא יֵאָכֵל". אֶלָּא שְׁמַע מִינַּהּ בִּתְרוּמָה. מַתְקִיף לַהּ רַב שֵׁישָׁא בְּרֵיהּ דְּרַב אִידִי: וּמִי מָצֵית אָמְרַתְּ תְּרוּמָה כְּתִיבָא הָכָא? וְהַתַּנְיָא:* °"דַּבֵּר אֶל בְּנֵי יִשְׂרָאֵל", ואֵין לִי אֶלָּא בְּנֵי יִשְׂרָאֵל, גִּיּוֹרֶת וְשִׁפְחָה מְשׁוּחְרֶרֶת מִנַּיִן — תַּלְמוּד לוֹמַר "אִשָּׁה". וְאִי סָלְקָא דַּעְתָּךְ בִּתְרוּמָה — גִּיּוֹרֶת וְשִׁפְחָה בְּנוֹת מֵיכַל תְּרוּמָה נִינְהוּ?! אָמַר רָבָא: וְלָא?! וְהָכְתִיב

ויקרא כב (at "ולא יאכל מן"); שם (at "ובא השמש"); שם יב (at "וכפר עליה"); שם (at "ביולדת"); שם ז (at "והבשר"); שם יב (at "דבר אל")

רש"י

בזרעו של אהרן. בזכרים ונקבות. דאילו קדשי קדשים הניתנים לכהנים – אין נאכלים אלא לזכרי כהונה. **ואימא**(א) חזה ושוק. דשלמים, הניתן לכהנים ונאכל לנשיהן, כדכתיב (ויקרא י) "אתה ובניך ובנותיך", והני הוא דאסר רחמנא לטמאים – משום דקדשים נינהו, אבל תרומה – לא: ומשני. **ליתא בחוזרת.** בת כהן אלמנה מישראל וזרע אין לה, דאמר בפרק "אלמנה" (לעיל סח:): כשהיא חוזרת – חוזרת לתרומה, ואין חוזרת לחזה ושוק. **וממאי דהאי עד אשר יטהר** עד דעביד הערב שמש. ותו לא, דאמר לעיל מחוסר כפורים מותר בתרומה. **זב בעל שתי ראיות.** לאו בר קרבן הוא, כדתניא במסכת מגילה (דף ח.): מנה הכתוב שתים וקראו טמא, שלש וקראו טמא, הא כיצד? שתים לטומאה, ושלש לקרבן, ומצורע מוסגר נמי לאו בר קרבן הוא, כדתנן התם: אין בין מצורע טהור מתוך הסגר לטהור מתוך החלט אלא תגלחת וצפרים, וכיון דתגלחת ליכא – קרבן נמי ליכא, דבהדי דתגלחת כתיב קרבן. **אבל דבר כפרה.** כגון זב בעל שלש ראיות, ומצורע מוחלט. **הד"ם ט"ב.** הבאת מקום, וידוי, אסור לאונן, ולבער ממנו בטומאה, ואוכלו בטומאת עצמו לוקה, וחייב בביעור. ה' – הבאה, ד' – וידוי, ס' – אסור לאונן, ט' – טומאה, ב' – ביעור. וכולהו ליתנהו בתרומה. **אמר קרא נפש.** בקרא ד"כי אם רחץ בשרו" כתיב "נפש כי תגע בו", אלמא: קרא קמא במעשר משתעי. **ואכתי.** אימא הני מילי דסגי בהערב שמש לתרומה – היכא דלאו בר כפרה הוא, דהא אמרת בזב בעל שתי ראיות ובמצורע מוסגר משתעי קרא. **אבל היכא דבר כפרה.** לא סגי ליה בהערב שמש, ולא אכיל בתרומה עד דמייתי כפרה. **תרי קראי כתיבי ביולדת.** דבת כפרה היא. **כיון שמלאו ימיה.** ארבעים לזכר ושמונים לנקבה – טהרה, והוא הערב שמש שלה, דמשעת טבילה לסוף שבעה לזכר ושבועים לנקבה עד אור הבאת קרבנותיה ליום מחר היא נקראת טבולת יום ארוך במסכת נדה (דף עא.), דומיא דכל מחוסרי כפרה הנקראים טבולי יום ארוך משעת טבילתם עד הערב שמש דליל הבאת קרבנותיהם למחרת. (הכא נמי הוי טבולת יום ארוך משעת טבילה עד סוף יומי הבאת קרבנותיה). **כאן לתרומה.** בהערב שמש. וליכא למימר כאן למעשר בהערב שמש, דהא אמרן לעיל: הא רחץ – טהור, דלא בעי הערב שמש. ולענין טבול יום – מה לי בר כפרה, מה לי לאו בר כפרה. **מכלל שהיא טמאה.** עד השתא. ואי סלקא דעתך קרא קמא דשרי למיכל מאורתא בקדשים. **קרי כאן והבשר אשר יגע בכל טמא לא יאכל.** והאי מחוסר כפורים טמא מקרי, כדכתיב "וטהרה" – מכלל שהיא טמאה. **אל בני ישראל אשה** כי תזריע. אין לי אלא בנות ישראל מטמאות בלידה.

והכתיב

תוספות

אינה בחוזרת. וא"ת: תרומה נמי, כשיש לה בן אינה בחוזרת? וי"ל: דאם מת חוזרת. **הא** רחץ טהור. ואע"ג דבההוא קרא כתיב "וטמאה עד הערב", איכא למימר דקאי אתרומה וקדשים. ומ"מ משמע הא רחץ – טהור. **הוי** אומר זה מעשר. אע"ג דקדשים קלים שוים בכל נפש, מסתברא קדשים דחמירי לא מישתרי בהו עד דמייתי כפרה. **אימא** ה"מ דלאו בר כפרה. אתרומה פריך, אבל מעשר, כיון דסגי בטבילה בלא הערב שמש, ולא בעי שיטהר לגמרי – ה"ה במידי דבר כפרה הוא. **ימי** טהרה. דהוה מצי למכתב: "ובמלאת לבן או לבת". **הנך** נפישן. ה"מ למימר כרת עדיפא. **מכלל** שהיא טמאה. תימה: דבפ"ב דזבחים (דף יט:) דרשי דמחוסר כפרה מחלל עבודה מ"וטהרה" – מכלל שהיא טמאה, וטבול יום דריש התם (דף יז.) "חלול" "חלול" מתרומה, דפסול בתרומה – מיחל עבודה כו'. ואמאי לא יליף בטבול יום נמי מ"ובא השמש וטהר" – מכלל שהוא טמא, כדאמר גבי מחוסר כפורים! ותירץ הרב רבינו חיים: ד"ובא השמש וטהר" – היינו טהר יומא, ולא טהר גברא, כדאמר בריש ברכות (דף ב.) ואע"ג דגבי יולדת כתיב "ובמלאת ימי טהרה" דמשמע מכלל שהיא טמאה – יולדת מחוסרת כפרה היא, ולא גמרי מינה לטבול יום בעלמא. וקרא(ב) ד"לא יאכל מן הקדשים עד אשר יטהר" איכא למימר נמי דתנא דזבחים מוקי לה בזב בעל ג' ראיות, דהוי מחוסר כפרה, כדתנא לקמן (דף עה.) ומיהו תימה: דגבי נגיעה כתיב "וטמא עד הערב וטהר" – מכלל שהוא טמא! ונראה לר"י: דאי לאו דגלי לן בטבול יום מ"ולא יחללו" דחשיב כטמא אע"ג דקלישא טומאתיה, לא הוה דרשינן לא בטבול יום ולא במחוסר כפורים מכלל שהיא טמאה, כיון דקלישא טומאתייהו. והא דקאמר התם לא לכתוב רחמנא בטבול יום ותיתי מהנך, אע"ג דאיצטריך למכתב טבול יום לגלויי אמחוסר כפורים – ה"ק: לא לכתוב בטבול יום, ובמחוסר כפורים יכתוב בפירוש! וא"ת: בפרק "ג' מינין" (נזיר דף מה.) דדרשי' "טמא יהיה" – לרבות טבול יום, "עוד טומאתו בו" – לרבות מחוסר כפורים לענין ביאת מקדש למה לי קרא, כיון דאיקרי טמא? ויש לומר: משום דבטמא הנכנס למקדש כתיב בטומאת מת "ולא יתחטא", וה"א דבחיטוי תליא מילתא, ומכי הזה שלישי ושביעי – תו לא מחייב אביאת מקדש. ואע"ג דאיתקוש קודש ומקדש אהדדי – לא הוה גמרינן להכי. וא"ת: וליפתוק מ"וטהרה" דהכא, ומ"לא יחללו" דזבחים, ונילף קדש ועבודה מדאיקרו טמאים לענין ביאת מקדש! ואר"י: דאי לאו קראי דהכא – לא הוה דרשינן התם "טמא יהיה" לרבות טבול יום כו', אלא הוה מוקמינן ליה לדרשא אחריתי. **קרי** כאן והבשר **אשר** יגע בכל **טמא** כו'. תימה לר"י: דה"ל למימר איקרי כאן וטומאתו עליו ונכרתה, דבטומאת הגוף(ג) קיימין! וי"ל: דלרבותא נקטיה, דאפילו טומאת בשר איכא. **ושפחה** מנין. אית ספרים דגרסי משוחררת. וכן נראה, מדפריך גירות ושפחה בנות מיכל תרומה נינהו? ואי כשאין משוחררת – בת מיכל תרומה היא, אם היא של כהן ומיהו, שאינה משוחררת נמי טמאה לידה, דאמר בפרק "ר' אליעזר דמילה" (שבת קלה:) לקח שפחה מעוברת וילדה אצלו – זהו יליד בית שנימול לח', אלא אותו שאמו טמאה לידה, ובפרק קמא דכריתות (דף ז:) נמי תנן: וכן שפחה, דמביאה קרבן ונאכל. ובתורת כהנים בהדיא גרסינן: גיורת ושפחה, בין משוחררת בין אינה משוחררת, מנין – ת"ל "אשה". ומיהו, תימה: היכי מתרביא שפחה מקרא דאשה? כיון דאיצטריך לגיורת ומשוחררת! ונראה, דשאינה משוחררת אתיא "לה" "לה" מאשה, כדמשמע בכריתות (ג"ז שם)*. **ושפחה** בנות מיכל תרומה נינהו. הך סוגיא דלא כרבי שמעון דשרי לעיל בפרק "הבא על יבמתו" (דף ס:) גיורת פחותה מבת ג' לכהן.

והכתיב

עין משפט נר מצוה

נז א מיי' פ"ו מהלכות תרומות הלכה ט:

נח ב מיי' שם הלכה ז:

נט ג מיי' פ"ג מהלכות מעשר שני הלכה ד סמג לאוין רסד:

ס ד מיי' פ"ז מהלכ' תרומות הלכה ב סמג לאוין רט:

סא ה מיי' פ"א מהלכ' מחוסרי כפרה הלכ' א ופי"ח מהלכות פסולי מוקדשין הלכה יד:

סב ו מיי' פ"ד מהלכ' איסורי ביאה הל' ב:

תוספות ישנים

גיורת ושפחה משוחררת מנין גרסינן אבל לא גרסינן שפחה ומשוחררת דא"כ מאי קא מתמה לקמן גיורת ושפחה בני מיכל תרומה נינהו ליקני אה"נ דשפחה אוכלת בתרומה כדכתיב קנין כספו ועוד שהרי הוקשה לאשה מדגמרינן לה לה מאשה אלא ודאי גרסינן שפחה משוחררת וניחא שפיר שאינה אוכלת בתרומה כיון דשחררה ולכהן לא חזיא א"נ אגב גיורת נקט שפחה. וגם י"ל דמיירי בנתגיירה גדולה דאי בפחותה מג' שנים ויום א' שפיר אכלה בתרומה לרשב"י שמכשירה לכהונה:

מסורת הש"ס

פסחים לה. נדה עא: [נגעים פי"ד מ"ג וע"ש בס"פ בהג"ה]

[סנהדרין פג: זבחים יט:]

[כריתות ז: ע"ש]

במ"ס אין זה

הגהות הב"ח

(א) ד"ה ואימא בחזה ובשוק דשלמים הניתנים לכהנים ונאכלים: (ב) תוס' ד"ה מכלל וכו' וקרא דבקדשים לא יאכל עד אשר יטהר: (ג) ד"ה קרי וכו' קיימינן וי"ל:

גליון הש"ס

גמ' חללה לאו זרעו דאהרן. עי' קדושין דף סו ע"ב תוס' ד"ה ואמרו:

[ועי' תוס' פסחים ע. ד"ה בשפחתו ותוס' ע"ז מב. ד"ה לידע ותוס' נדה טו: ד"ה בשפחתו וע"ע תוס' מנחות סח: ד"ה אין לי וכו' ותוס' סנהדרין פו. ד"ה בני ישראל ותוס' סוכה כח: ד"ה לרבות הגרים]

והכתיב °"בכל קדש לא תגע" *אלרבות התרומה! אלא: קרא מילי מילי קא חשיב. ותלתא קראי בתרומה למה לי? צריכי, דאי מ"עד אשר יטהר" לא הוה ידענא במאי, כתב רחמנא "ובא השמש וטהר". ואי כתב רחמנא "ובא השמש" – *ה"מ דלאו בר כפרה, אבל דבר כפרה – אימא עד דמייתי כפרה, כתב רחמנא "עד מלאת". ואי כתב רחמנא "עד מלאת" הוה אמינא: אפילו בלא טבילה, כתב רחמנא "עד אשר יטהר". ולהך תנא דפליג עליה דתנא דבי ר' ישמעאל, דאמר: בזב בעל ג' ראיות ובמצורע מוחלט הכתוב מדבר, והאי "עד אשר יטהר" עד דמייתי כפרה – תרי קראי בקדשים ל"ל? צריכי; דאי כתב רחמנא ביולדת – משום דמרובה טומאתה, אבל בזב – אימא לא. ואי כתב רחמנא בזב – דלא הותר מכללו, אבל יולדת אימא לא – צריכא. °"במים יובא וטמא עד הערב" למה לי? א"ר זירא: בלנגיעה. דתניא: "וטמא", יכול לכל – ת"ל "וטהר", אי "וטהר" יכול לכל – ת"ל "וטמא". הא כיצד? כאן – למעשר, גכאן – לתרומה. ואיפוך אנא! מסתברא, כי היכי דחמירא אכילה דתרומה מאכילה דמעשר ה"נ חמירא נגיעה דתרומה מנגיעה דמעשר. ואיבעית אימא: נגיעה דתרומה מהכא נפקא: (א) °"בכל קדש לא תגע" – *אזהרה לאוכל, או אינו אלא לנוגע? ת"ל "בכל קדש לא תגע ואל המקדש לא תבא" – מקיש קדש למקדש, מה מקדש – דבר שיש בו נטילת נשמה, אף קדש – דבר שיש בו נטילת נשמה, ובנגיעה נטילת נשמה ליכא, והאי דאפקיה בלשון נגיעה – הכי קאמר: נגיעה כאכילה.§ "פצוע דכא וכו'".§ מאן תנא משתמרת לביאה פסולה דאורייתא אכלה? א"ר אלעזר: במחלוקת שנויה, *ורבי אלעזר ורבי שמעון היא, ר' יוחנן אמר: אפי' תימא ר' מאיר, שאני הכא שכבר אכלה. ור' אלעזר: *שכבר אכלה לא אמרינן, דאי לא תימא הכי, בת ישראל שנשאת לכהן ומת בעלה – תאכל, שכבר אכלה. ורבי יוחנן: *התם – פקע קניינה, הכא – לא פקע קניינה.§ "איזהו פצוע".§ תנו רבנן: *דאיזהו פצוע דכא – כל שנפצעו ביצים שלו, ואפילו אחת מהן. ואפי' ניקבו, ואפילו נמוקו, ואפילו חסרו. אמר רבי ישמעאל בנו של ר' יוחנן בן ברוקה, שמעתי מפי חכמים בכרם ביבנה: כל שאין לו אלא ביצה אחת – אינו אלא סרים חמה, וכשר. סרים חמה ס"ד?! אלא: הרי הוא כסרים חמה, וכשר. וניקב לא מוליד? והא ההוא גברא דסליק לדיקלא וחרזיה

רש"י

והכתיב בכל קדש לא תגע. בההיא פרשתא, ואמר מר במסכת מכות (דף יד:): "בכל קדש" – לרבות התרומה, דאסורה בה כל ימי טוהר, שהיא טבולת יום(ב) לטומאת לידתה. ותלתא קראי בתרומה. "בקדשים לא יאכל עד אשר יטהר", ואוקימנא לעיל מיניה: בתרומה הכתוב מדבר, דבר השוה בזרעו של אהרן, "ובא השמש וטהר" "עד מלאת ימי טהרה". לא ידענא במאי. איזהו היא גמר טהרתו, דעל כרחך גמר טהרה משמע. ה"מ היכא דלאו בר כפרה. דהא כולה עניינא בבעל ג' ראיות ומצורע מוסגר וטמא שרץ ומת משתעי. כתב רחמנא עד מלאת. דאפי' יולדת, דבת כפרה היא – טהורה בהערב שמש. והאי עד אשר יטהר עד דמייתי כפרה. ועל כרחך בקודש מוקמת לה, דהא כתיב קרא אחרינא "ובא השמש וטהר" דמוקמת ליה בתרומה. תרי קראי. "עד אשר יטהר" "וכפר עליה וטהרה" בקדשים למה לי – לאשמועינן דעד דמייתי כפרה. מרובה טומאתה. שמנים יום לאכילת תרומה וקדשים. יולדת הותרה מכללה. שרואה דם וטהורה לבעלה. אבל זב לא הותר מכללו, דכל כמה דלא פסיק – טמא. במים יובא וטמא עד הערב. ע"כ לתרומה איירי, מדבעי הערב שמש למה לי תיפוק לי מ"ובא השמש וטהר". לנגיעה. דקרא דלעיל באכילה משתעי, כדכתיב (ויקרא כב) "ואחר יאכל מן הקדשים", והאי קרא בכלים משתעי, דנגיעה בעלמא היא. ואשמעינן כלי, וה"ה לאדם, טבול יום, לא יגע בתרומה. וטמא. "במים יובא וטמא", אף לאחר ביאת המים קראו טמא. יכול לכל. הוי טמא, ת"ל: "וטהר". מדלא כתיב "ויטהר", משמע דאמעיקרא קאי, קודם הערב שמש. ואי בעית אימא נגיעה דתרומה. לטבול יום מהכא נפקא, דתניא: "בכל קדש לא תגע" – אזהרה לאוכל, שלא תאכל בתרומה כל זמן שהיא טבולת יום ארוך. נטילת נשמה. הבא למקדש טמא – בכרת, שנאמ' (במדבר יט) "ונכרתה... כי את מקדש ה' טמא". אף קדש דבר שיש בו נטילת נשמה. דהיינו אכילה בטומאה, שהוא גבי קדש בכרת, ואוכל תרומה בטומאה במיתה, דכתיב (ויקרא כב) "ומתו בו כי יחללוהו". נגיעה כאכילה. האסור לאכול אסור ליגע. מאן תנא משתמרת לביאה פסולה אכלה. דקתני: ואם לא ידעה משנעשה פצוע דכא – הרי אלו יאכלו, אע"ג דמלפה ומשתמרת לביאתו. במחלוקת שנויה. בפרק "הבא על יבמתו" (לעיל נו:): אלמנה לכ"ג, גרושה וחלוצה לכהן הדיוט, מן האירוסין – לא יאכלו בתרומה, רבי אלעזר ורבי שמעון מכשירין. נפצעו. כמו פצע (שמות כא), מכת חרב וסכין. נמוקו. מחמת מכה נמוקו והוקטנו מאליהן. ואפילו חסרו. כל שהוא. בכרם. שהיו יושבים שורות שורות, ככרם הנטוע שורות שורות. סרים חמה ס"ד. הא סרים חמה בידי שמים (הוא) מחמת חולי, והאי לאו חולי הוא. כסרים חמה וכשר. דלא אסרה תורה אלא פצוע ודך וכרות. וחרזיה

תוספות

והכתיב בכל קדש לא תגע לרבות את התרומה. אע"ג דבנות מגע תרומה נינהו, האי "לא תגע" – באכילה איירי, כדאמר בסמוך ד"לא תגע" אזהרה לאוכל. ותימה: דלמה לי קרא הא אזהרה דתרומה נפקא לן מ"איש איש מזרע אהרן"? ומיהו, מצינו למימר: דאיצטריך למכתב נמי גבי יולדת; משום דהותרה מכללה, כדאמר בסמוך. אבל קשה: דהך דרשא לא אתיא לא כריש לקיש ולא כרבי יוחנן, דבפרק "כל הפסולין" (זבחים לג: ושם) דריש ר"ל: "לא תגע" – אזהרה לטמא שאכל את הקדש, ומדאפקי' בלשון נגיעה מפיק אזהרה לנוגע בקדש, ומרבויא ד"בכל" אזהרה לאוכל לפני זריקה. ולאזהרה לאוכל תרומה לא מוקי לה כלל, אלא מפיק לה מ"איש איש". ור' יוחנן מוקי "לא תגע" אזהרה לנוגע בתרומה, אבל לאוכל – לא מוקי! ותירץ ה"ר אפרים: דהכא, דמוקי לה אזהרה לאוכל תרומה, היינו למאן דמוקי קרא ד"איש איש מזרע אהרן" בזב בעל שלש ראיות, ו"עד אשר יטהר" – עד דמייתי כפרה, ולקדש, כדאמר בסמוך. וא"כ אזהרה לאוכל תרומה – לא נפקא אלא מהכא. ואע"ג דהכא פריך למאן דמוקי ההוא קרא בזב בעל שתי ראיות – מ"מ פריך שפיר, דהא איכא מאן דמוקי לה בתרומה. אע"ג דגיורת ושפחה לאו בנות מיכל תרומה נינהו, ואע"ג דבקדשים מצריך תרי קראי, חד בזב וחד ביולדת – גבי תרומה לא צריך, כיון דכבר חזינן דבאכילת קדש זב ויולדת שוין. ועוי"ל: דתרומה דלא תליא בכפרה לא בעי תרי קראי לזב ויולדת, אלא דוקא לקדש, שצריך להמתין אכפרה.

דאי מ"עד אשר יטהר" לא ידענא במאי. אי יטהר בטבילה לחודה, אי בהערב שמש, כתב רחמנא "ובא השמש וטהר" בתר "כי אם רחץ בשרו במים", לאורויי ד"עד אשר יטהר" דלעיל – בטבילה והערב שמש קאמר. ואי כתב רחמנא "עד מלאת" דהיינו נמי הערב שמש – ה"א דבלא טבילה קאמר, דבכולה פרשתא לא כתיב התם טבילה, כתב רחמנא "עד אשר יטהר" דמשמע טבילה, כדמפרשי קראי בתריה. ואי כתב רחמנא "ובא השמש" ולא כתב "עד מלאת" הוה אמינא: ה"מ – דלאו בר כפרה. וליכא למימר נמי דלכתוב "ובא השמש" ו"עד מלאת", ד"עד אשר יטהר" איצטריך לאזהרה לטבול יום דלאו בר כפרה. ואי כתב רחמנא "עד אשר יטהר" ו"עד מלאת", ולא כתב "ובא השמש", הוה אמינא: ד"עד אשר יטהר" – בטבילה לחודה במידי דלאו בר כפרה, והערב שמש – במידי דבר כפרה, כתב רחמנא "ובא השמש". א"נ: "ובא השמש וטהר" איצטריך לטהר יומא, כדאיתא בריש ברכות (דף ב.).

נגיעה דתרומה מהכא נפקא. תימה לר"י: כיון דמהכא נפקא, אם כן תקשה לן כדמעיקרא: "במים יובא וטמא עד הערב וטהר" למה לי? ועוד: דבפ' "אלו הן הלוקין" (מכות דף יד:) משמע דהך ברייתא דמוקמינן הכא לנגיעת תרומה דבקודש מיירי, דמייתי מינה סייעתא לריש לקיש דמוקי האי קרא ד"בכל קדש לא תגע" לאכילה דקדש ונגיעה דקדש! ונראה לר"י: דה"נ בקדשים מיתוקמא, ואתא לשנויי דלא נימא ואיפוך אנא, דכי היכי דגבי קדש החמיר בנגיעה כבאכילה, הכי נמי גבי תרומה.

כרות שפכה כל שנכרת הגיד. תימה לר"י: דלמאי נקט פליעה בביצים וכריתה בגיד, הא אמרי' בגמרא פלוע בכולן, דכא בכולן, כרות בכולן! ואמר ר"י: דמשום דגיד על ידי כריתה שופך, דבלא כריתה מקלח, נקט כרות שפכה בגיד.

ניקבו. וה"ה אפילו אחת מהן.

שאין לו אלא ביצה אחת אינו אלא כסרים חמה וכשר. תימה: דהא אמר מר כל שנפצעו ביציו, ואפילו אחת מהן! וליכא למימר דהכא בידי שמים – דאם כן אפילו שניהן נמי, כדאמרינן בסמוך גבי פלוע דכשר בידי שמים, ומסתמא הוא הדין כרות. ועוד: דבידי אדם נמי, הא חזינן כמה בני אדם שכורתין מהן ביצה אחת ומולידין, ולא מסתבר לומר לא וחזר על בניהם מאין הם! ואמר

תוספות ישנים

והא כתיב בכל קדש לא תגע לרבות את התרומה דאינה אוכלת בתרומה. וע"כ צ"ל דבאכילה איירי מדפריך תלמודא הכא מיניה דאי בנגיעה לא הוה פריך תלמודא מיניה שהרי גיורת ושפחה אין קפידא בנגיעתם אלא ודאי סבר רבה דבאכילה איירי. וגם נגיעה מפיק תלמודא לקמן מהכא מדאפקיה בלשון נגיעה וקשה דא"כ לא סבר רבה לא כר' יוחנן ולא כריש לקיש דרבי יוחנן מוקי להאי קרא לנגיעת תרומה ולאכילת קדש ולריש לקיש אצטריך קרא לאוכל בשר קדש ולנגיעתו ואומר ה"ר אפרים דסבר שפיר כריש לקיש דמוקים קרא לאוכל בשר קדש ומבכל מפיק אוכל בתרומה ואף לר' יוחנן טוכל לומר כן ודוחק. ועוד תירץ דהא משמע התם דמפקינן אכילה דתרומה מבקדשים לא יאכל עד שיטהר וא"כ י"ל דסוגיא דהתם הויא כמ"ד בזב בעל שתי ראיות הכתוב מדבר ור"ל עד שיטהר עד שיעריב שמשו. ומיירי בתרומה ובכל קדש לא תגע לאכילת קדשים אבל סוגיא דהכא אתיא כמ"ד בזב בעל שלש ראיות הכתוב מדבר ומאי עד אשר יטהר עד אשר יביא כפרתו. וא"כ מיירי קרא [דבקדשים לא יאכל] בקדשים אבל לא בתרומה ובכל קדש לא תגע לרבות את התרומה ואע"ג דהכא איירינן לתנא דבי רבי ישמעאל דאמר בזב בעל שתי ראיות הכתוב מדבר. מ"מ מוכח תלמודא דמצינן למימר מילי מילי קתני שהרי למ"ד בזב בעל ג' ראיות נמי צ"ל כן דתקשי לדידיה הא כתיב בכל קדש וכו' וצריך לו לתרץ מילי מילי קתני וה"נ נימא מילי מילי קתני: ואיפוך אנא וא"ת ומאי ס"ד הלא אסיקנא לעיל דתרומה חמורה משום מתפ"ז ונראה לרבינו נתנאל דדוקא גבי אכילה יש לנו לומר תרומה חמורה משום דבתרומה איכא מיתה באוכלה בטומאת הגוף ובמעשר ליכא אבל גבי נגיעה שמטמא גוף המעשר חמיר טפי מעשר מתרומה שהאוכל מעשר בטומאת עצמו לוקה לאיכא ביה לאו והאוכל תרומה בטומאת עצמה ליכא אלא עשה וא"ל כיון דנגיעה תהא אסורה במעשר היכי מצינו למימר שתהא אכילה מותרת י"ל כגון שתחב לו חבירו בבית הבליעה: ורבי אלעזר סבר אכלה

הגהות הב"ח

(א) גמ' מהכא נפקא דתניא בכל קדש: (ב) רש"י ד"ה והכתיב וכו' טבולת יום ארוך לטומאת לידתה הס"ד:

תוספות חד מקמאי

ת"ר איזהו פצוע דכא כל שנפצעו ביצים שלו ואפילו א' מהם ואפילו נמוקו ואפילו חסרו אר"י בנו של ר' יוחנן בן ברוקה שמעתי מפי חכמים בכרם ביבנה כל שאין לו אלא ביצה א' אינו אלא כסרים חמה וכשר והלכתא כר' ישמעאל והלכתא כת"ק דאמר אפילו אחת מהן דלא פליגי אהדדי כלל ואיתא להא [ואיתא להא] אם נפצע א' מהם פסול ואם נטלה א' מהם כשר מידי דהוי אכליות שאם נטלו הכליות כשרה ואם לקתה בכוליא א' טריפה:

מסורת הש"ס

א) מכות יד: שבועות ז.
כלפו' ה"א
מכות יד. זבחים לג:
[לעיל נו:]
[לעיל נז.]
[ג"ז"ש]
[תוספתא פ"ז]

עין משפט נר מצוה

סג א מיי' פ"ו מהל' מטמאי משכב ומושב הלכה ד:
סד ב ג מיי' פ"ז מהלכות אבות הטומאה הלכ' א והלכה ג:
סה ד מיי' פט"ז מהל' איסורי ביאה הלכה א סמג לאוין קכו טוש"ע אה"ע סימן ה סעיף ז:

תורה אור

וְחַרְזֵיהּ סִילְוָא בְּבֵיצִים, וּנְפַק מִינֵּיהּ כְּחוּט דְּמוּגְלָא, וְאוֹלֵיד. הָא שְׁלַח שְׁמוּאֵל לְקַמֵּיהּ דְּרַב, וַאֲמַר לֵיהּ: צֵא וְחַזֵּר עַל בָּנָיו מֵאַיִן הֵם. אָמַר רַב יְהוּדָה אָמַר שְׁמוּאֵל: [א]פְּצוּעַ דַּכָּא בִּידֵי שָׁמַיִם כָּשֵׁר. אֲמַר רָבָא: הַיְינוּ דְּקָרֵינַן "פְּצוּעַ" וְלָא קָרֵינַן *"הַפָּצוּעַ". בְּמַתְנִיתָא תָּנָא: נֶאֱמַר °"לֹא יָבֹא פְצוּעַ" וְנֶאֱמַר °"לֹא יָבֹא מַמְזֵר" מַה לְּהַלָּן בִּידֵי אָדָם — אַף כָּאן בִּידֵי אָדָם. אָמַר רָבָא: פָּצוּעַ בְּכוּלָּן, דַּךְ בְּכוּלָּן, כָּרוּת בְּכוּלָּן. פָּצוּעַ בְּכוּלָּן — [ב]בֵּין שֶׁנִּפְצַע הַגִּיד, בֵּין שֶׁנִּפְצְעוּ בֵּיצִים, בֵּין שֶׁנִּפְצְעוּ חוּטֵי בֵּיצִים. דַּךְ בְּכוּלָּן — בֵּין שֶׁנִּידַּךְ הַגִּיד, בֵּין שֶׁנִּידְּכוּ בֵּיצִים, בֵּין שֶׁנִּידְּכוּ חוּטֵי בֵּיצִים. כָּרוּת [בְּכוּלָּן] — בֵּין שֶׁנִּכְרַת הַגִּיד, בֵּין שֶׁנִּכְרְתוּ בֵּיצִים, בֵּין שֶׁנִּכְרְתוּ חוּטֵי בֵּיצִים. אֲמַר לֵיהּ הַהוּא מֵרַבָּנַן לְרָבָא: מִמַּאי דְּהַאי פְּצוּעַ דַּכָּא בְּאוֹתוֹ מָקוֹם? אֵימָא מֵרֹאשׁוֹ! אֲמַר לֵיהּ: מִדְּלָא מָנֵה בֵּיהּ דּוֹרוֹת, ש"מ — בְּאוֹתוֹ מָקוֹם. וְדִלְמָא הַאי דְּלָא מָנֵה בּוֹ דּוֹרוֹת — דְּאִיהוּ הוּא דְּאָסוּר, בְּרֵיהּ וּבַר בְּרֵיהּ — כָּשֵׁר? דּוּמְיָא דִּכְרוּת שָׁפְכָה, מַה כְּרוּת שָׁפְכָה בְּאוֹתוֹ מָקוֹם — אַף הַאי נַמִי בְּאוֹתוֹ מָקוֹם. וּכְרוּת שָׁפְכָה גּוּפֵיהּ, מִמַּאי דִּבְאוֹתוֹ מָקוֹם הוּא? אֵימָא מִשִּׁפְתֵיהּ! "שָׁפְכָה" כְּתִיב, בְּמָקוֹם שֶׁשּׁוֹפֵךְ. וְאֵימָא מֵחוֹטְמוֹ! מִי כְּתִיב "בְּשִׁפּוּךְ" "כְּרוּת שָׁפְכָה" כְּתִיב, מִי שֶׁעַל יְדֵי כְּרִיתָה שׁוֹפֵךְ, שֶׁלֹּא עַל יְדֵי כְּרִיתָה אֵינוֹ שׁוֹפֵךְ, אֶלָּא מְקַלֵּחַ, לְאַפּוּקֵי הַאי דְּאִידֵי וְאִידֵי שׁוֹפֵךְ הוּא. בְּמַתְנִיתָא תָּנָא: נֶאֱמַר "לֹא יָבֹא פְּצוּעַ דַּכָּא" וְנֶאֱמַר "לֹא יָבֹא מַמְזֵר" מַה לְּהַלָּן בְּאוֹתוֹ מָקוֹם — אַף כָּאן בְּאוֹתוֹ מָקוֹם. נִיקַּב לְמַטָּה מֵעֲטָרָה, שֶׁכְּנֶגְדּוֹ לְמַעְלָה מֵעֲטָרָה, סָבַר רַבִּי חִיָּיא בַּר אַבָּא לְאַכְשׁוּרֵי. א"ל רַבִּי אַסִּי: הָכִי אֲמַר ריב"ל: [ג]עֲטָרָה כָּל שֶׁהִיא מְעַכֶּבֶת.§ "וְאִם נִשְׁתַּיֵּיר מֵעֲטָרָה כו'".§ יָתֵיב רָבִינָא וְקָמִיבַּעְיָא לֵיהּ: מְלֹא הַחוּט שֶׁאָמְרוּ — [ד]עַל פְּנֵי כּוּלָּהּ אוֹ עַל פְּנֵי רוּבָּהּ? אֲמַר לֵיהּ *רָבָא תּוֹסְפָאָה לְרָבִינָא: מְלֹא הַחוּט עַל פְּנֵי [א] רוּבָּהּ, וּכְלַפֵּי רֵישָׁא. א"ר הוּנָא: [ה]כְּקוּלְמוֹס כְּשֵׁרָה, כְּמַרְזֵב — פְּסוּלָה. הַאי — שָׁלֵיט בָּהּ אֲוִירָא, וְהַאי — לָא שָׁלֵיט בָּהּ אֲוִירָא. וְרַב חִסְדָּא אֲמַר: כְּמַרְזֵב — כְּשֵׁרָה, כְּקוּלְמוֹס — פְּסוּלָה, הַאי — גָּרֵיד, וְהַאי — לָא גָּרֵיד. אֲמַר רָבָא: כְּוָותֵיהּ דְּרַב הוּנָא מִסְתַּבְּרָא, הַאי — לָא שָׁלֵיט בָּהּ אֲוִירָא, וְהַאי — שָׁלֵיט בָּהּ אֲוִירָא. אִי מִשּׁוּם גְּרִידוּתָא — מִידֵי דַּהֲוָה אַבַּרְזָא דְּחָבִיתָא. אֲמַר לֵיהּ רָבִינָא לְמָרֵימָר, הָכִי אֲמַר מָר זוּטְרָא מִשְּׁמֵיהּ דְּרַב פַּפָּא: הִלְכְתָא, בֵּין כְּקוּלְמוֹס בֵּין כְּמַרְזֵב — כְּשֵׁרָה. מִיהוּ, מִיבַּעְיָא לֵיהּ: לְמַטָּה מֵעֲטָרָה אוֹ לְמַעְלָה? פְּשִׁיטָא דִּלְמַעְלָה מֵעֲטָרָה, דְּאִי ס"ד לְמַטָּה מֵעֲטָרָה — אֲפִילּוּ נִכְרַת הַגִּיד נַמִי! וְרָבִינָא: לְשַׁבּוֹשֵׁי לְמָרֵימָר הוּא דְּבָעֵי. הַהוּא עוּבְדָּא דַּהֲוָה בְּמָתָא מְחַסְיָא, שַׁפְיֵיהּ מָר בַּר רַב אָשֵׁי כְּקוּלְמוֹס וְאַכְשְׁרֵיהּ. הַהוּא עוּבְדָּא דַּהֲוָה בְּפוּמְבְּדִיתָא אִיסְתַּתֵּים גּוּבְתָּא דְּשִׁכְבַת זֶרַע וְאַפֵּיק בִּמְקוֹם קְטַנִּים, סָבַר רַב בֵּיבַי בַּר אַבַּיֵי לְאַכְשׁוּרֵי, אֲמַר רַב פַּפִּי: מִשּׁוּם (א) דְּאָתוּ מִמּוּלָאֵי

דברים כג שם

רש"י

וְחַרְזֵיהּ סִילְוָא בְּבֵיצִים. נִקְּבוֹ קוֹץ בְּבֵיצָיו. לְשׁוֹן מַחֲרוֹזוֹת שֶׁל דָּגִים (ב"מ דף כא.) וּנְפַק מִינֵּיהּ. שִׁכְבַת זֶרַע. כְּחוּט דְּמוּגְלָא. כְּמִין לֵיחָה, וַאֲפִי' הָכִי אוֹלִיד בָּתַר הָכִי. מֵאַיִן הֵם. זָנְתָה אִשְׁתּוֹ. בִּידֵי שָׁמַיִם. ע"י רְעָמִים וּבָרָד, אוֹ מִמְּעֵי אִמּוֹ. אִי הֲוָה כְּתִיב הַפָּצוּעַ. הֲוֵי מַשְׁמַע הַפָּלוּעַ מֵעִיקָּרוֹ, כְּגוֹן מִמְּעֵי אִמּוֹ. בְּכוּלָּן. בֵּיצִים וְגִיד וְחוּטֵי בֵּיצִים, שֶׁהַבֵּיצִים תְּלוּיִן בָּהֶן בְּתוֹךְ הַכִּיס. מִדְּלָא מָנֵה בֵּיהּ דּוֹרוֹת שְׁמַע מִינָּהּ. מִדְּלָא כְּתִיבָא בֵּיהּ "עַד דּוֹר שְׁלִישִׁי" אוֹ "עֲשִׂירִי" כְּמוֹ שֶׁנֶּאֱמַר בְּמַמְזֵר וְעַמּוֹנִי וּמוֹאָבִי וּמִצְרִי — ש"מ מִשּׁוּם דְּלָאו בַּר אוֹלוּדֵי הוּא. אֵימָא מִשִּׁפְתֵיהּ. שֶׁשּׁוֹפְכִים רוֹק. כְּרוּת שָׁפְכָה(ג). וּפִיו אֵינוֹ שׁוֹפֵךְ, אֶלָּא זוֹרֵק לְמֵרָחוֹק. מִי כְּתִיב כְּרוּת בְּשִׁפּוּךְ. מִמָּקוֹם הָרָגִיל לִשְׁפּוֹךְ קוֹדֶם לָכֵן. שׁוֹפֵךְ. שׁוֹתֵת. אִידִי וְאִידִי. קוֹדֶם כְּרִיתָה וּלְאַחַר כְּרִיתָה. נִיקַּב לְמַטָּה מֵעֲטָרָה. בְּסוֹף הַגִּיד כְּלַפֵּי קַרְקַע, וְהוֹלֵךְ הַנֶּקֶב בַּאֲלַכְסוֹן, וְיוֹצֵא כְּנֶגְדּוֹ לְמַעְלָה מִן הָעֲטָרָה כְּלַפֵּי הַגּוּף. לְאַכְשׁוּרֵי. הוֹאִיל וְאֵין שְׁנֵי רָאשֵׁי הַנֶּקֶב לְמַעְלָה מֵעֲטָרָה, דְּכָל לְמַטָּה מֵעֲטָרָה בָּשָׂר בְּעָלְמָא הוּא, כִּדְקָתָנֵי מַתְנִיתִין: אִם נִשְׁתַּיֵּיר מִן הָעֲטָרָה מְלֹא הַחוּט — כָּשֵׁר. עֲטָרָה — שׁוּרָה גְּבוֹהָה הַמַּקֶּפֶת סְבִיבוֹת הַגִּיד. כָּל שֶׁהוּא. כֵּיוָן שֶׁהַנֶּקֶב עוֹבֵר דֶּרֶךְ עַל פְּנֵי כָּל הָעֲטָרָה, אֲפִי' נֶקֶב כָּל שֶׁהוּא מְעַכֶּבֶת תּוֹלַדְתּוֹ, וּפָסוּל. וְאִם נִשְׁתַּיֵּיר מֵעֲטָרָה כו'. מַתְנִי' הִיא (לעיל דף ע.), וְאַכְּרִיתָה קָאֵי.(ג) (פֵּירֵשׁ אַכְּרוּת שָׁפְכָה וְלָא אַפְּצוּעַ דַּכָּא). וּכְלַפֵּי רֹאשָׁהּ. לְצַד גּוּפוֹ. נִשְׁתַּיֵּיר מְלֹא הַשֵּׂעָר עַל פְּנֵי רוֹב הֶקֵּיפָהּ. אֲבָל אִם נֶחְתְּכָה כְּלַפֵּי הַגּוּף, וְנִשְׁתַּיֵּיר מְלֹא הַחוּט מִן הָעֲטָרָה עַל פְּנֵי הֶיקֵּף כָּל הַגִּיד בְּלִדָּהּ כְּלַפֵּי קַרְקַע — פָּסוּל. כְּקוּלְמוֹס. כְּחִיתּוּךְ קוּלְמוֹס, שֶׁמְּחַתְּכִין אֶת חוּדּוֹ בַּאֲלַכְסוֹן לִכְתּוֹב בּוֹ. כְּמַרְזֵב. שֶׁנֶּחְקַק כְּסִילוֹן, וְיֵשׁ לוֹ דְּפָנוֹת מִב' צְדָדִים וְהַחֲקָק בָּאֶמְצַע כְּמִין צִנּוֹר. כְּמַרְזֵב שָׁלֵיט בָּהּ אֲוִירָא. הָרוּחַ נִכְנָס לְתוֹךְ הַדְּפָנוֹת, וּמִתְקָרֵר הַגִּיד לְתוֹכוֹ, וְאֵין הַזֶּרַע מִתְבַּשֵּׁל. בְּקוּלְמוֹס. לֹא שָׁלֵיט אֲוִירָא בְּתוֹךְ הַגִּיד, וּמִתְבַּשֵּׁל הַזֶּרַע בְּחִימּוּם כְּהִלְכָתוֹ. הַאי גָּרֵיד. כְּמַרְזֵב גָּרֵיד שִׁכְבַת זֶרַע מִן הַגּוּף בִּשְׁעַת תַּשְׁמִישׁ, וּמַזְרִיעַ, שֶׁהֲרֵי לֹא נֶחְסַר הַגִּיד מֵעוֹבְיוֹ, וְנוֹגֵעַ בְּלִידֵי הָרֶחֶם וּמִתְחַמֵּם, וּמוֹצִיא וְיוֹרֶה כְּחֵץ. וְהַאי לָא גָּרֵיד. כְּקוּלְמוֹס, ע"י שֶׁנֶּחְסַר עוֹבְיוֹ וְאֵינוֹ נוֹגֵעַ בְּכוֹתְלֵי הָרֶחֶם — אֵין מִתְחַמֵּם כָּל כָּךְ, וְאֵין נִמְשָׁךְ מִתּוֹךְ הַגּוּף בְּקִילּוּחַ, אֶלָּא שׁוֹתֵת. מִידֵי דַּהֲוָה אַבַּרְזָא דְּחָבִיתָא. שֶׁקָּצָר וְדַק מִלְּפָנָיו, וְאֵינוֹ נוֹגֵעַ בְּכוֹתְלֵי נֶקֶב הֶחָבִית בְּפָנָיו, וּכְשֶׁהוּא תּוֹחֲבוֹ וּבָא עַד עָבְיוֹ — נוֹגֵעַ. כָּךְ, אע"ג שֶׁאֵין רֹאשׁ הַגִּיד נוֹגֵעַ מִפָּנָיו — מִתְחַמֵּם הוּא מֵחֲמַת נְגִיעַת אֲחוֹרָיו. אִית דְּאָמְרֵי: כְּקוּלְמוֹס גָּרֵיד — שִׁכְבַת זֶרַע מִמְּעֵי אִשָּׁה וּמוֹצִיאוֹ, וְאֵין נִקְלָט. בַּרְזָא דְּחָבִיתָא — שֶׁאֵין שִׁיפּוּעַ רֹאשׁוֹ נוֹגֵעַ בְּדוֹפְנֵי הֶחָבִית שֶׁבִּפְנִים. וַאֲפִילּוּ נִכְרַת נַמִי. כָּל הַגִּיד, דְּהָא תְּנַן: אִם נִשְׁתַּיֵּיר מֵעֲטָרָה מְלֹא הַחוּט — כָּשֵׁר, אע"פ שֶׁנֶּחְתַּךְ כֹּל שֶׁמֵּעֲטָרָה וּלְמַטָּה. לְשַׁבּוֹשֵׁי לְמָרֵימָר. לֵידַע אִם מְחוּדָּד הוּא לְהָשִׁיב עַל שְׁאֵלָתוֹ. הַהוּא עוּבְדָּא. דַּהֲוָה כְּמַרְזֵב. שַׁפְיֵיהּ. חָתַךְ הַבָּשָׂר מִכָּל צַד, וְנָטַל דּוֹפְנֵי מַרְזֵב וַעֲשָׂאוֹ כְּקוּלְמוֹס, וְאַכְשְׁרֵיהּ כְּרַב הוּנָא. גּוּבְתָּא. קָנֶה. נֶקֶב שֶׁרָאוּי לְהוֹצִיא בּוֹ זֶרַע נִסְתַּם, וְהָיָה מוֹצִיא קֶרִי דֶּרֶךְ מֵי רַגְלַיִם, דְּתַנְיָא בִּבְכוֹרוֹת (דף מד:): שְׁנֵי נְקָבִים יֵשׁ בָּאָדָם, אֶחָד מוֹצִיא שֶׁתֶן וְאֶחָד מוֹצִיא שִׁכְבַת זֶרַע, וּבֵינֵיהֶן כִּקְלִיפַּת הַשּׁוּם. קְטַנִּים. מֵי רַגְלַיִם. לְאַכְשׁוּרֵי. שֶׁהֲרֵי אֵין כָּאן לֹא פָּצוּעַ וְלֹא דַּךְ וְלֹא כָּרוּת. מִמּוּלָאֵי

תוספות

ואמר רבינו תם דיש לחלק בין ניטלה הבילה לפליעה. דכשניטלה לגמרי — מוליד, מידי דהוה אניטול הטחול (חולין דף נה.) דכשרה, וניקב בסומכיה — טריפה. והא דאמר לקמן בין שנכרתו בילים בין חוטי בילים — היינו דוקא שניהן, אבל נכרת אחת מן הבילים — כשר. ואף אם תמלי לומר דר' ישמעאל לפלוגי אתנא קמא אתי — הלכתא כוותיה, כיון ששמע מפי חכמים בכרם ביבנה, דהוה סמכא. כדאמר ב"החולץ" (לעיל מב:): ממתני' דכרמא הדר ביה. ובירושלמי נמי משמע דהלכה דכשר. אבל משמע דאין מוליד, דא"ר זירא: שמעתי שהלכה כרבי ישמעאל. ואמר נמי שמואל התם: אם יבא לפני בעל בילה אחת — אני מכשירו. א"ר יודן בר חנינא: ובלבד שלימין. אר"י: שיש לפרש בתרי גווני, כלומר: דוקא שנטלה האחת והאחת שלימה כשר, אבל נפלעה אפילו אחת — גרע טפי, כדפי'. אבל יותר נראה לר"י לפרש שהם שתי תיבות, ובלבד בשל ימין. וחומרא גדולה. וטוב להזהיר לרופאים לחתוך של שמאל אם אפשר. ומסיים דעובדא הוה קמיה דרבי אמי, א"ל: אין כרתי את שריי ליה, אלא הוי ידעה דלא מוליד. משמע דלכולהו הלכה כרבי ישמעאל דמכשר, ומשמע התם מתוך המסקנא דאיירי בידי אדם: **ניקב** למטה מן העטרה שכנגדו למעלה מן העטרה. ואר"י: דעל גב גיד העטרה מארכת, ובתחתונו של גיד הולכת ומתקצרת לראש הגויה. וקאמר ניקב למטה מן העטרה בעליונו של גיד, והנקב מפולש — והוי בתחתונו של גיד למעלה מן העטרה, לפי שמתקצרת שם. וקאמר: סבר רבי חייא לאכשורי, כיון דמצד אחד, דהיינו בעליונו, הוי למטה מעטרה. ומסיק דעטרה כל שהוא מעכבת, ופסול. כיון שמצד אחד הוא למעלה מן העטרה. ונראה דנקב מפולש בעינן. דאין לומר אפילו לא ניקב אלא עד חלל הגיד, ואפילו למטה מעטרה, פסול, כיון שאם היה נקב מעבר אל עבר היה בצד אחד למעלה מעטרה — דהא מכשרינן בסמוך כקולמוס וכמרזב, וכיון דאפי' נחתך לגמרי כשר — כל שכן ניקב: ממולאי

עין משפט נר מצוה

סו א מיי' פט"ז מהל' איסורי ביאה הלכה ח סמג לאוין קי טוש"ע אה"ע סימן ה סעיף י:

סז ב מיי' שם הלכה ג טוש"ע שם סעיף ב:

סח ג מיי' שם הלכה ה טוש"ע שם סעיף ה:

סט ד מיי' שם הלכה ד טוש"ע שם סעיף ב:

ע ה מיי' שם טוש"ע שם סעיף ג:

הגהות הב"ח

(א) גמ' משום דאתיתו ממולאי: (ב) רש"י ד"ה כרות שפכה כתיב ופיו: (ג) ד"ה ואם נשתייר וכו' קאי (פי' אכרות וכו' דכא) תא"מ. ונ"ב בס"א אינו ושום תלמיד הגיהו לפרש דברי רש"י:

גי' יעב"ץ רבה

[נ"ל פציע פי' פליע בידי שמים אבל פלוע כמו פרוע כדכתיב כי פרעה אהרן והוא דבר שנעשה בידי אדם ערוך ערך פלע בשם רבינו חננאל]

במ"ס אין זה

תוספות חד מקמאי

נקב (למעלה) [למטה] מעטרה שכנגדו למעלה מעטרה סבר ר' חייא לאכשורי. א"ל ר' אבא הכי אמר ריב"ל עטרה כל שהוא מעכבת: הא דתנן אם נשתייר מעטרה כחוט (בשר) [השערה כשר] אמר עלה בגמ' יתיב רבינא וקא מבעיא ליה מלא החוט שאמרו ע"פ כולה או ע"פ רובה. א"ל רבה תוספאה מלא החוט ע"פ רובה וכלפי ראשה אמר מר זוטרא משמיה דרבינא הלכתא בין כקולמוס בין כמרזב כשר מיהא קא מיבעיא ליה למטה מעטרה או למעלה מעטרה פשיטא דלמעלה מעטרה דאי למטה מעטרה אפילו נכרת. ההוא עובדא דהוה בפומבדיתא דאסתתם גובתא דשכבת זרע ואפיק במקום קטנים סבר רב ביבי בר אביי לאכשורי אמר רב פפי

הגהות הגר"א

[א] גמ' רובה. נ"ב גי' הרא"ש כולה. (ועמ"ש רבינו באה"ע סי' ה' סק"ו):

ממולאי. ממשפחה אומללה, מבית עלי. דאמרינן בפ"ק דר"ה (דף יח.): אביי ורבה מדבית עלי קאתו. מבשלה. מתבשל שכבת זרע ונגמר להוליד ולעשות פרי. ניקב. נקב קטן שנסתם בכל שהוא, ואין ניכר. רואים, אם גדול כ"כ שאם נקרי האיש הזה נקרע ומרחיב הנקב מחמת דוחק הזרע שמתאסף — פסול.

ממולאי פי' בקונטרס: מקוטעים, משפחה אומללה. וקשה: דהוה ליה למימר משום דאתון מולאי! ויש לפרש שהוא שם מקום, כדאמרינן בב"ר *ר"מ אזל לממלא, חזנהו דהוו שחורי ראש, אמר להו: מדבית עלי אתון, דכתיב "כל מרבית ביתך" וגו'.

תורה אור

*ממולאי אמריתו מילי מוליתא? [א]במקומה — מבשלה, שלא במקומה — לא מבשלה. אמר רב יהודה אמר שמואל: [ב]ניקב ונסתם, כל שאילו נקרי ונקרע פסול, ואי לאו כשר. הוי בה רבא: היכא? אילימא למטה מעטרה — אפי' נכרת נמי, [ג]אלא בעטרה עצמה. איתמר נמי, אמר רב מרי בר מר אמר מר עוקבא אמר שמואל: ניקב בעטרה עצמה ונסתם, כל שאילו נקרי ונקרע — פסול, ואי לאו — כשר. שלח ליה רבא בריה דרבה לרב יוסף: ילמדנו רבינו, היכי עבדינן? א"ל: מייתינן נהמא חמימא דשערי, ומנחינן ליה אבי פוקרי, ומקרי, וחזינן ליה. אמר אביי: אטו כ"ע יעקב אבינו הואי, דכתיב ביה (בראשית מט) °"כחי וראשית אוני" שלא ראה קרי מימיו? אלא אמר אביי: מעברינן קמיה בגדי צבעונין. אמר רבא: אטו כ"ע ברזילי הגלעדי הוא? אלא, מחוורתא כדשנין מעיקרא. ת"ר: *ניקב — פסול, מפני שהוא שותת. [ד]נסתם — כשר, מפני שהוא מוליד. וזהו פסול שחוזר להכשירו. זהו — למעוטי מאי? למעוטי קרום שעלה מחמת מכה בריאה, דאינו קרום. שלח ליה רב אידי בר אבין לאביי: היכי עבדינן? מייתינן שערתא, ומסרטינן ליה, ומייתינן תרבא ושייפינן, ומייתינן שומשנא גמלא ומנכתינן ליה, ופסקינן ליה לרישיה. ודוקא שערתא, אבל *פרזלא — מזרף זריף. וה"מ — קטן, אבל גדול — מיקפולי מיקפל. אמר רבה בר רב הונא: המטיל מים משתי מקומות — פסול. אמר רבא: לית הלכתא לא כברא ולא כאבא. ברא — הא דאמרן, אבא — דא"ר הונא: *נשים המסוללות זו בזו פסולות לכהונה. ואפילו לרבי אלעזר דאמר *פנוי הבא על הפנויה שלא לשם אישות עשאה זונה, ה"מ איש, אבל אשה — [ה]פריצותא בעלמא.

§ **מתני'** [ו]פצוע דכא וכרות שפכה מותרין בגיורת ומשוחררת, ואינן אסורין אלא מלבא בקהל, שנאמר (דברים כג) °"לא יבא פצוע דכא וכרות שפכה בקהל ה'".

§ **גמ'** בעו מיניה מרב ששת: פצוע דכא כהן, מהו בגיורת ומשוחררת? בקדושתיה קאי, ואסיר, או דלמא [ז]לאו בקדושתיה קאי, ושרי? א"ל רב ששת: תניתוה, [ח]פצוע דכא ישראל מותר בנתינה. ואי ס"ד בקדושתיה קאי — איקרי כאן (שם ז) °"לא תתחתן בם"! אמר רבא: אטו התם משום קדושה ולאו קדושה הוא? דלמא מוליד בן ואזיל פלח לעבודה זרה, (א) וה"מ — בגויותן, כי מגיירי — *בישראל שרו, ורבנן הוא דגזרו בהו, וכי גזרו בהו רבנן — בהנך דבני אולודי, אבל האי דלאו בר אולודי לא גזרו ביה רבנן. אלא מעתה, ממזר דבר אולודי — הכי נמי דאסיר? (ב) והא תנן: *[ט]ממזרים ונתינים מותרים לבא זה בזה! אלא: כי גזור רבנן — בכשרים, בפסולים לא גזור רבנן. הדר אמר רבא: לאו מילתא היא, (ג) בגויותן לית להו חתנות, נתגיירו — אית להו חתנות. מתיב רב יוסף: (מ"א ג) °"ויתחתן שלמה את בת פרעה מלך מצרים"! [י]גיורי גיירה. והא *[כ]לא קבלו גרים לא בימי דוד ולא בימי שלמה! מידי הוא טעמא — אלא לשולחן מלכים, הא

רש"י

היכא אילימא למטה מעטרה כו'. דהוא בראש הגיד. ולמעלה מעטרה ליכא לאוקומי, דהתם ודאי לא מקרע, שאין הזרע דוחה ומתאסף אלא אצל נקב יציאתו. היכי עבדינן. כי אתי לקמן לאורויי, היכי מייתינן ליה לידי קרי, דלחזי אי מיקרע, למיבדקיה ולאכשוריה? אבי פוקרי. נקב בית הרעי. ומחמת חמימותו הוא נקרי. כך שמעתי. ראשית אוני. היא היתה טפת קרי שיצאה ממנו ראשון, שלא ראה קרי מימיו, כלומר: דמצרכת ליה כולי האי. מעבירין לפניו בגדי צבעונים. של אשה, והוא מהרהר באשה, ונקרי. ברזילי הגלעדי. שטוף בזימה היה, דכתיב ביה: "אם יטעם עבדך", ואמרי' במסכת שבת בפ' "שואל אדם" (דף קנב.): שטוף בזימה היה, לפיכך קפצה עליו זקנה. דההיא אמתא דהויא בי רבי בת צ' ותרתין שנין, וטעמה קידרא. מפני שהוא שותת. שמחמימות התאוה יוצא דרך הנקב, (וכשהזרע יוצא דרך הנקב יציאתו) אין יורה כחץ וקי"ל (חגיגה דף טו.): שכבת זרע שאין יורה כחץ — אינו מזריע. למעוטי קרום שעלה מחמת מכה בריאה דאינו קרום. משום דהדר מיפחת. והיינו הנך סירכי דריאה דמיטרפא בהו חיותא. היכי עבדינן. רפואה לסתום גיד שניקב. שערתא. שעורה. ומסרטינן ליה. כל סביבות הנקב, כדי (ד) שיגליע ויוציא דם, ומתוך כך הוא מעלה ארוכה ובשר עולה. שומשנא גמלא. נמלה גדולה. ומנכתינן ליה. מניחין ראשה שם, ונושך, ונדבק ראשו בנקב. ופסקינן ליה לרישיה. להיות סתומה. וכל זמן שהוא הולך ובלה — הבשר עולה ומתחבר. מזרף זריף. עושה חבורה, אסגרטי"א בלע"ז. לישנא אחרינא: מזרף זריף — מעלה נפח, אופל"א בלע"ז. איקפולי מיקפל. לאחר שעלה ארוכה חוזר ונקלף ונסתר. המסוללות. דרך תשמיש זכר ונקבה, משפשפות נקבתן זו לזו. וכן המסוללת בבנה קטן דסנהדרין (דף סט:). פסולות לכהונה. משום זנות. **מתני'** מותרין בגיורת ומשוחררת. דלא איקרו קהל. **גמ'** כהן. [אבל כהן] כשר אסור בגיורת ומשוחררת משום זונה, °שנבעלה מקודם. פצוע דכא כהן. שאסור בישראלית, מהו לישא גיורת? פצוע דכא ישראל. ה"ג: פלוע דכא מותר בנתינה, ולא גרסינן כהן. נתינה. מז' אומות, מן הגבעונים. ואי ס"ד פצוע דכא בקדושתיה קאי. היכי שרי ישראל בנתינה? הא כתיב "לא תתחתן בם". אטו התם. דקאסר רחמנא להתחתן בגוים, משום קדושה ולאו קדושה הוא דליסרינהו אפילו נתגיירו, כגון נתינים שהם גרים? התם טעמא דלמא מוליד בר ופלח לעבודה זרה, הלכך קרא בגויותן כתיב, אבל נתגיירו — שרו, דהא דאמור רבנן ישראל כשר לא ישא נתינה — גזירה הוא דגזור, כדאמרינן בהאי פירקא (דף עח:): דוד גזר עליהן. וכי גזור רבנן בהני — דבני אולודי נינהו, דומיא דאיסור דאורייתא, דטעמא משום אולודי. אלא מעתה ממזר דבר אולודי הוא. ומוזהר על כל איסורין שבתורה, ומדאורייתא אסור בגויה, ה"נ דאסור מדרבנן בנתינה. בפסולין. כגון פלוע דכא וממזר לא גזור רבנן, משום דמילתא דלא שכיחא היא. א"נ שלא היתה(ה) זו גזירה משום איסור, אלא לפי שלא היו רחמנים, אמר דוד: אין ראוין להתערב ישראל בהן, לכך לא אסר את הפסולים. לאו מילתא היא דאמרי. דאוקימנא קרא בגויותן, דבגויותן לית להו חתנות. אלא ודאי קרא בגרים כתיב, ומשום קדושה היא. ומדשרינן פלוע דכא בנתינה — שמע מינה לאו בקדושתיה קאי. לא קבלו גרים כו'. קושיא הוא. מידי הוא טעמא. האי דלא קבלו גרים, אלא משום דלא הוו מגיירי אלא לשולחן מלכים, הא בת פרעה לאו צריכא להכי, שהרי בת מלך היתה.

ותיפוק

תוספות

שלא ראה קרי מימיו. ונתעברה מביאה ראשונה, שמיעכה באצבעה. כדאמרינן בתמר בפרק "ד' אחין" (לעיל לד:).

המסוללות. פירש ריב"ן: מטילות שכבת זרע שקבלו מבעליהן. ולא יתכן, דבפ' "במה אשה" (שבת דף סה. ושם) אמרי': *שמואל לא שביק להו לבנתיה דגנין גבי הדדי, משום דרב הונא, דאמר: נשים המסוללות כו'. ומשמע דלא היו נשואות, שהיו עדיין בבית שמואל! ולא יתכן נמי הא דפירש בקונטרס התם דפסולות לכהן גדול, דאע"ג דכהן גדול לא הוה בימי שמואל — מכל מקום מכוער הדבר, כיון שנפסלות בכך לכהן גדול. דהכא משמע דפסולות אף לכהן הדיוט משום זונה, מדקאמר: אפילו לרבי אלעזר דאמר פנוי כו', מכלל דרב הונא משום זונה פסיל להו.

בגויותן לית להו חתנות. והא דפריך בפ' "אין מעמידין" (ע"ז דף לו. ושם) בנותיהן דאורייתא נינהו, דכתיב "לא תתחתן בם" — אסיפא דקרא סמיך, דכתיב "בתו לא תקח לבנך". וכן בשילהי "האומר" בקדושין (דף סח: ושם) לא גרסינן התם לא יהא לך חיתון בהם, דלשון זה משמע ד"לא תתחתן" דריש. ור"ת הגיה: לא יהא לך ליקוחין בהן, ד"לא תקח" דריש, כדפרישית, ואיירי בגויותן. כדדרשינן: "כי יסיר" — לרבות כל המסירים, דלא שייך בגירות.

ותיפוק

עין משפט נר מצוה

[סדר חיי שרה פרשה נט]

עא א מיי' פט"ז מהל' איסורי ביאה הלכה ה סמג לאוין קי טוש"ע אה"ע סימן ה סעיף ו:

עב ב ג ד מיי' שם הלכה ה טוש"ע שם סעיף ז:

עג ה מיי' שם פרק כא הלכה ח סמג לאוין קכז טוש"ע שם סימן כ סעיף ב:

[נ"ל אבוה דשמואל]

עד ו ז ח מיי' שם פט"ז הלכה א סמג לאוין קיח טוש"ע שם סי' ה סעיף א:

עה ט מיי' שם פט"ו הלכה לג:

עו י מיי' שם פי"ג הלכה טז:

עז כ מיי' שם הלכה טו:

תוספות ישנים

ורבנן הוא דגזרו בהו. וא"ת והא קא חשיב באלו הן הלוקין נתינה. וי"ל דמכת מרדות קאמר ואגב ממזרת נקטא ולקמן אפרש בעז"ה:

תוספות חד מקמאי

משום דאתי ממולאי אמריתו [מילי] מוליתא במקומה מבשלה שלא במקומה לא מבשלה. אמר רב יהודה אמר שמואל ניקב ונסתם כל שאילו נקרי פי' רואה קרי ונקרע פסול ואי לאו כשר. הוו בה רבה אילימא למטה מעטרה אפלו נקרע נמי אלא למעלה מעטרה: היכי עבדינן מייתינן נהמא חמימא דשערי ומנחינן ליה אבי פוקריה ומקרי וחזינן ליה: בעו מיניה מרב ששת פצוע דכא מהו בגיורת בקדושתיה קאי ואסור או דלמא לאו בקדושתיה קאי ושרי אמר להו רב ששת תניתוה הפצוע דכא מותר בנתינה ואי ס"ד בקדושתיה קאי קרי כאן לא תתחתן בם אלא לאו ש"מ לאו בקדושתיה קאי. וכהן בגיורת ה"ל כישראל בנתינה. וכיון דפסק רבה אפי' בגירותן אית להו חתנות וכ"ש בגיותן אלמא מסקנא הכי דלאו בקדושתיה קאי והא דאמרי' לקמן דוד גזר עליהם דנתינים איכא למימר דפליג אדרבה וס"ל דלא תתחתן בם בגיותן הוא אבל בגירותן שרי ואתא דוד וגזר עליהם דאי ס"ל כרבה דבגירותן אמורה תורה לא תתחתן בם מה גזר דוד וכ"ת א"כ קשיא מתני' דאלו הן הלוקין דקתני הבא על הנתינה ומדקאמר הבא על הנתינה ולא קתני הבא על הגויה אלמא לכשנתגיירה עסקינן ואפ"ה לוקה אלמא נתגיירו אית להו חתנות וקשה למ"ד דוד גזר עליהם וי"ל ולטעמיך לטעמיה דרב' דס"ד מעיקרא דבגיותן אסרה תורה ולא בגירותן קשיא מתני' דאלו הן הלוקין אלא מאי אית לך למימר מאי לוקה מדרבנן ומשום שטפה דממזרת

תנא נתנה אע"ג דלא דמיא לה ולא אתיא מינה דומיא דחלוצה דאגב שטפה דגרושה תניא אע"פ שאינה אלא מדרבנן. ומיהו לא דמי אהדדי דחלוצה מגרושה אתיא כדאמרי' בעשרה יוחסין גרושה אין לי אלא גרושה חלוצה מנין ת"ל אשה ואסיקנא התם מדרבנן וקרא אסמכתא בעלמא אבל נתינה לא מממזרת קאתיא אפ"ה שטפיה בהדי ממזרת. הכא נמי למ"ד דוד גזר עליהם איכא לתרוצי הכי ורבינו יעקב ז"ל פי' נתינין דוד גזר עליהם שלא להפקיעם מידי שעבוד ישראל ושלא לשחררם. תניא בספרי לא יבוא ממזר בקהל ה' גם דור עשירי אין לי אלא עשירי מעשירי ואילך מנין נאמר כאן עשירי ונאמר בעמוני ומואבי עשירי מה להלן לעולם אף כאן לעולם:

אר"ל

מסורת הש"ס

עירובין כה: כתובות פה. ב"מ קטו. ב"ב קלה: קנח.

[תוספתא פ"י] חולין מח.

רש"ל מ"ז

[חולין עז.]

שבת סה.

לעיל נט: סא. סנהדרין נח. תמורה ל.

נ"א מישרא

קדושין סט.

רש"ל [לעיל כב:]

הגהות הב"ח

(א) גמ' פלח לעבודת כוכבים הוא והני מילי: (ב) שם הכי נמי דאסיר (והא תנן) תא"מ. וכ"ב ס"א אלמא תנן: (ג) שם לאו מילתא היא דאמרי בגיותן לית להו: (ד) רש"י ד"ה ומסרטינן וכו' כדי שיגליע נ"ב פי' לשון מוגלת: (ה) ד"ה בפסולין וכו' שלא היתה גזירה זו משום:

גליון הש"ס

רש"י ד"ה כהן וכו' שנבעלה מקודם. עיין תוס' לעיל סא ע"א ד"ה אין זונה.

עח א מיי' פי"ב מהל' איסורי ביאה הלכה יח סמג לאוין קיד טוש"ע אה"ע סימן ד סעיף ב:
עט ב מיי' שם הלכה יט טוש"ע שם סעיף ג:
פ ג מיי' פ"ה מהלכות מלכים הלכה ג:

תוספות ישנים

א) ובשלמא אי לאו גיירה ניחא שנשאה שלמה דכל זמן שלא נתגיירה לא שייך איסור דמצרית ראשונה ואיסור הבא על הנכרית דחייב משום נשג"א עדיין לא נתקן עד בית דינו של חשמונאי וגם קנאים פוגעין בו ליכא דלא שייך רק בצנעא אבל בפרהסיא לא ושמא שלמה בצנעא לקחה אבל כיון דגיירה קשה היכי נשאה דהא הויא לה מצרית ראשונה: **כדי** שיהא בן בני ראוי לבא בקהל. ותימה שהרי גם בנו מותר לבא בקהל דהא אמרינן בא סנחריב ובלבל כל העולם כולו. וי"ל שאני הכא משום (דאמרינן כה"ג) [דכתב בה"ג] שמצרים חזרו למקומן דכתיב מקץ ארבעים שנה אקבץ את מצרים ואע"ג דגבי עמון נמי כתיב ושבתי את שבות בני עמון התם לא כתיב שום זמן ושמא עדיין לא בא אבל גבי מצרים כתוב מקץ ארבעים שנה וא"כ מסתמא שבו למקומן. ובתוספתא קאמר בהדיא אמר לו ר"ע מנימין טעית בא סנחריב ובלבל כל העולם כולו ומ"מ פריך שפיר הכא וכי תימא הנך אזלו לעלמא וכו' שהרי בימי שלמה עדיין לא בלבל אותם סנחריב:

גמרא

הָא לָא צְרִיכָא לֵיהּ. [וְתֵיפּוֹק לֵיהּ] דְּהָא מִצְרִית רִאשׁוֹנָה הִיא! וְכִי תֵּימָא: הָנָךְ אָזְלֵי לְעָלְמָא וְהָנֵי אַחֲרִינֵי נִינְהוּ — וְהָא תַּנְיָא, *א"ר יְהוּדָה: מִנְיָמִין גֵּר מִצְרִי הָיָה לִי חָבֵר מִתַּלְמִידֵי ר"ע, אָמַר: אֲנִי מִצְרִי רִאשׁוֹן, וְנָשָׂאתִי מִצְרִית רִאשׁוֹנָה. אַשִּׂיא לִבְנִי מִצְרִית שְׁנִיָּה, כְּדֵי שֶׁיְּהֵא בֶּן בְּנִי רָאוּי לָבֹא בַּקָּהָל. אָמַר רַב פָּפָּא: אֲנַן מִשְּׁלֹמֹה לֵיקוּ וְנֵתִיב? שְׁלֹמֹה לָא נָסֵיב מִידֵי דִּכְתִיב בֵּיהּ °"מִן הַגּוֹיִם אֲשֶׁר אָמַר ה' אֶל בְּנֵי יִשְׂרָאֵל לֹא תָבֹאוּ בָהֶם וְהֵם לֹא יָבֹאוּ בָכֶם אָכֵן יַטּוּ אֶת לְבַבְכֶם אַחֲרֵי אֱלֹהֵיהֶם בָּהֶם דָּבַק שְׁלֹמֹה לְאַהֲבָה". אֶלָּא קַשְׁיָא "וַיִּתְחַתֵּן"! מִתּוֹךְ אַהֲבָה יְתֵירָה שֶׁאֲהֵבָהּ מַעֲלֶה עָלָיו הַכָּתוּב כְּאִילּוּ נִתְחַתֵּן בָּהּ. א"ל רָבִינָא לְרַב אַשִׁי: וְהָא אֲנַן (א) תְּנַן פְּצוּעַ דַּכָּא וּכְרוּת שָׁפְכָה — מוּתָּרִים בְּגִיּוֹרֶת וּמְשׁוּחְרֶרֶת, הָא בִּנְתִינָה אֲסִירֵי! א"ל: וְלִיטַעְמִיךְ, אֵימָא סֵיפָא: וְאֵינָן אֲסוּרִין אֶלָּא מִלָּבֹא בַּקָּהָל הָא בִּנְתִינָה — שָׁרוּ. *אֶלָּא, מֵהָא לֵיכָּא לְמִשְׁמַע מִינָּהּ.§

מתני' *א עַמּוֹנִי וּמוֹאָבִי אֲסוּרִים, וְאִיסּוּרָן אִיסּוּר עוֹלָם, אֲבָל נְקֵבוֹתֵיהֶם מוּתָּרוֹת מִיָּד. ב מִצְרִי וַאֲדוֹמִי אֵינָם אֲסוּרִים אֶלָּא עַד שְׁלֹשָׁה דוֹרוֹת, אֶחָד זְכָרִים וְאֶחָד נְקֵבוֹת. ר"ש מַתִּיר אֶת הַנְּקֵבוֹת מִיָּד. א"ר שִׁמְעוֹן: ק"ו הַדְּבָרִים: וּמָה אִם בְּמָקוֹם שֶׁאָסַר אֶת הַזְּכָרִים אִיסּוּר עוֹלָם — הִתִּיר אֶת הַנְּקֵבוֹת מִיָּד, מָקוֹם שֶׁלֹּא אָסַר אֶת הַזְּכָרִים אֶלָּא עַד שְׁלֹשָׁה דוֹרוֹת — אֵינוֹ דִּין שֶׁנַּתִּיר אֶת הַנְּקֵבוֹת מִיָּד? אָמְרוּ לוֹ: *אִם הֲלָכָה — נְקַבֵּל, וְאִם לְדִין — יֵשׁ תְּשׁוּבָה, אָמַר לָהֶם: לֹא כִּי, הֲלָכָה אֲנִי אוֹמֵר.§

גמ' מְנָא ה"מ? א"ר יוֹחָנָן: דְּאָמַר קְרָא °"וְכִרְאוֹת שָׁאוּל אֶת דָּוִד יוֹצֵא לִקְרַאת הַפְּלִשְׁתִּי אָמַר אֶל אַבְנֵר שַׂר הַצָּבָא בֶּן מִי זֶה הַנַּעַר, אַבְנֵר, וַיֹּאמֶר אַבְנֵר חֵי נַפְשְׁךָ הַמֶּלֶךְ אִם יָדָעְתִּי". וְלָא יָדַע לֵיהּ? וְהָכְתִיב °"וַיֶּאֱהָבֵהוּ מְאֹד וַיְהִי לוֹ נוֹשֵׂא כֵלִים"! אֶלָּא: אַאֲבוּהּ קָא מַשְׁאִיל. וְאָבִיו לָא יָדַע לֵיהּ? וְהָכְתִיב °"וְהָאִישׁ בִּימֵי שָׁאוּל זָקֵן בָּא בַאֲנָשִׁים". *וְאָמַר רַב וְאִיתֵימָא רַבִּי אַבָּא: זֶה יִשַׁי אֲבִי דָוִד שֶׁנִּכְנַס בְּאוּכְלוּסָא וְיָצָא בְּאוּכְלוּסָא! (ב) ה"ק שָׁאוּל: אִי מִפֶּרֶץ אָתֵי, אִי מִזֶּרַח אָתֵי? אִי מִפֶּרֶץ אָתֵי — מַלְכָּא הָוֵי, *ג שֶׁהַמֶּלֶךְ פּוֹרֵץ לַעֲשׂוֹת דֶּרֶךְ וְאֵין מְמַחִין בְּיָדוֹ, אִי מִזֶּרַח אָתֵי — חֲשִׁיבָא בְּעָלְמָא הָוֵי. מ"ט אֲמַר לֵיהּ שְׁאַל עֲלֵיהּ? דִּכְתִיב °"וַיַּלְבֵּשׁ שָׁאוּל אֶת דָּוִד מַדָּיו" — כְּמִדָּתוֹ, וּכְתִיב בֵּיהּ בְּשָׁאוּל °"מִשִּׁכְמוֹ וָמַעְלָה גָּבוֹהַּ מִכָּל הָעָם". א"ל דּוֹאֵג הָאֲדוֹמִי: עַד שֶׁאַתָּה מַשְׁאִיל עָלָיו אִם הָגוּן הוּא לְמַלְכוּת אִם לָאו, שְׁאַל עָלָיו אִם רָאוּי לָבֹא בַּקָּהָל אִם לָאו. מ"ט — דְּקָאָתֵי מֵרוּת הַמּוֹאֲבִיָּה. א"ל אַבְנֵר: תְּנֵינָא, *"עַמּוֹנִי" וְלֹא עַמּוֹנִית "מוֹאָבִי" וְלֹא מוֹאָבִית. אֶלָּא מֵעַתָּה "מַמְזֵר" וְלֹא מַמְזֶרֶת! "מַמְזֵר" כְּתִיב, מוּם זָר. "מִצְרִי" וְלֹא מִצְרִית! שָׁאנֵי הָכָא דִּמְפָרֵשׁ טַעֲמָא דִּקְרָא: °"עַל (ג) אֲשֶׁר לֹא קִדְּמוּ אֶתְכֶם בַּלֶּחֶם וּבַמַּיִם" — דַּרְכּוֹ שֶׁל אִישׁ לְקַדֵּם, וְלֹא דַּרְכָּהּ שֶׁל אִשָּׁה לְקַדֵּם. הָיָה לָהֶם לְקַדֵּם אֲנָשִׁים לִקְרַאת אֲנָשִׁים וְנָשִׁים לִקְרַאת נָשִׁים! אִישְׁתִּיק. מִיָּד: "וַיֹּאמֶר הַמֶּלֶךְ שְׁאַל אַתָּה בֶּן מִי זֶה הָעָלֶם". הָתָם קָרֵי לֵיהּ "נַעַר", הָכָא קָרֵי לֵיהּ "עֶלֶם", הָכִי קָא אָמַר לֵיהּ: הֲלָכָה נִתְעַלְּמָה מִמְּךָ, צֵא וּשְׁאַל בְּבֵית הַמִּדְרָשׁ, שָׁאַל, אָמְרוּ לֵיהּ: "עַמּוֹנִי" וְלֹא עַמּוֹנִית, "מוֹאָבִי" וְלֹא מוֹאָבִית.

אַקְשֵׁי

רש"י

וְתֵיפּוֹק לֵיהּ. דַּאֲפִי' (ד) גִּיּוֹרֶת מִצְרִית רִאשׁוֹנָה הִיא, וַאפ"ה קָרֵי לֵיהּ חֲתָנוּת. הָנָךְ אָזְלֵי לְעָלְמָא. מֵתוּ וְטָבְעוּ בִּימֵי פַרְעֹה, וְכִי אַזְהַר רַחֲמָנָא — מֵעֵרֶב רַב. וְהָנֵי אַחֲרִינֵי נִינְהוּ. אוּמּוֹת אֲחֵרִים בָּאוּ וְיָשְׁבוּ בְּאַרְצָם. אַשִּׂיא לִבְנִי מִצְרִית שְׁנִיָּה. שֶׁאִם אַשִּׂיאֶנּוּ מִצְרִית רִאשׁוֹנָה יְהֵא בְּנָהּ שֵׁנִי לָהּ, דְּאָמְרִינַן בְּפִירְקִין (לקמן עח.): הַלֵּךְ אַחַר פְּסוּלָן. אַלְמָא, לָא אָזְדוּ לְעָלְמָא, וְהָנֵי מִצְרִית נִינְהוּ. לָא נְסֵיב מִידֵי. אֶלָּא לִזְנוּת הָיָה מִתְכַּוֵּין. דָּבַק שְׁלֹמֹה לְאַהֲבָה. וְלֹא לְאִישׁוּת. וְהָא אֲנַן לָא תְּנַן הָכִי. כִּי הָךְ מַתְנִיתָא דְּקָתָנֵי לְעֵיל: פְּצוּעַ דַּכָּא מוּתָּר בִּנְתִינָה. גִּיּוֹרֶת וּמְשׁוּחְרֶרֶת אִין. דְּלְיִשְׂרָאֵל כָּשֵׁר נַמִי שָׁרְיָא. הָא בִּנְתִינָה אָסוּר. כְּיִשְׂרָאֵל מְעַלְיָא, דִּבְקְדוּשָּׁתֵיהּ קָאֵי. **מתני'** אִם הֲלָכָה. שְׁמַעְתָּא מֵרַבּוֹתֶיךָ, שֶׁהַנְּקֵבוֹת מוּתָּרוֹת מִיָּד בְּמִצְרִי וַאֲדוֹמִי — נְקַבֵּל מִמְּךָ. וְאִם לְדִין. שֶׁאַתָּה דָּן ק"ו מֵעַצְמְךָ — יֵשׁ תְּשׁוּבוֹת לְהָשִׁיב. וּבַגְּמָרָא מְפָרֵשׁ לָהּ. לֹא כִּי. אֲפִילּוּ אֲנִי דָּן מֵעַצְמִי — אֵין לָכֶם תְּשׁוּבָה, כִּדְמְפָרֵשׁ בַּגְּמָרָא. וּמ"מ, הֲלָכָה אֲנִי אוֹמֵר. **גמ'** וְלָא יָדַע לֵיהּ. שָׁאוּל לְדָוִד. בְּאוּכְלוּסָא. שַׂר עַל ס' רִבּוֹא. שֶׁהַמֶּלֶךְ פּוֹרֵץ. גְּדֵרוֹת שֶׁל אֲחֵרִים לַעֲשׂוֹת לוֹ דֶּרֶךְ קָצָר מִבֵּיתוֹ לְפַרְדֵּסוֹ אוֹ לְכַרְמוֹ. חֲשִׁיבָא בְּעָלְמָא הָוֵי. כִּדְמְפָ', דַּחֲזָא בֵּיהּ סִימָנֵי מַלְכוּת, הִלְכָּךְ לָא אֶפְשָׁר דְּלָא הָוֵי רֵישָׁא. מַאי טַעְמָא אֲמַר לֵיהּ שְׁאַל. מַאי חֲזָא דְּמִסְתְּפֵי מִינֵּיהּ מִמַּלְכוּתָא. מַמְזֵר כְּתִיב מוּם זָר. כָּל שֶׁיֵּשׁ בּוֹ מוּם זָרוּת.

אִם

תוספות

ותיפוק ליה משום דהויא מצרית ראשונה. פי' בקונט': ואפ"ה קרי ליה חתנות. וקשה: דפשיטא דשייך בה חתנות, דהא תפסי בה קידושין! ונראה דפריך: דהיאך נשאה שלמה? הא מצרית ראשונה הואי ואסורה בקהל(א)! **וכי** תימא הנך אזלו לעלמא. פי': אומה של מצרים, שאמר עליהם הכתוב "דור שלישי יבא להם" ולא שני — הלכו להתיישב בשאר ארצות, והני אחריני נינהו, שאומה אחרת נתיישבה שם. והאמר רבי יהודה: מנימין גר מצרי כו', ופשט לו דמנימין בא מארץ מצרים. דאי מן המצריים שנתיישבו בשאר ארצות — לא היה קורהו גר מצרי, שלא היו ידועים בשאר ארצות. **מנימין** גר מצרי כו'. וא"ת: ולמה לא היה מותר לבא בקהל? והלא אין מצריים במקומן, שכבר עלה סנחרב ובלבל כל העולם, ומטעם זה התיר ר' יהושע את יהודה גר העמוני במס' ידים (פ"ד מ"ד), ומייתי לה בפרק "תפלת השחר" (ברכות דף כח.) שאמר לו ר' יהושע: מותר אתה, שכבר עלה כו'. ובסוטה (דף ט. ושם) פי' בקונטרס: דתניא בתוספתא שאמר לו ר' עקיבא: מנימין טעית, שכבר עלה סנחריב ובלבל כל העולם. ובה"ג תירץ דמצרים שבו למקומן, דנתן להם הכתוב קצבה, כדכתיב (יחזקאל כט) "מקץ ארבעים שנה אקבץ את מצרים מן (ה) הגוים אשר נפוצו שם" ואע"ג דגבי עמון כתיב "ואחר כן אשיב את שבות בני עמון" — לא נתן להם קצבה. כמו שאמר רבי יהושע לר"ג במס' ידים (פ"ד מ"ד), אמר ליה ר' יהושע: והא כתיב "ושבתי את שבות ישראל ויהודה ועדיין לא שבו". והכי תניא בתוספתא דמסכת ידים בתר עובדא דיהודה גר העמוני, שהודה ר"ג לרבי יהושע, והותר לבא בקהל. אמר ליה ר"ג: גר מצרי כיוצא בזה. אמר ליה: למצרים נתן להם קצבה, ור"ע לא אסיק אדעתיה שנתן להם קצבה. וקשה לר"י על ההיא דברכות ומסכת ידים, דמשמע דסנחריב בלבל עמון, דהא כתיב בירמיה (מט) בעמון גבי חורבן שהחריבן נבוכדנצר "מדוע ירש מלכם את גד ועמו בעריו ישב וגו' הלילי חשבון כי שודדה וגו'" הרי משמע שבאותה שעה היו יושבים במקומם, ובאותה פרשה כתיב "ואחר כן אשיב את שבות בני עמון" — א"כ לא בלבלם סנחריב, ואם בלבלם — חזרו קודם שהחריבם נבוכדנצר! וכן משמע נמי ב"חלק" שבמקומם היו בימי נבוכדנצר, דאמר התם (סנהדרין דף צו:): עמון ומואב שכני בישי דישראל הוו, שלחו לנבוכדנצר תא(ו) עלייהו. ונראה לר"י דגבי יהודה גר עמוני אחורבן דנבוכדנצר סמיך, דנבוכדנצר נמי בלבל, אע"ג דאין מזכיר בסוטה (דף מו: ושם) אלא סנחריב, דקאמר: עלה סנחריב ולא בלבלה, נבוכדנצר ולא החריבה — היינו משום דסנחריב לא היה מחריב, אלא מעביר אותם לערים הגלת שלומים, ולכך לא הזכיר בו חורבן, אבל נבוכדנצר בלבל והחריב. ואינו תולה הבלבול בסנחריב בברכות ובמסכת ידים אלא משום שהתחיל הבלבול, ומשום דבלבל כל העולם כתיב *סתם (ישעיה י) "ואסיר גבולות עמים" — דמשמע בכל האומות, ועיקר מילתא אנבוכדנצר סמיך. וא"ת: הא דאמר במגילה (דף יב:) דאמרו לו סנהדרין לאחשורוש: זיל לגבי עמון ומואב דיתבי אדוכתייהו, דכתיב "שאנן מואב וגו'" והלא כבר החריבן נבוכדנצר, שהיה הרבה קודם אחשורוש! וי"ל: במילתא בעלמא הוא דאוקמוהו, כי לא מואבים היו אותם שנתיישבו שם אלא שאר אומות, ושמא גם ממואב היו מעורב בהם, והיו קורין להם מואבים. כמו בימי חכמים שהיו קורין ליהודה גר עמוני ועוד, שלא היה הדבר ברור אם שבו ואם לא שבו. ואף על פי שהגְלָם נבוכדנצר, מ"מ, לפי שלא גלו בימי סנחריב כשאר אומות אמרו לאחשורוש שעמד טעמם בם*. **שלמה** לא נסיב מידי. ד"בהם דבק שלמה לאהבה" כתיב, שלא היה אלא דרך אהבה, ולא דרך חתנות.

אם

הגהות הב"ח

(א) גמ' והא אנן לא תנן הכי פלוע: (ב) שם ויצא באוכלוסא (ה"ק שאול) תא"מ. ונ"ב ס"א ה"ק זיל שאל: (ג) שם טעמא דקרא על דבר אשר: (ד) רש"י ד"ה ותיפוק ליה וכו'. נ"ב ס"א דאפילו הוי גיורת הא הוי מצרית ראשונה ואסירא ליה: (ה) תוס' ד"ה מנימין וכו' את מצרים מן העמים אשר נפוצו שמה ואע"ג: (ו) בא"ד תא אסיק עלייהו:

מסורת הש"ס

תורה אור · רס"ל · מ"א יא · שמואל א יז · שם טז · ש"א יז · שם יז · שם ט · דברים כג

לקמן עח. סוטה ט. [תוספ' קדושין פ"ה] · [ברכות כה. ע"ש] · נזיר כג: הוריות י: · [כריתות טו:] · ברכות נח. · ב"ק ס: ב"ב קג: סנהדרין כ: · [לעיל סט. וש"נ] · נ"ל התם. יעב"ץ · [ועי' תוס' מגילה יב: ד"ה זיל ותוס' סוטה ט. ד"ה מנימין]

אַקְשֵׁי לְהוּ דּוֹאֵג כָּל הָנֵי קוּשְׁיָיתָא, אִישְׁתִּיקוּ, בָּעֵי לְאַכְרוּזֵי עֲלֵיהּ, מִיַּד °"וַעֲמָשָׂא בֶּן אִישׁ וּשְׁמוֹ יִתְרָא הַיִּשְׂרְאֵלִי אֲשֶׁר בָּא אֶל אֲבִיגַיִל בַּת נָחָשׁ", וּכְתִיב °"יֶתֶר הַיִּשְׁמְעֵאלִי" אָמַר רָבָא: מְלַמֵּד שֶׁחָגַר חַרְבּוֹ כְּיִשְׁמָעֵאל וְאָמַר: כָּל מִי שֶׁאֵינוֹ שׁוֹמֵעַ הֲלָכָה זוֹ — יִדָּקֵר בַּחֶרֶב, כָּךְ מְקוּבְּלַנִי מִבֵּית דִּינוֹ שֶׁל שְׁמוּאֵל הָרָמָתִי: *"עַמּוֹנִי" וְלֹא עַמּוֹנִית, "מוֹאָבִי" וְלֹא מוֹאָבִית. וּמִי מְהֵימַן? וְהָאָמַר רַבִּי אַבָּא אָמַר רַב: *[א]כָּל תַּלְמִיד חָכָם שֶׁמּוֹרֶה הֲלָכָה וּבָא, אִם קוֹדֶם מַעֲשֶׂה אֲמָרָהּ — שׁוֹמְעִין לוֹ, וְאִם לָאו — אֵין שׁוֹמְעִין לוֹ! שָׁאנֵי הָכָא, דְּהָא שְׁמוּאֵל וּבֵית דִּינוֹ קַיָּים. מִכָּל מָקוֹם קַשְׁיָא! (א) הָכָא תַּרְגְּמוּ: °"כָּל כְּבוּדָּה בַת מֶלֶךְ פְּנִימָה", בְּמַעְרְבָא אָמְרִי, וְאִיתֵימָא ר' יִצְחָק: אָמַר קְרָא °"וַיֹּאמְרוּ אֵלָיו אַיֵּה שָׂרָה אִשְׁתֶּךָ וגו'". כְּתַנָּאֵי: "עַמּוֹנִי" וְלֹא עַמּוֹנִית, "מוֹאָבִי" וְלֹא מוֹאָבִית, דִּבְרֵי רַבִּי יְהוּדָה, רַבִּי שִׁמְעוֹן אוֹמֵר: °"עַל דְּבַר אֲשֶׁר לֹא קִדְּמוּ אֶתְכֶם בַּלֶּחֶם וּבַמַּיִם" — דַּרְכּוֹ שֶׁל אִישׁ לְקַדֵּם וכו'. דָּרַשׁ רָבָא: מַאי דִּכְתִיב °"פִּתַּחְתָּ לְמוֹסֵרָי" אָמַר דָּוִד לִפְנֵי הקב"ה: רִבּוֹנוֹ שֶׁל עוֹלָם, שְׁנֵי מוֹסֵרוֹת שֶׁהָיוּ עָלַי פִּתַּחְתָּם, רוּת הַמּוֹאֲבִיָּה וְנַעֲמָה הָעַמּוֹנִית. דָּרַשׁ רָבָא: מַאי דִּכְתִיב °"רַבּוֹת עָשִׂיתָ אַתָּה ה' אֱלֹהַי נִפְלְאוֹתֶיךָ וּמַחְשְׁבוֹתֶיךָ אֵלֵינוּ", "אֵלַי" לֹא נֶאֱמַר אֶלָּא "אֵלֵינוּ", [א] מְלַמֵּד שֶׁהָיָה רְחַבְעָם יוֹשֵׁב בְּחֵיקוֹ שֶׁל דָּוִד, אָמַר לוֹ: עָלַי וְעָלֶיךָ נֶאֶמְרוּ שְׁתֵּי מִקְרָאוֹת הַלָּלוּ. דָּרַשׁ רָבָא: מַאי דִּכְתִיב °"אָז אָמַרְתִּי הִנֵּה בָאתִי בִּמְגִלַּת סֵפֶר כָּתוּב עָלָי", אָמַר דָּוִד: אֲנִי אָמַרְתִּי עַתָּה בָּאתִי, וְלֹא יָדַעְתִּי שֶׁבִּמְגִילַּת סֵפֶר כָּתוּב עָלַי. הָתָם כְּתִיב °"הַנִּמְצָאוֹת" הָכָא כְּתִיב °"מָצָאתִי דָּוִד עַבְדִּי בְּשֶׁמֶן קָדְשִׁי מְשַׁחְתִּיו". אָמַר עוּלָּא א"ר יוֹחָנָן: בַּת גֵּר עַמּוֹנִי כְּשֵׁרָה לִכְהוּנָּה. א"ל רָבָא בַּר עוּלָּא לְעוּלָּא: כְּמַאן? אִי כְּר' יְהוּדָה — הָא אָמַר: *בַּת גֵּר זָכָר כְּבַת חָלָל זָכָר. וְאִי כְּרַבִּי יוֹסֵי — פְּשִׁיטָא, הָא אָמַר: *אַף גֵּר שֶׁנָּשָׂא גִּיּוֹרֶת בִּתּוֹ כְּשֵׁרָה לִכְהוּנָּה! וְכ"ת: בְּהָנָךְ דִּרְאוּיִן לָבֹא בַּקָּהָל, אֲבָל הַאי דְּאֵין רָאוּי לָבֹא בַּקָּהָל — לָא, מְנָא לֵיהּ? דְּיָלֵיף מִכ"ג בְּאַלְמָנָה. *מַה לְּכ"ג בְּאַלְמָנָה שֶׁכֵּן בִּיאָתוֹ בַּעֲבֵירָה. חָלָל יוֹכִיחַ, מַה לְּחָלָל — שֶׁכֵּן יְצִירָתוֹ בַּעֲבֵירָה, כ"ג יוֹכִיחַ, *וְחָזַר הַדִּין, לֹא רְאִי זֶה כִּרְאִי זֶה, וְלֹא רְאִי זֶה כִּרְאִי זֶה, הַצַּד הַשָּׁוֶה שֶׁבָּהֶן: שֶׁאֵינוֹ בְּרוֹב קָהָל, וּבִתּוֹ פְּסוּלָה — אַף כָּאן, שֶׁאֵינוֹ בְּרוֹב קָהָל וּבִתּוֹ פְּסוּלָה. מַה לְּהַצַּד הַשָּׁוֶה שֶׁבָּהֶן שֶׁכֵּן יֵשׁ בָּהֶן צַד עֲבֵירָה — דִּלְמָא (ב) וַדַּאי בְּעַמּוֹנִי שֶׁנָּשָׂא בַּת יִשְׂרָאֵל קָאָמְרַתְּ, [ב]אע"ג דְּבִיאָתוֹ בַּעֲבֵירָה — בִּתּוֹ כְּשֵׁרָה? א"ל: אִין, דְּכִי אֲתָא רָבִין א"ר יוֹחָנָן: [ג]בַּת גֵּר עַמּוֹנִי וּבַת מִצְרִי שֵׁנִי, רַבִּי יוֹחָנָן אָמַר: כְּשֵׁרָה, וְר"ל אָמַר: פְּסוּלָה. ר"ל אָמַר פְּסוּלָה, דְּיָלֵיף לָהּ מִכ"ג בְּאַלְמָנָה. ר' יוֹחָנָן אָמַר כְּשֵׁרָה, דְּתָנֵי

אם קודם מעשה. שבאת הוראה לידו, אמרה ושנאה לתלמידיו בבית המדרש בשם רבו – שומעין לו בשעת הוראה. ואם לאו – אין שומעין לו. שמא מחמת מעשה הבא לידו אמרה. דהא שמואל ובית דינו קיים. ומילתא דעבידא לגלויי הוא, ולא משקר בה. הנה באהל. דאין דרך אשה לצאת מביתה. כתנאי. דאיכא דנפקא ליה מ"עמוני", ואיכא דנפקא ליה מ"על דבר". מוסרות. הן רצועות שקושרין בהן העול. פתחת. שהתרת את הנקבות. נעמה. אמו של רחבעם, וממנה יצאו מלכי בית דוד. נפלאותיך ומחשבותיך אלינו. עלי ועל רחבעם בן בני חשבת לטובה, כשהתרת את הנקבות. אני אמרתי. בשעה שנמשחתי: עתה באתי לגדולה, ומקרוב פסקו לי גדולה זו, ולא ידעתי שמימי אברהם נכתבה עלי במגילת ספר. בת גר עמוני. קא סלקא דעתך עמוני שנתגיירה אשתו עמו, והורתה ולידתה בקדושה. בת חלל. פסולה לכהונה, בפ' "עשרה יוחסין". ופלוגתא דרבי יהודה ור' יוסי בפרק "עשרה יוחסין". מנא ליה. מנא תיתי לן האי, דמשום דאין ראוי לבא בקהל בתו פסולה יותר משאר גרים, הואיל ונקבותיהן מותרות. מכהן גדול באלמנה. דהואיל ואינו ראוי בה בתו חללה ופסולה לכהונה. מה לכ"ג שכן ביאתו בעבירה. תאמר בעמוני שנשא עמונית שאין ביאתו בעבירה. חלל זכר יוכיח. שמותר בבת ישראל, ואין ביאתו בה בעבירה, ובתו פסולה לכהונה. מה לחלל שכן יצירתו בעבירה. שביאת אביו ואמו בעבירה, תאמר בעמוני שאין יצירתו בעבירה. כ"ג יוכיח. שאין יצירתו בעבירה, ובתו מאלמנה פסולה. הצד השוה שבהן שאינן ברוב קהל. אינן כשאר רוב ישראל, שהרי יש בכולן צד פגום: כהן גדול – ביאתו בעבירה, חלל – יצירתו בעבירה, עמוני – אינו ראוי לבא בקהל. צד עבירה. בת כהן גדול – יצירתה בעבירה, בת חלל – יצירת אביה בעבירה. תאמר בעמונית, שאין עבירה לא ביצירתה ולא ביצירת אביה, ופשיטא שכשרה. אמר ליה אין. ולקמן יליף "מעמיו". בת גר עמוני ומצרי שני. שנשאו בת ישראל, וביאתן בעבירה.

אם קודם מעשה אמרה שומעין לו. אר"ת: דהיינו דוקא היכא דהוא עצמו נוגע בדבר, כגון [יתרא] שהיה צריך לאותה הוראה, שהרי בת ישי נשא, כדכתיב "אשר בא אל אביגיל בת נחש", ואמרינן בפ"ק דבבא בתרא (דף יז. ושם): בת מי שמת בעטיו של נחש. וכן בפרק "נושאין על האנוסה" (לקמן דף צח. ושם) גבי גר שהעיד על אשתו ושבעה בניו, ובפ' "עשרה יוחסין" (קדושין דף ע:) גבי עובדא דרב יהודה, בכל דוכתא דמייתי לה היו הן צריכין לאותה הוראה. אבל אם אין צריכין לאותה הוראה – שומעין לו, אע"פ שלא אמרה עד שעת מעשה.

כתנאי עמוני ולא עמונית. וא"ת: לר' יהודה תקשי ליה מצרי ולא מצרית! ואמר ר"י דגבי עמוני ומואבי היה לו לקצר ולכתוב עמון ומואב. הלכך, מדכתיב "עמוני" ו"מואבי" אית לן למדרש דלמעט עמונית ומואבית קאתי, אבל מצרי אם היה כותב מצרים היה מאריך יותר. והא דכתיב "אדומי" ולא כתיב אדום – אגב "מצרי" כתיב "אדומי" א). **הכא** כתיב מצאתי דוד. אע"פ שדוד עצמו אמרה – ברוח הקודש אמרו.

מכהן גדול באלמנה מה לכ"ג כו'. תימה: דמייתי לרבי יוסי האי דינא דכ"ג באלמנה וחלל, דאפילו לרבי יהודה לית ליה האי דינא, משום דאיכא למיפרך כדפריך הכא: מה להצד השוה שבהן שכן יש בהן צד עבירה, כדאמר בפרק בתרא דקדושין (דף עח. ושם), – והוה ליה לאתויי דינא דדאין מיניה ר' יהודה, דבת גר זכר כבת חלל זכר מחלל ומצרי ראשון, כדאמר התם. ומיהו, לענין שאר בנות גרים איכא למימר לית ליה לרבי יוסי דינא דר' יהודה, דלא חשיב ליה צד השוה שאינו ברוב קהל – כיון דגר ראוי לקהל. וכן פירש בקונטרס התם ארבי אליעזר בן יעקב דפליג ארבי יהודה. אבל הכא, גר עמוני דחשיב הוא צד השוה כדאמר הכא, כיון דאין ראוי לבא בקהל, קשה: אמאי לא נדון לר' יוסי מחלל ומצרי ראשון שתפסל בת עמוני שנשא עמונית לכהן, אע"ג שראויה לבא בקהל? וי"ל: דקסבר ר' יוסי כיון דבת מצרי ראשון אינה ראויה לבא בקהל – אין לעשות צד השוה מפסול כהונה ופסול קהל ללמוד מהא בעלמא לפסול כהונה. ואין להקשות דנילף שפוסל גר בביאתו מחלל ומצרי ראשון, דהשתא יש לעשות צד השוה, כיון שאין אנו באין לעשות צד השוה ממנה ממה שבנותיהן פסולין זו לקהל וזו לכהונה, אלא ממה שאינו ברוב קהל, דגר חשוב ברוב קהל לרבנן, כדפרישית. ועוד: דמה להנך – שכן זרעם פסול, תאמר בגר – שבתו כשרה. אבל קשה: דמחזיר גרושתו ויבמה לשוק נילף שיפסלו בביאתן מחלל ומצרי ראשון! וצ"ל כמו שפירשנו בספ"ק (דף טו: ושם ד"ה מה) דלרבנן לא ילפינן מאיסור כהונה לעשותה חללה, דאין חללה אלא מאיסורי כהונה, ואפילו בהצד השוה מעלמא ומפסול כהונה. ורבי יהודה ודאי יליף במה הצד אפילו לפסול בביאתו, כדאמר בקידושין (דף עח.). **רבי** יוחנן אמר כשרה. תימה לר"י: היכי ילפינן לעיל ב"החולץ" (דף מה.) מק"ו דאלמנה דגוי ועבד הבא על בת ישראל הולד פגום? הא איכא למימר לרבי יוחנן בת גר עמוני שנשא בת ישראל יוכיח, שאיסורו שוה בכל ובתו כשרה! ולרבן שמעון בן גמליאל, דקאמר בפרק "אלמנה" (לעיל דף סט.) דגר עמוני אינו פוסל בביאתו – אתי שפיר, אבל לת"ק ורבי יוסי קשיא! ומיהו, ממצרי שני אין להקשות תוכיח, דמה למצרי שכן עשה. **ריש** לקיש אמר פסולה. הקשה הר' משה כהן: דלעיל (שם) משמע דלכולי עלמא בת עמון ומצרי שני כשרה לכהונה, דאמר: מאי איכא בין תנא קמא לר' יוסי? א"ר יוחנן: מצרי שני איכא בינייהו כו', לאפוקי מצרי שני דאין זרעו פסול כמו כהן גדול באלמנה. וגבי גר עמוני קאמר דאין כל זרעו פסול, אלמא בתו כשרה לכהונה! ואמר ר"י: דסוגיא דהתם ר' יוחנן קאמר ליה, דאמר הכא כשרה, אבל ריש לקיש דפוסל הכא יאמר דתנא קמא דפסיל התם היינו משום דזרעו פסול, ולא יפרש מילתיה דת"ק כמו שמפרש ר' יוחנן: מה כהן גדול שביאתו בעבירה כו', דא"כ הוה משמע דמודה לר' יוסי דמצרי שני אין זרעו פסול אלא לתנא קמא נמי הוה נקט במילתיה מה כהן גדול באלמנה שזרעו פסול כו', דסבירא ליה דבת גר עמוני ומצרי שני זרעו פסול. ור' יוסי דקאמר כל שזרעו פסול כו' וממעט מצרי שני – אליבא דנפשיה נקיט האי לישנא. מצרי

עין משפט נר מצוה

פא א טוש"ע י"ד סימן רמב סעיף לו בהג"ה:

פב ב ג מיי' פי"ט מהלכ' איסורי ביאה הלכה יג טוש"ע אה"ע סימן ד סעיף ו:

תוספות ישנים

א) עוי"ל דטעמא דר' יהודה דלא דרשינן ולא מצרית משום דכתיב גבי מצרי בנים אשר יולדו הכתוב תלאו בלידה א"כ גלי קרא דנקבות אסורות וכן אמרינן לקמן: **הצד** השוה שבהן שאינן ברוב קהל. וא"ת כיון דס"ד השתא שהדין זה גמור אמאי מכשיר ר' יוסי בת גר וגיורת לכהונה שהרי כמו כן אינן ברוב קהל שבאים מטפה פסולה. דמהאי טעמא פסיל לה ר' יהודה בפרק עשרה יוחסין ולא פרכינן התם עלה אלא מה להצד השוה שבהן שיש בהם צד עבירה ועדיין לא מסקינן אדעתין עד לקמן. וי"ל דלא חשיב רבי יוסי גר וגיורת אינן ברוב קהל כיון דלית בהו צד פגם כמו באלמנה לכ"ג שביאתו בעבירה וחלל יצירתו בעבירה ועמוני אסור בקהל: **מה** להצד השוה שבהן שכן יש בהם צד עבירה. וא"ת ולימא מצרי ראשון שנשא מצרית ראשונה יוכיח שאין בהם צד עבירה שהרי לא ביאתם ולא יצירתם היו בעבירה ואפ"ה בתה פסולה אף לקהל אף אני אביא גר עמוני שתפסל בתו לכל הפחות לכהונה דהכי נמי אמרינן בפרק עשרה יוחסין. וי"ל דלא חשבינן ליה הכא צד השוה משום שאינן שוין דחלל פסולה בתו לכהונה ולא לקהל ובמצרי פסולה בתו אף לקהל. ונראה לר"ס דר' יוחנן סבר כרשב"ג דאמר לעיל דגר עמוני אין פוסל אשה בביאתו וא"כ איכא למפרך מה להצד השוה שבהן שכן פוסלין אשה בביאתם תאמר בגר עמוני. וא"ת ומנא ליה לתלמודא הך טעמא וי"ל דמדמכשיר ר' יוחנן בת גר עמוני ולא קפסיל לה מהך דינא א"כ צריך לנו לומר דסבר כרשב"ג דלעיל דאי לאו הכי הוה פסיל לה ר' יוחנן מדינא דחלל ומצרי והא דקאמר הכא ואי כר' יוסי ר"ל אי סבר כר' יוסי דבת גר וגיורת כשרה פשיטא דבת עמוני כשרה דמהיכא נוכל לפוסלה אי מכ"ג באלמנה וכו' אבל כרבי יוסי ממש לא סבר דהא ר' יוסי פליג לעיל אדרשב"ג ור' יוחנן ס"ל כרשב"ג כדפרישית.

מסורת הש"ס

[לעיל סט. וש"נ]

קדושין ע: לקמן צח. בכורות לח:

[לעיל נז.] קדושין עז.

ג"ז שם

קדושין עח.

[קדושין כא. וש"נ]

הגהות הב"ח

(א) גמ' הכי תרגמו: (ב) שם דלמא בעמוני שנשא כצ"ל ותיבת ודאי נמחק:

הגהות מהר"ב רנשבורג

א] גמ' מלמד שהיה רחבעם יושב בחיקו של דוד. נ"ב עי' בעשרה מאמרות מאמר אם כל חי חלק ב' סי' יו"ד דף מז ע"ב ובפירוש יד יהודה שם:

דתני רבי זכאי קמיה דר' יוחנן: °"כי אם בתולה מעמיו יקח אשה" – להביא גיורת מכנה שהיא כשרה לכהונה. ואמר ליה: אני שונה "עמיו" "מעמיו" – להביא בתולה הבאה מב' עממין, ואת אמרת גיורת מכנה ותו לא? מאי שני עממין? אילימא עמוני שנשא עמונית, ומאי משני עממין, דזכרים אסורין ונקבות מותרות – היינו גיורת מכנה! אלא בעמוני שנשא בת ישראל. ואיכא דאמרי, אמר ליה: אני שונה "עמיו" "מעמיו" – להביא בתולה הבאה משני עממין, ומעם שיש בו שני עממין ואת אמרת גיורת מכנה ותו לא? ולהך לישנא, בת מצרי שני דכשרה לכהונה מנא ליה? וכי תימא דיליף מעמוני שנשא בת ישראל – מה לעמוני שנשא בת ישראל שכן נקבות מותרות! מצרי שני שנשא מצרית שניה יוכיח. מה למצרי שני שנשא מצרית שניה – שכן אין ביאתו בעבירה! עמוני שנשא בת ישראל יוכיח, וחזר הדין וכו'. °אמר רב יוסף: היינו דשמענא ליה לרב יהודה דאמר "עמיו" "מעמיו" ולא ידענא מאי קאמר. כי אתא רב שמואל בר יהודה אמר, הכי תנא קמיה: אשה עמונית כשרה, בנה מעמוני פסול, ובתה מעמוני כשרה, במה דברים אמורים – בעמוני ועמונית שנתגיירו, אבל בתה מעמוני – פסולה. אמר ליה: *פוק תני לברא. מאי דאמרת אשה עמונית כשרה – עמוני ולא עמונית, בנה מעמוני פסול, דהא עמוני הוא, ובתה מעמוני כשרה, למאי? אילימא לבא בקהל – השתא אמה כשרה, היא מיבעיא? אלא לכהונה. במה דברים אמורים – בעמוני ועמונית שנתגיירו, אבל בתה מעמוני – פסולה. מאי בתה מעמוני? אילימא עמוני שנשא עמונית – היינו גיורת מכנה. אלא, עמוני שנשא בת ישראל. א"ל: פוק תני לברא.§ "מצרי ואדומי אינן אסורין וכו'".§ מאי תשובה? אמר רבה בר בר חנה א"ר יוחנן: משום דאיכא למימר: עריות יוכיחו, שלא אסר בהן אלא עד שלשה דורות, אחד זכרים ואחד נקבות. מה לעריות שכן כרת. ממזר יוכיח. מה לממזר שכן אינו ראוי לבא בקהל לעולם, עריות יוכיחו. וחזר הדין, לא ראי זה כראי זה ולא ראי זה כראי זה, הצד השוה שבהן: שאסורין, ואחד זכרים ואחד נקבות, אף אני אביא מצרי ומצרית שיהיו אסורין, אחד זכרים ואחד נקבות. מה להצד השוה שבהן שכן יש בהן צד כרת. ורבנן: *מחלל, דחייבי עשה וכר' אליעזר בן יעקב. ומאי "לא כי"? הכי קאמר להו: לדידי – לא סבירא לי דר' אליעזר בן יעקב, לדידכו דסבירא לכו כר"א בן יעקב – הלכה אני אומר. תניא, אמר להן ר"ש: הלכה אני אומר. ועוד: מקרא מסייעני: "בנים" ולא בנות. ת"ר: "בנים" ולא בנות, דברי ר"ש. אמר ר' יהודה: הרי הוא אומר °"בנים אשר יולדו להם דור שלישי" – הכתוב תלאן בלידה. א"ר יוחנן: אי לאו דאמר ר' יהודה הכתוב תלאן בלידה – *לא מצא ידיו ורגליו בבית המדרש. כיון דאמר מר "קהל גרים איקרי קהל"

מצרי

תורה אור: ויקרא כא; דברים כג

[שבת קו. ב"ק לד: סנהדרין סב.]

[לעיל ס. לקמן פה:]

[גיטין מח.]

[לעיל נט: ס.]

רש"י

דתני רבי זכאי כו'. כלומר, מהאי כללא שמעינן ליה לרבי יוחנן דמכשיר. גיורת מכנה. ממכונה. כלומר, שאביה ואמה מעם אחד ונולדה בקדושה. לאפוקי גר עמוני שנשא בת ישראל, דלאו מכנה היא הואיל וביאתה בעבירה – בתו פסולה. עמיו מעמיו. מדמצי למכתב "בתולה עמיו יקח", וכתיב "מעמיו" – אפי' ממקצת עמיו ועם אחר, להביא בתולה הבאה משני עממין. ומהכא שמעינן ליה לרבי יוחנן דמכשיר: מאי שני עממין דקאמר אילימא כו'. איכא דאמרי. הכי קאמר ליה בהדיא להביא בתולה הבאה משני עממין מישראלית וגר, ואותו גר הוי מעם שיש בו שני עממין – דהיינו עמוני. ולהאי לישנא. דקתני בהדיא, דלא מרבי אלא בת עמוני, דקתני: מעם שיש בו שני עממין. בת מצרי שני. שנשא ישראלית, וביאתו בעבירה, מנא ליה לר' יוחנן דכשרה? מה לעמוני שכן נקבות. עמוניות מותרות מיד, תאמר במצרי שני שהחמיר בהם הכתוב לעשות נקבות כזכרים עד שלשה דורות? מצרי שני שנשא מצרית שניה יוכיח. שבתו כשרה, שהרי שלישית היא, ואע"פ שיש בהן צד חמור, כדקאמר, ואפילו הכי שריא, אף אני אביא את זו, הואיל והרי היא שלישית – כשרה לכהונה. וחזר הדין. הצד השוה שבהן שאינו בדור קהל ובתו כשרה. ולא ידענא מאי קאמר. מה הוה דריש בה. אבל השתא ידענא דלאכשורי בת עמוני שנשא בת ישראל קאתי. הכי תנא קמיה. רבי זכאי קמיה דר' יוחנן. אשה עמונית כו'. מפרש לה לקמיה. אמר ליה פוק תני לברא. דמאי דקאמר אשה עמונית כשרה לקהל שפיר קאמר, דעמוני ולא עמונית, ובנה מעמוני פסול לקהל (א) – דהא עמוני הוא. בתה מעמוני כשרה למאן אילימא לקהל השתא אמה. שלא נולדה בקדושה אמרת כשרה, בתה שנולדה בקדושה מיבעיא?! אלא לכהונה, והדר תני: במה דברים אמורים, בעמוני ועמונית שנתגיירו וילדה לו בת, דאין לידתה בעבירה, והיא גיורת מכנה, אבל בתה מעמוני פסולה, ומאי היא? אילימא בתה של עמונית מעמוני – היינו גיורת מכנה, והא אכשרת לה, דהא תני רישא בתה מעמוני כשרה! אלא ודאי סיפא דקא פסלת – בעמוני שנשא בת ישראל, משום דביאתו בעבירה. פוק תני לברא. דהא נמי כשרה, שהרי אני שונה עמיו מעמיו. עריות יוכיחו. שלא אסר בהן אלא שלשה דורות, בת בתו אסורה לו, והוא בכלל (דהויא דור שלישי), ועשה בהן נקבות כזכרים: בת בתו כבת בנו. שכן כרת. תאמר במצרי ואדומי שאינו אלא עשה – "דור שלישי יבא להם", ולא ראשון ושני, ולאו הבא מכלל עשה – עשה. הלכך לא נעשה בו נקבות כזכרים. ממזר יוכיח. שאין כרת בביאתו, ועשה בו בתו כבנו, דאחד ממזרת ואחד ממזר אסור. עריות יוכיחו. שכשרים לכל ישראל, חוץ מקרובים. צד כרת. שהרי ממזר, אע"פ שאין כרת בביאתו מ"מ יש כרת בלידתו, שנולד מאשה שהיא לאביו בכרת. ורבנן. דאמרי יש תשובה פרכין ליה לרבי שמעון מחלל דחייבי עשה, כגון כ"ג שנשא אנוסה או מפותה, שהיא עליו בעשה – "בתולה יקח", ולא בעולה – ואין כאן לאו דזונה, דליכא למ"ד ביאת פנויה זנות היא אלא רבי אלעזר, ולית הלכתא כוותיה, כדאמר בפרק "הבא על יבמתו" (דף סא:). וקאמר ר' אליעזר בן יעקב התם:* הנולד חלל. והכי פרכי ליה רבנן לרבי שמעון: עריות יוכיחו, מה לעריות שכן כרת – חלל דחייבי עשה יוכיח, שאין בו כרת, ואסורה הבת כבן. מה לחלל – שכן יצירתו בעבירה, לפיכך עשה נקבות כזכרים – עריות יוכיחו שאין יצירתם בעבירה, ואסר בת בתו כבת בנו. מאי לא כי. דמשמע: דאין תשובתכם תשובה. לא סבירא לי דר' אליעזר בן יעקב. דאין חלל מחייבי עשה. ומחלל דחייבי לאוין לא מצית למיפרך, דאיכא למיפרך: מה להנך – שכן לאו, תאמר במצרי ואדומי שהן עשה, ואין חמור. לדידכו נמי דסבירא לכו. יש חלל, הלכה אני אומר שהנקבות מותרות. אשר יולדו. כל הנולדים להם, אפילו נקבה במשמע. לישנא אחרינא: תלאן בלידה – תלה הבנים באם שיולדת אותם, דאם היא ראשונה – הבן שני, ואי לאו דנקבות אסורות – למאי הלכתא תלאן בלידה? אי לאו דאמר ר' יהודה הכתוב תלאן בלידה. ונקבות נמי אסורות. לא מצא ידיו ורגליו בבית המדרש. כלומר, לא היה יכול לעמוד בדבריו. כיון דאמר מר קהל גרים איקרי קהל. במס' קידושין (דף עג.), אי איתא דנקבות שריין לאלתר, הוו להו קהל ואסורות מצרית ראשונה ושניה למצרי ראשון ושני – במה יטהרו ויבואו לידי דור שלישי?

דאי

רס"ל מ"ז

תוספות

מצרי שני שנשא בת ישראל מנא ליה. תימה: מהיכי תיתי לה דתיפסל? אילימא מחלל ואלמנה מה להנך שכן לאו תאמר במצרי שכן עשה! ואמר רבינו יצחק דאתי מחלל דחייבי עשה כגון בעולה לכהן גדול וכראב"י דאמר יש חלל מחייבי עשה.

שכן יש בהן צד כרת. ותימה: דאליבא דרבי יוחנן קיימינן, ולדידיה אשכחן ממזר בלא צד כרת, דקסבר דיש ממזר מגוי ועבד הבא על בת ישראל! ועוד תימה: דהוה מצי למימר: מה להצד השוה שכן לאו, תאמר במצרי דליכא אלא עשה!

מחלל דחייבי עשה. הקשה ר"י ברבי מאיר: מכל מקום איכא למיפרך: מה להצד השוה שכן לאו, שאף באיסור חלל דחייבי עשה איכא לאו ד"חללה לא יקח"! ותירץ: דשמא חללה הבאה מחייבי עשה ליכא לאו אלא עשה לכהן הבא עליה א).

הלכה אני אומר. לאו הלכה למשה מסיני קאמר א], דאם כן – אמאי פליג עליה רבי יהודה? אלא הכי קאמר: הלכה אני אומר, כך קבלתי מרבותי.

מצרי

תוספות ישנים

פוק תני לברא. וא"ת היכי מצי פסיל ריש לקיש בת גר עמוני ובת מצרי שני הא לעיל משמע דליכא מאן דפסיל בסוף פ' אלמנה דקאמר מאי איכא בין ת"ק לר' יוסי וכו' לאפוקי מצרי שני דאין זרעו פסול. ולבתר כן נמי קאמר לאפוקי גר עמוני דאין כל זרעו פסול שהבנות כשרות. וא"ל דלעיל מיירי במצרי ומצרית עמוני ועמונית אבל בת עמוני וישראלית כי הכא איכא למימר דפסולה [דאי] אפשר לומר כן שהרי לעיל קאמר יליף מכ"ג באלמנה והיינו דאינסיב באיסור מינן כמו כן מיירי במצרי ועמוני דאינסיב בלא מינייהו וי"ל דסוגיא דלעיל אתיא כר' יוחנן דמכשיר הכא דהיינו רבי יוחנן דאמר לעיל מצרי ואדומי איכא בינייהו. אבל ריש לקיש מצי סבר דפליגי בהא. והא דקאמר ר' יוסי לעיל כל שזרעו פסול (אינו) פוסל וממעט מצרי [שני ר"י] אליבא דנפשיה קאמר אבל ת"ק סבר דבת גר מצרי שני ובת גר עמוני פסולות לכהונה וריש לקיש יסבור כמותן: מה להצד השוה שבהן שכן יש בהן צד כרת א"כ הוה מצי למיפרך אפילו לית בהו כרת מה להצד השוה שבהן שיש בהן צד לאו וא"ת לר' יוחנן דאמר גוי ועבד הבא על בת ישראל הולד ממזר א"כ מצינו ממזר שאין בו צד כרת. וי"ל דמ"מ ממזר דקרא בחייבי כריתות איירי. א"נ נראה לומר דמ"מ איכא למיפרך מה מה לעריות שיש בהן לאו תאמר במצרי שאין בו רק עשה: א) אכן תימה אמאי אין לאו בחללה בבעולה לכ"ג דהא כתיב כי אם בתולה מעמיו דמשמע ולא בעולה וסמיך ולא יחלל. וי"ל דקאי אחייבי לאוין דכתיבי בקרא אלמנה וגרושה וגו':

הגהות הב"ח

(א) רש"י ד"ה אמר ליה וכו' פסול לקהל נמי דהא:

גליון הש"ס

גמ' אמר רב יוסף הייני דשמענא. כעין זה שבת דף כח ע"ב לקמן דף פ ע"א:

הגהות מהר"ב רנשבורג

א] תד"ה הלכה כו' דא"כ אמאי פליג עליה רבי יהודה וכו'. כ"ב עי' יבין שמועה דף כז ע"א ובשו"ת חוות יאיר סי' קנב:

מצרי שני במאי יטהר? דלמא *דאי עבר ונסיב. – "דאי" לא כתיב קרא, הרי ממזר, דאי, וכתביה קרא! דאי לאיסורא – כתב, דאי להיתרא – לא כתב. הרי מחזיר גרושתו, דאי להיתרא, וכתביה! התם משום עיקר איסורא הוא דכתביה. ת"ר: אם נאמר בנים – למה נאמר דורות, ואם נאמר דורות למה נאמר בנים? אם נאמר בנים ולא נאמר דורות הייתי אומר: בן ראשון ושני – אסור, שלישי – מותר, לכך נאמר דורות. ואם נאמר דורות ולא נאמר בנים הייתי אומר: *לאותן העומדים על הר סיני, לכך נאמר בנים. "להם" – [א]מהם מנה, "להם" – [ב]הלך אחר פסולן. ואיצטריך למיכתב "להם" ואיצטריך למיכתב "אשר יולדו". דאי כתב רחמנא "אשר יולדו" ה"א: מבניהם מנה, כתב רחמנא "להם". ואי כתב רחמנא "להם" – ה"א: מצרית מעוברת שנתגיירה היא ובנה – חד, [ג]כתב רחמנא "אשר יולדו". ואיצטריך למיכתב "להם" הכא, ואיצטריך למיכתב "לו" גבי ממזר. דאי כתב רחמנא הכא – משום דבא מטיפה פסולה, אבל ממזר דבא מטיפה כשרה – אימא לא. ואי כתב רחמנא גבי ממזר – משום דאין ראוי לבא בקהל לעולם, אבל הכא – אימא לא, צריכא. אמר רבה בר בר חנה א"ר יוחנן: *מצרי שני שנשא מצרית ראשונה – בנה שלישי הואי. אלמא קסבר: בתר דידיה שדינן ליה, מתיב רב יוסף: רבי טרפון אומר: *[ד]יכולין ממזרים ליטהר, כיצד? ממזר נשא שפחה – הולד עבד, שחררו – נמצא בן חורין. אלמא בתר דידה שדינן ליה! שאני התם, דאמר קרא °"האשה וילדיה תהיה לאדוניה". שמות כא מתיב רבא, *אמר ר' יהודה: מנימין גר מצרי היה לי חבר מתלמידי רבי עקיבא, ואמר: אני מצרי ראשון, ונשאתי מצרית ראשונה, אשיא לבני מצרית שניה כדי שיהא בן בני ראוי לבא בקהל. ואי ס"ד בתריה דידיה שדינן ליה – אפילו ראשונה נמי! הא אמר ליה רבי יוחנן לתנא: תני ראשונה. כי אתא רב דימי אמר רבי יוחנן: *[ה]מצרי שני שנשא מצרית ראשונה – בנה שני הואי. אלמא: בתר אימיה שדינן ליה. אמר ליה אביי: אלא הא דאמר ר' יוחנן: *[ו]הפריש חטאת מעוברת וילדה, רצה – מתכפר בה, רצה – מתכפר בולדה. אי אמרת בשלמא עובר לאו ירך אמו הוא – הוה ליה כמפריש שתי חטאות לאחריות, ואמר רב אושעיא: [ז]הפריש שתי חטאות לאחריות – מתכפר באחת מהן, והשניה תרעה. אלא אי אמרת עובר ירך אמו הוא – הוה ליה ולד חטאת, [ח]וולד חטאת למיתה אזיל! אישתיק. א"ל: דלמא שאני התם, דכתיב: "אשר יולדו" – הכתוב תלאו בלידה? א"ל: *קרקפנא, חזיתיה לרישך ביני עמודי. כי אמר רבי יוחנן להא שמעתא, טעמא דכתיב "אשר יולדו", הא בעלמא – בתר אבוה שדינן ליה, אלא הא דאמר רבא: [ט]גויה מעוברת שנתגיירה – בנה אין צריך טבילה. אמאי אין צריך טבילה? וכי תימא משום דרבי יצחק, *דאמר רבי יצחק: [י]דבר תורה, רובו ומקפיד עליו חוצץ, רובו שאינו מקפיד עליו אינו חוצץ, והא

רש"י

דאי עבר ונסיב. או בת ישראל או גיורת. דאי לא כתב קרא. מידי דעל ידי עבירה קאתי – לא כתב קרא, למימר: "בנים אשר יולדו" כו'. דהא לא שכיח למיתי לידי דור שלישי. והרי ממזר. דאיהו לא הוי ממזר אלא ע"י עבירה, שבא אביו על חייבי כריתות, וכתביה קרא – "לא יבא ממזר". ואע"ג דלא שכיח, תורה אור איצטריך קרא למיכתביה, דלכי מיתרמי לא נטמע ביה. דאי להיתרא. כגון שלישי יבא וגו'. והרי מחזיר גרושתו. משניסת לאחר, דאי הוא, וכתב קרא להיתרא – דכתיב (דברים כד) "כי תועבה היא", ודרשינן (קידושין ד' עו.): היא תועבה, ואין בניה תועבין. התם משום עיקר איסורא כתביה. לאשמועינן דאיהי מיהא תועבה הויא. אם נאמר בנים כו'. לכתוב "בן שלישי יבא" וגו', או "דור שלישי יבא להם", ולא לכתוב "בנים". בן ראשון ושני. גר מצרי שנולדו לו שלשה בנים לאחר שנתגייר – הבן הראשון והשני יאסרו, והשלישי מותר. לכך נאמר דורות. לאשמועינן דכל בניו אסורים, ובני בנים מותרים. ואם נאמר דור שלישי ולא נאמר בנים. הייתי אומר, לאותם ישראלים העומדים על הר סיני הוא אומר: דור שלישי שלכם יבוא להם בקהל, כלומר: בכם ובבניכם – אסורין מצרי ואדומי, אבל בבני בנים – מותרים. ומשם והלאה מותרין מצריים אפילו גר ראשון. מהם מנה. הוא ראשון, בנו שני, ובן בנו מותר. להם הלך אחר פסולן. תרי "להם" כתיבי, ומשמע: הלך אחריהם. דאם נטמעו בכשרים, כגון מצרי שנשא ישראלית, וישראל שנשא מצרית – הלך אחריהן, והולד פסול עד דור שלישי. ואיצטריך למכתב להם. דמשמע דמהם מנה, ואיצטריך "אשר יולדו", דלא תימא אשר יולדו מבניהם מנה, וקשו קראי אהדדי. אלא למילתא אחריתי איצטריך. כתב רחמנא אשר יולדו. למימר דכל לידה דמגרות ואילך (א) חדא דרא היא. לו גבי ממזר. למימר הלך אחר פסולו, שאם נשא כשרה – בנו ממזר. מן טפה כשרה. מישראל טהור. שאני התם. גבי שפחה גזירת הכתוב היא, דולד שפחה כשפחה. אפי' ראשונה נמי. ישיא לבנו. רצה בה מתכפר. והולד ירעה. רצה מתכפר בולדה. והיא תרעה. אי אמרת בשלמא עובר לאו ירך אמו הוא. משום הכי, רצה – בולדה מתכפר, דהוי חשוב בשעת הפרשה כבהמה בפני נפשה, והוה ליה כמפריש ב' חטאות באחריות, שאם תאבד האחת – יתכפר בחברתה. וכי אמרינן ולד חטאת למיתה – היכא דאפריש בהמה ריקנית, ונתעברה וילדה. והשניה תרעה. וכי אמרינן (תמורה דף טז.) חטאת שכפרו בעליה למיתה אזלא – כגון שהפריש חטאת, ואבדה, והקריב אחרת תחתיה, ואחר כך נמצאת ראשונה. בלידה. הלך אחר האם. קרקפנא. אדם חשוב. בי עמודי. היכא דגרסי. כי אמר ר' יוחנן. ומפי השמועה אמרת, ולא מדעתך. אין צריך טבילה. לשום גירות, דסלקא ליה טבילה דאימיה. משום דר' יצחק דאמר דבר תורה רובו ומקפיד עליו חוצץ. והכא לא קפיד בהאי חציצה האי ולדא, דרביתיה הוא. ואע"ג דאמר התם גזרו על רובו שאין מקפיד כו' – הכא אוקימנא אדאורייתא. והא

תוספות

מצרי שני במה יטהר. וא"ת: ישא שתוקית, דהא ר' יהודה אית ליה בפ' "עשרה יוחסין" (קדושין עג.) בקהל ודאי הוא דלא יבא, הא בקהל ספק – יבא, והבן נמי יהא מותר לבא בקהל, דממזר ודאי הוא דלא יבא, הא ממזר ספק – יבא! ויש לומר: דשתוקין לא שכיחי. אי נמי: דממזרת דלא אפשר אלא באיסור חשיב דאי, ודאי לא כתיב. וא"ת: וישא נתינה והולד כשר לרבי יוחנן דאמר בסמוך: מצרי שני שנשא מצרית ראשונה – בנה שלישי הוי, דבתר דידיה שדינן! וי"ל: דר' יוחנן דהכא סבר כאידך דרבי יוחנן, דאמר רב דימי א"ר יוחנן: בנה שני הוי, דבתר דידה שדינן ליה. וא"ת: והא כתיב קרא דאי, לרבי יוחנן דדרשי לעיל (דף עז:) "מעמיו" לבת גר עמוני הבא על בת ישראל! וי"ל: דיתורא דקרא אתי שפיר לדאי, אבל פשטיה דקרא – לא.

הוה אמינא מצרית מעוברת שנתגיירה היא ובנה חד הוא כתב רחמנא "אשר יולדו". וא"ת: אי סבר כרבי יהודה – א"כ לימא דאיצטריך "אשר יולדו" לומר שהכתוב תלאן בלידה. ואי כרבי שמעון – היכי ס"ד דהיא ובנה חד הוא? כיון דקבר מצרי ולא מצרית! וי"ל: דקס"ד, כיון שהורתו בנכרית – חשיב דור ראשון. **חזיתיה** לרישך ביני עמודי. פירוש: רבך, דמצינו רבה שהלך ללמוד לפני רבי יוחנן, בשילהי כתובות (דף קיא.*). **בעלמא** בתר אבוה שדינן ליה. דעובר לאו ירך אמו הוא. והא דמשמע בסוף פרק שני דגיטין (דף כג: ושם) דאית ליה לרבי יוחנן דעובר ירך אמו הוא, גבי הא דקאמר נראין הדברים שעבד מקבל גט מיד רבו של חברו כו' – התם אליבא דרבי איירי, וגרסינן התם בסיפא: מאי טעמא דרבי. **אלא** הא דאמר רבא גויה מעוברת כו'. וא"ת: ומאי פריך מרבא? הא בהדיא אית ליה דעובר ירך אמו הוא בפ' "כל האסורין" (תמורה ל:) ובפרק "שור שנגח את הפרה" (ב"ק דף מז. ושם) דקאמר: היא וולדה נגחו, היא וולדה נרבעו! ואמר ר"י: שרוצה ליישב דברי רבא דהכא אפילו כרבי יוחנן.

רובו ומקפיד עליו חוצץ. לא כמו שפירש בקונטרס בפ"ק דסוכה (דף ו: ושם) דהיינו דוקא בשערו, אבל בגופו חוצץ אפילו מיעוטו שאין מקפיד, דא"כ, למה לי קרא לשערו דדרשינן (שם) "את בשרו" – את הטפל לבשרו, כיון דהלכה למשה מסיני נאמרה לו בפירוש: שערו רובו ומקפיד עליו כו'. ועוד מדקדק ר"ת: דאי בשערו דוקא – ה"ל למימר הכא: אימור דאמר רבי יצחק שערו, בשרו מי אמר? ומיהו, בלאו הכי פריך שפיר. מי

עין משפט נר מצוה

פג א מיי' פי"ב מהל' איסורי ביאה הלכ' יט סמג לאוין קיב טוש"ע אה"ע סימן ד סעיף ג:

פד ב מיי' שם טוש"ע שם סעיף ו:

פה ג מיי' שם הל' כ טוש"ע שם סעי' ד:

פו ד מיי' שם פט"ו הלכה ד סמג לאוין קיז טוש"ע שם סעיף כ:

פז ה מיי' שם פי"ב הלכה כ סמג שם קיב קטז טוש"ע שם סעיף ו:

פח ו מיי' פ"ד מהלכות פסולי המוקדשין הלכה ו:

פט ז מיי' שם הלכה ה:

צ ח מיי' שם הלכה א:

צא ט מיי' פי"ג מהל' איסורי ביאה הלכה ז סמג לאוין קטז טוש"ע י"ד סימן רסח סעיף ו:

צב י מיי' פ"א מהלכ' מקוואות הלכה יב סמג עשין רמח טוש"ע י"ד סימן קלח סעיף א:

מסורת הש"ס

[לעיל י.]

[ב"ב קכ.]

קדושין סז.

שם סט.

[לעיל עז: סוטה ע. תוספתא קדושין פ"ה]

לקמן פד:

תמורה [יט.] כה. [מנחות פח.]

ערכין כב: [וז"ל רש"י שם בעל הגולגולות כלומר אדם חשוב]

ערכין ד: סוכה ו: נדה סז:

[וע"ע תוספות עירובין כב: ד"ה קרקפנא]

הגהות הב"ח

(א) רש"י ד"ה כתב רחמנא וכו' ואילך תשבינן חדא דרא הס"ד ותיבת היא נמחק:

גליון הש"ס

גמ' מצרי שני במאי יטהר. עי' קדושין סז ע"א תוד"ה בנה שלישי: **שם** דאמר קרא האשה וילדיה. לעיל כב ע"ב: **שם** בנה אין צריך טבילה. עי' לעיל מז ע"ב תד"ה מטבילין אותו: **תד"ה** מצרי וכו' וא"ת וישא נתינה וכו' עי' טורי אבן מגילה יד ע"ב ד"ה דאגיירה:

תוספות ישנים

מצרי שני במאי יטהר. וא"ת ישא ממזרת תשיעית דאיכא מ"ד לקמן ממזרת לאחר עשרה דורות מותרת וא"כ כי ישא ממזרת תשיעית תהיה בתו כשרה כי עשירית תהיה וי"ל דמלתא דלא שכיחא הוא שיחי' כל כך ושיפרו וירבו עד עשרה דורות דאינם כל כך ידועים ואי אינם ידועים כל כך לא חיו ועוי"ל דהתינח הבת כשרה לאחר עשרה דורות אבל הבן שמא לא יוכשר דהא לא אמר לקמן אלא ממזרת דמותרת לאחר עשרה דורות אבל הזכר שמא לא יוכשר: **מצרי** שני שנשא מצרית ראשונה בנה שלישי הוי דהא דאמרינן לעיל הלך אחר פסוליהם היינו דוקא בעמוני ומצרי שנשא בת ישראל או איפכא אבל בעם אחד לא איירי לעיל: **לרישך** בי עמודי פ"ה אביי שהיה לפני רבי יוחנן ותימה דלא מצינו שעלה אביי לארץ ישראל. ונראה דר"ל לרישך רבה שהיה רבו של אביי והוא למד לפני ר' יוחנן כדאיתא פרק שני דייני גזלות ששלח אליו אחיו של רבה יש לך רב ומנו רבי יוחנן ואפשר שעלה ללמוד בפניו: **משום** דר' יצחק דאמר ר' יצחק [ד"ת] רובו ומקפיד עליו וכו' וזה אינו מקפיד ואע"ג דאמרינן התם גזרו על רובו שאינו מקפיד משום רובו המקפיד מ"מ איכא למימר דמשום מעלת גירות אוקמוה רבנן אדאורייתא:

עין משפט נר מצוה

צג א מיי' פ"ט מהל' עבדים הלכה ג סמג עשין רכ:

צד ב מיי' פי"ב מהלכ' איסורי ביאה הל' כ טוש"ע אה"ע סימן ד סעיף ז:

צה ג מיי' פט"ו מהלכ' איסורי ביאה הל' כא סמג לאוין קיז טוש"ע שם סעיף א:

צו ד מיי' שם פי"ב הלכה כב כג סמג שם טוש"ע שם:

מסורת הש"ס

וְהָא אָמַר רַב כַּהֲנָא כו' אֲבָל כּוּלּוֹ חוֹצֵץ. אע"ג דְּלָא מַקְפִּיד, וְהָכָא כּוּלּוֹ הוּא מְכוּסֶּה. דְּהַיְינוּ רְבִיתֵיהּ. וְלָאו חֲצִיצָה הִיא. **בָּאוּמּוֹת.** בְּשֶׁבַע אוּמּוֹת לְעִנְיַן "לֹא תְחַיֶּה כָּל נְשָׁמָה" הַלֵּךְ אַחַר הַזְּכָרִים, וּכְדִמְפָרֵשׁ לְקַמָּן. נִתְגַּיְּירוּ הַלֵּךְ אַחַר הַפָּגוּם שֶׁבִּשְׁנֵיהֶם. לְעִנְיַן יוֹחֲסִין, וּכְדִמְפָרֵשׁ. **לְאֶחָד** מִן הָאוּמּוֹת. שֶׁאֵינוֹ מִשִּׁבְעָה אוּמּוֹת, וְאֵינוֹ בִּכְלַל "לֹא תְחַיֶּה כָּל נְשָׁמָה". שֶׁאַתָּה רַשַּׁאי לִקְנוֹתוֹ בְּעֶבֶד. וְאִי אַתָּה מְצוּוֶּה לַהֲמִיתוֹ, דְּשָׁדֵינַן לֵיהּ בָּתַר אֲבוּהּ. ת"ל מִבְּנֵי הַתּוֹשָׁבִים. שֶׁבָּאוּ מֵאוּמּוֹת אֲחֵרִים, וְנַעֲשׂוּ אֲבוֹתָם תּוֹשָׁבִים בִּמְקוֹמְכֶם. מִן הַנּוֹלָדִים בְּאַרְצְכֶם. שֶׁאִמּוֹ מֵאַרְצְכֶם וִילָדַתּוּ שָׁם, וְלֹא מִן הַגָּרִים בְּאַרְצְכֶם שֶׁנּוֹלַד בְּמָקוֹם אַחֵר, שֶׁאִמּוֹ מִן שְׁאָר אוּמּוֹת וְאח"כ בָּא לָגוּר אֵצֶל אָבִיו בְּאַרְצְכֶם. דֶּרֶךְ אִשָּׁה לִהְיוֹת בִּמְקוֹמָהּ, וְדֶרֶךְ אִישׁ לִגְלוֹת. הִלְכָּךְ, הַנּוֹלָדִים בָּאָרֶץ – וַדַּאי אִמּוֹ מִשִּׁבְעָה אוּמּוֹת; אֲבָל הַנּוֹלָדִים בְּמָקוֹם אַחֵר – וַדַּאי אִמּוֹ מִשְּׁאָר אוּמּוֹת. וּמִסְתַּבְּרָא כִּי מַעֲטִינְהוּ קְרָא – הֵיכָא דַּאֲבִיו כְּנַעֲנִי. **אִילֵימָא בְּמִצְרִי שֶׁנָּשָׂא** עַמּוֹנִית. וְקָאָמַר דְּשָׁדֵינַן זַרְעָם אַחַר הָאָב, דַּאֲפִילּוּ יָלְדָה נְקֵבָה אֲסוּרָה עַד ג' דּוֹרוֹת, וְלָא שָׁדֵינַן לָהּ בָּתַר אִמָּהּ לְמִישְׁרְיֵיהּ לְאַלְתַּר, דְּעַמּוֹנִי וְלֹא עַמּוֹנִית. **מַאי פָּגוּם שֶׁבִּשְׁנֵיהֶם אִיכָּא.** דְּמַשְׁמַע דִּשְׁנֵיהֶם פְּגוּמִים, אֶלָּא שֶׁזֶּה פָּגוּם מִזֶּה. הָא עַמּוֹנִית לָא פְּגוּמָה מִידֵּי, דְּעַמּוֹנִי כְּתִיב וְלֹא עַמּוֹנִית! **אֶלָּא בְּעַמּוֹנִי שֶׁנָּשָׂא** מִצְרִית. דִּשְׁנֵיהֶם פְּגוּמִים, דְּמִצְרִית רִאשׁוֹנָה אֲסוּרָה. **אִי זָכָר הוּא.** אִם יוֹלֵד לָהֶם זָכָר. שַׁדְיֵיהּ בָּתַר עַמּוֹנִי. וְיֵאָסֵר לְעוֹלָם. **וְאִם נְקֵבָה הִיא שַׁדְיֵיהּ** בָּתַר מִצְרִית. וְתִהְיֶה מִצְרִית שְׁנִיָּה, וַאֲסוּרָה לְיִשְׂרָאֵל, וְלָא תִּשְׁדְּיֵיהּ בָּתַר עַמּוֹנִי לְאִישְׁתְּרוּיֵי לְאַלְתַּר מִשּׁוּם עַמּוֹנִית. **מַתְנִי'** נְתִינִים. גִּבְעוֹנִים שֶׁנִּתְגַּיְּירוּ בְּעָרְמָה בִּימֵי יְהוֹשֻׁעַ, וּנְתָנָם עֲבָדִים לְחוֹטְבֵי עֵצִים וְשׁוֹאֲבֵי מַיִם. **גמ'** גָּמַר עֲשִׂירִי עֲשִׂירִי מֵעַמּוֹנִי. בַּסִּפְרֵי: מָה עֲשִׂירִי הָאָמוּר בְּעַמּוֹנִי – עַד עוֹלָם, אַף עֲשִׂירִי הָאָמוּר בְּמַמְזֵר – עַד עוֹלָם. הִלְכָּךְ, מַה לְּהַלָּן זְכָרִים וְלֹא נְקֵבוֹת – אַף כָּאן כו'. מֵעֲשִׂירִי וְאֵילָךְ. דְּעַד עֲשָׂרָה דּוֹרוֹת, דְּאִיסּוּרָא בְּגוּפֵיהּ דְּמַמְזֵר כְּתִיב – לֵיכָּא לְמִגְמַר מֵעַמּוֹנִי, דִּנְקֵבוֹת מוּתָּרוֹת. דְּהָא מַמְזֵר מוּם זָר מַשְׁמַע,* וַאֲפִילּוּ נְקֵבוֹת. אֲבָל מֵעֲשִׂירִי וְאֵילָךְ, דְּאִיסּוּרָא בְּג"ש דְּעַמּוֹנִי וּמוֹאָבִי יָלֵיף, דְּהָא לָאו בְּמַמְזֵר כְּתִיבָא – הִלְכָּךְ הֶיתֵּירָא נַמִי לִנְקֵבוֹת מִינֵּיהּ יָלֵיף, דְּאָמַר: דּוּן מִינָּהּ וּמִינָּהּ, כְּדִלְקַמָּן. **הָא כְּמַאן** דְּאָמַר דּוּן מִינָּהּ וּמִינָּהּ. פְּלוּגְתָּא דְּר' אֱלִיעֶזֶר וְר' יְהוֹשֻׁעַ בְּ"הָעוֹר וְהָרוֹטֵב" (חולין קכ:). דּוּן מִינָּהּ וּמִינָּהּ. כִּי גָּמְרִינַן מִילְּתָא מִמִּילְּתָא בְּג"ש – גָּמְרִינַן לָהּ כּוּלָּהּ מִילְּתָא מִינָּהּ. **דּוּן מִינָּהּ וְאוֹקֵי בְּאַתְרָא.** לְמַאי דִּצְרִיכֵי גָּמְרִינַן, לְמַאי דְּלָא צְרִיכִינַן מוֹקְמִינַן בְּאַתְרָא. וְהָכָא, מַאי גְּזֵרָה שָׁוָה אִיכָּא? בְּמַמְזֵר לָא כְּתִיב "עַד עוֹלָם", וּבְעַמּוֹנִי וּמוֹאָבִי כְּתִיב "עַד עוֹלָם", וְיָלְפִינַן מַמְזֵר מֵעַמּוֹנִי בְּג"ש, כִּדְתָנֵי בְּסִפְרֵי דְּבֵי רַב: נֶאֱמַר כָּאן עֲשִׂירִי וְנֶאֱמַר לְמַטָּה עֲשִׂירִי, מָה עֲשִׂירִי הָאָמוּר לְמַטָּה עַד עוֹלָם, אַף עֲשִׂירִי הָאָמוּר כָּאן עַד עוֹלָם: ר"ל סָבַר כְּמַאן דְּאָמַר דּוּן מִינָּהּ וּמִינָּהּ: מַה לְּהַלָּן עַד עוֹלָם, אַף כָּאן עַד עוֹלָם. וּמִינָּהּ: מַה לְּהַלָּן זְכָרִים וְלֹא נְקֵבוֹת, אַף כָּאן זְכָרִים וְלֹא נְקֵבוֹת, מִדּוֹר עֲשִׂירִי וְאֵילָךְ הוּא דְּגָמְרִינַן, דְּהָא כָּל עֲשָׂרָה לָא אִיצְטְרִיכוּ לָן לְמֵילַף בְּג"ש. וְתַנָּא דִּידַן סָבַר לָהּ כְּמ"ד דּוּן מִינָּהּ וְאוֹקֵי בְּאַתְרָהּ. דּוּן מִינָּהּ: מַה לְּהַלָּן עַד עוֹלָם – אַף מַמְזֵר עַד עוֹלָם. וְאוֹקֵי בְּאַתְרָא כִּדְמְעִיקָּרָא י' דּוֹרוֹת דִּקְרָא, אֶחָד זְכָרִים וְאֶחָד נְקֵבוֹת, דִּכְתִיב מַמְזֵר מוּם זָר – הָכִי נַמִי עַד עוֹלָם דְּמַיְיתִינַן בְּג"ש, אֶחָד זְכָרִים וְאֶחָד נְקֵבוֹת. כָּךְ שָׁמַעְתִּי, וְכֵן עִיקָּר. וְיֵשׁ שֶׁמְּפָרֵשׁ לָהּ בְּלָשׁוֹן אַחֵר. מִי יִתֵּן לִי דּוֹר שְׁלִישִׁי. כְּלוֹמַר: דָּבָר שֶׁאִי אֶפְשָׁר הוּא. **לָא חַיֵּי.** שֶׁלֹּא יִטַּמְּעוּ בִּכְשֵׁרִים בְּדוֹרוֹתָיו. מַמְזֵר דִּידִיעַ. לַכֹּל בְּבֵרוּר – חַיֵּי הוּא וְדוֹרוֹתָיו, דְּלָא מִיטַּמְּעִי בֵּיהּ. **דְּלָא יְדִיעַ.** כְּלָל – לָא חַיֵּי, אֲפִילּוּ הוּא, שֶׁלֹּא יִשָּׂא כְּשֵׁרָה. דִּידִיעַ וְלָא יְדִיעַ. עַד תְּלָת דָּרֵי, דִּזְהִירֵי אִינָשֵׁי – חַיֵּי, טְפֵי – לָא חַיֵּי. דְּכֵיוָן דְּלָאו דָּבָר בָּרוּר הוּא, מִשְׁתַּכְּחָא מִילְּתָא. דָּוִד גָּזַר עֲלֵיהֶן כִּדְכְתִיב וְהַגִּבְעוֹנִים לֹא מִבְּנֵי יִשְׂרָאֵל הֵמָּה. כְּלוֹמַר: אֵינָם רְאוּיִין לָבֹא בַּקָּהָל. **אִישׁ מִתְהַלֵּל בְּמַתַּת שָׁקֶר.** שֶׁפּוֹסֵק וְאֵין נוֹתֵן, גּוֹרֵם לַעֲצִירַת גְּשָׁמִים: כֹּהֲנִים הָיוּ מְסַפְּקִין לָהֶם מָזוֹן לַגִּבְעוֹנִים, שֶׁהָיוּ חוֹטְבֵי עֵצִים וְשׁוֹאֲבֵי מַיִם לַמִּזְבֵּחַ, כִּדְכְתִיב בִּיהוֹשֻׁעַ (ט) "וְלֹא יִכָּרֵת מִכֶּם חוֹטְבֵי עֵצִים וְשׁוֹאֲבֵי מַיִם לְבֵית אֱלֹהָי". קָתָבַע. הַקָּדוֹשׁ בָּרוּךְ הוּא בִּכְבוֹד שָׁאוּל, שֶׁלֹּא נִסְפַּד כַּהֲלָכָה, וַהֲדַר קָתָבַע בְּפוּרְעָנוּתֵיהּ דְּשָׁאוּל "אֲשֶׁר הֵמִית" כו'. **בַּאֲשֶׁר מִשְׁפָּטוֹ.** בְּמָקוֹם שֶׁדָּנִים הָאָדָם – שָׁם מַזְכִּירִין פּוֹעַל צִדְקוֹתָיו.
תְּרֵיסַר

מִי יתן לי דור שלישי ואטהרנו. סתמא בעו מיניה, והשיב להם כן, ואם היה בידוע היה משיב להם דמותרת. דסבירא ליה לרבי אליעזר דון מינה ומינה בפרק "העור והרוטב" (חולין דף קכ:), ולא רצה לברר להם תשובתו שכן היה דרכו לדחות עצמו מן השואלים, כדאשכחן בפ' "הישן" (סוכה דף כח.).
ארמוני

וְהָא אָמַר רַב כַּהֲנָא: לֹא שָׁנוּ אֶלָּא רוּבּוֹ, אֲבָל כּוּלּוֹ – חוֹצֵץ! שָׁאנֵי עוּבָּר דְּהַיְינוּ רְבִיתֵיהּ. כִּי אֲתָא רָבִינָא א"ר יוֹחָנָן: *בָּאוּמּוֹת – הַלֵּךְ אַחַר הַזָּכָר, נִתְגַּיְּירוּ – הַלֵּךְ אַחַר פָּגוּם שֶׁבִּשְׁנֵיהֶם. "בָּאוּמּוֹת הַלֵּךְ אַחַר הַזָּכָר" – כִּדְתַנְיָא: *[א]מִנַּיִן לְאֶחָד מִן הָאוּמּוֹת שֶׁבָּא עַל הַכְּנַעֲנִית וְהוֹלִיד בֵּן, שֶׁאַתָּה רַשַּׁאי לִקְנוֹתוֹ בְּעֶבֶד – שֶׁנֶּאֱמַר °"וְגַם מִבְּנֵי הַתּוֹשָׁבִים הַגָּרִים עִמָּכֶם מֵהֶם תִּקְנוּ". יָכוֹל אֲפִי' אֶחָד מִן הַכְּנַעֲנִים שֶׁבָּא עַל אַחַת מִן הָאוּמּוֹת וְהוֹלִיד בֵּן שֶׁאַתָּה רַשַּׁאי לִקְנוֹתוֹ בְּעֶבֶד – ת"ל "אֲשֶׁר הוֹלִידוּ בְּאַרְצְכֶם" – מִן הַנּוֹלָדִים בְּאַרְצְכֶם, וְלֹא מִן הַגָּרִים בְּאַרְצְכֶם.§ "נִתְגַּיְּירוּ, הַלֵּךְ אַחַר פָּגוּם שֶׁבִּשְׁנֵיהֶם".§ בְּמַאי? אִילֵימָא בְּמִצְרִי שֶׁנָּשָׂא עַמּוֹנִית – מַאי פָּגוּם שֶׁבִּשְׁנֵיהֶם אִית בַּהּ? *עַמּוֹנִי וְלֹא עַמּוֹנִית! [ב]אֶלָּא בְּעַמּוֹנִי שֶׁנָּשָׂא מִצְרִית, אִי זָכָר הָוֵי – שַׁדְיֵיהּ בָּתַר עַמּוֹנִי, אִי נְקֵבָה הָוֵי – שַׁדְיֵיהּ בָּתַר מִצְרִית.§

מַתְנִי' [ג]מַמְזֵרִין [ד]וּנְתִינִין אֲסוּרִין, וְאִיסּוּרָן אִיסּוּר עוֹלָם, אֶחָד זְכָרִים וְאֶחָד נְקֵבוֹת.§

גמ' אָמַר רֵישׁ לָקִישׁ: מַמְזֶרֶת, לְאַחַר עֲשָׂרָה דּוֹרוֹת מוּתֶּרֶת. יָלֵיף עֲשִׂירִי עֲשִׂירִי מֵעַמּוֹנִי וּמוֹאָבִי, מַה לְּהַלָּן נְקֵבוֹת מוּתָּרוֹת – אַף כָּאן נְקֵבוֹת מוּתָּרוֹת. אִי, מַה לְּהַלָּן מִיָּד אַף כָּאן מִיָּד! כִּי אַהֲנֵי גְּזֵירָה שָׁוָה – מֵעֲשִׂירִי וְאֵילָךְ. וְהָאֲנַן תְּנַן: מַמְזֵרִים וּנְתִינִין אֲסוּרִין וְאִיסּוּרָן אִיסּוּר עוֹלָם, אֶחָד זְכָרִים וְאֶחָד נְקֵבוֹת! לָא קַשְׁיָא, הָא – כְּמַאן דְּאָמַר דּוּן מִינָּהּ וּמִינָּהּ, הָא כְּמַאן דְּאָמַר *דּוּן מִינָּהּ וְאוֹקֵי בְּאַתְרָא. שָׁאֲלוּ אֶת רַבִּי אֱלִיעֶזֶר: מַמְזֶרֶת לְאַחַר עֲשָׂרָה דָּרֵי מַהוּ? אָמַר לָהֶם: מִי יִתֵּן לִי דּוֹר שְׁלִישִׁי וַאֲטַהֲרֶנּוּ. אַלְמָא קָסָבַר מַמְזֵרָא לָא חַיֵּי, וְכֵן אָמַר רַב הוּנָא: מַמְזֵרָא לָא חַיֵּי, וְהָא אֲנַן תְּנַן: מַמְזֵרִין אֲסוּרִין וְאִיסּוּרָן אִיסּוּר עוֹלָם! אָמַר רַבִּי זֵירָא: לְדִידִי מְפָרְשָׁא לִי מִינֵּיהּ דְּרַב יְהוּדָה: דִּידִיעַ – חַיֵּי, דְּלָא יְדִיעַ – לָא חַיֵּי. דִּידִיעַ וְלָא יְדִיעַ – עַד תְּלָתָא דָּרֵי חַיֵּי, טְפֵי לָא חַיֵּי. הַהוּא דַּהֲוֵי בִּשְׁבָבוּתֵיהּ דְּר' אַמִי, אַכְרֵיז עֲלֵיהּ דְּמַמְזֵרָא הֲוָה. בָּכֵי וַאֲזַיל. אֲמַר לֵיהּ: חַיִּים נָתַתִּי לְךָ. אָמַר רַב חָנָא בַּר אַדָּא: *נְתִינִים – דָּוִד גָּזַר עֲלֵיהֶם, שֶׁנֶּאֱמַר °"וַיִּקְרָא הַמֶּלֶךְ לַגִּבְעוֹנִים וַיֹּאמֶר אֲלֵיהֶם וְהַגִּבְעוֹנִים לֹא מִבְּנֵי יִשְׂרָאֵל הֵמָּה וגו'". מַאי טַעְמָא גָּזַר עֲלַיְיהוּ – דִּכְתִיב °"וַיְהִי רָעָב בִּימֵי דָוִד שָׁלֹשׁ שָׁנִים שָׁנָה אַחַר שָׁנָה". שָׁנָה רִאשׁוֹנָה אָמַר לָהֶם: שֶׁמָּא עוֹבְדֵי עֲבוֹדָה זָרָה יֵשׁ בָּכֶם דִּכְתִיב °"וַעֲבַדְתֶּם אֱלֹהִים אֲחֵרִים וְהִשְׁתַּחֲוִיתֶם לָהֶם... וְעָצַר אֶת הַשָּׁמַיִם וְלֹא יִהְיֶה מָטָר וגו'" – בָּדְקוּ וְלֹא מָצְאוּ. שְׁנִיָּה אָמַר לָהֶם: שֶׁמָּא עוֹבְרֵי עֲבֵירָה יֵשׁ בָּכֶם, דִּכְתִיב °"וַיִּמָּנְעוּ רְבִיבִים וּמַלְקוֹשׁ לֹא הָיָה וּמֵצַח אִשָּׁה זוֹנָה הָיָה לָךְ וגו'" – בָּדְקוּ וְלֹא מָצְאוּ. שְׁלִישִׁית אָמַר לָהֶם: שֶׁמָּא פּוֹסְקֵי צְדָקָה בָּרַבִּים יֵשׁ בָּכֶם וְאֵין נוֹתְנִין, דִּכְתִיב °"נְשִׂיאִים וְרוּחַ וְגֶשֶׁם אָיִן אִישׁ מִתְהַלֵּל בְּמַתַּת שָׁקֶר" – בָּדְקוּ וְלֹא מָצְאוּ. אָמַר: אֵין הַדָּבָר תָּלוּי אֶלָּא בִּי, מִיָּד – "וַיְבַקֵּשׁ דָּוִד אֶת פְּנֵי ה'" מַאי הִיא? אָמַר רֵישׁ לָקִישׁ: שֶׁשָּׁאַל בָּאוּרִים וְתוּמִּים. מַאי מַשְׁמַע? א"ר אֶלְעָזָר: אָתְיָא "פְּנֵי" "פְּנֵי", כְּתִיב הָכָא "וַיְבַקֵּשׁ דָּוִד אֶת פְּנֵי ה'" וּכְתִיב הָתָם °"וְשָׁאַל לוֹ בְּמִשְׁפַּט הָאוּרִים לִפְנֵי ה'", "וַיֹּאמֶר ה' אֶל שָׁאוּל וְאֶל בֵּית הַדָּמִים עַל אֲשֶׁר הֵמִית הַגִּבְעוֹנִים". "אֶל שָׁאוּל" – שֶׁלֹּא נִסְפַּד כַּהֲלָכָה, "וְאֶל בֵּית הַדָּמִים" – "עַל אֲשֶׁר הֵמִית הַגִּבְעוֹנִים". וְכִי הֵיכָן *מָצִינוּ בְּשָׁאוּל שֶׁהֵמִית הַגִּבְעוֹנִים? אֶלָּא, מִתּוֹךְ שֶׁהָרַג נוֹב עִיר הַכֹּהֲנִים שֶׁהָיוּ מַסְפִּיקִין לָהֶם מַיִם וּמָזוֹן – מַעֲלֶה עָלָיו הַכָּתוּב כְּאִילּוּ הֲרָגָן. קָא תָּבַע אֶל שָׁאוּל שֶׁלֹּא נִסְפַּד כַּהֲלָכָה וְקָא תָּבַע עַל אֲשֶׁר הֵמִית הַגִּבְעוֹנִים?! אִין, דְּאָמַר רֵישׁ לָקִישׁ: מַאי דִּכְתִיב °"בַּקְּשׁוּ אֶת ה' כָּל עַנְוֵי הָאָרֶץ אֲשֶׁר מִשְׁפָּטוֹ פָּעָלוּ", בַּאֲשֶׁר מִשְׁפָּטוֹ – שָׁם פָּעֳלוֹ, אָמַר דָּוִד: שָׁאוּל נָפְקוּ לְהוּ
תְּרֵיסַר

תורה אור: ויקרא כה; שמואל ב כא; שם; דברים יא; ירמיה ג; משלי כה; במדבר כז; צפניה ב

קדושין סז.; ג"ז שם: סוטה ג:; [לעיל סט. וש"נ]; [ב"ק כה: סנהדרין מה: שבועות לג. זבחים לג: מנחות סב. קז. חולין קכ: נדה מג:]; [לעיל עו:]; ב"ק קיט.

[עי' תוס' לקמן עט. ד"ה ונתינים ותוספות כתובות כט. ד"ה אלו]

תוספות חד מקמאי

אר"ל ממזרת לאחר עשרה דורות מותרת יליף עשירי עשירי מעמוני מה להלן נקבות מותרות אף כאן נקבות מותרות. אי מה להלן מיד אף כאן מיד כי גמירי [ג"ש] מעשירי ואילך ולית הלכתא כר"ל דס"ל דון מינה ואוקי באתרא אלא כסתם מתני' דתנן ממזרים נתינים אסורים ומסיק דאסור לעולם אחד זכרים ואחד נקבות:

תְּרֵיסַר יַרְחֵי שַׁתָּא, אוְלָא דַּרְכֵּיהּ לְמִסְפְּדֵיהּ. נְתִינִים נִיקָרִינְהוּ וְנַפַּיְיסִינְהוּ, (א) ש"ב כא °"וַיִּקְרָא הַמֶּלֶךְ לַגִּבְעֹנִים וַיֹּאמֶר אֲלֵיהֶם מָה אֶעֱשֶׂה לָכֶם וּבַמָּה אֲכַפֵּר וּבָרְכוּ אֶת נַחֲלַת ה'. וַיֹּאמְרוּ לוֹ הַגִּבְעֹנִים אֵין לָנוּ כֶּסֶף וְזָהָב עִם שָׁאוּל וְעִם בֵּיתוֹ וְאֵין לָנוּ אִישׁ וגו' יֻתַּן לָנוּ שִׁבְעָה אֲנָשִׁים מִבָּנָיו וְהוֹקַעֲנוּם לַה' וגו'". מִיפַּיֵּים, וְלָא פַּיְיסִינְהוּ. אָמַר: בשְׁלֹשָׁה סִימָנִים יֵשׁ בְּאוּמָּה זוֹ: הָרַחֲמָנִים, וְהַבַּיְישָׁנִין, וְגוֹמְלֵי חֲסָדִים. רַחֲמָנִים — דְּכְתִיב דברים יג °"וְנָתַן לְךָ רַחֲמִים וְרִחַמְךָ וְהִרְבֶּךָ". בַּיְישָׁנִין — שמות כ דִּכְתִיב °"בַּעֲבוּר תִּהְיֶה יִרְאָתוֹ עַל פְּנֵיכֶם". בראשית יח גּוֹמְלֵי חֲסָדִים — דִּכְתִיב °"לְמַעַן אֲשֶׁר יְצַוֶּה אֶת בָּנָיו וְאֶת בֵּיתוֹ וגו'". כָּל שֶׁיֵּשׁ בּוֹ שְׁלֹשָׁה סִימָנִים הַלָּלוּ רָאוּי לְהִדָּבֵק בְּאוּמָּה זוֹ. ש"ב כא °"וַיִּקַּח הַמֶּלֶךְ אֶת שְׁנֵי בְּנֵי רִצְפָּה בַת אַיָּה אֲשֶׁר יָלְדָה לְשָׁאוּל אֶת אַרְמֹנִי וְאֶת מְפִבֹשֶׁת וְאֶת חֲמֵשֶׁת בְּנֵי מִיכַל בַּת שָׁאוּל אֲשֶׁר יָלְדָה לְעַדְרִיאֵל בֶּן בַּרְזִלַּי הַמְּחֹלָתִי". מַאי שְׁנָא הָנֵי? אָמַר רַב הוּנָא: הֶעֱבִירוּם לִפְנֵי אָרוֹן, כָּל שֶׁאָרוֹן קוֹלְטוֹ — לְמִיתָה, כָּל שֶׁאֵין אָרוֹן קוֹלְטוֹ — לְחַיִּים. מְתִיב רַב חָנָא בַּר קְטִינָא: שם °"וַיַּחְמֹל הַמֶּלֶךְ עַל מְפִבֹשֶׁת בֶּן יְהוֹנָתָן בֶּן שָׁאוּל"! שֶׁלֹּא הֶעֱבִירוֹ. וְכִי מַשּׂוֹא פָּנִים יֵשׁ בַּדָּבָר? אֶלָּא: שֶׁהֶעֱבִירוֹ וּקְלָטוֹ, וּבִקֵּשׁ עָלָיו רַחֲמִים וּפְלָטוֹ. וְאַכַּתִּי, מַשּׂוֹא פָּנִים יֵשׁ בַּדָּבָר? אֶלָּא שֶׁבִּקֵּשׁ רַחֲמִים שֶׁלֹּא יִקְלְטֶנּוּ הָאָרוֹן. וְהָא כְּתִיב דברים כד °"לֹא יוּמְתוּ אָבוֹת עַל בָּנִים *וגו'"! אָמַר רַבִּי חִיָּיא בַּר אַבָּא אָמַר רַבִּי יוֹחָנָן: מוּטָב שֶׁתֵּעָקֵר אוֹת אַחַת מִן הַתּוֹרָה, וְאַל יִתְחַלֵּל שֵׁם שָׁמַיִם בְּפַרְהֶסְיָא. שמואל ב כא °"וַתִּקַּח רִצְפָּה בַת אַיָּה אֶת הַשַּׂק וַתַּטֵּהוּ לָהּ אֶל הַצּוּר מִתְּחִלַּת קָצִיר עַד נִתַּךְ מַיִם עֲלֵיהֶם מִן הַשָּׁמָיִם וְלֹא נָתְנָה עוֹף הַשָּׁמַיִם לָנוּחַ עֲלֵיהֶם יוֹמָם וְחַיַּת הַשָּׂדֶה לָיְלָה". דברים כא וְהָא כְּתִיב °"לֹא תָלִין נִבְלָתוֹ עַל הָעֵץ"! אָמַר רַבִּי יוֹחָנָן מִשּׁוּם רַבִּי שִׁמְעוֹן בֶּן יְהוֹצָדָק: גמוּטָב שֶׁתֵּעָקֵר אוֹת אַחַת מִן הַתּוֹרָה וְיִתְקַדֵּשׁ שֵׁם שָׁמַיִם בְּפַרְהֶסְיָא. שֶׁהָיוּ עוֹבְרִים וְשָׁבִים אוֹמְרִים: מַה טִּיבָן שֶׁל אֵלּוּ? הַלָּלוּ בְּנֵי מְלָכִים הֵם. וּמָה עָשׂוּ? פָּשְׁטוּ יְדֵיהֶם בְּגֵרִים גְּרוּרִים. אָמְרוּ: אֵין לְךָ אוּמָּה שֶׁרְאוּיָה לְהִדָּבֵק בָּהּ כְּזוֹ. וּמָה בְּנֵי מְלָכִים כָּךְ, בְּנֵי הֶדְיוֹטוֹת עַל אַחַת כַּמָּה וְכַמָּה! וּמָה גֵּרִים גְּרוּרִים כָּךְ, יִשְׂרָאֵל עַל אַחַת כַּמָּה וְכַמָּה! מִיָּד נִתּוֹסְפוּ עַל יִשְׂרָאֵל מֵאָה וַחֲמִשִּׁים אֶלֶף, שֶׁנֶּאֱמַר מלכים א ה °"וַיְהִי לִשְׁלֹמֹה שִׁבְעִים אֶלֶף נוֹשֵׂא סַבָּל וּשְׁמֹנִים אֶלֶף חֹצֵב בָּהָר". וְדִלְמָא יִשְׂרָאֵל הֲווּ! לָא סָלְקָא דַּעְתָּךְ, דִּכְתִיב שם ט °"וּמִבְּנֵי יִשְׂרָאֵל לֹא נָתַן שְׁלֹמֹה עָבֶד". וְדִלְמָא *דוּגְזַר בְּעָלְמָא! אֶלָּא מֵהָכָא: ד"ה ב ב °"וַיִּסְפֹּר שְׁלֹמֹה כָּל הָאֲנָשִׁים הַגֵּרִים אֲשֶׁר בְּאֶרֶץ יִשְׂרָאֵל [וגו'] וַיִּמָּצְאוּ מֵאָה וַחֲמִשִּׁים אֶלֶף [וגו'] וַיַּעַשׂ מֵהֶם שִׁבְעִים אֶלֶף (נוֹשֵׂא) סַבָּל וּשְׁמֹנִים אֶלֶף חֹצֵב בָּהָר". וּנְתִינִים, דָּוִד גָּזַר עֲלֵיהֶם? מֹשֶׁה גָּזַר עֲלֵיהֶם, דִּכְתִיב דברים כט °"מֵחֹטֵב עֵצֶיךָ עַד שֹׁאֵב מֵימֶיךָ"! מֹשֶׁה גָּזַר לְהַהוּא דָּרָא, דָּוִד גָּזַר לְכוּלֵּי דָּרָא. וְאַכַּתִּי יְהוֹשֻׁעַ גָּזַר עֲלַיְיהוּ דִּכְתִיב יהושע ט °"וַיִּתְּנֵם יְהוֹשֻׁעַ בַּיּוֹם הַהוּא חֹטְבֵי עֵצִים וְשֹׁאֲבֵי מַיִם לָעֵדָה וּלְמִזְבַּח ה'"! דיְהוֹשֻׁעַ גָּזַר בִּזְמַן שֶׁבֵּית הַמִּקְדָּשׁ קַיָּים, דָּוִד גָּזַר בִּזְמַן שֶׁאֵין בֵּית הַמִּקְדָּשׁ קַיָּים. בִּימֵי

רש"י

תְּרֵיסַר יַרְחֵי שַׁתָּא. לָאו דַּוְקָא, דְּהָא קָרוֹב לִתְלָתִין שְׁנִין הוּא. שֶׁהֲרֵי סוֹף שְׁנוֹתָיו שֶׁל דָּוִד הָיָה, אֶלָּא לְפִי שֶׁאֵין דֶּרֶךְ כָּבוֹד לִסְפּוֹד אַחַר יב"ח, אַחַר שֶׁנִּתְקַבְּלוּ תַּנְחוּמִין עַל הַמֵּת, כִּדְאָמַר בְּמוֹעֵד קָטָן (דף כא:). אֵין לָנוּ. לִתְבּוֹעַ לְשָׁאוּל וּלְבֵיתוֹ לֹא כֶּסֶף וְלֹא זָהָב כִּי אִם נְפָשׁוֹת, וְאֵין לָנוּ לְהָמִית בִּשְׁאָר יִשְׂרָאֵל כִּי אִם בְּזַרְעוֹ. וְהוֹקַעֲנוּם. תּוֹרָה אוֹר תְּלִיָּיה. בְּאוּמָּה זוֹ. יִשְׂרָאֵל. הָרַחֲמָנִים כו'. וְהָנֵי גִּבְעוֹנִים, כֵּיוָן דְּלָא מְרַחֲמִי — אֵינָן רְאוּיִין לִידָּבֵק בָּהֶן. מִיָּד גָּזַר עֲלֵיהֶן דָּוִד. לְכָךְ נֶאֱמַר "וְהַגִּבְעוֹנִים לֹא מִבְּנֵי יִשְׂרָאֵל הֵמָּה". וַיַּחְמוֹל הַמֶּלֶךְ. וְאִי בְּאָרוֹן תַּלְיָא מִילְּתָא, כֵּיוָן דְּלָא קְלָטוֹ אָרוֹן — מַהוּ חֶמְלָתוֹ שֶׁל דָּוִד? וּמְשַׁנֵּי: שֶׁלֹּא הֶעֱבִירוֹ. וְכִי מַשּׂוֹא פָּנִים יֵשׁ בַּדָּבָר. וְכִי הָיָה לוֹ לְדָוִד לִישָּׂא פָּנִים בְּדִינֵי נְפָשׁוֹת? הָיָה לוֹ לְהַעֲבִיר אֶת כּוּלָּן. וְאַכַּתִּי מַשּׂוֹא פָּנִים יֵשׁ בַּדָּבָר. הוֹאִיל וּקְלָטוֹ אָרוֹן — לֹא הָיָה לוֹ לְהָמִית אַחֵר תַּחְתָּיו. וְאַל יִתְחַלֵּל שֵׁם שָׁמַיִם. שֶׁיִּהְיוּ הָאוּמּוֹת אוֹמְרִים: אֵין אוּמָּה זוֹ רְאוּיִין לִידָּבֵק בָּהּ, שֶׁהֲרֵי פָּשְׁטוּ יְדֵיהֶם בְּגֵרִים לִיטּוֹל מְזוֹנוֹתֵיהֶם, וְלֹא עָשׂוּ בָּהֶן נְקָמָה. עַד נִתַּךְ מַיִם עֲלֵיהֶם. עַד יְמוֹת הַגְּשָׁמִים לֹא נִיתְּנוּ לִקְבוּרָה. דוּגְזַר. שְׂכִירִים. אֶלָּא מֵהָכָא. "וַיִּסְפֹּר שְׁלֹמֹה (אֶת) כָּל הָאֲנָשִׁים וַיִּמָּצְאוּ מֵאָה וַחֲמִשִּׁים אֶלֶף וַיַּעַשׂ מֵהֶם שִׁבְעִים אֶלֶף (נוֹשֵׂא) סַבָּל". מֵחוֹטֵב עֵצֶיךָ. מִדְּקָרֵינְהוּ לְחוֹטְבֵי עֵצִים בְּאַנְפַּיְיהוּ — שְׁמַע מִינַּהּ לָאו בִּכְלַל יִשְׂרָאֵל נִינְהוּ, וְלָאו בִּכְלַל גֵּרִים, אֶלָּא עֲבָדִים. וַעֲבָדִים פְּסוּלִים נִינְהוּ, וְגִבְעוֹנִים חוֹטְבֵי עֵצִים נִינְהוּ, דִּלְהָכִי אַקְלִינְהוּ יְהוֹשֻׁעַ. מֹשֶׁה גָּזַר עֲלֵיהֶן לְהַהוּא דָּרָא. עַל חוֹטְבֵי עֵצִים שֶׁהָיוּ בְּיָמָיו. וַיִּתְּנֵם יְהוֹשֻׁעַ. אַלְמָא: עֲבָדִים נִינְהוּ, וִיהוֹשֻׁעַ לַדּוֹרוֹת הַבָּאִים גָּזַר, דִּכְתִיב (יהושע ט) "לֹא יִכָּרֵת מִכֶּם חוֹטְבֵי עֵצִים". בִּזְמַן שֶׁבִּהמ"ק קַיָּים. דִּכְתִיב (שם) "לְמִזְבַּח ה'". חֶלְקוֹ

תוספות

ארמוני ומפיבושת. אותו מפיבושת היה בן שאול. ואמר ר"ת: דהוא היה רבו של דוד, דאמר בפרק קמא דברכות (דף ד. ושם): שהיה מבייש פני דוד בהלכה. וגרס התם דלא מפיבושת שמו אלא איש בעל שמו. כי מפיבושת בן שאול נקרא איש בעל בדברי הימים, ולא כמה שכתוב בספרים איש בושת שמו, דלא מלינו בשום מקום איש בושת שנקרא מפיבושת, ואיש בושת נהרג בתחלת מלכות בית דוד, קודם מעשה הגבעונים. דליכא למימר דמפיבושת, בנו של יהונתן, היה רבו של דוד — דאותו לא מלינו בשום מקום שנקרא לא איש בושת ולא איש בעל. וא"ת: ולמה לא חלק לו כבוד לרבו לבקש עליו רחמים שלא יקלטנו הארון? וי"ל: דשמא בקש ולא נענה.

ותטהו לה אל הצור. אומר במדרש: אל הצור — שהצדיקה (ב) עליו הדין, ואמרה "הצור תמים פעלו". **דונגר** גרסי'. מדת שכירות. דדון לשון מדה כדאמר בבבא בתרא (ג) (דף ל:): וקרו ליה *דון פפא. **ונתינים** דוד גזר עליהן. ברים שמעתין פי' בקונטרס שגזר עליהן חתנות וכדכתיב: והגבעונים לא מבני ישראל המה וגו'. כלומר, אין ראויין להדבק בישראל. והשתא פריך: דמשה גזר עליהן עַבְדוּת ואסור משום "לא יהיה קדש"! ומשני. דמשה לא גזר אלא להההוא דרא, ויהושע בזמן שבהמ"ק קיים. ומלינו למימר דלא נאסרו בשום פעם משום "לא יהיה קדש" כיון דלא גזר עליהן עבדות אף בזמן שאין בית המקדש קיים, ודוד גזר עליהן חתנות ולא שעבדם לכולהו דרי. ואתי שפיר הא דאין בנתינים תורת עבדים, דתנן ב"אלו נערות" (כתובות דף כט. ושם) דהבא על הנתינה — יש לה קנס, ואילו בבא על השפחה — תנן דאין לה קנס. ואומר בירושלמי: אפי' משומרת שלא נבעלה. ועוד: דאם יש בהם תורת עבדות — ליתסרו חרורי בנתיני, דמשוחרר אסור בשפחה, כדאמר בשילהי האיש מקדש: אין ספק בשחרור שאינו נושא שפחה אין יכול. ובפרק "עשרה יוחסין" (קידושין דף סט.) קאמר דחרורי ונתיני מותרים לבא זה בזה. ועוד יש לפרש, דהכי פריך: ולא עבדות ממש משה גזר עליהן, ומסתמא גזר נמי שלא יתחתנו בהם, דאין נכון שיתחתנו בהם כיון דנראין כעבדים. ודוד נמי נוכל לומר דגזר עליהן עבדות כדי שלא יתחתנו בהם, והשתא פריך שפיר דמשה גזר עליהן, וניחא השתא הא דקאמר: בימי ר' בקשו להתיר נתינים — להפקיע שעבוד מהם, ועל ידי כן יהיה מותר להתחתן בהם. ומסיק דחלק מזבח מי יתיר. וכיון דאישתייר בהן שעבוד של חלק מזבח — אין הגון לידבק בהם. ופליגא דרבי חייא בר אבא, דאמר: חלק מזבח בזמן שאין בית המקדש קיים — מותר, ואם היו מפקיעין חלק עדה — היו מותרים לגמרי, ושוב לא יחול שום עבדות של חלק מזבח, אפילו לכשיבנה. ואין נראה לרבינו תם: דמדאורייתא אסירי בלאו ד"לא תתחתן" כדמסיק רבא לעיל (דף עו.), דבגירותן אית להו חתנות, ותנן (מכות דף יג.) "ואלו הן הלוקין: הבא על הממזרת ועל הנתינה". ומיהו: איכא למימר דנתינה אגב שיטפא דממזרת נקטה, וכן צריך לומר למאי דהוה בעי רבא למימר דבגירותן לית להו חתנות. דבכל דוכתא איירי בגירות גבי קנס, וב"עשרה יוחסין" (קידושין סט.) במתניתין. ונראה לרבינו תם: דדוד גזר עליהם שעבוד, והא דקאמר לעיל ראוי להדבק עם ישראל — היינו להיות בני חורין כמותן, אבל חתנות — אסור מדאורייתא. והא דקאמר בימי רבי בקשו להתיר נתינים — לא להתחתן בהם, אלא להפקיע עבודתם. ואמר להם רבי: חלק מזבח מי יתיר, הלכך אין לנו להתיר אפילו חלקנו, שלא ישתכח חלק מזבח. ופליגא דרבי חייא בר אבא, דאמר: חלק מזבח בזמן שאין בית המקדש קיים — מותר ממילא בלא שום התרה

עין משפט נר מצוה

צז א טוש"ע י"ד סימן שלא סעיף ב:
צח ב מיי' פי"ב מהל' איסורי ביאה הלכה כב ופי"ט הלכה יז:
צט ג מיי' פ"ב מהל' ממרים הלכה ד:
ק ד מיי' פי"ב מהל' איסורי ביאה הלכה כב כג:

[לפנינו איתא רוז פפא]

[עיקר הכוונה אסיפא דקרא איש בחטאו יומתו ועי' תוס' ע"ז לו: ד"ה דכתיב לא תתחתן וכ"כ תוס' בכתובות כט. סוף ד"ה אלו]

[גרסת הערוך רונגר פירוש לשון פרסי רון יום גר שכיר כלומר שכיר יום ועיין ב"ב קכב. שגם הרשב"ם בשם ר"ח כתב כך רונגר]

הגהות הב"ח

(א) גמ' ונפייסינהו מיד ויקרא: (ב) תוס' ד"ה ותטהו וכו' שהצדיקה עליהם הדין: (ג) ד"ה דונגר וכו' כדאמר בב"ב. נ"ב דף ל' ושם משמע דהיו גורסי' רוז פפא שוב מצאתי בב"ב דף קכב ע"א דצריך לגרוס רוזגר והוא שתי תיבות רוז פי' יום וגר פי' שכיר דהיינו שכיר יום וכן נ"ל דצ"ל כאן רוזגר דר"ל שכיר יום דתיבת דונגר אין לו פירוש כלל וא"כ גם שם ברשב"ם צ"ל רוז פפא וק"ל:

עין משפט נר מצוה

קא א מיי' פ"ו מהלכות יבום הלכה ד ח סמג עשין נא טוש"ע אה"ע סימן קעב סעיף ג:
קב ב ג מיי' שם הל' ב ח טוש"ע שם ס"א:
קג ד (מיי' פי"ז מהל' איסורי ביאה) טוש"ע שם:
קד ה מיי' פי"ח שם הלכה ג סמג לאוין קפא טוש"ע שם סי' ו סעיף א:
קה ו טוש"ע שם סימן קעב סעיף ג בהג"ה:
קו ז מיי' פ"ו מהלכות יבום הלכה ד טוש"ע שם סימן קעד סעיף ב:
קז ח מיי' שם טוש"ע שם סעיף א וסימן קעג סעיף ג:

גמרא

בימי רבי בקשו להתיר נתינים. אמר להם רבי: חלקנו נתיר, חלק מזבח מי יתיר? ופליגא דר' חייא בר אבא, דאמר ר' חייא בר אבא אמר ר' יוחנן: חלק עדה — לעולם אסור, חלק מזבח, בזמן שבית המקדש קיים — אסור, אין בית המקדש קיים — שרי.§ **מתני'** אמר רבי יהושע: שמעתי שהסרים חולץ וחולצין לאשתו, והסרים לא חולץ ולא חולצין לאשתו, ואין לי לפרש. א"ר עקיבא: אני אפרש: [א] סרים אדם — חולץ וחולצין לאשתו, מפני שהיתה לו שעת הכושר. *[ב] סרים חמה לא חולץ ולא חולצין לאשתו מפני שלא היתה לו שעת הכושר. ר' אליעזר אומר: לא כי, אלא: סרים חמה — חולץ וחולצין לאשתו, מפני שיש לו רפואה. סרים אדם — לא חולץ ולא חולצין לאשתו, מפני שאין לו רפואה. העיד ר' יהושע בן בתירא על בן מגוסת שהיה בירושלים סרים אדם, ויבמו את אשתו, לקיים דברי ר"ע. הסרים לא חולץ ולא מייבם, [ג] וכן איילונית לא חולצת ולא מתייבמת. [ד] הסרים שחלץ ליבמתו — לא פסלה, בעלה — פסלה, [ה] מפני שהיא בעילת זנות. וכן איילונית שחלצו לה אחין — לא פסלוה, בעלוה — פסלוה, מפני שבעילתה בעילת זנות.§ **גמ'** מכדי שמעינן לר"ע דאמר חייבי לאוין כחייבי כריתות דמו — וחייבי כריתות לאו בני חליצה וייבום נינהו! אמר ר' אמי: הכא במאי עסקינן — [ו] כגון שנשא אחיו גיורת. ור"ע סבר לה כר' יוסי, דאמר: *קהל גרים לא אקרי קהל. אי הכי יבומי נמי מייבם! אין הכי נמי ואיידי דאמר ר' יהושע חולץ אמר איהו נמי חולץ. דיקא נמי, דקתני: העיד ר' יהושע בן בתירא על בן מגוסת שהיה בירושלים סרים אדם, ויבמו את אשתו, לקיים דברי ר"ע. ש"מ. מתיב רבה: *[ז] פצוע דכא, וכרות שפכה, *סרים אדם, והזקן — או חולצין או מייבמין. כיצד? מתו ולהם נשים, ולהם אחין, ועמדו אחין ועשו מאמר בנשותיהן ונתנו גט או שחלצו — מה שעשו עשו, ואם בעלו — קנו. מתו אחין ועמדו הן ועשו מאמר בנשותיהן ונתנו גט או חלצו — מה שעשו עשו, [ח] ואם בעלו — קנו, ואסור לקיימן, משום שנאמר °"לא יבא פצוע דכא וכרות שפכה בקהל ה'". אלמא בקהל עסקינן! אלא אמר רבה: כגון שנפלה לו ולבסוף נפצע. אמר ליה אביי: וליתי איסור פצוע ונידחי עשה דייבום! מי לא תנן*, ר"ג אומר: אם מיאנה — מיאנה, ואם לאו — תמתין עד שתגדיל, ותצא הלזו משום אחות אשה. אלמא: אתי איסור אחות אשה ודחי, הכא נמי ניתי איסור פצוע ונידחי! אלא אמר רב יוסף: האי תנא — הך תנא דבי רבי עקיבא היא, דאמר: מחייבי לאוין דשאר הוי ממזר, מחייבי לאוין גרידי — לא הוי ממזר. איקרי כאן °"להקים לאחיו שם" והא לאו בר הכי הוא! אמר רבא: אם כן אין לך אשה שכשרה ליבם שלא נעשה בעלה סרים חמה שעה אחת קודם למיתתו. לר' אליעזר פירוקא דרבא פירכא היא! התם כחישותא דאתחילה ביה. היכי דמי סרים חמה? אמר רב יצחק בר יוסף אמר רבי יוחנן: כל שלא

תוספות

התרה. ואם היה מופקע מהם שעבוד לגמרי — שוב לא היה חל עוד עליהן. וא"ת: וכיון דנתיני אסירי מדאורייתא, מ"לא תתחתן", מאי שנא דמשוחרר מותר בהן ובשפחה אסור משום "לא יהיה קדש"? וי"ל: דלאו ד"לא תתחתן" איכא למילף משאר פסולי קהל, כגון ממזר עמוני ומואבי, דשרו בקהל גרים. אבל לאו ד"לא יהיה קדש" לא שייך למילף, דהא לא תפסי קדושין בשפחה, ולא הוי דומיא דשאר פסולים. ואם תאמר: ומ"ש דממזר מותר בשפחה, דתנן ב"האומר" בקידושין (דף סט.): ממזר נושא שפחה, אפי' לכתחלה, כדמוכח התם בגמרא! ואמר ר"ת: דלא שייך "לא יהיה קדש" בממזר, דעיקרו בא מקדישות, מאיסור דלא תפסי בו קידושין. ואין להאריך.

בימי ר' בקשו להתיר נתינים. אין זה מבטל דברי ב"ד חברו, דהפקר בית דין היה הפקר. **אי** הכי יבומי נמי תתייבם. פי': אא"ב בנשא ישראלית איירי, אע"ג דהיא שפיר מתייבמת — אז לא תקשי אמאי אין מייבם, שהרי הוא אסור בה, דהוי פצוע דכא. ואיידי דקאמר חולץ — קאמר נמי חולצין לאשתו. אבל כיון דאיירי בגיורת — איהו גופיה שרי לייבם.

ואיידי דאמר רבי יהושע חולץ כו'. וא"ת: ור' יהושע גופיה אמאי נקט חולץ כיון דאיירי בגיורת? אי משום דקסבר דקהל גרים איקרי קהל כדפירש בקונטרס — א"כ מאי קאמר ואין לי לפרש? האיכא למשמע מדאתניוהו חולץ וחולצין, ולא אתניוהו מייבם ומייבמין — ש"מ דבסרים אדם חולץ וחולצין! דאי בסרים חמה, א"כ אפי' לייבם נמי שרי! וי"ל: דרבי יהושע נקט חולץ וחולצין אגב דבעי למימרא לא חולץ ולא חולצין, דלא מצי למנקט לא מייבם ולא מייבמין, דהוי משמע יבומי הוא דלא, אבל מיחלץ שרי. מיהו, רבי עקיבא הוי מצי למיתני לא מייבם ולא מייבמין, דכיון דפירש הטעם משום שלא היה לו שעת הכושר — ממילא הוה ידענא דמיחלץ נמי לא חליץ, אלא אגב דנקט ר' יהושע חולץ נקט נמי ר' עקיבא.

אלמא בקהל עסקינן. וכרבי עקיבא אתיא: דסרים אדם בר חליצה ויבום הוא. ותימה: דלמא בהא לא סברה כרבי עקיבא דמשוי חייבין לאוין כחייבי כריתות? אבל

תוספות חד מקמאי

הא דתנן א"ר [יהושע] שמעתי שהסרים חולץ וחולצין לאשתו דוקא לענין חליצה ויבום דפליגי אבל לבוא בקהל דכ"ע סרים אדם אסור לבוא בקהל סרים חמה מותר לבוא בקהל וסרים אדם ופצוע דכא מותרים בגיורת דקהל גרים לא איקרי קהל וסרים אדם מותר לייבם את אשתו אם היא גיורת אע"פ שאין לו רפואה כיון שהיתה לו שעת הכושר דאי לא אזלינן לשעת הכושר אין לך אשה שכשרה ליבם (אלא) שלא נעשה בעלה סרים שעה א' קודם למיתתו וסרים חמה דקי"ל כר"ע דאינו חולץ ולא חולצין לאשתו דוקא שהוא לקוי ממעי אמו שלא היתה לו שעת הכושר ולא חיישי' שמא הבריא בינתיים בכוליה גופיה:

רש"י

חלקנו נתיר. דיכולין בית דין להתיר ולהפקיר חלקם של ישראל, דקי"ל (לקמן דף פט:): הפקר בית דין היה הפקר. **ופליגא** דר' חייא. האי דקאמר חלק המזבח מי יתיר, ואע"ג דמזבח בימי רבי לא הוה קאמר דחלק מזבח אסור — פליגא דרבי חייא. חלק עדה לעולם **אסור**. עד שיתירוהו. **מתני'** והסרים לא חולץ כו'. *דכתיב "לא ימחה שמו מישראל" — פרט לסרים ששמו מחוי. ואין לי לפרש. איני יודע אי זה סרים בן חליצה ואי זה פטור. סרים אדם. שנסתרס לאחר שנולד. סרים חמה. ממעי אמו. לקיים דברי ר"ע. עדות זו של רבי יהושע ב"ב — לקיים דברי ר"ע העיד. **לא** פסלה. מן הכהונה, שאין חליצתן חליצה. בעילת זנות. שאסורה לו משום אשת אח שלא במקום מצוה. **גמ'** כחייבי כריתות דמי. דא"ר עקיבא ב"החולץ" (לעיל מט.): יש ממזר מחייבי לאוין. וסרים אדם מחייבי לאוין הוא, דכתיב (דברים כג) "לא יבא פצוע דכא", והיכי קאמר ר"ע סרים [חולץ] את אשת אחיו? הא לא רמיא קמיה, ואדרבא קיימא כחייבי כריתות, וקאי עלה באיסור אשת אח. **ואיידי** דאמר ר' יהושע חולץ. דלרבי יהושע יבומי לא, דאית ליה קהל גרים מיקרי קהל. ומיהו, מיחלץ חלצה, דחייבי לאוין לר' יהושע בני חליצה נינהו. **דיקא** נמי. דלר' עקיבא יבומי נמי שרי, דקתני וכו' ויבמו את אשתו. סרים **אדם**. הואיל והיתה לו שעת הכושר, ור"ע היא. זקן. נקט ליה בהדי הנך משום דדמי להו, דהיתה לו שעת הכושר, והשתא פסק מלידה. ונתנו גט. כלומר או נתנו לה גט. מה שעשו עשו. וצריכות גט למאמרן, או אם נתנו גט אסורין שוב לייבמן. ואסור לקיימן. לאו אזקן קאי. שנפלה לו. והוזקקה לייבום. ולבסוף **נפצע**. דהשתא בעיא חליצה לאפקועי זיקה. דרבן גמליאל. בפרק ב"ש בגדולה שנפלה לפני בעל אחות קטנה. אלמא, אתי איסור אחות אשה ודחי, אע"ג דבשעת נפילה איחזיא. **אלא אמר** רב יוסף. שנפצע ואח"כ נפלה לו. ודקאמרת הא אית ליה לר"ע חייבי לאוין כחייבי כריתות — האי תנא דמתניתין הך תנא דבי ר"ע היא, דאמר ב"החולץ ליבמתו" (לעיל מט.) אי: זהו ממזר — כל שאר בשר שהוא בלא יבא, ודלא כרבי סימאי, דאמר (כתובות דף כט:): מן הכל היה עושה רבי עקיבא ממזר חוץ מאלמנה לכ"ג, שהרי אמרה תורה "לא יקח ולא יחלל". אבל מכל חייבי לאוין גרידי, אפילו ליכא קורבה — הולד ממזר. ופרכינן: ואמאי סרים חולץ ואפילו היתה לו שעת הכושר, איקרי כאן להקים כו'. **אמר** **רבא אם כן**. דשעת הכושר דמעיקרא לאו מילתא היא, הואיל ובשעת מיתה לא חזי — אין לך אשה כו'. סמוך למיתתו. ייסורי מיתה מתישים כחו, אלא אמרינן: הואיל ומעיקרא בר הקמה הוה — בת חליצה היא, הכא נמי לא שנא. לרבי אליעזר **פירוקא** דרבא **פירכא** היא. גמרא פריך: כלומר, האי פירוקא דרבא — פירכא היא לרבי אליעזר. דהא ודאי חזינן דשעת הכושר מילתא היא, ואמאי קאמר רבי אליעזר סרים אדם אין חולץ, דלא מהניא ליה שעת הכושר דמעיקרא? הא ודאי סריסות של מיתה אין לו רפואה — אפילו הכי מתייבמת האשה, משום שעת הכושר דמעיקרא. כחישותא **הוא** דאתחילה ביה. ולאו סרים הוא, אלא מיתה מכחשת כחו. היכי דמי סרים חמה. דקאמרת שלא היתה לו שעת הכושר. שלא

מסורת הש"ס

תורה אור

בכורות מב:

רש"ל

[קדושין עג.]

[תוס' פי"א] לעיל כ:

[עי' תוס' סוטה כו. ד"ה אשת]

דברים כג

לעיל יח. לקמן קט.

שם כה

גליון הש"ס

מתני' א"ר יהושע שמעתי. כעין זה פסחים נו ע"ב: **רש"י** ד"ה והסרים וכו' דכתיב לא ימחה וכו'. לעיל כד ע"א:

עין משפט
נר מצוה

[ועי' היטב נדה מז: בתוס' ד"ה לדברי ב"ה]

קח א מיי' פ"ב מהלכות איסורי מזבח הי"ב:

קט ב מיי' פ"ב מהל' אישות הל' ד יא סמג עשין כ טוש"ע אה"ע סימן קנה סעיף יב יג וסי' קעב סעיף ו:

קי ג (מיי' שם) טוש"ע שם סעיף יב בהג"ה:

קיא ד מיי' פ"ז מהל ממרים הלכה ה ו:

קיב ה מיי' פ"ב מהל אישות הלכה ה:

קיג ו מיי' שם הלכה ד יא טוש"ע שם סימן קנה סעיף יב:

קיד ז מיי' פ"א מהל' מילה הלכה יג ופכ"ה מהל' שבת הלכה ו טוש"ע א"ח סימן של סעיף ח וטוש"ע י"ד סי' רסו סעיף יא:

מסורת הש"ס

בכורות לח:

לקמן נז. ב"ב קנה: נדה מז:

[ביצה כח. כתובות סח.]

שבת קלו. ב"ב כ. [תוס' שבת פט"ז]

נ"ל שנה. יעב"ץ

שֶׁלֹּא רָאָה שָׁעָה אַחַת בְּבַשְׂרוּתוֹ. מְנָא יָדְעִינַן? אָמַר אַבַּיֵי: כָּל הַמַּטִּיל מַיִם וְאֵינוֹ עוֹשֶׂה כִּיפָּה. מִמַּאי הֲוַאי? דְּאָפְיָה אִימֵּיהּ בְּטִיהֲרָא וְשָׁתְיָא שִׁיכְרָא מַרְקָא. אֲמַר רַב יוֹסֵף: הַיְינוּ דְּשָׁמַעְנָא לְאַמִּי דַּאֲמַר "כָּל שֶׁמִּמְּעֵי אִמּוֹ לָקוּי" וְלָא יָדַעְנָא מַאי נִיהוּ. וְלֵיחוּשׁ שֶׁמָּא הִבְרִיא בֵּינְתַיִם? כֵּיוָן דִּתְחִלָּתוֹ וְסוֹפוֹ לָקוּי – לָא חָיְישִׁינַן. מְתִיב רַב מָרִי, *רַבִּי חֲנִינָא בֶּן אַנְטִיגְנוֹס אוֹמֵר: אבּוֹדְקִין אוֹתוֹ שָׁלֹשׁ פְּעָמִים בְּתוֹךְ שְׁמוֹנִים יוֹם! לְחַד אֵבֶר חָיְישִׁינַן, לְכוּלֵּיהּ גּוּפָא לָא חָיְישִׁינַן.§ "רַבִּי אֱלִיעֶזֶר אוֹמֵר לֹא כִּי וכו'".§ וּרְמִינְהוּ: *בֶּן בעֶשְׂרִים שָׁנָה וְלֹא הֵבִיא שְׁתֵּי שְׂעָרוֹת – יָבִיאוּ רְאָיָה שֶׁהוּא בֶּן עֶשְׂרִים, וְהוּא הַסָּרִיס, לֹא חוֹלֵץ וְלֹא מְיַיבֵּם. בַּת עֶשְׂרִים וְלֹא הֵבִיאָה שְׁתֵּי שְׂעָרוֹת – יָבִיאוּ רְאָיָה שֶׁהִיא בַּת עֶשְׂרִים, וְהִיא הָאַיְלוֹנִית, לֹא חוֹלֶצֶת וְלֹא מִתְיַיבֶּמֶת, דִּבְרֵי בֵּית הִלֵּל. וּבֵית שַׁמַּאי אוֹמְרִים: זֶה וָזֶה בְּנֵי שְׁמֹנֶה עֶשְׂרֵה. רַבִּי אֱלִיעֶזֶר אוֹמֵר: הַזָּכָר כְּדִבְרֵי ב"ה, וּנְקֵבָה כְּדִבְרֵי ב"ש, מִפְּנֵי שֶׁהָאִשָּׁה מְמַהֶרֶת לָבֹא לִפְנֵי הָאִישׁ. אָמַר רָמִי בַּר דִּיקוּלֵי אָמַר שְׁמוּאֵל: חָזַר בּוֹ ר' אֱלִיעֶזֶר. אִיבַּעְיָא לְהוּ: מֵהֵי הֲדַר בֵּיהּ? תָּא שְׁמַע, דְּתַנְיָא: רַבִּי אֱלִיעֶזֶר אוֹמֵר: סָרִיס חַמָּה חוֹלֵץ וְחוֹלְצִין לְאִשְׁתּוֹ, שֶׁכֵּן בְּמִינָן מִתְרַפְּאִין בַּאֲלֶכְּסַנְדְּרִיָּא שֶׁל מִצְרַיִם. רַבִּי אֶלְעָזָר אוֹמֵר: לְעוֹלָם לָא הֲדַר בֵּיהּ, וְכִי תְּנַן הַהִיא – לְעוֹנָשִׁין. אִיתְּמַר: אָכַל חֵלֶב, מִבֶּן שְׁתֵּים עֶשְׂרֵה [וְיוֹם אֶחָד] עַד בֶּן שְׁמֹנֶה עֶשְׂרֵה, וְנוֹלְדוּ בּוֹ סִימָנֵי סָרִיס, וּלְאַחַר מִכָּאן הֵבִיא שְׁתֵּי שְׂעָרוֹת. גרַב אָמַר: נַעֲשָׂה סָרִיס לְמַפְרֵעַ, וּשְׁמוּאֵל אָמַר: קָטָן הָיָה בְּאוֹתָהּ שָׁעָה. מַתְקִיף לָהּ רַב יוֹסֵף: לְרַב, אַיְלוֹנִית לְרַבִּי מֵאִיר יְהֵא לָהּ קְנָס! אֲמַר לֵיהּ אַבַּיֵי: מִקַּטְנוּתָהּ יָצְתָה לְבֶגֶר. א"ל: *כָּל כִּי הָנֵי מִילֵּי מַעַלְיָיתָא יִתְאַמְרוּ מִשְּׁמַאי. דְּתַנְיָא: אֵין הַסָּרִים נִידּוֹן כְּבֵן סוֹרֵר וּמוֹרֶה, דלְפִי שֶׁאֵין בֵּן סוֹרֵר וּמוֹרֶה נִידּוֹן אֶלָּא בַּחֲתִימַת זָקָן הַתַּחְתּוֹן; וְאֵין אַיְלוֹנִית נִידּוֹנֵית כְּנַעֲרָה הַמְאוֹרָסָה, השֶׁמִּקַּטְנוּתָהּ יָצְתָה לְבֶגֶר. אָמַר רַבִּי אַבָּהוּ: וסִימָנֵי סָרִיס וְאַיְלוֹנִית וּבֶן שְׁמֹנָה אֵין עוֹשִׂין בָּהֶן מַעֲשֶׂה עַד שֶׁיְּהוּ בֶּן עֶשְׂרִים. וּבֶן שְׁמֹנָה מִי קָחָיֵי? וְהָתַנְיָא: *זבֶּן שְׁמֹנָה – הֲרֵי הוּא כְּאֶבֶן, וְאָסוּר לְטַלְטְלוֹ, אֲבָל אִמּוֹ שׁוֹחָה עָלָיו וּמְנִיקָתוֹ

מִפְּנֵי

רש"י

שֶׁלֹּא רָאָה שָׁעָה אַחַת בְּבַשְׂרוּתוֹ. שֶׁלָּקָה מִמְּעֵי אִמּוֹ. כִּיפָּה. אדול"ר, שֶׁאֵין קִילּוּחַ הַשֶּׁתֶן הוֹלֵךְ לְמֵרָחוֹק כְּשֶׁהוּא מֵטִיל כְּלַפֵּי מַעְלָה, וְאֵין נַעֲשֶׂה כְּכִיפָּה. דְּאָפְיָה אִימֵּיהּ. לֶחֶם בְּתַנּוּר. בְּטִיהֲרָא. שֶׁמְּחַמְּמָתָהּ חוֹם הַתַּנּוּר וְחוֹם הַצָּהֳרַיִם. שִׁיכְרָא מַרְקָא. שֵׁכָר מָזוּג. וְאִיכָּא דְּאָמְרֵי: חָזָק. וְלָא יָדַעְנָא מַאי נִיהוּ. כְּלוֹמַר, וְלָא יָדַעְנָא מֵאַי הָוֵי. לִישָּׁנָא אַחֲרִינָא ה"ג: הַיְינוּ דְּשָׁמַעְנָא לְאַמִּי כָּל שֶׁמִּמְּעֵי אִמּוֹ לָקוּי וְלָא יָדַעְנָא מַאי הִיא. כְּלוֹמַר: לָא הֲוָה יָדַעְנָא הֵיכָא קָאֵי. אֲבָל הַשְׁתָּא וַדַּאי יָדַעְנָא דְּסָרִיס חַמָּה קָמְפָרֵשׁ וְאָזֵיל. וְלֵיחוּשׁ שֶׁמָּא הִבְרִיא בֵּינְתַיִם. שָׁעָה אַחַת, וְאִשְׁתַּכַּח דַּהֲוָה לֵיהּ שְׁעַת הַכּוֹשֶׁר. בּוֹדְקִין אוֹתוֹ. בִּבְכוֹרוֹת קָאֵי: חֲוַורְוַור וְהַמַּיִם הַקְּבוּעִים – הֲרֵי זֶה מוּם. וְאֵיזֶה הוּא חֲוַורְוַור הַקָּבוּעַ – כָּל שֶׁשָּׁהָה שְׁמוֹנִים יוֹם. רַבִּי חֲנִינָא בֶּן אַנְטִיגְנוֹס אוֹמֵר: בּוֹדְקִין אוֹתוֹ שָׁלֹשׁ פְּעָמִים בְּתוֹךְ פ' יוֹם: בְּרֹאשׁ פ', וּבְאֶמְצַע פ', וּבְסוֹף פ'. אֲבָל בִּבְדִיקָה תְּחִלָּה וָסוֹף לָא סַגִּי, שֶׁמָּא בֵּינְתַיִם עָבַר, וְנִמְצָא שֶׁאֵין קָבוּעַ. וְלָא אָמְרִינַן: הוֹאִיל וּתְחִלָּתוֹ וְסוֹפוֹ לָקוּי וַדַּאי לֹא עָבַר. לְחַד אֵבֶר. לָעַיִן. לְכוּלֵּיהּ גּוּפָא. סָרִיס חַמָּה מֵחֲמַת חוֹלִי כָּל הַגּוּף הוּא. יָבִיאוּ רְאָיָה. אִם ב"ד מַצְרִיכִין אֶת הַיְבָמָה לַחֲלוֹץ וּלְיַיבֵּם – יָבִיאוּ קְרוֹבֵי הַיְבָמָה רְאָיָה שֶׁהוּא בֶּן כ', וְתִיפָּטֵר בְּלֹא חֲלִיצָה וְיִבּוּם. וְהוּא הַסָּרִיס. כְּלוֹמַר, וְנוֹלְדוּ בּוֹ סִימָנֵי סָרִיס. וְהָכִי מְפָרֵשׁ בְּנִדָּה בְּפֶ' "יוֹצֵא דוֹפֶן" (דף מז:), דְּאִי לֹא נוֹלְדוּ לוֹ סִימָנֵי סָרִיס – אָמְרִינַן הַאי דְּלָא מַיְיתֵי מִשּׁוּם קַטְנוּת הוּא, וּמַחְזְקִינַן לֵיהּ כְּקָטָן עַד רוֹב שְׁנוֹתָיו. הַזָּכָר כְּדִבְרֵי ב"ה. אַלְמָא: לְר' אֱלִיעֶזֶר סָרִיס חַמָּה לָא חָלֵיץ. ת"ש כו'. כִּי מַתְנִי', וְסָמֵי הָךְ דִּלְעֵיל מִקַּמֵּי תַּרְתֵּי, וּשְׁמַע מִינָּהּ: מֵהַהִיא הֲדַר בֵּיהּ. אִי נַמִי, מִדְּקָא מַיְיתֵי מַעֲשֶׂה דַּאֲלֶכְּסַנְדְּרִיָּא לִדְבָרָיו, ש"מ: מֵהַהִיא דִּלְעֵיל הֲדַר בֵּיהּ. וּמִמַּתְנִיתִין לֵיכָּא לְמִיפְשַׁט הָכִי, דְּקָתָנֵי "שֶׁיֵּשׁ לוֹ רְפוּאָה", מִשּׁוּם דְּמַשְׁמַע דִּמְסַבְּרָא קָאָמַר הָכִי. וְכִי תְּנַן הַהִיא. הַזָּכָר כְּדִבְרֵי ב"ה לָאו לְמַאי דְּאָמְרֵי לֹא חוֹלֵץ, אֶלָּא לְאַשְׁמוּעֵי' דְּעַד שֶׁיְּהֵא בֶּן עֶשְׂרִים חָשְׁבִינַן לֵיהּ קָטָן, אִם לֹא הֵבִיא, וּמִכָּאן וְאֵילָךְ אָמְרִינַן גָּדוֹל הוּא אִם לֹא הֵבִיא, אֶלָּא שֶׁהוּא סָרִיס, וְחַיָּיב בָּעוֹנָשִׁין שֶׁבַּתּוֹרָה: אִיתְּמַר גָּרְסִינַן. מִבֶּן י"ב עַד י"ח. אַתִּינוֹקֶת קָאֵי כְּרַבִּי אֱלִיעֶזֶר, דְּאָמַר נְקֵבָה כְּבֵ"שׁ. וּמֵרֵישָׁא נַמִי שָׁמְעִינַן לֵיהּ, דְּקָאָמַר י"ב וְיוֹם אֶחָד, וְאִי בְּתִינוֹק – אֵין זְמַנּוֹ לְהָבִיא עַד י"ג שָׁנָה וְיוֹם אֶחָד, בְּפֶ' "יוֹצֵא דוֹפֶן" (נדה דף מו.). מִבֶּן י"ב. דְּפָחוֹת מִי"ג וְלֹא הֵבִיאָה וַדַּאי קְטַנָּה הִיא. דִּזְמַן הֲבָאַת ב' שְׂעָרוֹת לְתִינוֹקֶת מִי"ב וְאֵילָךְ, בְּפֶ' "יוֹצֵא דוֹפֶן" בְּמַסֶּכֶת נדה (שם). נַעֲשָׂה סָרִיס לְמַפְרֵעַ. אַיְּידֵי דְּאַיְירֵי בִּלְשׁוֹן זָכָר, קָתָנֵי סָרִיס כֵּיוָן שֶׁעָבְרָה* שְׁמֹנֶה עֶשְׂרֵה כְּרַבִּי אֱלִיעֶזֶר וְלֹא הֵבִיאָה, אע"פ שֶׁחָזַר וְהֵבִיא – אֵינוֹ כְּלוּם. דְּלָא אָמְרִינַן, כֵּיוָן דְּהַשְׁתָּא אַיְיתִי – אִיגְלַאי מִילְּתָא דְּעַד הַשְׁתָּא קָטָן הֲוָה, דְּבִשְׂעָרוֹת תַּלְיָא מִילְּתָא; אֶלָּא בְּסָרִיס מַחְזְקִינַן לֵיהּ, וְחָשְׁבִינַן לָהּ בַּת עוֹנָשִׁין מִשְּׁנֵים עָשָׂר וְאֵילָךְ, שֶׁהָיְתָה רְאוּיָה לְהָבִיא. דְּקָאָמַר, הַאי דְּלָא אַיְיתִי – מִשּׁוּם דְּסָרִיס הֲוָה. וְהָא דְּתַנְיָא לְקַמָּן דַּאֲפִילּוּ הֵבִיא לְאַחַר מִכָּאן הֲרֵי הוּא כְּסָרִיס לְכָל דְּבָרָיו – לְמַפְרֵעַ הוּא דְּקָאָמַר, וּמִשְּׁנֵים עָשָׂר הָוְיָא גְּדוֹלָה, וְסָרִיס הֲוָה. וּשְׁמוּאֵל אָמַר קָטָן הָיָה בְּאוֹתָהּ שָׁעָה. דְּלָא מַחְזְקִינַן לֵיהּ בְּגָדוֹל אֶלָּא מִשְּׁמוֹנֶה עָשָׂר וְאֵילָךְ, שֶׁהוּא מוּחְזָק בְּסָרִיס. וְהָא דְּתַנְיָא לְקַמָּן הֲרֵי הוּא כְּסָרִיס לְכָל דְּבָרָיו – מִכָּאן וּלְהַבָּא קָאָמַר, אֲבָל לְמַפְרֵעַ הָוֵי קָטָן. וְהוּא הַדִּין נַמִי דַּאֲפִילּוּ לֹא הֵבִיא לְאַחַר זְמַן קָחָשֵׁיב לֵיהּ שְׁמוּאֵל קָטָן עַד י"ח, וּמִשּׁוּם רַב נָקֵיט לֵיהּ, לְאַשְׁמוּעִינַן רְבוּתָא, דְּאע"ג דְּחָזַר וְהֵבִיא – סָרִיס הוּא. לְרַב. דְּאָמַר נַעֲשָׂה גָּדוֹל לְמַפְרֵעַ מִי"ב וְאֵילָךְ. אַיְילוֹנִית לְר"מ יְהֵא לָהּ קְנָס. חֲמִשִּׁים כֶּסֶף, אַלְמָה תַּנְיָא בְּמַסֶּכֶת כְּתוּבּוֹת (דף לה:): אַיְילוֹנִית אֵין לָהּ לֹא קְנָס וְלֹא פִּתּוּי, בְּ"אֵלּוּ נְעָרוֹת", וּמוֹקְמִינַן לָהּ כְּר"מ, דְּאָמַר קְטַנָּה אֵין לָהּ קְנָס, וְאַיְילוֹנִית, הוֹאִיל וְאֵין לָהּ שְׂעָרוֹת – קְטַנָּה הִיא בַּיָּמִים שֶׁהָיְתָה רְאוּיָה לְנַעֲרוּת, וְלָא אָמְרִינַן כֵּיוָן שֶׁעָבְרוּ י"ח וְלֹא הֵבִיאָה נַעֲשֵׂית גְּדוֹלָה לְמַפְרֵעַ לְחַיֵּיב קְנָס אֶת הָאוֹנְסָהּ בִּימֵי נַעֲרוּת. א"ל אַבַּיֵּי מִקַּטְנוּתָהּ יָצְתָה לְבֶגֶר. לְעוֹלָם נַעֲשֵׂית גְּדוֹלָה לְמַפְרֵעַ, וְהָא דְּאֵין לָהּ קְנָס לְר"מ – מִשּׁוּם דְּמִקַּטְנוּתָהּ יָצְתָה לְבֶגֶר. דְּנַעֲרוּת בְּסִימָנִים תְּלוּיִן, וְזוֹ שֶׁאֵין לָהּ סִימָנִים חָשְׁבִינַן כָּל יְמֵי קַטְנוּתָהּ קְטַנָּה, וּבִימֵי נַעֲרוּת – בּוֹגֶרֶת, וְזוֹ לְר"מ אֵין לָהּ קְנָס. אֲבָל לְרַבָּנַן אַיְילוֹנִית בִּימֵי קַטְנוּתָהּ יֵשׁ לָהּ קְנָס, דְּרַבָּנַן פְּלִיגֵי עֲלֵיהּ, וְאָמְרִי קְטַנָּה יֵשׁ לָהּ קְנָס. יְמֵי קַטְנוּת עַד שְׁנֵים עָשָׂר שָׁנָה וְיוֹם אֶחָד. א"ל. רַב יוֹסֵף שַׁפִּיר קָאָמְרַתְּ, וְכָל כִּי הָנֵי מִילֵּי מַעַלְיָיתָא כו'. סִימָנֵי סָרִים וְאַיְילוֹנִית אֵין עוֹשִׂין בָּהֶן מַעֲשֶׂה. לְהַחֲזִיקָם בִּגְדוֹלִים וְסָרִיסִים עַד שֶׁיִּהְיוּ בְּנֵי עֶשְׂרִים וְלֹא הֵבִיאוּ, וּמִשְּׁנֵים עָשָׂר עַד עֶשְׂרִים מְלַפְּפִים לָהֶם: אִם יָבִיאוּ – הֲרֵי הֵם קְטַנִּים עַד עַכְשָׁיו, וְאִם לֹא יָבִיאוּ – גְּדוֹלִים הֵם. וּבֶן ח'. שֶׁנּוֹלַד לְח' חֳדָשִׁים, אֵין עוֹשִׂין בּוֹ מַעֲשֶׂה לְהַחֲזִיקוֹ כְּבֶן קַיָּימָא בִּשְׁבִיל סִימָנִים. כְּלוֹמַר: אע"פ שֶׁגָּמְרוּ סִימָנֵי שְׂעָרוֹ וְצִפָּרְנָיו כְּשֶׁנּוֹלַד, אפ"ה לָא אָמְרִינַן בַּר קַיָּימָא הוּא וַדַּאי, עַד שֶׁיִּהְיֶה בֶּן עֶשְׂרִים שָׁנָה.

מִפְּנֵי

תוספות

אכל חלב מבן י"ב שנה ועד בן י"ח. *בנקבה איירי, וכר' אליעזר. ואיידי דנקט לשון זכר – נקט סימני סרים, ולא נקט סימני אילונית, דלא מסתבר למימר דסברי לה כב"ש. **ולאחר** מכאן הביא שערות. רבותא נקט, דאף על פי שהביא שערות לא אמרינן דאיגלאי מילתא למפרע שהיה קטן עד עכשיו שהביא שערות, אלא חשיב ליה גדול, לרב משתים עשרה ולשמואל מי"ח.

נעשה סרים למפרע. ולקי על חלב שאכל, דלא חשיב התראת ספק, אע"ג דבשעת התראה היה ספק שמא יביא שערות קודם י"ח, דהשתא מיהא איגלאי למפרע שהיה גדול בשעת התראה. ולא דמי להכה את זה וחזר והכה את זה (מכות טו.), דאף לאחר שהכה את שניהם לא ידיע איזהו אביו(א). **אילונית** לר"מ יהא לה קנס. לשמואל ניחא, כיון שימי קטנות נמשכים עד י"ח, א"כ אין כאן נערות, דימי נערות הם בששה חדשים הסמוכים לשתים עשרה, כשפוסקין אז ימי קטנות. אבל לרב יהא לה קנס, שפוסקין בזאת ימי קטנות כמו בשאר נשים. **והא** תניא בן שמונה אסור לטלטלו. ואם יכול להיות בר קיימא – לא היה אסור לטלטלו! ומשני: הב"ע – שגמרו סימנים. דע"י סימנים יש היכירא להוציאו מתורת נפל בכ' שנה(ב) לרבנן כדאשכחן לרבי, דכי גמרו סימנים חשיב בר קיימא בשלשים יום כשאר ולדות. ומילתיה דר' אבהו כרבנן. אבל אין לפרש דלרבנן אין יוצא לעולם מתורת נפל, ולרבי בכ' שנה, ור' אבהו כרבי, דא"כ, כי פריך ארבה תוספאה: כמאן – כרבי, הוה ליה למיפרך אר' אבהו דקאי כיה! ועוד: דאם כן רבה תוספאה אפילו כרבי לא אתי, דלא חשיב לר' בר קיימא לומר דאישתהי אלא ע"י הוכחה יתירא שחי כ' שנה(ב)! אלא נראה לר"י כדפירשנו ונראה דאפילו נגמרו סימנים דאסור לטלטלו, דבתוספתא, בתר ההיא דבן ח' הרי הוא כאבן ואסור לטלטלו, קתני: איזהו בן שמונה – שלא כלו לו חדשיו, והיינו אפילו גמרו, דאין יוצא מתורת נפל בשלשים יום אלא ע"י עשרים. ומילתא דלא שכיח היא, ואסור לטלטלו.

כיון

תוספות ישנים

ושמואל אמר קטן היה באותה שעה והא דאמרי' לקמן איזהו סרים חמה כל שהיה בן עשרים ולא הביא שתי שערות ואפי' הביא לאחר מכאן הרי הוא כסרים לכל דבריו וא"כ מחשבינן ליה כגדול וכן מחשבינן נקבה לי"ח כמו זכר לכ' שנה. י"ל דלקמן מיירי משעת שנת עשרים ואילך להחשיבו כסרים וא"ת במאי פליגי רב ושמואל אי לקרבן הא א"א לומר דהא לא הוו בזמן קרבן ואי ללקות איך מצי לקי התראת ספק היא [ועי' בתוספות ד"ה נעשה]: **א)** ובזה ניחא דלא דמי לאמרו לו אל תותיר דחשיב ליה תלמודא התראת ספק לפי שלעולם לא יתברר הדבר שתהא ההתראה התראת ודאי דבשעה שהתרו לו אל תותיר עדיין יש שהות ביום לאוכלה ובסוף היום ליכא למימר דה"א לאמנם אבל הכא מתברר הדבר שהיה גדול בשעה שאכל חלב וגם כי היתה ההתראה ודאית: **ב)** ועוד קשה דאמר לקמן כיון דליכא רשב"ג דאמר משתהי כרבים עבד וא"כ משמע דרשב"ג סבר כר' ולא נהירא שהרי רבי לא חשיב ליה בר קיימא עד שיהא בן עשרים ורשב"ג קאמר מכיון ששהה שלשים בר קיימא הוא:

תוספות חד מקמאי

א"ר אבהו סימני סרים ואילונית ובן שמונה אין עושין בהם מעשה עד שיהיו בן עשרים פרש"י סימני סרים ואילונית להחזיקם בגדולים ובן ח' [להחזיקו] בן קיימא אין עושין בהן מעשה עד שיהיו בן עשרים ופרכינן בן ח' מי קחיי והתניא בן ח' הרי הוא כאבן ואסור לטלטלו הב"ע בשלא גמרו סימניו ואיכא דאמרי' הב"ע כשנגמרו סימניו וזה וזה אחת היא דתניא איזהו בן ח' כל שלא כלו לו חדשיו

גליון הש"ס

גמ' אמר רב יוסף היינו דשמעתא כעין זה לעיל עז ע"ב שבת כח ע"ב:

מפני הסכנה. הכא במאי עסקינן (א) – כשגמרו סימניו. דתניא: *איזהו בן שמנה – כל שלא כלו לו חדשיו. רבי אומר: [א]סימנין מוכיחין עליו: שערו וצפרניו שלא גמרו. טעמא – דלא גמרו, הא גמרו – אמרינן: האי בר ז' הוא, ואישתהויי הוא דאישתהי, אלא הא דעבד *רבא תוספאה עובדא [ב]באשה שהלך בעלה למדינת הים, [א]ואישתהי עד תריסר ירחי שתא, ואכשריה, כמאן – כרבי דאמר משתהא? כיון דאיכא רבן שמעון בן גמליאל, דאמר משתהי – כרבים עבד. דתניא, *רשב"ג אומר: כל ששהה ל' יום באדם אינו נפל. ת"ר: *[ג]איזהו סריס חמה – כל שהוא בן עשרים ולא הביא שתי שערות, ואפילו הביא לאחר מכאן הרי הוא כסריס לכל דבריו. [ד]ואלו הן סימניו: כל שאין לו זקן, ושערו לקוי, ובשרו מחליק. רשב"ג אומר משום רבי יהודה בן יאיר: [ה]כל שאין מימיו מעלין רתיחות. ויש אומרים: [ו]כל המטיל מים ואין עושה כיפה. ויש אומרים: [ז]כל ששכבת זרעו דוחה. ויש אומרים: [ח]כל שאין מימי רגליו מחמיצין. אחרים אומרים: [ט]כל שרוחץ בימות הגשמים ואין בשרו מעלה הבל. רבי שמעון בן אלעזר אומר: [י]כל שקולו לקוי, ואין ניכר בין איש לאשה. [כ]ואיזו היא אילונית? כל שהיא בת עשרים ולא הביאה ב' שערות. ואפי' הביאה לאחר מכאן – הרי היא כאילונית לכל דבריה. [ל]ואלו הן סימניה: כל שאין לה דדים, ומתקשה בשעת תשמיש. רבן שמעון בן גמליאל אומר: [מ]כל שאין לה שיפולי מעים כנשים. רבי שמעון בן אלעזר אומר: [נ]כל שקולה עבה, ואינה ניכרת בין אשה לאיש. איתמר, סימני סרים, רב הונא אמר: עד שיהו כולם. רבי יוחנן אמר: [ס]אפי' באחד מהן. [ע]היכא דהביא שתי שערות[א] בזקן – כולי עלמא לא פליגי דעד שיהו כולן, כי פליגי – בשלא הביא. אלא הא דאמר להו רבה בר אבוה לרבנן: עיינו ביה ברב נחמן, אי בשרו מעלה הבל – איתיב ליה ברת – כמאן, כרב הונא?! לא, רב נחמן סיכי[ב] דיקנא הויא ליה. § "הסרים לא חולץ ולא מייבם וכן אילונית וכו'". § קתני סרים דומיא דאילונית, מה אילונית בידי שמים – אף סרים בידי שמים, וסתמא כרבי עקיבא, דאמר: בידי אדם – אין, בידי שמים – לא. § "הסרים שחלץ ליבמתו לא פסלה כו'". § טעמא דבעלה הוא, הא אחר – לא. לימא

מפני הסכנה. (ב) סכנת שניהם, הבן והאם, שלא ירבה חלב הדדין ותיאנס ותמות. טעמא דלא גמרו כו'. בניחותא, וסיומא דמילתא היא. בר שבעה הוא. ולשבעה נגמרה צורתו, אלא שנשתהא* וחזר. ואשמעינן רבי אבהו, דאפי' לרבי לא מחזקינן ליה כבר קיימא עד שיהא בן כ'. ואישתהי עד תריסר ירחי שתא. שלא חזר, (ג) וילדה אשתו לסוף שנתה. ואכשריה. רבא, דקסבר: משתהא הולד אחר גמר צורתו, וזה נשתהא ג' חדשים. ולא אמרי' לאחר שהלך בעלה נתעברה מאחר. כל ששהא שלשים יום באדם. שחיה שלשים יום. אינו נפל. ואפילו לא כלו לו חדשי עיבור. דאמרינן: לשבעה נגמרה צורתו, ואישתהי עד שמיני. להכי נקט באדם, דאילו בבהמה, קתני התם: שמנה ימים שהה – אין נפל. לקוי. רך. מחליק. חלק כבשר אשה. דרך בשר איש להיות שעיר = אשפר"א בלע"ז. רתיחות. אשקומ"א. כיפה. קילוח ארוך למרחוק. דוחה. שאינו קשור, אלא צלול כמים. מחמיצין. מסריחין כששוהים בכלי. הבל. חמימות כעין עשן. ומתקשה בשעת תשמיש. תשמיש קשה לה. שיפולי מעים. כמין כף למעלה מאותו מקום, כדאמר בפ' "יוצא דופן" (נדה דף מז:). איתיב ליה ברת. אלמא: כיון דליתנהו כולהו סימני סרים, דבצר ליה האי – לא מחזקינן ליה כסרים. סיכי דיקנא. יתדות הזקן. כלומר, בכמה מקומות הוה לו שער בזקנו. בידי אדם. כלומר, סריס אדם בעי חליצה, סריס חמה – לא. טעמא דבעלה הוא. דהויא זונה דנבעלה לאחי בעלה שלא במקום מצוה. והיא היתה עליו בכרת. פסולה

כיון דאיכא רשב"ג דאמר משתהי כו'. תימה: דהשתא משמע דפלוגתא דרשב"ג ורבנן בבן שמונה דחשיב בר קיימא לרשב"ג, ולא לרבנן, וקשיא לר"י: דלעיל ב"החולץ" (דף לו:) ובפ' "ר"א דמילה" (שבת דף קלה: ושם) משמע דפליגי איפכא, ובסתם וולדות. דלרשב"ג היכא דלא שהה – חשבינן ליה ספיקא, ולרבנן חשבינן ליה בר קיימא! ואמר ר"י: דמשמע ליה לגמרא דפליגי בתרתי, דעל כרחך רשב"ג איירי בבן שמנה, דמדתניא בתוספתא* בתר פלוגתא דרבי ורבנן דלעיל, ומדקאמר "כל ששהה" ולא נקט "אם שהה" – משמע דאתא לרבויי סתם וולדות, דאין יוצאין מתורת נפל אלא בשלשים יום. ועוד: דבתוספתא מסיים במילתיה דרשב"ג: שנאמר "ופדויו מבן חדש תפדה" – משמע דמיירי בסתם וולדות, מדמייתי קרא. ועוד: דאם לא בא להוסיף רשב"ג סתם וולדות – מה בא להוסיף על רבי? ואכתי קשיא לר"י הא דאיבעי לן בסוף "רבי אליעזר דמילה" (שם דף קלו.): מי פליגי רבנן עליה דרשב"ג בסתם וולדות או לא? ומדקדק מדאמר רב יהודה אמר שמואל הלכה כרשב"ג – מכלל דפליגי רבנן. ומאי ראיה היא? דלמא משום בן ח' בא לפסוק כמותו! ואמר ר"י: דקי"ל דשמואל בסתם וולדות פוסק כמותו. א"נ, דע"כ לא בבן שמנה פסק כמותו אלא בסתם וולדות, דבבן שמנה אין הלכה כמותו מדר' אבהו דהכא. ועוד: דאי בבן שמונה פוסק כמותו – הוה ליה למימר הלכה כרבי ורבן שמעון בן גמליאל. **עד** שיהא בכולן. אע"ג דאמרן לעיל דבעינן שיהא לקוי ממעי אמו, ויש סימנים שאין יכולין להוודע משנולד – מ"מ, כיון שניכר מיד שאין עושה כיפה, ושאר סימנים ניכרים כל אחד כשהוא בזמנו – הוכיח הראשון על האחרים שממעי אמו הוא לקוי, אלא שלא היו ראוין להיות ניכרים סמוך ללידתו. וא"ת: הא דאמרינן (לקמן דף קיא:*) קטן וקטנה לא חולצין ולא מייבמין, קטן – שמא ימצא סריס, כשמטיל מים ועושה כיפה – יחלוץ וייבם לרב הונא דאמר עד שיהא בכולן! *ואפילו אם יולדו כל הסימנים לאחר מכאן – אין בכך כלום, כיון שלא היה לקוי ממעי אמו! ואין לומר דבאותו קטן שיש בו סימני סרים שאין עושה כיפה קאמר דלא חולצין ולא מייבמין – דהא בכל דוכתא משמע דטעמא משום דחיישינן למיעוט. וזה היה תימה, דאותן שיש בהן סימני סרים בקטנותם – רובם מתקנין, ולאו סרים נינהו! ועוד: דלקמן בפרק "בית שמאי" (דף קיא:) משמע דבכל קטנים איירי רבי מאיר גבי יבם קטן שבא על יבמה גדולה תגדלנו, דקאמרינן: לימא מתניתין דלא כרבי מאיר כו'! ואמר ר"י: דהא דבעינן לעיל שיהו בו סימני סרים משנולד – היינו ליחשב ודאי סרים, אבל ספק סרים הוי, אף על פי שאין בו סימני סרים. וכן פירש רשב"ם ב"יוצא דופן" (נדה דף מז: ושם) גבי הא דאמר וכי לא נולדו בו סימני סרים עד כמה – עד רוב שנותיו. פירוש: עד רוב שנותיו אם לא הביא – הוי גדול ודאי וסרים ודאי. אבל קודם לכן – הוא קטן ויש לו דין בן תשעה מכ' ועד רוב שנותיו. ואם הביא ב' שערות מכ' ועד קודם רוב שנותיו – הוי גדול, ולא סרים. **דהביא** שתי שערות בזקן כולי עלמא לא פליגי עד שיהא בכולן. וא"ת: והא לעיל אמרינן בן עשרים ולא הביא שערות יביאו כו', הא הביא שערות קודם כ' – לא חשיב ודאי סרים, אע"פ שיש בו סימני סרים. ואם כן, מאי קאמר עד שיהא בכולן? אפילו כולן אין מועילין, דהא הביא שתי שערות בזקן! ואמר ר"י: דשערות דזקן אין מועילין לדין הבאת שתי שערות, אף על גב דבכל שאר מקומות בגוף מועילים. ואם תאמר: כיון דהביא שתי שערות בזקן – מאי קאמר עד שיהא בכולן? והלא אחד מן הסימנים הוא שאין לו זקן, והרי יש לו זקן! ואמר ר"י: דאין חשוב בהבאת שתי שערות לבד יש לו זקן אלא אם כן נתמלא זקנו. וא"ת: הא דאמר בפרק קמא דקדושין (דף לה: ושם) זקן האשה והסרים, ופירש בקונטרס: סרים חמה, היכי משכחת לה למ"ד עד שיהא בכולן? ואר"י: דהכא מיירי קודם כ', שכבר הוא סרים – ודאי אין בכך כלום. אבל מה שהביא אחר כ', **כי** פליגי בשלא הביא*. והא דקאמר רבי יוחנן אפי' באחד מהן – לא שילטרך סימן אחד בהדי האי, אלא בהאי לחודיה חשוב סרים. ואין לתמוה על הלשון, דבכי האי גוונא אמרי' ב"אלו טרפות" (חולין דף סג.): עוף הבא בסימן אחד טהור, *והני מילי דלא דריס, ועל כרחך הכי פירושו: הני מילי שאותו סימן הוא – דלא דריס. לימא

תוספות חד מקמאי

ר' אומר סימניו מוכיחין עליו שעריו וצפרניו טעמא דשלא גמרו סימניו הא גמרו סימניו אמרינן האי בן ז' הוא ואשתהויי אישתהי אלא הא דאמר רבא תוספאה עובדא הוה באשה שהלך בעלה למדינת הים ואשתהי עד תריסר ירחי שתא כמאן כר' דאמר אישתהי כיון דאיכא רשב"ג דאמר אישתהי כרבים עבד דתניא רשב"ג אומר כל ששהא ל' יום באדם [אינו] נפל לכאורה מסתבר' דשלש מחלוקות בדבר ת"ק דפליג אדר' ס"ל דבן ח' לא חיי בין נגמרו סמניו בין לא נגמרו ור' ס"ל דכשנגמרו מחייא חיי אלא שאין עושים מעשה להחזיקו כבן קיימא ודאי עד שיהא בן כ' ורשב"ג ס"ל כל ששהה שלשים יום באדם אינו נפל אפילו בשלא גמרו לו סימניו דאי אמרינן דרשב"ג דוקא בדנגמרו סימניו הוא דאמר כל ששהה ל' יום וכו' אבל לא גמרו אע"פ ששהה נפל הוא א) השתא י"ל אי בשנגמר סימניו אמרו שהה ל' יום אינו נפל שאם היה נפל אינו יכול לחיות ל' יום כש"כ כשלא נגמרו סימניו אם היה נפל אינו יכול לחיות ל' יום אלא משמע דס"ל לרשב"ג כל ששהה ל' יום אינו נפל בין גמרו בין לא גמרו ורשב"ג ורבנן בתרתי פליגי פליגי בבן ח' כדאמרי' ופליגי בספק בן ז' ספק בן ח' דאליבא דרבנן הולכין אחר רוב נשים דילדן ולד של קיימא ולרשב"ג ספק הוא ואפסיק הלכתא בפרק ר"א דמילה כרשב"ג ומשמע דבתרווייהו אפסיק הלכתא כרשב"ג בין בספק בן ח' בין בודאי בן ח' וממילא ש"מ דלית הלכתא כר' אבהו דאמר אין עושין בהם מעשה להחזיקו כבן קיימא עד שיהיה בן כ' דהא אפסיק הלכתא כרשב"ג דאמר כל ששהה ל' יום באדם אינו נפל דמשמע בודאי אינו נפל וולד של קיימא הוא. ויש לפרש מלתא דרשב"ג בתרתי בספק בן ח' אבל כל זמן שלא שהה ספקא הוה כי שהה ודאי בן קיימא הוי בן ח' בלא שהה ודאי נפל הוא בששהה ל' יום הוי ספק עד שיהיה בן כ' ולעולם לר' אבהו הלכה הוא והר' שמואל ב"ר דוד כתב ר' אמר חדא ורשב"ג אמר חדא ולא פליגי דר' לא אדכר כלל שהה ל' יום ס"ל דבשנגמר סימניו תליא מלתא בין שהה ל' יום בין לא שהה ודאי בן קיימא הוא ות"ק ס"ל דבן ח' שנגמרו סימניו מיחייא חיי אלא שאין מחזיקין אותו כבן קיימא ודאי עד שיהא בן כ' וי"מ דסימני בן ח' דקא"ר אבהו לאו להחזיקו כבן קיימא קאמר אלא לענין קטנות כשם שסימני סרים ואילונית קאמר לענין קטנות וגדלות כך בן ח' לענין קטנות ולכן פי' הרב א"ב ב"ד ז"ל וז"ל אמר אביי בן ח' שאין עושין מעשה עד שיהיה בן כ' כי העשרים שלו כי"ג של שאר תינוקת ולפני כ' שלו כלפני זמן של שאר תינוקת מפני דקותו וחולשתו ויש מי שאומר שאם לא הביא שתי שערות והוא בן כ' ה"ז סרים ואע"פ שלא הביא סימני סרים כי (היחוד) [האיחור] מוכיח עליו שהוא לקוי מבטן אמו ומעת לידתו ועכשיו נתגלה ספקו אבל קודם כ' שעדיין לא נתברר רעותו לא אבל אם הביא ב'

א) אולי צ"ל די"ל דאי בשנגמר סימניו אמרו ששהה ל' יום אינו נפל ה"ה בלא נגמר סימניו שאם היה נפל וכו'.

עין משפט נר מצוה

קטו א מיי' פ"א מהל' מילה הלכה יג טוש"ע י"ד סימן רסו סעיף יא.
קטז ב מיי' פט"ו מהל' איסורי ביאה הל' יט טור ש"ע אה"ע סי' ד סעיף יד:
[שבת פט"ז]
קיז ג מיי' פ"ב מהל' אישות הל"א טוש"ע שם סימן קעב סעיף ו וסי' קנה סעיף יב:
קיח דהווזחטי מיי' שם הל' יג טוש"ע שם סי' קעב סעיף ה:
[תוספתא פ"י]
קיט כ מיי' שם הל' ד טוש"ע שם סימן קעב סעיף ו:
קכ ל מ נ מיי' שם הל' ו טור ש"ע שם סימן קעב סעיף ד:
קכא ס ע טוש"ע שם סעיף א בהג"ה:
[ולעיל סא. ולקמן קיט.]
[ועמ"ש תוס' נדה לב. ד"ה שמא כו' דלא מועלת הבדיקה עד שהוא גדול בשנים]

מסורת הש"ס

ס"א וחיי
[תוספתא שבת פט"ז]
[עי' תוס' נדה כז. ד"ה אלא]
לעיל לו: שבת קלה: נדה מד: [תוס' לשבת פט"ז]

הגהות הב"ח
(א) גמרא הכא במאי עסקינן (כשגמרו סימניו) תא"מ ונ"ב הכי גרס ברי"ף הב"ע כשלא גמרו סימניו כו': (ב) רש"י ד"ה מפני הסכנה סכנת שניהם נ"ב ובמס' שבת דף קלה. פרש"י רק משום סכנת אם ע"ש ובתוס': (ג) ד"ה ואישתהי וכו' שלא חזר הבעל וילדה:

הגהות הגר"א
[א] גמ' בזקן. נמחק (ור"ל היכא דהביא ב"ש לאחר עשרים ועי' א"ר סוף פ"ה דנדה וא"צ לכל מה שדחקו התוס' בזה): [ב] שם דיקנא. נמחק:

גליון הש"ס
תד"ה כיון וכו' ואמר ר"י דקי"ל דשמואל וכו' עי' שבת ט ע"ב תד"ה הא לן וש"נ:

הגהות מהר"ב רנשבורג
א] גמ' ואשתהי עד תריסר ירחי שתא. נ"ב עי' ראב"ן דף קכב ע"א ומפרש מהיכן אתי הדבר והוא כשנתעברה ופגעה בסוס זכר תחלה:

[עי' תוס' קדושין לה: ד"ה סרי הוא]
[בחולין איתא והוא דלא דריס]

ליממא תיהוי תיובתא דרב המנונא, דאמר: *שומרת יבם שזינתה פסולה ליבמה! לא, הוא הדין אפילו לאחר נמי, ואיידי דתנא רישא בדידיה תנא נמי סיפא בדידיה. § "וכן איילונית שחלצו לה אחין כו'", § טעמא דבעלוה, הא לא בעלוה לא, כמאן — דלא כרבי יהודה, דאי רבי יהודה — *האמר: איילונית זונה היא. §

מתני' [א] סריס חמה כהן שנשא בת ישראל מאכילה בתרומה. רבי יוסי ור"ש אומרים: אנדרוגינוס כהן שנשא בת ישראל מאכילה בתרומה. ר' יהודה אומר: *טומטום שנקרע ונמצא זכר לא יחלוץ, מפני שהוא כסרים. *[ב] אנדרוגינוס נושא, אבל לא נישא. ר' *אליעזר אומר: [ג] אנדרוגינוס חייבין עליו סקילה כזכר. §

גמ' פשיטא! מהו דתימא: מוליד — מאכיל, שאינו מוליד — אינו מאכיל, קמ"ל. § "רבי יוסי ורבי שמעון אומרים אנדרוגינוס". § אמר ר"ל: מאכילה בתרומה, ואין מאכילה בחזה ושוק. רבי יוחנן אומר: אף מאכילה בחזה ושוק. ולריש לקיש, מאי שנא חזה ושוק, דאורייתא — תרומה נמי דאורייתא! הכא במאי עסקינן — בתרומה בזמן הזה, דרבנן. אבל בזמן שבהמ"ק קיים מאי — לא, אדתני: אין מאכילה בחזה ושוק, ליפלוג וליתני בדידה: בד"א בתרומה דרבנן, אבל בתרומה דאורייתא לא! הכי נמי קאמר: כשהוא מאכילה — מאכילה בתרומה בזה"ז, דרבנן, ואין מאכילה בזמן חזה ושוק, ואפילו בתרומה דרבנן, דלמא אתי לאוכלה בתרומה דאורייתא. ור' יוחנן אמר: אף מאכילה בחזה ושוק. א"ל ר' יוחנן לר"ל: מי סברת [ד] תרומה בזה"ז דרבנן? א"ל: אין, שאני שונה: [ה] עיגול בעיגולים עולה. אמר ליה: והלא אני שונה: חתיכה בחתיכות עולה. מי סברת "כל שדרכו לימנות" שנינו? "את שדרכו לימנות" שנינו. מאי היא? דתנן: *[ו] מי שהיו לו חבילי תלתן של כלאי הכרם — ידלקו. נתערבו באחרות —

רש"י

פסולה ליבמה. כאשת איש שזינתה, שאסורה לבעלה. וכיון דזונה היא — אסורה לכהונה. האמר איילונית זונה היא. בפרק "הבא על יבמתו" (לעיל דף סא.), ויליף לה מ"הזנו ולא יפרוצו". **מתני'** סרים חמה כהן וכו'. אבל סרים אדם מיפסל נמי פסיל לה מתרומה דהוי נשא, דהיינו פצוע דכא. לא יחלוץ. אם יש אח אחר. אבל לא נישא. שהוא כזכר, והשוכב עמו הרי הוא כבא על הזכר. רבי אליעזר אומר. בגמרא מפרש פלוגתייהו. **גמ'** מהו דתימא מוליד מאכיל. דדייקינן "ויליד ביתו הם יאכלו" — הראוי להוליד יאכיל. מאכילה בתרומה כו'. לקמן מפרש לה בתרומה בזמן הזה דרבנן, אבל במידי דאורייתא לא, מאי טעמא — ספק איש ספק אשה הוא. ה"נ קאמר כו'. והכי משתמע מילתיה דר"ל מאכילה בתרומה — כלומר בזה"ז, שאין נוהג אלא תרומה. ואינו מאכילה בכלום — בזמן שחזה ושוק נוהגין, דהיינו כשהמקדש קיים. אפי' בתרומה דרבנן. כגון תרומת פירות. הואיל ואיכא תרומה דאורייתא, כגון דגן תירוש ויצהר — גזרי'. אף מאכילה. דזכר מעליא הוא. מי סברת תרומה בזה"ז דרבנן. דקמוקמת לה למתניתין במידי דרבנן ואסרת לה בחזה ושוק. שאני שונה. ברייתא: עיגול של תרומה בטל במאה של חולין, או עיגול של תרומה טמאה בטל בק' עיגולים של תרומה טהורה. ואי תרומה בזמן הזה דאורייתא, כיון דעיגול דבר חשוב הוא ודרכו לימנות, לא בטיל, אף על גב דתרומת תאנים דרבנן, הואיל ותרומה דאורייתא נוהגת לא מבטלינן דרבנן, גזרה דרבנן אטו דאורייתא. אמר ליה והלא אני שונה כו'. כלומר: מי אית לך למיגזר בהא דרבנן אטו דאורייתא? אי נמי אתית לבטולי בדאורייתא — לאו איסורא הוא, שהרי אני שונה חתיכה של חטאת טמאה בטיל בטהורה, והכא מידי דאורייתא הוא. ואף על גב דדרכו לימנות, דמי סברת "כל שדרכו לימנות" שנינו דלא בטיל — "את שדרכו לימנות" במנין שנינו, שעשאוהו מיוחד למנין. אבל חתיכה ועיגול פעמים שהם נמכרים באומד, אף על גב דרגילים לימנות, הואיל ואינן מיוחדים בכך — בטלין. תלתן. פניגר"י. מין קטנית הוא, ולמתק הקדירה בא. ידלקו. כלאים בשריפה, דכתיב (דברים כב) "תוקדש" — תוקד אש.

תוספות

לימא תיהוי תיובתא דרב המנונא כו'. וא"ת: לעיל בפ"ק (דף טו:) דקאמר לרות מתיירא אני, בני צרות מעיד אני לכם, לרב המנונא מבני צרות לפשוט שהצרות פטורות מחליצה ומן היבום, שאם היו זקוקות לאחין, א"כ היו בני צרות פסולות מק"ו דאלמנה. דליכא למפרך מה לאלמנה שכן היא עצמה מתחללת — שגם היבמה שזינתה מתחללת לרב המנונא! ואמר ר"י: דמה דפשט להם בני צרות — בזה לא היה מתיירא, שאם יקפידו עליו — יאמר שאין הלכה כרב המנונא. **ואין** מאכילה בזמן חזה ושוק אפילו בתרומה דרבנן. בפרק שני דכתובות (דף כה.) גבי מאי גדולה חזקה, דקאמר: ואיבעית אימא בתרומה דרבנן — אכלי, דאורייתא — לא אכלי. ההיא שינויא לא הויא כסוגיא דהכא, דגזרינן דרבנן אטו דאורייתא. והא דאמר ב"אלו עוברין" (פסחים דף מד.), גבי שתי מדוכות: הנא לתרומת תבלין דרבנן, ולא גזרין אטו דאורייתא — אמר ר"י דשאני התם דאקראי בעלמא, ולא איתחזק איסורא, דאימור תרומה לתוך תרומה נפלה. אבל עיגול בעיגולים דהכא, אע"ג דאקראי בעלמא — איתחזק איסורא. והא דפריך לקמן (דף פב.) דרבי יוחנן אדרבי יוחנן מברייתא דשתי קופות — הו"מ לשנויי בתרומת פירות דרבנן, כי ההיא דפסחים, אלא דמשני לה שפיר. וא"ת: ומי דחקו לר"ל דלא אכלה בתרומה בזמן חזה ושוק? ואור"י: משום דשמעינן לר' יוסי דאמר אנדרוגינוס ספיקא הוי, דקאמר (א) שלא הכריעו בו חכמים אם הוא זכר אם הוא נקבה. וא"ת: והא לר' יוסי תרומה בזמן הזה דאורייתא, כדמוכח ברייתא דסדר עולם דמייתי לקמן בשמעתין! וי"ל: דקסבר ר"ל דר' יוסי תנא לה ולא סבר לה, דכה"ג אשכחן בפרק "יוצא דופן" (נדה דף מו:) ועוד: לפי שהיה שונה אליבא דר' יוסי עיגול בעיגולים עולה. ורבי יוחנן אית ליה לקמן (דף פב:) דתני לה וסבר לה, כדדייק ממתניתין, דמשוי ליה רבי יוסי לאנדרוגינוס ודאי זכר, מדקתני נושא, ומינה מותבינן לקמן (שם) לריש לקיש, ולדידיה ליתא לברייתא מקמי מתני'.

אמר ליה ר' יוחנן לר"ל מי סברת תרומה בזמן הזה דרבנן. אע"ג דר' יוחנן גופיה אית ליה לקמן (שם) דלרבנן תרומה בזה"ז דרבנן — הכא אליבא דר' יוסי קיימי, וה"ק: מי סברת דלר' יוסי תרומה בזה"ז דרבנן? והשתא צ"ל דהא דמהדר ליה ר"ל אני שונה עיגול בעיגולים עולה — אליבא דרבי יוסי היה שונה. **שאני** שונה עיגול בעיגולים עולה כו'. וא"ת: אכתי, דלמא אע"ג דהוי דאורייתא עולה, משום דסבר כרבנן דאמרי אינו מקדש אלא ו' דברים בלבד? ואר"י: דא"כ ה"ל למינקט מידי דאורייתא, כגון בילת טריפה שנתערבה, ומדנקט עיגול בעיגולים ש"מ משום דתרומה דרבנן, אבל במידי דאורייתא אסור כל שדרכו. **והלא** אני שונה חתיכה בחתיכות עולה. היינו מתני' דמייתי בסמוך דחתיכה של חטאת וכו'. תימה: מנא ליה דאתיא כר' יוסי? דלמא רבנן היא דאמרי אינו מקדש אלא ו' דברים בלבד! וי"ל: חדא, דבר פלוגתיה דר' יהודה הוא רבי יוסי. ועוד: מאי איריא דנקט חתיכה, דהוי כל שדרכו לימנות? הוה ליה למינקט מילתא דהוי את שדרכו כיון דאין מקדש אלא ששה דברים, ומדנקט חתיכה דוקא — ש"מ דוקא חתיכה, דהויא "כל שדרכו" עולה, אבל "את שדרכו" — אוסר. וה"נ הוה מצינן לשנויי לר"ל דשפיר דייק מהסיא דעיגול בעיגולים, דעל כרחך לא אתי כרבנן, מדנקט עיגול דהויא "כל שדרכו", ולא נקט "את שדרכו". **מאי** היא דתנן מי שהיו לו חבילי תלתן כו'. וא"ת: לר"ל, כיון דתרומה בזמן הזה דרבנן, אלמא בטלה קדושת הארץ — א"כ כלאי הכרם נמי דרבנן, ואמאי תני "כל שדרכו"? הא בדרבנן אין אוסר "כל שדרכו"! ואין לומר דלר"מ תרומה בזמן הזה דאורייתא — דהא שמעינן ליה לר"מ דעיגול בעיגולים עולה, בריש מסכת ביצה (דף ג:) גבי ליטרא קליעות כו'! וי"ל: דכלאי הכרם חדא דרבנן, דבזמן בהמ"ק הוי דאורייתא. אבל עיגול — תרתי דרבנן, חדא — דבטלה קדושת הארץ, ועוד — דאפילו בזמן בית המקדש תרומת תאנים דרבנן. אי נמי, חבילי תלתן הוי "את שדרכו". והכי פירושו: שהיה ר"מ אומר "כל שדרכו" בדאורייתא מקדש, ולכך דין הוא ד"את שדרכו" יקדש אפי' בדרבנן, כגון חבילי תלתן: **נתערבו** באחרות. אמר ר"ת: דלא גרסי' ואחרות באחרות — מדפריך ב"התערובת" (זבחים דף עד. ושם) לשמואל דאסר ספק ספיקא בעבודה זרה מברייתא שמתרת, ולא משכח דקאי כשמואל אלא ר' יהודה בברייתא, שאוסר אפי' בשאר איסורין ספק ספיקא. ושמואל סבר כוותיה בחדא בעבודה זרה, ופליג בשאר איסורין. ואי הוה גרס הכא ובע"ז ובכל דוכתי דכי הך משנה ואחרות באחרות — הוה ליה לאתויי לשמואל סייעתא מכל הנך משניות! וי"מ: דאפילו גרס בכל הנך משניות ואחרות באחרות לא היה יכול להביא ראיה מהם לשמואל דאסר ספק ספיקא, דדלמא הכי קאמר: וכל האחרות שנתערבו באחרות, דליכא אלא חד ספיקא. ויש חידוש יותר בנתערב שתי פעמים מבנתערב פעם אחת, דאף על גב דאיכא תרי רובי — אסיר. דגבי שאר מילי אוסרין חד רובא ושרינן תרי רובי, כגון גבי יוחסין, בסוף פ"ק דכתובות (דף טו. ושם) דאמר: הולכין אחר רוב העיר, והוא דאיכא רוב סיעה בהדה, ואין הולכין אחר רוב העיר גרידתא, ורוב סיעה גרידתא*.

כולן

עין משפט נר מצוה

קכב א מיי' פ"ז מהל' תרומות הלכה יד סמג לאוין רמח טוש"ע יו"ד סימן שלג.
קכג ב ג מיי' פ"א מהלכות איסורי ביאה הלכה טו.
קכד ד מיי' פ"א מהל' תרומות [ו] סמג עשין [...] טוש"ע יו"ד סימן שלג סעיף ב.
קכה ה מיי' פי"ד מהל' תרומות הלכה ב.
קכו ו טוש"ע יו"ד סימן רצו סעיף ג.

תוספות ישנים

א"ל אין שאני שונה (לעיל) עיגול בעיגולין עולה וצ"ל לפי אשר פירשנו א) דר"ל שאני שונה דרבי יוסי סבר עיגול בעיגולין עולה וא"כ ע"כ תרומה בזמן הזה דרבנן דאי מדאורייתא לא הוה עולה דהוי דבר שבמנין דלא בטיל וא"ת אפילו תרומה בזה"ז דאורייתא ניחא שפיר דעולה משום דעיגול הוי תרומת פירות דהייא מדרבנן אף בזמן (שאין) שביהמ"ק קיים וי"ל דאם איתא דתרומה בזה"ז דאורייתא הוה גזרינן דרבנן אטו דאורייתא. וא"ת ומנא לן דר' יוסי קאמר לה וי"ל משום דר' יהודה פליג עלה בסיפא מכלל דת"ק דידיה הוי ר' יוסי דסתמא הוא בר פלוגתיה וקשה לרבינו נתנאל שיטתא דא דא"כ הול"ל (למכתב) הכא מי סברת דר' יוסי סבר תרומה בזמן הזה דרבנן. ועוד דהו"ל לר"ל להשיב אה"נ משום ברייתא דלקמן דר' יוסי אומר אנדרוגינוס בריה בפני עצמה היא דחשיב ליה ספק וא"כ צריך לנו לומר מאכילה בתרומה ולא בחזה ושוק וטעמא משום דתרומה בזמן הזה דרבנן. ועוד קשה דא"כ דידע תלמודא מתניתין דלקמן דאמר ר' יוסי אנדרוגינוס בריה בפ"ע וספק הוא לא הוה קאמר [illegible]

[illegible]

[illegible]

[וע"ע תוספות ביצה ג: ד"ה ואחרות ותוספות ע"ז מט. ד"ה נתערבו ותוספות סנהדרין פ. ד"ה ואחרים ותוספות זבחים עב. ד"ה נתערבו]

[illegible] דמשנה היא בתרומות ומדסתם רבי כר"מ (לא"כ) [אליבא דר'] יהושע פ"ק דביצה אם יש שם מאה פומין יעלו ודאי הכי הלכתא דעגול בעגולין עולה וא"כ הוי תרומה בזה"ז דרבנן ומש"ה עולה אע"פ שהוא דבר שבמנין וא"ת הלא [illegible] סבר תרומה בזה"ז לדאורייתא ואפ"ה קאמר יעלו י"ל דהיינו טעמא דר"מ משום דקא בעי דבר שבמנין ואיסורי הנאה אבל כי ליכא אלא חד מינייהו סבר דבטל אבל (לר"מ) [לרבי] שסתם משנה דתרומות דעיגול בעיגולין עולה כר"מ [illegible] ג) כמותו מטעמא דאיהו סבר דבעינן דבר שבמנין ואיסורי הנאה ולריש לקיש הוי טעמא דעולה משום דתרומה בזמן הזה דרבנן וא"ת ומנא ליה לר"ל הא דלמא סתם רבי כר"מ ומטעמיה דקא בעי תרתי דבר שבמנין ואיסורי [illegible] וי"ל ודאי לא אפשר לומר שהרי הלכתא הוא דלא בעינן תרתי דהא סתם לן מתני' בפרק גיד הנשה דחתיכת דג טמא ונבילה לא בטלה אע"ג דבהנאה שריא וניחא דקאמר לקמן מאי חתיכה ולא בעי מאי עיגול דמשנה ידועה היא בפ"ק

[illegible] לפי מה שפי' בתוס' לעיל ד"ה אמר דר"י מיירי אליבא דר' יוסי. ב) ואף דג"ה נוהג גם בחיה מ"מ שמנו של גיד משום לתא דחלב גזרו ולא משום גיד וכ"כ הרשב"א בתו"ה האחרון דף ק"ח דפוס ברלין לחד פירושא. ועי' בשו"ת הרדב"ז ח"ב סימן תר"ע ואמנם ק"ק דהא במקום [illegible] למגזר משום לדאורייתא מודה ר"ל וצ"ע. ג) נ"ל לאו מטעמיה סתם כמותו דר"מ סבר דבעינן דבר שבמנין.

תוספות חד מקמאי

[illegible]ערות בזמנו הרי הוא כשאר תינוקת ומסתברא כפי' קמא דאי כפי' בתרא הכי איבעי ליה למימר בן ח' כיון [illegible]ה בן כ' עושים בו מעשה וחז"ל לא עלה פירושו כלום לבן ח': **הא** דתנן סרים שחלץ ליבמתו לא פסלה מן [illegible]נה בעלה פסלה דוקא בעלה הוא הא אחר לא פסלה מן האחים דלית הלכתא כרב (הונא) [המנונא] דאמר [illegible]ת יבם שזינתה אסורה ליבמה דגרסינן בסוטה פרק היה מביא אמרי במערבא לית הלכתא כרב המנונא. תנן [illegible] בפרק בתרא דבכורים אנדרוגינוס יש בו דרכים שוה לאנשים ויש בו דרכים שוה לנשים ויש בו דרכים שוה [illegible]שים ולנשים ויש בו דרכים [שאינו שוה לא לאנשים ולא לנשים] שוה לאנשים כיצד מטמא בלובן כאנשים [illegible] ליבום כאנשים ומתעטף ומסתפר כאנשים ונושא ואינו נישא כאנשים וחייב בכל מצות האמורות בתורה [illegible]שים כיצד הוא שוה לנשים מטמא בדם כנשים ואינו מתיחד עם האנשים כנשים ואינו עובר על בל

תקיפו ועל בל תשחית ועל בל תטמא למתים כנשים ופסול לעדות כנשים ואינו [נבעל] בעבירה כנשים ונפסל מן הכהונה כנשים כיצד שוה לאנשים ולנשים חייב על הכאתו ועל קללתו כאנשים ונשים וחייבים על נזקו בין מזיק בין ניזק כאנשים וכנשים וההורגו שוגג גולה מזיד נהרג כאנשים ונשים וחולק בקדשי הגבול כאנשים ונשים ונוחל בכל נחלות כאנשים ונשים ואם אמר הריני נזיר שזה איש ואשה ה"ז נזיר כיצד אינו שוה לא לאנשים ולא לנשים אין חייבין לא על קללתו ולא על הכאתו לא כאנשים ולא כנשים ולא נערך לא כאנשים ולא כנשים ואם אמר הריני נזיר שזה לא איש ולא אשה אינו נזיר ר"מ אומר אנדרוגינוס בריה בפני עצמה היא ולא יכלו חכמים להכריע עליו אם זכר אם נקבה אבל טומטום אינו כן פעמים שהוא איש פעמים שהוא אשה כתבתי זו המשנה [מפני] שהיא צריכה תלמוד במקצת דברים שיש בה ובתוספתא דבכורים פ' בתרא

קכז א מיי' פט"ו מהל' מאכלות אסורות הלכה יד:
קכח ב מיי' שם פט"ז הלכה ט טוש"ע יו"ד סימן קי סעיף א:
קכט ג מיי' פ"ו מהל' פסולי המוקדשין הלכה כג:
קל ד מיי' שם הל' כד:

כּוּלָּן יִדָּלְקוּ, דִּבְרֵי ר' מֵאִיר. וְחכ"א: אאֵיעָלוּ בְּאֶחָד וּמָאתַיִם, שֶׁהָיָה ר"מ אוֹמֵר: כָּל שֶׁדַּרְכּוֹ לִימָּנוֹת מְקַדֵּשׁ, וְחכ"א: אֵינוֹ מְקַדֵּשׁ אֶלָּא שִׁשָּׁה דְּבָרִים בִּלְבָד. ר"ע אוֹמֵר בשִׁבְעָה. אֵלּוּ הֵן: אֱגוֹזֵי פֶרֶךְ, וְרִמּוֹנֵי בָדָן, וְחָבִיּוֹת סְתוּמוֹת, וְחִלְפֵי תְרָדִין, וְקוּלְחֵי כְרוּב, וּדְלַעַת יְוָנִית. וְר"ע מוֹסִיף אַף כִּכָּרוֹת שֶׁל בעה"ב. הָרְאוּיִן לְעָרְלָה – עָרְלָה, לְכִלְאֵי הַכֶּרֶם – כִּלְאֵי הַכֶּרֶם. ר' יוֹחָנָן סָבַר: "אֶת שֶׁדַּרְכּוֹ לִימָּנוֹת" שָׁנִינוּ, וְרֵישׁ לָקִישׁ סָבַר: "כָּל שֶׁדַּרְכּוֹ לִימָּנוֹת" שָׁנִינוּ. מַאי חֲתִיכָה? דְּתַנְיָא: גחֲתִיכָה שֶׁל חַטָּאת טְמֵאָה שֶׁנִּתְעָרְבָה בְּמֵאָה חֲתִיכוֹת שֶׁל חַטָּאוֹת טְהוֹרוֹת, וְכֵן פְּרוּסָה שֶׁל לֶחֶם הַפָּנִים טְמֵאָה שֶׁנִּתְעָרְבָה בְּמֵאָה פְּרוּסוֹת שֶׁל לֶחֶם הַפָּנִים טְהוֹרוֹת – תַּעֲלֶה. רַבִּי יְהוּדָה אוֹמֵר: לֹא תַּעֲלֶה. אֲבָל דחֲתִיכָה שֶׁל חַטָּאת טְהוֹרָה שֶׁנִּתְעָרְבָה בְּמֵאָה חֲתִיכוֹת שֶׁל חוּלִּין טְהוֹרוֹת, וְכֵן פְּרוּסָה שֶׁל לֶחֶם הַפָּנִים טְהוֹרָה שֶׁנִּתְעָרְבָה בְּמֵאָה פְּרוּסוֹת שֶׁל חוּלִּין טְהוֹרוֹת – דִּבְרֵי הַכֹּל לֹא תַּעֲלֶה. קָתָנֵי מִיהַת רֵישָׁא תַּעֲלֶה! אָמַר רַבִּי חִיָּיא בְּרֵיהּ דְּרַב הוּנָא: בְּנִימּוֹחָה. אִי הָכִי מַאי טַעֲמָא דְּר' יְהוּדָה? רַבִּי

כּוּלָּן יִדָּלְקוּ. דְּלָא בָּטְלֵי, כִּדְקָתָנֵי טַעְמָא שֶׁהָיָה רַבִּי מֵאִיר אוֹמֵר כָּל שֶׁדַּרְכּוֹ לִימָּנוֹת מְקַדֵּשׁ אֶת הַמִּתְעָרֵב עִמּוֹ, וְאֵין בָּטֵל בְּרוֹב. שֶׁכִּלְאֵי הַכֶּרֶם כְּדָבָר שֶׁאֵין בְּמִנְיָן בְּטֵלִין בְּאֶחָד וּמָאתַיִם, כִּדְאָמַר בִּפְסָחִים בְּ"אֵלּוּ עוֹבְרִין" (דף מח:): "מִן הַמָּאתַיִם" – מִמּוּתָּר שְׁתֵּי מֵאוֹת שֶׁנִּשְׁתַּיְּירוּ בַּבּוֹר, מִיכָּן לְעָרְלָה וְכִלְאֵי הַכֶּרֶם שֶׁבְּטֵלִים בְּמָאתַיִם. מְקַדֵּשׁ. מָאתַיִם אוֹ שְׁלֹשׁ מֵאוֹת, דְּלָא בָּטֵל. פֶּרֶךְ. מָקוֹם. הָרְאוּיִן לְעָרְלָה. כְּגוֹן אֱגוֹזִים וְרִימּוֹן וְחָבִיּוֹת – מְקַדְּשִׁין וְאוֹסְרִין אֶת הַכְּשֵׁרִים מִשּׁוּם עָרְלָה. הָרְאוּיִן לְכִלְאֵי הַכֶּרֶם. כְּגוֹן תְּרָדִין וּכְרוּב וּדְלַעַת. רַבִּי יוֹחָנָן סָבַר אֶת שֶׁדַּרְכּוֹ לִימָּנוֹת. שֶׁמְּיוּחָד בְּמִנְיָן, שָׁנִינוּ דְּלָא בָּטֵל. הִלְכָּךְ, חֲתִיכוֹת וְעִיגּוּלִים, אע"ג שֶׁדַּרְכָּן לִימָּנוֹת, הוֹאִיל שֶׁדַּרְכָּן נַמִּי לִימָּכֵר בְּאוֹמֶד – בָּטְלֵי. וְר"ל סָבַר כָּל שֶׁדַּרְכּוֹ לִימָּנוֹת. אֲפִילּוּ לִפְרָקִים שָׁנִינוּ דְּלָא בָּטֵיל. הִלְכָּךְ, עִיגּוּל, אִי ס"ד תְּרוּמָה בִּזְמַן הַזֶּה דְּאוֹרַיְיתָא – לָא הָיָה בָּטֵיל. ר' יְהוּדָה אוֹמֵר לֹא תַּעֲלֶה. דְּקָסָבַר ר' יְהוּדָה בְּכָל דּוּכְתָּא מִין בְּמִינוֹ לָא בָּטֵיל. דִּבְרֵי הַכֹּל לֹא תַּעֲלֶה. ת"ק מוֹדֶה, הוֹאִיל וְאֶפְשָׁר לְמוֹכְרָן לְכֹהֵן בְּהֶפְסֵד מוּעָט, וַחֲתִיכָה וּפְרוּסָה דַּרְכָּן לִימָּנוֹת – מִשּׁוּם הֶפְסֵד מוּעָט לָא מְבַטְּלִינַן אִיסּוּרָא דְּאוֹרַיְיתָא. וְאע"ג דְּעִיגּוּל בָּטֵל בְּחוּלִּין, וְלָא מְזַבְּנִינַן לֵיהּ לְכֹהֵן – הָתָם הוּא דְּעִיגּוּל גּוּפֵיהּ תְּרוּמָה דְּרַבָּנַן הִיא. וְרֵישָׁא תַּעֲלֶה – דְּאֵין לָהֶם תַּקָּנָה אֶלָּא שְׂרֵיפָה, וְאִיכָּא הֶפְסֵד קֳדָשִׁים. קָתָנֵי מִיהַת רֵישָׁא תַּעֲלֶה. קַשְׁיָא לְר"ל, דְּאָמַר: כָּל שֶׁדַּרְכּוֹ לִימָּנוֹת שָׁנִינוּ, דְּהָא הָכָא דַּרְכָּן לִימָּנוֹת – וּבָטֵיל. רַבִּי

כולן ידלקו. וליכא למימר דלניידינהו, דגזרינן שמא יבואו עשרה בני אדם בבת אחת כו', כדאמר בריש פ' "התערובות" (זבחים דף עג: ושם). וא"ת: ומ"ש דלא פליג ר' אליעזר הכא, וכן אכל הנהו דמס' ערלה (בפ"ג מ"ו), כדקאמר לענין עבודה זרה בסוף "כל הצלמים" (ע"ז דף מט:) דיוליך הנאה ליס המלח! ומיהו, רבינו שמואל פירש שם דה"ה בכל איסורין. ונראה דדוקא גבי עבודה זרה אית ליה הכי, משום דתופסת את דמיה, וכשמוליך הנאה נראה כאילו הוליך האיסור. ועוד יש לפרש: דדוקא בתנור שהסיקו בעצי עבודה זרה ואפה בו את הפת, ונטל ממנה ככר וארג בו את הבגד אמרינן יוליך הנאה ליס המלח, כשנתערב, לפי שאין ממשות האיסור בעין. וההוא דאיתערב לו חביתא דחמרא, דקאמר (שם) דיוליך הנאה – היינו משום דאין נהנה מגוף האיסור, דאסור בשתיה, אלא או למכור או ליתן לפועליו. וא"ת: ומה טעם לא אמרי' בכל הנך דמס' ערלה (פ"ג מ"ו) ימכרו כולן לגוי חוץ מדמי איסור שבו, כדאמר רשב"ג בפרק בתרא דמס' ע"ז (דף עד. ושם) גבי יין נסך? בירושלמי פריך לה, ומשני: דחיישינן בכולהו אם ימכור לגוי שמא יחזור וימכור לישראל. וכן בפת ובגד דפרק "כל הצלמים" (שם דף מט:), אע"ג דפת של גוי אסור, כיון דשרי בהנאה חיישינן שמא יקנה ממנו ישראל ליתן לפועליו. ומבית דההוא גברא, אם היה חפץ למכור כל יינו ביחד – ה"ה דהוה מצי למכור חוץ מדמי איסור שבו.

פרך. פירש בקונטרס: שם מקום. ור"י אומר: על שם שנפרכים, כדאמר בפסיקתא דפרשתא "ויהודה וישראל רבים" אחר פרשת "כי תשא", דריש "על אל גנת אגוז ירדתי" שנמשלו ישראל לאגוז שיש בו ג' מינים: של פרך – שנפרך מעצמו. ככרות של בעל הבית. אבל של נחתום שהם קטנות – אפי' ר"מ מודה דלא מקדש, דהא תנן במס' ערלה (פ"ג מ"ז) דמעלה באחד ומאתים. והא דמשמע לקמן דחתיכה של לחם הפנים לא בטלה בשל חולין – שאני לחם הפנים דחשיב טפי, וראוי להתכבד בו. ואפה בו את הפת דפ' "כל הצלמים" (ע"ז דף מט:) דקתני נתערבה באחרות כולן אסורות – צריך לאוקמא בככרות של בעל הבית*. הראויה לערלה ערלה. בירושלמי מדקדק: אמאי לא תני נמי הראוי לתרומה תרומה, דכיון דחשיבי לא בטלי באחד ומאה? ומשני: משום דכולהו שייכי בתרומה, ולא מצי למיתני הראוי לתרומה תרומה. ועוד מצי לשנויי דהאי תנא תרתי אית ליה: דבר שבמנין ואיסור הנאה, כדאמר בפ' בתרא דמסכת ע"ז (דף עד.) אמתניתין דהתם. רבי יוחנן אומר את שדרכו למנות שנינו. בירושלמי משמע דלא הוי אלא עשרה דברים "את שדרכו". ונראה דהיינו אותן ששה דברים דקאמרי רבנן, ותבילי תלתן הרי שבעה, ובגד שצבעו בקליפי ערלה, וכובע מלא הסיט בקליפי ערלה, וארגו בבגד, ותרי מילי חשיבי – הרי ט', ואורג מלא הסיט מצמר הבכור בבגד ואית דחשיב ככרות של בעל הבית בעשירית, וקשה לר"י: דהא איכא טובא: טבעות וכוסות של עבודה זרה ד"התערובות" (זבחים עד.), וכל הנהו דתנן בפרק בתרא דמסכת ע"ז (דף עד. שם): יין נסך ועורות לבובין וכו', וקאמר התם דהאי תנא תרתי אית ליה: דבר שבמנין ואיסורי הנאה, וכל הנהו הוו "את שדרכו", דאי לאו הכי – תקשה ההיא משנה לרבי יוחנן! ודוחק לומר דתנא דליטרא קציעות היא, דא"כ הוה ליה לאקשויי ולשנויי הכי, כדפריך אההיא ד"התערובות" ובריש מסכת ביצה (דף ג: ושם). ועוד נראה דעדיפי מ"את שדרכו", מדפריך התם: וליתני נמי אגוזי פרך ורמוני באדן, וליתני נמי ככרות של בעל הבית! ומשני אכולהו: הא תנא ליה התם. ומחבילי תלתן דחשיב הכא ברישא לא פריך, משמע דכרבנן בעי לאוקמי דלא סגי להו ב"את שדרכו". ואמר רבינו יצחק: דבירושלמי לא חשיב אלא אותן שנוייס שם במסכת ערלה (פ"ג), אבל אכתי איכא טובא. וא"ת: יין נסך דחשיב התם במסכת ע"ז – ע"כ בחביות סתומות איירי, דהא כרבנן בעי לאוקמיה, וא"כ אמאי חשיב לה, הא תנא ליה במסכת ערלה? ואמר רבינו יצחק: דאיצטריך לאשמועינן דמתמרינן ביין נסך, ואע"ג דלא כתיב איסוריה בדאורייתא אלא מדברי קבלה. או שמא אשמועינן דדוקא ביין נסך מחמרינן, ולא בסתם יינן. ואם בסתם יינן הוי דינא הכי – כ"ש דאיצטריך לאשמועינן משום סתם יינן. א"נ, אשמועינן דלא שרי על ידי פדיון, לאפוקי מדר' אליעזר. וא"ת: והא קתני שור הנסקל, ובפ' "התערובות" (זבחים עב. ושם) משמע דשור הנסקל וטלאות המתות לא חשיבי אפילו כחבילי תילתן! ואמר ר"י: דדוקא מטלאות מתות, הן כבשות קטנות, פריך ב"התערובות", דלא חשיב שבמנין לפי שרגילים למכור כל העדר יחד. ואפילו יתשב כשהוא שחוט כחתיכה הראויה להתכבד בה – כשהוא חי גריע טפי. אבל שור הנסקל שהוא גדול – חשיב הוא אפילו אליבא דרבנן. ובירושלמי מוקי ההיא דפרק בתרא דמסכת ע"ז בשור הנסקל שחוט, דראוי להתכבד בו. ומיהו, אמר ר"י: דלפי הש"ס שלנו משמע שמעמידה בחי, דבפ' "התערובות" (שם דף עא:) עביד צריכותא ממתני' דהתם לאשמועינן שור הנסקל שנתערב בקדשים, ודפרק בתרא דמס' ע"ז לאשמועינן שור הנסקל בחולין, ואי בחתיכה איירי ההוא דמס' ע"ז לא הוה צריך לטעמא דהפסד קדשים דקאמר התם. רבי יהודה אומר לא תעלה. פי' בקונטרס: משום דקסבר מין במינו לא בטיל. ואין נראה, דדוקא בדבר המתערב אית ליה לר' יהודה דמין במינו לא בטיל, כמו שאפרש בסמוך. אלא הכא טעמא דר' יהודה דקסבר: כל שדרכו למנות לא בטיל. דר' יהודה לטעמיה דאמר בליטרא קציעות דלא בטלה, בריש "התערובות" (שם עג.) ובריש מס' ביצה (דף ד. ושם). וכי מוקי לה בנימוחה, הוא דקאמר דטעמא דר' יהודה משום דמין במינו לא בטיל. דברי הכל לא תעלה. נראה לפרש דטעמא דסיפא שנתערבה בשל חולין, משום דלאמר שנתבטלה ראויה להתכבד בה, לפיכך לד"ה לא בטלה. אבל רישא, שנתערבה בחתיכות טהורות של חטאות, דכי נמי תעלה אין ראויה להתכבד בה, דלא שייך כיבוד בפני כהנים במקדש. ולהכי לת"ק תעלה, דהוי "כל שדרכו". והא דפליגי בתוספתא במס' תרומות (פ"ה) *בחתיכה של חטאת, בין טהורה בין טמאה שנתערבה בחולין, דרבנן אמרי תעלה, ור' יהודה אומר לא תעלה, צריך לאוקומה בנימוחה, ור' יהודה לטעמיה, דאמר (חולין קח.): מין במינו לא בטל. וק"ק: לפי זה, אמאי לא נקט טמאה בשל חולין – ד"ה לא תעלה. דאין לומר דטהורות בטהורות עדיפא ליה, דמשמע דלא צריך האי טעמא אלא לר"לא)! ונראה דלר' יוחנן הוי חידוש טפי לאשמועינן דבר שבמנין, ולא איסור הנאה דמקדש, מבטמאה דהוי דבר שבמנין ואיסור הנאה דאין חידוש כל כך. והא דלא חשיב במסכת ע"ז חתיכה של חטאת טמאה בשל חולין, דההוא תנא תרתי אית ליה, כדקאמר התם – איכא למימר דבקדשים לא איירי. ולפי טעמא שבקונטרס שתולה בהפסד מועט – לא מצי למינקט בסיפא טמאה בחולין*.

רבי

[ועי' היטב תוספות זבחים עב: ד"ה אף בכרות]

ולפנינו איתא פרוסה של לחם הפנים שנתערבה

[ועי' תוס' זבחים עב. ד"ה וליבטלו וכו' הגיהו טעמו ופירושו של רש"י בתימה גם הוסיפו שם עוד בענין דהכא ע"ש]

תוספות ישנים

בפ"ק דביצה מתניא דר"מ קאמר אם יש שם מאה פומין יעלו: רשב"ל אומר כל שדרכו למנות שנינו. וא"ת והרי קתני חבילי תלתן דהוי את שדרכו לימנות וי"ל דקסבר רשב"ל דאהדרבה מ"ה הדר ותנא שהיה ר"מ אומר שלא נטעה לומר דוקא חבילי תלתן דהוי את שדרכו והא דנקט חבילי תלתן דהוי את שדרכו ולא נקט דבר דהוי כל שדרכו משום דמדרבנן הוי דקנבוס ולוף אסרה תורה מש"ה בעינן את שדרכו ולרבי יוחנן דאמר את שדרכו לימנות שנינו צריך ליתן טעם למה חזר ושנה שהיה ר"מ אומר וכו' שהרי הזכיר חבילי תלתן דהוי את שדרכו וי"ל דסד"א דדוקא חבילי תלתן דלא הוי רק מדרבנן כדפרישית אמרי' דוקא את שדרכו מקדש אבל כל שדרכו לא אבל איסורא דאורייתא מקדש אף כל שדרכו להכי הדר ותנא כללא דבכל ענין לא מקדש אלא את שדרכו א"נ סד"א דוקא חבילי תלתן דאסירי בהנאה דכלאי הכרם אסירי בהנאה אמרי' דמקדש אבל במלתא דקריא בהנאה לא מקדש אף את שדרכו קמ"ל. וא"ת לרשב"ל אמאי אמרי' הכא בחבילי תלתן דמקדש הלא לא אסירי רק מדרבנן וא"כ הו"ל כמו עיגול בעיגולים דסבר ריש לקיש שולה משום דתרומה בזמן הזה דרבנן וי"ל שאני חבילי תלתן דאסירי בהנאה ותשיבי כמו איסורי דאורייתא י"מ דטעמא דשולה עיגול בעיגולים משום דהוי תרומה בזה"ז דרבנן ותרומת פירות דרבנן ולא נסירא דטעם דתרומת פירות דרבנן לא מעלה ולא מוריד דאי הוי תרומה בזה"ז דאורייתא הוה גזרי' דרבנן אטו דגן דהוי תרומה דאורייתא: קתני מיהא רישא תעלה אע"ג דהויא דאורייתא וקשיא לריש לקיש דאמר לעיל עיגול בעיגולין שולה משום דתרומה בזמן הזה דרבנן דהכא בדאורייתא נמי אמרי' תעלה פ"ה והא דאמרי' בסיפא לא תעלה הייתו משום טעמא דכי נמי אמרי' לא תעלה ליכא הפסד כל כך שהרי התטאת והחולין ראויה לכהנים וכו'. וא"ת א"כ מאי פריך מהכא לריש לקיש הלא שפיר קאמר דשוכח תרומה בזמן הזה דרבנן דעיגול בעיגולין שולה דאי מדאורייתא לא הוה שולה שהרי אין בו הפסד מרובה דהא חזו לכהן אף אם לא תעלה. ונ"ל טעמא דסיפא דאמרי' לא תעלה משום דאי תתבטל הויא חתיכה הראויה להתכבד בפני האורחים ותפיכה הראויה להתכבד לא בטלה [ועי' בתוס' כאן: א) ועוד י"ל דרבותא אשמעינן דאע"ג דהויא טהורה ואינה אסורה אלא לזרים וכ"ש טמאה שאינה ראויה אף לכהנים והוי כענין דאמרינן לקמן טהורה מטהורה עדיפא ליה למילף: א' הכי מאי טעמא דרבי יהודה. אא"כ דמיירי בקלא נטוהה ניחא טעמא דרבי יהודה כדפרישית לעיל דדבר שבמנין לא בטיל אבל כיון דאיירי בנימוחו מאי טעמא דרבי יהודה:

תוספות חד מקמאי

בתרא גרסינן אנדרוגינוס יש בו דרכים שוה לאנשים ויש בו דרכים שוה לנשים ויש בו דרכים שוה לא לאנשים ולא לנשים ויש בו דרכים שוה לאנשים ולנשים שוה לאנשים מטמא בלובן כאנשים נושא אבל לא נישא כאנשים ואינו מתיחד עם נשים כאנשים ואינו ניזון עם בנות כאנשים ואינו נעטף ומספר כאנשים ואין מטמא ועובר על בל תקיף ועל בל תשחית כאנשים וחייב על כל מצות האמורות בתורה כאנשים דרכים שוה לנשים מטמא באודם כנשים ואינו מתיחד עם אנשים כנשים ואינו זקוק ליבום ואינו מחלק בקדשי הקדשים כנשים ואינו חולק עם בנים כנשים ופסול לעדות כנשים ופסול לכהונה כנשים דרכים ששוה לאנשים ולנשים חייבים על נזקו כאנשים ונשים וההורגו במזיד נהרג בשוגג גולה לערי מקלט ואמו יושבת עליו דם טומאה כאנשים וכנשים ואם אמר הריני נזיר שזה איש ואשה ה"ז נזיר דרכים שאינו שוה לא לאנשים ולא לנשים אין חייבים על טומאתו ואין שורפין על טומאתו ואינו מבורך לא לאנשים ולא לנשים ואם אמר הריני נזיר שאין זה לא איש ולא אשה ה"ז נזיר ר' יוסי אומר אנדרוגינוס בריה בפ"ע היא ולא יכלו חכמים להכריע אם איש אם אשה אבל טומטום אינו כן אלא או ספק איש או ספק אשה וכ"כ הראב"ד בפירושיו וכתב בזה הלשון שכתבתי זו התוספתא אע"פ ששלשה [דברים] יש בה שאין בירור פי' אצלם כמו ואינו נעטף ומספר כאנשים ואינו נבעל בעבירה כנשים ואינו מברך לא לאנשים ולא לנשים אלו ג' דברים אין בירורם אצלם ואצלנו ובעל הלכות גדולות הכי אמר זו התוספתא דאנדרוגינוס בהלכות יבמות וכתב א) אינו נעטף באבילות ואינו מספר כנשים ואינו נבעל בעבירה ופסול מן התרומה כנשים וקי"ל אע"ג דאין חולקים תרומה לאנדרוגינוס אבל משגרי' לו לביתו כדאיתא בפ' נושאין דאנדרוגינוס אוכל בתרומה ואינו אוכל בקדשים ואינו נבעל בעבירה דחשבינן ליה כחללה ונפסל מן התרומה ולדידי נמי משמע אין מברך לאנשים ולא לנשים משום דבריה בפני עצמה היא ע"כ:

א) בכה"נ לפנינו (ונדפס בסוף כרך ברכות) איתא ומתעטף באבילות ואינו מספר כאנשים וכו' וכן נ"ל גם כאן.

רַבִּי יְהוּדָה לְטַעְמֵיהּ, דְּאָמַר: *מִין בְּמִינוֹ לָא בָּטֵיל. אֲבָל לֹא נִימּוֹחַ מַאי, לֹא תַּעֲלֶה — אַדְּתָנֵי: אֲבָל חֲתִיכָה שֶׁל חַטָּאת טְהוֹרָה שֶׁנִּתְעָרְבָה בְּמֵאָה חֲתִיכוֹת שֶׁל חוּלִּין טְהוֹרוֹת לֹא תַּעֲלֶה — נִיפְלוֹג וְנִיתְנֵי בְּדִידָהּ: בד"א בְּשֶׁנִּימּוֹחָה, אֲבָל לֹא נִימּוֹחָה — לֹא תַּעֲלֶה! טְהוֹרוֹת בִּטְהוֹרוֹת עָדִיף לֵיהּ. ולר"ל, מַאי שְׁנָא רֵישָׁא ומ"ש סֵיפָא? א"ר שֵׁישָׁא בְּרֵיהּ דְּרַב אִידִי: רֵישָׁא בְּטוּמְאַת מַשְׁקִין דְּרַבָּנַן, סֵיפָא דְּאוֹרָיְיתָא. אֲבָל טוּמְאַת שֶׁרֶץ מַאי, לֹא תַּעֲלֶה — אַדְּתָנֵי סֵיפָא: אֲבָל חֲתִיכָה שֶׁל חַטָּאת טְהוֹרָה שֶׁנִּתְעָרְבָה בְּמֵאָה חֲתִיכוֹת שֶׁל חוּלִּין טְהוֹרוֹת לֹא תַּעֲלֶה — נִיפְלוֹג וְלִיתְנֵי בְּדִידָהּ: בַּמֶּה דְּבָרִים אֲמוּרִים בְּטוּמְאַת מַשְׁקִין, אֲבָל בְּטוּמְאַת שֶׁרֶץ לֹא! טְהוֹרָה בִּטְהוֹרוֹת עָדִיף לֵיהּ. רַבָּה אֲמַר: רֵישָׁא — אִיסּוּר לָאו, סֵיפָא — אִיסּוּר כָּרֵת. וְהָא רַבָּה הוּא דַּאֲמַר: כָּל *בְּדאוֹרָיְיתָא — לָא שְׁנָא אִיסּוּר לָאו וְלָא שְׁנָא אִיסּוּר כָּרֵת! קַשְׁיָא. רַב אַשִׁי אֲמַר: סֵיפָא — מִשּׁוּם דְּהָוֵי לֵיהּ *דָּבָר שֶׁיֵּשׁ לוֹ מַתִּירִין, [א]וְכָל דָּבָר שֶׁיֵּשׁ לוֹ מַתִּירִין — אֲפִילּוּ בְּאֶלֶף לָא בָּטֵיל. וְהָא דְּרַב אַשִׁי *בְּדוּתָא הִיא. לְמַאן? אִי לְכֹהֵן — מִישְׁרָא שָׁרֵי, אִי לְיִשְׂרָאֵל — לְעוֹלָם אָסוּר. אֶלָּא הָא דְּרַב אַשִׁי בְּדוּתָא הִיא. וְסָבַר ר' יוֹחָנָן תְּרוּמָה בִּזְמַן הַזֶּה דְּאוֹרָיְיתָא? וְהָתַנְיָא: *[ב]שְׁתֵּי קוּפּוֹת, אַחַת שֶׁל חוּלִּין וְאַחַת שֶׁל תְּרוּמָה, וְלִפְנֵיהֶם שְׁתֵּי סְאִין, אַחַת שֶׁל חוּלִּין וְאַחַת שֶׁל תְּרוּמָה, וְנָפְלוּ אֵלּוּ בְּתוֹךְ אֵלּוּ — הֲרֵי אֵלּוּ מוּתָּרִים, שֶׁאֲנִי אוֹמֵר: תְּרוּמָה לְתוֹךְ תְּרוּמָה נָפְלָה, וְחוּלִּין בְּתוֹךְ חוּלִּין נָפְלוּ. וְאָמַר רֵישׁ לָקִישׁ: וְהוּא שֶׁרַבּוּ חוּלִּין עַל הַתְּרוּמָה. וְר' יוֹחָנָן אָמַר: [ג]אע"פ שֶׁלֹּא רַבּוּ חוּלִּין עַל הַתְּרוּמָה. בִּשְׁלָמָא לְרֵישׁ לָקִישׁ — קָסָבַר: בִּדְרַבָּנַן נַמִי רִבּוּיָא הוּא דְּבָעֵינַן. אֶלָּא לְרַבִּי יוֹחָנָן, קַשְׁיָא! הָא מַנִּי — רַבָּנַן הִיא, וְאָנָא

רש"י

ר' יְהוּדָה לְטַעְמֵיהּ. בְּ"כִיסּוּי הַדָּם" וּבְ"הַקּוֹמֶץ". אַדְּתָנֵי אֲבָל חֲתִיכָה כו'. דְּמַשְׁמַע טַעְמָא מִשּׁוּם דְּהֶפְסֵד מוּעָט הוּא, נִפְלוֹג בְּדִידָהּ, וְאע"ג דְּלֵיכָּא תַּקַּנְתָּא – לָא בָּטְלָה. טְהוֹרָה בִּטְהוֹרָה עֲדִיפָא לֵיהּ. לְאַשְׁמוּעִינַן, דְּאע"ג דִּשְׁתֵּיהֶן טְהוֹרוֹת וְשַׁיָּיךְ בְּהוּ בִּיטּוּלָא טְפֵי, דְּאַשְׁכַּחַן בְּמַסֶּכֶת תְּרוּמוֹת (פ"ה מ"ג) דִּתְרוּמָה טְהוֹרָה בְּחוּלִּין טְהוֹרִין הַכֹּל מוֹדִין שֶׁעוֹלִין, וּבִתְרוּמָה טְמֵאָה בִּטְהוֹרָה חֲלוּקִים ב"ש וב"ה (שם מ"ד). וְעוֹד, דְּנִימּוֹחָה וַאפ"ה לֹא תַּעֲלֶה. וּלְר"ל מַאי שְׁנָא רֵישָׁא ומ"ש סֵיפָא. בִּשְׁלָמָא לְר' יוֹחָנָן דְּמוֹקֵי לָהּ בִּשְׁלֵימָה, סֵיפָא, כֵּיוָן דְּהֶפְסֵד מוּעָט הוּא, לָא מְבַטְּלִינַן חֲתִיכָה שְׁלֵימָה, הוֹאִיל וְדַרְכּוֹ לִימָּנוֹת. וְאַף עַל גַּב דִּלְר' יוֹחָנָן עִיגּוּל דִּתְרוּמָה בָּטֵל בְּחוּלִּין, דְּקָא מְהַדַּר לְר"ל וַהֲלֹא אֲנִי שׁוֹנֶה כו', מִכְּלָל דְּמוֹדֶה בְּעִיגּוּל דְּבָטֵיל מִשּׁוּם הֶפְסֵד מוּעָט – בַּחֲתִיכָה מוֹדֶה דְּיָהֲבִינַן כּוּלְּהוּ לְכֹהֵן, הוֹאִיל וְהִיא גּוּפָהּ דְּאוֹרָיְיתָא לָא חָיְישִׁי' לְהֶפְסֵד מוּעָט. אֶלָּא לְר"ל דְּאָמַר מִידֵי דְּאוֹרָיְיתָא לָא בָּטֵיל, וְהָכָא מִשּׁוּם דְּנִימּוֹחַ לָא חָשִׁיב תּוּ אִיסּוּר דִּילָהּ, וּבָטְלָה – סֵיפָא אַמַּאי לֹא תַּעֲלֶה? הָא לֵיתָא לְאִיסּוּרָא בְּעֵינֵיהּ! אָמַר רַב שֵׁישָׁא בְּרֵיהּ דְּרַב אִידִי. לְעוֹלָם בְּנִימּוֹחָה, וְרֵישָׁא בְּטוּמְאַת מַשְׁקִין דְּרַבָּנַן, כְּגוֹן שֶׁנִּטְמְאָה חֲתִיכָה עַל יְדֵי מַשְׁקִין טְמֵאִין, שֶׁנָּגְעוּ בִּכְלִי. דְּמִדְּאוֹרָיְיתָא אֵין מַשְׁקֶה מְטַמֵּא כְּלִי, וְאע"ג דְּאִיכָּא לְמִיגְזַר מִשּׁוּם טוּמְאָה דְּאוֹרָיְיתָא – מוֹדֶה רֵישׁ לָקִישׁ דְּבָטֵיל, הוֹאִיל וְאֵין דַּרְכּוֹ לִימָּנוֹת. וְסֵיפָא. קָדָשִׁים לְזָר אִיסּוּר דְּאוֹרָיְיתָא הוּא, וּמִידֵי דְּאוֹרָיְיתָא מִין בְּמִינוֹ לְהַאי תַּנָּא סְבִירָא לֵיהּ דְּלָא בָּטֵיל, אֲפִילּוּ שֶׁאֵין דַּרְכּוֹ לִימָּנוֹת. לִיפְלוֹג וְלִיתְנֵי בְּדִידָהּ. בְּטוּמְאָה וְטָהֳרָה, כִּדְנָקַט מִילְּתֵיהּ וְאָתֵי. מַאי שְׁנָא דִּשְׁבַקֵיהּ תַּנָּא לְמִילְּתֵיהּ לְמִנְקַט חוּלִּין וְקָדָשִׁים? טְהוֹרוֹת בִּטְהוֹרוֹת עֲדִיפָא לֵיהּ. וְנִיחָא לֵיהּ לְתַנָּא לְמִיתְנֵי טְהוֹרוֹת בִּטְהוֹרוֹת, דְּשַׁיָּיךְ בְּהוּ בִּיטּוּלָא טְפֵי, כִּדְפָרִישִׁי' לְעֵיל. וַאפ"ה אָזְלִינַן לְחוּמְרָא, הוֹאִיל וְאִיסּוּר דְּאוֹרַיְי'. אִיסּוּר לָאו. טוּמְאַת בְּשַׂר קָדָשִׁים לְאוֹכְלוֹ בְּלָאו "וְהַבָּשָׂר אֲשֶׁר יִגַּע בְּכָל טָמֵא" (ויקרא ז). סֵיפָא. קָדָשִׁים בְּחוּלִּין אָתֵי לִידֵי כָּרֵת, דְּאָכֵיל לְהוּ בְּטוּמְאַת הַגּוּף וְטוּמְאַת הַגּוּף בְּכָרֵת, דִּכְתִיב "וְהַנֶּפֶשׁ אֲשֶׁר תֹּאכַל בָּשָׂר". וּלְעוֹלָם בְּשֶׁנִּימּוֹחָה. ל"א: לְעוֹלָם בְּשֶׁלֹּא נִימּוֹחָה, וְעִיגּוּל הַיְינוּ טַעְמָא דְּר"ל דְּבִדְאוֹרָיְיתָא לָא בָּטֵיל, דְּכֵיוָן דִּתְרוּמָה לְזָר בְּמִיתָה כְּכָרֵת דָּמְיָא. וְהָא רַבָּה הוּא דַּאֲמַר. בְּפֶרֶק בַּתְרָא (דף קיט.). כָּל בִּדְאוֹרָיְיתָא. (לָא בָּטֵיל) ל"ש אִיסּוּר לָאו ל"ש אִיסּוּר כָּרֵת אִם חָשׁוּ רַבָּנַן לְכָרֵת חָשׁוּ נַמִי לְלָאו, וַעֲבוּד תַּקַּנְתָּא. רַב אַשִׁי אֲמַר. בְּנִימּוֹחָה. וְסֵיפָא הָוֵי דָּבָר שֶׁיֵּשׁ לוֹ מַתִּירִין, דְּמוּתָּרִין לְכֹהֵן. בְּדוּתָא הִיא. דְּהָא דְּקי"ל (ביצה דף ג:): דָּבָר שֶׁיֵּשׁ לוֹ מַתִּירִין לָא בָּטֵיל – כְּגוֹן דְּמִתְּשַׁרְיָא לְמָחָר לְמַאן דַּאֲסִירָא לֵיהּ הַשְׁתָּא, כְּגוֹן בֵּיצָה שֶׁנּוֹלְדָה בְּיוֹם טוֹב. מִישְׁרָא שָׁרֵי. אֲפִילּוּ הַשְׁתָּא. הֲרֵי אֵלּוּ. הַחוּלִּין מוּתָּרִין לְזָר. וְהוּא שֶׁרַבּוּ חוּלִּין. שֶׁבְּקוּפַּת חוּלִּין. עַל הַתְּרוּמָה. שֶׁבַּסְּאָה תְּרוּמָה. הִלְכָּךְ תָּלֵינַן בְּ"שֶׁאֲנִי אוֹמֵר חוּלִּין לְתוֹךְ חוּלִּין נָפְלוּ", דְּאִי נַמִי הָוֵי אִיפְכָא וְנָפְלָה סְאָה תְּרוּמָה בְּקוּפַּת חוּלִּין – בָּטְלָה בְּרוּבָּא. אַף עַל פִּי שֶׁלֹּא רַבּוּ. דְּסָמְכִינַן אַ"שֶׁאֲנִי אוֹמֵר". אֶלָּא לְר' יוֹחָנָן קַשְׁיָא. דְּמִי תָּלֵינַן לְקוּלָּא בְּאִיסּוּר דְּאוֹרָיְיתָא.

תוספות

רבי יהודה לטעמיה דאמר מין במינו לא בטיל. דוקא בדבר לח ומתערב אית ליה לר' יהודה דלא בטיל, דומיא דדם הפר ודם השעיר דיליף מינה ר' יהודה ב"הקומץ רבה" (מנחות דף כב. ושם). אבל בדבר יבש – לא, דר' יהודה גופיה אית ליה בפ' "נוטל" (שבת דף קמא:) דמעלין את המדומע בק"א ואפי' מין במינו, כדמשמע גבי ליטרא קציעות. ונבלה ב"הקומץ רבה" (מנחות דף כג. ושם) דאיכא למאן (א) דלא בטל – היינו בנימוחה, וסברא הוא דדבר המתערב מתפשט טעם האיסור בכל ההיתר ולא בטל. אבל דבר יבש – האיסור מונח במקומו, אלא שאין ניכר היכן הוא. והא דשילהי בילה (דף לח: ושם) דאמר דחיטין ושעורים בטלים לרבי יהודה, ולא חטין בחטין – בקמח איירי, דאל"כ, חטין בשעורין אמאי בטל? והלא ניכרים הן. ועוד נראה, דאפילו קמח, כיון שלונן הוא ואין טעם מתפשט – בטל. דאי לאו הכי – אפילו קמח חטין וקמח שעורים מין במינו הוא לרבא, דאזיל בתר שמא, בפרק בתרא דע"ז (דף סו. ושם), כמו חמירא דחיטי וחמירא דשערי. אלא התם ברותח איירי. וב"הקומץ רבה" (מנחות דף כג. ושם) דאמר דמנחות שנתערבו לא בטילי לרבי יהודה – התם נמי, מתוך שומנן מתרככין ונותנין טעם זה בזה. א"נ: כשיאפה אותן – יתנו טעם זה בזה*.

טהורות בטהורות עדיף ליה. דאע"פ שאין איסורה אלא לזרים – אפ"ה חמירא ולא בטלה. וכ"ש טמאה, דאיסורה אף לכהנים. ובקונטרס פירש טעם אחר.

בטומאת משקין דרבנן. וקסבר רב שישא בריה דרב אידי דרבנן לא פליגי אדרבי יהודה דאמר מין במינו לא בטל – אלא בדרבנן, אבל בדאורייתא – מודו דלא בטלה. אבל לא נימוחה, כיון דכל שדרכו לימנות מקדש – אף בטומאה דרבנן לא בטל, כמו תרומה בזמן הזה. דאי הויא דאורייתא – לא הוה עיגול בעיגולים עולה, אע"ג דתרומת פירות דרבנן.

רישא איסור לאו סיפא וכו'. אמאי דאוקמינן בנימוחה קאי. ובקונטרס פירש דאתי לפרושי בשלא נימוחה, ועיגול היינו טעמא דר"ל – דמדאורייתא לא בטיל, כיון דתרומה לזר במיתה – ככרת דמיא. ותבילי תלתן של כלאי הכרם, אע"ג דאיסור לאו הויא – מ"מ לא בטל משום דהוי "את שדרכו". ודוקא ב"כל שדרכו" הוא דמפליג רבה בין איסור לאו לאיסור כרת. ואע"ג דעלה קתני שהיה ר"מ אומר "כל שדרכו" לימנות מקדש – יש לפרש כעין שפי' לעיל, דה"ק: שהיה ר"מ אומר כל שדרכו לימנות מקדש באיסור כרת או באיסור מיתה, והואיל וכן – דין הוא שיקדש "את שדרכו" אפילו באיסור לאו. ומיהו לא יתכן כלל לפרש כן, דהא חתיכה של חטאת טהורה בחולין עדיפא אפילו מ"את שדרכו" כדפרישית לעיל, מטעם דראויה להתכבד. ומשמע דוקא משום דהוי איסור כרת לא בטל, אבל איסור לאו – בטל.

משום דהוי ליה דבר שיש לו מתירין. למאי דקטעי רב אשי קשה: עיגול בעיגולים אמאי עולה? דאפילו בדרבנן שמעינן ליה לרב אשי (ביצה דף ד.) דדבר שיש לו מתירין לא בטל! ויש להעמיד ההיא דעיגול בעיגולין בתרומה טמאה דאין לה מתירין. ומיהו קשה: למאי דס"ד השתא, אמאי תרומה טהורה עולה בק"א?

שתי קופות אחת של חולין. הקשה הר"ר שמואל מאכוז: אדמקשה מברייתא – לותיב ממתני' דתרומות (ריש פ"ז (מ"ה)) דתנן: ב' קופות, אחת של חולין ואחת של תרומה, שנפלה סאה של תרומה לתוך אחת מהן, ואין ידוע לאיזה מהן נפלה, הריני אומר: לתוך תרומה נפלה. והוו להו לרבי יוחנן ור"ל לאיפלוגי עלה! והשיב ר"י דמשום רבותא דר' יוחנן מייתי ברייתא, דאפילו בב' קופות ושתי סאין, דליכא למימר כולי האי אוקי חולין אחזקייהו, דמה שנפל בקופה של חולין ספק הוא ואין לו חזקת היתר – שרי בה רבי יוחנן בלא רבייה. ואפשר דבשעה אחת אפילו ר"ל שרי בלא רבייה, דסמכינן אחזקת חולין שבקופה, ומוקי לה אחזקתייהו. ולהכי לא פליגי אמתניתין אלא אברייתא. אלא לר' יוחנן מאי איכא למימר. פירוש: כיון דתרומה בזמן הזה דאורייתא – היכי סמכינן א"שאני אומר" להתיר בלא רבייה? תימה: למאי דסלקא דעתך השתא דתרומה בזמן הזה דאורייתא – אפילו הוה מוקי לה רבי יוחנן כשרבו, תקשי ליה: היכי סמכינן א"שאני אומר" כיון דאית ליה לרבי יוחנן בריש "אלו עוברין" (פסחים דף מד. ושם) כזית בכדי אכילת פרס דאורייתא! דהכי פריך לה התם, ומתוך קושיא זו משני התם: הכ"ע – בתרומה בזמן הזה דרבנן! ויש לומר: דה"מ למימר וליטעמיך. והתם נמי הוה מצי למימר: וליטעמיך, אפילו כזית בכדי אכילת פרס דרבנן תקשי אמאי אמרינן "שאני אומר" כיון דרבי יוחנן מוקי לה הכא בלא רבייה. וכן דרך הש"ס בכמה מקומות.

ירושה

עין משפט נר מצוה

קלא א מיי' פ"א מהל' יו"ט הלכה כ סמג עשין עה טור ש"ע י"ד סימן קב סעיף א:

קלב ב ג מיי' פי"ג מהלכות תרומות הלכה יד טוש"ע י"ד סימן קיא סעיף א:

[ועי' אריכות בזה בתוס' מנחות כב: ד"ה ור"י סבר ותוס' זבחים עג. ד"ה ר"י אומר]

תוספות ישנים

רבא אמר רישא איסור לאו פי' משו"ה אמרינן ברישא תעלה דהא נמי כי תעלה לא תאכל רק לכהנים א) וליכא אלא לאו דטומאה אבל בסיפא אי אמרינן דתעלה בחולין תאכל לישראל ואוכל אותם בטומאת הגוף כי אינו נזהר לאכול חולין בטומאת הגוף ואיכא כרת באכילת קדשים בטומאת הגוף:

א) נ"ל וליכא כאן אלא לאו דטומאת בשר.

הגהות הב"ח

(א) תוס' ד"ה ר' יהודה וכו' דאיכא למאן דאמר דלא בטל:

מסורת הש"ס

זבחים עט. מנחות כב: כג: חולין ק. קח.

לקמן קיט. [ושם איתא רבא]

[ביצה ג: לט. ב"מ נג.]

[עמ"ש על הגליון ב"מ ט.]

פסחים ט: מד. נזיר לו: [תוס' תרומות סוף פ"ו]

תורה אור

וַאֲנָא דַּאֲמָרִי כְּרַבִּי יוֹסֵי, דְּתַנְיָא* בְּסֵדֶר עוֹלָם °"אֲשֶׁר יָרְשׁוּ אֲבוֹתֶיךָ וִירִשְׁתָּהּ" — יְרוּשָּׁה רִאשׁוֹנָה וּשְׁנִיָּה יֵשׁ לָהֶן, וּשְׁלִישִׁית אֵין לָהֶן. וְא"ר יוֹחָנָן: מַאן תְּנָא סֵדֶר עוֹלָם — רַבִּי יוֹסֵי. וְסָבַר רַבִּי יוֹחָנָן בְּדְרַבָּנַן לָא בָּעֵינַן רִבּוּיָא? וְהָא תְּנַן: *אמִקְוֶה שֶׁיֵּשׁ בּוֹ אַרְבָּעִים סְאָה מְכוּוָּנוֹת, נָתַן סְאָה וְנָטַל סְאָה כָּשֵׁר, וְא"ר יְהוּדָה בַּר שֵׁילָא אָמַר ר' אַסִי א"ר יוֹחָנָן: עַד רוּבּוֹ. מַאי לָאו — דְּנִשְׁתַּיֵּיר רוּבּוֹ? לָא, דְּלָא נִשְׁקוֹל רוּבּוֹ. וְאִיבָּעֵית אֵימָא: שָׁאנֵי הָכָא, דְּאִיכָּא לְמֵימַר "שֶׁאֲנִי אוֹמֵר". *תְּנַן: "אַנְדְּרוֹגִינוֹס נוֹשֵׂא"! תְּנֵי: "אִם נָשָׂא". וְהָא "נוֹשֵׂא" קָתָנֵי! וְלִיטַעֲמִיךְ, מַאי "אֲבָל לֹא נִישָּׂא"? אֶלָּא מַאי "נִישָּׂא" דִּיעֲבַד — "נוֹשֵׂא" נַמִי דִּיעֲבַד. אָמְרִי: לָא, "נוֹשֵׂא" — לְכַתְּחִלָּה מַשְׁמַע, "אֲבָל לֹא נִישָּׂא" — דִּיעֲבַד נַמִי לָא. וְהָא מִדְּקָתָנֵי סֵיפָא רַבִּי אֱלִיעֶזֶר אוֹמֵר: אַנְדְּרוֹגִינוֹס חַיָּיבִין עָלָיו סְקִילָה כְּזָכָר, מִכְּלָל דְּת"ק סְפוּקֵי מְסַפְּקָא לֵיהּ! בֵּין לְמָר בֵּין לְמָר מִפְשַׁט פְּשִׁיטָא לֵיהּ, אִיכָּא בֵּינַיְיהוּ סְקִילָה מִשְּׁנֵי מְקוֹמוֹת: דְּמָר סָבַר חַיָּיבִין עָלָיו סְקִילָה מִשְּׁנֵי מְקוֹמוֹת, וּמָר סָבַר — בכְּזָכָר. אֲמַר רַב: לֵיתָא

רש"י

וַאֲנָא אָמֵינָא לְרַבִּי יוֹסֵי. דְּהָא מַתְנִי' ר' יוֹסֵי קָאָמַר לָהּ אַנְדְּרוֹגִינוֹס כֹּהֵן וכו', וּלְדִידֵיהּ אָמֵינָא אַף מַאֲכִילָהּ בְּחָזֶה וְשׁוֹק. דְּהָא תְּרוּמָה נַמִי לְר' יוֹסֵי דְּאוֹרַיְיתָא הִיא אַף בַּזְּמַן הַזֶּה. יְרוּשָּׁה רִאשׁוֹנָה. בִּימֵי יְהוֹשֻׁעַ הָוְיָא יְרוּשָּׁה, וְכֵן שְׁנִיָּה דְּבִימֵי עֶזְרָא. דִּכְשֶׁגָּלוּ גָּלוּת רִאשׁוֹנָה בָּטְלָה קְדוּשַּׁת הָאָרֶץ. שְׁלִישִׁית אֵין לָהֶם. כְּלוֹמַר, לָא בָּעֵי לְמֶהְדַּר וּמֵירְתָא, דִּירוּשָּׁה עוֹמֶדֶת הִיא. וְאַשְׁמְעִינַן הַאי קְרָא דְּלָא בָּטְלָה קְדוּשַּׁת הָאָרֶץ בְּגָלוּת טִיטוּס. וְסָבַר ר' יוֹחָנָן כו'. קס"ד הַאי דְּמוֹתֵיב דְּטַעְמָא דְּר' יוֹחָנָן לָאו מִשּׁוּם דְּסָמֵיךְ אַ"שֶּׁאֲנִי אוֹמֵר", אֶלָּא מִשּׁוּם דְּאִי הָוֵי נַמִי אִיפְכָא לָא אִיכְפַּת לָן, דְּלָא בָּעֵינַן רִבּוּיָא בִּדְרַבָּנַן, אֶלָּא מִכִּי אִיעֲרַב בָּטֵיל לֵיהּ. נָתַן סְאָה וְנָטַל סְאָה כָּשֵׁר. גַּבֵּי שְׁאָר מַשְׁקִין ומֵי פֵּירוֹת וְתֶמֶד שֶׁהֶחְמִיץ קָאֵי, בְּמַסֶּ' מִקְוָאוֹת. וְאַשְׁמוּעִי' דְּאַע"ג דְּחָזַר וְנָטַל, וְאִיכָּא לְמֵימַר הָא חָסֵר לֵיהּ מִקְוֶה, שֶׁהַסְּאָה הַזֹּאת אֵין מַשְׁלִימַתּוּ, שֶׁאֵין רְאוּיָה לְמִקְוֶה, אפ"ה כָּשֵׁר. דְּמִכִּי יָהֲבוּ לְגַבֵּיהּ בָּטֵל לֵיהּ, וְהָווּ לְהוּ אַרְבָּעִים וְחַד, כּוּלָּן רְאוּיִן, וְכִי שָׁקַל חַד סְאָה — פָּשׁוּ אַרְבָּעִים. אֲבָל אִיפְכָא לָא, דְּכִי נָטַל סְאָה בְּרֵישָׁא — חָסֵר לֵיהּ, וְכִי הֲדַר מַלְיֵיהּ הָוֵה לֵיהּ מִקְוֶה חָסֵר, דְּמַשְׁקִין הַלָּלוּ אֵין מַשְׁלִימִין אֶת הַמִּקְוֶה. מַאי לָאו דְּנִשְׁתַּיֵּיר רוּבּוֹ. עַד י"ט סְאָה יָכוֹל לַעֲשׂוֹת כֵּן, אֲבָל טְפֵי — לָא. דְּבָעֵינַן דְּנֶיהֱוֵי רוּבָּא מֵי גְשָׁמִים. אַלְמָא, אע"ג דִּפְסוּל שְׁאִיבָה דְּרַבָּנַן — בָּעֲיָא רוּבָּא בְּכַשְׁרוּת. דְּלָא נִשְׁקוֹל רוּבָּא. אֲבָל עַד פַּלְגָא שַׁפִּיר דָּמֵי. וְאִיבָּעֵית אֵימָא. לְעוֹלָם בָּעֵינַן רִבּוּיָא בִּדְרַבָּנַן, וְהַאי דְּקָאָמַר אע"פ שֶׁלֹּא רַבּוּ חוּלִּין — מִשּׁוּם דְּתָלֵינַן אַ"שֶּׁאֲנִי אוֹמֵר חוּלִּין לְתוֹךְ חוּלִּין נָפְלוּ" וְאֵין כָּאן אִיסּוּר. אֲבָל הָכָא לֵיכָּא לְמֵימַר "שֶׁאֲנִי אוֹמֵר" כה"ג, דְּהָא מַיָּא מִיַּד מִבַּלְבְּלֵי, וְלֵיכָּא לְמֵימַר חָזַר וּנְטָלָהּ. תְּנַן אַנְדְּרוֹגִינוֹס נוֹשֵׂא לְכַתְּחִלָּה. אַלְמָא זָכָר מְעַלְיָא הוּא, וְקַשְׁיָא לְרֵישׁ לָקִישׁ, דְּאָמַר: אֵין מַאֲכִיל בְּחָזֶה וְשׁוֹק. תְּנֵי אִם נָשָׂא נָשׂוּי. דְּבָעֲיָא גִּיטָּא מִינֵּיהּ מִשּׁוּם סָפֵק זָכָר, וּלְעוֹלָם סְפֵיקָא הוּא. מַאי אֲבָל לֹא נִישָּׂא. (א) מַשְׁמַע דִּיעֲבַד: ה"ג. נוֹשֵׂא נַמִי דִּיעֲבַד אָמְרִי לָא נוֹשֵׂא לְכַתְּחִלָּה אֲבָל לֹא נִישָּׂא דִּיעֲבַד נַמִי לָא. וּלְעוֹלָם קָשֶׁה לֵיהּ לְר"ל, וְדַיְיקָא כְּר' יוֹחָנָן. וּמוֹתְבִי' לְר' יוֹחָנָן: וְהָא מִדְּקָתָנֵי סֵיפָא כו'. מִשְּׁנֵי מְקוֹמוֹת. אֲפִי' בְּנַקְבוּתוֹ, וְטַעְמָא מְפָרֵשׁ לְקַמָּן מִקְּרָא בִּשְׁמַעְתִּין. וְר"א סָבַר כְּזָכָר. בִּמְקוֹם זַכְרוּת אִין, בִּמְקוֹם נַקְבוּת — לָא. לֵיתָא

תוספות

ירושה ראשונה ושניה יש להן כו'. פר"ח: ראשונה – ירושת אברהם יצחק ויעקב, שניה – ירושת יהושע. ומשם ואילך – קדושה לעולם. ולא יתכן לפרש כן, דבסוף פרק "יוצא דופן" (נדה דף מז. ושם) מפליג רבי יוסי בין תרומה לחלה, וא"כ קדושה שניה היא קדושת עזרא, דבקדושת עזרא שייך לחלק בין תרומה לחלה, משום דגבי חלה כתיב "בבואכם" וכי אסקינהו עזרא – לאו כולהו סלוק. עוד שאל ה"ר שמואל מאניוב את ר"י: דהכא קאי ר' יוחנן כר' יוסי דירושה ראשונה ושניה יש להם, דקדושה ראשונה לא קדשה לעתיד לבא, ובפרק "השוחט והמעלה" (זבחים דף קז:) קאמר הש"ס לר' יוחנן דקדשה לעתיד! והשיב ר"י: דלמעשרות ודאי לא קדשה הארץ לעתיד, אבל קדושת ירושלים והבית – קדשה, שקדושת מחיצות קיימא כל שעה, מ"אשר לו חומה", דדרשי' במגילה (דף י: ושם): אע"פ שאין לו עכשיו והיה לו קודם לכן. אי נמי, קדושת ירושלים משום דאיקרי נחלה – אין לה הפסק. א"נ: משום דכתיב (תהלים קלב) "זאת מנוחתי עדי עד". ואתי שפיר, דבפ"ק דמגילה (דף י.) בעי למימר דקסבר רבי אליעזר קדושה ראשונה קדשה לשעתה, וקדשה לעתיד ורבי יהושע אית ליה התם בהדיא הכי, א) ובריש בילה (דף ד.) אית להו דליטרא קליעות בטלה – ואם כן סברי דתרומה בזמן הזה דרבנן, ובטלה קדושת הארץ. וכן לר"ל, ר' יוסי סבר דתרומה בזמן הזה דרבנן, ובפ' "קדשי קדשים" (זבחים דף ס: ושם) גרס בכל הספרים: א"ר יוסי משום ר' ישמעאל כו' לעולם קסבר קדשה לעתיד! אלא יש לחלק בין קדושת הארץ למחיצות. עוד שאלו: דהכא משמע דסבר רבי יוחנן דקדושת הארץ דאורייתא, ובמדרש רות משמע דהוי דרבנן? דקאמר ר' יוחנן: מעשרות, כיון שגלו – נפטרו, והם חייבו עצמן מאליהן! והשיב ר"י: דאיכא למימר דהא דקאמר הכא ואנא דאמר כר' יוסי – לאו משום דסבר ר' יוחנן כוותיה, אלא משום דאליבא דר' יוסי דאנדרוגינוס דמתני' קיימי. ועוד אר"י: דאין נראה שום חכם יאמר שקדושת הארץ בזמן בית שני למעשרות ולכל מצות התלויות בארץ היתה מדרבנן. והיא דמדרש(ב) – איכא לאוקמי במעשר פירות. וה"ק: כיון שגלו – נפטרו ממעשר דאורייתא, והם חייבו עצמן מאליהם כשחזרו יותר ממה שהיו חייבים בתחלה, שהוסיפו מעשר פירות. ועוד אר"י: מתוך הירושלמי דשביעית *פ"י דהכי פירושו: כיון שגלו – נפטרו, שקדושה ראשונה לא קדשה לעתיד, ולא היה חובה להם לקדש את כל א"י, כדאמר (חולין דף ז.) הרבה כרכים כו'. וכמו שהניחו במקלת – היו רשאין להניח הרבה יותר, או שמא הכל אם היו רוצים, ואעפ"כ חייבו עצמן מאליהן וקדשו – וכיון שקדשו – קדשה מן התורה.

נתן סאה ונטל סאה כשר. קשה: דנהי דשאיבה דרבנן, כדאמר בפרק "המוכר את הבית" (ב"ב דף סו: ושם), מי פירות מיהא פסולין מדאוריי' לטבול בהן, כדמוכח פ"ק דפסחים (דף יז: ושם) דאמר: משקי בי מטבחיא בקרקע טהורים. אמר רב פפא: לא אמרן אלא מים, אבל דם – לא. ומים נמי לא אמרן אלא דהוו רביעית, דחזיא להטביל מחטין וצנורות כו'. משמע דדם לא חזי להטביל בו. ועוד: אמרי' ב"כסוי הדם" (חולין דף פד. ושם) דג' "מים" כתיבי, וממעטינן מי פירות. והיכי פריך מהכא דמדרבנן בעיא ריבויא, ואמי פירות בהדיא קתני לה, כדפי' בקונטרס! וי"ל: דפריך משום דקא פסיק ותני עד רובו אפילו למחטין וצנורות, דמדאורייתא לא בעי מ' סאה. ונהי דכשמי פירות רוב מתבטלים המים במי פירות, ופסול מדאורייתא אף למחטין, מ"מ במחצה על מחצה מיהא מדאורייתא כשר למחטין, ומדרבנן הוא דבעינן רבייה. ועוד י"ל: דמדאורייתא קמא קמא בטיל, ואפ"ה בעינן רובא, לכך פריך שפיר. א"נ: קאי נמי אמקוה שיש בו מים, דקתשיב במס' מקוואות (פ"ז מ"ב), ואכולהו קא"ר יוחנן עד רובו(ב).

אמר רבי יוחנן עד רובו. משמע דברובו לא אמרינן ראשון ראשון בטל. וכן בפרק "במה אשה" (שבת דף סה: ושם) גבי אבוה דשמואל דעבד להו לבנתיה מקוואות ביומי ניסן שלא ירבו נוטפים על הזוחלים. ובפ' "הנודר מן הירק" (נדרים נז:) בצל שעקרו בשביעית ונטעו בשמינית ורבו גידוליו על עיקרו – מותר. ותימה: דבפרק בתרא דמסכת ע"ז (דף עג.) א"ר יוחנן: המערה יין נסך מחבית לבור, אפילו כל היום כולו – ראשון ראשון בטל! ונראה לר"י: דההיא דמס' ע"ז דאמרינן ראשון ראשון בטל – היינו דוקא עד ס', אבל אם אין ס' מן ההיתר – לא, דה"א להתבטל כיון שיש נ"ט לבסוף. דהא טעם כעיקר מן התורה הוא כדאמר ב"אלו עוברין" (פסחים דף מד: ושם) ובפרק "ג' מינים" (נזיר דף לז: ושם). ומ"מ, אע"ג דאיכא ס' מן ההיתר, אי לאו דנפול קמא קמא היה נאסר, כגון אם היה נופל בבת אחת, או אם היה מערה בדבר דנפיש עמודיה טפי מפי חבית, דלא נפיש עמודיה טפי *מצירצור קטן. דיין נסך החמירו יותר מבשאר איסורים, כדתנן התם (ע"ז דף עד.) שהוא בכל שהוא, וקסבר רבי יוחנן דכי איכא למימר ראשון בטל באיסורא לגו היתירא, ולא נפיש עמודיה שבטל והולך עד ס', ולא אמרינן שיאסור בכל שהוא, דלמתניתין דהתם קאי, וכי פריך התם ממתני' דיין נסך אוסר בכל שהוא, מאי לאו דנפול איסורא לגו היתירא – לא הוה מצי לשנויי דאיירי בנפיש עמודיה מפי חבית, דהא כל שהוא קתני, דלא נפיש. והא דפריך עלה מיין במים בנ"ט מאי לאו דנפול חמרא דאיסורא לגו מיא דהיתירא, אע"ג דרבי יוחנן נמי לא קאמר דבטל אלא עד ס' – לא פריך אלא מכח רישא, מדסיפא איסורא לגו היתירא – רישא נמי איסורא לגו היתירא, וקתני בכל שהוא. ומסיק דכולה מתניתין היתירא לגו איסורא. ומ"מ אמת הוא דבנ"ט אסור בכל ענין, בין איסורא לגו היתירא בין איפכא.

דלא נשקול רובא. תימה: היכי מצי למימר הכי, הא תנן במס' מקוואות (פ"ד מ"ד): מים שאובין ומי גשמים שהן מתערבות בחצר ובמערה עד מעלות המערה, אם רוב כשר – כשר, אם רוב פסול – פסול, מחצה על מחצה – פסול. אימתי – בזמן שהן מתערבין עד שלא הגיעו למקוה כו'. משמע בהדיא דשאובין דרבנן בעי רבייה!

תנן אנדרוגינוס נושא. פירוש: דמשמע נשואין גמורים, והרי הוא כזכר, ומאכיל בתרומה דאורייתא. דאי לא הוו נשואין ודאין ה"ל למימר אנדרוגינוס שקדש – קידושיו קידושין. ומשני: תני אם נשא – דיעבד, ולישנא דלכתחלה דהך סוגיא היינו פי' נישואין ודאין. אבל אין לפרש דמדקדק מדשרי לכתחלה לישא, ולא אסרינן ליה לכתחלה מספק נשים המסוללות זו בזו, דמאחר דמאכיל לר"ל בתרומה בזמן הזה דרבנן – לא מסתבר לאוסרו בתחלה מטעם זה. ועוד יש לפרש: דאנדרוגינוס נושא משמע דחייב לישא, דמיפקד אפריה ורביה. וא"ת: והיכי פריך מאנדרוגינוס נושא אמילתיה דרבי יוסי? וצריך לדחוק: שהוא סיום מילתיה דרבי יוסי, אף על פי שרבי יהודה מפסיק בינתים.

עין משפט נר מצוה

קלג א מיי' פ"ד מהל' מקואות הלכה ז סמג עשין רמח טוש"ע י"ד סימן רא סעיף כד:

קלד ב מיי' פ"א מהל' איסורי ביאה הלכה טו:

תוספות ישנים

א) עוי"מ דהא דקאמר התם קדושה ראשונה קדשה לעתיד לבא לאו דוקא אלא ר"ל קדושה שניה וכר' יוסי דהכא דתני סדר עולם וסבר תרומה בזמן הזה מן התורה ומ"מ קרי לה ראשונה אע"פ דמיירי בקדושה שקידש עזרא לפי שהיא ראשונה לנו: **ב)** ותימה דהא לא אמרינן קמא קמא בטיל רק עד שעים תדע דאל"כ אם יערה אדם כל היום חלב בקדרה לא יאסור וצ"ל דהכא לא הוי רק מדרבנן שהרי אין כאן שיעור לאסור שאפילו כי נתן סאה ונטל סאה עד רובו א"א שכל הפעמים שנוטל הסאה מן המקוה שלא יתערב בהם מעט ממי פירות אשר נתן בתוך המקוה וא"כ אפילו יתר ממנו היה לנו להכשיר שאף עד יתר מרובו יש בתוך המקוה יתר מרובו ממים גמורים ואפ"ה (לא) גזור רבנן לפי שהוא נראה כרובו ומש"ה א) לא שרינן יותר מרובו אלמא מדרבנן בעי רבייה: אלא מאי נישא דיעבד. ותימה אמאי לא אמרינן שיועילו נשואין להאכילו בתרומה דרבנן אם כהן נשאו כמו שאנו אומרים שאוכלת אשתו בשביל קדושין בתרומה דרבנן והלא כיון דספיקא הוא היה לנו לומר זה כזה וי"ל דלא דמי דהא אם נחשבו כזכר אין תקלה בדבר דחומרא הוי דחייבין עליו סקילה אבל אם אנו אומרים שהוא נישא לאכול בתרומה דרבנן ונחשוב אותו כנקבה יש חשש איסור בדבר דא"כ לא יתחייב סקילה כזכר:

א) נראה דל"ל ומשו"ה לא שרינן רק עד רובו אלמא דגם בדרבנן בעי רבייה.

מסורת הש"ס

דברים ל

נדה מז:

זבחים כב. מקוואות פ"ז מ"ב

לעיל פא.

הגהות הב"ח

(א) רש"י ד"ה מאי אבל וכו' דמשמע: (ב) תוס' ד"ה ירושה וכו' דמדרש רות איכא לאוקמי:

גליון הש"ס

רש"י ד"ה נתן סאה וכו' ומי פירות וכו'. עי' זבחים דף עח ע"ב תוד"ה דלי שיש בו יין וכו':

נ"ל נראה דהכי. יעב"ץ

[אלא כצ"ל ועי' בתוס' ע"ז עג ד"ה ודוקא וק"ל]

ליתא לברייתא מקמי מתניתין. דתניא, *רבי יוסי אומר: [א]אנדרוגינוס בריה בפני עצמה הוא, ולא הכריעו בו חכמים אם זכר אם נקבה. אדרבה, ליתא לברייתא מקמי מתניתין! *מדשבקיה רבי יוסי לבר זוגיה, ש"מ הדר ביה. ושמואל אמר: ליתא לברייתא מקמי מתניתין. אדרבה, ליתא למתניתין מקמי ברייתא, דהא שמעינן ליה לשמואל *דחייש ליחידאה! הני מילי כי לא מתעקרא מתניתין, אבל כי מתעקרא מתניתין — לא חייש. אמרי בי רב משמיה דרב: הלכה כרבי יוסי באנדרוגינוס ובהרכבה. ושמואל אמר: בקושי ובקידוש. אנדרוגינוס — הא דאמרן, הרכבה — דתנן: *[ב]אין נוטעין, ואין מבריכין, ואין מרכיבין ערב שביעית פחות משלשים יום לפני ראש השנה. ואם נטע והבריך והרכיב — יעקור. *רבי יהודה אומר: כל הרכבה שאינה קולטת בשלשה ימים — שוב אינה קולטת. רבי יוסי ור' שמעון אומרים: [ג]שתי שבתות. ואמר ר"נ אמר רבה בר אבוה: לדברי האומר שלשים — צריך שלשים ושלשים, לדברי האומר שלשה — צריך שלשה ושלשים, לדברי האומר שתי שבתות — [ד]צריך שתי שבתות ושלשים. ושמואל אמר: בקושי וקידוש. קושי — דתנן: *כמה יהא קישויה? ר"מ אומר: או ארבעים או חמשים יום, רבי יהודה אומר: דייה חדשה, רבי יוסי ור' שמעון אומרים: [ה]אין קישוי יותר משתי שבתות. קידוש — דתנן: *המסכך גפנו על גבי תבואתו של חבירו הרי זה קידש, וחייב באחריותו, *דברי רבי מאיר. רבי יוסי ורבי שמעון אומרים:

רש"י

ליתא למתני'. דקתני לר' יוסי אנדרוגינוס מאכיל את אשתו בתרומה. מקמי ברייתא. דקתני לר' יוסי ספיקא הוא. מדשבקיה רבי יוסי לר' שמעון בן זוגיה. דאיירי בהדיה במתני', ואיירי בברייתא לחודיה — ש"מ הדר ביה. ולאו תנאי היא, דאיכא סמי תנא דברייתא מקמי תנא דמתני', דאי תנאי היא — תרווייהו הוה תני להו נמי בברייתא, ומפיק לדרבי שמעון כדאפכא לדרבי יוסי. דחייש ליחידאה. דאמר שמואל ב"החולץ" (לעיל דף מא.): הלכה כרבי יהודה בשומרת יבם שקדש אחיו את אחותה. ואיהכא אמרינן לה במס' מגילה בפ' "הקורא" (דף יח:). הלכה כרבי יוסי. דמתני'. ואמרי בי רב היינו רב הונא, כדלקמן. ופליג אדאמרן לעיל אליבא דרב ליתא למתניתין, ובהרכבה לקמן מפרש לה. וכן קושי וקידוש, ובכולהו איירי רבי שמעון בהדיה. הלכך מסתברא דאדר' יוסי דבמתני' קאי דאיירי רבי שמעון בהדיה. יעקור. דקא קלטה בשביעית, דאין הרכבה קולטת בפחות משלשים יום. צריך שלשים ושלשים. כדי שתקלוט שלשים לפני שביעית. דכל שלשים לפני שביעית כשביעית דמו, דנפקא לן מ"בחריש ובקציר תשבות" ב"מקשין בית השלחין" (מ"ק ג:). ג' ול'. ג' לקליטה, שתקלוט קודם זמן האיסור. כמה יהא קישויה. דקיי"ל (נדה דף לו:) בנדה דאורייתא: המקשה בתוך י"א שבין נדה לנדה, ורואה דם ג' ימים רצופים מחמת צער וולדה — אינה באה לידי זיבה להיות צריכה ספירת ז' נקיים כיולדת בזוב, אלא ימי טומאת לידה כיולדת גרידתא. דתניא (שם) "כי יזוב זוב דמה" — דמה מחמת עצמה, ולא מחמת ולד. וכמה יהא קישויה דאמרי' מחמת ולד הוא — אפילו מ' או חמשים יום קודם לידה. דייה חדשה. חדש תשיעי שהיא יולדת בו, ופעמים שאין יותר מיום או יומים. כגון שילדה בב' בחדש, אין הולד מטהר אלא דמים שראתה מר"ח ואילך, שאין באה על ידו לזיבה אם לא ראתה ג' ימים רצופים קודם ר"ח. דקסבר ר' יהודה: שיפורא גרים (שופר שבית דין תוקעים לקידוש (א) גורם הקישוי). ופעמים שהוא מטהר את כל החדש, כגון אם ילדה בסופו ואין הטהרה אלא מזיבה, אבל מנדה — אינו מטהרה בימי נדה. ואם שפתה מן הצער סמוך ללידה יום אחד — אף מזיבה לא טהרה, והרי היא יולדת בזוב וצריכה ז' נקיים, דאיגלאי מילתא דצער קמא לאו מחמת ולד הוה. קידש. לשון "פן תקדש" (דברים כב) — אסר תבואת חברו, וחייב לשלם. אמרי

תוספות

בריה בפני עצמה כו'. אר"י: דהאי בריה לא הוי פירושו כגון בריה שבמקומות אחרים, שאינו ספק. אלא בריה דקאמר הכא היינו שהוא ספק, כדקאמר ולא הכריעו בו כו'. וכן משמע ב"המפלת" (נדה דף כח.) דאמר רב: טומטום ואנדרוגינוס שראו לובן או אודם אין שורפין עליו את התרומה, ראו לובן ואודם כאחת שורפין עליו את התרומה. אלמא בהדיא משוי ליה רב ספיקא. והיינו ע"כ כר' יוסי דברייתא, דלר' יוסי דמתני' זכר הוא. וקשה: דבתוספתא דבכורים (פ"ב) מסיים בהך ברייתא דשמעתין: אבל טומטום אינו כן, אלא או ספק איש או ספק אשה. מכלל דאנדרוגינוס לא הוי ספק, אלא אינו לא איש ולא אשה. ועוד: מדלת"ק דר' יוסי דתוספתא דבכורים הוי אנדרוגינוס ספק, ומטמא באודם כנשים ובלובן כאנשים — מכלל דלר' יוסי לא הוי ספק! ואר"י: דהתם ה"פ: אבל טומטום אינו כן, כמו אנדרוגינוס שהוא ספק מחמת שהוא בריה משונה, משום שיש לו זכרות ונקבות והוא ספק לעולם, אבל טומטום אינו כן, אלא ספק שהוא איש ודאי או אשה ודאית, אלא שהוא מכוסה ואין ניכר. ואם קדש, ונקרע ונמצא זכר — אגלאי מילתא דמתחלה היה זכר ודאי. וכן אם נתקדשה ונמצאת נקבה. ור' יוסי לא פליג את"ק קמא, אלא לפרושי טעמא דת"ק קמא קאתי, אע"ג דקתני ר' יוסי אומר. אי נמי, כולה ר' יוסי היא, ותני שרבי יוסי אומר. ועי"ל: דפליג אמאי דקאמר ת"ק קמא (שם) הריני נזיר שזה איש ואשה, פירוש: שניהם, בין איש בין אשה, הרי זה נזיר. ועלה פליג ר' יוסי, שאין חשוב איש ואשה אלא או זה או זה. ות"ק סבר שחשוב שניהם, במקצת כאיש ובמקצת הוא כאשה. וקאמר נמי ת"ק: הריני נזיר שאין זה לא איש ולא אשה — הרי זה נזיר, לפי שאין זה לא איש גמור ולא אשה גמורה. רבי יוסי לבר זוגיה כו'. תימה: דלמא הדר ביה מברייתא לגבי ר' שמעון דמתניתין? כי מתעקרא מתני' לא חייש. ואע"ג דכמה משניות סוברות דאנדרוגינוס ספק, בפ' "אם לא הביא" (שבת דף קלד:) וב"המפלת" (נדה דף כח. ושם) ובפרק "על אלו מומין" (בכורות דף מב. ושם) — מ"מ, לר' יוסי אנדרוגינוס הוא זכר, שהמשנה היא עיקר מן הברייתא. ומ"מ דייק שפיר לקמן דאנדרוגינוס לשמואל זכר הוא, אע"ג דכמה משניות סברי דספיקא הוי, דאם איתא דסבר כהנהו משניות לא היה אומר דליתא לברייתא, דכיון שתופס אותה סברא עיקר היה לו לומר דברייתא היא עיקר שאומרת כן לרבי יוסי.

הלכה כר' יוסי באנדרוגינוס. פירש בקונטרס: דכרבי יוסי דמתניתין פסק. דבכל הנך מילי דחשיב הכא: אנדרוגינוס, הרכבה, וקושי, וקידוש — כולם משניות הם, ואיירי ר' שמעון בהדי רבי יוסי. ש"מ דאאנדרוגינוס דמתני' קאי. ועוד: דאמרי בי רב — היינו רב הונא, ושמעי' ליה לרב הונא דאמר לקמן משמיה דרב אנדרוגינוס חייבין עליו סקילה משני מקומות(ב), ופליגי אדאמרן לעיל אליבא דרב דליתא למתני', מדקאמר דליתא — משמע דסבר כברייתא, כדמדקדק לקמן אדשמואל דסבר כר' יוסי דמתני' מדקאמר ליתא לברייתא. והיא דהמפלת — סבר רב נמי כר' יוסי דברייתא גבי טומטום ואנדרוגינוס שראו לובן או אודם. והשתא אמוראי נינהו ואליבא דרב. לדברי האומר שלשים צריך ל' ושלשים. פר"ת: דלאו אשביעית קאי. דלענין נטיעה(ג) ליכא תוספת שביעית. לאסור נטיעה הנקלטת בתוספת שביעית אלא לענין ערלה קאמר, וה"ק: לדברי האומר שלשים לקליטה — צריך לגבי ערלה שלשים ושלשים. ואר"י דסוגיא דפ"ק דר"ה (דף י: ושם) מוכחת כן, גבי הא דתניא: אחד הנוטע ואחד המבריך ואחד המרכיב ערב שביעית שלשים יום לפני ר"ה — עלתה לו שנה, ומותר לקיימן בשביעית כו'. ודייק התם דלא מיתוקמא כרבי אליעזר דאמר שלשים יום בשנה חשובים שנה, משום דלדידיה שלשים ושלשים בעי. ומוקי לה כרבי מאיר, דאמר יום אחד בשנה חשוב שנה, דיום שלשים עולה לכאן ולכאן. ואם איתא דרב נחמן אמר רבה בר אבוה אשביעית קאי — שפיר מיתוקמא ההיא דאחד הנוטע כר' אליעזר, ולא הזכיר התנא אלא שלשים שנחשבים שנה, ואותן שלשים של קליטה לא הזכיר, כמו שבמתני' דאין נוטעים דמייתי הזכיר ל' של קליטה ושייר שלשים של התוספת הנחשבין שנה: קידוש דתנן כו'. אע"ג דפסקי' ב"הגוזל" (ב"ק דף ק. ושם) כי הך דר' מאיר דדאין דינא דגרמי, מ"מ אפשר דהלכה כר' יוסי בהא דקאמר לא קידש. ואפשר דר' יוסי מודה לר' מאיר, דאם קידש — דחייב באחריותו. והתם לא מייתי אלא דמהכא שמעינן דדאין דינא דגרמי, ולענין דינא דגרמי הוא דפסקינן כותיה בעלמא, אבל הכא — הלכה כר' יוסי דלא קידש. המסכך הוא הדין הזורע, בההוא עובדא דמייתי רבי יוסי בסיפא, אלא נקט המסכך משום רבותא דרבי מאיר, דאף במסכך אסור. רבי יוסי אומר כו'. בסיפא מייתי רבי יוסי מעשה באחד שזרע כרמו של חברו, והתיר רבי עקיבא. אם בזריעת תבואה, דהוי כלאים דאורייתא, התיר — אם כן הא דאמר ב"הקומץ זוטא" (מנחות דף טו. ושם): מעשה באחד שזרע כרמו של חברו סמדר, ואסרו חכמים את הזרעים והתירו הגפנים, ומשמע(ג) דבשאר זרעים דהוו דרבנן איירי, אבל בקנבוס ולוף או ה' המינים שהם כלאים דאורייתא — היו אוסרים גם הגפנים שאינן של זרוע — אם כן לא אתיא ההיא דמנחות כרבי יוסי, אף על גב דפסיק שמואל כותיה אלא כרבנן. ורב הונא אמר רב אמר נמי בסמוך דאין הלכה כרבי יוסי. והא דלא מוקי התם כרבי יוסי ונימא דהתירו הגפנים אפילו בכלאים דאורייתא — היינו משום דקסבר דלרבי יוסי אפילו זרעים מותרים. דכיון דמן התורה אין אדם אוסר (ג) בכלאים דבר שאינו שלו — אין כאן כלאים, והכל מותר.
אין

מסורת הש"ס

[תוספתא דבכורים פ"ב]
[לעיל ס:]
[מגילה יח:]
שביעית פ"ב מ"ו ר"ה י:
[פסחים נה.]
נדה לו:
ב"ק ק. כלאים פ"ז מ"ד
[במשנה כלאים וכן בירושלמי ליתא דברי ר"מ וכן מוכח מתוס' דב"ק ק. ד"ה מחלוקת וכו' דסתם משנה ר"מ וכו' וכן בהרא"ש ליתא]

עין משפט נר מצוה

קלה א מיי' פ"ב מהל' אישות הלכה כד ופ"ב מהלכות נזירות הלכה י:
קלו ב ג ד מיי' פ"ג מהלכות שמיטה ויובל הלכה יא סמג לאוין רסו:
קלז ה מיי' פ"ז מהל' איסורי ביאה הלכה א סמג לאוין קיא:

תוספות ישנים

מדשבקיה ר' יוסי לבר זוגיה וא"ת ומנלן דברייתא עיקר דלמא ר' יוסי אמר הברייתא ברישא ושמע לר' שמעון הא דמתני' וסברה ואמר נמי כוותיה והדר ביה מברייתא ומתני' עיקר ואין זה קושיא דהא לשמואל הא דמתני' קדמה לברייתא כנ"ל. עוד אומר רבינו נתנאל מדקאמר ולא הכריעו בו חכמים משמע דשמעיה לחכמים שהכריעו בו לעשותו כזכר והוא לא חשיב ליה הכרעה ברורה דמשמע ולא הכריעו בו מתחלה הכריעו הוא והיינו מר' שמעון שהכריעו בו לחשבו כזכר והוא לא סבר כן: א) ורא"ה לדבר דכרבי יוסי דמתני' פסיק דאי כרבי יוסי דברייתא תרתי דרב למה לי לומר הלכה כר' יוסי: ב) י"ל מההיא דלקמן דהא דקאמר חייבין עליו מב' מקומות היינו משום יהודה דאמר דמרבינן ליה ומ"ש קשיא דהא ודאי לאו זכר הוא רבייה קרא אבל יש לדחות דודאי גבי סקילה שאני משום דגלי קרא דמשמע נמי אשכחא לר' יהודה אמר לעיל דאנדרוגינוס שקידש קידושיו ספק ספק איש ספק אשה ובפ' ר' אליעזר דמילה משמע דשרי אנדרוגינוס בשבת וא"ל ודאי טעמא משום דגלי קרא יהודה דהמול יכול כל זכר לרבות ליה גבי סקילה שאני דגלי קרא: ג) ועוד ראיה דאמרינן פ"ק דר"ה והדוחן והשומשמין שהשרישו יום אחד לפני ר"ה מתעשרין לשעבר ומותרין מיד בשביעית אלמא לא בעינן כלל (תוספתא) רק בחריש ובקציר תשבות אפילו ארבעים וג' יום פירשתי בנדה: המסכך גפנו פירשתי פ"ק דב"ק:

הגהות הב"ח

(א) רש"י ד"ה דייה חדשה כו' שב"ד תוקעין לקידוש החדש: (ב) תד"ה ר"י כו' והתירו הגפנים ומשמע התם וכו': (ג) בא"ד אין אדם אוסר דבר שאינו שלו כצ"ל ותיבת בכלאים נמחק:

עין משפט
נר מצוה

קלח א מיי' פ"ה מהל' כלאים הלכה ח טוש"ע י"ד סימן לנו סעיף ז:
קלט ב מיי' פ"א מהל' איסורי ביאה הלכה טו:
קמ ג מיי' פ"ג מהל' איסורי מזבח הל' ו והלכה יא ופ"ז מהל' פסולי המוקדשין הלכה ד:
קמא ד מיי' פ"ג מהל' איסורי מזבח הלכה ג:

ᵃאֵין אָדָם אוֹסֵר דָּבָר שֶׁאֵינוֹ שֶׁלּוֹ. אִיבַּעְיָא לְהוּ: בְּאַנְדְּרוֹגִינוֹס מַה לִּי אָמַר שְׁמוּאֵל? ת"ש, דַּאֲמַר שְׁמוּאֵל לְרַב עָנָן: לֵיתָא לְבָרַיְיתָא מִקַּמֵּי **מתני'**. הַרְכָּבָה מַה לִּי אָמַר שְׁמוּאֵל? תָּא שְׁמַע, דְּא"ל שְׁמוּאֵל לְרַב עָנָן: תְּנֵי כְּמַאן דַּאֲמַר שְׁלֹשָׁה וּשְׁלֹשִׁים. קוֹשִׁי מַה לִּי אָמַר רַב? תֵּיקוּ. קִידּוּשׁ מַה לִּי אָמַר רַב? אָמַר רַב יוֹסֵף: ת"ש, דְּאָמַר רַב הוּנָא אָמַר רַב: אֵין הֲלָכָה כְּרַבִּי יוֹסֵי. אֲמַר לֵיהּ אַבַּיֵי: מַאי חֲזֵית דְּסָמְכַתְּ אַהָא, סְמוֹךְ אַהָא דַּאֲמַר רַב אַדָּא אָמַר רַב הֲלָכָה כְּרַבִּי יוֹסֵי! *אָמְרִי בֵּי רַב מַנּוּ — רַב הוּנָא, וְרַב הוּנָא אָמַר: אֵין הֲלָכָה.§ "רַבִּי יְהוּדָה אוֹמֵר טוּמְטוּם וכו'".§ א"ר אַמִי: מַאי עָבֵיד לֵיהּ רַבִּי יְהוּדָה לְטוּמְטוּם דְּבִירִי דְּאוֹתְבוּהּ אַבֵּי כּוּרְסֵיהּ וְאִיקְּרַע, וְאוֹלִיד שְׁבַע בְּנִין? וְר' יְהוּדָה א"ל: חֲזֵר עַל בָּנָיו מֵאַיִן הֵם. תַּנְיָא, ר' יוֹסֵי בְּר' יְהוּדָה אוֹמֵר: *טוּמְטוּם לֹא יַחֲלוֹץ, שֶׁמָּא יִקָּרַע וְנִמְצָא סָרִיס חַמָּה. אַטּוּ כָּל דְּמִקְּרַע זָכָר הָוֵי? הָכִי קָאָמַר: שֶׁמָּא יִקָּרַע וְנִמְצָא נְקֵבָה, (א) וַאֲפִילּוּ נִמְצָא זָכָר — שֶׁמָּא יִמָּצֵא סְרִיס חַמָּה. מַאי בֵּינַיְיהוּ? אָמַר רָבָא: לִפְסוֹל בִּמְקוֹם אַחִין, וְלַחֲלוֹץ שֶׁלֹּא בִּמְקוֹם אַחִין, אִיכָּא בֵּינַיְיהוּ. אָמַר רַב שְׁמוּאֵל בַּר יְהוּדָה א"ר אַבָּא אֲחוּהּ דְּר' יְהוּדָה בַּר זַבְדִּי ᴮאָמַר רַב יְהוּדָה אָמַר רַב: אַנְדְּרוֹגִינוֹס חַיָּיבִין עָלָיו סְקִילָה מִשְּׁתֵּי מְקוֹמוֹת. מֵיתִיבֵי, *רַבִּי אֱלִיעֶזֶר אָמַר: אַנְדְּרוֹגִינוֹס חַיָּיבִין עָלָיו סְקִילָה כְּבְזָכָר, ᵇבד"א בְּזַכְרוּת שֶׁלּוֹ, אֲבָל בְּנַקְבוּת שֶׁלּוֹ — פָּטוּר! הוּא דְּאָמַר כִּי הַאי תַּנָּא, דְּתַנְיָא, רַבִּי סִימַאי אוֹמֵר: אַנְדְּרוֹגִינוֹס חַיָּיבִין עָלָיו סְקִילָה מִשְּׁתֵּי מְקוֹמוֹת. מ"ט דְּרַבִּי סִימַאי? אָמַר רָבָא: בַּר הַמְדוּרֵי אַסְבְּרָא לִי: °"וְאֶת זָכָר לֹא תִשְׁכַּב מִשְׁכְּבֵי אִשָּׁה" (ויקרא יח), אֵי זֶהוּ זָכָר שֶׁיֵּשׁ בּוֹ שְׁנֵי מִשְׁכָּבוֹת — הֱוֵי אוֹמֵר זֶה אַנְדְּרוֹגִינוֹס. וְרַבָּנַן? אע"ג דְּאִית בֵּיהּ שְׁנֵי מִשְׁכָּבוֹת, "אֶת זָכָר" כְּתִיב, וְרַבָּנַן, זָכָר גְּרֵידָא מְנָא לְהוּ? (ב) מֵ"אִשָּׁה". בְּאִשָּׁה שֶׁלֹּא כְּדַרְכָּהּ מְנָא לְהוּ? *מִ"וְּאִשָּׁה". אָמַר רַב שֵׁיזְבִי אָמַר רַב חִסְדָּא: ᴰלֹא לַכֹּל א"ר אֱלִיעֶזֶר אַנְדְּרוֹגִינוֹס זָכָר מְעַלְּיָא הוּא, שֶׁאִם אַתָּה אוֹמֵר כֵּן — בְּמוּקְדָּשִׁין יִקְדַּשׁ. וּמְנָלַן דְּלָא קָדֵשׁ — דְּת"ר: *ᶜהַנִּרְבָּע, וְהַמּוּקְצֶה, וְהַנֶּעֱבָד, וְהָאֶתְנָן, וּמְחִיר, וְטוּמְטוּם, וְאַנְדְּרוֹגִינוֹס מְטַמְּאִין בְּגָדִים אַבֵּית הַבְּלִיעָה. רַבִּי אֱלִיעֶזֶר אוֹמֵר: טוּמְטוּם וְאַנְדְּרוֹגִינוֹס אֵין מְטַמְּאִין בְּגָדִים אַבֵּית הַבְּלִיעָה. שֶׁהָיָה ר"א אוֹמֵר: כָּל מָקוֹם שֶׁנֶּאֱמַר זָכָר וּנְקֵבָה — ᵈאַתָּה מוֹצִיא טוּמְטוּם וְאַנְדְּרוֹגִינוֹס מִבֵּינֵיהֶם, וְעוֹף, הוֹאִיל וְלֹא נֶאֱמַר בּוֹ זָכָר וּנְקֵבָה — אִי אַתָּה מוֹצִיא טוּמְטוּם וְאַנְדְּרוֹגִינוֹס מִבֵּינֵיהֶם.§ אר"נ בַּר יִצְחָק: אַף אֲנַן נַמִי תְּנֵינָא, *רַבִּי אֱלִיעֶזֶר אוֹמֵר:

הַכִּלְאַיִם

אָמְרִי בֵּי רַב. דַּאֲמוּר לְעֵיל: הֲלָכָה כְּר' יוֹסֵי בְּאַנְדְּרוֹגִינוֹס וּבְהַרְכָּבָה, דְּקָמִיבָּעֲיָא לוֹ אַלִּיבַּיְיהוּ: קִידּוּשׁ מַאי? מַנּוּ רַב הוּנָא. בְּפ"ק דְּסַנְהֶדְרִין (דף יז:). וְרַב הוּנָא הָא קָאָמַר אֵין הֲלָכָה. אע"ג דְּמַשְׁנֵינַן הָתָם: "אָמְרִי בֵּי רַב" — רַב הַמְנוּנָא, הַיְינוּ הֵיכָא דְּאָמַר רַב הוּנָא דְּאָמְרִי בֵּי רַב, דְּמוֹכְחָא מִילְּתָא דְּאַחֲרִינָא קָאָמַר, אֲבָל הֵיכָא דְּאִיתְּמַר סְתָמָא — וַדַּאי הָוֵי רַב הוּנָא. **טוּמְטוּם** דְּבִירִי. שֶׁהָיָה בְּאוֹתוֹ מָקוֹם, וְאוֹלֵיד ז' בָּנִים, אַלְמָא לָאו סָרִיס הוּא. מֵאַיִן הֵם. אִשְׁתּוֹ זִינְּתָה. **אַטּוּ** כָּל דְּמִקְּרַע זָכָר מִשְׁתַּכַּח. דְּלָא מְסַפְּקָא לֵיהּ לְרַבִּי יוֹסֵי בְּרַבִּי יְהוּדָה בִּנְקֵבָה, אֶלָּא לְסָרִיס הוּא דְּחָיֵישׁ. וְדִינוֹ כְּסָרִיס, דְּלָא חוֹלֵץ וְלֹא מְיַיבֵּם: ה"ק שֶׁמָּא יִקָּרַע וְיִמָּצֵא נְקֵבָה, וַאֲפִילּוּ נִמְצָא זָכָר — שֶׁמָּא יִמָּצֵא סָרִיס חַמָּה. **מַאי** בֵּינַיְיהוּ. מַאי אִיכָּא בֵּין ר' יוֹסֵי בְּרַבִּי יְהוּדָה לַאֲבוּהּ? לִפְסוֹל בִּמְקוֹם אַחִין. אִם יֵשׁ אַחִין שְׁלֵימִים עִמּוֹ וְחָלַץ לָהּ טוּמְטוּם, לְרַבִּי יְהוּדָה דְּאָמַר שֶׁהוּא כְּסָרִיס — מַחֲזִיק לֵיהּ בְּסָרִיס וַדַּאי, וְלֹא פְּסָלָהּ עַל הָאַחִין, וּמִתְיַיבֶּמֶת. וּלְר' יוֹסֵי שֶׁמָּא קָתָנֵי, סְפֵיקָא הוּא וּפְסָלָהּ עַל הָאַחִין, דִּלְמָא לָאו סָרִיס הֲוָה וַחֲלִיצָה הִיא. וְלַחֲלוֹץ שֶׁלֹּא בִּמְקוֹם אַחִין. אִם אֵין שָׁם אָח אֶלָּא הוּא, לְרַבִּי יְהוּדָה לָא בָּעֲיָא חֲלִיצָה מִינֵּיהּ, לְרַבִּי יוֹסֵי בְּרַבִּי יְהוּדָה בָּעֲיָא חֲלִיצָה מִסָּפֵק. זֶה אַנְדְּרוֹגִינוֹס. וְעַל שְׁנֵי מִשְׁכָּבוֹת הִזְהִיר הַכָּתוּב. וְאֶת זָכָר כְּתִיב. וְה"ק: אֶת זַכְרוּתוֹ שֶׁל מִי שֶׁיֵּשׁ בּוֹ שְׁנֵי מִשְׁכָּבוֹת לֹא תִּשְׁכַּב. וְרַבָּנַן זָכָר גְּרֵידָא מְנָא לְהוּ. בִּשְׁלָמָא לְר' סִימַאי "וְאֶת זָכָר" — כָּל זְכָרִים בְּמַשְׁמַע, "מִשְׁכְּבֵי" — לְרַבּוֹת מִשְׁכַּב שֵׁנִי שֶׁל אַנְדְּרוֹגִינוֹס. אֶלָּא לְרַבָּנַן, דְּמִיבָּעֵי לְהוּ "זָכָר" לְמַעוּטֵי נַקְבוּת דְּאַנְדְּרוֹגִינוֹס, זָכָר גְּרֵידָא מְנָא לְהוּ? שֶׁלֹּא כְּדַרְכָּהּ מְנָא לְהוּ. בֵּין לְמַר בֵּין לְמַר דְּהָוְיָא בֵּיהּ לְעִנְיַן עוֹנְשִׁין שֶׁל עֲרָיוֹת, הוֹאִיל וּמַפְּקֵי לְהַאי "מִשְׁכְּבֵי" לְאַנְדְּרוֹגִינוֹס. בְּמוּקְדָּשִׁים יִקְדַּשׁ. לִיקָּרֵב: הָרוֹבֵעַ ל"ג, שֶׁאֵין לְךָ עוֹף רוֹבֵעַ אִשָּׁה. הַנִּרְבָּע וְהַמּוּקְצֶה כו'. בִּמְלוּקִין דְּקָדָשִׁים קָמַיְירֵי. מְטַמְּאִין בְּגָדִים כו'. כְּדִין נִבְלַת עוֹף טָהוֹר. דְּכֵיוָן דְּאֵין רְאוּיִין לְהַקְרָבָה, כִּדְתַנְיָא: "מִן הַבְּהֵמָה" — לְהוֹצִיא רוֹבֵעַ וְנִרְבָּע כו', בִּתְמוּרָה בְּפֶ' בַּתְרָא (דף כח.) וּמְלִיקָתוֹ נְבֵלָה. מוּקְצֶה. שֶׁהִקְצָהוּ וְיִחֲדוּ לְתִקְרוֹבֶת עֲבוֹדָה זָרָה. נֶעֱבָד. שֶׁהִשְׁתַּחֲוָה לוֹ וַעֲשָׂאוֹ עֲבוֹדָה זָרָה: נִבְלַת עוֹף טָהוֹר אֵין לָהּ טוּמְאָה אֶלָּא בְּבֵית הַבְּלִיעָה, כְּדִכְתִיב (ויקרא כב) "לֹא יֹאכַל לְטָמְאָה בָהּ". אַתָּה מוֹצִיא טוּמְטוּם וְאַנְדְּרוֹגִינוֹס מִבֵּינֵיהֶן. כִּדְדָרְשִׁינַן (נדה דף כח:): זָכָר וַדַּאי, נְקֵבָה וַדָּאִית, וְלֹא טוּמְטוּם וְאַנְדְּרוֹגִינוֹס. אַלְמָא לְרַבִּי אֱלִיעֶזֶר לָא קָדְשֵׁי.

אין אדם אוסר דבר שאין שלו. וא"ת: ומ"ש מנותן נבלה או חלב בתבשיל של חברו שנאסר? ואר"י: דבדבר התלוי במחשבה הוא דאמר הכי, כגון משתחוה לבהמת חברו דספ"ב דחולין (דף מ. ושם), דאפי' עשה בה מעשה כגון ששחטה איכא למ"ד דלא אסרה. ואיסור כלאים נמי תלוי במחשבה, כדאמר במס' כלאים (פ"ה מ"ו), גבי הרואה ירק, כשהגיע אלקטנו, אפילו הוסיף מאתים מותר, לכשאחזור אלקטנו – אסור א). ומטעם זה מפרש ר"ת דנקט ב"הגוזל" (ב"ק דף ק: ושם): נתייאש הימנה ולא גדרה, דוקא נתייאש, אבל לא נתייאש, שהיה עוסק בגדר ולא הספיק לגדור עד שהוסיף מאתים – לא קידש. **אמרי** בי רב מנו רב הונא. פירש בקונטרס: אע"ג דמשנינן בספ"ק דסנהדרין (דף יז: ושם) אמרי בי רב – רב המנונא, היינו היכא דאמר רב הונא אמרי בי רב, דמוכחא מילתא דלאו רב הונא הוא. אבל סתמא הוא רב הונא. אע"ג דרב המנונא תלמיד חבר דרב חסדא הוה, ורב חסדא תלמיד חבר דרב הונא, כדמוכח בריש "הדר" (עירובין דף סג: ושם), ולא יתכן שיאמר רב הונא משמיה דרב המנונא, שהיה תלמידו – ע"כ תרי רב המנונא הוו. דאשכחן רב המנונא שהיה תלמיד של רב, כדאמר ב"הגוזל קמא" (ב"ק דף קו.): מכדי רב המנונא תלמידיה דרב הוה. ובפ' "חלון" (עירובין עו:) גבי סולם המצרי: לא שמיע לך הא דאמר רב אחא בר אדא אמר רב המנונא אמר רב. וב"כיצד מעברין" (שם דף נד.) א"ל רב לרב המנונא: ברי, מדאית לך אוטיב לך. וקשה לר"ת על פירוש הקונטרס: דאם כן, כי פריך התם אמאי דאמר שלחו מתם – רבי יוסי בר חנינא, מחכו עלה במערבא – ר' אלעזר. והא שלחו מתם לדברי רבי יוסי בר חנינא! ומשני: אלא איפוך. מאי דוחקיה לאפוכי תרוייהו? לימא: היכא דמוכח – הוי רבי אלעזר, אבל סתמא – הוי רבי יוסי בר חנינא, ולעולם מחכו עלה רבי אלעזר! ועוד: דכיון דקאמר התם אלא רב המנונא – משמע דהדר ביה לגמרי. דה"ל למימר: היכא דמוכחא שאני! ורבינו תם מפרש: אלא רב המנונא, פי': בכל מקום שתמצא(ג) רב הונא אמרי בי רב, לא תימא רב הונא, אלא אימא: אמר רב המנונא אמרי בי רב. והא דאשכחן בפרק "ארבע מיתות" (סנהדרין דף נז.) דפליגי אמרי בי רב ארב הונא ורב יהודה וכולהו תלמידי דרב – דלמא הא דידיה והא דרביה. וק"ק: דבפ' "המזבח מקדש" (זבחים פז.) אמר: אמרי בי רב מ"ט דרב חסדא, ורב הונא רבו של רב חסדא היה, ותימה הוא שבא לפרש את דבריו*). **שמא** יקרע ונמצא נקבה. פי' ר"ח, וכן גרס בבכורות בפרק "על אלו מומין" (דף מב:): שמא יקרע וימצא נקבה, ואם ימצא זכר – שמא ימצא סריס. ותימה לר"י: מנא ליה הא? דלמא ה"ק: שמא ימצא נקבה, ואם ימצא זכר – ודאי ימצא סריס, כרבי יהודה דמתני'! וי"ל: דהא לא מצינא למימר, דא"כ מאי נפקא מינה במאי דקאמר בין כך ובין כך אין ראוי כלל ליבם, וה"ל למימר: טומטום הרי הוא כסריס. **לא** לכל אמר רבי אליעזר אנדרוגינוס זכר הוא שאם אתה אומר כן במוקדשים יקדש. שאל הר' שמואל בחור מר"י: דבפרק "מי שמת" (ב"ב דף קמ:) קאמר רבא: לעולם דוחין אותו, ויש לו. וסיפא רשב"ג היא, דתניא: ילדה טומטום ואנדרוגינוס, רשב"ג אומר: אין קדושה חלה עליהן. היכי מדמי קדשים לשאר דוכתי? דלמא בעלמא סבר דספיקא הוא, אבל קדשים בעינן שלא יהא בו ספיקא, כדקאמר רבי אליעזר הכא, וזכר מפורסם ונקבה מפורסמת – למעוטי טומטום! והשיב ר"י: דגרס התם דתנן, כדגריס רבינו שמואל. ומייתי ראיה דבריה(ד) הוי, דאי ספיקא הוי – ליקדוש קדושת פה, אע"פ שנתמעט מהקרבה, דלא יהא אלא דיקלא בעלמא. אלא ודאי לא הוי לא זכר ולא נקבה, ולכך לא חלה עליו קדושת פה, שאמר: אם זכר – עולה, אם נקבה – של זבחי שלמים. ול"ג דתניא, כמו שגורס הר"א בן מאגש, ואומר דתניא גבי בכור. דלא היה לו לרבא להניח המשנה ולהביא הברייתא שאין להוכיח ממנה. ואין להאריך ב).

מטמאין בגדים אבית הבליעה. טריפה לא חשיב הכא, דפליגי בה ר"מ ורבי יהודה ורבי יוסי בזבחים בפרק "חטאת העוף" (דף סט:) במולק ונמצא טרפה אם היא מטמאה בגדים. והתם נמי מפרש דכל שפסולו בקדש – אין מטמא בגדים:

רבי אליעזר אומר טומטום ואנדרוגינוס אין מטמאין בגדים. מצי למימר דה"ה דכשרים להקרבה, כדקאמר: דאין אתה יכול להוציא טומטום ואנדרוגינוס מביניהם. אלא איידי דנקט ת"ק מטמאין – נקט נמי איהו אין מטמאין. או שמא מדרבנן אסורים להקרבה.

לא

*) [ובזבחים פז. כתבו ישוב נכון]

תוספות ישנים

א) שוי"ל דשאני כלאים דכתיב בהו שקך לא תזרע כלאים א) דמשמע דבעינן שיהא שלו: **הנרבע.** ולא גרסינן הרובע דבעוף איירינן שמטמא בגדים אבית הבליעה ובעוף לא שייך רובע: **שהיה** ר' אליעזר אומר כל מקום שנאמר זכר ונקבה אתה מוציא טומטום ואנדרוגינוס מביניהם פירוש כל מקום דאיכא תרי זכר ממעטינן אנדרוגינוס מיתור דזכר וזה אתה מוציא פירוש אתה ממעט ועוף הואיל ולא נאמר בו זכר ונקבה אי אתה מוציא טומטום ואנדרוגינוס מביניהם וה"ה נמי אם נאמר בו זכר ולא יהא מיותר. ורבנן דפליגי עליה וממעטי עוף טומטום ואנדרוגינוס ואע"ג דלא כתיב גבי קרבן עוף לא זכר ולא נקבה אלמא סבירא להו דטומטום ואנדרוגינוס בריות נינהו דאי ספיקא נינהו ליקרוב שלא הקפיד הכתוב בין זכר ונקבה: **ב)** ועוד נראה לפרש התם פירוש אחר דלעולם לא נפרש כרשב"ם דפי' דס"ל לרשב"ג שהוא בריה אלא ה"ק וסיפא דקאמר טומטום אינו נוטל כלום כרשב"ג דאמר אין קדושה חלה עליו ואע"ג דהוי או זכר או נקבה ואפ"ה לא קדשי אלמא אמרינן לדעת המקדיש כן הוא לאמר אם ילדה הבהמה זכר רוצה לומר זכר ודאי אם ילדה נקבה נקבה ודאית ה"נ אם ילדה זכר יטול מנה זכר מבורר קאמר ונקבה מבוררת קאמר אבל לעולם סבר שפיר רשב"ג דספיקא הוא אבל ודאי זכר לא הוי מדקאמר דאין קדושה חלה עליו משמע שום קדושה (אלא קודשין) [אין בו] דאע"ג דשאר בעלי מומין קודשין לאסור בגיזה ועבודה אף לאחר שנפדו כדאמרינן תזבח ולא גיזה וכו' מ"מ הני כדיקלא בעלמא נינהו ולא חלה עלייהו קדושה כלל:

א) ואף דהך קרא גבי כלאי זרעים כתיב מ"מ לר' יאשיה גם בכלאי הכרם אינו חייב רק עד שיהי' בו כלאי זרעים ועי' בירושלמי פ"ז דכלאים ה"ג ול"ע.

גליון הש"ס

גמ' אמר רב יהודה אמר רב אנדרוגינוס חייבין עליו סקילה. בתוספות בדף זה ע"א ד"ה הלכה כר"י וכן בראשונים הגי' כאן אמר רב הונא אמר רב: **שם** לא לכל אמר ר' אליעזר אנדרוגינוס. עי' נדה כח ע"ב תד"ה אמר עולא:

מסורת הש"ס

[סנהדרין יז:]
[תוס' פי"א בכורות מב:]
[תוספתא פ"י]
ס"א מואת
[בכורות מב. ע"ש זבחים פה:]
בכורות שם תמורה יא

הגהות הב"ח

(א) גמ' ונמצא נקבה ואם: (ב) שם ורבנן זכר גרידא מנ"ל מואת אשה שלא כדרכה מנ"ל מאשה: (ג) תד"ה אמרי בי רב וכו' אמר רב הונא אמרי כו': (ד) ד"ה לא כו' ומייתי ראייה דבריה בפני עצמה היא דאי כו':

הכלאים וטרפה, ויוצא דופן, טומטום ואנדרוגינוס — לא קדושין ולא מקדשין. ואמר שמואל: לא [א]קדושין — בתמורה, ולא מקדשין — בעושה תמורה, ש"מ.§ "ר' אליעזר אומר: חייבין עליו סקילה כזכר".§ תניא, א"ר: כשהלכתי ללמוד תורה אצל ר' אלעזר בן שמוע, חברו עלי תלמידיו כתרנגולים של בית בוקיא, ולא הניחוני ללמוד אלא דבר אחד במשנתינו: רבי אליעזר אומר: אנדרוגינוס חייבין עליו סקילה כזכר.§

הדרן עלך הערל

*יש מותרות לבעליהן ואסורות ליבמיהן, מותרות ליבמיהן ואסורות לבעליהן, מותרות לאלו ולאלו, ואסורות לאלו ולאלו. ואלו מותרות לבעליהן ואסורות ליבמיהן: כהן הדיוט שנשא את האלמנה ויש לו אח כ"ג; חלל שנשא כשרה ויש לו אח כשר; ישראל שנשא בת ישראל ויש לו אח ממזר; ממזר שנשא ממזרת ויש לו אח ישראל — מותרות לבעליהן ואסורות ליבמיהן. ואלו מותרות ליבמיהן ואסורות לבעליהן: כ"ג שקידש את האלמנה ויש לו אח כהן הדיוט; כשר שנשא חללה ויש לו אח חלל; ישראל שנשא ממזרת ויש לו אח ממזר; ממזר שנשא בת ישראל ויש לו אח ישראל — מותרות ליבמיהן ואסורות לבעליהן. ואלו אסורות לאלו ולאלו: כהן גדול שנשא את האלמנה ויש לו אח כהן גדול או כהן הדיוט; כשר שנשא חללה ויש לו אח כשר; ישראל שנשא ממזרת ויש לו אח ישראל; ממזר שנשא בת ישראל ויש לו אח ממזר — אסורות לאלו ולאלו. ושאר כל הנשים מותרות לבעליהן וליבמיהן. שניות מד"ס: שנייה לבעל ולא שנייה ליבם — [ב]אסורה לבעל ומותרת ליבם. שנייה ליבם ולא שנייה לבעל — אסורה ליבם ומותרת לבעל. שנייה לזה ולזה — אסורה לזה ולזה. [ג]אין לה לא כתובה, ולא פירות, ולא מזונות, ולא בלאות, והולד כשר, [ד]וכופין אותו להוציא. *[ה]אלמנה לכ"ג, גרושה וחלוצה לכהן הדיוט, ממזרת ונתינה לישראל, בת ישראל לנתין ולממזר — יש להן כתובה.§ **גמ'** מאי איריא דתני נשא, ליתני קידש! וכ"ת: טעמא דנשא, דהוה ליה עשה ולא תעשה, אבל קידש אתי עשה ודוחה לא תעשה — והא כולה פירקין עשה ולא תעשה הוא, ולא אתי עשה ודחי לא תעשה! משום דקבעי למיתני סיפא: "כ"ג שנשא את האלמנה" דוקא נשא — דשוייה חללה, אבל קידש — שריא ליה, תנא נמי רישא "נשא". ואדתני משום סיפא — ליתני משום מציעתא: "כ"ג שקידש את האלמנה ויש לו אח כהן הדיוט"! אלא משום בת בוקתא. דקבעי למיתני: "חלל שנשא כשרה", טעמא — דנשא, דשוייה חללה. אבל קידש — שריא ליה, משום הכי קתני "נשא". ומאי איריא דקתני "אלמנה", ליתני "בתולה"! וכי

רש"י

כלאים. פסול להקרבה, דכתיב (ויקרא כב) "שור או כשב" – פרט לכלאים, "כי יולד" – פרט ליוצא דופן. והני חמשה יליף ר' אליעזר מקראי בתמורה בפ' "יש בקרבנות" דלא חייל קדושה עליהן. ואע"ג דשאר פסולי הקרבה, כגון רובע ונרבע מוקצה ונעבד ואתנן ומחיר חיילא עלייהו קדושת הגוף, וצריכין מום קבוע ליפדות עליו, ולאחר פדיון אסורין בגיזה ועבודה – הני לא חיילי עלייהו אלא קדושת דמים, כדיקלא בעלמא, ונפדין בלא מום, ומותרין בגיזה ועבודה לאחר פדיונן. לא קדושין בתמורה. לא מיבעיא תחלת הקדש דלא קדשי, דאפי' בעל מום שקדם מומו להקדשו לא נחתא ליה קדושת הגוף, כדאמר בבכורות בפ"ב (דף יד.), אלא אפילו אם המיר קודש בהן – הני לא מקדשי, דאילו בעל מום חיילא עליה קדושת הגוף ליאסר בגיזה ועבודה אף משיפדה, דכתיב (ויקרא כז) "טוב ברע אם המר ימירנו", אפילו הכי אהני לא חיילא ואין מקדש לעשות תמורה, אם הם קדושים והמיר חולין בהם – אינן עושין תמורה. והתם מותבינן במסכת תמורה: וכי מאחר שאין קדושין היאך מקדישין? אי אתה מוצא אלא במקדיש בהמה ואח"כ נטרפה, במקדיש ולד ויצא דרך דופן. אבל כלאים וטומטום ואנדרוגינוס שנפסלו משעת יצירתם – אי אתה מוצא שיקדיש אלא בולדות קדשים, שהיתה אמן קדושה, ומה תקנתם – ירעו ויסתאבו ויפדם ויאכלם, והטריפה תקבר. של בית בוקיא. בקיאים וחריפים, ואין מניחין תרנגול נכרי ביניהם.

[נדרים ב:]

הדרן עלך הערל

יש מותרות. כהן הדיוט שנשא את האלמנה. ה"ה לבתולה, דכשמת נעשית אלמנה, ואסורה לכ"ג אחיו. ובגמרא פריך: ליתני בתולה. אח כשר. כהן, אסור לייבמה, שנתחללה בביאת חלל, כדילפינן מ"ובת כהן כי תהיה לאיש זר" בפ' "אלמנה" (לעיל סח.), וחלל מותר בכשרה. שקידש. אבל נשא – נתחללה בביאתו, ואסורה ליבמה הדיוט. שנייה לבעל ולא שנייה ליבם. אם אמו של בעל ולא של יבם, כגון שהיה אחיו מן האב ולא מן האם. ולא פירות. אין משלם לה פירות נכסי מלוג שאכל משלה. ואף על גב דקי"ל בכתובות (דף מז:) תקנו פרקונה תחת פירות נכסי מלוג שהוא אוכל, כדתנן (שם דף נא.): לא כתב לה "דאם תשתבאי אפרקינך" – חייב לפדותה, שהוא תנאי ב"ד, וזו אין חייב לפדותה, דלא קרינן ביה "ואותביניך לאנתו" – אפי' הכי לא ישלם לה פירות שאכל משלה, כדמפרש בגמ' (לקמן דף פט.): תנאי כתובה ככתובה דמי. וכי היכי דקנסוה רבנן דלא גביא מיניה כתובת נכסי צאן ברזל שהכניסה לו משלה בתורת כתובה – קנסוה נמי דלא תגבה מיניה פירות שאכל בתנאי כתובה של פירקונה, שהוא תנאי ב"ד שאין כתוב בשטר כתובה. ולא מזונות. לא מיבעיא היכא דיתבה תותיה דלא קיימינן ליה לזונה, דהא ב"עמוד והוצא" קאי, אלא אפילו אם הלך למדינת הים, ולותה ואכלה – לא משלם. וא"ת: ה"ה לכשרה, דהא קי"ל (בכתובות דף קז.) כמ"ד הניח מעותיו על קרן הצבי – לאו מילתא היא ולא דמי: התם קתני (שם דף קז:) מי שהלך למדינת הים ועמד אחד ופרנס אשתו, שלא הלוה לה כלום אלא בשביל בעלה פרנסה, דהתם מאחן תבע? היא לא לותה, הוא לא בקש הימנו – הילכך מלוה הוא דאבד. אבל היכא דהלוה לה בתורת הלואה – הוא תובעה, והיא תובעת את בעלה, ומשלם, כדאמר לקמן בגמרא, ושמא תתאלמן או תתגרש ותשלם משלה, דתנן (ב"ק דף פז.): נתגרשה האשה, נשתחרר העבד – חייבין לשלם. ולא בלאות. אם עדיין יש לה בלאות ושחקים מן בגדים שהכניסה לו – אינה נוטלתן כשיוצאה, דקנסוה רבנן. אלמנה לכ"ג כו'. מפרש בגמרא טעמא. **גמ'** מאי איריא דתני נשא. הגה"ה(א) אלמנה קאי. ליתני קידש. דהא נמי מותרת לבעלה ואסורה ליבמה. דהוה ליה עשה. "בתולה מעמיו יקח" (ויקרא כא) ולא בעולה. ולא תעשה "אלמנה לא יקח" (שם). ואין עשה דיבום דוחה את לא תעשה ועשה. אבל קידש הדיוט בתולה אלמנה מן האירוסין, ומת גם הוא באירוסין – מייבם לה כ"ג, דאתי עשה ודחי לא תעשה דאלמנה. והא כוליה פירקין. עשה דיבום ולא תעשה דאיסור הוא דרמו אהדדי, ולא אתי עשה דיבום ודחי ללאו דאיסור, כגון ממזרת לישראל, או ממזר לישראלית, וכן חללה לכהן, ומ"ט – דהא נפקא לן בפ"ב (לעיל כ.) מ"ועלתה יבמתו השערה". אבל קידש שריא ליה. ליבם הדיוט. ואדתני. נשא משום סיפא דמתני', ניתני קידש משום מליעתא, דקתני: כ"ג שקידש, דלא מצי למיתני נשא: ה"ג. אלא משום בת בוקתא. הא דתני נשא ברישא דפרקין משום בת בוקתא, כלומר: השנויה בגלה, חלל שנשא כשרה כו'. ליתני בתולה. וכשמת נעשית אלמנה. נישואין

תוספות

לא קדושין כו'. והא דלא חשיב נרבע ומוקצה ואתנן ומחיר – משום דהנהו קדושין ומקדישין, כדמוכח בתוספתא (דתמורה פ"ד).

רבי אליעזר גר' *במשנתינו, וכן בההיא דאין מטמא בגדים, (ב)וההיא דלא קדושין ולא מקדישין בבכורות (דף מג.) ובתמורה (דף יא.):

הדרן עלך הערל

יש מותרות. פי' הר"ר יהודה בר' י"ט: דכן דרך התנא, לאחר שפי' הלכות המסכתא חוזר ושונה אותם בלשון קצר, כדי שיהיו מסודרים בידך ושמורים בפה ובלב. ועוד אמר ר"י: דנקטינהו לכולהו משום בבא דאסורות לבעליהן ומותרות ליבמיהן. דאע"ג דמכה בעל (דמית קמייבם) – לא אסרי לה אינם, אע"ג דאסורות לבעליהן. מאי איריא דתני נשא כו'. בשאר מקומות אין דרך הש"ס לדקדק בזה, דבפרק "ד' אחין" (לעיל כו.) שונה בכמה מקומות נשואין שתי אחיות, והכא דייק משום דבמליעתא קידש קתני. והא כוליה פירקין לא תעשה הוא. פי' בקונטרס: כגון ממזרת לישראל וחללה לכהן. ואין נראה, דבחללה נמי איכא(ג) עשה ד"קדושים יהיו"! אלא אאיסור ממזרות קאי שנזכר בכמה בבות. ולא אתי עשה ודחי לא תעשה. אף על גב דלאו דאלמנה אינו שוה בכל, וגרע טפי – מ"מ מייתי ראיה, כיון דגזרינן ביאה ראשונה אטו ביאה שנייה בלאו השוה בכל – ה"ה דגזרינן אפי' שאינו שוה בכל. וכי

עין משפט נר מצוה

קמב א מיי' פ"א מהל' תמורה הלכה יז:

ע' תוי"ט

א ב מיי' פ"ו מהלכות יבום הלכה יג סמג עשין נא נב טוש"ע אה"ע סימן קעד סעיף ב:

ב ג מיי' פכ"ד מהלכות אישות הלכה ב סמג עשין מח טוש"ע שם סי' קטז סעיף ד:

ג ד מיי' שם סמג עשין שם טוש"ע שם סי' קנד סעיף כ:

ד ה מיי' שם הלכה ז סמג שם טוש"ע שם סי' קטז סעי' א ועי' בכ"מ:

ס"א רמיין קמי יבם:

תוספות ישנים

לא קדושין בתמורה לא מיבעיא תחלת הקדש דלא קדשה אלא אפי' סוף הקדש כגון תמורה לא מתפסא בקדושת תמורה ואע"ג דבעלי מומין נתפסין בתמורה כדכתיב טוב ברע או רע בטוב דר"ל בעלי מומין בתמימין מ"מ א) איכא התם קרא בהני דלא חלה עלייהו קדושה כלל: ולא מקדישין והתם קאמר וכי מאחר שאין קדושין היאך מקדישין ומשני טריפה המקדיש בהמ' ואח"כ נטרפה הקדיש ולד ויצא דרך דופן וטומטום ואנדרוגינוס משכחת לה בולדות קדשים וכמ"ד ולדות קדשים במעי אמן הן קדושים ומכלהו נמי נוכל ליישב כן דמיירי שהם ולדות קדושים ואח"כ נולד בהם הפסול וקדושים כדפריסית דולדות קדשים במעי אמן הם קדושים כנ"ל:

א) אולי צ"ל מ"מ התם איכא קרא אבל בהני לא חלה וכו'

כתובות ק: לקמן פה.

תוספות חד מקמאי

כתב הרב אלפס דאלמנה לכ"ג גרושה וחלוצה לכהן הדיוט כשלא הכיר בה אין לה כתובה אבל תוספת יש לה ומסיק דתום' נמי אין לה דכי אקני לה אדעתא למיקם קמיה אדעתא דלמשקל ולמפק לא אקני לה. ויש לתת טעם לדברי הרב מהא דאמרינן בפרק אע"פ הל' כר' אליעזר בן עזריה שלא כתב לה [אלא] על מנת לכונסה ומבעיא לן התם חיבת חופה קונה או חיבת ביאה קונה. אלמא תום' משום חיבת ביאה או משום חיבת חופה הראויה לביאה כתב לה הלכך אפי' בשלא הכיר בה משום חיבת ביאה אקני לה אבל כתובה משום תקנה היא באלמנה לכ"ג לא תקינו ואיהו נמי לא כתב לה כתובה אלא אדעתא דתקנתא דתקינו רבנן כתובה אדעתא דנשואי היתר ולאו אדעתא דנשואי איסור כיון דקי"ל (לקמן פ"ה ע"ב) הלכה כר' מחבירו הלכך טעמא דאלמנה לכ"ג [יש לה כתובה] משום דדברי תורה אינם צריכים חזוק. ש"מ דה"ה לממזרת ונתינה לישראל ומחזיר גרושתו משנשאת וספק סוטה וסוטה ודאית כולן יש להן כתובה כשהכיר בה ואע"ג דקי"ל דאשה שזנתה תחת בעלה אין לה כתובה ה"מ כשאין רוצה לקיימה אחרי שידע שזנתה אבל זה שידע שזנתה וקיימה א"נ כשהחזירה אחר שגירשה יש לה כתובה אליבא דר' ואליבא דרשב"א לית לה כתובה מפני שהיא מרגילתו דהא לא פסיל לה דהא לתרומה ולכהונה הא אפסלה לה בזנות והלכה כר': מתני'

הגהות הב"ח

(א) רש"י ד"ה מאי איריא כו'. אנשא דרישא קאי ותיבת אלמנה נמחק: (ב) תום' ד"ה ר"א וכו' דאין מטמא בגדים וכן בההיא לא קדושין: (ג) ד"ה והא כוליה וכו' עשה דקדושים. נ"ב תימה לי דהרי גם בכ"ג איכא עשה זו דקדושים כדלעיל דף כ' וא"כ שפיר מקשה מחללה דאם היה זה עשה א"כ גם בקידש הוה ל"ת ועשה ופריך זה בדרך ממ"נ אלא בודאי דזה נקרא איסור מצוה כדלעיל דף כ' דחזר ממה שאמר דהוה איסור קדושה ולכאורה יש ליישב דדוקא גבי אלמנה לכ"ג חזר הגמ' דאינו גבה עשה דקדושים אבל גבי חללה לכהן הדיוט דזה הפסוק קדושים יהיו לאלהיהם כתיב שם אין ספק דהוה עשה ואחר העיון יראה דזה אינו דהא להדיא אי' בקדושין דף ע"ח כשלא גמר ביאתו נעשית לכ"ג מיד חללה בהערלה ע"ש דהיא משנה מפורשת בהבא על יבמתו דאלמנה לכ"ג נעשי' חללה מיד ממילא בגמר ביאה איכא עשה דקדושים יהיו לכהנים גבי חללה ואיך אפשר לייבם אלמנה הא א"כ נגמור ביאתו הא עובר בעשה דקדושים:

וְכִי תֵּימָא קָסָבַר הַאי תַּנָּא נִישּׂוּאִין הָרִאשׁוֹנִים מַפִּילִין – הֲרֵי חָלָל שֶׁנָּשָׂא כְּשֵׁרָה, וְלָא אָמְרִינַן נִישּׂוּאִין הָרִאשׁוֹנִים מַפִּילִין! הָא וַדַּאי מִשּׁוּם סֵיפָא, מִשּׁוּם דְּקָבָעֵי לְמִיתְנָא סֵיפָא "כ"ג שֶׁנָּשָׂא אֶת הָאַלְמָנָה וְיֵשׁ לוֹ אָח כ"ג אוֹ כֹּהֵן הֶדְיוֹט", דַּוְקָא אַלְמָנָה, אֲבָל בְּתוּלָה חַזְיָא לֵיהּ, מִשּׁוּם הָכִי קָתָנֵי "אַלְמָנָה". מַתְקִיף לָהּ רַב פַּפָּא: אִם אִיתָא לְהָא דְּכִי אֲתָא רַב דִּימִי אֲמַר ר' יוֹחָנָן: *מִצְרִי שֵׁנִי שֶׁנָּשָׂא מִצְרִית רִאשׁוֹנָה – בְּנָהּ שֵׁנִי הָוֵי, לִתְנֵי נַמִי: מִצְרִי שֵׁנִי שֶׁנָּשָׂא שְׁתֵּי מִצְרִיּוֹת, אַחַת רִאשׁוֹנָה וְאַחַת שְׁנִיָּה, וְהָיוּ לוֹ בָּנִים מֵרִאשׁוֹנָה (א) וּשְׁנִיָּה, אִי נְסוּב כִּי אוֹרְחַיְיהוּ – מוּתָּרוֹת לְבַעֲלֵיהֶן וַאֲסוּרוֹת לִיבְמֵיהֶן, וְאִי אֵיפּוּךְ וּנְסוּב – מוּתָּרוֹת לִיבְמֵיהֶן וַאֲסוּרוֹת לְבַעֲלֵיהֶן, מוּתָּרוֹת לְאֵלּוּ וּלְאֵלּוּ – גִּיּוֹרוֹת, אֲסוּרוֹת לְאֵלּוּ וּלְאֵלּוּ – אַיְלוֹנִיּוֹת! *תָּנָא וְשִׁיֵּיר. מַאי שִׁיֵּיר דְּהַאי שִׁיֵּיר? שִׁיֵּיר פְּצוּעַ דַּכָּא. אִי מִשּׁוּם פְּצוּעַ דַּכָּא – לָאו שִׁיוּרָא, דְּהָא תָּנָא לֵיהּ חַיָּיבֵי לָאוִין! אַטּוּ חַיָּיבֵי לָאוִין מִי לָא קָתָנֵי וַהֲדַר תָּנֵי? וְהָא קָתָנֵי "כֹּהֵן הֶדְיוֹט שֶׁנָּשָׂא אַלְמָנָה, וְחָלָל שֶׁנָּשָׂא כְּשֵׁרָה"! הַהוּא אִיצְטְרִיכָא לֵיהּ לְאַשְׁמוּעִינַן כְּדְרַב יְהוּדָה אָמַר רַב, *דְּאָמַר רַב יְהוּדָה אָמַר רַב: אלֹא הוּזְהֲרוּ כְּשֵׁרוֹת לְהִנָּשֵׂא לִפְסוּלִין. וְהָא קָתָנֵי "חָלָל שֶׁנָּשָׂא כְּשֵׁרָה, וְיִשְׂרָאֵל שֶׁנָּשָׂא בַּת יִשְׂרָאֵל וְיֵשׁ לוֹ אָח מַמְזֵר"! הָא נַמִי לָא מְהַדַּר מִיתְנָא הִיא, דְּאַשְׁמוּעִינָן לָאו שֶׁאֵין שָׁוֶה בַּכֹּל וְקָמַשְׁמַע לָן לָאו הַשָּׁוֶה בַּכֹּל. הָא קָתָנֵי יִשְׂרָאֵל שֶׁנָּשָׂא מַמְזֶרֶת וְיֵשׁ לוֹ אָח יִשְׂרָאֵל, (וּמַמְזֵר שֶׁנָּשָׂא מַמְזֶרֶת וְיֵשׁ לוֹ אָח יִשְׂרָאֵל!) רש"ל מ"ז אֶלָּא לָאו שְׁמַע מִינָּהּ תָּנָא וְשִׁיֵּיר, ש"מ. § גּוּפָא, אָמַר רַב יְהוּדָה אָמַר רַב: לֹא הוּזְהֲרוּ כְּשֵׁרוֹת לְהִנָּשֵׂא לִפְסוּלִין. לֵימָא מְסַיַּיע לֵיהּ: "חָלָל שֶׁנָּשָׂא כְּשֵׁרָה". מַאי לָאו: כֹּהֶנֶת [הָרְאוּיָה לוֹ], וּמַאי "כְּשֵׁרָה", כְּשֵׁרָה לִכְהוּנָּה? לָא, יִשְׂרְאֵלִית, וּמַאי "כְּשֵׁרָה" – כְּשֵׁרָה לַקָּהָל. אִי הָכִי, יֵשׁ לוֹ אָח כָּשֵׁר נַמִי – כָּשֵׁר לַקָּהָל, מִכְּלָל דְּהוּא פָּסוּל לַקָּהָל?! אֶלָּא לָאו – כֹּהֵן, וּמִדְּהוּא כֹּהֵן – הִיא כֹּהֶנֶת! מִידֵּי אִירְיָא? הָא כִּדְאִיתָא וְהָא כִּדְאִיתָא. מְתִיב רָבִין בַּר נַחְמָן "לֹא יִקָּחוּ" "לֹא יִקָּחוּ" – מְלַמֵּד שֶׁהָאִשָּׁה מוּזְהֶרֶת עַל יְדֵי הָאִישׁ! אָמַר רָבָא: כָּל הֵיכָא דְּהוּא מוּזְהָר – הִיא מוּזְהֶרֶת, וְכָל הֵיכָא דְּהוּא לָא מוּזְהָר – הִיא לָא מִזְדַּהֲרָא. וְהָא מֵהָכָא נָפְקָא: מִדְּרַב יְהוּדָה אָמַר רַב נָפְקָא! דְּאָמַר רַב יְהוּדָה אָמַר רַב, וְכֵן תָּנָא דְּבֵי רַבִּי יִשְׁמָעֵאל: °"אִישׁ אוֹ אִשָּׁה כִּי יַעֲשׂוּ מִכָּל חַטֹּאת הָאָדָם" – *בהִשְׁוָה הַכָּתוּב אִשָּׁה לְאִישׁ לְכָל עוֹנָשִׁין שֶׁבַּתּוֹרָה! אִי מֵהַהִיא הֲוָה אָמִינָא: לָאו הַשָּׁוֶה בַּכֹּל, אֲבָל לָאו שֶׁאֵינוֹ שָׁוֶה בַּכֹּל – לָא.

וַהֲרֵי

רש"י

נִישּׂוּאִין הָרִאשׁוֹנִים. שֶׁנְּשָׂאָהּ אָח שֶׁמֵּת, מַפִּילִין אוֹתָהּ לְיִיבּוּם. וּבָתַר הָהִיא שַׁעְתָּא, אָזְלִינַן וְאִי לָאו אַלְמָנָה מֵאַחֵר הֲוַאי – שָׁרֵינַן לָהּ לְכ"ג יְבָמָהּ. וְהָא תָּנָא חָלָל שֶׁנָּשָׂא כְּשֵׁרָה. וְאָסַר לָהּ לְיַיבּוּמֵי לְאָח כָּשֵׁר. דַּוְקָא אַלְמָנָה. שֶׁנִּתְחַלְּלָה בְּבִיאָתוֹ וְנֶאֶסְרָה לְאָחִיו הַהֶדְיוֹט אֲבָל בְּתוּלָה חַזְיָא לָהּ לְהִתְיַיבֵּם. אִם אִיתָא לְהָא דְּרַב דִּימִי. אִם הֲלָכָה כְּמוֹתוֹ. מֵרִאשׁוֹנָה וּמִשְּׁנִיָּה. דְּהָוֵה לְהוּ דּוֹר שְׁלִישִׁי וְדוֹר שֵׁנִי. נְסִיב כִּי אוֹרְחַיְיהוּ. שְׁלִישִׁי נָשָׂא יִשְׂרְאֵלִית, וְשֵׁנִי מִצְרִית שְׁנִיָּה – אֲסוּרוֹת לִיבָמֵיהֶן. דִּשְׁלִישִׁי יִשְׂרָאֵל הוּא, וְאָסוּר בִּשְׁנִיָּה. דְּמִצְרִי וַאֲדוֹמִי אֶחָד זְכָרִים וְאֶחָד נְקֵבוֹת אֲסוּרִין עַד דּוֹר שְׁלִישִׁי, וְשֵׁנִי אָסוּר בְּיִשְׂרְאֵלִית. אִי אֵיפּוּךְ וּנְסוּב. שֶׁנָּשָׂא שְׁלִישִׁי שְׁנִיָּה, וְשֵׁנִי נָשָׂא יִשְׂרְאֵלִי'. גִּיּוֹרֶת. מוּתֶּרֶת לִשְׁלִישִׁי, דְּיִשְׂרָאֵל הוּא. וְלַשֵּׁנִי – דִּקְהַל גֵּרִים לָא אִיקְּרִי קָהָל, וְלָא קָרֵינַן שְׁלִישִׁי יָבֹא בַּקָּהָל וְלֹא שֵׁנִי – דְּזוֹ לָאו קָהָל הֲוַאי. וְאִם נָשָׂא הָאַחֵר גִּיּוֹרֶת וּמֵת – מוּתֶּרֶת לִיבָמָהּ (ב) כְּבַעֲלָהּ. אֲסוּרוֹת לְאֵלּוּ וְאֵלּוּ אַיְילוֹנִית. יִשְׂרְאֵלִית, אִם שֵׁנִי נָשָׂא יִשְׂרְאֵלִית וְהִיא אַיְילוֹנִית – אֲסוּרָה לוֹ, מִשּׁוּם דְּיִשְׂרְאֵלִית הִיא. וּכְשֶׁמֵּת – אֲסוּרָה לִיבָמָהּ מִשּׁוּם "אֲשֶׁר תֵּלֵד" – פְּרָט לְאַיְילוֹנִית שֶׁאֵינָהּ יוֹלֶדֶת. שִׁיֵּיר פְּצוּעַ דַּכָּא. דַּהֲוָה מָצֵי לְמִיתְנֵי בֵּיהּ כּוּלְּהוּ, (ג) פְּצוּעַ דַּכָּא שֶׁנָּשָׂא יִשְׂרְאֵלִית אֲסוּרָה לְבַעְלָהּ וּמוּתֶּרֶת לִיבָמָהּ כָּשֵׁר, וְהַכָּשֵׁר שֶׁנָּשָׂא כְּשֵׁרָה וְיֵשׁ לוֹ אָח פְּצוּעַ דַּכָּא – אֲסוּרָה לִיבָמָהּ וּמוּתֶּרֶת לְבַעְלָהּ. פְּצוּעַ דַּכָּא שֶׁנָּשָׂא יִשְׂרְאֵלִית וְיֵשׁ לוֹ אָח פְּצוּעַ דַּכָּא – אֲסוּרָה לְבַעְלָהּ וְלַיָּבָם, גִּיּוֹרֶת – מוּתֶּרֶת לָזֶה וְלָזֶה. הַהוּא. דְּחָלָל שֶׁנָּשָׂא כְּשֵׁרָה אִיצְטְרִיךְ לֵיהּ. וּבְכֹהֶנֶת עָסְקִינַן, וְלָאו מִשּׁוּם אֲסוּרָה לִיבָמָהּ אֶלָּא מִשּׁוּם מוּתֶּרֶת לְבַעְלָהּ. וְקָמַשְׁמַע לָן דְּלֹא הוּזְהֲרוּ כְּשֵׁרוֹת וְכֹהֲנוֹת מִלִּינָּשֵׂא לִפְסוּלִין, לַחֲלָלִין שֶׁמּוּתָּרִין בְּיִשְׂרָאֵל. וְאַע"פ שֶׁהַכֹּהֵן הוּזְהַר בַּחֲלָלָה – כֹּהֲנוֹת לֹא הוּזְהֲרוּ בַּחֲלָלִים. מַאי כְּשֵׁרָה כְּשֵׁרָה לִכְהוּנָּה. דְּקַיְימָא לָן: כֹּהֵן, כָּל זְמַן שֶׁמּוּצָא לִישָּׂא בַּת כֹּהֵן – לֹא יִשָּׂא בַּת יִשְׂרָאֵל, דְּאָמַר בִּפְסָחִים: סְעוּדַּת הָרְשׁוּת – בַּת יִשְׂרָאֵל לְכֹהֵן, בְּ"אֵלּוּ עוֹבְרִין" (דף מט.). לֹא יִקָּחוּ. לָמָּה לִי לְמִכְתַּב "לֹא יִקָּחוּ" תְּרֵי זִימְנֵי? לְהַזְהִיר הָאִשָּׁה עַל יְדֵי הָאִישׁ קס"ד. לְהַזְהִיר כְּשֵׁרוֹת שֶׁלֹּא יִנָּשְׂאוּ לַחֲלָלִים. אָמַר רָבָא כָּל הֵיכָא כו'. וְהַאי קְרָא לָאו לְהַזְהִיר כְּשֵׁרוֹת אָתֵי, אֶלָּא (ד) פְּסוּלוֹת שֶׁלֹּא לִינָּשֵׂא לִכְשֵׁרִים. שֶׁכְּשֵׁם שֶׁהַכֹּהֵן מוּזְהָר שֶׁלֹּא לִיקַּח זוֹנָה וַחֲלָלָה, כָּךְ הִיא מוּזְהֶרֶת שֶׁלֹּא תִּשָּׂאֵנוּ. וְכָל הֵיכָא דְּהוּא לֹא מוּזְהָר. כְּגוֹן חָלָל בִּכְשֵׁרָה. עוֹנָשִׁים. לָאו וְכָרֵת. אֲבָל עֲשֵׂה – לָא הָוֵי עוֹנֶשׁ. הִלְכָּךְ, מִצְוַת עֲשֵׂה שֶׁהַזְּמַן גְּרָמָא – נָשִׁים פְּטוּרוֹת. אֲבָל לֹא תַעֲשֶׂה, בֵּין שֶׁהַזְּמַן גְּרָמָא בֵּין שֶׁלֹּא הַזְּמַן גְּרָמָא – נָשִׁים חַיָּיבוֹת. לָאו. דִּכְהוּנָּה אֵינוֹ שָׁוֶה בַּכֹּל, שֶׁאֵין נוֹהֵג בְּיִשְׂרָאֵל. הִילְכָּךְ, אִי לָא אַשְׁמְעִי' "לֹא יִקָּחוּ" – הֲוָה אָזְלִי' לְקוּלָּא, וּמִיפְּטְרוּ נָשִׁים.

וַהֲרֵי

תוספות

וכי תימא קסבר האי תנא דנישואין הראשונים מפילין. תימה: דבכה"ג לא אמרינן בשום דוכתא נישואין מפילין, דלהחמיר הוא דאמר הכי, לאסור כנס ואח"כ גירש, "בפ"ד אחין" (לעיל ל:) אבל להקל לא אשכחן? ועוד: דאפי' לאחר מיתה אמרי' ב"הערל" (לעיל עט:), כשנפלה לו ואח"כ נפצע, דחייל איסור פליעה! וי"ל: דבלאו הכי פריך לה מגופה.

אי נסוב כי אורחייהו מותרות לבעליהן ואסורות ליבמיהן. לא שנשא שני שניה ושלישי שלישית – דא"כ שתיהן מותרות לבעליהן וליבמיהן, דהא קסבר דקהל גרים לא אקרי קהל, כדקאמר מותרות לאלו ולאלו גיורות. אלא בן השנייה שהוא שלישי נשא ישראלית, והיינו כי אורחייהו שהוא מותר בה. ואר"י: דאסורות ליבמיהן לא קאי אתרוייהו, דאשת שני שהיא שנייה מותרת ליבמה, דקהל גרים לא איקרי קהל. ומשום אשת שלישי שהיא ישראלית נקט אסורות ליבמיהן. וכן הא דקאמר אי אפוך מותרות ליבמיהן ואסורות לבעליהן – נמי לא קאי אלא אאשת מצרי שני שנשא ישראלית, ומשום הכי נקט כה"ג אי נסוב כי אורחייהו אי אפוך ונסוב – דלא מצי למינקט כולה מילתא בחד גברא. וקאי מעיקרא אאשת שלישי, ובתר הכי קאי אאשת שני. וא"ת: ואמאי לא נקט דליהוי קאי אתרוייהו, כגון מצרי שני שנשא ישראלית ומצרית ראשונה, דהשתא אחד מהם ישראל גמור ואחד מצרי שני, נסוב כי אורחייהו – שתיהן אסורות ליבמיהן, אפוך ונסוב – אסורות לבעליהן! וי"ל: דבן הישראלית ממצרי שני אין חשוב ישראל לענין קהל, אלא חשיב קהל גרים. וא"ת: אפי' ליתא לדרב דימי, ליתני ישראל שנשא שתי נשים, מצרית ראשונה וישראלית והיו לו בנים משתיהן, דבן מצרית – מצרי שני, ובן ישראלית – ישראל, נסוב כי אורחייהו – אסורות ליבמיהן, אפוך ונסוב – אסורות לבעליהן! וכ"ת דלא תני הכי לפי שנישואי מצרית הוי באיסור – והא קתני ממזר וחלל שנשאו באיסור? א) ואומר ר"י: דלא פריך אלא ממה ששייר דברים של חידוש. דאם איתא לדרב דימי היה לו לכוללה במשנתנו, ולהכי, כי משני שייר פצוע דכא, פריך: הא תנא ליה חייבי לאוין ואין זה חידוש. ולבסוף מסיק דמ"מ שיורא הוא. והא דלא קאמר שייר גרושה זונה ונתינה – משום דלא חשיב להו שיורא, דכיון דתנא חללה הוא הדין גרושה וזונה, ונתינה הוי בכלל ממזרת, דהכל ענין אחד. וא"ת: ומאי מקשה לרב דימי? לימא דלא תני הכי משום דבפלוגתא לא קמיירי, דאיכא למ"ד קהל גרים מיקרי קהל! ועוד: דר' שמעון מתיר הנקבות מיד! ויש לומר: דעדיפא משני. ועוד: דמתני' איירי בפלוגתא, דקסבר קידושין תופסין בחייבי לאוין, דקתני בחייבי לאוין אסורות לבעליהן ומותרות ליבמיהן, משמע דשייך בהו ייבום – אלמא תפסי בהו קידושין. **שייר** פצוע דכא. אפי' נפצע לאחר שנשאה לא מיתסרא בהכי ליבם שאין פצוע דכא, ולא אמרינן במותר לה נאסרה כו' – דלא שייך אלא כשנעשה באשה שום מעשה דנאסרת בכך לבעל, כגון סוטה ומחזיר גרושתו דפ"ק (דף יא:)*. **וקמשמע** לן לאו השוה בכל. משום מותרות ליבמיהן איצטריך לאשמועינן בלאו השוה בכל דאי משום אסורות ליבמיהן כיון דאשמועינן בלאו שאין שוה בכל – כל שכן בלאו השוה בכל.

אלא לאו ש"מ תנא ושייר. וא"ת: והא "אלו" קתני! דהכי פריך בפ"ק דקידושין (דף טז: ושם) גבי "ואלו שמעניקין להן" וגבי "אלו דברים שאין להם שיעור" בשלהי פרקא (שם דף מ.) ואר"י: דהכא לא נקט "אלו" אלא לפרושי הא דקתני ענייניס הרבה ברישא: יש מותרות, יש אסורות, ולהכי לא שייך למפרך. ועוד: דבכל מקום ששונה שני עניינים אלו ואלו, שיש ואלו שאין משייר, אע"ג דתני אלו, כי ההיא ד"אלו נערות שיש להן קנס" (כתובות דף כט.) דשייר מצרי ואדומי ופסול כהונה, וב"מזבח מקדש" (זבחים דף פד.) דתנן: "אלו שפסולן בקדש", ולא חשיב ניתנים למעלה שנתנן למטה כו' בחוץ בפנים, בפנים בחוץ, ופסח וחטאת ששחטן שלא לשמן, דחשיב להו ברייתא (שם)*.

ולותה

עין משפט נר מצוה

ה א מיי' פי"ט מהלכות איסורי ביאה הל' יא סמג לאוין קכא קכב טור ש"ע אה"ע סי' ז סעיף כב וסימן ב סעיף ג:
ו ב מיי' פי"ז שם הל' ה:

תוספות ישנים

א) וי"ל דהא לא קשה מידי דאי ליתא לדרב דימי אין למפרך ליתני כדפרישית דהא לא הוה קמ"ל רבותא [בזה] דפשיטא דהיכא דהאחד ישראל והאחד מצרי הלך אחר פסולו אבל פריך שפיר תלמודא דאם איתא לדרב דימי הו"ל למיתני מצרי שני שנשא שתי מצריות וכו' ולאשמעינן רבותא דהיכא נמי שהאיש והאשה פסולים הלך אחר הפסול יותר דזה לא שמעינן: **ומאי** כשרה כשרה לכהונה. פי' כהנת וקרי לה כשרה משום דמצוה לכהן לישא כהנת כדאמרי' בפרק ואלו עוברין: **לכל** עונשין בלאוין קאמר דבמצות עשה אינן שוין שהרי מצות עשה שהז"ג נשים פטורות:

גליון הש"ס

גמ' כל היכא דהוא מוזהר. עי' חגיגה דף יד ע"ב תוד"ה בסולה ובנדרים בת"י דף ל ע"ב ד"ה חזרו לומר:

מסורת הש"ס

תורה אור

לעיל עח.

סוכה נב. ושם נסמן

[לקמן פה.] קדושין עג. עו.

במדבר ה

ב"ק טו. תמורה ב: קדושין לה. פסחים מג. נדה מח: סוכה כח:

[ע' היטב תוס' סוטה ו. ד"ה אשת כהן]

[וע"ע תוס' כתובות כט. בסוף ד"ה ועל הכותית ותוס' זבחים פד. ד"ה הכן ותוס' שבועות לט. ד"ה ואלו נאמרין ועוד שם בשבועות מד: ד"ה כל הנשבעין ועי' היטב תוס' שבת עה. ד"ה חסר אחת]

הגהות הב"ח

(א) גמ' מראשונה ומשניה: (ב) רש"י ד"ה גיורת וכו' ליבמה כבעלה: (ג) ד"ה שייר וכו' כולהו כמו כן פצוע דכא: (ד) ד"ה אמר רבא וכו' אלא להזהיר פסולות:

וַהֲרֵי טוּמְאָה, דְּלָאו שֶׁאֵין שָׁוֶה בַּכֹּל, וְטַעֲמָא דִּכְתַב רַחֲמָנָא "בְּנֵי אַהֲרֹן" [א]וְלֹא בְּנוֹת אַהֲרֹן, הָא לָאו הָכִי – ה"א: נָשִׁים חַיָּיבוֹת. מַאי טַעֲמָא – לָאו מִשּׁוּם דְּרַב יְהוּדָה אָמַר רַב? לָא, דְּגָמְרִינַן מִ"לֹּא יִקָּחוּ". אִיכָּא דְּאָמְרִי: קִיחָה אִיצְטְרִיכָא לֵיהּ, ס"ד אָמִינָא: לִיגְמַר מִטּוּמְאָה, קָמַשְׁמַע לָן. רַב פַּפָּא וְרַב הוּנָא בְּרֵיהּ דְּרַב יְהוֹשֻׁעַ אִיקְלְעוּ (א) לְהִינְצְבוּ, לְאַתְרֵיהּ דְּרַב אִידִי בַּר אָבִין. בָּעוּ מִינַּיְיהוּ: הוּזְהֲרוּ כְּשֵׁרוֹת לְהִנָּשֵׂא לִפְסוּלִין אוֹ לֹא? אֲמַר לְהוּ רַב פַּפָּא: תְּנֵיתוּהָ, *עֲשָׂרָה יוּחֲסִין עָלוּ מִבָּבֶל: כֹּהֲנִים, לְוִיִּם, וְיִשְׂרְאֵלִים, חֲלָלִים, גֵּרִים, וַחֲרוּרִים, וּמַמְזֵרִים, נְתִינִים, שְׁתוּקֵי, וַאֲסוּפֵי; [ב]כֹּהֲנִים, לְוִיִּם, יִשְׂרְאֵלִים, מוּתָּרִין לָבֹא זֶה בָּזֶה. [ג]לְוִיִּם, יִשְׂרְאֵלִים, חֲלָלִים, גֵּרִים, חֲרוּרִים – מוּתָּרִין לָבֹא זֶה בָּזֶה; גֵּירֵי, חֲרוּרֵי, [ד]וּמַמְזֵרֵי, נְתִינֵי, שְׁתוּקֵי, וַאֲסוּפֵי – מוּתָּרִים לָבֹא זֶה בָּזֶה, וְאִילּוּ כֹּהֲנוֹת לְחָלָל – לָא קָתָנֵי. א"ל רַב הוּנָא בְּרֵיהּ דְּרַב יְהוֹשֻׁעַ: כָּל הֵיכָא דְּהָנֵי נָסְבֵי מֵהָנֵי וְהָנֵי נָסְבֵי מֵהָנֵי – קָתָנֵי. כֹּהֵן, כֵּיוָן דְּאִילּוּ בָּעֵי לְמִינְסַב חֲלָלָה אֲסִירָא לֵיהּ – לָא קָתָנֵי. אָתוּ לְקַמֵּיהּ דְּרַב אִידִי בַּר אָבִין, אֲמַר לְהוּ: דַּרְדְּקֵי, הָכִי *אָמַר רַב יְהוּדָה אָמַר רַב: לֹא הוּזְהֲרוּ כְּשֵׁרוֹת לִינָּשֵׂא לִפְסוּלִים. § "שְׁנִיּוֹת מִדִּבְרֵי סוֹפְרִים וכו'". § בָּעוּ מִינֵּיהּ בְּנֵי בִּירִי מֵרַב שֵׁשֶׁת: שְׁנִיָּה לַבַּעַל וְלֹא שְׁנִיָּה לַיָּבָם, יֵשׁ לָהּ כְּתוּבָּה מִיָּבָם אוֹ לֹא? *כֵּיוָן דְּאָמַר מָר כְּתוּבָּתָהּ *עַל נִכְסֵי בַּעְלָהּ הָרִאשׁוֹן – לֵית לָהּ, אוֹ דִּלְמָא: כֵּיוָן *דְּאִילּוּ לֵית לָהּ מֵרִאשׁוֹן תַּקִּינוּ לָהּ רַבָּנַן מִשֵּׁנִי – אִית לָהּ? אֲמַר לְהוּ רַב שֵׁשֶׁת: תְּנֵיתוּהָ, כְּתוּבָּתָהּ עַל נִכְסֵי בַּעְלָהּ הָרִאשׁוֹן, וְאִם הָיְתָה שְׁנִיָּה לַבַּעַל – אֲפִי' מִיָּבָם אֵין לָהּ. מִכְּלָל דְּאִיכָּא דְּאִית לָהּ מִיָּבָם? חַסּוּרֵי מִיחַסְּרָא וְהָכִי קָתָנֵי: *כְּתוּבָּתָהּ עַל נִכְסֵי בַּעְלָהּ הָרִאשׁוֹן, וְאִי לֵית לָהּ מֵרִאשׁוֹן – תַּקִּינוּ לָהּ מִשֵּׁנִי, [ה]וְאִם הָיְתָה שְׁנִיָּה לַבַּעַל – אֲפִי' מִיָּבָם אֵין לָהּ. § בְּעָא מִינֵּיהּ רַבִּי אֶלְעָזָר מֵרַבִּי יוֹחָנָן: אַלְמָנָה לְכ"ג, גְּרוּשָׁה וַחֲלוּצָה לְכֹהֵן הֶדְיוֹט – יֵשׁ לָהֶן מְזוֹנוֹת אוֹ אֵין לָהֶן מְזוֹנוֹת? הֵיכִי דָּמֵי, אִילֵימָא דְּיָתְבָה תּוּתֵיהּ – בַּ"עֲמוֹד וְהוֹצֵא" קָאֵי, מְזוֹנוֹת אִית לָהּ?! לָא צְרִיכָא שֶׁהָלַךְ הוּא לִמְדִינַת הַיָּם, וְלָוְתָה וְאָכְלָה, מַאי? מְזוֹנֵי תְּנַאי כְּתוּבָּה נִינְהוּ, מִדְּאִית לָהּ כְּתוּבָּה – אִית לָהּ מְזוֹנֵי, אוֹ דִּלְמָא: כְּתוּבָּה דִּלְמִשְׁקַל וּמֵיפַק – אִית לָהּ, מְזוֹנֵי דִּלְמָא תִּיעַכַּב גַּבֵּיהּ – לֵית לָהּ? א"ל: [ו]לֵית לָהּ. וְהָתַנְיָא: יֵשׁ לָהּ! [ז]כִּי תַּנְיָא הַהִיא – לְאַחַר מִיתָה. אִית דְּאָמַר, אֲמַר לֵיהּ: תַּנְיָא יֵשׁ לָהּ. הָא בַּ"עֲמוֹד וְהוֹצֵא" קָאֵי! וְאֶלָּא הָתַנְיָא יֵשׁ לָהּ! כִּי תַּנְיָא הַהִיא – לְאַחַר מִיתָה. ת"ר: *[ח]אַלְמָנָה לְכֹהֵן גָּדוֹל, גְּרוּשָׁה וַחֲלוּצָה לְכֹהֵן הֶדְיוֹט – יֵשׁ לָהּ כְּתוּבָּה, פֵּירוֹת, מְזוֹנוֹת, בְּלָאוֹת, [ט]וְהִיא פְּסוּלָה וּוְלָדָהּ פָּסוּל, [י]וְכוֹפִין אוֹתוֹ לְהוֹצִיא. שְׁנִיּוֹת מִדִּבְרֵי סוֹפְרִים – אֵין לָהּ כְּתוּבָּה, לֹא פֵּירוֹת, לֹא מְזוֹנוֹת וְלֹא בְּלָאוֹת, [כ]וְהִיא כְּשֵׁירָה וּוְלָדָהּ כָּשֵׁר, וְכוֹפִין אוֹתוֹ לְהוֹצִיא. אָמַר ר"ש בֶּן אֶלְעָזָר: מִפְּנֵי מָה אָמְרוּ: אַלְמָנָה לְכ"ג יֵשׁ לָהּ כְּתוּבָּה – מִפְּנֵי שֶׁהוּא פָּסוּל וְהִיא פְּסוּלָה, וְכ"מ שֶׁהוּא פָּסוּל וְהִיא פְּסוּלָה

קָנְסוּ

רש"י

וַהֲרֵי לָאו דְּטוּמְאָה. דְּאֵין שָׁוֶה בַּכֹּל, דְּאֵין יִשְׂרָאֵל מוּזְהָרִין שֶׁלֹּא לִיגַּע, דִּכְתִיב (ויקרא כא) "אֱמוֹר אֶל הַכֹּהֲנִים" – כֹּהֲנִים מוּזְהָרִין וְלֹא יִשְׂרָאֵל. לָאו מִשּׁוּם דְּרַב יְהוּדָה. אַלְמָא אֲפִי' לָאו שֶׁאֵין שָׁוֶה בַּכֹּל נָפְקָא לָן מֵהָתָם דְּנָשִׁים חַיָּיבוֹת. **לָא** דְּגָמְרִי מִ"לֹּא יִקָּחוּ". כְּלוֹמַר, מֵ"אִישׁ אוֹ אִשָּׁה" לָא נָפְקָא לָן אֶלָּא לָאו הַשָּׁוֶה בַּכֹּל, וְהָא דְּאִיצְטְרִיךְ לְמַעוּטֵי וְלֹא בְּנוֹת אַהֲרֹן – מִשּׁוּם דְּאִי לָא מַעֲטִי' הֲוָה גָּמְרִינַן מִ"לֹּא יִקָּחוּ" דִּמְחַיֵּיב לְנָשִׁים אַלָּאו שֶׁאֵין שָׁוֶה בַּכֹּל. **אִיכָּא דְּאָמְרִי** קִיחָה **אִיצְטְרִיךְ** לֵיהּ. לְמִיכְתַּב, דִּבְלָאו שֶׁאֵין שָׁוֶה בַּכֹּל נָשִׁים מוּזְהָרוֹת. וְאַף ע"ג דְּמִדְּרַב יְהוּדָה מִשְׁתַּמְעָא, סד"א לִיגְמַר מִטּוּמְאָה, דְּלָאו שֶׁאֵין שָׁוֶה בַּכֹּל הוּא וְנָשִׁים פְּטוּרוֹת: ה"ג. כֹּהֲנִים לְוִיִּם וְיִשְׂרְאֵלִים מוּתָּרִין **לָבֹא** זֶה בָּזֶה לְוִיִּם וְיִשְׂרְאֵלִים חֲלָלֵי גֵּירֵי חֲרוּרֵי מוּתָּרִין **לָבֹא** זֶה בָּזֶה. אֲבָל כָּהֲנֵי בַּחֲלָלֵי, וַחֲלָלֵי בְּכֹהֲנוֹת – לָא. **אֲמַר** לֵיהּ **רַב הוּנָא**. לְעוֹלָם חֲלָלֵי בְּכֹהֲנוֹת שַׁפִּיר דָּמֵי. וְהָא דְּלָא תְּנַנְהוּ – מִשּׁוּם דְּכָהֲנֵי בַּחֲלָלֵי אֲסִירִי, לָא פְּסִיקָא לֵיהּ. דְּכָל הֵיכָא דְּהָנֵי נָסְבִי מֵהָנֵי וְהָנֵי מֵהָנֵי קָתָנֵי וכו'. בְּנֵי בִּירִי. מָקוֹם. כֵּיוָן דְּאָמַר מָר. (לעיל דף לח.) כְּתוּבָּתָהּ שֶׁל יְבָמָה עַל נִכְסֵי בַּעְלָהּ הָרִאשׁוֹן, לֵית לָהּ מִיָּבָם. וְאע"ג דְּהָא מֵרִאשׁוֹן לֵית לָהּ. **אוֹ** **דִּלְמָא** כֵּיוָן דְּאִי לֵית לָהּ. לִיבָמָה דְּעָלְמָא מֵרִאשׁוֹן, כְּגוֹן דְּלֵית לֵיהּ נְכָסִים – תַּקִּינוּ לָהּ רַבָּנַן מִשֵּׁנִי, וְהָא נַמִּי לֵית לָהּ מֵרִאשׁוֹן, הִילְכָּךְ אִית לָהּ מִיָּבָם. כְּתוּבָּתָהּ עַל נִכְסֵי בַּעְלָהּ הָרִאשׁוֹן. אַכָּל יְבָמוֹת קָאֵי, וְקָתָנֵי: אִם הָיְתָה שְׁנִיָּה לַבַּעַל – אֲפִי' מִיָּבָם אֵין לָהּ, ש"מ. מִכְּלָל **דְּאִיכָּא** דְּאִית לָהּ מִיָּבָם. בִּתְמִיָּה. כְּלוֹמַר, בְּעָיָין אִיפְשִׁיטָא, מִיהָא לִישָּׁנָא דִּבְרַיְיתָא קַשְׁיָא, דְּקָתָנֵי: אֲפִילּוּ מִיָּבָם אֵין לָהּ, וּמַשְׁמַע מִדְּקָתָנֵי אֲפִי' – מִכְּלָל דְּאִיכָּא יְבָמָה אַחֲרִיתִי דְּאִית לָהּ כְּתוּבָּה מִיָּבָם, וְהָא קָתָנֵי רֵישָׁא כְּתוּבָּתָהּ עַל נִכְסֵי בַּעְלָהּ הָרִאשׁוֹן. תַּקִּינוּ לָהּ מִשֵּׁנִי. כְּדֵי שֶׁלֹּא תְּהֵא קַלָּה בְּעֵינָיו לְהוֹצִיאָהּ. מְזוֹנֵי תְּנַאי כְּתוּבָּה נִינְהוּ. שֶׁכָּךְ כָּתַב לָהּ בִּכְתוּבָּה: אַתְּ תְּהֵא יָתְבָא בְּבֵיתִי וּמִתְזְנָא מִנִּכְסַי כָּל יְמֵי מֵיגַר אַרְמְלוּתִיךְ. לְאַחַר מִיתָה. אִם מֵת וְלֹא גֵּירְשָׁהּ – יֵשׁ לָהּ מְזוֹנוֹת כָּל יְמֵי אַלְמְנוּתָהּ כִּשְׁאָר אַלְמָנָה. דִּמְזוֹנֵי תְּנַאי כְּתוּבָּה, וְהָכָא לֵיכָּא לְמִיגְזַר דִּלְמָא תִּתְעַכֵּב גַּבֵּיהּ. וְיֵשׁ לָהּ פֵּירוֹת. שֶׁאַף עַל פִּי שֶׁאָכַל אֶת הַפֵּירוֹת, כֵּיוָן דְּשֶׁלֹּא כַּדִּין אֲכָלָן, שֶׁהֲרֵי לֹא הָיָה לוֹ בָּהּ נִישּׂוּאִין מֵעוֹלָם. וְאַף עַל גַּב דְּאָמְרִינַן (כתובות עט:) גַּבֵּי כְּשֵׁרָה, מַה שֶּׁאָכַל אָכַל וּמַה שֶּׁהוֹצִיא הוֹצִיא – הָכָא קָנְסִינַן לֵיהּ דִּמְשַׁלֵּם אֲפִי' מַה שֶּׁאָכַל, מִפְּנֵי שֶׁהוּא מַרְגִּילָהּ לַעֲבֵירָה: ה"ג, וְכֵ"ן מָצָאתִ"י בִּתְשׁוּבַ"ת הַגְּאוֹנִי"ם. מִפְּנֵי שֶׁהוּא פָּסוּל וְהִיא פְּסוּלָה וְכָל מָקוֹם שֶׁהוּא פָּסוּל וְהִיא פְּסוּלָה קָנְסוּ אוֹתוֹ רַבָּנַן כְּתוּבָּה. וְהָכִי פֵּירוּשָׁ': מִפְּנֵי שֶׁהוּא פָּסוּל, כִּדְתְנַן בִּבְכוֹרוֹ' (מה:): הַנּוֹשֵׂא נָשִׁים בַּעֲבֵירָה – פָּסוּל (ב) עַד שֶׁיִּדּוֹר הֲנָאָה, וְהִיא פְּסוּלָה עַל יָדוֹ.

קָנְסוּ

קדושין סט.

[לעיל פד: וש"נ]

[כתובות נג:]

[לעיל לח. כתובות פ:]

[לעיל לט. כתובות פב:]

כתובות פב: לעיל לט.

לעיל פז. כתובות ק: [תוספתא פ"ב ע"ש]

תוספות

ולותה ואכלה מאי. אי לותה ואכלה קודם שפסקו לה ב"ד – לא היה הבעל חייב לשלם, אפי' לותה בב"ד, כדפירש ר"ת בסוף כתובות (דף קז. ושם) גבי קדמו ב"ד ופסקו, מה שפסקו – פסקו. והכא מיבעיא ליה אם יש לב"ד לפסוק לה מזונות כשהלך בעלה למדינת הים, ותלוה ותאכל כשאר נשים, או לא.

אלמנה לכ"ג יש לה פירות. לאביי, דאמר בפרק "נערה שנתפתתה" (שם נא: ושם*) אלמנה לכ"ג, נשבית – חייב לפדותה, דקרינא וכהנת "אהדרנתיך למדינתיך" הוי פירות כמשמעו, דין פירות דהיינו פירקונה דהוי תחת פירות. ובשניה דקתני אין לה פירות – הוי נמי דין פירות, דאם נשבית אינו חייב לפדותה, אע"ג דהבעל אוכל פירות. כי ההיא ד"האשה רבה" (לקמן פט.) דתנא נמי: אין לה פירות ומזונות כו'. ואמר עלה בירושלמי: שאינה יכולה להוציא ממנו הפירות שאכל. א"ר חנינא: הא דתימא – כשאכל עד שלא בא הראשון כו'. ולרבא דאמר התם אלמנה לכ"ג דאינו חייב לפדותה נראה לר"י לפרש: יש לה פירות – דאם נשבית משלם הבעל הפירות שאכל לפדותה בהם. אבל מה שפרקונה יתר על דמי פירות שאכל – לא יהיב. ובשניות, אפילו דמי הפירות שאכל לא יהיב. ומתוך פירוש הקונטרס משמע שאין לבעל פירות באלמנה כלל, ואפילו לא נשבית – חייב להחזיר פירות שאכל, דפי' יש לה פירות – שאף על פי שאכל פירות – כיון דשלא כדין אכלן – משלם. ואליבא דרבא דכתובות פירש כן. אך נראה לר"י כמו שפי', דלא משלם בעל אלא לצורך פרקונה כשנשבית. וכן פירש הריב"ן.

בלאות. פי' בקונטרס במשנתינו גבי שניה דאין לה בלאות, שאם יש לה עדיין בלאות ושחקים מבגדים שהכניסה לו – אינה נוטלתן כשיוצאה, דקנסא קנסו חכמים. ואין נראה לר"י, דבהדיא משמע בסוף "אלמנה ניזונית" (כתובות קא. ושם) דדוקא מה שבלה ואין בעין – אין לה, אבל מה שבעין – שקלה. והיכא דאיירי באותן שהן עדיין בעין – רגיל לפרש "בלאותיה קיימין", כדאמר התם" זינתה – הפסידה בלאותיה קיימין. וכן בסוף "אף על פי" (שם סג:) גבי מורדת. אבל ק"ק, כיון דקתני באלמנה שיש לה פירות – היינו בלאות. כיון דאיירי בבלאות שאין קיימין כדאמר התם (כתובות עט: קא.) עיילא ליה גלימא – פירא הוי, ומכסי בה ואזיל עד דבלי*.

וכל מקום שהוא פסול והיא פסולה. פי' בקונטרס: שהוא פסול – שנושא אותה בעבירה, כדתנן בבכורות (דף מה:) ולא תרוייהו בעי, אלא אם הוא פסול או היא פסולה – קנסו אותו, דלא מרגלא ליה, כיון דמיפסל בהכי חד מינייהו, כדאמר בסמוך: ממזרת ונתינה איכא בינייהו. ופריך: ולר"א דאמר הרי זה עבד וממזר – הא לא מרגלא ליה! והתם בעל לא מיפסיל, דהא בישראל לא שייך למימר שיפסל על ידה. ואיהי נמי לא מיפסלא בהכי, דהא מעיקרא מיפסלא וקיימא. אלא משום זרע לחוד מנעה, ולא מרגלא ליה, שיראה להרגילו כיון שזרעו נפסל על ידה.

א) ומיהו, קשה: דקאמר בעולה לכ"ג איכא בינייהו כו', ואמאי מרגלא ליה? והא הוא נפסל על ידה, שנושא נשים בעבירה, ויראה להרגילו! ור"ת מפרש: דהוא פסול דקאמר – אולד קאי. ובפסלות דידה לחוד, אפילו במקום שהולד כשר – לא מרגלא ליה, כדאמרינן. ולרבי מתיא בן חרש דקאמר אפילו הלך כו' עשאה זונה – הא לא מרגלא ליה. ויש ספרים דגרסי: הוא כשר והיא פסולה, וכן בתוספתא דמכילתין בפ"ב.

ממזרת

עין משפט נר מצוה

ז א מיי' פ"ב מהל' אבל הלכה ו סמג עשין נח ולאוין רלה טוש"ע יו"ד סי' שעג סעיף ב:

ח ב מיי' פי"ט מהלכות איסורי ביאה הל' טו טוש"ע אה"ע סימן ח סעיף א:

[גנ. ד"ה ממזרת]

ט ג מיי' שם הלכה טז טוש"ע שם סעי' ב ג:

י ד מיי' פרק ט"ו שם הלכה לג:

יא ה מיי' פ"ב מהלכות יבום הלכה יז טוש"ע שם סי' קסח סעיף ט:

יב ו ז ח מיי' פרק כ"ד מהל' אישות הלכה ד טוש"ע שם סימן קטז סעיף א:

יג ט מיי' פי"ט מהלכות איסורי ביאה הל' ג סמג לאוין קכב טוש"ע שם סי' ז סעיף יב:

יד י מיי' פכ"ד מהל' אישות הל' ד טוש"ע שם סי' קנד סעיף כ:

טו כ מיי' פי"ח מהל' איסורי ביאה הל' ד ופי"ט הלכה ח טוש"ע שם סימן ז סעיף יט:

תוספות ישנים

מתני' ולא מזונות ומיירי בלותה ואכלה דאל"ה פשיטא דהא בעמוד והוצא קאי מזוני אית לה אלא מיירי שהלך בעלה למדי"ה ולותה ואכלה וא"ת אפ"ה מאי אריא משום שהיא פסולה אפילו כשרה נמי אמרינן הניח מעותיו על קרן הצבי אותו האיש שהלוה לה א) כדאמרי' הלך בעלה למדי"ה ועמד איש אחד ופרנס אותה הניח מעותיו על קרן הצבי וי"ל ה"מ היכא דלא מסר לה דרך הלואה אלא מסר בגלל בעלה ואין לו לאיש לתבוע לא לבעל ולא לאשה שהרי האיש לא שם במלוה לכן. והאשה לא שאלה מאתו. אבל הכא שלותה ממנו לא הניח מעותיו על קרן הצבי אלא המלוה תובע את האשה והאשה תובעת את בעלה וגם אם נתגרשה האשה משלמת המזונות לאיש שלוה לה והכא בשניה לא ישלם הבעל מזונות שלותה ואכלה ולא נהירא דדומיא דאמרינן בשניה אין לה מזונות קאמר באלמנה לכה"ג יש לה מזונות ובגמרא משמע דאלמנה לכה"ג אין לה מזונות בלותה ואכלה אלא נראה דבשניה לית לה מזונות אף לאחר מיתת הבעל דקנסינן ליה. אבל באלמנה לכה"ג יש לה מזונות בלאחר מיתה כדמשמע בגמרא: **א)** ואין להקשות ממה דמשמע מההיא דהיכא דפסל זרע לא מרגלא ליה והכא פ"ה שהוא פסול הבעל. דאל"ל דמודה רש"י דפסול זרע הוי שפיר פיסול בעל ולא מרגלא ליה:

א) נ"ל כדתנן בכתובות בפרק שני דייני גזירות (דף ק"ז ע"ב) מי שהלך בעלה וכו'

הגהות הב"ח

(א) גמ' איקלעו להנצבו לאתריה דרב אידי: (ב) רש"י ד"ה ה"ג וכו' הנושא נשים בעבירה פסול לעבודה עד שידור הנאה והיא פסולה חללה וכל מקום שהוא פסול על ידה או היא פסולה על ידו קנסו וכו':

טז א מיי' פכ"ד מהל' איסורי ביאה הלכה ז:
יז ב מיי' פ"א מהלכות מעשר הלכה ב סמג עשין קלה:

קָנְסוּ אוֹתוֹ כְּתוּבָּה. וּמִפְּנֵי מָה אָמְרוּ שְׁנִיּוֹת מִדִּבְרֵי סוֹפְרִים אֵין לָהֶן כְּתוּבָּה – מִפְּנֵי שֶׁהוּא כָּשֵׁר וְהִיא כְּשֵׁרָה, וְכָל מָקוֹם שֶׁהוּא כָּשֵׁר וְהִיא כְּשֵׁרָה קָנְסוּ אוֹתָהּ כְּתוּבָּה. רַבִּי אוֹמֵר: אהַלָּלוּ דִּבְרֵי תוֹרָה – *וְדִבְרֵי תוֹרָה אֵין צְרִיכִין חִיזּוּק, וְהַלָּלוּ דִּבְרֵי סוֹפְרִים – וְדִבְרֵי סוֹפְרִים צְרִיכִין חִיזּוּק. דָּבָר אַחֵר: זֶה – הוּא מַרְגִּילָהּ, וְזוֹ – הִיא מַרְגִּילָתוֹ. דָּבָר אַחֵר מַאן קָתָנֵי לָהּ? אִיכָּא דְּאָמַר: ר"ש בֶּן אֶלְעָזָר קָתָנֵי לָהּ, וּמַה טַּעַם קָאָמַר: מַה טַּעַם אָמְרוּ הוּא פָּסוּל וְהִיא פְּסוּלָה קָנְסוּ אוֹתוֹ כְּתוּבָּה – מִפְּנֵי שֶׁהוּא מַרְגִּילָהּ, וּמַה טַּעַם הוּא כָּשֵׁר וְהִיא כְּשֵׁרָה קָנְסוּ אוֹתָהּ כְּתוּבָּה – מִפְּנֵי שֶׁהִיא מַרְגִּילָתוֹ. אִיכָּא דְּאָמַר: רַבִּי קָתָנֵי לָהּ, וַחֲלוּצָה קָא קַשְׁיָא לֵיהּ: וְהָא חֲלוּצָה דְּרַבָּנַן וְאִית לָהּ כְּתוּבָּה! הֲדַר אֲמַר: כֵּיוָן דְּפָסֵיל לָהּ (א) מִדְּרַבָּנַן, זֶה – הוּא מַרְגִּילָהּ, וְזוֹ – הִיא מַרְגִּילָתוֹ. מַאי אִיכָּא בֵּין רַבִּי לְרַבִּי שִׁמְעוֹן בֶּן אֶלְעָזָר? אֲמַר רַב חִסְדָּא: מַמְזֶרֶת וּנְתִינָה לְיִשְׂרָאֵל אִיכָּא בֵּינַיְיהוּ. מ"ד דְּאוֹרַיְיתָא הָא נַמִי דְּאוֹרַיְיתָא, מ"ד מִפְּנֵי שֶׁהוּא מַרְגִּילָהּ, הָא הִיא מַרְגְּלָא לֵיהּ. *וּלְרַבִּי אֱלִיעֶזֶר, דַּאֲמַר: הֲרֵי זֶה עֶבֶד וּמַמְזֵר, הָא לָא מַרְגְּלָא לֵיהּ וְלָא מִידֵּי! אֶלָּא אֲמַר רַב יוֹסֵף: מַחֲזִיר (ב) גְּרוּשָׁה מִשֶּׁנִּיסֵּת אִיכָּא בֵּינַיְיהוּ. מַאן דַּאֲמַר דְּאוֹרַיְיתָא – הָא נַמִי דְּאוֹרַיְיתָא, וּמַאן דַּאֲמַר מִפְּנֵי שֶׁהוּא מַרְגִּילָהּ – הָא הִיא מַרְגְּלָא לֵיהּ. וּלְרַבִּי עֲקִיבָא, דְּאָמַר *יֵשׁ מַמְזֵר מֵחַיָּיבֵי לָאוִין, הָא לָא מַרְגְּלָא לֵיהּ וְלָא מִידֵּי! אֶלָּא, אֲמַר רַב פַּפָּא: בְּעוּלָה לְכ"ג אִיכָּא בֵּינַיְיהוּ. מַאן דַּאֲמַר דְּאוֹרַיְיתָא – הָא נַמִי דְּאוֹרַיְיתָא, וּמַאן דַּאֲמַר מִפְּנֵי שֶׁהוּא מַרְגִּילָהּ – הָא הִיא מַרְגְּלָא לֵיהּ. *וּלְר' אֱלִיעֶזֶר בֶּן יַעֲקֹב, דְּאָמַר: יֵשׁ חָלָל מֵחַיָּיבֵי עֲשֵׂה, הָא לָא מַרְגְּלָא לֵיהּ וְלָא מִידֵּי! אֶלָּא אֲמַר רַב אַשִׁי: מַחֲזִיר סָפֵק סוֹטָתוֹ אִיכָּא בֵּינַיְיהוּ. מ"ד דְּאוֹרַיְיתָא – הָא נַמִי דְּאוֹרַיְיתָא, ומ"ד מִפְּנֵי שֶׁהוּא מַרְגִּילָהּ – הָא הִיא מַרְגְּלָא לֵיהּ. וּלְר' מַתְיָא בֶּן חָרָשׁ, דַּאֲמַר: *אֲפִי' הָלַךְ בַּעְלָהּ לְהַשְׁקוֹתָהּ וּבָא עָלֶיהָ בַּדֶּרֶךְ – עֲשָׂאָהּ זוֹנָה, הָא לָא מַרְגְּלָא לֵיהּ וְלָא מִידֵּי? אֶלָּא, אֲמַר מָר בַּר רַב אַשִׁי: סוֹטָה וַדַּאי אִיכָּא בֵּינַיְיהוּ.§ **מתני'** בַּת יִשְׂרָאֵל מְאוֹרֶסֶת לְכֹהֵן, מְעוּבֶּרֶת מִכֹּהֵן, שׁוֹמֶרֶת יָבָם לְכֹהֵן, וְכֵן בַּת כֹּהֵן לְיִשְׂרָאֵל – לֹא תֹאכַל בִּתְרוּמָה. בַּת יִשְׂרָאֵל מְאוֹרֶסֶת לְלֵוִי, מְעוּבֶּרֶת מִלֵּוִי, שׁוֹמֶרֶת יָבָם לְלֵוִי, וְכֵן בַּת לֵוִי לְיִשְׂרָאֵל – לֹא תֹאכַל בְּמַעֲשֵׂר. בַּת לֵוִי מְאוֹרֶסֶת לְכֹהֵן, מְעוּבֶּרֶת מִכֹּהֵן, שׁוֹמֶרֶת יָבָם לְכֹהֵן, וְכֵן בַּת כֹּהֵן לְלֵוִי – לֹא תֹאכַל לֹא בִּתְרוּמָה וְלֹא בְּמַעֲשֵׂר.§ **גמ'** וְתֵהֵא זָרָה, בזָרָה מִי לָא אָכְלָה בְּמַעֲשֵׂר?! אֲמַר רַב נַחְמָן אֲמַר שְׁמוּאֵל: הָא מַנִּי – ר"מ הִיא, דְּאָמַר: *מַעֲשֵׂר רִאשׁוֹן אָסוּר לְזָרִים. דְּתַנְיָא:

תְּרוּמָה

קָנְסוּ אוֹתוֹ כְּתוּבָּה. כְּלוֹמַר לֹא קְנָסוּהָ מִשְׁאָר כָּל הַנָּשִׁים. וְהַאי דִּקְנָסוּהָ רַבָּנַן לִשְׁנִיָּה כְּתוּבָּה – כְּדֵי שֶׁלֹּא תִּתְעַכֵּב אֶצְלוֹ הוּא. דְּכֵיוָן דְּלָא תֶּיהֱוֵי לָהּ כְּתוּבָּה מִינֵּיהּ, שָׁבְקָא לֵיהּ וְנָפְקָא. אֲבָל הָכָא לָא צְרִיךְ, דְּמִמֵּילָא שָׁבְקָא לֵיהּ. דְּכֵיוָן דְּהוּא נִפְסָל עַל יָדָהּ – יֵשׁ קְטָטָה בֵּינֵיהֶם. וְכֵן כְּשֶׁהִיא נִפְסֶלֶת עַל יָדוֹ. **זֶה הוּא מַרְגִּילָהּ.** אַלְמָנָה לְכ"ג, גְּרוּשָׁה וַחֲלוּצָה לְכֹהֵן הֶדְיוֹט – הוּא מַרְגִּילָהּ וּמְסִיתָהּ לִינָּשֵׂא לוֹ. **וְזוֹ** – שְׁנִיָּה, דְּכֵיוָן דְּלָא הִיא מִיפַּסְלָא וְלָאו זַרְעָהּ מִיפְּסִיל, וְלָא מַפְסְדָה מִידֵּי בְּבִיאָתוֹ – הִיא מַרְגִּילָתוֹ. שֶׁהָאִשָּׁה רוֹצָה לְהִנָּשֵׂא יוֹתֵר מִן הָאִישׁ. **אִיכָּא דַּאֲמַר רַבִּי קָתָנֵי לָהּ.** שֶׁנָּתַן טַעַם לִדְבָרָיו מִפְּנֵי שֶׁהֵן שֶׁל תּוֹרָה. וְקָשֶׁה לֵיהּ: וְהָא חֲלוּצָה לְכֹהֵן לָאו דְּאוֹרַיְיתָא אֶלָּא דְּרַבָּנַן, כִּדְאָמַר (ג) בְּפ' יוֹחֲסִין (קדושין עח.) מִ"וְאִשָּׁה גְּרוּשָׁה" מְרִיבּוּיָא דְּוָי"ו, וּמוֹקְמִינַן לָהּ מִדְּרַבָּנַן וּקְרָא אַסְמַכְתָּא בְּעָלְמָא, וְקָתָנֵי מַתְנִיתִין דְּאִית לָהּ כְּתוּבָּה. **הֲדַר אֲמַר כֵּיוָן דְּפָסֵיל לָהּ** מִתְּרוּמָה דְּרַבָּנַן כו'. וְהַיְינוּ דָּבָר אַחֵר דְּקָאָמַר. **הָא הִיא מַרְגְּלָא לֵיהּ.** הוֹאִיל וְאֵינָהּ גְּרוּעָה מֵחֲמָתוֹ טְרַחָא וּמְהַדְּרָא לִינָּשֵׂא לְיִשְׂרָאֵל, כְּדֵי לְהַעֲלוֹת זַרְעָהּ. וְאַע"ג דִּבְנָהּ נַמִי מַמְזֵר, דְּקַיְ"ל (לעיל דף עח.) הַלֵּךְ אַחַר פְּסוּלָן – אֲפִילּוּ הָכִי, כֵּיוָן דְּאִיכָּא תַּקַּנְתָּא לְמַמְזֵרִים כְּר' טַרְפוֹן. דְּאָמַר בְּקִידּוּשִׁין (דף סט.): יְכוֹלִין מַמְזֵרִים לִיטָּהֵר – טְרַחָא וּמִיפַּסְּקָא לְיִשְׂרָאֵל. **וּלְרַבִּי אֱלִיעֶזֶר.** דִּפְלִיג עֲלֵיהּ דְּרַבִּי טַרְפוֹן (שם), וְאָמַר: מַמְזֵר שֶׁנָּשָׂא שִׁפְחָה וְהוֹלִיד בֵּן – אֵינוֹ נִטְהַר מִן הַמַּמְזֵרוּת בִּשְׁבִיל עַבְדוּתוֹ, וַהֲוֵה עֶבֶד וּמַמְזֵר, הָא כֵּיוָן דְּלֵיכָּא תַּקַּנְתָּא לְזַרְעָהּ – לָא מְהַדְּרָא לְמִיפְסַל זַרְעֵיהּ דְּגַבְרָא, לְפִי שֶׁהִיא מַקְנִיטָתוֹ תָּמִיד. **מַחֲזִיר גְּרוּשָׁתוֹ. מִשֶּׁנִּיסֵּת. בְּעוּלָה.** פְּנוּיָה, לְכֹהֵן גָּדוֹל. **עֲשֵׂה אִיכָּא** – בְּתוּלָה וְלֹא בְּעוּלָה, וְלָאו הַבָּא מִכְּלַל עֲשֵׂה – עֲשֵׂה. וְלָאו דְּזוֹנָה לֵיכָּא הָכָא, דְּאֵין זוֹנָה אֶלָּא הַנִּבְעֶלֶת בִּיאָה אֲסוּרָה. **וּלְר' אֱלִיעֶזֶר בֶּן יַעֲקֹב.** בְּ"הַבָּא עַל יְבִמְתּוֹ" (לעיל ס.). **סָפֵק סוֹטָה.** שֶׁקִּינֵּא לָהּ וְנִסְתְּרָה, וְקָאֵי עֲלָהּ בְּאִיסּוּרָא דְּאוֹרַיְיתָא, דִּכְתִיב "וְנִטְמָאָה" שְׁנֵי פְּעָמִים, אֶחָד לַבַּעַל וְאֶחָד לַבּוֹעֵל. **הָא לָא מַרְגְּלָא לֵיהּ.** דְּנִיחָא לָהּ לִשְׁתּוֹת בְּרֵישָׁא, דְּלָא לִיפַּסְלָא מִכְּהוּנָּה. **סוֹטָה וַדַּאי.** אֵשֶׁת אִישׁ שֶׁזִּינְּתָה, דַּאֲסִירָא לֵיהּ מִדְּאוֹרַיְיתָא, כִּדְכְתִיב (במדבר ה) "וְהִיא לֹא נִתְפָּשָׂה", דְּמַשְׁמַע: הוֹאִיל וְלֹא נֶאֶנְסָה – אֲסוּרָה. וְאִי קַשְׁיָא: הָא נַמִי חַיָּיבֵי לָאוִין הִיא, לְרַבָּנַן דִּפְלִיגֵי עֲלֵיהּ דְּר' יוֹסֵי בֶּן כֵּיפַר בְּפ"ק (לעיל יא:), דְּאָמְרֵי: "אַחֲרֵי אֲשֶׁר הוּטַּמָּאָה" לְרַבּוֹת סוֹטָה. וְלִיפְרַךְ: וּלְר"ע דְּאָמַר יֵשׁ מַמְזֵר כו'! – לָאו פִּירְכָא הוּא, דְּאִיכָּא לְתָרוּצֵי דְּהָא אָמְרִינַן לְעֵיל בְּ"הַחוֹלֵץ" (דף מט:): הַכֹּל מוֹדִים בְּבָא עַל הַסּוֹטָה שֶׁאֵין הַוָּלָד מַמְזֵר. **מתני' לֹא תֹאכַל בִּתְרוּמָה.** כְּדִתְנַן בְּפ' "אַלְמָנָה" (לעיל דף סז:): הָעוּבָּר וְהַיָּבָם וְהָאֵירוּסִין – פּוֹסְלִין וְלֹא מַאֲכִילִין. **לֹא תֹאכַל בְּמַעֲשֵׂר.** בַּגְּמָ' פָּרֵיךְ: זָרָה גּוּפָהּ מִי לָא אָכְלָה בְּמַעֲשֵׂר? **לֹא בִּתְרוּמָה וְלֹא בְּמַעֲשֵׂר.** תְּרוּמָה כְּדַאֲמַרַן, דִּלְוִיָּה נַמִי לְעִנְיַן תְּרוּמָה זָרָה הִיא, מַעֲשֵׂר מְפָרֵשׁ בַּגְּמָ'. **גמ' מי לא אכלה במעשר.** "כָּל זָר לֹא יֹאכַל קֹדֶשׁ" כְּתִיב (ויקרא כב), וּמַעֲשֵׂר רִאשׁוֹן לָאו קֹדֶשׁ אִיקְרִי.

תְּרוּמָה

ממזרת ונתינה איכא בינייהו. שיכול לטהר את בניו ע"י שפחה. ואע"פ שאין יכול לטהר את הנקבות, כדאמר בסוף "האומר" בקידושין (דף סט.) במה תטהר את הנקבות – סבורה היא שלא יקפיד, כיון שיכול לטהר את הזכרים. ואלמנה לכ"ג גרושה וחלוצה לכהן הדיוט, דמשמע דלא מרגלא ליה משום פסול זרעה שהם חללים, אע"פ שבני ישראל – מקוה טהרה לחללות, ובנות ישראל מקוה טהרה לחללים לרבי דוסתאי ברבי ינאי (קדושין דף עז.) – מכל מקום מקפיד הוא על בניו שאינם כהנים, ויראה להרגילו.

ולרבי עקיבא דאמר יש ממזר מחייבי לאוין הא לא מרגלא ליה. הו"מ למימר דר' עקיבא כר' טרפון, דאמר (שם דף סט.) ממזר נושא שפחה, ואיכא בינייהו ממזרת ונתינה כדלעיל, וא"ת: ומאי קשיא ליה! דלר"ע, כיון דלא תפסי בה קידושין – א"כ אינה אשתו, ואין שייך לקונסו שיתן לה כתובה, דאפילו גט לא בעיא מיניה, כדאמר ב"החולץ" (לעיל דף מט. ושם) וי"ל: דלאו משום כתובה ומזונות פריך, אלא משום פירות ובלאות, שאין לה להפסיד כיון דלא מרגלא ליה. **ולרבי** מתיא בן חרש כו' הא לא מרגלא ליה. פי' בקונטרס: דניחא לה לשתות ברישא, דלא ליפסלה לכהונה. וקשה: דכיון דגירשה – לאו בת שתיה? כדמוכח בסוף "האשה רבה" (לקמן צה. ושם) דקאמר: מאי איריא בא עליה, אפי' נתן לה גט נמי. ואפי' אמר איני משקה נמי, פי': דשוב אינה שותה. ועוד קשיא לפי' הקונט': דמאי איריא דפריך לרבי מתיא בן חרש – לרבנן נמי תיקשה, דלא מרגלא ליה, שרוצה לשתות תחלה להיות מותרת לכהונה. דאם יבא עליה – שוב לא ישקנה, דלא הוי מנוקה מעון, ואין המים בודקין אותה! אלא יש לומר: דלרבנן ניחא ליה, דהא לאו בת שתיה היא, כיון שגירשה. אבל לרבי מתיא בן חרש שנעשית זונה – לא מרגלא ליה, אע"ג דבלאו הכי היתה פסולה לכהונה מ"ונטמאה", ועוד: דגרושה היא ובתרומה נמי אסירא וקיימא, שהיא זרה, מכל מקום, פסול של זנות גנאי הוא לה ולא מרגלא ליה. ובפרק "עשרה יוחסין" (קדושין עז:) נמי חמיר ליה פסול של זנות טפי משאר איסורי כהונה, הואיל ושם זנות פוסל בישראל. ועוד: לא מרגלא ליה משום דאיכא השתא תרי לאוי.

תרומה

תוספות ישנים

ממזרת ונתינה איכא בינייהו למ"ד מפני שמרגילה זו היא מרגילתו וא"ל הלא הוי ממזר י"ל לאפשר לטהרו כדאמרינן יכולים ממזרים ליטהר כילד ממזר נושא שפחה הולד עבד שחררו הולד בן חורין ותימה מאי קאמר זו היא מרגילתו הלא אין מרווחת בו כלום שהרי אף אם תנשא לממזר יכולה ליטהר בנה כלפריקית וי"ל דמ"מ היא מרגילתו שיקרא זרעה על שם ישראל גמור ולמורי הא"י נראה דאין אנו צריכים לזה אף אם אינה מרווחת כלום הכשר בדבר מ"מ מרגלא ליה כדאמרי' יותר ממה שהאיש רוצה לישא אשה רוצה להנשא וכן פ"ה לעיל. וכן מוכח בתלמודא דבשניה אמרינן לעיל קנסוה בכתובתה אע"פ שאינה מוספת שום הכשר אלא משום שהיא רוצה להנשא יותר מהאיש. וא"ת א"כ מאי פריך אחרי כן ולר' אליעזר דאמר ה"ז עבד וממזר הא לא מרגלא ליה. ומאי קא פריך הלא מ"מ אינה נפסדת כלום בדבר שהרי גם אם תנשא לממזר כדינה יהיה בנה ממזר. ואי משום דלא מרווחא שום הכשר הלא פי' דמ"מ מרגלא ליה משום שרוצה להנשא. וי"ל דשפיר פריך לר' אליעזר דאמר ה"ז עבד וממזר א"כ איכא פסול לבעל שעל (ידה) [ידו] א) הוי זרעו נפסל וא"כ לא מרגלא ליה כדאמרינן לעיל כ"מ שהוא פסול והיא פסולה קנסו אותו שהוא מרגילה והיא אינה מרגילתו: **סוטה** ודאי איכא בינייהו דלמ"ד מפני שמרגילה זו היא מרגילתו ואי תקשי הדרא קושיא לדוכתין ולר' עקיבא דאמר יש ממזר מחייבי לאוין הא לא מרגלא ליה שהרי היא סוטה ודאי וחייבי לאוין היא לרבנן דפליגי עליה דר' יוסי בן כיפר ואמרי אחרי אשר הוטמאה לרבות סוטה שהוסתרה וי"ל דהא אמרינן לעיל הכל מודים בבא על הסוטה שאין הולד ממזר ואפי' ר"ע מודה:

א) אינו מובן שהרי אם היתה נישאת לממזר ג"כ היה הזרע נפסל א"כ הפסול אינו על ידו ואולי דר"ל כיון דהזרע ישאר בפסולו אינה מרגלתו בשביל שהיא רוצה להנשא וצ"ע

[ר"ה יט. תענית יז:]

[קדושין סט.]

לעיל מט.

[לעיל ס. עז:]

לעיל סח:

[לעיל עד. כתובות כו.]

הגהות הב"ח

(א) גמ' כיון דפסיל לה מתרומה דרבנן זהו מרגילה: (ב) שם מחזיר גרושתו איכא בינייהו כצ"ל ותיבת משניסת נמחק: (ג) רש"י ד"ה איכא דאמר וכו' כדאמר בעשרה. נ"ב ומייתי לה לעיל פ"ב דף כב.:

תורה אור

א תְּרוּמָה לְכֹהֵן ב וּמַעֲשֵׂר רִאשׁוֹן לְלֵוִי, דִּבְרֵי רַבִּי מֵאִיר. רַבִּי אֶלְעָזָר בֶּן עֲזַרְיָה מַתִּירוֹ לְכֹהֵן. מַתִּירוֹ — מִכְּלָל דְּאִיכָּא מַאן דְּאָסַר? אֶלָּא אֵימָא: נוֹתְנוֹ אַף לְכֹהֵן. מ"ט דְּר' מֵאִיר? אֲמַר רַב אַחָא בְּרֵיהּ דְּרַבָּה מִשְּׁמֵיהּ דִּגְמָרָא: (במדבר יח) °"כִּי אֶת מַעְשַׂר בְּנֵי יִשְׂרָאֵל אֲשֶׁר יָרִימוּ לַה' תְּרוּמָה", מַה תְּרוּמָה אֲסוּרָה לְזָרִים — אַף מַעֲשֵׂר רִאשׁוֹן אָסוּר לְזָרִים. אִי מַה תְּרוּמָה חַיָּיבִין עָלָיו מִיתָה וְחוֹמֶשׁ — אַף מַעֲשֵׂר חַיָּיבִין עָלָיו מִיתָה וְחוֹמֶשׁ? אָמַר קְרָא (ויקרא כב) °"וּמֵתוּ בוֹ כִּי יְחַלְּלֻהוּ" "וְיָסַף חֲמִישִׁיתוֹ עָלָיו", "בּוֹ" — וְלֹא בְּמַעֲשֵׂר, "עָלָיו" — וְלֹא עַל מַעֲשֵׂר. וְרַבָּנַן: מַה תְּרוּמָה טוֹבֶלֶת — אַף מַעֲשֵׂר רִאשׁוֹן נַמִי טוֹבֵל. וּכְדְתַנְיָא, רַבִּי יוֹסֵי אוֹמֵר: ג יָכוֹל לֹא *יְהֵא חַיָּיב אֶלָּא עַל טֶבֶל שֶׁלֹּא הוּרַם מִמֶּנּוּ כָּל עִיקָּר, הוּרַם מִמֶּנּוּ תְּרוּמָה גְּדוֹלָה וְלֹא הוּרַם מִמֶּנּוּ מַעֲשֵׂר רִאשׁוֹן, מַעֲשֵׂר רִאשׁוֹן וְלֹא מַעֲשֵׂר שֵׁנִי, וַאֲפִי' מַעֲשַׂר עָנִי — מִנַּיִן? ת"ל (דברים יב) °"לֹא תוּכַל לֶאֱכוֹל בִּשְׁעָרֶיךָ" וּלְהַלָּן הוּא אוֹמֵר (שם כו) °"וְאָכְלוּ בִשְׁעָרֶיךָ וְשָׂבֵעוּ", מַה "שְּׁעָרֶיךָ" הָאָמוּר לְהַלָּן מַעְשַׂר עָנִי, אַף "שְׁעָרֶיךָ" הָאָמוּר כָּאן מַעְשַׂר עָנִי, וְאָמַר רַחֲמָנָא "לֹא תוּכַל". וְאִי מֵהָתָם הֲוָה אָמִינָא לְלָאו, אֲבָל מִיתָה לֹא, קמ"ל. לִישָּׁנָא אַחֲרִינָא: מַעֲשֵׂר רִאשׁוֹן דְּטָבֵיל מִדְּרַבִּי יוֹסֵי נָפְקָא! אִי מֵהַהִיא — ה"א: לְלָאו, אֲבָל מִיתָה לָא, ד קמ"ל. בְּמַאי אוֹקִימְתָּא — כְּר' מֵאִיר, אֵימָא סֵיפָא: "בַּת לֵוִי מְאוֹרֶסֶת לְכֹהֵן, וּבַת כֹּהֵן לְלֵוִי — לֹא תֹּאכַל לֹא בִּתְרוּמָה וְלֹא בְּמַעֲשֵׂר". הָכָא מַאי זָרוּת אִיכָּא? אֲמַר רַב שֵׁשֶׁת: מַאי "אֵינָהּ אוֹכֶלֶת" דְּקָתָנֵי — אֵינָהּ נוֹתֶנֶת רְשׁוּת לִתְרוֹם, מִכְּלָל דִּנְשׂוּאָה נוֹתֶנֶת רְשׁוּת? אִין, וְהָתַנְיָא: (במדבר יח) °"וַאֲכַלְתֶּם אוֹתוֹ בְּכָל מָקוֹם אַתֶּם וּבֵיתְכֶם" — לִימֵּד עַל נְשׂוּאָה בַּת יִשְׂרָאֵל שֶׁנּוֹתֶנֶת רְשׁוּת לִתְרוֹם. אַתָּה אוֹמֵר רְשׁוּת לִתְרוֹם, אוֹ אֵינוֹ אֶלָּא לֶאֱכוֹל? אָמַרְתָּ תְּרוּמָה חֲמוּרָה אוֹכֶלֶת, מַעֲשֵׂר הַקַּל — לֹא כָּל שֶׁכֵּן?! אֶלָּא, לִימֵּד עַל נְשׂוּאָה בַּת יִשְׂרָאֵל שֶׁנּוֹתֶנֶת רְשׁוּת לִתְרוֹם. מָר בְּרֵיהּ דְּרַבָּנָא אָמַר: לוֹמַר שֶׁאֵין חוֹלְקִין לָהּ מַעֲשֵׂר בְּבֵית הַגְּרָנוֹת. הָנִיחָא לְמַאן דְּאָמַר *מִשּׁוּם יִיחוּד, אֶלָּא לְמַאן דְּאָמַר מִשּׁוּם גְּרוּשָׁה — גְּרוּשָׁה בַּת *(לֵוִי מִי לָא אָכְלָה בְּמַעֲשֵׂר? וְלִיטַעֲמִיךְ, גְּרוּשָׁה בַּת כֹּהֵן מִי לָא אָכְלָה בִּתְרוּמָה?) אֶלָּא, גְּזֵירָה מִשּׁוּם גְּרוּשָׁה בַּת יִשְׂרָאֵל. אִי הָכִי, מַאי אִירְיָא מְאוֹרֶסֶת? אֲפִי' נְשׂוּאָה נַמִי! אַיְּידֵי דְּתָנָא רֵישָׁא מְאוֹרֶסֶת תָּנָא נַמִי סֵיפָא מְאוֹרֶסֶת. *תָּנוּ רַבָּנַן: תְּרוּמָה לְכֹהֵן וּמַעֲשֵׂר רִאשׁוֹן לְלֵוִי, דִּבְרֵי רַבִּי עֲקִיבָא. רַבִּי אֶלְעָזָר בֶּן עֲזַרְיָה אוֹמֵר: לְכֹהֵן

רש"י

תְּרוּמָה לְכֹהֵן. נְתִינָתָהּ לְכֹהֵן, וּמַעֲשֵׂר רִאשׁוֹן לְלֵוִי. קָתָנֵי מַעֲשֵׂר לְלֵוִי דּוּמְיָא דִּתְרוּמָה לְכֹהֵן, מַה תְּרוּמָה אֲכִילָתָהּ כִּנְתִינָתָהּ, לְכֹהֵן וְלֹא לְזָר, אַף מַעֲשֵׂר לְלֵוִי אֲכִילָתוֹ לְלֵוִי וְלֹא לְזָר. דְּאִי לָאו הָכִי סְבִירָא לֵיהּ לְר' מֵאִיר, תְּרוּמָה לְמַאי קָתָנֵי? נְהִי דְּמַעֲשֵׂר אִיצְטְרִיכָא לֵיהּ לְאוֹרוּיֵי דְּלָא יָהֲבִינַן לֵיהּ לְכֹהֵן כְּר' אֶלְעָזָר בֶּן עֲזַרְיָה, אֶלָּא תְּרוּמָה ל"ל? וְעוֹד: מִדְּקָמְהַדַּר לֵיהּ ר"א לְשׁוֹן הֶיתֵּר, מִכְּלָל דְּר"מ נַמִי בְּאִיסּוּר וְהֶיתֵּר אַיְירֵי. מִכְּלָל דְּאִיכָּא לְמַאן דְּאָסַר. מַעֲשֵׂר לְכֹהֵן לֶאֱכוֹל? בִּתְמִיָּה. וְהָא וַדַּאי כֹּהֲנִים לָאו זָרִים נִינְהוּ, כִּדְאָמַר לְקַמָּן דְּכֹהֲנִים אִיקְרוּ לְוִיִּם. נוֹתְנוֹ אַף לְכֹהֵן. כִּדְקָאָמַר לְקַמָּן טַעְמָא. מִשְּׁמֵיהּ דִּגְמָרָא. כָּךְ קִיבֵּל מֵרַבּוֹ, וְרַבּוֹ מֵרַבּוֹ, עַד ר"מ שֶׁשָּׁמַע מִשְּׁמוֹ. וְלָאו מִן דַּעְתֵּיהּ קָמְפָרֵשׁ לְטַעֲמָא דְּר"מ. מַה תְּרוּמָה טוֹבֶלֶת. שֶׁכָּל זְמַן שֶׁלֹּא הוּפְרְשָׁה חַיָּיבִין מִיתָה עַל אֲכִילָתוֹ שֶׁל טֶבֶל, דְּהָא מִיתָה כְּתִיב בֵּיהּ. אַף מַעֲשֵׂר רִאשׁוֹן טוֹבֵל. וְאַע"ג דִּבְדִידֵיהּ לֵיכָּא מִיתָה — חַיָּיבִין מִיתָה עַל הַטֶּבֶל, שֶׁלֹּא הוּפְרַשׁ מַעֲשֵׂר רִאשׁוֹן מִמֶּנּוּ. אוֹ אֲפִילוּ מַעְשַׂר עָנִי. דְּקִיל כִּצְדָקָה בְּעָלְמָא, דְּלָאו צַד קְדוּשָּׁה אִית בֵּיהּ. וְאָכְלוּ בִשְׁעָרֶיךָ. בַּשָּׁנָה הַשְּׁלִישִׁית מִשְׁתַּעֵי קְרָא: הָכִי גָּרְסִינַן: וְקָאָמַר רַחֲמָנָא לָא תֵּיכוֹל וְאִי מֵהָתָם ה"א לְלָאו אֲבָל מִיתָה לָא קמ"ל. מַאי אֵינָהּ אוֹכֶלֶת דְּקָתָנֵי. כּוּלָּהּ מַתְנִי' לְגַבֵּי מַעֲשֵׂר. אֵינָהּ נוֹתֶנֶת רְשׁוּת. לִשְׁלוּחָהּ לִתְרוֹם מַעֲשֵׂר שֶׁל אָרוּס, וּלְהָרִים מִמֶּנּוּ תְּרוּמַת מַעֲשֵׂר, וַהֲוָה לֵיהּ כְּתוֹרֵם שֶׁלֹּא מִדַּעַת. וַאֲכַלְתֶּם אוֹתוֹ בְּכָל מָקוֹם אַתֶּם וּבֵיתְכֶם. הִשְׁוָה הַכָּתוּב אִשְׁתּוֹ לוֹ, לִימֵּד עַל בַּת יִשְׂרָאֵל נְשׂוּאָה לְלֵוִי כו': ה"ג. מָר בְּרֵיהּ דְּרָבִינָא אָמַר לוֹמַר שֶׁאֵין חוֹלְקִין לָהּ מַעֲשֵׂר בְּבֵית הַגְּרָנוֹת הָנִיחָא לְמ"ד מִשּׁוּם יִיחוּד אֶלָּא לְמ"ד מִשּׁוּם גְּרוּשָׁה גְּרוּשָׁה בַּת לֵוִי מִי לָא אָכְלָה בְּמַעֲשֵׂר? וְלִיטַעֲמִיךְ, גְּרוּשָׁה בַּת כֹּהֵן מִי לָא אָכְלָה בִּתְרוּמָה? אֶלָּא גְּזֵירָה מִשּׁוּם גְּרוּשָׁה בַּת יִשְׂרָאֵל. וְה"פ: רֵישָׁא — כִּדְאוֹקִימְנָא בַּאֲכִילָה מַמָּשׁ, וְר"מ. וְסֵיפָא, בַּת לֵוִי לְכֹהֵן וּבַת כֹּהֵן לְלֵוִי דְּקָתָנֵי לְגַבֵּי מַעֲשֵׂר — לוֹמַר שֶׁאֵין חוֹלְקִין לָהּ מַעֲשֵׂר בְּבֵית הַגְּרָנוֹת בְּלֹא בַּעְלָהּ, וְה"ה לִנְשׂוּאָה. וּלְקַמָּן פָּרֵיךְ: אֲפִי' נְשׂוּאָה נַמִי! הָנִיחָא לְמ"ד. בְּפֶרֶק "נוֹשְׂאִין עַל הָאֲנוּסָה" (לקמן דף ק.) מִשּׁוּם יִיחוּד אֵין חוֹלְקִין תְּרוּמָה לְאִשָּׁה בַּגּוֹרֶן, אֶלָּא לְמ"ד טַעְמָא מִשּׁוּם גְּרוּשָׁה, שֶׁמָּא יְגָרְשֶׁנָּה בַּעְלָהּ וּתְהֵא זָרָה וְאֵין הַכֹּל יוֹדְעִים וְיַחְזְרוּ וְיִתְּנוּ תְּרוּמָה לְזָרָה. גְּרוּשָׁה בַּת לֵוִי מִי לָא אָכְלָה בְּמַעֲשֵׂר. וְאַמַּאי בַּת לֵוִי שֶׁנִּתְאָרְסָה לְכֹהֵן דְּקָתָנֵי אֵין חוֹלְקִין לָהּ מַעֲשֵׂר בַּגּוֹרֶן בִּשְׁבִיל בַּעְלָהּ, אַמַּאי גְּזוּר בָּהּ רַבָּנַן? הָא אִי נַמִי מְגָרֵשׁ לָהּ — שַׁפִּיר קָאָכְלָה מַעֲשֵׂר. וְלִיטַעֲמִיךְ גְּרוּשָׁה בַּת כֹּהֵן מִי לָא אָכְלָה בִּתְרוּמָה. כְּלוֹמַר, וְלִיטַעֲמִיךְ דְּמוֹתְבַתְּ אַמַּתְנִיתִין לְגַבֵּי מַעֲשֵׂר — ה"נ בְּפֶרֶק "נוֹשְׂאִין" (שם) דְּאִיתְּמַר עִיקַּר מִילְּתָא, דְּקָתָנֵי: אִשָּׁה אֵין חוֹלְקִין לָהּ תְּרוּמָה עַל הַגּוֹרֶן, וּפָרְשִׁינַן טַעְמָא מִשּׁוּם גְּרוּשָׁה, וְלָא פָּלֵיג בֵּין בַּת יִשְׂרָאֵל לְכֹהֵן וּבַת כֹּהֵן לְכֹהֵן. גְּרוּשָׁה בַּת כֹּהֵן מִי לָא אָכְלָה בִּתְרוּמָה? אֶלָּא גְּזֵירָה מִשּׁוּם גְּרוּשָׁה בַּת יִשְׂרָאֵל. וּמַאן דְּגָרֵיס אִיפְּכָא לָא מִיתּוֹקְמָא כְּלָל, דְּהָכִי מָלֵי פָּרֵיךְ מִתְּרוּמָה דְּמַתְנִי' דְּקָתָנֵי בַּת כֹּהֵן לְלֵוִי לֹא תֹּאכַל בִּתְרוּמָה? הָא וַדַּאי שַׁפִּיר קָתָנֵי דְּאִיפַּסְלָה בַּאֲרוּסֶיהָ, וְטַעְמָא לָאו מִשּׁוּם שֶׁמָּא תִּתְגָּרֵשׁ הוּא. אַיְּידֵי דְּתָנָא רֵישָׁא מְאוֹרֶסֶת. לְגַבֵּי אֲכִילָה מַמָּשׁ, דְּהָתָם דַּוְקָא מְאוֹרֶסֶת. דִּגְבֵי בַּת כֹּהֵן לְיִשְׂרָאֵל וּלְלֵוִי לְעִנְיַן תְּרוּמָה, וּבַת לֵוִי לְיִשְׂרָאֵל לְעִנְיַן מַעֲשֵׂר, אַשְׁמוּעִינַן דְּפָסֵיל לָהּ אֵירוּסִין. וְגַבֵּי בַּת יִשְׂרָאֵל לְכֹהֵן וּלְלֵוִי וּבַת לֵוִי לְכֹהֵן אַשְׁמוּעִינַן דְּלָא מוֹכְלֵי לָהּ. תָּנָא נַמִי סֵיפָא — בַּת כֹּהֵן לְלֵוִי, וּבַת לֵוִי לְכֹהֵן לְעִנְיַן חֲלוּקָה דְּמַעֲשֵׂר, מְאוֹרֶסֶת.

לְכֹהֵן

תוספות

תרומה לכהן ומעשר ראשון ללוי. פי' בקונטרס: דדייק, מדקתני מעשר ראשון ללוי דומיא דתרומה לכהן דאכילתה כנתינתה. דאי לאו הכי – תרומה למאי קתני לה. וקשה: דא"כ לימא נמי ר"ע היא, דקתני נמי לקמן כי האי לישנא! ואי משום דסתם משנה רבי מאיר – הא אמרינן (סנהדרין דף פו.) וכולהו אליבא דר"ע. ומדמהדר נמי ר"א לשון היתר – אין לדקדק, דדלמא הא דאיירי ר"מ באיסור והיתר היינו בתרומה דאסורה ללוי ושריא לכהן! ופירש ריב"ן: דגרסינן בהדיא בדברי ר"מ מעשר ראשון אסור לזרים. **רבי** אלעזר מתירו לכהן. ל"ג בן עזריה, דר"א בן עזריה °קדים טובא לר"מ. ולקמן בברייתא דר"ע גרס ר' אלעזר בן עזריה, דהוא בר פלוגתיה. **מה** תרומה טובלת. פי' בקונטרס: בשלא הופרשה חייבין מיתה על אכילתו של טבל, דהא תרומה מיתה כתיבא ביה. וקשה לר"י: מעשר ראשון נמי כתיבא ביה תרומת מעשר! ועוד: אי מטעם זה – לא ליתסר טבל לכהן כיון דתרומה שריא ליה! ופי' ריב"ן: משו' דדרשי' בפ' "הנשרפין" (סנהדרין פג. ושם) "ולא יחללו את קדשי בני ישראל אשר ירימו" – בעתידים לתרום הכתוב מדבר, ויליף חילול(א) מתרומה: **אף** מעשר ראשון טובל. אבל איסור זרות לא ילפינן לרבנן. אע"ג דאין היקש למחצה, כיון דלא מצי לאקושי לגמרי לאסור אף ללוים כמו תרומה. ועוד: דמיסתבר לאוקומי היקישא אמאי דאסר קרא בדוכתא אחרינא, כמו טבל דילפינן בסמוך מ"לא תוכל לאכול" ואית ביה לאו, ואתא היקישא לאתויי נמי מיתה. אבל לאוקומי בה איסורא דלא אשכחן – לא מקשינן. **אי** מהתם ה"א ללאו. ומהיקישא לא הוה שמעי' ללאו ומיתה, אי לאו דאשמעינן לאו מהכא, כדפי'. ועוד: דאיצטריך "לא תוכל לאכול" למעשר עני דטביל. וא"ת: מנ"ל דטבל מעשר עני במיתה? הא לא אתקש לתרומה! וי"ל: דשמא אין בו מיתה.א] אי נמי, כיון שאין חלוק משאר טבל לענין אזהרה – ה"ה לענין מיתה.

מאי אינה אוכלת דקתני אינה נותנת רשות לתרום. פי' בקונטרס: דקאי אכולה מתניתין לגבי מעשר, דאינה נותנת רשות. וקשה לרבינו יצחק: דהוה ליה למימר: אלא אמר רב ששת, כיון דהדר ביה משינויא קמא! ועוד: דכיון דכל לא תוכל היינו דאינה נותנת רשות – הוה ליה למיתני בהדיא הכי! ועוד: דליתני אפילו בת לוי ללוי! ועוד: דמעוברת מה שייך למיתני לענין נתינת רשות! ואר"י: דלרב ששת נמי מפרש רישא דמתני' כדאמרן, ועיקר מתני' אתא לאשמועינן איסור אכילה. וכן בסיפא: בת לוי לכהן, בת כהן ללוי – איצטריך לאשמועינן דלא תאכל בתרומה. דסלקא דעתך שלא יפסול בת כהן מן התרומה, כיון דאוכלת מעשר האסור לזרים. ומעשר נקט לענין נתינת רשות, ואגב תרומה נקט לשון "לא תאכל", והוא הדין אפילו בת לוי ללוי ובת כהן לכהן, – אין נותנת רשות, אלא איידי דנקט בת לוי לכהן ובת כהן ללוי לענין אכילה, איירי בהו נמי לענין נתינת רשות.

מאי

עין משפט נר מצוה

יח א מיי' פ"ו מהל' תרומות הל"א ופ"ב הלכ' יד סמג לאוין רנב:
יט ב מיי' פ"א מהל' מעשר הלכה א סמג עשין קלג:
כ ג ד מיי' פ"י מהלכות מאכלות אסורות ה"כ:

תוספות ישנים

או א) היכי הלא אפילו מעשר עני. דאין בו קדושה כלל: אף שעריך האמור כאן מעשר עני. וא"ת ומעשר ראשון מנלן אי מכ"ש דמעשר עני הא איכא למיפרך מה למעשר עני שכן אין מוסרין מן הדין וי"ל דאין זה אלא גלוי מלתא בעלמא: אי מההיא ה"א ללאו וכו' וא"ת כיון דידעי' [דחייב] מיתה נ"ל קרא ללאו. וי"ל דאצטריך קרא דלא תוכל למעשר ראשון בו קדושה וא"ת ומיתה מנלן למעשר עני דממעשר ראשון לא ילפינן ליה שהרי אין במעשר עני קדושה וי"ל כיון שראינו שמעשר ראשון ומעשר עני שוין לענין לאו ה"ה לענין מיתה שאין חלוק בהם: ה"נ מר בריה דרבינא אמר לומר שאין חולקין לה מעשר בבית הגרנות. הגיחא למ"ד משום יחוד אלא למ"ד משום גרושה פי' שמא יגרשנה בעלה ותהא זרה והעולם לא ידעו ויתנו לה תרומה: גרושה בת לוי מי לא אכלה במעשר וא"כ אפילו תתגרש יכולה לאכול: ולטעמיך גרושה בת כהן מי לא אכלה בתרומה. פי' מאי אמרי' לקמן אין חולקין תרומה בבית הגרנות ולא חלקו הספר בשום נשים משמע דאף בת כהן ומאי אמרו אין חולקין לה מי לא אכלה בתרומה ואפי' אם נתגרשה. י"ג איפכא אלא למ"ד משום גרושה גרושה בת כהן מי לא אכלה בתרומה ולטעמיך גרושה בת לוי מי לא אכלה במעשר. ומאי אמרינן במתני' בת כהן מאורסת ללוי לא תאכל בתרומה ולטעמיך גרושה בת לוי מי לא אכלה במעשר. ולא נהירא פירוש זה דמאי קשיא ליה מתניתין דאמאי אין בת כהן ללוי לא תאכל בתרומה שלא טעמא רבה איכא משום דאיפסלה באירוסין פוסלין ולאו טעמא משום גרושה גרושה כו' ע"כ לשונו.

א) נ"ל מעשר ראשון ולא מעשר שני אפילו מעשר עני מנין וכו'.

גליון הש"ס

תוס' ד"ה רבי אלעזר וכו' קדים טובא לרבי מאיר וכו'. עיין בכבוד שור ריש ברכות:

מסורת הש"ס

מכות טז:

[לקמן ק.]

נ"א בת כהן מי לא אכלה בתרומה וליטעמיך גרושה בת לוי מי לא אכלה במעשר

כתובות כו. ב"ב פא: חולין קלא. ע"ש

הגהות הב"ח

(א) תוס' ד"ה מה וכו' ויליף חילול חילול מתרומה:

הגהות מהר"ב לנדא

א) תוס' ד"ה אי וכו' דשמא אין בו מיתה. נ"ב עי' ברמב"ם פ"י מהלכות מ"א ה"כ אבל במדרש הלכה בפסוק גלתה יהודה משמע מפורש שחייב מיתה:

כא א מיי' פ"א מהל' מעשר הלכה ד:
כב ב מיי' פ"ו מהל' תרומות הל' ג טור יו"ד סי' שלא:
כג ג מיי' שם הל' יב:
כד ד מיי' שם הל' יז:

לכהן. לכהן ולא ללוי?! אימא: אף לכהן. מאי טעמא דר' עקיבא – דכתיב °"ואל הלוים תדבר ואמרת אליהם" (במדבר יח), בלוים קא משתעי קרא. ואידך – כדר' יהושע ב"ל, דאמר ר' יהושע ב"ל: *בעשרים וארבעה מקומות נקראו כהנים "לוים", וזה אחד מהם: °"והכהנים הלוים בני צדוק" (יחזקאל מד). ור"ע: הכא לא מצית אמרת, דכתיב °"ואכלתם אותו בכל מקום" (במדבר יח) – מי שיכול לאוכלו בכל מקום, יצא כהן שאין יכול לאוכלו בבית הקברות. ואידך: כל היכא דבעי, דלא בעי חומה, ואי אכיל ליה בטומאת הגוף – לא לקי. ההיא גינתא דהוה שקיל רבי אלעזר בן עזריה מעשר ראשון מינה, אזל ר"ע אהדריה לפתחא לבי קברי. אמר[א]: עקיבא בתרמילו ואנא חיי! איתמר, מפני מה קנסו לוים במעשר? פליגי בה רבי יונתן וסביא. חד אמר: [א]שלא עלו בימי עזרא, וח"א: כדי שיסמכו כהנים עליו בימי טומאתן. בשלמא למאן דאמר שלא עלו – משום הכי קנסינהו. אלא למ"ד כדי שיסמכו עליו כהנים בימי טומאתן – משום כהנים קנסינהו ללוים? אלא: כולי עלמא קנסא שלא עלו בימי עזרא, והכא בהא קמיפלגי; מר סבר: קנסא לעניים, ומר סבר: כהנים בימי טומאתן עניים נינהו. *(בשלמא למאן דאמר קנסא לעניים – משום הכי אהדריה ר"ע לפתחא לבי קברי. אלא למאן דאמר לכהנים – אמאי אהדריה לפתחא לבי קברי?) הכי קאמר ליה: אי דקא אתית בתורת קנסא – אית לך, ואי קא אתית בתורת חלוקה – לית לך. ומנא לן דלא סליקו בימי עזרא – דכתיב °"ואקבצם אל הנהר הבא על אהוא ונחנה שם ימים שלשה ואבינה בעם ובכהנים ומבני לוי לא מצאתי שם" (עזרא ח). אמר רב חסדא: בתחלה לא היו מעמידים שוטרי' אלא מן הלוים, שנאמר °"ושוטרים הלוים לפניכם" (דה"ב יט), עכשיו אין מעמידין שוטרים אלא מישראל, שנאמר *"ושוטרים הרבים בראשיכם" (פסוק זה לא נמצא בתנ"ך).§

מתני' [ב]בת ישראל שניסת לכהן – תאכל בתרומה. [ג]מת ולה הימנו בן – תאכל בתרומה. ניסת ללוי תאכל במעשר. מת ולה הימנו בן תאכל במעשר. [ד]ניסת לישראל – לא תאכל לא בתרומה ולא במעשר. מת ולה הימנו בן – לא תאכל לא בתרומה ולא במעשר. מת בנה מישראל תאכל במעשר. מת בנה מלוי תאכל בתרומה. מת בנה מכהן לא תאכל לא בתרומה ולא במעשר. בת

רש"י

לכהן ולא ללוי. בתמיה. הא ודאי קרא לוים קאמר. בני צדוק. ולדוק כהן הוה, וקרא לבניו "הלוים". ר"א בן עזריה. כהן הוה, כדאמר בברכות (דף כז:) דהוא עשירי לעזרא. עקיבא בתרמילו. משום דר"ע *רעיא דכלבא שבוע הוה [כתובות סב:]. תרמילו. חמת של עור, בשטייל"א בלע"ז, ורועה נותן בה פתו ותולה בצוארו. מפני מה קנסו לוים במעשר. לאו לעיל קאי, דטעמא דהכא לאו משום קנסא, אלא משום דכהנים נמי לוים איקרו, כדאמרן. אלא דאמר בכמה דוכתין בהתלמוד בתר דקנסינהו עזרא (חולין דף קלא:), ובמסכת סוטה (דף מז:) תנן: יוחנן כ"ג העביר הודיית המעשר, ואמר: מפני שאין מפרישין אותו כתקנן, דרחמנא אמר יהבה ללוים ואנן יהבינן לכהנים. והכא נקט לה משום דקבעי למיפרך עלה מהא דרבי עקיבא, דאהדריה לפתחא לבי קברי. אלא ר' עקיבא מ"ט אהדריה כו'. למ"ד קנסא לכהנים קפריך: אם איתא דתקנתא לכהנים הואי – מי הוה מהדר ר"ע לפתחא לבי קברי? נהי נמי דקרא בלוים כתיב, מיהו ר"ע לבתר דקנסינהו עזרא הוה. ושוטרים הרבים בראשיכם. דהיינו ישראל, שהם רבים מלוים. **מתני'** ניסת ללוי. אחר שילדה מכהן. תאכל במעשר. ולא בתרומה, דהדר הויא זרה. מת ולה הימנו בן תאכל במעשר. בשביל בנה. והאי בן פסיל לה מתרומה, שהרי יש לה זרע מן הזר, וכתיב (ויקרא כב) "וזרע אין לה ושבה", והרי יש לה זרע. ואע"ג דקרא בבת כהן כתיב – מרבינן מיניה בגמרא נמי בת ישראל האוכלת בשביל בנה כהן, וניסת לזר ומת, שחוזרת ואוכלת בשביל בנה. הלכך, כי היכי דבת כהן כי אית לה זרע מישראל לא הדרה, בת ישראל (א) האוכלת בשביל בנה כהן, נמי, כי אית לה זרע בין מלוי או מישראל – לא הדרה אוכלת בשביל בנה כהן. בת

תוספות

מאי טעמא דר"ע. לכאורה נראה דר"מ ור"א פליגי בפלוגתא דר"ע ור' אלעזר בן עזריה, דר"מ דלעיל כר"ע, ותימה: דבפ' "המוכר את הספינה" (ב"ב פא: ושם) אמר דיהיב ליה לכהן, וכר' אלעזר בן עזריה. והתם מתרץ לה בין לר"מ בין לרבנן! וי"ל: דאליבא דרבנן מוקי לה התם כר"א בן עזריה. אבל לר"מ אית ליה לאוקומי בתר דקנסינהו עזרא, דלכ"ע לכהן. ואפילו למ"ד קנסא לעניים – יכול ליתן לכהן עני.

מי שיכול לאוכלו בכל מקום. וא"ת: לר"מ דאוסר לזרים, מ"ט דמעשר ללוי ולא לכהן? דלא מצי דריש כר"ע מי שיכול לאוכלו בכל מקום – דמההוא טעמא דאסור לזרים אסור לאוכלו נמי בטומאת הגוף, וא"א לאוכלו בבית הקברות. וי"ל: דאע"ג דאסור לזרים גזירת הכתוב הוא "ואכלתם אותו בכל מקום". [בכורות ז. חולין כד. [תמיד כז.]]

מפני מה קנסו לוים במעשר. פי' ר"י: *דלא מצינו בהדיא, אלא מצינו בעזרא "והיה הכהן בן אהרן עם הלוים במעשר הלוים". ואיכא למימר דהכי קאמר: כשיבאו הלוים לחלוק בבית הגרנות – יבואו עמהם הכהנים. וקשה: דלר' אלעזר בן עזריה דלא שקלי לוים כלל בתר קנסא, אלא כהנים, הא לא משתמע מההוא קרא! דהא ליכא למימר שהיו הכהנים עם הלוים לקבל מהם מעשר משלהם, דהא בשלהם לא קנסום, כדמוכח בפ' "הזרוע" (חולין דף קלא:) וי"ל: דלר"א בן עזריה לא נמנעו הלוים מכל וכל מלילך לבית הגרנות לחלוק במעשר, כדמוכח פ"ב דכתובות (דף כו. ושם) וכ"ש בימי עזרא, שעדיין לא פשט הקנס. ולכך נאמר שילך הכהן עם הלוים. ולמ"ד קנסא לעניים – נקט כהן עם הלוים, משום דשכיחי עניי כהנים טפי, לפי שאין עסוקין במלאכה אלא בעבודת בית המקדש, וגם אין להם קרקעות. וה"ה עניי ישראל, למ"ד מעשר מותר לזרים. והר' יוסף אומר: דנפקא לן מדכתיב במלאכי (ג) "הביאו את כל המעשר אל בית האוצר" דבית האוצר הוא לשכה שתקן עזרא לתת שם תרומת כהנים, כדכתיב בעזרא (נחמיה י) וכיון שמצוה לתת שם מעשר – אם כן של כהנים הוא, וקי"ל (מגילה דף טו.) מלאכי זה עזרא. ולמ"ד קנסא לעניים – מצוה לתת לכהנים משום דעניים שכיחי בהו, כדפרישית. [וכן פרש"י בחולין קלא: ד"ה בתר]

מר סבר קנסא לעניים. דוקא, ולא לכהנים עשירים. ואליבא דר"ע פליגי, דלר"א בן עזריה דשקלי כהנים מן התורה – אפי' עשירים, בתר דקנסינהו נמי דהוי לכהן ולא ללוי, כדמוכח ב"הזרוע" (חולין קלא:) ובפרק ב' דכתובות (דף כו. ושם) שקלי נמי כהנים עשירים, דלדידהו לא קניס עזרא שהרי עלו. וקנסא לעניים דקאמר הכא אין לפרש דוקא לעניי לוים ולא עניי ישראל וכהנים – דא"כ נשתכרו עניי לוים במה שלא עלו. ועוד: דמשמע הכא דאי הוו כהנים בימי טומאתן עניים – הוו שקלי לכ"ע, אע"ג דמדאורייתא לר"ע ללוי ולא לכהן. אלא ודאי, עניים דקאמר – אפילו עניי ישראל וכהנים. ומיהו, למ"ד מעשר ראשון אסור לזרים – אין נראה שינתן לעניי ישראל כדי למוכרו, דמילתא דאתי לידי תקלה לא הוו מתקני רבנן, דאיכא למיחש דלמא אתי למיכליה. וכה"ג אמרינן בפ"ב דכתובות. (שם) ונראה דלר"ע לא הפקיע עזרא כח הלוים מכל וכל להשוותן לכהן ולישראל, שלא יטלו מעשר אלא עניים ולא עשירים. אלא: לוים, בין עניים בין עשירים היו נוטלים לעולם, כדמשמע בכמה דוכתין שהיו נוטלין בתורת לויות, דתנן בגיטין (דף ל.): המלוה מעות את הכהן ואת הלוי להיות מפריש: עליהן, (ב) ואיתא בגמרא: (שם:) ישראל שאמר לבן לוי כור מעשר לאביך בידי, וב"הזרוע" (חולין קלא:) ובפ"ב דכתובות (דף כו:) פריך התלמוד מעשר ראשון ללוי הוא! וטעמא: כיון דמעיקרא היה המעשר של לוים לבדם לר"ע – דיין שיקנסום ליתן גם לאחרים עמהם, למר לעניים ולמר לכהנים, וסתמא בכל דוכתא כר"ע. ולר"א בן עזריה דאמר מדאורייתא אף לכהן – בתר קנסא לכהן דוקא, כדאמר בפ' שני דכתובות. (שם) ולדידיה דוקא מעשר ראשון חזקה לכהונה, ולא לר"ע. תדע, דלמ"ד לעניים – היאך יהיה חזקה לכהונה? ולר"א בן עזריה מה שבטל יוחנן את הודוי (סוטה דף מז:) אף על פי שדינו היה לכהנים כמו ללוים – מכל מקום, כיון דנצטוו לתתו אף ללוים "כי שכר הוא לכם חלף עבודתכם" (במדבר יח) כשמפקיעין אותו מלוים לתת כולו לכהנים – אין זה כמצותו. **ומבני** לוי לא מצאתי שם. והא דתנן בקדושין (דף סט.) עשרה יוחסין עלו מבבל, וקחשיב לוים, וקרא נמי כתיב (עזרא א) "ויקומו ראשי האבות ליהודה ובנימין והלוים וגו'" אלמא עלו! פרש"י ב"עשרה יוחסין" (שם) דאותן לוים שעלו עמו היו קלועי בהונות, כשאמר להם נבוכדנצר שירו לנו משיר ציון עמדו וקצצו בהונותיהן, ואמרו: איך נשיר את שיר ציון. ולפי שלא מצא שם ראויים לשיר עמד וקנסם. ואפילו למאן דאמר עיקר שיר בפה – מכל מקום הקפיד, משום דאיכא נמי מצוה בכלים.

ואימא

תוספות ישנים

(**נחזור** לראשונות) [ואידך] כריב"ל דאמר בעשרה מקומות וכו' והקשה הר' שמואל מאיוור"א היכי מצינן למימר דהאי קרא מיירי בכהנים והכתיב בההוא ענינא ונתתם ממנו תרומת ה' לאהרן הכהן וא"כ בלוים מיירי שנותנים תרומת מעשר לכהן דאי בכהנים הא לא מחייבי להפרישה דשלהם היא. וא"ל דמ"מ איירי קרא גם בלוים דלוים כתיבי אכן גם בכהנים איירי. זה א"א לומר. דא"כ מאי מוכח ר' עקיבא מואכלתם אותו בכל מקום דלא איירי קרא בכהנים הא כיון דאיירי קרא בלוים וכהנים מצינן למיקם ואכלתם אותו אלוים ושמא י"ל דשפיר איירי בכהני' ור"ל ונתתם אותו לאהרן הכהן כלומ' ונתתם שצריך שיהא נתון כבר ממנו תרומת ה' שהפריש' הישראל או הלוי מן המעשר עוד אומר מורי ראש"י דלעולם נאמר דאיירי קרא גם בלוים ובכהנים ומ"מ קרא דונתתם אלוים קאי ואין להקשות א"כ היכי מוכח רבי עקיבא מואכלתם אותו דלא מיירי קרא בכהנים כיון דאיירי קרא בתרוייהו מצינו למיקם ואכלתם בלוים אבל לעולם איירי קרא אף בכהנים וי"ל דזה לא קשה מידי דהא ודאי כולי קרא לא איירי אלא בלוים אליבא דר' עקיבא שהרי ואכלתם אותו בכל מקום נתינת טעם הוא לכל הפסוק דהכי משמע דכתיב ואכלתם אותו בכל מקום חלף עבודתכם באהל מועד וא"כ הפסוק נותן טעם לדבריו שיאכלו כל אותם הנזכרים למעלה חלף העבודה וא"כ כל הפסוק דכתיב לעיל מיניה דואכלתם לא איירי אלא במה שהפסוק דואכלתם מדבר. וקרא דואכלתם לא מצי מיירי בכהנים דהא כתיב בכל מקום כדמפרש תלמודא מי שיכול לאכלו וכו' [הרי] דלא איירי כלל בכהנים אליבא דר"ע כ"נ לראש"י: **ומר** סבר דוקא לענים נראה דפליגי אליב' דר"ע דאמר דקודם הקנס היה ללוי ולא לכהן אבל לרבי אליעזר דאמר דקודם הקנס היה לכהן וללוי א"כ יחלוקו אליבא דידיה ויאמרו קנסא לעניים פירוש [לכהנים וללוים עניים ולאידך מ"ד] לכהנים בימי טומאתן לבד וא"כ עשירים כהנים נקנסו והלא מה פשעו ומה חטאתם הלא לא קנס עזרא רק לוים משום טעמא דמפרש אלא נראה דאליבא דר"ע פליגי. ונראה דהלכה כרבי עקיבא דהא פליגי אליביה וכזה ניחא מההיא דמעשה שהיו באים בספינה שנתן רבן גמליאל המעשר ראשון לר' יהושע בן חנניה שהיה לוי ואמאי הלא קנסינהו עזרא ורבי [גמליאל] לאחר קנסא הוה. אלא ודאי לרבי עקיבא ניחא דמתחלה היה ללוי דווקא ועזרא קנסינהו ונתנו לכהן וללוי עניים ורבי יהושע עני היה ורבי אליעזר סבר שהיה בתחלה לכהן וללוי ולבתר קנסא היה לכהן דווקא. וכמו כן ניחא הא דאמרינן יוחנן כהן גדול ביטל את הוידוי משום דקרא משמע שנותנו ללוי דוקא ולבתר קנסא היה לכהן וללוי: **שנאמר** שוטרים בראשיכם. אין זה פסוק בכל המקרא. ושמא היינו דכתיב ואשימם בראשיכם (דברים א) א):

א) ר"ל דבריש' דקרא כתיב שם הבו לכם אנשים וגו' וידועים לשבטיכם אלמא דמישראל מיירי

הגהות הב"ח

(א) רש"י ד"ה מת ולה הימנו וכו' בת ישראל נמי האוכלת בשביל בנה כהן כי אית לה כצ"ל: (ב) תוס' ד"ה מר סבר וכו' מפריש עליהן וכן התם בגמרא:

הגהות מהר"ב רנשבורג

א] גמ' אמר עקיבא בתרמילו ואנא חיי. עיין במהרש"א בחדושי אגדות:

ס"א אלא רבי עקיבא מ"ט אהדריה לפתחא לבי קברא

תוספות חד מקמאי

מתני' בת ישראל שנשאת לכהן אוכלת בתרומה מת ויש לה ממנו בן תאכל בתרומה. נשאת ללוי תאכל במעשר מת ולה ממנו בן תאכל במעשר. נשאת לישראל לא תאכל לא בתרומה ולא במעשר. מת ולה ממנו בן לא תאכל לא בתרומה ולא במעשר. מת בנה מישראל תאכל במעשר. מת בנה מלוי תאכל בתרומה. מת בנה מכהן לא תאכל לא בתרומה ולא במעשר בת כהן שנשאת לישראל לא תאכל בתרומה מת ולה הימנו בן לא תאכל בתרומה נשאת ללוי תאכל במעשר. מת ולה הימנו בן תאכל במעשר נשאת לכהן תאכל בתרומה מת ולה הימנו בן תאכל בתרומה מת בנה מכהן לא תאכל בתרומה מת בנה מלוי לא תאכל במעשר מת בנה מישראל חוזרת לבית אביה ואוכלת בתרומה וע"ז נאמר ושבה אל בית אביה כנעוריה:

תורה אור

אבת כהן שניסת לישראל לא תאכל בתרומה. במת, ולה הימנו בן, לא תאכל בתרומה. ניסת ללוי, תאכל במעשר. מת, ולה הימנו בן, תאכל במעשר. גניסת לכהן, תאכל בתרומה. מת, ולה הימנו בן, תאכל בתרומה. מת בנה מכהן, לא תאכל בתרומה. מת בנה מלוי, לא תאכל במעשר. מת בנה מישראל, חוזרת לבית אביה, ועל זו נאמר °"ושבה אל בית אביה כנעוריה מלחם אביה תאכל".§ **גמ'** "מת בנה מלוי תאכל בתרומה", דהדרא אכלה משום בנה מנלן? *אמר ר' אבא אמר רב: "בת" "ובת". כמאן — כר"ע דדריש ווי? אפילו תימא רבנן, כולא "ובת" קרא יתירא הוא. תנו רבנן: דכשהיא חוזרת — *חוזרת לתרומה, ואינה חוזרת לחזה ושוק. אמר רב חסדא אמר רבינא בר שילא: מאי קרא — °"היא בתרומת הקדשים לא תאכל" — *במורם מן הקדשים לא תאכל. רב נחמן אמר רבה בר אבוה: ה"מלחם" — ולא כל לחם, פרט לחזה ושוק. מתקיף לה רמי בר חמא: אימא פרט להפרת נדרים! אמר רבא: כבר פסקה תנא דבי רבי ישמעאל. *דתנא דבי ר' ישמעאל: °"ונדר אלמנה וגרושה יקום עליה" מה ת"ל? והלא מוצאה מכלל אב ומוצאה מכלל בעל! ואלא, הרי שמסר האב לשלוחי הבעל, או שמסרו שלוחי האב לשלוחי הבעל, ונתארמלה או נתגרשה בדרך — היאך אני קורא בה, בית אביה של זו או בית בעלה של זו? אלא לומר לך: כיון שיצאה שעה אחת מרשות האב שוב אינו יכול להפר. רב ספרא אמר: "מלחם אביה תאכל" — לחם ולא בשר. רב פפא אמר: "מלחם אביה תאכל" — לחם הקנוי לאביה, פרט לחזה ושוק דמשלחן גבוה קא זכו. ורבא אמר: °"ואת חזה התנופה ואת שוק התרומה תאכלו... אתה ובניך ובנותיך אתך" — בזמן שאתך. אמר רב אדא בר אהבה: תנא, כשהיא חוזרת לבית אביה — חוזרת לתרומה, ואינה חוזרת לחזה ושוק. יבשביל בנה — חוזרת אף לחזה ושוק. אזל רב מרדכי אמרה לשמעתא קמיה דרב אשי. אמר: מהיכא קא מתרביא, מ"ובת" — מי עדיפא לה מינה? התם כתיבי מיעוטי, הכא לא כתיבי מיעוטי.§ "בת כהן שניסת לישראל וכו'".§ ת"ר: "ושבה אל בית אביה" — פרט חלשומרת יבם, "כנעוריה" — טפרט למעוברת. והלא דין הוא: ומה במקום שלא עשה ולד מן הראשון כולד מן השני לפוטרה מן הייבום — עשה עובר כילוד, מקום שעשה ולד מן הראשון כולד מן השני לפוסלה מן התרומה — אינו דין שנעשה עובר כילוד?! לא, מה לי עשה עובר כילוד, לענין ייבום, שהרי עשה מתים כחיים, נעשה עובר כילוד, לענין תרומה, שלא עשה מתים כחיים?! ת"ל: "כנעוריה" — פרט למעוברת. ואיצטריך למכתב (א) מעוברת ואיצטריך למכתב "וזרע אין לה", *דאי כתב רחמנא "וזרע אין לה" — מעיקרא חד גופא והשתא תרי גופי, אבל מעוברת, דמעיקרא חד גופא והשתא חד גופא — אימא תיכול, צריכא. ואי כתב רחמנא מעוברת, דמעיקרא גופא

סריקא

רש"י

בת כהן שניסת לישראל לא תאכל בתרומה. דפסיל לה, (ג) מדקאמר רחמנא "וזרע אין לה ושבה", מכלל דבחיי בעלה לא אכלה. מת בנה מכהן לא תאכל בתרומה. דפסיל לה לוי. **גמ'** דהדרא אכלה משום בנה. דקתני מתניתין גבי בת ישראל: מת בנה מלוי — תאכל בתרומה בשביל בנה. מנלן. דזרה האוכלת בשביל בנה, וניסת לזר, ומת, שחוזרת ואוכלת. בת ובת. "ובת כהן כי תהיה אלמנה וגרושה" (ויקרא כב). כרבי עקיבא דדריש ווי. בפרק "ד' מיתות" (סנהדרין נא:) א"ל ר"ע: ישמעאל אחי, "בת" "ובת" אני דורש. כוליה קרא ובת יתירא הוא. דכתיב לעיל מיניה "ובת כהן כי תהיה לאיש זר", וסמיך ליה "ובת כהן כי תהיה אלמנה", ומצי למיכתב וכי תהיה אלמנה וגרושה, ואנא ידענא דבבת כהן משתעי, דהא מיניה סליק. כשהיא חוזרת כו'. אקרא קאי, "ובת כהן כי תהיה אלמנה וגרושה וזרע אין לה" כשהיא חוזרת לבית אביה — חוזרת לתרומה כו', אבל אוכלת בשביל בנה דמתניתין — חוזרת אף לחזה ושוק, כדאמר לקמן. במורם מן הקדשים. חזה ושוק. מדהוה מצי למכתב "בקדשים", וכתב "בתרומת" — למורם הוא דאתא, והאי "לא תאכל" — לעולם הוא. ולא תימא ביושבת תחת בעלה ישראל, כדמשמע קרא "ובת כהן כי תהיה לאיש זר" כו', דהא אוקימנא להאי קרא בפרק "אלמנה" (לעיל סח.) בנבעלה לפסול לה, כגון נתין וממזר וחלל שפסיל עולמית. וכהנת דמנסבא לזר דלא אכלה — מ"ושבה אל בית אביה" ילפינן, מכלל דמעיקרא לא אכלה. ומילתיה דרב חסדא מ"בתרומת" נפקא, דא"כ דכוליה קרא לנבעלה לפסול לה אתא — ליכתוב בקדשים לא תאכל, מאי "בתרומת"? שמע מינה הכי קאמר: יש לך אחרת שאוכלת בקדשים, כגון תרומה, ואינה אוכלת במורם, ואי זו? — זו חוזרת, דסמיך לה "ובת כהן כי תהיה אלמנה" והכי תרילנא להא מילתא בפרק "אלמנה" (לעיל דף סח:). מלחם ולא כל לחם פרט לחזה ושוק. והאי "לחם" — כל מאכל משמע, כדכתיב (דניאל ה) "בלשאצר מלכא עבד לחם רב", הילכך איצטריך מיעוטא. ואימא פרט להפרת נדרים. ולא תימא, כי היכי דלענין תרומה הדרא למילתא קמייתא, תיהדר נמי לענין נדרים. מוצאה מכלל אב כו'. ומי יפר לה. בית אביה של זו. הואיל ולא יצתה לגמרי, ויכול האב להפר. או בית בעלה של זו. והרי היא *כשאר אלמנה ואין האב מפר, לכך יצא מקרא הזה לומר לך: כיון שיצתה כו': תרומה היא קנויה לכהנים, שאינה שירי שלחן מלך, אבל שירי קדשים — הרי הן כמשאת מאת פני אלהים, שהן שירי שלחנו. כשהיא חוזרת. בת כהן, אבל בת ישראל החוזרת לאכול בתרומה בשביל בנה, כגון ילדה מכהן וניסת לישראל ומת — חוזרת אף לחזה ושוק, דגבי בת כהן כתיבי מיעוטי. פרט לשומרת יבם. שאינה חוזרת לבית אביה, דהא אגידא ביה. כנעוריה. בזמן שהיא ריקנית, כעין נעוריה, פרט למעוברת. והלא דין הוא. ולמה לי קרא? ומה במקום שלא עשה ולד מן הראשון כולד מן שני — ניסת לאחד וילדה לו ומת, וניסת לאחר ומת בלא בנים, צריכה ייבום, ולא פטרה ולד שיש לה מן הראשון. עשה עובר כולד. שאם היתה מעוברת פטורה, דכתיב (דברים כה) "בן אין לו" — עיין עליו בכל ענייניס. מקום שעשה ולד כו'. בת כהן שניסת לישראל, וילדה לו ומת, וניסת לאחר ומת בלא בנים, עדיין היא אסורה בתרומה משום ולד מן הראשון, דהא כתיב "וזרע אין לה", והרי יש לה. לענין ייבום שהרי עשה מתים כחיים. מת בעלה ואח"כ מת בנה, הרי הוא כחי, ואינה חוזרת להתייבם, כדאמרן בשמעתין "דרכיה דרכי נועם". לענין תרומה שלא עשה מתים כחיים. בת כהן שילדה מישראל, ומת בעלה, ואח"כ בנה — חוזרת לבית אביה. וכולהו נפקי מקראי בשמעתין. ואיצטריך למכתב כנעוריה. למעוטי מעוברת, ואיצטריך למיכתב "וזרע אין לה" למעוטי יש לה ולד ילוד.

סריקא

תוספות

ואימא פרט להפרת נדרים. פי' בקונט': דלא תימא כי היכי דלענין תרומה הדרא למילתא קמייתא הדרא נמי לענין נדרים. ולפי טעם זה היה נראה דפריך אכל נשואה, אפילו נכנסה לחופה ונבעלה, דא נתארמלה — תיהדר למילתא קמייתא. ועל זה צ"ל: הא כבר פסקה תנא דבי רבי ישמעאל, דמשמע דפשיטא לי' בלא שום דרשה שמוצאה מכלל אב ומכלל בעל, ולא הדרא, ולא איצטריך ליה קרא אלא למסר האב לשלוחי הבעל, דסלקא דעתך דתיהדר משום דאכתי לא נשאת. **אלמנה** וגרושה מה תלמוד לומר. תימה: דאיצטריך לכדדרשינן בפרק נערה דנדרים (דף פח:). **היאך** אני קורא. היכא דנתארמלה או נתגרשה הוא דאיצטריך קרא, שאין האב יכול להפר, דה"א שתועיל כאן חזרה, הואיל ולא היתה כאן יציאה גמורה. אבל כל זמן שלא נתארמלה פשיטא דאין יכול להפר, מכיון שמסר האב לשלוחי הבעל, בלאו האי קרא דמ"לזנות בית אביה" נפקא בכתובות בפ' "נערה" (דף מח:), כדדרשי' התם: פרט לשמסר האב לשלוחי הבעל, ונדרים נמי גמרי' מהתם. **התם** כתיבי מיעוטי הכא לא כתיבי מיעוטי. תימה לר"י: בשלמא לכל הנך אמוראי דדרשי משאר קראי דכתיב בהו אביה — אתי שפיר, דמיעוטי כתיב גבי אביה דוקא. אבל לרבינא בר שילא, דדריש מ"היא בתרומת הקדשים" מאי משמע דההיא בחוזרת לבית אביה מיירי? וי"ל: כיון דכתב רישיה דקרא "ובת איש כהן" — נראה דבחוזרת לרשות אביה מיירי. ומיהו, קשה למאן דדריש מלחם ולא מבשר, דלגבי בנה נמי כתיב "ילידי ביתו הם יאכלו בלחמו" ודרשינן (לעיל דף סז.): ילוד מאכיל, והוה לן למימר: בלחמו ולא בבשרו.

הדרן עלך יש מותרות

עין משפט נר מצוה

כה א מיי' פ"ו מהל' תרומות הלכה ה טוי"ד סי' שלח:
כו ב מיי' שם הלכה יג והלכה ח:
כז ג מיי' שם הל' יח:
כח ד ה מיי' שם הל"ז:
כט ו טוש"ע י"ד סימן רלד סעיף יב:
ל ז מיי' פ"ו מהל' תרומות הלכה יח ועי' בכ"מ:
לא ח מיי' שם פ"ח הלכה ה:
לב ט מיי' שם הל"ב:

תוספות ישנים

במורם מן הקדשים לא תאכל. מדלא כתיב בקדשים וכתיב בתרומת הקדשים משמע במורם מן הקדשי' וא"ל דהיינו דוקא בעודה לאיש זר לא תאכל דהכי כתיב בקרא ובת כהן כי תהיה לאיש זר וגו' אבל כי גרשה או מת תאכל דהא מלאיש זר דהכא שמעינן כי נבעלה לנתין ולממזר פסלה לעולם והא דלא אכלה אף בתרומה דבית אביה ביושבת תחת בעלה נפקא לן מדכתיב ושבה אל בית אביה מכלל דמעיקרא לא אכלה וא"כ לא שמעינן ליה מהכא דלא תאכל בחזה ושוק בעודה לאיש זר דהא אף בתרומה דעלמא לא אכלה מקרא דושבה אל בית אביה כנעוריה וא"כ קרא דבתרומת קדשים לא תאכל לא איירי אלא בחוזרת: [שייך לע"ב] **ת"ל** וזרע אין לה והא אין לה. הקשה הר"ס כי היכי דאמרינן גבי יבום פי' דנעשה מתים כחיים משום דרכיה דרכי נועם ומפרשי' הא דכתיב ובן אין לו בשעת מיתה אבל אם יש לו בן בשעת מיתה ומת מהני כחיים לפוטרה מן היבום כמו כן נימא לגבי תרומה מק"ו ונפרש וזרע אין לה שעת מיתה אבל כי יש לה זרע בשעת מיתה מן הזר אע"ג דמית אח"כ לא תשוב לתרומת בית אביה. וי"ל שאני התם גבי יבום דגלי קרא דכתיב דרכיה דרכי נועם ומפיק לקרא מפשטיה אבל גבי תרומה אין לנו מק"ו להוציא קרא מפשטיה דפשטיה משמע וזרע אין לה כל זמן שאין לה זרע תחזור. עוד נראה לרשב"י דדוקא גבי יבום משמע שפיר קרא ובן אין לו בשעת מיתה דהא כתיב כי ישבו אחים יחדו ומת אחד מהם ובן אין לו בשעת מיתה ואם יש לו בשעת מיתה אין זה בן אין לו כי מת. אבל גבי תרומה בדידה תלה הכתוב וא"כ משמע בכל עת שלא יהיה לה זרע תשוב לתרומת בית אביה דהא בכל עת שמת זרעה נשארה אלמנה וגרושה וזרע אין לה ובהכי אמר קרא דתיכול בתרומה דכי נשא כ"נ לרשב"י: **האשה** וכו' ממזר מזה ומזה. הרב ר' אליהו הזקן היה ר"ל הא דקאמר במתני' הולד משני הוי ממזר היינו דוקא כשבא עליה קודם שנתגרשה מן הראשון אבל אם נתגרשה ובא

עליה השני אחרי כן לא הוי הולד ממזר. ול"נ א) לר"י כיון דאין לחלק מן הראשון בין בא עליה קודם שנתגרשה מן השני בין לאחר שנתגרשה דהא גירושי השני לא מעלין ולא מורידין שהרי קנסא הוא. כמו כן אין לחלק בשני דבכל ענין הוי הולד ממזר מטעם קנס: **ודלמא** משום דאשתיק ושתיקה כהודאה דמיא. וא"ת ומעיקרא מאי ס"ד דבעי להוכיח דעד א' מהימן מאי קאמ' הא אשתיק מהימן אפי' אמ' איני יודע מהימן. וי"ל דאה"נ דאישתיק לאו דוקא אלא ה"ה אמ' איני יודע מדנקט והלה אומר לא אכלתי. משמע דוקא משום דלא (אמר) אכלתי דקאמ' דידע שפיר דלא אכל והשתא קא דחי דקאמ' ודילמא משום דאשתיק והא דנקט והלה אומ' לא אכלתי לא ידעתי שאכלתי: **רבי** מאיר מחייב. וא"ת ... חובה שייך הכא הלא אמרי' חייבי חטאות ואשמות אין ממשכנין אותן. וי"ל ה"מ היכא שהוא מודה שהוא חייב דודאי כיון שהוא מודה שהוא חייב ישלם דהא לכפרה אתו. אבל הכא שאומר לאינו חייב ודאי לא יפרע אם לא משכנו: **אם** ... מזיד הייתי. והתם פריך מאי מגו הוא הלא אין אדם משים עצמו רשע. ומשני דר"ל דמתרלינן דבוריה דאמרי' דר"ל לא אכלתי שוגג אלא מזיד. וא"ת ונשלינן ליה. וי"ל דעביד איניש דמכסי חטאיה כדכתיב אשרי נשוי פשע כסוי חטאה:
א) עי' לקמן ע"ב בתוס' חד מקמאי שהאריך ג"כ בזה

[לעיל סח: סט.]
לעיל סח:
ג"ז שם כתובות כה. קדושין סט:
כתובות מט.
ס"א כשאר
נדה מד.

הגהות הב"ח

(א) גמ' למכתב כנעוריה למעוטי מעוברת ואיצטריך וכו' אין לה למעוטי ולד דלא כתב רחמנא כו' למעוטיה: (ב) רש"י ד"ה בת כהן וכו' לה ישראל מדקאמר:

האשה . איידי דאיירי לעיל ב"יש מותרות" בפסול תרומה ומעשר, קתני נמי הא פירקא בתריה, דאיירי נמי בהכי. דקתני: היתה בת לוי – נפסלה מן המעשר, בת כהן – מן התרומה.

הולד ממזר מזה ומזה. אר"י: דאפילו לאחר שנתן הראשון גט הוי ממזר מן השני, מידי דהוה אראשון, *שהולד ממזר ממנו.

מכלל דרישא ברשות ב"ד ובעד אחד, אלמא עד אחד מהימן מנלן. לאו דס"ד השתא דעד אחד מהימן מדאורייתא, הא דקרי ליה ברשות ב"ד – לפי שיש דברים שאין נאמן להם, וצריכה לישאל לב"ד להתירה לינשא על פיו. אבל בשנים – הדבר ידוע שהיא מותרת, ואע"ג דסבור עכשיו דנאמן מן התורה כמו שנים – מ"מ אסורה לחזור, (ג) דבעד אחד הוה לה למידק, אע"פ שהאמינתו תורה.

רבי מאיר מחייב. וממשכנים אותו אם אומר שלא *להביא. ולא דמי לשאר (ג) חייבי חטאות, דניחא להו בכפרה, ולא בעי משכוני*.

ומה

סְרִיקָא. רֵיקָה, כְּמוֹ אִילָן סְרָק (ב"ב דף מ:). וְלֹא נַעֲשֶׂה מֵתִים כְּחַיִּים. וְתַחֲזוֹר לְזִיקָה אִם יָמוּת בְּנָהּ לְאַחַר זְמַן. דְּרָכֶיהָ דַּרְכֵי נוֹעַם. וְזוֹ שֶׁהָיָה לָהּ בֵּן וְלֹא נִזְקְקָה לְיָבָם, וְנִישֵּׂאת לַשּׁוּק וּמֵת בְּנָהּ – אִם תֹּאמַר תַּחֲלוֹץ, הֲרֵי הִיא מִתְגַּנָּה עַל בַּעְלָהּ. הִילְכָּךְ, עַל כָּרְחָךְ "בֵּן אֵין לוֹ" – בִּשְׁעַת מִיתָה קָאָמַר, וַהֲרֵי יֵשׁ לוֹ.

תורה אור

סְרִיקָא וְהַשְׁתָּא גּוּפָא מַלְיָא. אֲבָל "זֶרַע אֵין לָהּ", דְּמֵעִיקָּרָא גּוּפָא סְרִיקָא, וְהַשְׁתָּא גּוּפָא סְרִיקָא – אֵימָא לָא, צְרִיכָא.§ סימ"ן: אמר ליה לא נעש"ה מעשי"ה במית"ה נעש"ה ולא נעשה בולד יבם ותרומה יבום ותרומה. סימ"ן.§ אָמַר לֵיהּ רַב יְהוּדָה מִדְּאִסְקַרְתָּא לְרָבָא לֹא נַעֲשָׂה מֵתִים כְּחַיִּים לְעִנְיַן יִבּוּם מִקַּל וָחוֹמֶר: וּמַה בְּמָקוֹם שֶׁעָשָׂה וָלָד מִן הָרִאשׁוֹן כְּוָלָד מִן הַשֵּׁנִי לְפוֹסְלָהּ מִן הַתְּרוּמָה – לֹא עָשָׂה מֵתִים כְּחַיִּים, מָקוֹם שֶׁלֹּא עָשָׂה וָלָד מִן הָרִאשׁוֹן כְּוָלָד מִן הַשֵּׁנִי לְפוֹטְרָהּ מִן הַיִּבּוּם – אֵינוֹ דִּין שֶׁלֹּא נַעֲשָׂה מֵתִים כְּחַיִּים?! ת"ל °"דְּרָכֶיהָ דַרְכֵי נוֹעַם וְכָל נְתִיבוֹתֶיהָ שָׁלוֹם". *וְנַעֲשָׂה מֵתִים כְּחַיִּים לְעִנְיַן תְּרוּמָה מִק"ו: וּמַה בְּמָקוֹם שֶׁלֹּא עָשָׂה וָלָד מִן הָרִאשׁוֹן כְּוָלָד מִן הַשֵּׁנִי לְפוֹטְרָהּ מִן הַיִּבּוּם – עָשָׂה מֵתִים כְּחַיִּים, מָקוֹם שֶׁעָשָׂה וָלָד מִן הָרִאשׁוֹן כְּוָלָד מִן הַשֵּׁנִי לְפוֹסְלָהּ מִן הַתְּרוּמָה – אֵינוֹ דִּין שֶׁנַּעֲשָׂה מֵתִים כְּחַיִּים?! ת"ל °"וְזֶרַע אֵין לָהּ" – וְהָא אֵין לָהּ. וְנַעֲשָׂה וָלָד מִן הָרִאשׁוֹן כְּוָלָד מִן הַשֵּׁנִי לְעִנְיַן יִבּוּם מִק"ו: וּמַה בְּמָקוֹם שֶׁלֹּא עָשָׂה מֵתִים כְּחַיִּים לְעִנְיַן תְּרוּמָה – עָשָׂה וָלָד מִן הָרִאשׁוֹן כְּוָלָד מִן הַשֵּׁנִי – מָקוֹם שֶׁעָשָׂה מֵתִים כְּחַיִּים לְעִנְיַן יִבּוּם אֵינוֹ דִּין שֶׁנַּעֲשָׂה וָלָד מִן הָרִאשׁוֹן כְּוָלָד מִן הַשֵּׁנִי?! ת"ל °"וּבֵן אֵין לוֹ" – וְהָא אֵין לוֹ. וְלֹא נַעֲשָׂה וָלָד מִן הָרִאשׁוֹן כְּוָלָד מִן הַשֵּׁנִי לִתְרוּמָה מִק"ו: מַה בְּמָקוֹם שֶׁעָשָׂה מֵתִים כְּחַיִּים לְפוֹטְרָהּ מִן הַיִּבּוּם לֹא עָשָׂה וָלָד מִן הָרִאשׁוֹן כְּוָלָד מִן הַשֵּׁנִי – מָקוֹם שֶׁלֹּא עָשָׂה מֵתִים כְּחַיִּים לְעִנְיַן תְּרוּמָה אֵינוֹ דִּין שֶׁלֹּא נַעֲשָׂה וָלָד מִן הָרִאשׁוֹן כְּוָלָד מִן הַשֵּׁנִי?! תַּלְמוּד לוֹמַר "אֵין לָהּ" – וְהָא יֵשׁ לָהּ:

משלי ג | ס"א אבל | ויקרא כב | דברים כה

הדרן עלך יש מותרות

הדרן עלך יש מותרות

הָאִשָּׁה שֶׁהָלַךְ בַּעְלָהּ לִמְדִינַת הַיָּם, וּבָאוּ וְאָמְרוּ לָהּ "מֵת בַּעְלִיךְ" וְנִיסֵּת, וְאח"כ בָּא בַּעְלָהּ – תֵּצֵא מִזֶּה וּמִזֶּה, וּצְרִיכָה גֵּט מִזֶּה וּמִזֶּה, וְאֵין לָהּ כְּתוּבָּה, וְלֹא פֵּירוֹת, וְלֹא מְזוֹנוֹת, וְלֹא בְּלָאוֹת לֹא עַל זֶה וְלֹא עַל זֶה. וְאִם נָטְלָה מִזֶּה וּמִזֶּה – תַּחֲזִיר. וְהַוָּלָד מַמְזֵר מִזֶּה וּמִזֶּה. וְלֹא זֶה וָזֶה מִטַּמֵּא לָהּ. וְלֹא זֶה וָזֶה זַכָּאִים לֹא בִּמְצִיאָתָהּ, וְלֹא בְּמַעֲשֵׂה יָדֶיהָ, וְלֹא בַּהֲפָרַת נְדָרֶיהָ. הָיְתָה בַּת יִשְׂרָאֵל – נִפְסְלָה מִן הַכְּהוּנָּה, וּבַת לֵוִי – מִן הַמַּעֲשֵׂר, וּבַת כֹּהֵן – מִן הַתְּרוּמָה. וְאֵין יוֹרְשִׁין שֶׁל זֶה וְיוֹרְשִׁין שֶׁל זֶה יוֹרְשִׁין אֶת כְּתוּבָּתָהּ. וְאִם מֵתוּ – אָחִיו שֶׁל זֶה וְאָחִיו שֶׁל זֶה חוֹלְצִין וְלֹא מְיַבְּמִין. ר' יוֹסֵי אוֹמֵר: כְּתוּבָּתָהּ עַל נִכְסֵי בַּעְלָהּ הָרִאשׁוֹן. רַבִּי אֶלְעָזָר אוֹמֵר: הָרִאשׁוֹן זַכַּאי בִּמְצִיאָתָהּ וּבְמַעֲשֵׂה יָדֶיהָ וּבַהֲפָרַת נְדָרֶיהָ. רַבִּי שִׁמְעוֹן אוֹמֵר: בִּיאָתָהּ אוֹ חֲלִיצָתָהּ מֵאָחִיו שֶׁל רִאשׁוֹן פּוֹטֶרֶת צָרָתָהּ, וְאֵין הַוָּלָד מִמֶּנּוּ מַמְזֵר. וְאִם נִיסֵּת שֶׁלֹּא בִּרְשׁוּת – מוּתֶּרֶת לַחֲזוֹר לוֹ. נִיסֵּת עַל פִּי ב"ד – תֵּצֵא, וּפְטוּרָה מִן הַקָּרְבָּן. לֹא נִיסֵּת עַל פִּי ב"ד – תֵּצֵא, וְחַיֶּיבֶת בְּקָרְבָּן. יָפֶה כֹּחַ ב"ד, שֶׁפּוֹטְרָהּ מִן הַקָּרְבָּן. הוֹרוּהָ ב"ד לִינָּשֵׂא, וְהָלְכָה וְקִלְקְלָה – חַיֶּיבֶת בְּקָרְבָּן, שֶׁלֹּא הִתִּירוּהָ אֶלָּא לִינָּשֵׂא.§ **גמ'** מִדְּקָתָנֵי סֵיפָא "נִישֵּׂאת שֶׁלֹּא בִּרְשׁוּת מוּתֶּרֶת לַחֲזוֹר לוֹ" – שֶׁלֹּא בִּרְשׁוּת ב"ד, אֶלָּא בְּעֵדִים. מִכְּלָל דְּרֵישָׁא – בִּרְשׁוּת ב"ד, וּבְעֵד אֶחָד, אַלְמָא: עֵד אֶחָד נֶאֱמָן. וּתְנַן נָמֵי: "הוּחְזְקוּ לִהְיוֹת מַשִּׂיאִין עֵד מִפִּי עֵד, וְאִשָּׁה מִפִּי אִשָּׁה, וְאִשָּׁה מִפִּי עֶבֶד וּמִפִּי שִׁפְחָה". אַלְמָא: עֵד אֶחָד מְהֵימַן. וּתְנַן נָמֵי: "עֵד אֶחָד אוֹמֵר "אָכַלְתָּ חֵלֶב", וְהוּא אוֹמֵר "לֹא אָכַלְתִּי" – פָּטוּר. טַעְמָא דְּאָמַר "לֹא אָכַלְתִּי", הָא אִישְׁתִּיק – מְהֵימַן, אַלְמָא: עֵד אֶחָד מְהֵימַן מִדְּאוֹרָיְיתָא. מְנָא לַן? דְּתַנְיָא: °"אוֹ הוֹדַע אֵלָיו חַטָּאתוֹ" – וְלֹא שֶׁיּוֹדִיעוּהוּ אֲחֵרִים. יָכוֹל אע"פ שֶׁאֵינוֹ מַכְחִישׁוֹ? הָא פָּטוּר – תַּלְמוּד לוֹמַר "אוֹ הוֹדַע אֵלָיו" – מ"מ. הֵיכִי דָּמֵי? אִילֵימָא דְּאָתוּ תְּרֵי וְלָא קָא מַכְחִישׁ לְהוּ – קְרָא לְמָה לִי? אֶלָּא לָאו – חַד, וְכִי לָא קָא מַכְחִישׁ לֵיהּ – מְהֵימַן, ש"מ: עֵד אֶחָד נֶאֱמָן. וְדִלְמָא שָׁאנֵי הָתָם מִשּׁוּם דְּקָא שָׁתֵיק, *)וּשְׁתִיקָה כְּהוֹדָאָה דָּמְיָא! תֵּדַע, דְּקָתָנֵי סֵיפָא: אָמְרוּ שְׁנַיִם "אָכַלְתָּ חֵלֶב" וְהוּא אוֹמֵר: "לֹא אָכַלְתִּי" – פָּטוּר. רַבִּי מֵאִיר מְחַיֵּיב. אָמַר ר' מֵאִיר: קַל וָחוֹמֶר, (א) אִם הֱבִיאוּהוּ שְׁנַיִם לִידֵי מִיתָה חֲמוּרָה – לֹא יְבִיאוּהוּ לִידֵי קָרְבָּן הַקַּל? אָמְרוּ לוֹ: מָה אִם יִרְצֶה לוֹמַר "מֵזִיד הָיִיתִי"! רֵישָׁא

כריתות יא: | ויקרא ד | כריתות יא:

*) [ולקמן צא. ב"מ כו: ב"ח לח:]

מ"ט

הָאִשָּׁה. בָּאוּ וְאָמְרוּ לָהּ כו'. [illegible]

[ע' תוספות זבחים עז: ד"ה כל חלב ותוס' חולין כג: ד"ה ופסול]

גליון הש"ס
תוס' ד"ה הולד ממזר וכו' שהולד ממזר ממנו. עי' לעיל דף מט ע"ב תוד"ה סוטה נמי:

תוספות חד מקמאי

פרק האשה רבה הא דתנן הולד ממזר מזה ומזה אמרינן בגמ' משני ממזר מדאורייתא ומותר בממזרת וראשון ממזר מדרבנן ואסור בישראלית ובממזרת נמי אסור דאין ב"ד מתנין לעקור דבר מן התורה בידים אלא בשב ואל תעשה כגון שופר ולולב שאין דוחים את השבת וכיוצא בהן אבל לעשות סג ונדרים לפי השעה והזמן יש להן סג ולעקור דבר מן התורה בידים והפקר ב"ד היה הפקר אפילו לעקור בידים. והוי יודע הא דקתני הולד ממזר מזה ומזה דוקא כשהורה הראשון בלא גט מהשני הוא שהולד ממזר מדרבנן אבל לאחר גט השני נהי שאסורה לחזור לו אבל אינו ממזר אפי' מדרבנן וכן שני אם הודיה לאחר שנתן לה הראשון גט אף על פי שאסור לעכבה בידו מהו אין הולד ממזר דתנן בהאי פרקין אמרו לה מת בעלך ונשאת ואח"כ אמרו לה קיים היה באותה שעה תצא מזה ומזה והולד ראשון ממזר והאחרון אינו ממזר וכיון דלאחר מיתת הא' אינו ממזר כך לאחר גט הראשון אינו ממזר אפי' דרבנן ומותר בישראלית. וי"מ לעולם הוי ממזר מן השני אפי' לאחר גט הראשון הא דקתני סיפא גבי קיים היה באותה שעה האחרון אינו ממזר הכי קאמר אינו ממזר מדאורייתא אלא מדרבנן. וראיתם הא דפרכי' בשמעתא [קף לן] דעד אחד ביבמה וכ"ת לא דק הא מדקתני סיפא הראשון ממזר והאחרון אינו ממזר ש"מ דוקא קתני ומפרש הכי מדקתני סיפא האחרון אינו ממזר ומאי אינו ממזר מדאורייתא אבל מדרבנן הוי ממזר מכלל דרישא דקתני ממזר מדאורייתא קאמר וזה הפי' רחוק מן הדעת מאד בכמה תשובות. הרא דהכי פשיטא ליה מאי אינו ממזר מדאורייתא אלא מדרבנן ועוד אם איתא דאחרון ממזר מדרבנן ליתני הולד ראשון ואחרון ממזר כדקתני רישא הולד ממזר מזה ומזה דפירשו לראשון מדרבנן ולשני מדאורייתא' והכא נמי ליתני הכי ועוד דקתני סיפא גבי מתה אשתו הולד ראשון ממזר והאחרון אינו ממזר וכי היכי דאחרון אינו ממזר דהתם מותר בישראלית ה"נ האי אינו ממזר כלל אפי' דרבנן א). (עין לעיל סוף פ' החולץ גבי הכל מודים בבא ג) ועוד דלא אשכחן בשום דוכתא על הנדה ועל הסוטה וכו' דאין הולד ממזר בעולם דליתני (אינו) [דהוי] ממזר שהו' שכ' הרב המחבר ז"ל דעל הסוטה הדך נישאין ממזר מדרבנן) ועוד אם איתא הוי ממזר מדרבנן וצ"ע (א"ש) [א"כ] והא דקתני רישא הולד ממזר מזה ומזה אפי' לאחר גט ראשון הא דאמרינן בגמ' בשלמא משני הוי ממזר אלא מראשון אמאי הא אשתו מעליותא היא וקא שרי ליה בממזרת הו"ל לאקשויי משני אמאי הולד ממזר משני לאחר שנתן לה גט הראשון ועוד והא ק"ל דאין ממזר מסוטה. ורואה אני הדברים ק"ו ומה בעל דאיכא לאו דאחרי אשר הוטמאה לרבות סוטה שנסתרה ועשה הטמאה נטמאה ג' פעמים א' לבעל וא' לבועל אפ"ה לא הוי ממזר מדרבנן. וכ"ת והא דאמרי' אין ממזר מסוטה מדאורייתא קאמר אבל מדרבנן הוי ממזר הא לא מצית אמרת דהא אמרי' בפ' יש מותרות סוטה והיית איכא בינייהו ואם איתא שהוא ממזר מדרבנן הא לא מתגלא ליה שהרי זרעה פסול מדרבנן אלא לאו ש"מ שאין בזרעה שום ממזרות לא מדאורי' ולא מדרבנן ואם מבעל אין בה שום ממזרות כ"ש מבועל ומה' כיון שנפסלה מהתרומה כדדרשי' א' לבעל וא' לבועל וא' לתרומה כ"ש (לתרומה) [לכהונה] מק"ו ומה גרושה שמותרת בתרומה אסורה לכהן זו שאסורה בתרומה אינו דין שאסורה לכהן והאי ק"ו איתא בפ' אלמנה גבי נבעלה לפסול לה ואע"ג דפסולה לכהונה (לא) [מ"מ] מתגלא שהרי פסולה ועומדת היא משעת זנותה. מ' צד ממזרות ליכא לא מבעל ולא מבועל לאחר גט ולא לפסול חלל בזרעה אם בעלה ישראל וליכא ספיקא בהא. והא דפרכי' בשמעתי' דעד א' ביבמה והא מדקתני סיפא הראשון והאחרון אינו ממזר ש"מ [דוקא] קתני לאו מאחרון קא פריך אלא מראשון קפריך דכי היכי דראשון ממזר דקתני בסיפא מדאורי' קאמר ה"נ הולד ראשון ואחרון ממזר דקתני רישא גבי יבמה מדאורייתא קאמר ואע"ג דהולד ממזר מזה ומזה דקתני רישא הוי פרושו לשני מדאורייתא ולראשון מדרבנן ואם כן אופריך ליה מסיפא לסייעי' מרישא דקתני הולד ממזר מזה ומזה שא' מהם ממזר מדרבנן התם כיון (דמשמע) [דמשני] ממזר מדאורייתא קתני הולד ממזר מזה ומזה אבל הכא שהראשון ה"ל ספק ממזר לא הו"ל למתני הולד ראשון ואחרון ממזר ומשום הכי אקשי' ליה מסיפא דקתני הראשון ממזר והאחרון אינו ממזר דכי היכי דהראשון דקתני סיפא דוקא ה"נ ראשון ואחרון דרישא דוקא וזה הפי' העיקר ואין ספק בדבר דליכא צד ממזרות אפי' מדרבנן לאחר נתינת הגט לא לראשון ולא לשני. והכא דאיכא חד שהוא דלא מת לא תנשא לכתחילה משום לזות שפתים ואם נשאת לא תצא אפילו לא נשאת לא' מעידיה דאמר עולא כל מקום (שהאמינה) [שהאמינה] תורה עד א' הרי כאן שנים ואם באו שנים ואמרו מת וב' אמרו לא מת אם לא נשאת לא תנשא ואם נשאת לא' מעידיה או אפי' נשאת לא' מעידיה ולא אמרה איזה ברי לי אם נשאת תצא. כיון דעד השתא הבא עליה באשם תלוי קאי ומכאן ואילך ה"ל מזיד בספק א"א ואם נשאת לא' מעידיה ואמרה ברי לי פלוגתא דרבנן ור' מנחם בר יוסי דלרבנן לא תצא והלכתא כותייהו אבל בנשאת עפ"י עדים שנית ואח"כ באו עדים שהוא חי אפי' לר"מ בר יוסי לא תצא אם נשאת לא' מעידיה ואמרה ברי לי ואם בא עד א' כשר מעיקרא והעיד שמת אפי' ק' נשים העידו שלא מת כפלגא ופלגא דמי אם העידו בבת א' ואם באו בזה אח"ז והתחילה עפ"י עד א' כשר הרי הוא כשנים. ואם באו ק' נשים אח"כ לומר לא מת כעד א' דמין ואין דבריו של א' במקום שנים. ואם באותה אשה א' מעיקרא והתירה לינשא על פיה ואח"כ באו ב' (עדים) [נשים] ואמ' לא מת הולכים אחר רוב דעות. עשו שתי נשים כאשה א' כשני (נשים). [אנשים באיש אחד] ואפי' נשאת לא' מעידיה וא' ברי לי תצא. ואמר רב אשי לקלא לא חיישינן. פי' אם לאחר שנשאה עפ"י עד א' יצא עליה [קול] שלא מת לא חיישינן ולא תצא:

א) [illegible] ב) [illegible]